*Major Problems in American Colonial History*

# MAJOR PROBLEMS IN AMERICAN HISTORY SERIES

GENERAL EDITOR

THOMAS G. PATERSON

# *Major Problems in American Colonial History*

SECOND EDITION

DOCUMENTS AND ESSAYS

EDITED BY

## KAREN ORDAHL KUPPERMAN

NEW YORK UNIVERSITY

HOUGHTON MIFFLIN COMPANY     BOSTON   NEW YORK

Editor-in-Chief: Jean L. Woy
Senior Associate Editor: Frances Gay
Associate Project Editor: Amy Johnson
Associate Production/Design Coordinator: Jodi O'Rourke
Assistant Manufacturing Coordinator: Andrea Wagner
Senior Marketing Manager: Sandra McGuire

Cover Designer: Sarah Melhado Bishins
Cover Image: Giraudon/Art Resource, William Penn's Treaty with the Indians

Note regarding the icon: The icon is the signature of Solomon of the Mohegan nation, which was affixed
to a petition the Mohegans sent to the King. See pages 375–378.

Printed in the U.S.A.

Library of Congress Catalog Card Number: 99-71980

ISBN: 0-395-93676-4

123456789-CRS-03 02 01 00 99

# Contents

CHAPTER 4
## *New England: The Settlement of Puritan Colonies*
### *Page 87*

CHAPTER 5
## *New England: Growth and Conflict*
### *Page 118*

CHAPTER 9

*Expansion in the South: Hopes and Realities*

Page 255

CHAPTER 10

*Slave Life and Culture*

Page 286

CHAPTER 13

## *New Realities in the Backcountry*

Page 400

CHAPTER 14

## *Colonial America at Mid-Century*

Page 435

# *Preface*

The colonial period may seem remote to many Americans because of the way the study of the era has been constructed. Teachers and scholars have long focused almost exclusively on the English colonies, seeing other peoples and regions as peripheral to the story. Such an approach no longer satisfies either historians or the public. We are increasingly aware that the roots of modern life lie deep in the past, and that America was multicultural from the beginning. The founding period saw colonies within the future United States established by Spain, France, the Netherlands, and Sweden, as well as by England. Even the colonies established by English companies were populated by people from many parts of the Old World, creating a rich mix of traditions and assumptions. No longer does the colonial story focus exclusively on English transplantation and agency.

Historians also now question a narrative that posits a steady movement of culture and civilization from east to west, with regions added to the account as the frontier of civilization arrives at their boundaries. They now recognize the activities of Europeans all around the edges of the continent and moving into the interior from the north. Santa Fe, Jamestown, and Quebec were founded virtually simultaneously in the first decade of the seventeenth century, and St. Augustine preceded them all by half a century. Nor do historians any longer construe Indian societies as outside the story until they come face to face with Europeans. Presenting their role as purely oppositional no longer makes sense. In short, a satisfying version of the colonial period recognizes all participants as actors and views the entire region of the future United States as the stage on which events transpired. This new approach creates daunting problems of organizing and presenting a mass of new research, but it also offers an exciting opportunity to reconfigure the founding period.

Meeting the challenge has been made difficult by the fragmentation plaguing colonial history. Scholars traditionally have focused their work on a single region, usually the Chesapeake, New England, or the Middle Colonies, implicitly endorsing the idea that each area was quite different from the others and that only the English-dominated east coast matters. Such an approach has left little opening for comparative work or for a search for common themes. As historians have sought to weave in those people formerly excluded from the story—women, American Indians, Africans, and non-English Europeans—they typically have placed these experiences in the same constrictive regional framework.

This second edition, in which 75 percent of the essays are new, seeks to open our definition of American colonial history to regions and peoples left out of the traditional, English-centered approach. Scholarly work exists to create a new, more integrated early American past, but instructors are faced with the task of locating this work in a wide variety of sources and academic languages. One of these scholarly approaches is ethnohistory. Ethnohistorians are producing a substantial body of scholarship revealing Native Americans as dynamic actors in the historical drama, pointing both to the vitality of the entities that grew up in the regions beyond European settlements and to the survival of Indian groups within the established colonies. Native responses changed as the context in which they found themselves developed through time and space. This edition presents several examples of new ethnohistorical thinking that are woven through the chapters rather than being segregated in a single discussion. The essays by Bruce G. Trigger and Paul A. Robinson in Chapter 2 both examine the Indian response to the European presence, and the range of methods American natives used to deal with novel situations. Jill Lepore's essay in Chapter 5 explores the situation of John Sassamon in Puritan New England, a man thoroughly educated in both Indian and Christian English ways. As the frontier of settlement and contact pressed west, native groups faced new challenges and created new responses. Some of these are explored in Gregory E. Dowd's essay in Chapter 13 about religious revivals among displaced Indians in the Ohio Valley and the ways they wove together the traditional and the new.

The westward movement of Europeans and Indians opened new kinds of roles and demands for settlers and natives. Much new scholarship focuses on these frontier actors. In Chapter 1, Colin G. Calloway surveys the way all American societies had changed and adapted by the end of the colonial period. The article by James H. Merrell in Chapter 13 examines processes of adaptation through the career of Andrew Montour and other culture brokers like him in eighteenth-century western Pennsylvania. Warren R. Hofstra's essay in Chapter 12 looks at the threat of frontier warfare perceived by settlers and officials and the kinds of imperial policies that were created to deal with it.

Much of the new scholarship looks at the presence and activities of people from all over the Old World. In Chapter 6, essays by Ramón A. Gutiérrez and David J. Weber focus on New Mexico and the relationship between Pueblo Indians and Spanish imperial and religious leaders—a relationship destroyed during the Pueblo Revolt of 1680. Several new essays examine aspects of large-scale immigration. In Chapter 1, Nicholas P. Canny looks broadly at the reasons for emigration throughout the colonial period. Others illuminate the issues by focusing on particular waves of immigration. James Horn's essay in Chapter 3 discusses the development of tobacco in Virginia and the interaction between economic success and large-scale immigration from England in the seventeenth century. Marianne Wokeck's essay in Chapter 7 focuses on eighteenth-century German immigration and the various ways migrants were recruited, channeled, and financed.

New work also emphasizes that forced migrants from Africa, despite their enslavement, responded creatively to their changed contexts. In Chapter 10, Ira Berlin's new essay examining the varieties within the experience of American slaves joins Philip D. Morgan's article from the first edition; together they give a more rounded understanding of slavery as it developed in the colonial period. Jack P. Greene's new essay in Chapter 8 examines the ways in which the Caribbean slavery experience shaped the development of the lower South. Greene's essay is paired with a new essay by Karen Ordahl Kupperman on England's dreams for rich colonies in the Caribbean and the thinking on which colonial planning was based. In Chapter 9, the institution of slavery in the lower South during a later period is the topic of Alan Gallay's essay from the first edition.

This edition of *Major Problems in American Colonial History* also presents new work in religious history. In Chapter 4, Mark A. Peterson examines the old idea that Puritanism and economic endeavor were basically incompatible and that economic success spelled the decline of piety. In Chapter 5, Jane Kamensky presents a new article that is a contribution to the history of women as well as to religious history. This article looks at women accused of witchcraft and the kind of challenge to the standing religious and civil order they represented. In Chapter 11, Timothy D. Hall and Frank Lambert offer challenging new interpretations of the Great Awakening and the experience of Americans who responded to it.

Finally, this editon presents scholarship on the issues of empire. Essays in Chapter 12 by Alison M. Olson and Warren R. Hofstra offer insight into transatlantic communication and influence, and discuss how governments on both sides of the Atlantic responded to challenges. Chapter 14 offers new essays by T. H. Breen and John M. Murrin, both giving analyses of the formation of American identity in the middle of the eighteenth century and the ways in which American colonists experienced European products, culture, and demands.

*Major Problems in American Colonial History,* by bringing together work by scholars who seek to integrate previously neglected topics and regions, as well as by historians who have pursued more traditional themes, seeks to contribute to the creation of a more representative and coherent field. Like other volumes in the series, it offers teachers and students a combination of scholarly essays and primary sources. Most of the essays are recent publications that explore the issues and problems engaging the present generation of scholars and teachers. Noteworthy for their clarity, these recent essays relate their themes to the established concerns of colonial historians and offer bridges between new and old approaches.

The primary sources presented here develop or illustrate the themes of the essays and allow students to read firsthand colonial men's and women's own descriptions of their experiences and motivations. Sources include the letters and reports of ordinary men and women from all groups and regions as well as of colonial leaders, plus oral traditions, sermons, court records, government documents, newspaper accounts, and travel guides. The diversity and abundance of first-person testimony that survives is the best evidence of the importance of America in European eyes. Even though the colonial period is the farthest from the modern classroom in time, the experiences of men, women, and children caught up in an unprecedented undertaking for which no reliable cultural road maps existed takes on a sense of immediacy when students confront the actors speaking for themselves. (In cases where archaic spelling makes primary texts unapproachable, the spelling has been modernized.) Chapter introductions and document and essay headnotes set the topics in historical perspective and identify key questions and approaches. Bibliographies at the end of each chapter suggest readings for further exploration.

Work on the table of contents for this second edition began while I was the Times Mirror Foundation Distinguished Fellow at the Huntington Library. My interaction with the outstanding scholars attracted to this library gave me important perspectives on the way the field is developing, and their generosity is deeply appreciated. Many colleagues have helped shape this edition, especially in offering the fruits of their experience in using the first edition. I would like to thank the following reviewers who gave me helpful comments on revising the table of contents: Robert A. Becker, Louisiana State University; Jonathan M. Chu, University of Massachusetts, Boston; Matthew Dennis, University of Oregon; Timothy Hall, Central Michigan University; Richard Johnson, University of Washington; Gloria

Main, University of Colorado, Boulder; Debra Myers, Long Island University; June Namias, University of Alaska, Anchorage; Edwin J. Perkins, University of Southern California; John E. Selby, College of William and Mary; Rebecca S. Shoemaker, Indiana State University; and J. Russell Snapp, Davidson College. I would also like to thank all the people who helped me on the first edition: Robert A. Becker, Richard L. Haan, Dan M. Hockman, Gregory H. Nobles, Alan Rogers, Rebecca S. Shoemaker, and Rosemarie Zagarri. My research assistants, Michael LaCombe and Joel Budd, have given me invaluable help in locating sources and in preparing the manuscript. Joel Kupperman read and discussed many essays, helping me consider their suitability for an undergraduate audience. I have very much enjoyed working with Frances Gay, Senior Associate Editor in History at Houghton Mifflin, and have appreciated the shaping influence of Thomas G. Paterson, the Series Editor, and Jean Woy, Editor-in-Chief, History and Political Science, at Houghton Mifflin.

K. O. K.

# CHAPTER
## 1

# The Meaning
# of the American Experiment

Almost five centuries have passed since the first voyage of Christopher Columbus across the Atlantic, and the revelation to both hemispheres of unknown lands and peoples. European statesmen, merchants, and scholars, spurred on by the Renaissance quest for knowledge and aided by the newly invented printing press, eagerly sought information about the new-found lands across the sea. Those who traveled to America were urged by their friends and sponsors to write about what they saw. Thus we have accounts from people of all levels from common seamen to highly trained scholars as they all tried to fit the lands and peoples they saw into some framework that made sense.

Europeans pushed out from their ports in an enthusiasm for trade that took in the whole world. All kinds of new opportunities presented themselves. New merchant communities brought luxury goods and hastened a revolution in standards of living in Europe. Ordinary people found opportunities for advancement denied them in their former homes, and hundreds of thousands emigrated to America. Many—especially single young men and some young women—came voluntarily in search of opportunities. Others came in family groups partly for economic betterment and partly with the goal of living according to their own lights in communities of like-minded people. Of these voluntary migrants, some experienced failure and early death while others found the secure footing they sought. Success in these cases usually meant being able to worship and work as they chose and to pass a modest economic base, usually a farm, on to their children.

Many thousands of others came involuntarily and had no choice about their destination or their fate after arrival. Some of these were Europeans from the bottom of the society, the "scum" as some writers called them, and some of these achieved the same success as many voluntary migrants. However, the majority of those who arrived involuntarily were Africans who were forced into slavery in a system that was doubly alien to them. After the first few decades, these had no hope of any advance in their position, as they were slaves for life, and the only legacy they could pass on to their children and grandchildren was enslavement.

Old World migrants to America intruded on native societies that were highly developed and whose relationship to the environment was sophisticated. Settlers

1

*became pupils of their Indian neighbors and learned slowly and painfully how to grow American crops and how to negotiate the American landscape. While we are accustomed to think of powerful and technologically advanced Europeans overwhelming American Indian cultures, the reality was more complicated. The devastating impact of Old World diseases did more to undermine native societies than European technology, and made ruthless Old World styles of warfare even more destructive.*

*Indian societies did not disappear. Rather, they adapted, and often the price they paid for survival was very high. The Europeans and Africans who came to America also adapted. None of their societies was merely a replica of the cultures from which they came. The experience of America was transforming for all participants, and even the Old World was changed by it in ways that participants may have only dimly realized.*

 E S S A Y S

Traditionally historians have treated the events discussed here as the "discovery of the New World" by Europeans, implying passivity on the part of the American natives. The older view has implicitly seen the flow of culture as one-way, east to west, and has assumed that the main story is the European conquest. More recently historians have begun to emphasize that the confrontation was nothing less than a collision of biospheres, a bringing together of plants and animals from two formerly isolated worlds with enormous and entirely unforeseen consequences. This was an event that can occur only once in the history of our planet. Though the participants were only dimly aware of the great drama in which they played roles, the documents they left provide evidence for environmental historians such as Alfred Crosby of the University of Texas to reshape our understanding of its consequences. He does so in the first essay.

In the second essay, Nicholas Canny of the National University of Ireland, Galway, assesses the overall nature of European immigration to America in the colonial period and demonstrates that it extended and broadened a pattern of movement within Europe that proceeded alongside colonization of America. In the third essay, Colin Calloway of Dartmouth College stands on the western shore of the Atlantic and views the newcomers and their impact from that vantage point. He looks at the mixing of people from all over the Old World and their interaction with American Indian societies, and assesses both the ingredients in that mixing and the nature of the cultures and societies that resulted.

## Colonization as a "Swarming"

### ALFRED CROSBY

None of the major genetic groupings of humankind is as oddly distributed about the world as European, especially western European, whites. Almost all the peoples we call Mongoloids live in the single contiguous land mass of Asia. Black Africans are

Alfred W. Crosby, "Ecological Imperialism: The Overseas Migration of Western Europeans as a Biological Phenomenon," *The Texas Quarterly,* 21(1978), 103–117. Reprinted with permission of Alfred W. Crosby.

divided between three continents—their homeland and North and South America—but most of them are concentrated in their original latitudes, the tropics, facing each other across one ocean. European whites were all recently concentrated in Europe, but in the last few centuries have burst out, as energetically as if from a burning building, and have created vast settlements of their kind in the South Temperate Zone and North Temperate Zone (excepting Asia, a continent already thoroughly and irreversibly tenanted). In Canada and the United States together they amount to nearly 90 percent of the population; in Argentina and Uruguay together to over 95 percent; in Australia to 98 percent; and in New Zealand to 90 percent. The only nations in the Temperate Zones outside of Asia which do not have enormous majorities of European whites are Chile, with a population of two-thirds mixed Spanish and Indian stock, and South Africa, where blacks outnumber whites six to one. How odd that these two, so many thousands of miles from Europe, should be exceptions in *not* being predominantly pure European.

Europeans have conquered Canada, the United States, Argentina, Uruguay, Australia, and New Zealand not just militarily and economically and technologically—as they did India, Nigeria, Mexico, Peru, and other tropical lands, whose native people have long since expelled or interbred with and even absorbed the invades. In the Temperate Zone lands listed above Europeans conquered and triumphed demographically. These, for the sake of convenience, we will call the Lands of the Demographic Takeover.

There is a long tradition of emphasizing the contrasts between Europeans and Americans—a tradition honored by such names as Henry James and Frederick Jackson Turner—but the vital question is really why Americans are so European. And why the Argentinians, the Uruguayans, the Australians, and the New Zealanders are so European in the obvious genetic sense.

The reasons for the relative failure of the European demographic takeover in the tropics are clear. In tropical Africa, until recently, Europeans died in droves of the fevers: in tropical America they died almost as fast of the same diseases, plus a few native American additions. Furthermore, in neither region did European agricultural techniques, crops, and animals prosper. Europeans did try to found colonies for settlement, rather than merely exploitation, but they failed or achieved only partial success in the hot lands. The Scots left their bones as monument to their short-lived colony at Darien at the turn of the eighteenth century. The English Puritans who skipped Massachusetts Bay Colony to go to Providence Island in the Caribbean Sea did not even achieve a permanent settlement, much less a Commonwealth of God. The Portuguese who went to northeastern Brazil created viable settlements, but only by perching themselves on top of first a population of native Indian laborers and then, when these faded away, a population of laborers imported from Africa. They did achieve a demographic takeover, but only by interbreeding with their servants. The Portuguese in Angola, who helped supply those servants, never had a breath of a chance to achieve a demographic takeover. There was much to repel and little to attract the mass of Europeans to the tropics, and so they stayed home or went to the lands where life was healthier, labor more rewarding, and where white immigrants, by their very number, encouraged more immigration.

In the cooler lands, the colonies of the Demographic Takeover, Europeans achieved very rapid population growth by means of immigration, by increased life span, and by maintaining very high birthrates. Rarely has population expanded more rapidly than it did in the eighteenth and nineteenth centuries in these lands. It is these lands, especially the United States, that enabled Europeans and their overseas offspring to expand from something like 18 percent of the human species in 1650 to well over 30 percent in 1900. Today 670 million Europeans live in Europe, and 250 million or so other Europeans—genetically as European as any left behind in the Old World—live in the Lands of the Demographic Takeover, an ocean or so from home. What the Europeans have done with unprecedented success in the past few centuries can accurately be described by a term from apiculture: They have swarmed.

They swarmed to lands which were populated at the time of European arrival by peoples as physically capable of rapid increase as the Europeans, and yet who are now small minorities in their homelands and sometimes no more than relict populations. These population explosions among colonial Europeans of the past few centuries coincided with population crashes among the aborigines. If overseas Europeans have historically been less fatalistic and grim than their relatives in Europe, it is because they have viewed the histories of their nations very selectively. When he returned from his world voyage on the *Beagle* in the 1830s, Charles Darwin, as a biologist rather than a historian, wrote, "Wherever the European has trod, death seems to pursue the aboriginal."

Any respectable theory which attempts to explain the Europeans' demographic triumphs has to provide explanations for at least two phenomena. The first is the decimation and demoralization of the aboriginal populations of Canada, the United States, Argentina, and others. The obliterating defeat of these populations was not simply due to European technological superiority. The Europeans who settled in temperate South Africa seemingly had the same advantages as those who settled in Virginia and New South Wales, and yet how different was their fate. The Bantu-speaking peoples, who now overwhelmingly outnumber the whites in South Africa, were superior to their American, Australian, and New Zealand counterparts in that they possessed iron weapons, but how much more inferior to a musket or a rifle is a stone-pointed spear than an iron-pointed spear? The Bantu have prospered demographically not because of their numbers at the time of first contact with whites, which were probably not greater per square mile than those of the Indians east of the Mississippi River. Rather, the Bantu have prospered because they survived military conquest, avoided the conquerors, or became their indispensable servants—and in the long run because they reproduced faster than the whites. In contrast, why did so few of the natives of the Lands of the Demographic Takeover survive?

Second, we must explain the stunning, even awesome success of European agriculture, that is, the European way of manipulating the environment in the Lands of the Demographic Takeover. The difficult progress of the European frontier in the Siberian *taiga* or the Brazilian *sertão* or the South African *veldt* contrasts sharply with its easy, almost fluid advance in North America. Of course, the pioneers of North America would never have characterized their progress as easy: Their lives were filled with danger, deprivation, and unremitting labor: but as a group they always succeeded in taming whatever portion of North America they wanted within a few decades and usually a good deal less time. Many individuals among them failed—they were driven mad by blizzards and dust storms, lost their crops to locusts and their flocks to cougars and wolves, or lost their scalps to understandably inhospitable Indians—but as a group they always succeeded—and in terms of human generations, very quickly.

In attempting to explain these two phenomena, let us examine four categories of organisms deeply involved in European expansion: (1) human beings; (2) animals closely associated with human beings—both the desirable animals like horses and cattle and undesirable varmints like rats and mice; (3) pathogens or microorganisms that cause disease in humans; and (4) weeds. Is there a pattern in the histories of these groups which suggests an overall explanation for the phenomenon of the Demographic Takeover or which at least suggests fresh paths of inquiry?

Europe has exported something in excess of sixty million people in the past few hundred years. Great Britain alone exported over twenty million. The great mass of these white emigrants went to the United States, Argentina, Canada, Australia, Uruguay, and New Zealand. (Other areas to absorb comparable quantities of Europeans were Brazil and Russia east of the Urals. These would qualify as Lands of the Demographic Takeover except that large fractions of their populations are non-European.)

In stark contrast, very few aborigines of the Americas, Australia, or New Zealand ever went to Europe. Those who did often died not long after arrival. The fact that the flow of human migration was almost entirely from Europe to her colonies and not vice versa is not startling—or very enlightening. Europeans controlled overseas migration, and Europe needed to export, not import, labor. But this pattern of one-way migration is significant in that it reappears in other connections.

The vast expanses of forests, savannas, and steppes in the Lands of the Demographic Takeover were inundated by animals from the Old World, chiefly from Europe. Horses, cattle, sheep, goats, and pigs have for hundreds of years been among the most numerous of the quadrupeds of these lands, which were completely lacking in these species at the time of first contact with the Europeans. By 1600 enormous feral herds of horses and cattle surged over the pampas of the Río de la Plata (today's Argentina and Uruguay) and over the plains of northern Mexico. By the beginning of the seventeenth century packs of Old World dogs gone wild were among the predators of these herds.

In the forested country of British North America population explosions among imported animals were also spectacular, but only by European standards, not by those of Spanish America. In 1700 in Virginia feral hogs, said one witness, "swarm like vermaine upon the Earth," and young gentlemen were entertaining themselves by hunting wild horses of the inland counties. In Carolina the herds of cattle were "incredible, being from one to two thousand head in one Man's Possession." In the eighteenth and early nineteenth centuries the advancing European frontier from New England to the Gulf of Mexico was preceded into Indian territory by an avant-garde of semiwild herds of hogs and cattle tended, now and again, by semiwild herdsmen, white and black.

The first English settlers landed in Botany Bay, Australia, in January of 1788 with livestock, most of it from the Cape of Good Hope. The pigs and poultry thrived; the cattle did well enough; the sheep, the future source of the colony's good fortune, died fast. Within a few months two bulls and four cows strayed away. By

1804 the wild herds they founded numbered from three to five thousand head and were in possession of much of the best land between the settlements and the Blue Mountains. If they had ever found their way through the mountains to the grass-lands beyond, the history of Australia in the first decades of the nineteenth century might have been one dominated by cattle rather than sheep. As it is, the colonial government wanted the land the wild bulls so ferociously defended, and considered the growing practice of convicts running away to live off the herds as a threat to the whole colony; so the adult cattle were shot and salted down and the calves captured and tamed. The English settlers imported wooly sheep from Europe and sought out the interior pastures for them. The animals multiplied rapidly, and when Darwin made his visit to New South Wales in 1836, there were about a million sheep there for him to see.

The arrival of Old World livestock probably affected New Zealand more radi-cally than any other of the Lands of the Demographic Takeover. Cattle, horses, goats, pigs and—in this land of few or no large predators—even the usually timid sheep went wild. In New Zealand herds of feral farm animals were practicing the ways of their remote ancestors as late as the 1940s and no doubt still run free. Most of the sheep, though, stayed under human control, and within a decade of Great Britain's annexation of New Zealand in 1840, her new acquisition was home to a quarter million sheep. In 1974 New Zealand had over fifty-five million sheep, about twenty times more sheep than people.

In the Lands of the Demographic Takeover the European pioneers were accom-panied and often preceded by their domesticated animals, walking sources of food, leather, fiber, power, and wealth, and these animals often adapted more rapidly to the new surroundings and reproduced much more rapidly than their masters. To a certain extent, the success of Europeans as colonists was automatic as soon as they put their tough, fast, fertile, and intelligent animals ashore. The latter were sources of capital that sought out their own sustenance, improvised their own protection against the weather, fought their own battles against predators and, if their masters were smart enough to allow calves, colts, and lambs to accumulate, could and often did show the world the amazing possibilities of compound interest.

The honey bee is the one insect of worldwide importance which human beings have domesticated, if we may use the word in a broad sense. Many species of bees and other insects produce honey, but the one which does so in greatest quantity and which is easiest to control is a native of the Mediterranean area and the Middle East, the honey bee (*Apis mellifera*). The European has probably taken this sweet and short-tempered servant to every colony he ever established, from Arctic to Antarctic Circle, and the honey bee has always been one of the first immigrants to set off on its own. Sometimes the advance of the bee frontier could be very rapid: The first hive in Tasmania swarmed sixteen times in the summer of 1832.

Thomas Jefferson tells us that the Indians of North America called the honey bees "English flies," and St. John de Crèvecoeur, his contemporary, wrote that "The Indians look upon them with an evil eye, and consider their progress into the inte-rior of the continent as an omen of the white man's approach: thus, as they discover the bees, the news of the event, passing from mouth to mouth, spreads sadness and consternation on all sides."

Domesticated creatures that traveled from the Lands of the Demographic Takeover to Europe are few. Australian aborigines and New Zealand Maoris had a few tame dogs, unimpressive by Old World standards and unwanted by the whites. Europe happily accepted the American Indians' turkeys and guinea pigs, but had no need for their dogs, llamas, and alpacas. Again the explanation is simple: Europeans, who controlled the passage of large animals across the oceans, had no need to reverse the process.

It is interesting and perhaps significant, though, that the exchange was just as one-sided for varmints, the small mammals whose migrations Europeans often tried to stop. None of the American or Australian or New Zealand equivalents of rats have become established in Europe, but Old World varmints, especially rats, have colonized right alongside the Europeans in the Temperate Zones. Rats of assorted sizes, some of them almost surely European immigrants, were tormenting Spanish Americans by at least the end of the sixteenth century. European rats established a beachhead in Jamestown, Virginia, as early as 1609, when they almost starved out the colonists by eating their food stores. In Buenos Aires the increase in rats kept pace with that of cattle, according to an early nineteenth-century witness. European rats proved as aggressive as the Europeans in New Zealand, where they completely replaced the local rats in the North Islands as early as the 1840s. Those poor creatures are probably completely extinct today or exist only in tiny relict populations.

The European rabbits are not usually thought of as varmints, but where there are neither diseases nor predators to hold down their numbers they can become the worst of pests. In 1859 a few members of the species *Orytolagus cuniculus* (the scientific name for the protagonists of all the Peter Rabbits of literature) were released in southeast Australia. Despite massive efforts to stop them, they reproduced—true to their reputation—and spread rapidly all the way across Australia's southern half to the Indian Ocean. In 1950 the rabbit population of Australia was estimated at 500 million, and they were outcompeting the nation's most important domesticated animals, sheep, for the grasses and herbs. They have been brought under control, but only by means of artificially fomenting an epidemic of myxomatosis, a lethal American rabbit disease. The story of rabbits and myxomatosis in New Zealand is similar.

Europe, in return for her varmints, has received muskrats and gray squirrels and little else from America, and nothing at all of significance from Australia or New Zealand, and we might well wonder if muskrats and squirrels really qualify as varmints. As with other classes of organisms, the exchange has been a one-way street.

None of Europe's emigrants were as immediately and colossally successful as its pathogens, the microorganisms that make human beings ill, cripple them, and kill them. Whenever and wherever Europeans crossed the oceans and settled, the pathogens they carried created prodigious epidemics of smallpox, measles, tuberculosis, influenza, and a number of other diseases. It was this factor, more than any other, that Darwin had in mind as he wrote of the Europeans' deadly tread.

The pathogens transmitted by the Europeans, unlike the Europeans themselves or most of their domesticated animals, did at least as well in the tropics as in the temperate Lands of the Demographic Takeover. Epidemics devastated Mexico, Peru, Brazil, Hawaii, and Tahiti soon after the Europeans made the first contact with aboriginal populations. Some of these populations were able to escape demographic defeat because their initial numbers were so large that a small fraction was still sufficient to maintain occupation of, if not title to, the land, and also because the mass of Europeans were never attracted to the tropical lands, not even if they were partially vacated. In the Lands of the Demographic Takeover the aboriginal populations were too sparse to rebound from the onslaught of disease or were inundated by European immigrants before they could recover.

The First Strike Force of the white immigrants to the Lands of the Demographic Takeover were epidemics. A few examples from scores of possible examples follow. Smallpox first arrived in the Río de la Plata region in 1558 or 1560 and killed, according to one chronicler possibly more interested in effect than accuracy, "more than a hundred thousand Indians" of the heavy riverine population there. An epidemic of plague or typhus decimated the Indians of the New England coast immediately before the founding of Plymouth. Smallpox or something similar struck the aborigines of Australia's Botany Bay in 1789, killed half, and rolled on into the interior. Some unidentified disease or diseases spread through the Maori tribes of the North Island of New Zealand in the 1790s, killing so many in a number of villages that the survivors were not able to bury the dead. After a series of such lethal and rapidly moving epidemics, then came the slow, unspectacular but thorough cripplers and killers like venereal disease and tuberculosis. In conjunction with the large numbers of white settlers these diseases were enough to smother aboriginal chances of recovery. First the blitzkrieg, then the mopping up.

The greatest of the killers in these lands was probably smallpox. The exception is New Zealand, the last of these lands to attract permanent European settlers. They came to New Zealand after the spread of vaccination in Europe, and so were poor carriers. As of the 1850s smallpox still had not come ashore, and by that time two-thirds of the Maori had been vaccinated. The tardy arrival of smallpox in these islands may have much to do with the fact that the Maori today comprise a larger percentage (9 percent) of their country's population than that of any other aboriginal people in any European colony or former European colony in either Temperate Zone, save only South Africa.

American Indians bore the full brunt of smallpox, and its mark is on their history and folklore. The Kiowa of the southern plains of the United States have a legend in which a Kiowa man meets Smallpox on the plain, riding a horse. The man asks, "Where do you come from and what do you do and why are you here?" Smallpox answers, "I am one with the white men—they are my people as the Kiowas are yours. Sometimes I travel ahead of them and sometimes behind. But I am always their companion and you will find me in their camps and their houses." "What can you do?" the Kiowa asks. "I bring death," Smallpox replies. "My breath causes children to wither like young plants in spring snow. I bring destruction. No matter how beautiful a woman is, once she has looked at me she becomes as ugly as death. And to men I bring not death alone, but the destruction of their children and the blighting of their wives. The strongest of warriors go down before me. No people who have looked on me will ever be the same."

In return for the barrage of diseases that Europeans directed overseas, they received little in return. Australia and New Zealand provided no new strains of pathogens to Europe—or none that attracted attention. And of America's native diseases none had any real influence on the Old World—with the likely exception of venereal syphilis, which almost certainly existed in the New World before 1492 and probably did not occur in its present form in the Old World.

Weeds are rarely history makers, for they are not as spectacular in their effects as pathogens. But they, too, influence our lives and migrate over the world despite human wishes. As such, like varmints and germs, they are better indicators of certain realities than human beings or domesticated animals.

The term "weed" in modern botanical usage refers to any type of plant which—because of especially large numbers of seeds produced per plant, or especially effective means of distributing those seeds, or especially tough roots and rhizomes from which new plants can grow, or especially tough seeds that survive the alimentary canals of animals to be planted with their droppings—spreads rapidly and outcompetes others on disturbed, bare soil. Weeds are plants that tempt the botanist to use such anthropomorphic words as "aggressive" and "opportunistic."

Many of the most successful weeds in the well-watered regions of the Lands of the Demographic Takeover are of European or Eurasian origin. French and Dutch and English farmers brought with them to North America their worst enemies, weeds, "to exhaust the land, hinder and damnify the Crop." By the last third of the seventeenth century at least twenty different types were widespread enough in New England to attract the attention of the English visitor, John Josselyn, who identified couch grass, dandelion, nettles, mallowes, knot grass, shepherd's purse, sow thistle, and clot burr and others. One of the most aggressive was plantain, which the Indians called "English-Man's Foot."

European weeds rolled west with the pioneers, in some cases spreading almost explosively. As of 1823 corn chamomile and maywood had spread up to but not across the Muskingum River in Ohio. Eight years later they were over the river. The most prodigiously imperialistic of the weeds in the eastern half of the United States and Canada were probably Kentucky bluegrass and white clover. They spread so fast after the entrance of Europeans into a given area that there is some suspicion that they may have been present in pre-Colombian America, although the earliest European accounts do not mention them. Probably brought to the Appalachian area by the French, these two kinds of weeds preceded the English settlers there and kept up with the movement westward until reaching the plains across the Mississippi.

Old World plants set up business on their own on the Pacific coast of North America just as soon as the Spaniards and Russians did. The climate of coastal southern California is much the same as that of the Mediterranean, and the Spaniards who came to California in the eighteenth century brought their own Mediterranean weeds with them via Mexico: wild oats, fennel, wild radishes. These plants, plus those brought in later by the Forty-niners, muscled their way to dominance in the coastal grasslands. These immigrant weeds followed Old World horses, cattle, and sheep into California's interior prairies and took over there as well.

The region of Argentina and Uruguay was almost as radically altered in its flora as in its fauna by the coming of the Europeans. The ancient Indian practice, taken up immediately by the whites, of burning off the old grass of the pampa every year, as well as the trampling and cropping to the ground of indigenous grasses and forbs by the thousands of imported quadrupeds who also changed the nature of the soil with their droppings, opened the whole countryside to European plants. In the

1780s Félix de Azara observed that the pampa, already radically altered, was chang-ing as he watched. European weeds sprang up around every cabin, grew up along roads, and pressed into the open steppe. Today only a quarter of the plants growing wild in the pampa are native, and in the well-watered eastern portions, the "natural" ground cover consists almost entirely of Old World grasses and clovers.

The invaders were not, of course, always desirable. When Darwin visited Uruguay in 1832, he found large expanses, perhaps as much as hundreds of square miles, monopolized by the immigrant wild artichoke and transformed into a prickly wilderness fit neither for man nor his animals.

The onslaught of foreign and specifically European plants on Australia began abruptly in 1778 because the first expedition that sailed from Britain to Botany Bay carried some livestock and considerable quantities of seed. By May of 1803 over two hundred foreign plants, most of them European, had been purposely introduced and planted in New South Wales, undoubtedly along with a number of weeds. Even today so-called clean seed characteristically contains some weed seeds, and this was much more so two hundred years ago. By and large, Australia's north has been too tropical and her interior too hot and dry for European weeds and grasses, but much of her southern coasts and Tasmania have been hospitable indeed to Europe's willful flora.

Thus, many—often a majority—of the most aggressive plants in the temperate humid regions of North America, South America, Australia, and New Zealand are of European origin. It may be true that in every broad expanse of the world today where there are dense populations, with whites in the majority, there are also dense populations of European weeds. Thirty-five of eighty-nine weeds listed in 1953 as common in the state of New York are European. Approximately 60 percent of Canada's worst weeds are introductions from Europe. Most of New Zealand's weeds are from the same source, as are many, perhaps most, of the weeds of south-ern Australia's well-watered coasts. Most of the European plants that Josselyn listed as naturalized in New England in the seventeenth century are growing wild today in Argentina and Uruguay, and are among the most widespread and troublesome of all weeds in those countries.

In return for this largesse of pestiferous plants, the Lands of the Demographic Takeover have provided Europe with only a few equivalents. The Canadian water weed jammed Britain's nineteenth-century waterways, and North America's horse-weed and burnweed have spread in Europe's empty lots, and South America's flow-ered galinsoga has thrived in her gardens. But the migratory flow of a whole group of organisms between Europe and the Lands of the Demographic Takeover has been almost entirely in one direction. Englishman's foot still marches in seven league jackboots across every European colony of settlement, but very few Ameri-can or Australian or New Zealand invaders stride the waste lands and unkempt backyards of Europe.

European and Old World human beings, domesticated animals, varmints, pathogens, and weeds all accomplished demographic takeovers of their own in the temperate, well-watered regions of North and South America, Australia, and New Zealand. They crossed oceans and Europeanized vast territories, often in informal cooperation with each other—the farmer and his animals destroying native plant cover, making way for imported grasses and forbs, many of which proved more nourishing to domesticated animals than the native equivalents: Old World pathogens, sometimes carried by Old World varmints, wiping out vast numbers of aborigines, opening the way for the advance of the European frontier, exposing more and more native peoples to more and more pathogens. The classic example of symbiosis between European colonists, their animals, and plants comes from New Zealand. Red clover, a good forage for sheep, could not seed itself and did not spread without being annually sown until the Europeans imported the bumblebee. Then the plant and insect spread widely, the first providing the second with food, the second carrying pollen from blossom to blossom for the first, and the sheep eating the clover and compensating the human beings for their effort with mutton and wool.

There have been few such stories of the success in Europe of organisms from the Lands of the Demographic Takeover, despite the obvious fact that for every ship that went from Europe to those lands, another traveled in the opposite direction.

The demographic triumph of Europeans in the temperate colonies is one part of a biological and ecological takeover which could not have been accomplished by human beings alone, gunpowder notwithstanding. We must at least try to analyze the impact and success of all the immigrant organisms together—the European portmanteau of often mutually supportive plants, animals, and microlife which in its entirety can be accurately described as aggressive and opportunistic, an ecosystem simplified by ocean crossings and honed by thousands of years of competition in the unique environment created by the Old World Neolithic Revolution.

The human invaders and their descendants have consulted their egos, rather than ecologists, for explanations of their triumphs. But the human victims, the aborigines of the Lands of the Demographic Takeover, knew better, knew they were only one of many species being displaced and replaced; knew they were victims of something more irresistible and awesome than the spread of capitalism or Christianity. One Maori, at the nadir of the history of his race, knew these things when he said, "As the clover killed off the fern, and the European dog the Maori dog—as the Maori rat was destroyed by the Pakeha (European) rat—so our people, also, will be gradually supplanted and exterminated by the Europeans." The future was not quite so grim as he prophesied, but we must admire his grasp of the complexity and magnitude of the threat looming over his people and over the ecosystem of which they were part.

## In Search of a Better Home?

NICHOLAS P. CANNY

One of the more piquant entries in the records of the General Court of Colonial Virginia is that concerning the case of Thomas Hall who claimed to be both man and woman. The issue came to court because Hall had taken to wearing women's clothing when in search of sexual adventure, and because he had denied the findings of a series of self-appointed physical inspectors who had pronounced that he was "a perfect man". The court ordered a further examination of his privates, and satisfied

Nicholas Canny, "In Search of a Better Home? European Overseas Migration, 1500–1800," in Nicholas Canny, ed., *Europeans on the Move: Studies on European Migration, 1500–1800* (Oxford: Oxford University Press, 1994), 263–283.

itself that Hall had the physical attributes of a man. However, in the face of Hall's insistence that he also possessed female sexual organs and did not have "the use of the man's part", it was decreed by the court that Hall was both man and woman, and that he should thereafter go dressed in man's apparel, "only his head to be attired in a coyfe and croscloth with an apron before him". This case, which may warrant the attention of historians of sexuality, is of relevance to our present purpose because the details provided by Hall of his career, prior to the court hearing of 1629, gives us an insight into the extent to which regular geographic movement in search of employment was the dominating feature of the lives of those who became servants in seventeenth-century Virginia.

In his testimony Hall stated that he had been born in Newcastle upon Tyne, had been christened Thomasine, and had been dressed in "women's apparell" until the age of twelve. Then he was sent to London, where he lived with an aunt until "Cales accon", by which we can take him to have meant one of the three expeditions to La Rochelle mounted by the English between 1625 and 1627. On that occasion Hall's brother was conscripted into the navy, and our hero or heroine, wishing to join the fray, cut his hair, assumed men's clothing, "and went over as a soldier in the Isle of Ree being in the habit of a man". On his return from the front, Hall disembarked at Plymouth, where he again dressed himself in woman's attire, took up a woman's employment, "and made bone lace and did other work with his needle". "Shortly after" he perceived new opportunity in a ship which was bound from Plymouth to Virginia, so he changed "into the habit of a man", and enlisted as a servant for the colony. There he appears to have changed his employer as frequently as he did his attire, until the court order of 1629 required that he remain attached to one place and "give sureties for good behaviour from one quarter court to another".

Hall's mobility, which we can detail because of the testimony which he gave in court, was remarkable but not exceptional, as is clear from recent published work on the spatial mobility of England's poor during the early modern centuries. What is most significant is that his restlessness long pre-dated his voyage to America; it also emerges from his account that his ultimate journey to Virginia took place only because of the chance arrival at Plymouth of a ship bound for America. It is also clear from Hall's statement that his every move was explained by his quest for work; and it appears that his occasional switches between male and female attire, at least while he was in Europe, were an expedient to procure profitable employment. Perhaps it was only his arrival in the overwhelmingly male settler community in Virginia which suggested to Hall that sexual adventure, as well as economic advantage, could be gained by his assuming the appearance of a woman.

While few of the surviving records concerning European ventures overseas are as colourful as that which relates to Thomas Hall, its real significance is that it illustrates the point that the promotion of English settlement in North America served principally to broaden the range of destinations open to those who were already extremely mobile in search of employment. What these possibilities were in the seventeenth century emerges clearly from another document, this time the will of Mascall Giles, a clergyman from Wartling, Sussex. Giles made provision for three children in his will: a son Edward, a daughter Mercy, and a son Samuel. Mercy appears to have been his favourite child, and seemed destined to remain in England with a legacy of £60, which was to become hers either on her twenty-first birthday or on the day of her marriage. The son Edward was the least favoured, and was awarded "5*s* and no more, unless he is transported into New England, Virginia or the Barbados to serve a master for a term of years", after which term of service he would receive a further £3. The other son, Samuel, was given title to the £50 which the Reverend Giles had "adventured on the service of Ireland", presumably the Cromwellian settlement, on condition that "he goes over and lives there, and gives his sister Mercy the property called Sparthan in Ditchling".

Opportunities such as these were to alter and extend geographically over the next two centuries, but all Englishmen who, like the Reverend Giles, were concerned to find a niche for their children during those two centuries, could rely on the overseas territories which were then coming under English government control to provide fresh career openings for their sons, if not for their daughters. Similar opportunities were open to the sons of other European colonizing powers of the early modern centuries, and some European groups which ventured overseas, most notably the Spaniards, actually improved their circumstances in a rapid and enduring manner. . . .

All the major colonizing powers (including even France if we take account of the Huguenots who left France, and the foreign nationals who were attracted to service in the French army) were therefore responsible for promoting or triggering large-scale European migrations during the sixteenth, seventeenth, and eighteenth centuries. Some of this was low-risk betterment migration, but most of it was a high-risk subsistence migration. Migration of the first kind usually involved artisans and professionals, who decided to uproot themselves not because they were destitute but because they realized that their talents would fetch better rewards abroad than they would at home. By contrast, migration of the second kind usually involved people with low levels of skill, who resorted to emigration probably because of the meagre conditions and limited opportunities that existed in their home societies. Those involved in betterment emigration, such as the Spanish settlers in New Spain of the sixteenth and seventeenth centuries and the English migrants to the Middle Atlantic colonies of the eighteenth century, usually came from colonizing powers, whereas those associated with subsistence emigration, whether into the armies of the great European powers or to low-lying tropical colonies, usually came from impoverished areas of Europe which were not directly involved with colonization. Such distinctions are not absolute, however, and we find that some of the emigration from England to its colonies and most of that of Portugal can be depicted as subsistence migration. On the other hand, we also find that some eighteenth-century migrants from Scotland and Ireland, two countries associated with subsistence migration, were in fact professionals who quickly becames involved in the promotion of colonial ventures. It would be equally invalid to depict betterment emigration as motivated entirely by pull factors and subsistence migration by push factors. Those professionals and artisans who embarked for foreign destinations where they hoped to better themselves were usually aware that opportunities at home were shrinking for people with their precise skills. To this extent such people could be said to have been pushed to emigrate, although they usually had a fairly clear understanding of what to expect at the other end. Betterment emigrants can certainly be portrayed as reasonably well informed about what lay ahead of them, but those who became subsistence emigrants were not entirely ignorant of their possibilities of success either. Would-be emigrants were always eager for information about the places where they hoped to settle or anxious to learn of the careers that they hoped to pursue. In general, they expected those of their community who had preceded them to provide them with some knowledge of their experiences. The fact that such considerations played a role in helping the poor and destitute to arrive at a decision shows that the pull factor exerted some influence on them too. It should be remembered, however, that the existence of poverty did not always result in emigration, and that dislocations have occurred in European society which have resulted in famine rather than mass emigration. This prompts the conclusion that emigration occurs only where knowledge of better prospects exists, and where transport is in place to convey prospective migrants to their new home. Indeed, the transport factor was so important that it appears from the experience of the early modern centuries that persistent long-distance migration occurred only where it was profitable for merchants to promote it. Here, European exploitation of the resources of America, North and South, was crucial, because the existence of cargo vessels to convey the commodities of America to Europe provided cheap berths for Europeans who wished to travel in the opposite direction.

The two factors—information and transport—are especially important in explaining the decided shifts in mass migration patterns that occurred over time. The Portuguese, as we saw, were especially attracted to Asia and Africa during their earlier phase of colonial endeavour, and apparently had a low opinion of the opportunities which America offered. The balance in Portuguese migration had shifted decidedly in favour of South America by the eighteenth century, because people had become informed of the mining opportunities that existed there and because transport to America was more readily available. Similarly in the case of German Rhineland migration. This was an area that had experienced rapid population increase during the fifteenth and sixteenth centuries, and was persistently troubled by religious turmoil and military invasion during the next two centuries. The initial outlets were the Netherlands, which frequently led to Asia, and the underpopulated areas of eastern Europe, which had been undergoing a process of planned development, linked to German migration, for centuries. Then, suddenly in the eighteenth century, the possibility of emigrating to the Middle Atlantic colonies of North America presented itself, and increasing numbers were willing to gamble on this new prospect and reject the advice of their social leaders. They were ready to do so because the promoters of this venture engaged upon an effective propaganda campaign and because transport was readily available through the ports of the Netherlands. This eighteenth-century migration quickly established its own stock-factor, which made it self-sustaining and which facilitated the great German emigration to North America of the nineteenth century. The pattern of Irish Catholic migration is remarkably similar with a well-established popular movement to continental military service gradually giving way in the eighteenth century to a sizeable emigration to North America. Once more, the shift occurred because people had become aware of the opportunities that North America offered and because cheap shipping was available. Favourable mortality rates in North America ensured that enduring kinship and communal connections between home and migrant communities were quickly established, thereby preparing the way for the mass Irish exodus to North America of the nineteenth century. Such examples could be multiplied: together they make the point that the European encounter with America at the end of the fifteenth century increased the migration opportunities open to Europeans, already a very mobile people, but that American destinations became preferred by European migrants only after it had become clear that they presented better opportunities than existed elsewhere, and after it became feasible to travel to those destinations in large numbers.

It was only for the Spaniards that America became the land of opportunity so soon after first contact with it. For most other migrating peoples in western Europe—Scots, Irish, English, Germans, and Portuguese—America did not present decidedly better prospects than more traditional destinations until some point in the middle of the eighteenth century. Until then, the vast majority of Europeans who left their homelands were bound for destinations either within Europe itself or within the continents of Africa and Asia which had been attracting significant European settlement since at least the eleventh century. This more traditional type of migration greatly expanded, first, because the increased scale of warfare within Europe created more demand for fighting men, and second, because growing European knowledge of the coastal areas of Africa and Asia created new trading opportunities for Europeans which, when exploited, had to be serviced and defended. The vast majority of people who headed for these more traditional destinations seem to have been motivated by the desire to find an acceptable occupation niche which would provide them with some opportunity of improving their circumstances should they return to their country or village of origin. We know, in a way that these migrants did not, that the statistical probability of their realizing their ambitions was very remote; but they knew, in a way that we can hardly appreciate, that their sights would always remain fixed on their place of origin and that it was only there that they could conceive themselves making a permanent home.

Those Europeans of the sixteenth, seventeenth, and even the early eighteenth centuries who struck out for the more speculative prospects that America offered do not appear to have been motivated in a significantly different way from those who migrated across frontiers within Europe or travelled to Africa or Asia. It is true that a significant minority of Spaniards and some English groups crossed the Atlantic in family units, thereby suggesting that their ambition from the outset was to establish a new and better home in America than was possible for them in Europe. Historians who have studied such family migrants, however, find that their eyes too remained firmly fixed on their places of origin, and that some of them returned enriched to Europe to enjoy a social position that had previously been denied them. The fact that the overwhelming majority of Europeans who travelled to America during this long period were young, single, and male suggests that their ambitions would not have been different from the very similar element who found their way into European armies or to trading outposts in Africa and Asia. Those who went to America were also driven by need and by the spirit of adventure, and we can take it that their hope, when they set out from home, was to make their fortune and return. Some, as we know, realized this ambition, while the vast majority failed dismally; yet a third element met with modest success which made it possible for them to get married and establish a home and family albeit in a foreign location rather than their place of origin. This occurred only where the local environment and economy facilitated the establishment of a colony of settlement, and such colonies were rare indeed before the eighteenth century.

Colonies of settlement in the Americas became much more numerous after the mid-eighteenth century, and the ambitions of European migrants began to change accordingly. The emergence of such colonies, which attracted an ever increasing percentage of European migrants to American destinations from the middle of the eighteenth century, is explained partly by the fact that settlers had overcome the environmental hazards that had previously made life so perilous for Europeans, but partly also because the promoters of European colonies had found non-European peoples—American Indian and African, or (in the nineteenth century) Chinese and Indian workers—to undertake the more arduous employments in various American locations. The promoters of European trade and empire in Asia had resort to similar strategems, which goes to prove that European involvement overseas had increasing global consequences. European ventures overseas had been global from the outset, in that Europeans willingly ventured to, and established themselves in, all parts of the world that were accessible to them; but their endeavours assumed a still more global dimension when the deployment of African and Asian labour forces became necessary to the fulfilment of European colonial ambitions.

Such labour deployment, which spelled disaster for the non-Europeans involved, made life in the colonies less taxing for European settlers, and this was immediately reflected in the more even sex ratio among Europeans migrating to American destinations after about 1750. A better sex balance was achieved initially by the inclusion of more family units among the emigrants; but the nineteenth century witnessed the departure from Europe for American destinations of increasing numbers of young single women, although in all cases, except the Irish emigration of the nineteenth century, men remained a distinct majority. This phenomenon is presumably explained by a growing awareness among Europe's poor that they could better improve their circumstances by emigrating permanently to America rather than hankering after some dramatic reversal of their fortunes at home. While an increasing number of emigrants thought in this way, not all were in agreement with them, and many Europeans, throughout the nineteenth century, still engaged on long-distance migration with a view to making their fortune abroad and returning to invest their earnings in their local community. The difference in this respect from the earlier centuries was that a greater number of those who set out with this ambition in mind had the opportunity to realize it. Another aspect of continuity into the nineteenth century was that the inter-continental migration of Europeans was occurring simultaneously with long-distance and seasonal migration within Europe itself. Such migration seems also to have increased in scale during the nineteenth century, and improved transport facilities meant that migratory workers within Europe could travel longer distances within Europe or could even cross the Atlantic on a seasonal itinerary.

Why individuals chose one form of emigration over another must remain speculative, because appraisals of motivation were seldom stated at the moment when emigrants departed from home. Because of such uncertainties, the concern of the essays in this volume has been to establish what can be known with some certainty about the entire phenomenon of European overseas migration, 1500–1800. The questions that have been answered—how many people went? from what countries? of what gender and quality? and to what destinations?—raise another set of questions that have not been addressed. Most of these relate to the consequences for Europe of the loss of population through emigration. In some societies, contemporary observers welcomed the departure of young unemployed adult men, who might otherwise have been a threat to the social order, and, as Louis Cullen has pointed out in relation to Ireland, the emigration of younger sons was sometimes perceived as necessary for the economic survival of their relatives. The departure of young men in their productive years must also have created labour shortages in particular regions, unless those departing were replaced by workers who moved in to take their place. The numbers who left Ireland in the seventeenth century were certainly made good by the settlement there of English and Scots, and those who left the Netherlands for overseas destinations were consistently replaced by migratory workers of various kinds. This still leaves open the question of how Scotland compensated for the loss of so many of its young men in the prime of life, and we are left wondering whether the African slaves who were set to farming in Portugal were as efficient workers as the young Portuguese men who ventured their lives abroad. And even if we ignore the economic consequences for various European societies of the loss of those who must have been their most venturesome, imaginative risk-takers, what about the social consequences? The steady outflow of young men (few of whom ever returned) from a narrow population base must have deprived many young women in Europe of the opportunity to marry, and must have had grave demographic consequences for particular areas within Europe if not for Europe in general. The fact that these questions now come to mind is in itself proof that a collective investigation of Europeans on the move, 1500–1800, was long overdue.

## New Peoples and New Societies

### COLIN G. CALLOWAY

Europeans came to America to create new societies. Their invasions added new peoples to the human landscape. However, the conquest of North America was not a simple process in which Indian peoples were removed and their places taken by European and African immigrants. Europeans might aspire to displace Indians and create societies that were pristine duplicates of Old World societies, but they could not. They occasionally uncovered disturbing evidence that the societies they were trying to destroy were in some respects superior to their own. The mingling and mixing of peoples produced new kinds of people and societies, different from what had existed in North America and in Europe. Many of the new societies were embryonic and did not necessarily survive as permanent communities, but they were part of the landscape of early America. European colonists encountered and constructed new social and physical environments.

Although English colonists often went to great lengths to avoid "miscegenation" and protect their supposed racial purity, they could not prevent the mixing of peoples that occurred throughout North America as Indians, Europeans, and Africans met and intermarried. Surveying the Carolina backcountry in the eighteenth century, for

Colin Calloway, *New Worlds for All: Indians, Europeans, and the Remaking of Early America*, pp. 178–94. © 1997. Johns Hopkins University Press. Reprinted by permission.

example, historical geographer D. W. Meinig found that it was "a loose pattern of ethnic districts," comprising English and Scottish traders, mixed-blood packers and hunters, "remnants and renegades" from half a dozen Indian tribes, various religious sects from northern Europe, and so forth. Slave-holding Carolina brought Indians, Europeans, and Africans into close working relationships that demanded development of new ways of living. "Nor was this vital process simply an encounter among three peoples," writes Meinig. "There were Europeans from several sources, especially England, Ireland, and France, as well as Whites with years of experience in the West Indies, local Indians, Indian slaves from various inland tribes, and Blacks from many parts of Africa, some of whom had spent some seasons or years in the American tropics." Colonial society differentiated these peoples into categories by race, status, occupation, wealth, and privilege, but in daily life they worked closely together in an emerging regional economy. In such conditions, a considerable amount of racial mixing inevitably occurred. On the other edge of the continent, the northwestern Pacific coast sea otter trade attracted English, Yankee, Spanish, and Russian traders and sailors, on ships that sometimes included Africans, Asians, and Sandwich Islanders among their crews. These men met, and often mated with, Chinooks, Nootkas, Bella Coolas, Aleuts, and others, leaving a mixed progeny.

Some people advocated racial intermarriage as a way of alleviating ethnic and cultural conflicts and accelerating a union of Indian and European societies. The French experimented with racial intermixing as an instrument of empire building "in order that . . . they may form only one people and one blood." Puritan minister Cotton Mather referred disparagingly to the war parties that raided New England from Canada in the seventeenth century as composed of "half Frenchified Indians and half Indianized French." Even in Anglo-America, there were proponents of "miscegenation." English traveler John Lawson recommended coexistence and intermarriage as the best way to avoid conflict, "civilize" Indians, and gain knowledge of the Indians' skill in medicine and surgery. They would "become as one People with us," he said. One hundred years later, Thomas Jefferson echoed Lawson's sentiments. At a reception for visiting Delaware, Mahican, and Munsee Indians in 1802, the president held out the promise of a new union of new people if the Indians would agree to live under American law and institutions: "You will unite yourselves with us, join in our great councils and form one people with us, and we shall all be Americans; you will mix with us by marriage, your blood will mix with ours, and will spread, with ours, over this great island." Jeffersonian philanthropists urged racial blending, to incorporate Indians into the new society, but the realities of Indian-white dealings and American Indian policy in the early republic tended to exclude rather than include Indians. Racial intermarriages did occur, but they gave rise to epithets like "squaw man" and "half-breed," and families with Indian ancestry often denied that component of their heritage.

Sometimes the offspring of Indian and European parents developed their own communities and their own ethnic identity. In the southern Appalachians, the Melungeons developed from a frontier population of Indian, African, and European people. The Lumbees of North Carolina, who survive today as the largest Indian group east of the Mississippi and the largest tribe not formally recognized by the federal government, intermarried with outsiders from first contacts. One theory traces their origins to English colonists from Roanoke and Croatan Indians near Cape Hatteras; other theories suggest Cherokee, Tuscarora, or Siouan origins.

Throughout New France, trappers and traders lived with Indian women, producing whole communities of people of mixed ancestry. Originally applied to the offspring of French fathers and Cree Indian mothers, the term "Métis" came to refer to all children of Franco-Indian unions. Métis peoples developed their own distinct cultures and ways of life, and they were important in the history of the Canadian West. . . .

Intercourse and intermarriage between Indians and Europeans occurred most often in areas of Spanish colonization. The author of one chronicle of the de Soto expedition of 1539–43 was a Peruvian mestizo, Garcilaso de la Vega, known as "the Inca." The son of a Spanish conquistador and an Incan noblewoman, he was "the first of a new race of people born of unions between the Spanish conquerors and the Native American peoples they conquered." Spanish conquistadors in the Southeast abducted Indian women, and intercourse was common and intermarriage not unusual at Spanish frontier posts, where there were few Hispanic women, but Indian women went regularly to trade. After English and Indian raids from the north destroyed the Spanish missions in Florida in 1704, refugee Indians flooded into St. Augustine, joining the Spanish and Indian communities there. In 1736, as many as 1,350 Indian people lived in half a dozen towns around St. Augustine. The city had an Indian church. Spaniards and Indians traded, worked out labor arrangements, lived together, and intermarried. . . . St. Augustine parish records show that marriages took place with some regularity between both free and slave blacks and Indian men and women from the mid-seventeenth century onward. . . .

When Juan de Oñate established the first permanent European colony in New Mexico, he hoped to keep Indian and Spanish peoples and societies separate, and for a long time people were officially either Indians or Spanish. However, Santa Fe was 1,500 miles and six months' travel from Mexico City, and Hispanic settlers in New Spain's isolated northern province, in historian Andrew Knaut's words, "could not escape almost total immersion in the ways and beliefs of the land's overwhelming Pueblo majority." Interaction and intercourse produced new ways of living and new kinds of people that strained to the breaking point Spanish attempts to preserve ethnic and cultural separation. As intermarriage increased, people of mixed ancestry proliferated—as early as 1671, a Franciscan complained that "all the pueblos are full of friars' children." Spaniards created new categories to identify and define the "new" people. The child of a Spanish father and an Indian mother was a mestizo; the child of a Spanish father and black mother was a mulatto; the offspring of a mestizo father and a Spanish woman were castizos, and so on. Obsessed with maintaining their status in the New World, Spaniards in eighteenth-century New Mexico distinguished between Spaniards born in Old Spain and those born in New Spain, between Indians who spoke Spanish and those who did not. . . .

English colonial authorities also passed legislation to regulate the status of mixed and nonmixed groups of people. In Virginia, Indian people declined in number and African slaves increased, causing the English more concern with maintaining their position. They placed Indians in the inferior category of nonwhites, curtailing their ability to bear arms, to testify in court, to marry freely, and not to be enslaved. In 1691, Virginia passed a law prohibiting whites from intermarrying with "Negroes, Mulattoes and Indians." Indians were expected to occupy society's lowest ranks, along with slaves and "Free Negroes." In 1705, Virginia included Indians among the people subject to its "black code." As elsewhere in the South, white society moved to create a biracial system, and Indian people found themselves consigned to the wrong side of the dividing line: in white eyes and according to white laws, they were "black."

Whatever the status race-conscious whites accorded them, Indian people of mixed ancestry became a permanent and growing part of the mosaic of American society. Indeed, as their numbers plummeted, intermarriage was one way of bolstering population in those Indian societies that were matrilineal: children of an Indian mother were considered members of her clan and tribe, no matter who the father was. However, intermarriage is a two-way street: Indian populations displayed growing evidence of European ancestry, and many Europeans who were becoming Americans had Indian ancestors, whether or not they admitted it.

The new societies that Indian people inhabited after European invasion often were falling apart. Economic dependency, alcoholism, demographic disaster, political realignment according to European rather than Indian interests, and steady cultural assault, all served to destabilize Native communities. Indians' traditions, political structures, social arrangements, and values, which had provided guidance and unity in the past, faced unprecedented challenges. Some communities disappeared from history as tribes, and their members resurfaced in colonial society and colonial records as "people of color," or poor people of Indian descent, petitioning the authorities for relief or trying to eke out a living. Theirs was a new world of poverty, dependence, and debt, and they lived subject to colonial laws rather than by tribal custom.

Indian-European interactions produced new peoples, and they produced new communities. Europeans created the concept of "Indian"; European pressures also created new Indian "tribes." . . . The repercussions of European invasion, warfare, disease, and Christianity, which dislocated Indian peoples throughout North America, generated new communities and shattered old ones. Many tribes were postcontact creations: either they emerged out of the demographic chaos produced by European invasion or they existed first in the minds of Europeans who needed some organizing label for the bewildering array of family bands, clans, temporary and permanent alliances, coalitions of villages, and loose confederacies they encountered in Indian America. Unaccustomed to dealing with fluid band societies, Europeans pressed Indians to centralize and function as political units, and some Indian groups came to operate like the "tribes" Europeans assumed they were.

The Spanish invasion of the Southeast in the sixteenth century produced massive transformations in Indian societies. "When first encountered by Europeans," writes Jerald T. Milanich, "the native peoples of interior La Florida must have been incredible to behold." Powerful Mississippian chiefs demanded tribute and redistributed resources among their followers. Costumed in magnificent feather cloaks and beautifully crafted accoutrements reflecting their high status, they went in canopied litters carried on their subjects' shoulders and met the Europeans. Great chiefdoms, like Coosa in Georgia, held more than thirty thousand inhabitants. Populous towns contained plazas and temples built atop earthen mounds. By the late seventeenth century, the powerful chiefs and their densely settled chiefdoms had disappeared; only mounds and overgrown ruins remained in silent testimony to the civilizations that had once flourished there. The Indians who survived the Spanish onslaught "reorganized themselves to meet the challenges of the modern world." When the French and the English penetrated the southern interior, refugees from the chiefdoms and new immigrants had rebuilt, or were rebuilding, new societies from the ruins. Living in relatively small villages, Indian people banded together in loose confederacies, becoming the Catawbas, Creeks, Cherokees, Choctaws, Chickasaws, and other tribes and confederacies of the South. The Indian peoples encountered when English traders first penetrated the Southeast after the founding of Charleston (1670) were already "postcontact" societies.

The new societies of North America were ethnically as well as tribally mixed. Indian communities that adopted captives added a European strand to their social fabric. And many new communities, especially on the frontier, were almost from their beginnings multiethnic societies. Arriving at Charlestown, New Hampshire, then the northern frontier of New England, as a girl in 1744, Susanna Johnson found nine or ten families living in cabins, and numerous Indians "associated in a friendly manner with the whites." Looking back in her old age to that time, she recalled: "In these days there was such a mixture on the frontiers of savages and settlers, without established laws to govern them, that the state of society cannot easily be described." In 1774, Governor Patrick Tonyn of Florida said the Indians in his colony were "settled amongst our Plantations, they have daily intercourse with them, and are as it were a People interwoven with us." . . .

. . . Many towns and settlements that grew into America's cities began life as trading posts, which by their nature encouraged close interaction of Indians and Europeans. Schenectady, New York, for example, was on the overland route between Iroquois villages and Dutch settlements on the Hudson River. The community of Dutch origins and Dutch people was frequented by Iroquois Indians, French trappers, African slaves, and, from the 1690s, English soldiers and settlers. Like neighboring Albany, it was a community "where whites and Indians lived together, traded with each other, slept in the same rooms, and ate at the same table." Countless cities, towns, and villages across America began in similar fashion, springing up or emerging from existing Indian settlements at the junction of trade routes that brought together disparate peoples. Quebec, Montreal, Albany, Philadelphia, Pittsburgh, Charleston, Detroit, St. Louis, and many others all, at one time or another, depended on the fur trade and the Indians who provided most of its pelts and its man- and woman-power. French outposts in the Midwest were often cosmopolitan communities where Frenchmen met Indians from far and near, as well as people from different parts of Europe and Africa. Detroit, a multiethnic metropolis in the twentieth century, was a multiethnic community in the eighteenth century. When Sieur de la Mothe Cadillac founded Detroit in 1701, he planned to settle Indians and Europeans together, so that they would intermarry and form one people. A visitor to Fort Pitt in 1772 described the future city of Pittsburgh as a village of about forty log houses, the headquarters of the Indian traders, and "the resort of Indians of different & distant tribes." Auguste Chouteau and his younger brother, Pierre, the

"Founding Family of St. Louis," established a family fortune and a city's future on the basis of trade with the Indians of the Mississippi and Missouri Valleys. . . .

Not only did Indians and Europeans create new societies in the new world that emerged after contact, but existing societies experienced significant changes and responded to new influences. Those were greatest for Indian societies, of course, but Indian ways left subtle imprints in the societies of the Europeans who sought to displace them. . . .

   . . . Even as Europeans sought to displace and destroy Indian societies, some found much to admire. Indian ways seemed to infiltrate their own societies, and, at the very least, they were exposed to Indian ideas and social values. To say that American democracy emerged as a synthesis of European and Indian political traditions may be an overstatement, but to deny it may be placing too much weight on the written record: ideas and customs tend to seep subtly from one group to another rather than being formally acknowledged. Such indirect influences are difficult to establish with certainty, but they would be in keeping with the flow of Indian ways into Euro-American societies.

   Many have attributed to American Indians an impact on European social thought. From Roger Williams and the baron de Lahontan in the seventeenth century, to Thomas Jefferson and Benjamin Franklin in the eighteenth, and on to the present, numerous writers have found much to admire in Indian societies. French missionary Marc Lescarbot compared the social ills of European society with the merits he found in Micmac communities: "If only through considerations of humanity, and because these people of whom we shall treat are men like ourselves, we have reason to be roused with the desire of understanding their modes of life." Montaigne, Rousseau, and others used Indian society—that is, their understanding of it—as a yardstick by which to judge European civilization. . . .

   Certainly, some American colonists and European philosophers were impressed by the freedom, egalitarianism, and communal ethics they saw in Indian society. Indians lived in functioning democracies, enjoyed "natural" rights and freedom, and were not burdened by "unnatural" monarchy and government oppression. Roger Williams noted that Indian chiefs in New England led by "gentle persuasion" and would do nothing "unto which the people are averse." Daniel Gookin agreed that Indian sachems won and retained support by "acting obligingly and lovingly unto their people, lest they should desert them." William Penn said that Indian chiefs "move by the Breath of their People." Trader James Adair, who lived among the Indians of the Southeast before the Revolution, said the Indians' "whole constitution breathes nothing but liberty." Trader John Long said the Iroquois "laugh when you talk to them of Kings; for they cannot reconcile the idea of submission with the dignity of man." Cadwallader Colden said that each Iroquois nation was "an Absolute Republick by itself, governed in all Publick affairs of War and Peace by the Sachems or Old Men, whose Authority and Power is gained by and consists wholly in the opinions of the rest of the Nation in their Wisdom and Integrity. They never execute their Resolutions by Compulsion or Force Upon any of their People." A French officer, writing in the closing years of the French regime, commented that Frenchmen who lived among Indians found greater freedom than they had ever been accustomed to: "'Liberty,' they say, 'is no where more perfectly enjoyed, than where no subordination is known, but what is recommended by natural reason, the veneration of old age, or the respect of personal merit.'" A Mohawk said more simply: "We have no forcing rules or laws amongst us."

Indian communities were living proof that human beings could construct and maintain societies based on liberty, examples of political systems where those who governed derived their authority from the people. Some colonists went to live in these societies, and some writers advocated injecting healthy doses of Indian-style freedom and equality into their own ailing societies. John Lawson maintained that Indians were "the freest People in the World," and he urged settlers to emulate their ways.

Some Europeans saw in Indian societies practices that put "civilization" to shame. Father Claude Chauchetière was impressed by the sharing, hospitality, and patience in dealing with children he witnessed in Indian communities. "In fine," he said, "all our fathers and the French who have lived with the savages consider that life flows on more gently among them than with us." Crèvecoeur maintained that Indians had "in their social bond something singularly captivating, and far superior to anything to be boasted of among us." In marked contrast to Europe, where wealth and poverty existed side by side, Recollect missionary Gabriel Sagard reported that the Hurons "make hospitality reciprocal and are so helpful to one another that they provide for the needs of all, so that there are no poor beggars in any of their towns and villages." William Wood, in *New England's Prospect,* reported that the Indians were "reddy to communicate the best of their wealth to the mutual good of one another." Roger Williams pointed out that, in contrast to European society, Indians had "no beggars amongst them, nor fatherlesse children unprovided for." Revolutionary writer Thomas Paine said that Indian societies lacked "any of those species of human misery which poverty and want present to our eyes in all the towns and streets of Europe."

Sharing in Indian societies was not an ideal; it was an obligation. People acquired honor and established reciprocal relations by giving things away, not by accumulating them. Observing how an item given to an Indian "may pas twenty hands before it sticks," William Penn said, "Wealth circulateth like the blood, all parts partake." Refusal to share was regarded as antisocial, even hostile behavior: in 1712, Cree Indians around Hudson Bay killed seven Frenchmen who would not share food and ammunition with a band of Indians who were on the verge of starvation. Indians thought Europeans were selfish and uncaring; many Europeans felt that Indians who gave things away and failed to "get ahead" were "shiftless" and "improvident."

Many Indian societies also accorded women and children a measure of respect unusual in Europe. In societies where women produced food as well as prepared it, their economic role seems to have translated into higher status than that of their European or colonial counterparts. Iroquoian women in particular exerted an influence undreamed of by Europeans. "All real authority is vested in them," wrote Joseph François Lafitau in the seventeenth century. "The land, the fields, and their harvest all belong to them. They are the souls of the Councils and the arbiters of peace and of war. . . . The children are their domain, and it is through their blood that the order of succession is transmitted." While women gave and sustained life, raising crops and rearing children in the villages, men took life, fighting and hunting away from the villages.

Gender relations often changed after contact with Europeans. Women's participation in public affairs sometimes declined, since Europeans insisted on dealing with men, and the new demands generated by the fur trade and the increased absences of men on hunting and war expeditions placed additional economic burdens on women. Europeans interpreted egalitarian gender relations as a lack of social and family hierarchy, and they sought to subordinate women in their program of restructuring Indian societies along European lines: men, not clan mothers, must dominate society.

European travelers frequently noted that Indian people were indulgent parents, eschewing corporal punishment in child-rearing. Cabeza de Vaca said, "These people love their offspring more than any in the world and treat them very mildly." What attracted de Vaca in the sixteenth century, however, alarmed Puritans in the seventeenth century. They feared the effects of the New World and its Indian inhabitants, and they worried that in building a new "civilization" in America, they might become like the Indians they sought to displace. The Puritan minister Cotton Mather lamented that "tho' the first English planters of this country had usually a government and a discipline in their families that had a sufficient severity in it, yet, as if the climate had taught us to Indianize, the relaxation of it is now such that it seems wholly laid aside, and a foolish indulgence to children is become an epidemical miscarriage of the country, and like to be attended with many evil consequences." Increase Mather also lamented the decline of family government and the indulgence of parents and masters toward children and servants: "Christians in this Land, have become too like unto the Indians," he said. Subordination of children, as of women, was part of the invaders' agenda for Indian society. Nevertheless, travelers noted, backcountry settlers often seemed to follow Indian examples in their indulgent treatment of children. . . .

The egalitarian nature of Indian societies was antagonistic to the class societies of Europe. Individual freedom threatened to undermine patterns of hierarchy, discipline, and self-restraint. To contemporaries, the freedom of Indian society was largely inherent in what they saw as a wilderness environment, where land was plentiful and colonial authority was weak. In the seventeenth century, William Hubbard worried that the settlers scattered along New England's frontier "were contended to live without, yea, desirous to shake off all *yoake of Government,* both *sacred* and *Civil,* and so *Transforming* themselves as much as well they could into the manners of the Indians they lived amongst." In the 1750s, Louis Antoine de Bougainville complained that Montcalm's soldiers became "corrupted . . . by the example of the Indians and Canadians, breathing an air permeated with independence."

The patterns of communal sharing, leadership dependent upon the good will of one's followers, individual liberty, and egalitarian relations that typified many Indian societies contrasted starkly with the vision of society articulated by John Winthrop in a sermon to fellow Puritans aboard the *Arbella:* "God Almighty . . . hath so disposed of the Condition of mankind, as in all times some must be rich[,] some poor, some high and eminent in power and dignity; others mean and in subjection." The collision and occasional fusion of different concepts of society is part of the American historical experience, but how far European colonists, or American founding fathers, went in adopting Indian ways as they modified Winthrop's vision is difficult to say. Awareness and even admiration of Indian political systems and social ethics did not mean that Europeans would adopt them as permanent features of the new societies they were creating. Immigrants tended to cling to many of their own ways and to adopt new ways of life when and for as long as it suited them to do so. . . . In the end, European imperial ambitions, settlement patterns, laws, and institutions prevailed at the expense of idealistic notions that a truly new world could be created that incorporated the best of Indian and European societies. Ultimately, the invaders of North America succeeded in their goal of building new societies that were more like their old ones in Europe than the Native societies they encountered in America.

Nevertheless, those societies developed where Native American roots ran deep. How much of what was new in them derived from the human environment and how much from the physical is difficult to ascertain, but the early settlers themselves often regarded Indians and "wilderness" as inseparable. European colonists, like the Indians whose world they invaded, were compelled to combine old and new ways, to experiment and innovate as well as adhere to traditions for guidance. Although many social experiments did not endure, by the end of the colonial era, Europeans, Indians, and Africans had all created new societies. Each one, in James Merrell's words, was "similar to, yet very different from, its parent culture." The New England town meeting is a far cry from Winthrop's vision of an ordered and orderly society and displays more attributes of Algonkian government by consensus than of Puritan government by the divinely ordained.

## FURTHER READING

Ida Altman and James Horn, *"To Make America": European Emigration in the Early Modern Period* (1991).

James Axtell, *The Invasion Within: The Contest of Cultures in Colonial North America* (1985).

K. R. Andrews, N. P. Canny, and P. E. H. Hair, eds., *The Westward Enterprise: English Activities in Ireland, the Atlantic, and America, 1480–1650* (1978).

Bernard Bailyn, "The Idea of Atlantic History," *Itinerario,* 20 (1996), 19–44.

———, *Voyagers to the West: Emigration from Britain to America on the Eve of the Revolution* (1986).

Marilyn C. Baseler, *"Asylum for Mankind": America 1607–1800* (1998).

William Cronon, *Changes in the Land: Indians, Colonists, and the Ecology of New England* (1983).

Alfred Crosby, *The Columbian Exchange: Biological and Cultural Consequences of 1492* (1972).

———, *Ecological Imperialism: The Biological Expansion of Europe, 900–1900* (1986).

David Hackett Fischer, *Albion's Seed: Four British Folkways in America* (1989).

Gregory H. Nobles, *American Frontiers: Cultural Encounters and Continental Conquest* (1997).

Edmundo O'Gorman, *The Invention of America: An Inquiry into the Historical Nature of the New World and the Meaning of Its History* (1961).

David Beers Quinn, *North America from Earliest Discovery to First Settlements: The Norse Voyages to 1612* (1977).

———, *England and the Discovery of America, 1481–1620* (1974).

# American Natives' Response

# to the European Presence

*C*

*How do we know what the Americans thought as they saw their land and life being inundated by Europeans moving in? Many kinds of sources exist for this period, but all require interpretation. One fruitful source is the writings of the colonists, but since the Indians left no written sources these documents give us only one side of the dialogue. Many of these writers were very conscientious in transmitting their observations but we have only what the newcomers thought the Indians were thinking and feeling, and their interpretations—and their ambitions—colored everything they wrote. Another source is the natives' own oral tradition. Some of this is embedded in the European written sources. The information these documents presented almost all came from Native Americans who told them about their own society and its traditions. Other elements of the oral tradition that confirm the early accounts were written down by people, Indians and Europeans, during the colonial period and later; some are even being transmitted and written down today. A third source is archaeology, which has been especially important in the eastern part of North America in recent decades. Archaeologists' findings offer ways to revisit the early documents and judge their accuracy. Thus our ability to understand the early contact period, and especially what the Indians thought about the transformation of their lives and environments in it, is better today than earlier in the twentieth century.*

*The documents written by Europeans represent a variety of experiences and viewpoints. Often we have several different representations of a single period or event, and are thus able to play sources off against each other. As they wrote about Native Americans' religion, marriage customs, law, inheritance, and food, partly with a view to gauging how ripe they were for conversion, the Europeans were inventing a kind of ethnology—a new science of humankind.*

*Europeans were aware that the Indians were also analyzing the newcomers, attempting to fit them into a framework from their own experience. The Americans were interested in acquiring articles, particularly equipment and weapons of metal,*

*that the newcomers offered in exchange for their furs and precious metals. Trade
quickly became the chief medium of cultural exchange, and the Europeans tended to
assume that a purely economic exchange had been established in which products of
equal value were exchanged on a rational basis. But the Indians may have seen this
trade very differently. Historians and anthropologists interpret the evidence in various ways as they attempt to understand the Americans' view of the new relationships.*

*The influx of European articles, which Indians valued for their usefulness and
meaning within their own cultures, allowed natives whose proximity to the settlements gave them first access to the trade goods to become more powerful than before.
Native groups and leaders, such as the Narragansetts led by Miantonomi and
Canonicus, emerged as leading trading partners. But ultimately many of these early
allies became powerful opponents as they realized earlier than others the price of cooperation and settlement.*

## D O C U M E N T S

Indian interpretations of the coming of European explorers and colonists were gathered by reporters throughout the colonial period. The legend of Maushop and his
disgust at the new presence was one that appeared in many forms; one version is
document 1. One of the earliest documents of encounters between Europeans and
Americans was Alvar Nuñez Cabeza de Vaca's account, document 2, of his eight-
year journey on foot from the Texas coast where he and his companions were shipwrecked across the Southwest to Mexico in 1527–1536. He was accompanied by
two Spaniards and an African named Estevánico. As Cabeza de Vaca interpreted
their encounters, the party was called on again and again to cure natives they encountered, and their successes led the Americans to revere them. In 1841 the Reverend
John Heckewelder recorded a native oral tradition, also dating back to this early period, that reported Indian amazement when they saw the first Europeans in New
York's Hudson River area. This record, document 3, argues that good relations were
established, but in the final paragraph the account shows the Europeans tricking the
Indians into giving up land. Father Paul LeJeune, a member of the Jesuit mission to
Quebec, collected a similar native oral tradition in document 4 which conveys their
first impressions of the newcomers.

William Wood was an early settler in Massachusetts Bay, and in document 5 he
wrote of the period when the southern New England Algonquians and the colonists
were both trying to understand what their future relationships would be. Wood was told
a tradition of the Indians' first notions of the Europeans similar to those given to Heckewelder and LeJeune. The existence of these traditions shows that the Americans had a
well-developed system of recording and transmitting their own lore over many generations. Wood also went on to describe various tribes, and their relationships, and he was
interested in how Indians organized their lives within their own villages. This curiosity
led him to judge harshly what he saw as the poor treatment of Indian women in that society. Wood wrote just before the first great conflict in New England, the Pequot War of
1636–1637. Miantonomi was an ally of the English in that war, but within a few years
he believed that the English and the Indians could not coexist. He believed that the
strength of the English came from their solidarity, and in document 6, he called for all
the Indians to unite as the English did.

# 1. Maushop Leaves New England:
## An Indian Legend About Colonization, 1787

On the west end of Martha's Vineyard, are high cliffs of variegated coloured earths, known by the name of *Gayhead*. On the top of the hill is a large cavity, which has the appearance of the crater of an extinguished volcano, and there are evident marks of former subterraneous fires. The Indians who live about this spot have a tradition that a certain deity resided there before the Europeans came into America, that his name was *Maushop;* that he used to step out on a ledge of rocks which ran into the sea, and take up a whale, which he broiled for his own eating on the coals of the aforesaid volcano, and often invited the Indians to dine with him, or gave them the relicks of his meal. That once to show their gratitude to *Maushop* for his very great kindness to them, they made an offering to him of all the tobacco which grew upon the island in one season. This was scarcely sufficient to fill his great pipe, but he received the present very graciously, smoked his pipe, and turned out the ashes of it into the sea, which formed the island of Nantucket. Upon the coming of the Europeans into America, *Maushop* retired in disgust, and has never since been seen.

# 2. Alvar Nuñez Cabeza de Vaca Acts
## As a Curer and Shaman Across
## the American Southwest, 1527–1536

### Our Cure of Some of the Afflicted

That same night of our arrival, some Indians came to Castillo and told him that they had great pain in the head, begging him to cure them. After he made over them the sign of the cross, and commended them to God, they instantly said that all the pain had left, and went to their houses bringing us prickly pears, with a piece of venison, a thing to us little known. As the report of Castillo's performances spread, many came to us that night sick, that we should heal them, each bringing a piece of venison, until the quantity became so great we knew not where to dispose of it. We gave many thanks to God, for every day went on increasing his compassion and his gifts. After the sick were attended to, they began to dance and sing, making themselves festive, until sunrise; and because of our arrival, the rejoicing was continued for three days.

When these were ended, we asked the Indians about the country farther on, the people we should find in it, and of the subsistence there. They answered us, that throughout all the region prickly-pear plants abounded; but the fruit was now gathered and all the people had gone back to their houses. They said the country was very cold, and there were few skins. Reflecting on this, and that it was already winter, we resolved to pass the season with these Indians. . . .

Indian Legend of the Giant Maushop, and the Origin of the Island of Nantucket, *Columbian Magazine,* 1787, 525.

The Relation of Alvar Núñez Cabeza de Vaca, 1527–1536, from F. W. Hodge and T. H. Lewis, *Spanish Explorers in the Southern United States, 1528–1543* (New York, 1906).

## The Coming of Other Sick to Us the Next Day

The next day morning, many Indians came, and brought five persons who had cramps and were very unwell. They came that Castillo might cure them. Each offered his bow and arrows, which Castillo received. At sunset he blessed them, commending them to God our Lord, and we all prayed to Him the best we could to send health; for that He knew there was no other means, than through Him, by which this people would aid us, so we could come forth from this unhappy existence. He bestowed it so mercifully, that, the morning having come, all got up well and sound, and were as strong as though they never had a disorder. It caused great admiration, and inclined us to render many thanks to God our Lord, whose goodness we now clearly beheld, giving us firm hopes that He would liberate and bring us to where we might serve Him. For myself I can say that I ever had trust in His providence that He would lead me out from that captivity, and thus I always spoke of it to my companions.

The Indians having gone and taken their friends with them in health, we departed for a place at which others were eating prickly pears. These people are called Cuthalchuches and Malicones, who speak different tongues. Adjoining them were others called Coayos and Susolas, who were on the opposite side, others called Atayos, who were at war with the Susolas, exchanging arrow shots daily. As through all the country they talked only of the wonders which God our Lord worked through us, persons came from many parts to seek us that we might cure them. At the end of the second day after our arrival, some of the Susolas came to us and besought Castillo that he would go to cure one wounded and others sick, and they said that among them was one very near his end. Castillo was a timid practitioner, most so in serious and dangerous cases, believing that his sins would weigh, and some day hinder him in performing cures. The Indians told me to go and heal them, as they liked me; they remembered that I had ministered to them in the walnut grove when they gave us nuts and skins, which occurred when I first joined the Christians. So I had to go with them, and Dorantes accompanied me with Estevanico. Coming near their huts, I perceived that the sick man we went to heal was dead. Many persons were around him weeping, and his house was prostrate, a sign that the one who dwelt in it is no more. When I arrived I found his eyes rolled up, and the pulse gone, he having all the appearances of death, as they seemed to me and as Dorantes said. I removed a mat with which he was covered, and supplicated our Lord as fervently as I could, that He would be pleased to give health to him, and to the rest that might have need of it. After he had been blessed and breathed upon many times, they brought me his bow, and gave me a basket of pounded prickly pears.

The natives took me to cure many others who were sick of a stupor, and presented me two more baskets of prickly pears, which I gave to the Indians who accompanied us. We then went back to our lodgings. Those to whom we gave the fruit tarried, and returned at night to their houses, reporting that he who had been dead and for whom I wrought before them, had got up whole and walked, had eaten and spoken with them and that all to whom I had ministered were well and much pleased. This caused great wonder and fear, and throughout the land the people talked of nothing else. All to whom the fame of it reached, came to seek us that we should cure them and bless their children. . . .

## 3. Manhattan's Natives Express Wonder at the First Arrival of Europeans, Printed in 1818

The Lenni Lenape claim the honour of having received and welcomed the Europeans on their first arrival in the country, situated between New England and Virginia. It is probable, however, that the Mahicanni or Mohicans, who then inhabited the banks of the Hudson, concurred in the hospitable act. The relation I am going to make was taken down many years since from the mouth of an intelligent Delaware Indian, and may be considered as a correct account of the tradition existing among them of this momentous event. I give it as much as possible in their own language.

A great many years ago, when men with a white skin had never yet been seen in this land, some Indians who were out a fishing, at a place where the sea widens, espied at a great distance something remarkably large floating on the water, and such as they had never seen before. These Indians immediately returning to the shore, apprised their countrymen of what they had observed, and pressed them to go out with them and discover what it might be. They hurried out together, and saw with astonishment the phenomenon which now appeared to their sight, but could not agree upon what it was; some believed it to be an uncommonly large fish or animal, while others were of opinion it must be a very big house floating on the sea. At length the spectators concluded that this wonderful object was moving towards the land, and that it must be an animal or something else that had life in it; it would therefore be proper to inform all the Indians on the inhabited islands of what they had seen, and put them on their guard. Accordingly they sent off a number of runners and watermen to carry the news to their scattered chiefs, that they might send off in every direction for the warriors, with a message that they should come on immediately. These arriving in numbers, and having themselves viewed the strange appearance, and observing that it was actually moving towards the entrance of the river or bay; concluded it to be a remarkably large house in which the Mannitto (the Great or Supreme Being) himself was present, and that he probably was coming to visit them. By this time the chiefs were assembled at York island, and deliberating in what manner in which they should receive their Mannitto on his arrival. Every measure was taken to be well provided with plenty of meat for a sacrifice. The women were desired to prepare the best victuals. All the idols or images were examined and put in order, and a grand dance was supposed not only to be an agreeable entertainment for the Great Being, but it was believed that it might, with the addition of a sacrifice, contribute to appease him if he was angry with them. The conjurers were also set to work, to determine what this phenomenon portended, and what the possible result of it might be. To these and to the chiefs and wise men of the nations, men, women, and children were looking up for advice and protection. Distracted between hope and fear, they were at a loss what to do; a dance, however, commenced in great confusion. While in this situation, fresh runners arrive declaring it to be a large house of various colours, and crowded with living creatures. It appears now to be certain, that it is the great Mannitto, bringing them some kind of

John Heckewelder, "Indian Tradition of the First Arrival of the Dutch on Manhatten Island," *Collections of the New-York Historical Society,* I (1841), 69–74.

game, such as he had not given them before, but other runners soon after arriving declare that it is positively a house full of human beings, of quite a different colour from that of the Indians, and dressed differently from them; that in particular one of them was dressed entirely in red, who must be the Mannitto himself. They are hailed from the vessel in a language they do not understand, yet they shout or yell in return by way of answer, according to the custom of their country; many are for running off to the woods, but are pressed by others to stay, in order not to give offence to their visitor, who might find them out and destroy them. The house, some say, large canoe, at last stops, and a canoe of a smaller size comes on shore with the red man, and some others in it; some stay with his canoe to guard it. The chiefs and wise men, assembled in council, form themselves into a large circle, towards which the man in red clothes approaches with two others. He salutes them with a friendly countenance, and they return the salute after their manner. They are lost in admiration; the dress, the manners, the whole appearance of the unknown strangers is to them a subject of wonder; but they are particularly struck with him who wore the red coat all glittering with gold lace, which they could in no manner account for. He, surely, must be the great Mannitto, but why should he have a white skin? Meanwhile, a large *Hackhack* is brought by one of his servants, from which an unknown substance is poured out into a small cup or glass, and handed to the supposed Mannitto. He drinks—has the glass filled again, and hands it to the chief standing next to him. The chief receives it, but only smells the contents and passes it on to the next chief, who does the same. The glass or cup thus passes through the circle, without the liquor being tasted by any one, and is upon the point of being returned to the red clothed Mannitto, when one of the Indians, a brave man and a great warrior, suddenly jumps up and harangues the assembly on the impropriety of returning the cup with its contents. It was handed to them, says he, by the Mannitto, that they should drink out of it, as he himself had done. To follow his example would be pleasing to him; but to return what he had given them might provoke his wrath, and bring destruction on them. And since the orator believed it for the good of the nation that the contents offered them should be drunk, and as no one else would do it, he would drink it himself, let the consequence be what it might; it was better for one man to die, than that a whole nation should be destroyed. He then took the glass, and bidding the assembly a solemn farewell, at once drank up its whole contents. Every eye was fixed on the resolute chief, to see what effect the unknown liquor would produce. He soon began to stagger, and at last fell prostrate on the ground. His companions now bemoan his fate, he falls into a sound sleep, and they think he has expired. He wakes again, jumps up and declares, that he has enjoyed the most delicious sensations, and that he never before felt himself so happy as after he had drunk the cup. He asks for more, his wish is granted; the whole assembly then imitate him, and all become intoxicated.

After this general intoxication had ceased, for they say that while it lasted the whites had confined themselves to their vessel, the man with the red clothes returned again, and distributed presents among them, consisting of beads, axes, hoes, and stockings such as the white people wear. They soon became familiar with each other, and began to converse by signs. The Dutch made them understand that they would not stay here, that they would return home again, but would pay them another visit the next year, when they would bring them more presents, and stay with them awhile; but as they could not live without eating, they should want a little land of them to sow seeds, in order to raise herbs and vegetables to put into their broth. They went away as they had said, and returned in the following season, when both parties were much rejoiced to see each other; but the whites laughed at the Indians, seeing that they knew not the use of the axes and hoes they had given them the year before; for they had these hanging to their breasts as ornaments, and the stockings were made use of as tobacco pouches. The whites now put handles to the former for them, and cut trees down before their eyes, hoed up the ground, and put the stockings on their legs. Here, they say, a general laughter ensured among the Indians, that they had remained ignorant of the use of such valuable implements, and had borne the weight of such heavy metal hanging to their necks, for such a length of time. They took every white man they saw for an inferior Mannitto attendant upon the supreme Deity who shone superior in the red and laced clothes. As the whites became daily more familiar with the Indians, they at last proposed to stay with them, and asked only for so much ground for a garden spot as, they said, the hide of a bullock would cover or encompass, which hide was spread before them. The Indians readily granted this apparently reasonable request; but the whites then took a knife, and beginning at one end of the hide, cut it up to a long rope, not thicker than a child's finger, so that by the time the whole was cut up, it made a great heap; they then took the rope at one end, and drew it gently along, carefully avoiding its breaking. It was drawn out into a circular form, and being closed at its ends, encompassed a large piece of ground. The Indians were surprised at the superior wit of the whites but did not wish to contend with them about a little land, as they had still enough themselves. The white and red men lived contentedly together for a long time, though the former from time to time asked for more land, which was readily obtained, and thus they gradually proceeded higher up the Mahicannittuck, until the Indians began to believe that they would soon want all their country, which in the end proved true.

## 4. Canadian Natives Recount Their Traditions of the First Sight of Men Dressed in Iron, 1633

. . . Pierre Pastedechouan has told us that his grandmother used to take pleasure in relating to him the astonishment of the Natives, when they saw for the first time a French ship arrive upon their shores. They thought it was a moving Island; they did not know what to say of the great sails which made it go; their astonishment was redoubled in seeing a number of men on deck. The women at once began to prepare houses for them, as is their custom when new guests arrive, and four canoes of Savages ventured to board these vessels. They invited the Frenchmen to come into the houses which had been made ready for them, but neither side understood the other.

---

"Relation of Father Paul LeJeune," 1633, in Reuben Gold Thwaites, ed., *The Jesuit Relations,* 73 vols. (Cleveland, 1896–1901). vol. 5, 119–121.

They were given a barrel of bread or biscuit. Having brought it on shore they examined it; and, finding no taste in it, threw it into the water. In a word, they were as much astonished as was the King of Calecut, in olden times, when he saw the first European ship nearing his shores; for, having sent some one to investigate the character and appearance of the men brought by that great house of wood, the messengers reported to their master that these men were prodigious and horrible; that they were dressed in iron, ate bones, and drank blood. They had seen them covered with their cuirasses, eating biscuits, and drinking wine. Our Savages said the Frenchmen drank blood and ate wood, thus naming the wine and the biscuits.

Now as they were unable to understand to what nation our people belonged, they gave them the name which has since always clung to the French, *ouemichtigouchiou;* that is to say, a man who works in wood, or who is in a canoe or vessel of wood. They saw our ships, which were made of wood, their little canoes being made only of bark. . . .

## 5. William Wood Describes Indian Responses to the English Presence in New England, and Predicts Future Relationships, 1634

### Of Their Wondering at the First View of Any Strange Invention

These Indians being strangers to arts and Sciences, and being unacquainted with the inventions that are common to a civilized people, are ravisht with admiration at the first view of any such sight: They tooke the first Ship they saw for a walking Iland, the Mast to be a Tree, the Saile white Clouds, and the discharging of Ordinance for Lightning and thunder, which did much trouble them, but this thunder being over, and this moving Iland stedied with an Anchor, they manned out their cannowes to goe and picke strawberries there, but being saluted by the way with a broad side, they cried out, what much hoggery, so bigge walke, and so bigge speake, and by and by kill; which caused them to turne back, not daring to approach till they were sent for. They doe much extoll and wonder at the English for their strange Inventions, especially for a Wind-mill, which in their esteeme was little lesse than the worlds wonder, for the strangenesse of his whisking motion, and the sharpe teeth biting the corne (as they terme it) into such small peeces; they were loath at the first to come neere to his long armes, or to abide in so tottering a tabernacle, though now they dare goe any where so farre as they have an English guide. The first plow-man was counted little better than a Juggler: the Indian seeing the plow teare up more ground in a day, than their Clamme shels could scrape up in a month, desire to see the workemanship of it, and viewing well the coulter and share, perceiving it to be iron, told the plow-man, hee was almost Abamocho, almost as cunning as the Devill; but the fresh supplies of new and strange objects hath lessen'd their admiration, and quickned their inventions, and desire of practising such things as they see, wherein they expresse no small ingenuitie, and dexterity of wit, being neither

---

William Wood, *New Englands Prospect* (London, 1634), 61–62, 77–78, 94–97.

furthered by art, or long experience. It is thought they would soon learne any mechanicall trades, having quicke wits, understanding apprehensions, strong memories, with nimble inventions and a quicke hand in using of the Axe or hatchet, and such like tooles.

## Of the Pequants and Narragansetts, Indians Inhabiting Southward

The Pequants be a stately warlike people, of whom I never heard any misdemeanour; but that they were just and equall in their dealings; not treacherous either to their Country-men, or English: Requiters of courtesies, affable towards the English. Their next neighbours the Narragansetts, be at this present the most numerous people in those parts, the most rich also, and the most industrious; being the storehouse of all such kind of wild Merchandize as is amongst them. These men are the most curious minters of their Wampompeage and Mowhakes, which they forme out of the inmost wreaths of Periwinkle-shels. The Northerne, Easterne, and Westerne Indians fetch all their Coyne from these Southerne Mint-masters. From hence they have most of their curious Pendant & Bracelets; from hence they have their great stone-pipes, which wil hold a quarter of an ounce of Tobacco, which they make with steele-drils and other instruments; such is their ingenuity & dexterity, that they can imitate the English mold so accurately, that were it not for matter and colour it were hard to distinguish them; they make them of greene, & sometimes of blacke stone; they be much desired of our English Tobaconists, for their rarity, strength, handsomnesse, and coolnesse. Hence likewise our Indians had their pots wherein they used to seeth their victuals before they knew the use of Brasse. Since the English came, they have employed most of their time in catching of Beavers, Otters, and Musquashes, which they bring downe into the Bay, returning backe loaded with English commodities, of which they make a double profit, by selling them to more remote Indians, who are ignorant of what they make them pay, so making their neighbours ignorance their enrichment. Although these be populous, yet I never heard they were desirous to take in hand any martiall enterprize, or expose themselves to the uncertain events of warre: wherefore the Pequants call them Women-like men; but being uncapable of a jeare, they rest secure under the conceit of their popularitie, and seeke rather to grow rich by industrie, than famous by deeds of Chevalry.

## Of the Aberginians or Indians Northward

First of their [the Indians'] stature, most of them being between five or six foot high, straight bodied, strongly composed, smooth-skinned, merry countenanced, of complexion something more swarthy than Spaniards, black haired, high foreheaded, black eyed, out-nosed, broad shouldered, brawny armed, long and slender handed, out breasted, small waisted, lank bellied, well thighed, flat kneed, handsome grown legs, and small feet. In a word, take them when the blood brisks in their veins, when the flesh is on their backs and marrow in their bones, when they frolic in their antic deportments and Indian postures, and they are more amiable to behold (though only in Adam's livery) than many a compounded fantastic in the newest fashion.

It may puzzle belief to conceive how such lusty bodies should have their rise and daily supportment from so slender a fostering, their houses being mean, their lodging as homely, commons scant, their drink water, and nature their best clothing. In them the old proverb may well be verified: *Natura paucis contenta* ["Nature is satisfied with a few things"], for though this be their daily portion they still are healthful and lusty. I have been in many places, yet did I never see one that was born either in redundance or defect a monster, or any that sickness had deformed, or casualty made decrepit, saving one that had a bleared eye and another that had a wen on his cheek. The reason is rendered why they grow so proportionable and continue so long in their vigor (most of them being fifty before a wrinkled brow or gray hair bewray their age) is because they are not brought down with suppressing labor, vexed with annoying cares, or drowned in the excessive abuse of overflowing plenty, which oftentimes kills them more than want, as may appear in them. For when they change their bare Indian commons for the plenty of England's fuller diet, it is so contrary to their stomachs that death or a desperate sickness immediately accrues, which makes so few of them desirous to see England.

Their swarthiness is the sun's livery, for they are born fair. Their smooth skins proceed from the often annointing of their bodies with the oil of fishes and the fat of eagles, with the grease of raccoons, which they hold in summer the best antidote to keep their skin from blistering with the scorching sun, and it is their best armor against the mosquitoes, the surest expeller of the hairy excrement, and stops the pores of their bodies against the nipping winter's cold.

Their black hair is natural, yet it is brought to a more jetty color by oiling, dyeing, and daily dressing. Sometimes they wear it very long, hanging down in a loose, disheveled, womanish manner; otherwhile tied up hard and short like a horse tail, bound close with a fillet, which they say makes it grow the faster. They are not a little fantastical or custom-sick in this particular, their boys being not permitted to wear their hair long till sixteen years of age, and then they must come to it by degrees, some being cut with a long foretop, a long lock on the crown, one of each side of his head, the rest of his hair being cut even with the scalp. The young men and soldiers wear their hair long on the one side, the other side being cut short like a screw. Other cuts they have as their fancy befools them, which would torture the wits of a curious barber to imitate. But though they be thus wedded to the hair of their head, you cannot woo them to wear it on their chins, where it no sooner grows but it is stubbed up by the roots, for they count it as an unuseful, cumbersome, and opprobrious excrement, insomuch as they call him an Englishman's bastard that hath but the appearance of a beard, which some have growing in a staring fashion like the beard of a cat, which makes them the more out of love with them, choosing rather to have no beards than such as should make them ridiculous. . . .

## Of Their Women, Their Dispositions, Employment, Usage by Their Husbands, Their Apparell, and Modesty

To satisfy the curious eye of women readers, who otherwise might think their sex forgotten or not worthy a record, let them peruse these few lines wherein they may see their own happiness, if weighed in the woman's balance of these ruder Indians who scorn the tutorings of their wives or to admit them as their equals—though their qualities and industrious deservings may justly claim the preeminence and command better usage and more conjugal esteem, their persons and features being every way correspondent, their qualifications more excellent, being more loving, pitiful, and modest, mild, provident, and laborious than their lazy husbands.

Their employments be many: first their building of houses, whose frames are formed like our garden arbors, something more round, very strong and handsome, covered with close-wrought mats of their own weaving which deny entrance to any drop of rain, though it come both fierce and long, neither can the piercing north wind find a cranny through which he can convey his cooling breath. They be warmer than our English houses. At the top is a square hole for the smoke's evacuation, which in rainy weather is covered with a pluver [rain cover]. These be such smoky dwellings that when there is good fires they are not able to stand upright, but lie all along under the smoke, never using any stools or chairs, it being as rare to see an Indian sit on a stool at home as it is strange to see an Englishman sit on his heels abroad. Their houses are smaller in the summer when their families be dispersed by reason of heat and occasions. In winter they make some fifty or threescore foot long, forty or fifty men being inmates under one roof. And as is their husbands' occasion, these poor tectonists [builders or carpenters] are often troubled like snails to carry their houses on their backs, sometime to fishing places, other times to hunting places, after that to a planting place where it abides the longest.

Another work is their planting of corn, wherein they exceed our English husbandmen, keeping it so clear with their clamshell hoes as if it were a garden rather than a corn field, not suffering a choking weed to advance his audacious head above their infant corn or an undermining worm to spoil his spurns. Their corn being ripe they gather it, and drying it hard in the sun convey it to their barns, which be great holes digged in the ground in form of a brass pot, sealed with rinds of trees, wherein they put their corn, covering it from the inquisitive search of their gourmandizing husbands who would eat up both their allowed portion and reserved seed if they knew where to find it. But our hogs having found a way to unhinge their barn doors and rob their garners, they are glad to implore their husbands' help to roll the bodies of trees over their holes to prevent those pioneers whose thievery they as much hate as their flesh.

Another of their employments is their summer processions to get lobsters for their husbands, wherewith they bait their hooks when they go afishing for bass or codfish. This is an everyday's walk, be the weather cold or hot, the waters rough or calm. They must dive sometimes over head and ears for a lobster, which often shakes them by their hands with a churlish nip and bids them adieu. The tide being spent, they trudge home two or three miles with a hundredweight of lobsters at their backs, and if none, a hundred scowls meet them at home and a hungry belly for two days after. Their husbands having caught any fish, they bring it in their boats as far as they can by water and there leave it: as it was their care to catch it, so it must be their wives' pains to fetch it home, or fast. Which done, they must dress it and cook it, dish it, and present it, see it eaten over their shoulders; and their loggerships having filled their paunches, their sweet lullabies scramble for their scraps. In the summer these Indian women, when lobsters be in their plenty and prime, they dry them to keep for winter, erecting scaffolds in the hot sunshine, making fires likewise underneath them (by whose smoke the flies are expelled) till the substance remain hard and dry. In this manner they dry bass and other fishes without salt, cutting them very thin to dry suddenly before the flies spoil them or the rain moist them, having a special care to hang them in their smoky houses in the night and dankish weather.

In summer they gather flags [probably cattail], of which they make mats for houses, and hemp and rushes, with dyeing stuff of which they make curious baskets with intermixed colors and protractures [drawings or designs] of antic imagery. These baskets be of all sizes from a quart to a quarter [eight bushels], in which they carry their luggage. In winter they are their husbands' caterers, trudging to the clam banks for their belly timber, and their porters to lug home their venison which their laziness exposes to the wolves till they impose it upon their wives' shoulders. They likewise sew their husbands' shoes and weave coats of turkey feathers, besides all their ordinary household drudgery which daily lies upon them, so that a big belly hinders no business, nor a childbirth takes much time, but the young infant being greased and sooted, wrapped in a beaver skin, bound to his good behavior with his feet up to his bum upon a board two foot long and one foot broad, his face exposed to all nipping weather, this little papoose travels about with his bare-footed mother to paddle in the icy clam banks after three or four days of age have sealed his pass-board and his mother's recovery.

For their carriage it is very civil, smiles being the greatest grace of their mirth; their music is lullabies to quiet their children, who generally are as quiet as if they had neither spleen or lungs. To hear one of these Indians unseen, a good ear might easily mistake their untaught voice for the warbling of a well-tuned instrument, such command have they of their voices.

These women's modesty drives them to wear more clothes than their men, having always a coat of cloth or skins wrapped like a blanket about their loins, reaching down to their hams, which they never put off in company. If a husband have a mind to sell his wife's beaver petticoat, as sometimes he doth, she will not put it off until she have another to put on. Commendable is their mild carriage and obedience to their husbands, notwithstanding all this—their [husband's] customary churlishness and savage inhumanity—not seeming to delight in frowns or offering to word it with their lords, not presuming to proclaim their female superiority to the usurping of the least title of their husband's charter, but rest themselves content under their helpless condition, counting it the woman's portion.

Since the English arrival, comparison hath made them miserable, for seeing the kind usage of the English to their wives, they do as much condemn their husbands for unkindness and commend the English for their love, as their husbands—commending themselves for their wit in keeping their wives industrious—do condemn the English for their folly in spoiling good working creatures. These women resort often to the English houses, where *pares cum paribus congregatae* ["equals gathered with equals"], in sex I mean, they do somewhat ease their misery by complaining and seldom part without a relief. If her husband come to seek for his squaw and begin to bluster, the English woman betakes her to her arms, which are the warlike ladle and the scalding liquors, threatening blistering to the naked runaway, who is soon expelled by such liquid comminations.

In a word, to conclude this woman's history, their love to the English hath deserved no small esteem, ever presenting them something that is either rare or desired, as strawberries, hurtleberries, raspberries, gooseberries, cherries, plums, fish, and other such gifts as their poor treasury yields them. But now it may be that this relation of the churlish and inhumane behavior of these ruder Indians towards their patient wives may confirm some in the belief of an aspersion which I have often heard men cast upon the English there, as if they should learn of the Indians to use their wives in the like manner and to bring them to the same subjection—as to sit on the lower hand and to carry water and the like drudgery. But if my own experience may out-balance an ill-grounded scandalous rumor, I do assure you, upon my credit and reputation, that there is no such matter, but the women find there as much love, respect, and ease as here in old England. I will not deny but that some poor people may carry their own water. And do not the poorer sort in England do the same, witness your London tankard bearers and your country cottagers? But this may well be known to be nothing but the rancorous venom of some that bear no good will to the plantation. For what need they carry water, seeing everyone hath a spring at his door or the sea by his house?

Thus much for the satisfaction of women, touching this entrenchment upon their prerogative, as also concerning the relation of these Indian squaws.

## 6. Miantonomi Calls for Algonquian Unity Against the English, 1643

A while after this came Miantenomie from Block-Island to Mantacut with a troop of men . . . ; and instead of receiving presents, which they used to do in their progress, he gave them gifts, calling them brethren and friends, for so are we all Indians as the English are, and say brother to one another; so must we be one as they are, otherwise we shall be all gone shortly, for you know our fathers had plenty of deer and skins, our plains were full of deer, as also our woods, and of turkies, and our coves full of fish and fowl. But these English having gotten our land, they with scythes cut down the grass, and with axes fell the trees; their cows and horses eat the grass, and their hogs spoil our clam banks, and we shall all be starved; therefore it is best for you to do as we, for we are all the Sachems from east to west, both Moquakues and Mohauks joining with us, and we are all resolved to fall upon them all, at one appointed day; and therefore I am come to you privately first, because you can persuade the Indians and Sachem to what you will, and I will send over fifty Indians to Block-Island, and thirty to you from thence, and take an hundred of Southampton Indians with an hundred of your own here; and when you see the three fires that will be made forty days hence, in a clear night, then do as we, and the next day fall on and kill men, women, and children, but no cows, for they will serve to eat till our deer be increased again. . . .

# E S S A Y S

The American Indians' world was completely transformed by the coming of Europeans—first by the trade initiated by early encounters and the diseases inadvertently in-

Miantonomo's statement in Lion Gardiner's relation, Massachusetts Historical Society *Collections,* 3rd ser., III (1833), 154.

troduced by explorers and fishermen and later by the arrival of permanent settlers. Our ability to understand how the Indians understood these early relationships and why many apparently welcomed the newcomers and cooperated with them is limited by the fact that our sources are primarily the documents written by Europeans. When they estimated the natives' response to them, the writers often reflected their own hopes as much as the realities, especially when they asserted that the Indians revered them and saw their technology and accomplishments as supernatural in origin. However, these same documents also give us the raw materials for better understanding. These accounts often embody much native knowledge, as Americans informed the writers and helped to shape what they wrote about Indian culture and history. They therefore allow scholars to read for the native voice amid the European writing. In recent decades, archaeology has also enhanced our ability to interpret the early accounts.

Fundamental questions remain as readers attempt to understand those lost early relationships. Did the Indians' cultural assumptions determine the way they responded and limit their ability to understand what would happen? In the first essay anthropologist Bruce Trigger of McGill University assesses the relative value of interpretations that stress such cultural relativism as opposed to interpretations that assume that all people were making rational choices based on economic and political considerations. What does each construction offer to us as we try to imagine those early relations? In the second essay Paul A. Robinson, the principal/state archaeologist with the Rhode Island Historical Preservation Commission looks at the choices that confronted the Narragansetts when English settlers first began to change the terms of life in southern New England. How did the beginning of English settlement affect the status of Miantonomi's Narragansetts who, as William Wood pointed out, were so well placed to profit in the early wampum trade? How was Miantonomi thinking about his people's options as he chose alliance with the New England colonists rather than with the Pequots who opposed them? Why, when Miantonomi tried to form an alliance to resist the newcomers in the aftermath of the Pequot War of 1636–1637, did other tribes refuse to join them?

## Native North American Responses to Europeans: Romantic Versus Rationalistic Interpretations

### BRUCE G. TRIGGER

. . . [B]oth history and anthropology are being strongly influenced by the resurgence of cultural relativism, which accords to the beliefs transmitted within specific cultures a preeminent role as determinants of human behavior. This view has challenged and largely eclipsed the rationalist claim that human behavior is shaped mainly by calculations of individual self-interest that are uniform from one culture to another. Studies of how native peoples perceived the first Europeans they encountered will probably be strongly influenced by this shift in emphasis. I wish to investigate in this paper whether it is sound to assign cultural relativism a dominant role in the discussion of this issue. To answer that question, I will examine the conflicting claims of cultural relativists and rationalists and the utility of each position for interpreting the historical evidence. I will seek to demonstrate that, while

Bruce G. Trigger, "Early Native American Responses to European Contact: Romantic versus Rationalistic Interpretations," *Journal of American History,* 77(4), March 1991, pp. 1195–1215. Copyright © 1991 by the Organization of American Historians. Reprinted by permission.

cultural beliefs may have significantly influenced Indian reactions in the early stages of their encounters with Europeans, in the long run rationalist calculations came to play a preponderant role, and I will document how this cognitive reorganization occurred. . . .

The most persistent manifestation of these preconceptions has been the conflict between romantic and rationalist explanations of human behavior. For over two centuries the romantic approach has emphasized contingently variable cultural patterns as the principal determinants of human behavior, while rationalism has assigned the major role to practical, or universal, human reason. On first inspection, these two views would appear to be complementary rather than antithetical. Although the varied behavior of different groups often appears to reflect idiosyncratic cultural premises, few scholars would deny that rational calculation plays a significant role in human behavior. . . .

The long-term alliances between idealism and romanticism and between materialism and rationalism are not historical accidents. Reason always serves some end. It may be used to promote goals that are wholly determined by the idiosyncrasies of a specific cultural system. Alternatively, it may allow the pursuit of more practical goals that sustain or alter a society's relationship to the physical world and that create new patterns for the production, distribution, and control of matter, energy, and information. While no process of reasoning occurs independently of culture, practical reason has the capacity to transcend culture. By mutual agreement the universalistic processes are termed rationalistic, and the privileging of them constitutes the basis of a materialistic view of human behavior. Some societies clearly are more consciously oriented toward such a privileging of practical reason than are others.

Anthropologists agree that individuals are born into cultural traditions that have been shaped by centuries of development, and each of which is unique in many respects. They also acknowledge that cultural traditions are "sense-making systems," systems that shape people's perceptions and values and hence influence their reactions to new experiences in important ways. More extreme versions of cultural relativism maintain that cultural patterns determine human behavior and view individuals as conceptually trapped within specific cultural traditions. . . .

The major alternative to this romantic view is the rationalistic philosophy that anthropology borrowed from the French Enlightenment. It stresses the universality of human nature and maintains that through the exercise of reason human groups at the same general level of development will respond in a similar way to the same kinds of challenges. Rationalists recognize that many of the problems that confront large hierarchical societies are radically different from those that must be resolved by small-scale ones. While this evolutionary perspective implies that the problems that must be solved change as societies become more complex, it does not posit that the basic methods for doing this change. Instead a rationalist approach sees the ability to calculate that is common to all human beings as playing a major role in shaping the behavior of all human groups and posits that on the basis of such calculations the most important cultural variations and changes can be explained. . . . In the late nineteenth and early twentieth centuries, racists believed that "primitive" groups were biologically less capable of rational thought and behavior than were "civilized" ones; but anthropologists, both before and since, have stressed the equal intelligence and rational capacity of all human groups. Rationalism underlies all modern cultural evolutionary approaches, which emphasize the uniformity of cultures at the same level of development regardless of the cultural traditions to which they belong. It is also congenial to a materialistic interpretation of human behavior, which assumes that human beings are likely to be most calculating, and hence least culture-bound, with respect to those matters that relate most directly to their material well-being. . . .

The problem that confronts historians and anthropologists is not simply to agree that relativistic and rational factors both play roles in human behavior but to determine what roles and how those factors fit together in the larger totality of behavior. Romantics tend to believe that early contact between Europeans and native Americans can best be explained as an interaction between cultures, or more specifically between mentalities. . . . For rationalists such relations can be accounted for more effectively in terms of economic and political considerations. All of these factors were at work in concrete situations; what is disputed is which, if either, of them more effectively determined what happened. This is not a matter of analytical preference; it addresses fundamental issues concerning the nature of human behavior and how cultural change comes about.

In the rest of this paper, I will attempt to assess the relative value of romantic and rationalist approaches for explaining the behavior of native North Americans in their earliest encounters with Europeans. In encountering Europeans after 1492, native Americans experienced novel challenges of both a practical and a cognitive sort. They clearly had well-established traditions of intertribal diplomacy, which guided their relations with neighboring groups. These traditions combined rationalistic calculations with culturally influenced objectives. At the same time, each culture possessed beliefs about the creation and nature of the universe that, while having adaptive significance, were far more independently determined by cultural traditions than were aspects of culture that were subjected to practical application on a regular basis. With the exception of sporadic contacts with the Norse in Newfoundland and the eastern Arctic, none of the native Americans had ever previously had to deal with anything like the bearded, white-skinned beings who began haunting their seacoasts. The latter's huge ships, abundant metal goods, brightly colored clothes, and thundering guns and cannons placed them in a different category from any known or imaginable native group. So too did the extreme self-confidence and arrogance with which the Europeans frequently conducted themselves. How were native peoples to interpret such strangers as they appeared with increasing frequency along their coasts, giving away trinkets, carrying off native people, and leaving behind unknown diseases, before coming into closer contact as shipwrecked sailors, traders, would-be conquerors, and finally settlers?

## First Perceptions

Indian folk traditions, often recorded generations after the events occurred, suggest that native North Americans believed the first European ships they saw to be floating islands inhabited by supernatural spirits and sometimes covered by white clouds (sails) from which lightning and thunder (cannons) were discharged, or else the mobile dwelling places of powerful spirits whom they prepared to welcome with sacrifices, food, and entertainment. These stories indicate that there was much about Europeans that offered itself to supernatural interpretation in terms of native religious concepts.

European records of early contacts with native Americans appear to corroborate the claim that in numerous instances native people interpreted the newcomers as supernatural. The Spanish who explored and settled the Caribbean islands in the late fifteenth century were convinced that native beliefs in their divinity were a source of power that they could use to control these people. In 1492 Christopher Columbus concluded that the inhabitants of the Bahamas believed that he had come from the sky. The Spanish recounted natives holding prisoners under water to determine whether Europeans were immortal. Accounts derived from Spanish and Aztec sources provide detailed descriptions of how native religious beliefs played a major role in the subjugation of one of the most populous and complex societies in the New World by a handful of European intruders. . . .

The accounts of the explorations of Jacques Cartier, Álvar Núñez Cabeza de Vaca, and Hernando de Soto described isolated instances when the Indians brought the sick of their communities to them and requested that they heal them. This suggests that these leaders were regarded as powerful shamans, if not as divinities, by native peoples in widely separated parts of North America. Native people are also reported to have worshiped and brought offerings to crosses erected by Francisco Vázquez de Coronado in what was to be the southwestern United States and to a large stone column put up by Jean Ribault in Florida, although it is possible that at least in the Southwest such behavior was motivated more by political than by religious considerations. . . .

Europeans were prepared to exploit North American Indian beliefs in their supernatural powers. Sometimes the deaths of early European explorers and settlers were concealed in the hope that Indians might continue to believe that they were immortal. In the course of their *entrada* into what is now the southeastern United States, de Soto and his followers, drawing upon their experiences in Mexico and Peru, claimed that he was the Child of the Sun and in that capacity had a claim upon the obedience of local chiefs.

Many cultural relativists assume that these scattered pieces of evidence provide insights into how native North Americans generally perceived Europeans in the early stages of their encounter. They take it for granted that similar culturally conditioned beliefs determined native responses in many other instances of early contact, but that such beliefs either were less obvious or failed to be recorded by less sensitive or less interested European observers. This is a highly suppositious conclusion. Moreover, most of the native accounts of what happened were recorded long after the event, and many are clearly influenced by European values and religious concepts. While detailed ethnographic analysis has revealed undeniably traditional elements in some of these tales, it is dangerous to overgeneralize from them about how native peoples first perceived Europeans, especially when we consider the great variability in specific beliefs from one culture to another.

The total corpus of documentary evidence that religious beliefs played an important and widespread role in influencing native behavior is in fact very limited.

For the most part, native American relations with Europeans are portrayed as having been governed by relatively straightforward concerns with exchange and defense. While some of the survivors of the Pánfilo de Narváez expedition found roles for themselves as shamans and traders among the hunter-gatherers of Texas, perhaps because they were not equipped to play an effective part in subsistence activities, hundreds of shipwrecked Spanish sailors were enslaved by chiefs in Florida. Did this plethora of prosaic accounts result from many European recorders failing to understand Indian behavior? The written historical evidence is inadequate to supply a definitive answer. In those cases where religious behavior is specifically ascribed to native people in sixteenth-century accounts, there is the equally difficult problem of the extent to which European observers uncritically ascribed their own ethnocentric views about non-Christian religious beliefs to native people, thereby either misinterpreting their actions or ascribing religious motives to them in situations where those did not apply. . . .

## Seventeenth-Century Pragmatism

In any discussion of how native peoples perceived Europeans, the far more abundant data from the seventeenth century are of vital importance. If native beliefs continued to play a preponderant role in determining native reactions to Europeans so long after first contact, it would reinforce the assumption that they had done so during the previous century. Recent historical and ethnographic research has challenged established rationalistic interpretations of native dealings with Europeans during the seventeenth century. In particular, a growing commitment to romantic and cultural relativist explanations of human behavior has led an increasing number of historians and anthropologists to reject the proposition that European goods had more than symbolic value to native peoples so long as their societies maintained any semblance of independence from European control. . . .

These arguments ignore a solid body of evidence that by the beginning of the seventeenth century the bulk of trade between Europeans and Indians was not in glass beads, other ornaments, and liquor. The first Indians who traded with Europeans may have hung metal axes and hoes on their chests as ornaments and used stockings as tobacco pouches. Yet, by the 1620s, the Montagnais at Tadoussac, near the mouth of the St. Lawrence River, were using large quantities of clothing, hatchets, iron arrowheads, needles, sword blades, ice picks, knives, kettles, and preserved foods that they purchased from the French. For some purposes, especially in wet weather, woolen clothing proved superior to their traditional skin garments. They had also ceased to manufacture birchbark baskets and stone axes. In the 1630s the Mohawks, who lived close to the Dutch traders at Fort Orange (now Albany), continued to produce their own food but were purchasing a wide range of clothing and metalware from Europeans. By the early 1640s, they owned more than three hundred guns, which had been paid for partly with skins they had seized from neighboring tribes. The Hurons, who lived much farther inland and had considerable transportation problems, were more selective in their purchases of European goods. They were primarily interested in obtaining metal cutting tools. In particular they wanted knives of all sizes, axes, and iron arrowheads. They also purchased guns, when the French were willing to sell them, and copper and brass kettles. The latter were easier to transport than their heavy and fragile clay cooking pots, and when they were worn out, they could be cut up and used as raw material to manufacture metal arrowheads and cutting tools as well as ornaments. In addition, Huron traders carried home glass beads and metal bracelets, which weighed relatively little. They do not appear to have purchased much cloth or many items of clothing, and unlike the coastal tribes, they did not seek alcoholic beverages when they came to trade. In selecting European goods, the Hurons showed a marked preference for tools with cutting edges that were superior to their own and that replaced native implements such as stone axes that took a long time to manufacture.

Among the Huron, Iroquois, and other Iroquoian-speaking peoples, a stone- and bone-based technology did not completely disappear until the late seventeenth century. . . . They also continued to manufacture pottery vessels until then, and the arrival of metal cutting tools seems to have resulted in a florescence of bone work- ing. Yet, well before 1650, there was a marked decline in the frequency of stone tools among these groups. This suggests that by 1636 the Hurons were sufficiently dependent on the French for metal cutting tools that one of their chiefs, Aenons, was not exaggerating when he said that if his people "should remain two years with- out going down to Quebec to trade, they would find themselves reduced to such ex- tremities that they might consider themselves fortunate to join with the Algonquins and to embark in their canoes." It is clear from the context of this report that Aenons was referring to the necessity of securing European goods, not to maintaining a mil- itary alliance against the Iroquois.

From the first arrival of the Jesuit missionaries in the 1620s, the Hurons and their neighbors regarded them as shamans. Beginning in the late 1630s, many Indians concluded that these priests were sorcerers or malevolent spirits, who were responsible for the great epidemics of European diseases that afflicted the native people of the region at that time. The Indians probably also continued to believe that the French, who were able to manufacture such large quantities of metal goods, must possess great supernatural power. Yet in their eyes this did not make Euro- peans intrinsically different from the Indians, who were also able to practice witchcraft and whose amulets and relations with appropriate spirits enabled them to hunt, fish, and move about on snowshoes and in canoes more effectively than Europeans did. Ordinary Frenchmen who traded, traveled, lived with Indian fami- lies, and even intermarried with them were viewed as regular human beings. They had been observed to become ill and die, and a few of them had even been killed by the Indians. The slowness of most Europeans to master native languages and skills led many Indians to conclude that on the whole Europeans were slow-witted, which accorded with the traditional Iroquoian belief that hairy people were unin- telligent.

The Indians were also appalled by what they saw as the greed, violence, and bad manners of the French, which all were recognizable, if negatively valued, pat- terns of human behavior. Huron chiefs felt confident of their ability to outwit and manipulate French traders and officials, even when they were becoming politically and economically reliant on them. All of this suggests that by the seventeenth cen- tury the fur-trading peoples of the northern Woodlands regarded most, if not all, Europeans as human beings who were different from themselves and in some respects more powerful, but with whom they could interact on a normal basis.

## Cognitive Reorganization

It is thus evident that at some point those native groups that initially reacted to Europeans primarily on the basis of their traditional religious beliefs came to regard Europeans as human beings with whom, while continuing to take account of their special customs and sensibilities, they could do business as they did with any other foreign group. The Indians' increasing familiarity with Europeans led to a "cognitive reorganization" in which the rational component inherent in the mental processes of every human being began to play the dominant role in guiding native relations with Europeans, while religious beliefs ceased to play the important part that in many cases they had done in the early stages of the encounter. The key factor in bringing about this transformation was the Indians' observation and rational evaluation of European behavior. This development accords with the general principle that whenever culturally transmitted beliefs are employed to guide human behavior, they are subject to rational scrutiny on the basis of the resulting performance; where those beliefs encourage counterproductive behavior, the evaluation may result in their being rejected, revised, or judged inapplicable. In the case of early encounters between Indians and Europeans, the question remains: Under what circumstances did this cognitive reorganization occur?

Some answers are provided by historical data from the early sixteenth century. When Giovanni da Verrazzano visited the relatively sheltered Narragansetts of southern New England in 1524, he found them anxious to obtain blue beads as well as bells and other trinkets made of copper. They were not interested in steel or iron objects, mirrors, or cloth. This suggests that these Indians were interested only in objects that had precise counterparts in their traditional system of belief and exchange. By contrast, Indians living farther north along the coast of Maine, who presumably had more contact with European fishermen and their goods (they were wearing European copper beads in their ears), were far less trustful of Verrazzano and his crew and would take in exchange for their goods only "knives, fish-hooks, and sharp metal." Likewise, the Micmacs that Jacques Cartier encountered in Chaleur Bay in 1534 not only indicated very clearly that they wished to barter their furs with the French but also sought hatchets, knives, and other ironware, as well as beads, in exchange. The following year the Iroquoians of Hochelaga, on Montreal Island, seemed pleased with any European goods that Cartier gave them, while those who lived at Stadacona, within the limits of modern Quebec City, and who appear already to have had limited access to European goods being traded by Breton fishermen at the Strait of Belle Isle, sought hatchets, knives, and awls from the French, as well as beads and other trinkets.

While the more isolated Hochelagans brought their sick to Cartier for him to heal, the Stadaconans, on being informed by two of their boys (whom Cartier had kidnapped and taken to France the previous year) that the goods he was trading were of little value in his own country, demanded more of those goods in exchange from the French. At the same time it was the Stadaconans who cured Cartier's crew of the scurvy that was afflicting them. Cartier had attempted to conceal the sickness and deaths among his men, not because he believed the Stadaconans thought the French to be immortal, but because he feared they might attack if they realized how defenseless these intruders were. Soon after Cartier's visit, a large quantity of iron-ware was reported being taken to the Strait of Belle Isle to trade for furs.

These data indicate that while groups such as the Narragansetts of Rhode Island and the Hochelagans of the upper St. Lawrence (who were remote from European fishermen at Cape Breton and the Strait of Belle Isle) were pleased to secure glass beads and copper and tin trinkets, bands that lived closer to these trading areas were anxious to obtain metal cutting tools as early as the 1520s and 1530s. The latter groups also appear to have already adopted a naturalistic view of Europeans. This suggests that if many Indian groups initially viewed Europeans as supernatural beings, upon closer contact this interpretation was replaced by the conclusion that Europeans were human beings like themselves. At the same time, European metal cutting tools came to be universally valued for their utilitarian advantages. While iron knives may have performed no more efficiently than did stone hide scrapers, they cut better and were more durable and easier to keep sharp than were stone tools. Metal tools also performed better as perforators, needles, and projectile points than did the stone and bone tools the Indians had used theretofore. It was for practical reasons that coastal peoples soon were putting iron tools at the top of their shopping lists. Glass beads and scraps of copper continued to dominate the indirect trade with the interior, but by the beginning of the seventeenth century native groups living as far inland as the lower Great Lakes were seeking metal cutting tools in preference to all other European goods. This suggests that, whatever native people initially believed about Europeans and the goods they brought with them, it did not take long after the development of reasonably regular direct contact for them to conclude that Europeans were human beings like themselves and to appreciate the practical advantages of iron cutting tools, metal kettles, and to a lesser extent woolen clothing.

These observations may help to interpret the records of other major encounters between Europeans and native North Americans in the early sixteenth century. The native rulers who lived in the path of de Soto's pillaging expedition through what is now the southeastern United States adopted various strategies to placate, deflect, defeat, or speed him on his way. Yet overwhelmingly they conducted their relations with him in terms of what must have been the normal idiom of intergroup diplomacy in that region of hierarchical societies. De Soto was treated as a powerful chief with whom an alliance might be desirable or submission inevitable, but only rarely was he recorded as having been approached as a shaman and asked to cure the sick. Moreover, on at least two occasions rulers pointedly rejected claims that he possessed supernatural powers, including the panic-stricken assertion by his successor Luis de Moscoso that de Soto had not died but gone to the sky for a few days to visit the gods. The Indian ruler of Guachoya, mocking the latter tale, promised to offer two human sacrifices in honor of de Soto—a tradition in that area at the burial of neighboring chiefs. It would appear that previous contacts with shipwrecked Spanish sailors, would-be conquerors such as Juan Ponce de Leon and Pánfilo de Narváez, and colonists such as Lucas Vázquez de Ayllón had provided the native people living on the periphery of this densely settled region with an opportunity to assess Europeans and that the results of their observations were transmitted inland through the diplomatic networks linking adjacent tribes and chiefdoms. Despite the devastating effects of the Spanish plundering and burning of their settlements, the Indians of what is now the southeastern United States quickly took advantage of new resources that were presented to them; hogs, for example, were soon being eaten. . . .

The available evidence for the sixteenth century suggests that, whatever the initial Indian understanding of Europeans, a relatively short period of direct contact between the two groups resulted in a naturalistic interpretation of the newcomers. It also led to a growing demand for some European tools, which were seen as allowing tasks to be performed more effectively than did traditional stone and bone tools. These shifts involved the Indians' rationally assessing the performance of persons and goods and a desire to adopt a technology that would reduce their expenditure of energy on some routine tasks and improve the quality of their products. This technology was adopted as soon as it became available on a regular basis, even though it rendered native groups reliant on European suppliers.

The first impressions that native peoples had of Europeans and the initial strategies that these peoples devised for dealing with them seem to have been strongly influenced by their traditional beliefs. In some situations these strategies crucially shaped relations between the two groups. Where contact remained limited or indirect, initial interpretations persisted without significant modification for long periods. As relations became more direct and intense, it appears that these interpretations were rapidly modified by rational assessments of what Europeans were like and what they had to offer. In at least some areas, these assessments spread inland ahead of European exploration. This appears to have happened more quickly in densely settled regions than in more thinly populated ones.

This utilitarian assessment of European technology does not mean that native people did not continue to assign their own social meanings to European goods or that native belief systems did not play a major role in determining how native people viewed Europeans or how European goods were used in religious contexts such as burials. On the contrary, there is evidence that basic native belief systems remained intact for long periods. This does not, however, rule out the importance of a rationalist perspective for understanding major aspects of native behavior, contrary to what more extreme relativists seek to maintain.

## Conclusion

It is impossible to understand native American responses to their contact with Europeans in the early sixteenth century without a detailed knowledge of native cultures. Amerindian world views appear to have played an important role in structuring their initial understanding of these encounters, and this in turn influenced how native people behaved in these situations. The little that we know about these world views suggests that they varied from one region or ethnic group to another and that even adjacent, highly similar world views could, depending on historically contingent situations, structure native interpretations of contact in different ways. From the beginning some interpretations of Europeans were probably more "rational" than others.

Nevertheless, in areas where contact became frequent, it does not appear to have been long before all native perceptions and behavior were significantly influenced by rational appraisals of Europeans and what they had to offer. The long-term evidence indicates that economic determinists were not mistaken when they claimed that native people appreciated the material benefits to be derived from many items of European technology and that they sought to utilize this technology even at the cost of growing dependence upon their European trading partners. Native leaders also learned from observation to understand the motivations of the different European groups with whom they interacted and to devise strategies for coping with their demands. Native people were not constrained by their traditional beliefs to the extent that a rational assessment of the dangers and opportunities of the novel situations in which they found themselves was precluded. In general these assessments appear to have been strong enough to survive the psychological disruptions that must have accompanied the unprecedented epidemics of European diseases that afflicted native North Americans in the course of the sixteenth and seventeenth centuries.

If, in the long run, native people failed to devise strategies that could halt European aggression, it was not because they were unable to understand European behavior from a rational point of view. They failed because they were overwhelmed by European technological superiority, by growing numbers of European settlers as their own populations declined because of European diseases, and by increasing dependence upon European technology. They also failed because they were unable to modify their social organizations and values quickly enough to compete with the more disciplined European societies that were seeking to dominate and exploit North America. In North American Indian societies, decision making depended upon a slow process of achieving consensus, while European ones had evolved complex hierarchies of authority and command. Native groups therefore had less political maneuverability and less potential for concerted action when competing with Europeans. The creation of such structures, involving as it did the formation of new institutions and new patterns of behavior, was a slow process, even when the need for change was clearly perceived. Native societies became increasingly dependent upon European ones and were dominated by them because they lacked time to develop the human and material resources required to compete with them, not because of their incapacity to understand in rational terms what was happening to them.

Although the examples in this paper have been drawn from North America, these conclusions should apply equally to relations between European colonists and native groups elsewhere in the Americas and around the world. . . . Had relations between Europeans and native peoples been determined mainly by their respective ideologies, much more variation could be expected.

While cultural relativists have expanded our understanding of how in the beginning native reactions to Europeans were conditioned by their cultural beliefs, this approach must not undermine our appreciation of the ability of native people to monitor new situations and to devise strategies that allowed them to respond in a rational fashion to the opportunities as well as the disruptive challenges of a European presence. While the importance of native beliefs should never be underestimated, in the long run a rationalist and materialist analysis of cultural interaction seems to explain far more about what happened to native people following European contact than does an analysis that assigns primary explanatory power to their traditional beliefs.

# Lost Opportunities: Miantonomi
# and the English in Narragansett Country

### PAUL A. ROBINSON

. . . Though Miantonomi's birth date was not recorded, he was one of the first Narragansett leaders to come of age in a world shaped by Europeans as well as Indians. His protector, teacher, and uncle, Chief Sachem Canonicus, was reportedly in his fifties when Plymouth was settled in 1620 and close to seventy when he granted Roger Williams permission to settle in Narragansett Country in 1637. Miantonomi was perhaps thirty years younger than his uncle, in his late teens in 1616, when the first of several deadly epidemics ravaged Indian communities from the Penobscot River in Maine to southeastern Massachusetts. These epidemics left much of the area depopulated and open for English settlement by 1620. Plymouth, for example, was founded near the site of a village decimated by disease and abandoned by survivors.

English accounts indicate that the epidemics left the Narragansetts and other Indian communities on the western side of Narragansett Bay untouched. William Bradford, the governor of Plymouth Colony, was one of many English to contrast the carnage on the Bay's east side with the lack of pestilence farther west. Writing in 1621, he reported that east of Narragansett Bay the "soil was good and the people not many, being dead and abundantly wasted . . . the Narragansetts had not been at all touched by this wasting plague."

The epidemics were a turning point in the Indian history of the region. Large areas of coastal New England were depopulated, enabling the English to land unopposed and establish permanent villages. Epidemic contagion also changed the way surviving Indians thought about themselves and other Indian groups. The deadly effects of the epidemics caused some to doubt the power of local medicine people; others blamed themselves for the diseases and examined their behavior to discover what had caused the spirits to harm their people so terribly.

Some Indians believed that powerful Narragansett medicine people had halted the sickness at the borders of Narragansett Country. A Narragansett burning ritual was credited particularly with keeping the sickness and death away from Narragansett families. Unlike most people to the east, who were shaken and confused by the epidemics, the Narragansetts may have felt reassured by their escape. Such feelings may have been heightened when some survivors urged their leaders to emulate the Narragansett burning ritual. With the Indian population decimated to the east, the epidemics left the Narragansetts and several allied communities west of Narragansett Bay positioned to play a dominant role in English-Indian relations in southern New England.

In early winter of 1621–22, Canonicus announced the Narragansett claim to dominance in the region by sending a gift of several arrows wrapped in the skin of a rattlesnake to Governor Bradford of the newly established Plymouth Colony. Advised by Tisquantum (Squanto), Bradford viewed the act as a Narragansett attempt to "domineer and lord" over Indian communities in the region by openly challenging the power of the newcomers. He responded in kind by filling the snake skin with bullets and returning it to Canonicus. Canonicus, however, refused to accept the snake skin and returned it to Plymouth.

Through this mutual act of rejection, each party signalled its refusal to submit to the other. Gifts or presents were used by Indian people to establish and represent symbolically social and political obligations. Acceptance of gifts inferred acceptance of obligations to givers. Gift rejection symbolized denial of an obligation. Colonial officials quickly became quite adept in using gift exchange to establish and maintain relations of mutual obligation with Indian people.

The English were not the only Europeans the Narragansetts were dealing with at the time of the snakeskin incident. Dutch traders from New Amsterdam, for example, sailed regularly to Narragansett Bay to obtain purple and white shell beads known as wampum. Highly valued by interior fur-producing tribes, these beads served as currency with which Dutch and English traders obtained pelts for export back to Europe. . . .

The shells used for making beads were particularly plentiful in this area. Responding to European demand, Pequot, Narragansett, and Long Island Indian communities became involved in the production and distribution of the beads. . . .

Plymouth became involved in the wampum trade in 1628, when Dutch merchants, operating with the understanding that the English would stay out of Narragansett Bay, provided Governor Bradford with wampum worth fifty pounds sterling to trade with Indians at Kennebec. The Indians at Kennebec first refused attempts by Plymouth traders to engage in wampum exchange. Two years later, however, Bradford reported that the Indians "could scarce ever get enough" of the shell beads.

Bradford's account of the beginning of the wampum trade is important because it described what the governor called the "Great Alteration." More recently, historian Neal Salisbury has called it the "wampum revolution." Bradford noted that Plymouth colonists trading wampum possessed an overwhelming advantage over other traders not having shell beads in their inventories. He wrote,

> And strange it was to see the great alteration it made in a few years among the Indians themselves; for all the Indians of these parts, and the Massachusetts, had none or very little of it, but the sachems and some special persons that wore a little of it for ornament. Only it was made and kept among the Narragansetts and Pequots, which grew rich and potent by it. . . . But after it grew to be a commodity in these parts, these Indians fell into it also, and to learn how to make it; for the Narragansetts do gather the shells of which they make it from their shores.

Puritan officials noted that the wampum trade was an important factor in the growing strength and political importance of the Narragansetts: Bradford observed that the trade had made the Narragansetts "rich and potent," and in 1634 William Wood of Massachusetts Bay described the Narragansetts as "curious minters" of wampum, "the most rich also; and the most industrious; being the storehouse of all such kind of wild merchandise as is among them."

Seemingly satisfied with their relations with the Dutch, the Narragansetts initially showed little interest in trading with Plymouth; in 1623, they rejected the offers of a trading party from Plymouth, and Bradford's accounts of the years immediately following mention little of the Narragansetts. It was not until 1631 that they established regular relations with the English, and interestingly, they chose to establish relations with the newly arrived Massachusetts Bay colonists rather than with their more entrenched, closer Plymouth neighbors. Visited by one of Canonicus's sons, the Massachusetts Bay settlers formalized the new arrangement with mutual exchanges of gifts, dinner, and hospitality.

Miantonomi followed his cousin's 1631 visit to Boston with one of his own the following year. According to Governor Winthrop, Miantonomi and his party were treated well: they were feted at a formal dinner and "made much of." But, in what may be the first recorded instance of cultural misunderstanding between the English and the Narragansetts, three of Miantonomi's men created a stir among the Puritans when they attempted "to break into a neighbor's house" during sermon hour.

Although it is possible that larceny was on the minds of these men, it is more likely that they were simply behaving as they might have done had they been visiting an Indian house. Roger Williams, in *A Key into the Language of America,* first published in 1643, gave the impression that Narragansett doors were rarely closed; friends and strangers alike could come and go at will. "In this respect," Williams wrote, "they are remarkably free and courteous, to invite all strangers in; and if any come to them upon any occasion they request them to come in, if they come not in of themselves."

If the "housebreak" attempt was, in fact, a cultural misunderstanding, it was one of the first of many misunderstandings, large and small, intentional and unintentional, that in time caused Miantonomi to rethink his relationship with the English. And as the relationship deteriorated, Roger Williams, once full of good fellowship for Miantonomi, began to see him instead as "proud and angry and covetous and filthy, hating, and hateful." . . .

By the end of the decade, Narragansett fortunes and those of most other southern New England Indian communities were in decline. A second major epidemic hit southern New England in 1633 and 1634. This time, the sickness (smallpox) penetrated Narragansett Country and swept west through Connecticut. As numbers of native people decreased, more English towns were established.

Indian people initially saw advantages in having English neighbors living nearby. Traders were especially welcome. In 1634, Narragansett sachems unsuccessfully tried to persuade John Oldham to establish a trading post in Narragansett Bay on Dutch Island. Three years later, Roger Williams became the first European allowed to set up a permanent post in the heart of Narragansett Country when he moved from Providence to Cocumscussoc.

Relations between the new neighbors did not proceed without incident. Narragansetts, led by Canonicus and Miantonomi, soon found themselves embroiled in English politics. These interests came to affect internal Narragansett policies as English influence and power increased.

Although direct documentation is lacking, records describing Pequot policy indicate that the Pequots came to a clear understanding of the dangers of European settlement before their neighbors. In the summer of 1636, the Pequots were at war with the Dutch, fighting the Narragansetts, and under tribute demands from the English. They approached the Narragansetts, appealing for unity against the colonists. Informed of the overture by Narragansett sachems, Bradford was told that the Pequot envoys declared to the Narragansetts that "the English were strangers and began to overspread their country, and would deprive them thereof in time, if they were suffered to grow and increase; and if the Narragansetts did assist the English to subdue [the Pequots], [the Narragansetts] did but make way for their own overthrow, for if [the Pequots] were rooted out, the English would soon take occasion to subjugate them."

Six years later, Miantonomi would say essentially the same thing at Montauk. In 1636, however, Canonicus and Miantonomi decided that there was more to be gained in siding with the English. In October, Miantonomi traveled to Massachusetts Bay and promised Narragansett support to the English against the Pequots. In return, he hoped to increase his people's power by gaining control over some of the Pequots' wampum trade. In May 1637, Narragansett warriors joined Mohegan and Niantic men in the English attack on the Pequot fortified village at Mystic. When English soldiers turned the attack into a slaughter, the Narragansetts complained bitterly that what the Puritans had done was "naught," that it was evil and had killed too many people.

Less than a month before the massacre, Miantonomi had visited Roger Williams at his house in Providence and sought reassurance that the English would not harm Pequot women and children. In a May 1 letter to officials at Massachusetts Bay, Williams passed along Miantonomi's counsel concerning the planned attack. Williams wrote that "it would be pleasing to all natives, that women and children be spared." That the English not only did not spare women and children but went out of their way to kill them was, to Miantonomi and many other Indian participants, an egregious and fearful act that made it clear that these Puritans could not be trusted. . . .

Narragansett power eroded in the years following the end of the Pequot War. Nearby Indian communities that accepted Narragansett hegemony prior to the Mystic massacre first questioned and later defied Narragansett domination. The political power of the Narragansetts over adjacent communities such as Shawomet, Coweset, and Pawtuxet had been based, in part, on Narragansett ability to influence English policy. The massacre dispelled that notion. Abandoned by former allies and tributaries, the Narragansetts found themselves increasingly unable to resist Puritan demands or obtain justice in Puritan councils.

Problems with the English centered on what Miantonomi and Canonicus considered Puritan violations of their October 22, 1636 agreement to assist the English in the war against the Pequots. Copies of this agreement have not survived and Winthrop's recollection of its terms was partial and perhaps fallacious. From Miantonomi's point of view, the slaughter of women and children at Mystic was a serious infraction, and Williams's letters after the massacre suggest that other problems were also on Miantonomi's mind. In one letter, Williams conveyed Miantonomi's claim that he had not received a promised musket.

More serious disagreements arose over the disposition of the Pequot survivors. Williams met with Canonicus and Miantonomi during the summer of 1637 to let the sachems know of Winthrop's displeasure over the protection of Pequot war refugees by Narragansetts and Niantics. According to Winthrop, the Narragansetts had agreed not to do this without the consent of Massachusetts. Miantonomi denied holding Pequots, claimed to have been "faithful and honest," and confronted Williams with ten instances of English dishonesty "since these [Pequot] wars." Miantonomi remarked to Williams, "Did ever friends deal so with friends?" Canonicus complained as well that "although he and Miantonomi had paid many hundred fathom [of wampum] to their soldiers, as Mr. Governor did, yet he had not received one yard of bead nor a Pequot."

Although frustrated at the failure of the English to make good on promises, the Narragansett leaders still worked to advance and protect English interests. These were now represented by Roger Williams at Providence and, in the heart of Narragansett Country, by his and other English trading posts at Cocumscussoc. In working to further the interests of Williams and other English people, Miantonomi and Canonicus ultimately undermined the interests of their former Indian allies. Two incidents occurring shortly after the Mystic massacre illustrate how the Narragansett leaders subordinated basic Indian social and political values to English interests.

In May of 1638, Williams described an incident involving a Pequot man named Wequashcook who had helped the English at Mystic and a Coweset man named Weeokamin, who blamed Wequashcook for the loss of two of his sons in the "Pequot Wars." Assaulted by Weeokamin while visiting a friend at Coweset, Wequashcook lost his coat "and other small things." Wequashcook complained to Williams, who asked the Narragansett leaders to intervene. According to Williams, Canonicus and Miantonomi responded quickly: "Canonicus sent his son and Miantonomi his brother (Yotash) who went to Coweset and demanded the reasons of such usage and the goods and so came to my house causing the goods to be restored, professing the sachem's ignorance and sorrow for such passages and giving charge to all natives for their safe travel."

Three months later a Nipmuc man was robbed and killed by four English colonists after visiting Narragansett. The murderers made off with five fathoms of wampum and three coats. Responding quickly, Miantonomi managed to prevent friends of the murdered man from avenging the killing. Williams reported the incident: "The natives, friends of the slain Penowanyanquis, had consultation to kill an English man in revenge. Miantonomi heard of it and desired that the English would be careful on the highways and sent himself express threatenings to them etc. and informed them that Mr. Govr would see justice done."

These incidents reveal a contradiction between an essential structural principle, that the sachem's power and authority was based in persuasion and consensus-building, and acts of officially sanctioned coercion against individuals and families. Unlike the English, who considered killings of individuals as crimes against the state, traditional Indian beliefs viewed murder as an act against the family of the victim. Just as it was the obligation of the European state to deal with the killer, it was the obligation of the Indian family to seek retribution from relatives of the killer.

The maintenance of the Narragansett social order now seemed to rest not on what Roger Williams termed the "gentle persuasion" of the sachems, but on mollification of English officials and acquiescence to English demands. In the cases of Weeokamin and Penowanyanquis, Miantonomi indicated his willingness to use threats of violence to prevent Indians within his sphere of influence from carrying out actions considered natural and necessary, thus advancing English aims. Acting like an English leader, he placed himself and those associated with him within the English system of rules and government.

Perhaps Miantonomi and Canonicus hoped Williams would help them in their relations with Massachusetts Bay. In November 1637, the sachems conveyed Prudence Island to Winthrop and Williams for twenty fathoms of wampum and two coats. The exchange, Williams observed, was a gift, not a sale. Williams wrote, "truth is, not a penny was demanded . . . and what was paid was only a gratuity." In the context of native gift exchange and the social obligation it imposed on Winthrop and Williams, the gift of land was difficult, perhaps impossible, to match. It appears likely that Miantonomi was trying to control the English by gifting them into debt.

Dependent on Narragansett goodwill for security, Williams might have honored such an obligation. Living far from Narragansett Country, Winthrop had no intention of doing so and considered the transaction a sale with no strings attached. The English from Massachusetts Bay neither lived up to Miantonomi's idea of exchange nor honored the pledges they had made to secure Narragansett assistance against the Pequots. Allowed to incorporate captured Pequot people, Wequashcook and Uncas gained power and influence at Narragansett expense. At the same time, English authorities insisted that Narragansett sachems continue to be responsible for the acts of these now independent communities. In 1638, for example, Massachusetts Bay levied a 100 pound fine on the Narragansetts for injuries sustained by a cow and some horses caught in Coweset traps. In 1640, Rhode Island held the Narragansetts responsible for damage caused by fires set by their neighbors.

The years 1640 to 1642 were filled with rumors of a region-wide Indian conspiracy against the English. Narragansetts were thought to be at the center of these plans. Records document constant maneuvering by the Indians and the English to maintain advantage in an increasingly hostile environment. These same records chronicle the slow but relentless erosion of Narragansett influence with the English. In nearly every encounter, the English offended, insulted, or threatened Narragansett people. Responding as best they could, the Narragansetts were forced ultimately to appease their English neighbors. Angered and alienated, Miantonomi began to try to undermine the strong position that he had helped the English attain.

In September 1640, Winthrop wrote that "there was some rumor of the Indians plotting mischief against the English." Earlier that year, Bradford wrote to Winthrop that Miantonomi had sent "a great present of wampum to the Mohawks, to aid him against the English and that it was accepted, and aid promised." Similar news coming from colonial authorities in Connecticut prompted the Bay Colony to strengthen its defenses and confiscate the powder and shot of local Indians. Miantonomi was summoned to Boston. Arriving in October, he was compelled to answer questions about the alleged conspiracy.

Miantonomi asked Roger Williams, a man he apparently trusted, to act as his translator during these interrogations. But, banished from Boston five years earlier, Williams could not accompany Miantonomi. Unable to proceed without an interpreter, the English offered him a "Pequot maid" to translate. The English had made a similar offer earlier that summer and knew that Miantonomi might find the offer insulting. Winthrop's description of the meeting conveyed how dramatically the English style in dealing with the Narragansetts had changed since the visits in 1631 and 1632:

> [Miantonomi] refused to treat with us by our Pequot interpreter . . . and the governor [Thomas Dudley] being as resolute as he, refused to use any other interpreter, thinking it a dishonor to us to give so much way to them. [Miantonomi then acted in a "rude manner"] whereof the governor informed the general court, and would show him no countenance, nor admit him to dine at our table, as formerly he had done, till he had acknowledged his failing, etc., which he readily did . . . and did speak to our committees and us by a Pequot maid who could speak English perfectly.

The English then read the provisions of the 1636 agreement to Miantonomi. This time, however, they added that he would be responsible for damage to English livestock caused by Indian traps set by Indian people from communities that no longer recognized Miantonomi as their leader. Miantonomi had come to Boston to answer questions about an alleged conspiracy, was treated roughly, and departed with an extra "English" responsibility that he could not carry out.

The year before, in May 1639, Miantonomi had brought gifts to Winthrop: wampum from Canonicus and himself and a basket for Mrs. Winthrop from Miantonomi's wife, Wawaloam. With these gifts, Miantonomi asked that he be given both Pequot survivors and free use of Pequot land. Accepting the gifts, Winthrop gave Miantonomi neither Pequots nor guarantees of hunting rights. To make matters worse, a year earlier, Uncas had visited Boston bearing a gift of wampum and had left with a red coat, corn for the journey home, and a letter of protection. According to Winthrop, Uncas "departed very joyful." So when Miantonomi returned home from Boston in 1640 with (in Winthrop's words) "an injury in his breast," the vise had tightened from the east and the west.

Given the circumstances, it is understandable why rumors of a Narragansett-led conspiracy became common. Confirmation of these rumors finally emerged when reports of Miantonomi's visit to Montauk reached Massachusetts in August 1641.

Unlike his previous visits to Monauk, on this visit Miantonomi brought rather than took gifts. Distributing them to the Montauks, he appealed to them to join him and others against the English: "for so are we all Indians, as the English are, and say brother to one another; so must we be one as they are, otherwise we shall be all gone shortly." Miantonomi's call for unity was not heeded. The Montauks instead reported Miantonomi's speech to officials of the newly formed United Colonies of New England. As their first official act, they arranged to allow Uncas to assassinate Miantonomi.

Avenging Miantonomi's death became an unfulfilled Narragansett obsession. His death, moreover, ended any hope of unification against the English, a hope that had already become slim. Miantonomi's influence and his ability to pull together communities in the region had been lost since the summer of 1637, when the Narragansetts and their then-allies participated with the English in an English war. For Miantonomi and other Narragansetts, the opportunities presented by English settlement had instead become a disaster. The Pequot warning about the dangers of the "English strangers" was heard too late.

# FURTHER READING

Kathleen J. Bragdon, *Native People of Southern New England, 1500–1650* (1996).

Frederic W. Gleach, *Powhatan's World and Colonial Virginia: A Conflict of Cultures* (1997).

Shepard Krech III, *Indians, Animals, and the Fur Trade: A Critique of Keepers of the Game* (1981).

Calvin Martin, *The Keepers of the Game: Indian-Animal Relationships and the Fur Trade* (1978).

Christopher L. Miller and George R. Hamell, "A New Perspective on Indian-White Contact: Cultural Symbols and Colonial Trade," *Journal of American History,* 73 (1986), 311–328.

Martin H. Quitt, "Trade and Acculturation at Jamestown, 1607–1609: The Limits of Understanding," *William and Mary Quarterly,* 3rd ser., LII (1995), 227–258.

Helen C. Rountree, ed., *Powhatan Foreign Relations, 1500—1722* (1993).

Neal Salisbury, "The Indians' Old World: Native Americans and the Coming of Europeans," *William and Mary Quarterly,* 3rd ser., LIII (1996), 435–458.

———, *Manitou and Providence: Indians, Europeans, and the Making of New England, 1500–1643* (1982).

Gordon M. Sayre, *Les Sauvages Américains: Representations of Native Americans in French and English Colonial Literature* (1997).

# CHAPTER
## 3

# *Virginia and Maryland: The Beginnings of English America*

English colonization differed from the successful Spanish model in that it was fostered by private enterprise. The royal government issued patents, but ventures were entirely planned and financed by joint-stock companies, corporations created for the purpose. Some of these companies were very small groups of wealthy men, but the Virginia Company, sponsor of the first successful colony, set the price of each share relatively low and opened membership to a wide variety of investors across the country.

Such innovation was necessary because founding a colony was immensely expensive. Stocking a venture with settlers and supplying them over the years until they built infrastructure and became able to feed themselves involved constant outlay. Backers expected much more than mere self-sufficiency. They had hazarded their money with the expectation of receiving a return on their investment, and settlers were therefore under overwhelming pressure to find or develop a product of value.

The earliest returns came from furs and fish, but neither required an expensive colony to support it. Settlers and backers quickly realized that no gold or other easy wealth existed; if colonies were to succeed, they must develop a true commodity to be produced by their own labor. After a decade of hardship, Virginia colonists began to cultivate tobacco in earnest, and this crop became the Chesapeake's gold. Then the key need was for labor to till the region's abundant land and this labor was provided by adapting an English institution, temporary servitude. In England most young men and women spent their adolescence in a series of annual contracts as servants before marrying and setting up on their own, usually in their mid-twenties. In America they served a term of several years to pay for their passage. The payoff was a grant of land of their own when the term was up, something which most could never attain in England where inflation and population explosion limited opportunities.

In the course of the later seventeenth century temporary servitude of English men and women who were destined to become landowners and full members of society was largely replaced by permanent servitude (slavery) of African men and women who were forever excluded from membership in Chesapeake society, and thus opportunities available to European servants declined. Historians continue to

*debate how and why this transition, with implications so momentous for American
history, came about.*

 ## D O C U M E N T S

Captain John Smith is one of the most famous names associated with early colonization.
During Jamestown's first year he explored Chesapeake Bay, in the course of which he
was captured and brought before the region's paramount chief, Powhatan. The famous
episode in which the chief's young daughter Pocahontas saved his life was probably a
symbolic death and rebirth as an Indian. It was followed by his adoption as a sub-chief
or werowance under Powhatan. Smith, who wrote about himself in the third person,
used his capacity to communicate by writing and using examples of European technology to dazzle his captors. Smith wrote in document 1 of his accomplishments as President of the colony, especially in forcing the unwilling colonists to work and feed
themselves. Incidentally he wrote of the introduction of destructive rats, and of the
colonists' learning from the Indians how to cope with the new environment. Finally he
described the terrible starving time after he had been forced out of the colony.

By 1620 the Virginia Company, with tobacco established as a cash crop, offered
every immigrant a headright—guaranteed land. Walter Woodward offers in document 2
a satire on this campaign, presenting it as a modern condominium offering. Richard
Frethorne, who went to Virginia as a servant, wrote his parents in 1623 about the
colonists' distress and his desire to come home. Frethorne's letter, document 3, was
written in the aftermath of the concerted Indian attack of 1622. Despite reports of suffering, servants continued to immigrate. *A Relation of Maryland* (1635) published a
blank indenture form, document 4, providing for a servant to serve "according to the
custom of the country;" recruits were often illiterate and could not read what they
signed. Document 5 shows George Alsop answering the charge that servitude was almost like slavery in the Chesapeake. Finally, at the beginning of the eighteenth century
in document 6, Robert Beverley reflected on the institution of servitude, temporary and
permanent, on which the English society and economy of the Chesapeake was built.

## 1. Captain John Smith Analyzes the Human Scene, Both English and Indian, in Early Jamestown, 1624

And now the winter approaching, the rivers became so covered with swans, geese,
ducks, and cranes, that we daily feasted with good bread, Virginia peas, pumpkins,
and putchamins [persimmons], fish, fowl, and diverse sorts of wild beasts as fat as we
could eat them: so that none of our Tuftaffaty humorists desired to go for *England.*

But our *Comedies* never endured long without a *Tragedy;* some idle exceptions
being muttered against Captain *Smith,* for not discovering the head of *Chickahama-
nia* river, and [being] taxed by the Council, to be too slow in so worthy an attempt.
The next voyage he proceeded so far that with much labour by cutting of trees in-

---

Some of the spelling in this document has been modernized.

Captain John Smith, "Generall Historie of Virginia, New England, and the Summer Isles" in Edward
Arber and A. G. Bradley, eds., *Travels and Works of Captain John Smith,* (Edinburgh: John Grant,
1910), II, 394–402, 471–473, 498–499.

sunder he made his passage; but when his Barge could pass no farther, he left her in a broad bay out of danger of shot, commanding none should go ashore til his return: himself with two English and two Savages went up higher in a Canoe; but he was not long absent, but his men went ashore, whose want of government gave both occasion and opportunity to the Savages to surprise one *George Cassen,* whom they slew, and much failed not to have cut of[f] the boat and all the rest. . . .

Six or seven weeks those Barbarians kept him prisoner, many strange triumphs and conjurations they made of him, yet he so demeaned himself amongst them, as he not only diverted them from surprising the Fort, but procured his own liberty, and got himself and his company such estimation amongst them, that those Savages admired him more than their own Quiyouckosucks. . . .

He demanding for their Captain, they showed him *Opechankanough,* King of *Pamavnkee,* to whom he gave a round Ivory double compass Dial. Much they marveled at the playing of the Fly and Needle, which they could see so plainly, and yet not touch it, because of the glass that covered them. But when he demonstrated by that Globe-like Jewel the roundness of the earth, and skies, the sphere of the Sun, Moon, and Stars, and how the Sun did chase the night round about the world continually; the greatness of the Land and Sea, the diversity of Nations, variety of complexions, and how we were to them *Antipodes,* and many other such like matters, they all stood as amazed with admiration.

Notwithstanding, within an hour after they tied him to a tree, and as many as could stand about him prepared to shoot him: but the King holding up the Compass in his hand, they all laid down their Bows and Arrows, and in a triumphant manner led him to *Orapaks,* where he was after their manner kindly feasted, and well used.

Their order in conducting him was thus; Drawing themselves all in file, the King in the middle had all their Pieces and Swords borne before him. Captain *Smith* was led after him by three great Savages, holding him fast by each arm: and on each side six went in file with their Arrows nocked. But arriving at the Town [*Orapaks*] (which was but only thirty or forty hunting houses made of Mats, which they remove as they please, as we our tents) all the women and children staring to behold him, the soldiers first all in file . . . and on each flank, officers as Sergeants to see them keep their orders. A good time they continued this exercise, and then cast themselves in a ring, dancing in such several Postures, and singing and yelling out such hellish notes and screeches; being strangely painted, every one his quiver of Arrows, and at his back a club; on his arm a Fox or an Otter's skin, or some such matter for his vambrace [armor for forearm]; their heads and shoulders painted red, . . . which Scarlet-like colour made an exceeding handsome show; his Bow in his hand, and the skin of a Bird with her wings abroad dried, tied on his head, a piece of copper, a white shell, a long feather, with a small rattle growing at the tails of their snak[e]s tied to it, or some such like toy. All this while *Smith* and the King stood in the middest guarded, as before is said: and after three dances they all departed. *Smith* they conducted to a long house, where thirty or forty tall fellows did guard him: and ere long more bread and venison was brought him than would have served twenty men. I think his stomach at that time was not very good; what he left they put in baskets and tied over his head. About midnight they set the meat again before him, all this time not one of them would eat a bit with him, till the next morning they brought him as much more; and then did they eat all the old, and reserved the new as they had done the other, which made him think they would fat him to eat him. Yet in this desperate estate to defend him from the cold, one *Mao-cassater* brought him his gown, in requital of some beads and toys *Smith* had given him at his first arrival in *Virginia*. . . .

. . . [His captors] made all the preparations they could to assault *James* town, craving his advice; and for recompence he should have life, liberty, land, and women. In part of a Table book [tablet] he wrote his mind to them at the Fort, what was intended, how they should follow that direction to affright the messengers, and without fail send him such things as he wrote for. And an Inventory with them. The difficultie and danger, he told the Savages, of the Mines, great guns, and other Engines exceedingly affrighted them, yet according to his request they went to *James* town, in as bitter weather as could be of frost and snow, and within three days returned with an answer.

But when they came to *Jame[s]* town, seeing men sally out as he had told them they would, they fled: yet in the night they came again to the same place where he had told them they should receive an answer, and such things as he had promised them: which they found accordingly, and with which they returned with no small expedition, to the wonder of them all that heard it, that he could either divine, or the paper could speak. . . .

After this they brought him a bag of gunpowder, which they carefully preserved till the next spring, to plant as they did their corn; because they would be acquainted with the nature of that seed. . . .

At last they brought him to *Werowocomoco* where was *Powhatan* their Emperor. Here more than two hundred of those grim Courtiers stood wondering at him, as he had been a monster; till *Powhatan* and his train had put themselves in their greatest braveries. Before a fire upon a seat like a bedstead, he sat covered with a great robe, made of *Rarowcun* [raccoon] skins, and all the tails hanging by. On either hand did sit a young wench of 16 or 18 years, and along on each side the house, two rows of men, and behind them as many women, with all their heads and shoulders painted red; many of their heads bedecked with the white down of Birds; but every one with something: and a great chain of white beads about their necks.

At his entrance before the King, all the people gave a great shout. The Queen of *Appamatuck* was appointed to bring him water to wash his hands, and another brought him a bunch of feathers, instead of a Towel to dry them: having feasted him after their best barbarous manner they could, a long consultation was held, but the conclusion was, two great stones were brought before *Powhatan:* then as many as could laid hands on him, dragged him to them, and thereon laid his head, and being ready with their clubs, to beat out his brains, *Pocahontas* the King's dearest daughter, when no entreaty could prevail, got his head in her arms, and laid her own upon his to save him from death: whereat the Emperour was contented he should live to make him hatchets, and her bells, beads, and copper; for they thought him aswell of all occupations as themselves. For the King himself will make his own robes, shoes, bows, arrows, pots; plant, hunt, or do anything so well as the rest. . . .

Two days after [7 *Jan.* 1608], *Powhatan* having disguised himself in the most fearfulest manner he could, caused Captain *Smith* to be brought forth to a great house in the woods, and there upon a mat by the fire to be left alone. Not long after from behind a mat that divided the house, was made the most dolefulest noise he ever heard; then Powhatan more like a devil than a man, with some two hundred more as black as himself, came unto him and told him now they were friends, and presently he should go to *James* town, to send him two great guns, and a grindstone, for which he would give him the Country of *Capahowosick,* and forever esteem him as his son *Nantaquoud.* . . .

Now ever once in four or five days, *Pocahontas* with her attendants, brought him so much provision, that saved many of their lives, that else for all this had starved with hunger. . . .

His relation of the plenty he had seen, especially at *Werawocomoco,* and of the state and bounty of *Powhatan,* (which till that time was unknown) so revived their dead spirits (especially the love of *Pocahontas*) as all men's fear was abandoned. . . .

### What was done in three months having Victuals. The Store devoured by Rats, how we lived three months of such natural fruits as the Country afforded.

Now we so quietly followed our business, that in three months we made three or four Last of Tar, Pitch, and Soap ashes; produced a trial of Glass; made a Well in the Fort of excellent sweet water, which till then was wanting; built some twenty houses; re-covered our Church: provided Nets and Weirs for fishing; and to stop the disorders of our disorderly thieves, and the Savages, built a Blockhouse in the neck of our Isle, kept by a Garrison to entertain the Savages' trade, and none to pass nor repass Savage nor Christian without the president's order. Thirty or forty Acres of ground we digged and planted. Of three sows in eighteen months, increased 60 and odd Pigs. And near 500 chickens brought up themselves without having any meat given them: but the Hogs were transported to Hog Isle: where also we built a block-house with a garrison to give us notice of any shipping, and for their exercise they made Clapboard and wainscot, and cut down trees.

We built also a fort for a retreat near a convenient River upon a high command-ing hill, very hard to be assaulted and easy to be defended; but ere it was finished this defect caused a stay.

In searching our casked corn, we found it half rotten, and the rest so consumed with so many thousands of Rats that increased so fast, but their original was from the ships, as we knew not how to keep that little we had. This did drive us all to our wits end, for there was nothing in the country but what nature afforded.

Until this time *Kemps* and *Tassore* were fettered prisoners, and did double task and taught us how to order and plant our fields: whom now for want of victual we set at liberty, but so well they liked our company they did not desire to go from us. . . .

And to express their loves, for 16 days continuance, the Country people brought us (when least) 100 a day, of Squirrels, Turkeys, Deer and other wild beasts.

But this want of corn occasioned the end of all our works, it being work suffi-cient to provide victual. . . .

Till this present, by the hazard and endeavors of some thirty or forty, this whole Colony had ever been fed. We had more Sturgeon, than could be devoured by Dog and Man, of which the industrious by drying and pounding, mingled with Caviar, Sorél and other wholesome herbs would make bread and good meat: others would gather as much *Tockwhogh* roots in a day as would make them bread a week, so that of those wild fruits, and what we caught, we lived very well in regard of such a diet.

But such was the strange condition of some 150, that had they not beene forced *nolens, volens,* perforce to gather and prepare their victual they would all have starved or have eaten one another. Of those wild fruits the Savages often brought us, and for that the president would not fulfill the unreasonable desire of those distracted Gluttonous Loiterers, to sell not only our kettles, hoes, tools, and iron, nayswords, pieces, and the very Ordnance and houses, might they have prevailed to have been but Idle: for those Savage fruits, they would have had imparted all to the Savages, especially for one basket of Corn they heard of to be at *Powhatans,* fifty miles from our Fort. . . .

. . . [H]e argued the case in this manner.

> Fellow soldiers, I did little think any so false to report, or so many to be so simple to be persuaded, that I either intend to starve you, or that *Powhatan* at this present hath corn for himself, much less for you; or that I would not have it, if I knew where it were to be had. Neither did I think any so malicious as now I see a great many; yet it shall not so passionate me, but I will do my best for my most maligner. But dream no longer of this vain hope from *Powhatan,* nor that I will longer forbear to force you from your Idleness, and punish you if you rail. But if I find any more runners for Newfoundland with the Pinnace, let him assuredly look to arrive at the Gallows. You cannot deny but that by the hazard of my life many a time I have saved yours, when (might your own wills have prevailed) you would have starved; and will do still whether I will or not; But I protest by that God that made me, since necessity hath not power to force you to gather for yourselves those fruits the earth doth yield, you shall not only gather for yourselves, but those that are sick. As yet I never had more from the store than the worst of you: and all my English extraordinary provision that I have, you shall see me divide it amongst the sick.
>
> And this Savage trash you so scornfully repine at; being put in your mouths your stomachs can digest: if you would have better, you should have brought it; and therefore I will take a course you shall provide what is to be had. The sick shall not starve, but equally share of all our labors; and he that gathereth not every day as much as I do, the next day shall be set beyond the river, and be banished from the Fort as a drone, till he amend his conditions or starve. . . .

Now we all found the loss of Captain *Smith,* yea his greatest maligners could now curse his loss: as for corn provision and contribution from the Savages, we had nothing but mortal wounds, with clubs and arrows; as for our Hogs, Hens, Goats, Sheep, Horse, or what lived, our commanders, officers and Savages daily consumed them, some small proportions sometimes we tasted, till all was devoured; then swords, arms, pieces, or any thing, we traded with the Savages, whose cruel fingers were so oft imbrewed in our blood, that what by their cruelty, our Governours indiscretion, and the loss of our ships, of five hundred within six months after Captain *Smith's* departure, there remained not past sixty men, women and children, most miserable and poor creatures; and those were preserved for the most part, by roots, herbs, acorns, walnuts, berries, now and then a little fish: they that had starch in these extremities, made no small use of it; yea, even the very skins of our horses.

Nay, so great was our famine, that a Savage we slew and buried, the poorer sort took him up again and eat him; and so did diverse one another boiled and stewed with roots and herbs: And one amongst the rest did kill his wife, powdered [*salted*] her, and had eaten part of her before it was known; for which he was executed, as he well deserved: now whether she was better roasted, boiled or carbonado'd [grilled], I know not; but of such a dish as powdered wife I never heard of.

This was that time, which still to this day we called the starving time; it were too vile to say, and scarce to be believed, what we endured: but the occasion was our own, for want of providence industry and government, and not the barrennesse and defect of the Country, as is generally supposed; . . . Yet had we been even in Paradise itselfe with these Governours, it would not have been much better with us; yet there was amongst us, who had they had the government as Captain *Smith* appointed, but that they could not maintain it, would surely have kept us from those extremities of miseries. This in ten days more, would have supplanted us all with death. . . .

## 2. Jamestown Estates: A Modern Parody, 1991

# JAMESTOWN ESTATES

*For As Little As £10 12s. 6d., You, Too, Can Own A Share of Paradise.*

From the moment the gentle, southern breezes waft your pinnace to the verdant, gardenlike shore, you'll know this is where you belong. Jamestown Estates, where only a few are living a life those in England can hardly imagine.

Jamestown Estates — another proud project of the Virginia Company — combines the best in colonial living with the excitement, adventure, and opportunity for which the Virginia Company is famous.

At Jamestown Estates, your every need is provided for in an environment that shows how caring people can live in symbiotic dominance of nature. And only Jamestown Estates offers an exclusive low cholesterol meal plan, the Sure-Fit™ exercise program, and a unique "Friends Together" living arrangement. In all details, Jamestown Estates is designed with your peace and well-being in mind. Each of our charming, thatch-roofed cottages — which you will share with congenial, adventuresome people just like yourself (specially designed to maximize both privacy and interpersonal contact) — has a spectacular river view. At Jamestown Estates, nature itself invites you to relax, reflect, converse with new-found friends, and share stories of your New World experiences, while becoming the sort of person you've always wanted to be. But it's not all play at Jamestown Estates — not by a long shot. For Jamestown Estates offers one of the most active labor markets in the New World. Whatever you do, you can do it better here.

Our employment office has many people anxious to welcome you to our growing work force.

No single ad can tell you all the remarkable things you'll want to know about Jamestown Estates. Consider, however, some of these exceptionally valuable Jamestown Pluses:

• 24-hour security, palisaded grounds.
• Hunting, fishing right on premises. Native guides teach you to hunt like a lord.
• The Sotweed Garden Center — learn how to plant like a pro. No experience necessary.
• Regularly scheduled "Trash For Treasure" excursions to the nearby Pamunkey Flea Market. Come & "Meet the Chief."
• And, as a special bonus to those who visit Jamestown Estates soon, we are introducing a new program called the Headright System* — your chance to receive 50 acres of land just for bringing yourself (or someone you know) to experience this new world of opportunity.
• Coming with a group? Ask about our Particular Plantations™ Program. Build your private world right here in our new one.

Finally, for those who appreciate the phenomenal profit potential of New World investment, there is the chance to secure shares in the Virginia Company itself, — a once in a lifetime time opportunity — starting at just £10 12s. 6d. To find out more, contact your nearest friendly, knowledgeable Virginia Company Representative.

---

**\* Headright™ and Headright System™ are registered trademarks of the Virginia Company. Offer void where prohibited.**

## Virginia  A WHOLE NEW WORLD

---

Walter Woodward, "Jamestown Estates," *William and Mary Quarterly,* 3d ser., XLVII (1991), 116–117. Reprinted by permission.

# 3. Richard Frethorne Begs His Parents for Support, 1623

Loving and kind father and mother, my most humble duty remembered to you hoping in God of your good health, as I my self am at the making hereof, this is to let you understand that I your Child am in a most heavy Case by reason of the nature of the Country is such that it Causeth much sickness, as the scurvy and the bloody flux [dysentery], and divers other diseases, which maketh the body very poor, and Weak, and when we are sick there is nothing to Comfort us; for since I came out of the ship, I never ate any thing but peas and loblollie (that is water gruel) as for deer or venison I never saw any since I came into this land, there is indeed some fowl, but We are not allowed to go and get it, but must Work hard both early and late for a mess of water gruel, and a mouthful of bread, and beef, a mouthful of bread for a penny loaf must serve for 4 men which is most pitiful if you did know as much as I, when people cry out day, and night, Oh that they were in England without their limbs and would not care to lose any limb to be in England again, yea though they beg from door to door, for we live in fear of the Enemy every hour, yet we have had a Combat with them on the Sunday before Shrovetide, and we took two alive, and make slaves of them, but it was by policy, for we are in great danger, for our Plantation is very weak, by reason of the dearth, and sickness, of our Company, for we came but Twenty for the merchants, and they half dead Just; as we look every hour When two more should go, yet there came some for other men yet to live with us, of which there is but one alive, and our Lieutenant is dead, and his father, and his brother, and there was some 5 or 6 of the last year's 20 of which there is but 3 left, so that we are fain to get other men to plant with us, and yet we are but 32 to fight against 3000 if they should Come, and the nighest help that We have is ten miles of us, and when the rogues overcame this place last, they slew 80 persons. How then shall we doe for we lie even in their teeth, they may easily take us but that God is merciful, and can save with few as well as with many; as he showed to Gilead and like Gilead's soldiers if they lapped water, we drink water which is but Weak, and I have nothing to Comfort me, nor there is nothing to be gotten here but sickness, and death, except that one had money to lay out in some things for profit; But I have nothing at all, no not a shirt to my backe, but two Rags nor no Clothes, but one poor suit, nor but one pair of shoes, but one pair of stockings, but one Cap, but two bands, my Cloak is stolen by one of my own fellows, and to his dying hour would not tell me what he did with it but some of my fellows saw him have butter and beef out of a ship, which my Cloak I doubt [think] paid for, so that I have not a penny, nor a half penny Worth to help me to either spice, or sugar, or strong Waters, without the which one cannot live here, for as strong beer in England doth fatten and strengthen them so water here doth wash and weaken these here, only keep life and soul together. But I am not half a quarter so strong as I was in England, and all is for want of victuals, for I do protest unto you, that I have eaten more in a day at home than I have allowed me here for a Week. You have given more than my day's allowance to a beggar at the door; and if Mr. Jackson had not relieved me, I should be in a poor Case, but he like a father and she like a loving mother doth still help me, for when we

---

Some of the spelling in this document has been modernized.

Richard Frethorne to his mother and father, March-April, 1623. In Susan M. Kingsbury, ed., *Records of the Virginia Company*, IV (Washington, U.S. Govt. Printing Office, 1935), 58–62.

go up to James Town that is 10 miles of us, there lie all the ships that Come to the land, and there they must deliver their goods, and when we went up to Town as it may be on Monday, at noon, and come there by night, then load the next day by noon, and go home in the afternoon, and unload, and then away again in the night, and be up about midnight, then if it rained, or blowed never so hard we must lie on the boat on the water, and have nothing but a little bread, for when we go into the boat we have a loaf allowed to two men, and it is all if we stayed there 2 days, which is hard, and must lie all that while in the boat, but that Goodman Jackson pitied me and made me a Cabin to lie in always when I come up, and he would give me some poor Jacks [fish] home with me which Comforted me more than peas, or water gruel. Of they be very godly folks, and love me very well, and will do any thing for me, and he much marveled that you would send me a servant to the Company. He sayeth I had been better knocked on the head, and Indeed so I find it now to my great grief and misery, and saith, that if you love me you will redeem me suddenly, for which I do entreat and beg, and if you cannot get the merchants to redeem me for some little money then for God's sake get a gathering or entreat some good folks to lay out some little sum of money, in meal, and Cheese and butter, and beef, any eating meat will yield great profit, oil and vinegar is very good, but father there is great loss in leaking, but for God's sake send beef and Cheese and butter or the more of one sort and none of another, but if you send Cheese it must be very old Cheese, and at the Cheesemonger's you may buy good Cheese for two pence farthing or half-penny that will be liked very well, but if you send Cheese you must have a Care how you pack it in barrels, and you must put Cooper's chips between every Cheese, or else the heat of the hold will rot them, and look whatsoever you send me be it never so much, look what I make of it. I will deal truly with you. I will send it over, and beg the profit to redeem me, and if I die before it Come I have entreated Goodman Jackson to send you the worth of it, who hath promised he will. If you send you must direct your letter to Goodman Jackson, at James Town, a Gunsmith. . . . Good Father do not forget me, but have mercy and pity my miserable Case. I know if you did but see me you would weep to see me, for I have but one suit, but it is a strange one, it is very well guarded, wherefore for God's sake pity me. I pray you to remember my love to all my friends, and kindred, I hope all my Brothers and sisters are in good health, and as for my part I have set down my resolution that certainly Will be, that is, that the Answer of this letter will be life or death to me, there good Father send as soon as you can, and if you send me any thing let this be the mark.

ROT                                    RICHARD FRETHORNE
                                       Martin's Hundred

## 4. A Blank Servant Indenture Form, 1635

The forme of binding a servant.

This Indenture *made the*          *day of*
                    *in the*
*yeere of our Soueraigne Lord King* Charles, *&c.*
*betweene*                          *of the one*
*party, and*                        *on the*
*other party,* Witneſſeth, *that the said*
              *doth hereby covenant promise, and*
*grant, to and with the said*
*his Executors and Aſſignes, to serve him from*
*the day of the date hereof, vntill his first and*
*next arrivall in* Maryland; *and after for and*
*during the tearme of          yeeres, in such*
*service and imployment, as he the said*
              *or his aſſignes shall there im-*
*ploy him, according to the custome of the Countrey*
*in the like kind. In consideration whereof, the said*
                    *doth promise*
*and grant, to and with the said*
              *to pay for his paſſing, and to*
*find him with Meat, Drinke, Apparell and Lodg-*
*ing, with other neceſſaries during the said terme;*
*and at the end of the said terme, to giue him one*
*whole yeeres provision of Corne, and fifty acres of*
*Land, according to the order of the countrey. In*
*witneſſe whereof, the said*
*hath hereunto put his hand and seale, the day and*
*yeere aboue written.*

Sealed and delivered in
        the preſence of          H

The uſuall terme of binding a ſervant, is for
five yeers; but for any artificer, or one that ſhall
deſerve more then ordinary, the Adventurer
ſhall doe well to ſhorten that time, and adde
encouragements of another nature (as he ſhall
ſee cauſe) rather then to want ſuch uſefull men.

---

Blank indenture form in Anon. [Father Andrew White], *A Relation of Maryland* (London, 1635, 1966), 53–54.

## 5. George Alsop Argues That Servants in Maryland Have a Good Deal, 1666

*The necessariness of Servitude proved, with the common usage of Servants in Mary-Land, together with their Priviledges.*

. . . There is no truer Emblem of Confusion either in Monarchy or Domestick Governments, then when either the Subject, or the Servant, strives for the upper hand of his Prince, or Master, and to be equal with him, from whom he receives his present subsistance: Why then, if Servitude be so necessary that no place can be governed in order, nor people live without it, this may serve to tell those which prick up their ears and bray against it, That they are none but Asses, and deserve the Bridle of a strict commanding power to rein them in: For I'me certainly confident, that there are several Thousands in most Kingdoms of Christendom, that could not at all live and subsist, unless they had served some prefixed time, to learn either some Trade, Art, or Science, and by either of them to extract their present livelihood.

Then methinks this may stop the mouths of those that will undiscreetly compassionate them that dwell under necessary Servitudes; for let but Parents of an indifferent capacity in Estates, when their Childrens age by computation speak them seventeen or eighteen years old, turn them loose to the wide world, without a seven years working Apprenticeship (being just brought up to the bare formality of a little reading and writing) and you shall immediately see how weak and shiftless they'le be towards the maintaining and supporting of themselves; and (without either stealing or begging) their bodies like a Sentinel must continually wait to see when their Souls will be frighted away by the pale Ghost of a starving want.

Then let such, where Providence hath ordained to life as Servants, either in England or beyond Sea, endure the pre-fixed yoak of their limited time with patience, and then in a small computation of years, by an industrious endeavour, they may become Masters and Mistresses of Families themselves. And let this be spoke to the deserved praise of Mary-Land, That the four years I served there were not to me so slavish, as a two years Servitude of a Handicraft Apprenticeship was here in London. . . . Not that I write this to seduce or delude any, or to draw them from their native soyle, but out of a love to my Countrymen, whom in the general I wish well to, and that the lowest of them may live in such a capacity of Estate, as that the bare interest of their Livelihoods might not altogether depend upon persons of the greatest extendments. . . .

They whose abilities cannot extend to purchase their own transportation over into Mary-Land, (and surely he that cannot command so small a sum for so great a matter, his life must needs be mighty low and dejected) I say they may for the debarment of a four years sordid liberty, go over into this Province and there live plentiously well. And what's a four years Servitude to advantage a man all the remainder of his dayes, making his predecessors happy in his sufficient abilities, which he attained to partly by the restrainment of so small a time?

Now those that commit themselves unto the care of the Merchant to carry them over, they need not trouble themselves with any inquisitive search touching their

---

George Alsop, "A Character of the Province of Maryland, 1666," in C. C. Hall, ed., *Narratives of Early Maryland* (New York: Charles Scribner's Sons, 1910; copyright renewed Barnes and Noble, 1946), 354–360.

Voyage; for there is such an honest care and provision made for them all the time they remain aboard the Ship, and are sailing over, that they want for nothing that is necessary and convenient.

The Merchant commonly before they go aboard the Ship, or set themselves in any forwardness for their Voyage, has Conditions of Agreements drawn between him and those that by a voluntary consent become his Servants, to serve him, his Heirs or Assigns, according as they in their primitive acquaintance have made their bargain, some two, some three, some four years; and whatever the Master or Servant tyes himself up to here in England by Condition, the Laws of the Province will force a performance of when they come there: Yet here is this Priviledge in it when they arrive, If they dwell not with the Merchant they made their first agreement withall, they may choose whom they will serve their prefixed time with; and after their curiosity has pitcht on one whom they think fit for their turn, and that they may live well withall, the Merchant makes an Assignment of the Indenture over to him whom they of their free will have chosen to be their Master, in the same nature as we here in England (and no otherwise) turn over Covenant Servants or Apprentices from one Master to another. Then let those whose chaps are always breathing forth those filthy dregs of abusive exclamations, . . . against this Country of Mary-Land, saying, That those which are transported over thither, are sold in open Market for Slaves, and draw in Carts like Horses; which is so damnable as untruth, that if they should search to the very Center of Hell, and enquire for a Lye of the most antient and damned stamp, I confidently believe they could not find one to parallel this: For know, That the Servants here in Mary-Land of all Colonies, distant or remote Plantations, have the least cause to complain, either for strictness of Servitude, want of Provisions, or need of Apparel: Five dayes and a half in the Summer weeks is the alotted time that they work in; and for two months, when the Sun predominates in the highest pitch of his heat, they claim an antient and customary Priviledge, to repose themselves three hours in the day within the house, and this is undeniably granted to them that work in the Fields.

In the Winter time, which lasteth three months (*viz.*) December, January, and February, they do little or no work or imployment, save cutting of wood to make good fires to sit by, unless their Ingenuity will prompt them to hunt the Deer, or Bear, or recreate themselves in Fowling, to slaughter the Swans, Geese, and Turkeys (which this Country affords in a most plentiful manner:) For every Servant has a Gun, Powder and Shot allowed him, to sport him withall on all Holidayes and leasurable times, if he be capable of using it, or be willing to learn. . . .

. . . He that lives in the nature of a Servant in this Province, must serve but four years by the Custom of the Country; and when the expiration of his time speaks him a Freeman, there's a Law in the Province, that enjoyns his Master whom he hath served to give him Fifty Acres of Land, Corn to serve him a whole year, three Sutes of Apparel, with things necessary to them, and Tools to work withall; so that they are no sooner free, but they are ready to set up for themselves, and when once entred, they live passingly well.

The Women that go over into this Province as Servants, have the best luck here as in any place of the world besides; for they are no sooner on shoar, but they are courted into a Copulative Matrimony, which some of them (for aught I know) had they not come to such a Market with their Virginity might have kept it by them until it had been mouldy. . . . Men have not altogether so good luck as Women in this kind, or natural preferment, without they be good Rhetoricians, and well vers'd in the art of perswasion, then (probably) they may ryvet themselves in the time of their Servitude into the private and reserved favour of their Mistress, if Age speak their Master deficient.

In short, touching the Servants of this Province, they live well in the time of their Service, and by their restrainment in that time, they are made capable of living much better when they come to be free; which in several other parts of the world I have observed, That after some servants have brought their indented and limited time to a just and legal period by Servitude, they have been much more incapable of supporting themselves from sinking into the Gulf of a slavish, poor, fettered, and intangled life, then all the fastness of their pre-fixed time did involve them in before. . . .

## 6. Robert Beverley Points Out the Benefits of Servitude, 1705

Their Servants, they distinguish by the Names of Slaves for Life, and Servants for a time.

Slaves are the Negroes, and their Posterity, following the condition of the Mother, according to the Maxim, *partus sequitur ventrem* [status proceeds from the womb]. They are call'd Slaves, in respect of the time of their Servitude, because it is for Life.

Servants, are those which serve only for a few years, according to the time of their Indenture, or the Custom of the Country. The Custom of the Country takes place upon such as have no Indentures. The Law in this case is, that if such Servants be under Nineteen years of Age, they must be brought into Court, to have their Age adjudged; and from the Age they are judg'd to be of, they must serve until they reach four and twenty: But if they be adjudged upwards of Nineteen, they are then only to be Servants for the term of five Years.

The Male-Servants, and Slaves of both Sexes, are imployed together in Tilling and Manuring the Ground, in Sowing and Planting Tobacco, Corn, &c. Some distinction indeed is made between them in their Cloaths, and Food; but the Work of both, is no other than what the Overseers, the Freemen, and the Planters themselves do.

Sufficient Distinction is also made between the Female-Servants, and Slaves; for a White Woman is rarely or never put to work in the Ground, if she be good for any thing else: And to Discourage all Planters from using any Women so, their Law imposes the heaviest Taxes upon Female-Servants working in the Ground, while it suffers all other white Women to be absolutely exempted: Whereas on the other hand, it is a common thing to work a Woman Slave out of Doors; nor does the Law make any distinction in her Taxes, whether her Work be Abroad, or at Home.

Because I have heard how strangely cruel, and severe, the Service of this Country is represented in some parts of *England;* I can't forbear affirming, that the work

Robert Beverly, *The History and Present State of Virginia,* 1705, rev. 1722 (1722 ed. repr. Charlottesville: University of Virginia Press, 1947), 271–274.

of their Servants, and Slaves, is no other than what every common Freeman do's. Neither is any Servant requir'd to do more in a Day, than his Overseer. And I can assure you with a great deal of Truth, that generally their Slaves are not worked near so hard, nor so many Hours in a Day, as the Husbandmen, and Day-Labourers in *England*. An Overseer is a Man, that having served his time, has acquired the Skill and Character of an experienced Planter, and is therefore intrusted with the Direction of the Servants and Slaves.

But to compleat this account of Servants, I shall give you a short Relation of the care their Laws take, that they be used as tenderly as possible.

### By the Laws of their Country

1. All Servants whatsoever, have their Complaints heard without Fee, or Reward; but if the Master be found Faulty, the charge of the Complaint is cast upon him, otherwise the business is done *ex Officio.*
2. Any Justice of Peace may receive the Complaint of a Servant, and order every thing relating thereto, till the next County-Court, where it will be finally determin'd.
3. All Masters are under the Correction, and Censure of the County-Courts, to provide for their Servants, good and wholsome Diet, Clothing, and Lodging.
4. They are always to appear, upon the first Notice given of the Complaint of their Servants, otherwise to forfeit the Service of them, until they do appear.
5. All Servants Complaints are to be receiv'd at any time in Court, without Process, and shall not be delay'd for want of Form; but the Merits of the Complaint must be immediately inquir'd into by the Justices; and if the Master cause any delay therein, the Court may remove such Servants, if they see Cause, until the Master will come to Tryal.
6. If a Master shall at any time disobey an Order of Court, made upon any Complaint of a Servant; the Court is impower'd to remove such Servant forthwith to another Master, who will be kinder; Giving to the former Master the produce only, (after Fees deducted) of what such Servants shall be sold for by Publick Outcry.
7. If a Master should be so cruel, as to use his Servant ill, that is faln Sick, or Lame in his Service, and thereby render'd unfit for Labour, he must be remov'd by the Church-Wardens out of the way of such Cruelty, and boarded in some good Planters House, till the time of his Freedom, the charge of which must be laid before the next County-Court, which has power to levy the same from time to time, upon the Goods and Chattels of the Master; After which, the charge of such Boarding is to come upon the Parish in General.
8. All hired Servants are intituled to these Priviledges.
9. No Master of a Servant, can make a new Bargain for Service, or other Matter with his Servant, without the privity and consent of a Justice of Peace, to prevent the Master's Over-reaching, or scareing such Servant into an unreasonable Complyance.
10. The property of all Money and Goods sent over thither to Servants, or carry'd in with them; is reserv'd to themselves, and remain intirely at their disposal.
11. Each Servant at his Freedom, receives of his Master fifteen Bushels of Corn, (which is sufficient for a whole year) and two new Suits of Cloaths, both Lin-

nen and Woollen; and then becomes as free in all respects, and as much entit-
uled to the Liberties, and Priviledges of the Country, as any other of the Inhabitants or Natives are.

12. Each Servant has then also a Right to take up fifty Acres of Land, where he can
find any unpatented: But that is no great Privilege, for any one may have as
good a right for a piece of Eight.

This is what the Laws prescribe in favour of Servants, by which you may find,
that the Cruelties and Severities imputed to that Country, are an unjust Reflection.
For no People more abhor the thoughts of such Usage, than the *Virginians,* nor take
more precaution to prevent it.

## E S S A Y S

During the first half of the seventeenth century tens of thousands of young English men
and women were willing to emigrate to the colonies because of the growth of poverty
and constriction of opportunity at home. They continued to come even after the risks,
particularly the high disease and death rates in the southern colonies, came to be known.
Peopling the colonies with single young servants, many of whom would not live to
complete their terms, had immense consequences. Imbalanced sex ratios, along with
postponement of marriage and childbearing until terms ended, meant that many died
without reproducing and the colonist population was composed largely of immigrants
until almost the end of the century. In the first essay Lois Green Carr, the historian of
Maryland's St. Mary's City Commission, and Lorena S. Walsh, historial researcher at
Colonial Williamsburg, consider the consequences for the women who were recruited
for the Chesapeake. They focus on whether women's status was enhanced in the frontier setting. How does their description compare to William Wood's anger over Indian
women's treatment in Chapter 2?

In the second essay historian James Horn, Director of the International Center for
Jefferson Studies at Monticello, explores the intertwined relationship between the growing tobacco economy and changing forms of servitude in the Chesapeake over the seventeenth century. This interaction produced the society and economy that typified the
region and created its characteristic institutions.

## The Experience of White Women in the Chesapeake

### LOIS GREEN CARR AND LORENA S. WALSH

Four facts were basic to all human experience in seventeenth-century Maryland.
First, for most of the period the great majority of inhabitants had been born in what
we now call Britain. Population increase in Maryland did not result primarily from
births in the colony before the late 1680s and did not produce a predominantly native population of adults before the first decade of the eighteenth century. Second,
immigrant men could not expect to live beyond age forty-three, and 70 percent

Lois Green Carr and Lorena Walsh. "The Planter's Wife: The Experience of Women in Seventeenth-
Century Maryland," *William and Mary Quarterly,* 3d ser., XXXIV (1977), 542–565. Reprinted by permission of the authors and the publisher.

would die before age fifty. Women may have had even shorter lives. Third, perhaps 85 percent of the immigrants, and practically all the unmarried immigrant women, arrived as indentured servants and consequently married late. Family groups were never predominant in the immigration to Maryland and were a significant part for only a brief time at mid-century. Fourth, many more men than women immigrated during the whole period. These facts—immigrant predominance, early death, late marriage, and sexual imbalance—created circumstances of social and demographic disruption that deeply affected family and community life.

We need to assess the effects of this disruption on the experience of women in seventeenth-century Maryland. Were women degraded by the hazards of servitude in a society in which everyone had left community and kin behind and in which women were in short supply? Were traditional restraints on social conduct weakened? If so, were women more exploited or more independent and powerful than women who remained in England? Did any differences from English experience which we can observe in the experience of Maryland women survive the transformation from an immigrant to a predominantly native-born society with its own kinship networks and community traditions? The tentative argument put forward here is that the answer to all these questions is Yes. There were degrading aspects of servitude, although these probably did not characterize the lot of most women; there were fewer restraints on social conduct, especially in courtship, than in England; women were less protected but also more powerful than those who remained at home; and at least some of these changes survived the appearance in Maryland of New World creole communities. However, these issues are far from settled, and we shall offer some suggestions as to how they might be further pursued.

Maryland was settled in 1634, but in 1650 there were probably no more than six hundred persons and fewer than two hundred adult women in the province. After that time population growth was steady; in 1704 a census listed 30,437 white persons, of whom 7,163 were adult women. Thus in discussing the experience of white women in seventeenth-century Maryland we are dealing basically with the second half of the century.

Marylanders of that period did not leave letters and diaries to record their New World experience or their relationships to one another. Nevertheless, they left trails in the public records that give us clues. Immigrant lists kept in England and documents of the Maryland courts offer quantifiable evidence about the kinds of people who came and some of the problems they faced in making a new life. Especially valuable are the probate court records. Estate inventories reveal the kinds of activities carried on in the house and on the farm, and wills, which are usually the only personal statements that remain for any man or woman, show something of personal attitudes. . . .

Whatever their status, one fact about immigrant women is certain: many fewer came than men. Immigrant lists, headright lists, and itemizations of servants in inventories show severe imbalance. On a London immigrant list of 1634–1635 men outnumbered women six to one. From the 1650s at least until the 1680s most sources show a ratio of three to one. From then on, all sources show some, but not great, improvement. Among immigrants from Liverpool over the years 1697–1707 the ratio was just under two and one half to one.

Why did not more women come? Presumably, fewer wished to leave family and community to venture into a wilderness. But perhaps more important, women were not as desirable as men to merchants and planters who were making fortunes raising and marketing tobacco, a crop that requires large amounts of labor. The gradual improvement in the sex ratio among servants toward the end of the century may have been the result of a change in recruiting the needed labor. In the late 1660s the supply of young men willing to emigrate stopped increasing sufficiently to meet the labor demands of a growing Chesapeake population. Merchants who recruited servants for planters turned to other sources, and among these sources were women. They did not crowd the ships arriving in the Chesapeake, but their numbers did increase.

To ask the question another way, why did women come? Doubtless, most came to get a husband, an objective virtually certain of success in a land where women were so far outnumbered. The promotional literature, furthermore, painted bright pictures of the life that awaited men and women once out of their time; and various studies suggest that for a while, at least, the promoters were not being entirely fanciful. Until the 1660s, and to a less degree the 1680s, the expanding economy of Maryland and Virginia offered opportunities well beyond those available in England to men without capital and to the women who became their wives.

Nevertheless, the hazards were also great, and the greatest was untimely death. Newcomers promptly became ill, probably with malaria, and many died. What proportion survived is unclear; so far no one has devised a way of measuring it. Recurrent malaria made the woman who survived seasoning less able to withstand other diseases, especially dysentery and influenza. She was especially vulnerable when pregnant. Expectation of life for everyone was low in the Chesapeake, but especially so for women. A woman who had immigrated to Maryland took an extra risk, though perhaps a risk not greater than she might have suffered by moving from her village to London instead.

The majority of women who survived seasoning paid their transportation costs by working for a four- or five-year term of service. The kind of work depended on the status of the family they served. A female servant of a small planter—who through about the 1670s might have had a servant—probably worked at the hoe. Such a man could not afford to buy labor that would not help with the cash crop. In wealthy families women probably were household servants, although some are occasionally listed in inventories of well-to-do planters as living on the quarters—that is, on plantations other than the dwelling plantation. Such women saved men the jobs of preparing food and washing linen but doubtless also worked in the fields. In middling households experience must have varied. Where the number of people to feed and wash for was large, female servants would have had little time to tend the crops. . . .

An additional risk for the woman who came as a servant was the possibility of bearing a bastard. At least 20 percent of the female servants who came to Charles County between 1658 and 1705 were presented to the county court for this cause. A servant woman could not marry unless someone was willing to pay her master for the term she had left to serve. If a man made her pregnant, she could not marry him unless he could buy her time. Once a woman became free, however, marriage was clearly the usual solution. Only a handful of free women were presented in Charles

County for bastardy between 1658 and 1705. Since few free women remained either single or widowed for long, not many were subject to the risk. The hazard of bearing a bastard was a hazard of being a servant.

This high rate of illegitimate pregnancies among servants raises lurid questions. Did men import women for sexual exploitation? Does John Barth's Whore of Dorset have a basis outside his fertile imagination? In our opinion, the answers are clearly No. Servants were economic investments on the part of planters who needed labor. A female servant in a household where there were unmarried men must have both provided and faced temptation, for the pressures were great in a society in which men outnumbered women by three to one. Nevertheless, the servant woman was in the household to work—to help feed and clothe the family and make tobacco. She was not primarily a concubine. . . .

A female servant paid dearly for the fault of unmarried pregnancy. She was heavily fined, and if no one would pay her fine, she was whipped. Furthermore, she served an extra twelve to twenty-four months to repay her master for the "trouble of his house" and labor lost, and the fathers often did not share in this payment of damages. On top of all, she might lose the child after weaning unless by then she had become free, for the courts bound out bastard children at very early ages. . . .

Were women sold for wives against their wills? No record says so, but nothing restricted a man from selling his servant to whomever he wished. Perhaps some women were forced into such marriages or accepted them as the least evil. But the man who could afford to purchase a wife—especially a new arrival—was usually already an established landowner. Probably most servant women saw an opportunity in such a marriage. In addition, the shortage of labor gave women some bargaining power. Many masters must have been ready to refuse to sell a woman who was unwilling to marry a would-be purchaser.

If a woman's time was not purchased by a prospective husband, she was virtually certain to find a husband once she was free. . . . In the four counties of the lower Western Shore only two of the women who left a probate inventory before the eighteenth century are known to have died single. Comely or homely, strong or weak, any young woman was too valuable to be overlooked, and most could find a man with prospects.

The woman who immigrated to Maryland, survived seasoning and service, and gained her freedom became a planter's wife. She had considerable liberty in making her choice. There were men aplenty, and no fathers or brothers were hovering to monitor her behavior or disapprove her preference. This is the modern way of looking at her situation, of course. Perhaps she missed the protection of a father, a guardian, or kinfolk, and the participation in her decision of a community to which she felt ties. There is some evidence that the absence of kin and the pressures of the sex ratio created conditions of sexual freedom in courtship that were not customary in England. A register of marriages and births for seventeenth-century Somerset County shows that about one-third of the immigrant women whose marriages are recorded were pregnant at the time of the ceremony—nearly twice the rate in English parishes. There is no indication of community objection to this freedom so long as marriage took place. No presentments for bridal pregnancy were made in any of the Maryland courts.

The planter's wife was likely to be in her mid-twenties at marriage. . . .

Because of the age at which an immigrant woman married, the number of children she would bear her husband was small. She had lost up to ten years of her childbearing life—the possibility of perhaps four or five children, given the usual rhythm of childbearing. At the same time, high mortality would reduce both the number of children she would bear over the rest of her life and the number who would live. One partner to a marriage was likely to die within seven years, and the chances were only one in three that a marriage would last ten years. In these circumstances, most women would not bear more than three or four children—not counting those stillborn—to any one husband, plus a posthumous child were she the survivor. The best estimates suggest that nearly a quarter, perhaps more, of the children born alive died during their first year and that 40 to 55 percent would not live to see age twenty. Consequently, one of her children would probably die in infancy, and another one or two would fail to reach adulthood. Wills left in St. Mary's County during the seventeenth century show the results. In 105 families over the years 1660 to 1680 only twelve parents left more than three children behind them, including those conceived but not yet born. The average number was 2.3, nearly always minors, some of whom might die before reaching adulthood.

For the immigrant woman, then, one of the major facts of life was that although she might bear a child about every two years, nearly half would not reach maturity. The social implications of this fact are far-reaching. Because she married late in her childbearing years and because so many of her children would die young, the number who would reach marriageable age might not replace, or might only barely replace, her and her husband or husbands as child-producing members of the society. Consequently, so long as immigrants were heavily predominant in the adult female population, Maryland could not grow much by natural increase. It remained a land of newcomers. . . .

A hazard of marriage for seventeenth-century women everywhere was death in childbirth, but this hazard may have been greater than usual in the Chesapeake. Whereas in most societies women tend to outlive men, in this malaria-ridden area it is probable that men outlived women. Hazards of childbirth provide the likely reason that Chesapeake women died so young. Once a woman in the Chesapeake reached forty-five, she tended to outlive men who reached the same age. Darrett and Anita Rutman have found malaria a probable cause of an exceptionally high death rate among pregnant women, who are, it appears, peculiarly vulnerable to that disease. . . .

However long they lived, immigrant women in Maryland tended to outlive their husbands—in Charles County, for example, by a ratio of two to one. This was possible, despite the fact that women were younger than men at death, because women were also younger than men at marriage. Some women were widowed with no living children, but most were left responsible for two or three. These were often tiny, and nearly always not yet sixteen.

This fact had drastic consequences, given the physical circumstances of life. People lived at a distance from one another, not even in villages, much less towns. The widow had left her kin 3,000 miles across an ocean, and her husband's family was also there. She would have to feed her children and make her own tobacco crop. Though neighbors might help, heavy labor would be required of her if she had no servants, until—what admittedly was usually not difficult—she acquired a new husband.

In this situation dying husbands were understandably anxious about the welfare of their families. Their wills reflected their feelings and tell something of how they regarded their wives. In St. Mary's and Charles counties during the seventeenth century, little more than one-quarter of the men left their widows with no more than the dower the law required—one-third of his land for her life, plus outright ownership of one-third of his personal property. If there were no children, a man almost always left his widow his whole estate. Otherwise there were a variety of arrangements.

During the 1660s, when testators begin to appear in quantity, nearly a fifth of the men who had children left all to their wives, trusting them to see that the children received fair portions. Thus in 1663 John Shircliffe willed his whole estate to his wife "towards the maintenance of herself and my children into whose tender care I do Commend them Desireing to see them brought up in the fear of God and the Catholick Religion and Chargeing them to be Dutiful and obedient to her." As the century progressed, husbands tended instead to give the wife all or a major part of the estate for her life, and to designate how it should be distributed after her death. Either way, the husband put great trust in his widow, considering that he knew she was bound to remarry. Only a handful of men left estates to their wives only for their term of widowhood or until the children came of age. When a man did not leave his wife a life estate, he often gave her land outright or more than her dower third of his movable property. Such bequests were at the expense of his children and showed his concern that his widow should have a maintenance which young children could not supply.

A husband usually made his wife his executor and thus responsible for paying his debts and preserving the estate. Only 11 percent deprived their wives of such powers. In many instances, however, men also appointed overseers to assist their wives and to see that their children were not abused or their property embezzled. Danger lay in the fact that a second husband acquired control of all his wife's property, including her life estate in the property of his predecessor. Over half of the husbands who died in the 1650s and 1660s appointed overseers to ensure that their wills were followed. Some trusted to the overseers' "Care and good Conscience for the good of my widow and fatherless children." Others more explicitly made overseers responsible for seeing that "my said child . . . and the other [expected child] (when pleases God to send it) may have their right Proportion of my Said Estate and that the said Children may be bred up Chiefly in the fear of God." A few men—but remarkably few—authorized overseers to remove children from households of stepfathers who abused them or wasted their property. On the whole, the absence of such provisions for the protection of the children points to the husband's overriding concern for the welfare of his widow and to his confidence in her management, regardless of the certainty of her remarriage. Evidently, in the politics of family life women enjoyed great respect. . . .

What happened to widows and children if a man died without leaving a will? There was great need for some community institution that could protect children left fatherless or parentless in a society where they usually had no other kin. By the 1660s the probate court and county orphans' courts were supplying this need. If a man left a widow, the probate court—in Maryland a central government agency—usually appointed her or her new husband administrator of the estate with power to pay its creditors under court supervision. Probate procedures provided a large measure of protection. These required an inventory of the movable property and careful accounting of all disbursements, whether or not a man had left a will. William Hollis of Baltimore County, for example, had three stepfathers in seven years, and only the care of the judge of probate prevented the third stepfather from paying the debts of the second with goods that had belonged to William's father. As the judge remarked, William had "an uncareful mother." . . .

. . . Every year the county courts were expected to check on the welfare of orphans of intestate parents and remove them or their property from guardians who abused them or misused their estates. From 1681, Maryland law required that a special jury be impaneled once a year to report neighborhood knowledge of mistreatment of orphans and hear complaints.

This form of community surveillance of widows and orphans proved quite effective. In 1696 the assembly declared that orphans of intestates were often better cared for than orphans of testators. From that time forward, orphans' courts were charged with supervision of all orphans and were soon given powers to remove any guardians who were shown false to their trusts, regardless of the arrangements laid down in a will. The assumption was that the deceased parent's main concern was the welfare of the child, and that the orphans' court, as "father to us poor orphans," should implement the parent's intent. In actual fact, the courts never removed children—as opposed to their property—from a household in which the mother was living, except to apprentice them at the mother's request. These powers were mainly exercised over guardians of orphans both of whose parents were dead. The community as well as the husband believed the mother most capable of nurturing his children.

Remarriage was the usual and often the immediate solution for a woman who had lost her husband. The shortage of women made any woman eligible to marry again, and the difficulties of raising a family while running a plantation must have made remarriage necessary for widows who had no son old enough to make tobacco. One indication of the high incidence of remarriage is the fact that there were only sixty women, almost all of them widows, among the 1,735 people who left probate inventories in four southern Maryland counties over the second half of the century. Most other women must have died while married and therefore legally without property to put through probate.

One result of remarriage was the development of complex family structures. Men found themselves responsible for stepchildren as well as their own offspring, and children acquired half-sisters and half-brothers. Sometimes a women married a second husband who himself had been previously married, and both brought children of former spouses to the new marriage. They then produced children of their own. The possibilities for conflict over the upbringing of children are evident, and crowded living conditions, found even in the households of the wealthy, must have added to family tensions. Luckily, the children of the family very often had the same mother. In Charles County, at least, widows took new husbands three times more often than widowers took new wives. The role of the mother in managing the relationships of half-brothers and half-sisters or stepfathers and stepchildren must have been critical to family harmony.

Early death in this immigrant population thus had broad effects on Maryland society in the seventeenth century. It produced what we might call a pattern of serial polyandry, which enabled more men to marry and to father families than the sex ratios otherwise would have permitted. It produced thousands of orphaned children who had no kin to maintain them or preserve their property, and thus gave rise to an institution almost unknown in England, the orphans' court, which was charged with their protection. And early death, by creating families in which the mother was the unifying element, may have increased her authority within the household. . . .

So far we have considered primarily the experience of immigrant women. What of their daughters? How were their lives affected by the demographic stresses of Chesapeake society?

One of the most important points in which the experience of daughters differed from that of their mothers was the age at which they married. In this woman-short world, the mothers had married as soon as they were eligible, but they had not usually become eligible until they were mature women in their middle twenties. Their daughters were much younger at marriage. A vital register kept in Somerset County shows that some girls married at age twelve and that the mean age at marriage for those born before 1670 was sixteen and a half years. . . .

Not only did native girls marry early, but many of them were pregnant before the ceremony. Bridal pregnancy among native-born women was not as common as among immigrants. Nevertheless, in seventeenth-century Somerset County 20 percent of native brides bore children within eight and one half months of marriage. This was a somewhat higher percentage than has been reported from seventeenth-century English parishes.

These facts suggest considerable freedom for girls in selecting a husband. Almost any girl must have had more than one suitor, and evidently many had freedom to spend time with a suitor in a fashion that allowed her to become pregnant. . . .

Native girls married young and bore children young; hence they had more children than immigrant women. This fact ultimately changed the composition of the Maryland population. Native-born females began to have enough children to enable couples to replace themselves. These children, furthermore, were divided about evenly between males and females. By the mid-1680s, in all probability, the population thus began to grow through reproductive increase, and sexual imbalance began to decline. In 1704 the native-born preponderated in the Maryland assembly for the first time and by then were becoming predominant in the adult population as a whole. . . .

## Tobacco and the Peopling of Virginia

### JAMES HORN

. . . As the numbers of Indians inhabiting the Chesapeake rapidly declined, the white population grew by leaps and bounds, from 105 men and boys who settled at

---

From *Adapting to a New World: English Society in the Seventeenth-Century Chesapeake* by James Horn. Copyright © 1994 by the University of North Carolina Press. Used by permission of the publisher.

Jamestown in 1607 to about 900 in 1620, 8,000 in 1640, 25,000 in 1660, 60,000 in 1680, and 85,000 by 1700. Virginia was the most populous of the mainland colonies throughout the century, although dwarfed by the scale of demographic growth in the Caribbean. In both Virginia and Maryland the flow of immigrants surged after 1650. During the 1630s and 1640s immigration averaged about 8,000–9,000 per decade, but from 1650 to 1680, 16,000–20,000 people entered the Chesapeake each decade—the equivalent of the population of England's second city, Bristol. Half the total number of immigrants who settled along the tobacco coast in the seventeenth century arrived in these three decades.

Despite this impressive growth, immigrants did not enter a healthy environment. Whereas about 120,000 settlers immigrated to the Chesapeake over the whole century, the white population in 1700 was not even 90,000. Unlike the northern colonies, growth in the South was sustained only by continuous immigration to compensate for the massive wastage of life and, increasingly after 1675, a significant movement of people out of the region. Contemporaries were well aware of the deleterious effect of the Chesapeake environment on English settlers. Colonists, wrote George Gardyner in 1650, were subject to "much sickness or death. For the air is exceeding unwholesome, insomuch as one of three scarcely liveth the first year at this time." . . .

. . . Mortality rates in the tidewater, however, were even greater. Up to 40 percent of new arrivals may have died in their first couple of years, commonly of a variety of ailments associated with malaria and intestinal disorders. Malaria occasionally reached pandemic proportions among settlers and frequently left survivors in poor health, easy prey to a variety of other diseases. Even if the outcome was not fatal, most immigrants experienced a period of sickness (seasoning) in their first year. Moving to Virginia and Maryland, like moving from the provinces to London, was risky and amounted to a calculated gamble on survival. For those who survived and lived long enough, the rewards could be considerable, but that very success was predicated in part on a rapid turnover of population caused by the high death rate.

Natural population growth was retarded also by the considerable sexual imbalance that existed throughout the century. Chesapeake society was dominated by males not only in the conventional sense but simply in sheer numbers. At no time in the century did the sex ratio improve upon two to three men for every woman. Such an imbalance had far-reaching practical effects (quite apart from the psychological stress it must have caused). A shortage of women restricted family formation and forced many males to remain single. More than a quarter of men from the lower Western Shore of Maryland who died leaving estates between 1658 and 1705 were unmarried. The problem was exacerbated by the relatively late age at which women married. Since the vast majority of women arrived in the Chesapeake as servants and were usually obliged to finish their term of service before marrying, they were unable to take a husband until their mid-twenties: about the same age they would have married in England. . . .

One of the most obvious differences between English and New World society immediately apparent to early settlers and, indeed, its main attraction was an "abundance of land and absence of people." Covering about half the land area of England, the Chesapeake had a population at midcentury that could have quite easily been accommodated in a small English county or London suburb. . . . Low population density was a function of both the small size of local populations and a scattered pattern of settlement. Given the cheapness of land and the nature of the economy, it made sense for planters to take up large tracts of land (by European standards) and seat themselves on or near convenient shipping routes. Water carriage not only provided the best means of transporting bulky tobacco leaf packed in hogsheads, but it was also favored by English merchants, who preferred to trade directly with individual producers: manufactured goods, liquor, and servants brought from London, Bristol, or other outports could be exchanged on the spot for tobacco. The system bypassed the need for market towns in the tidewater, because trade was as dispersed as settlement.

An unfortunate consequence, as commentators never tired of repeating, was that Chesapeake society failed to develop urban communities. "Townes and Corporations have likewise been much hindred," Anthony Langston wrote of Virginia in the 1650s,

> by our manner of seating the Country; every man having Liberty . . . to take up Land (untaken before) and there seat, build, clear, and plant without any manner of restraint from the Government in relation to their Religion, and gods Service, or security of their persons, or the peace of the Country, so that every man builds in the midst of his own Land, and therefore provides beforehand to take up so much at the first Patent, that his great Grandchild may be sure not to want Land to go forward with any great design they covet, likewise the conveniency of the River from Transportation of their Commodities, by which meanes they have been led up and down by these famous rivers . . . to seate in a stragling distracted Condition leaving the inside of the Land from the Rivers as wast for after Comers.

Thirty years later, the French Huguenot Durand of Dauphine commented, there was "neither town nor village in the whole country, save one named Gemston [Jamestown], where the Council assembles. All the rest is made up of single houses, each on its own plantation." In 1678, Charles, Lord Baltimore, described St. Mary's City, the capital of Maryland, as consisting of "not above thirty houses, and these at considerable distances from each other." No other place in the province was even worthy of being called a town.

In terms of first impressions, it is worth stressing that to English eyes what was missing in Virginia's and Maryland's landscape was as significant as what was present. Immigrants, whether from urban or rural backgrounds, were used to living in a society where there was a hierarchy of interdependent and interrelated communities: village, market town, provincial capital, and city. Few people in England lived more than a few miles from a local town—an hour, if that, by road or across country. Along the tobacco coast, only the cluster of dwellings and other buildings located in the colonies' capitals resembled small towns, and for most of the century even they were nearer in size, if not character, to English villages. The absence of towns inclined English commentators to view the Chesapeake as undeveloped and uncivilized. Missing, too, was the bustle of fairs and market days, crowded taverns and inns, and busy roads bringing people and goods to trade. Approximations existed, but nothing that could compare to the crowd of people and places familiar to

English men and women in their native communities. Getting used to the *absence* of significant aspects of everyday life that were taken for granted in England was probably the most difficult part of adapting to conditions in the Chesapeake.

## Tobacco and the Chesapeake Economy

Little can be understood of the development of Virginia and Maryland society without reference to tobacco. Considered a luxury in the early seventeenth century, it could be produced cheaply in the tidewater and sold initially for a handsome profit in European markets. From the early 1620s, when extensive production began, tobacco governed the character and pace of immigration, population growth, settlement patterns, husbandry and land use, transatlantic trade, the development of the home market, manufactures, opportunity, standards of living, and government policy. Settlers used leaf as local money, paid their taxes, extended credit, settled debts, and valued their goods in it. "We have [no] trade at home and abroad," a contemporary stated at the end of the century, "but that of Tobacco . . . [it] is our meat, drink, clothes, and monies." Without tobacco, a very different kind of society would have evolved.

The advantages of tobacco production were many: its yield per acre was high, and its keeping qualities were good; it fetched a better price per pound than English grains, and the soils and climate of the Chesapeake were, for the most part, suitable for its cultivation. A plantation required relatively little capital to set up, and a man's labor, or that of his family and a couple of servants, was sufficient to run it. Last, there was a potentially expansive market for tobacco in England, which the monopoly granted to the Virginia Company in 1619 recognized and protected. The very success of the "Weede," in fact, would later cause problems in both colonies owing to overproduction. . . .

. . . The creation of a mass market was crucial, because without it Chesapeake tobacco would have remained a high-priced luxury item in limited demand. Consequently, there would have been no expansion of output and, therefore, no need for significant population growth. Stagnation set in after 1680 because planters were unable to lower the costs of production any further: freight charges ceased to fall as quickly after 1660, the amount of tobacco being produced by each worker reached a maximum such that increased productivity required more labor (more capital investment), and the price of both land and servants rose steadily in the 1670s and 1680s. Any economies in the costs of transportation and marketing of leaf could no longer be passed on to the consumer; instead, they helped planters absorb rising production costs. The result was thirty years of depression until the end of the War of Spanish Succession and renewed demand after 1715. . . .

## Inequality and Opportunity

Chesapeake society differed from that of England in many important respects. Entire sections of English society were missing. There was little in the Chesapeake to attract men of established fortune from the parent country, despite the efforts of promotional writers to convince them otherwise. In the absence of towns and industry and with a relatively small, dispersed population, Virginia and Maryland did not require (and could not support) the range of specialist trades and crafts to be found at home. Consequently, social status associated with most Old World occupations was not transferred to the New. Colonial society lacked the complexity and subtlety of European social hierarchies.

Yet this is not to imply that the Chesapeake developed as a rough-hewn, undifferentiated society. As in England, those with the greatest estates were judged the fittest to govern, and the precept that political power followed economic power was generally accepted, if not always practiced. The absence of a traditional ruling class undoubtedly weakened social cohesion and was exacerbated by the high turnover of officeholders owing to heavy mortality, the difficulty of establishing ruling dynasties, and the return of gentry to England. In these uncertain conditions, it is hardly surprising that colonial rulers appealed time and time again to English precedents to justify and legitimize their actions. Assemblies were loosely modeled on Parliament, county courts on quarter sessions, and the church (in Virginia, not Maryland) on parochial organization in England. Virginia governors were enjoined in their oath of office to adhere as closely as possible "to the common law of England, and equity thereof." Justices were commanded to "do justice as near as may be" to English precedent and were granted extensive powers similar to those of their counterparts in English shires. Injunctions and appeals to the past, to tradition, were intoned endlessly throughout the century. . . .

. . . Inevitably, colonial officials encountered serious difficulties in trying to recreate, overnight, governing institutions that had evolved over centuries in England. Neither Virginia nor Maryland developed viable manorial structures, and in both colonies the county court absorbed the functions of English borough, manor, and church courts, becoming the key governing institution at the local level. The rich particularity of the past could not be replicated in America; what emerged were compromises and approximations.

Chesapeake society, therefore, developed as a simplified version of English society, but also a highly aberrant one. One of the most obvious social differences was the presence of slaves. Numerically insignificant throughout most of the century, the black population increased enormously in the final two decades. From a couple of thousand in 1670 (6 percent of the total population), numbers shot up to about thirteen thousand (13 percent of the population) by 1700. Half the bound labor force was enslaved by the beginning of the eighteenth century.

As suggested earlier, English attitudes toward blacks were molded by a similar ragbag of racial and cultural prejudice adopted against Indians and other alien peoples. They were savage, heathen, lascivious, shifty, lazy, and apelike, in every way inferior to whites. Apart from emigrants from London or Bristol, most settlers probably encountered blacks for the first time in the Chesapeake and in this context made the indelible connection between slavery and race. Yet, like English reactions to Indians, the everyday response to blacks was more complex than the general framework of prejudice and institution of slavery might lead one to expect. Especially in the early years of settlement, down to 1660, when numbers were small and blacks worked alongside servants and masters to bring in the tobacco crop, relations between the two races may have been relatively relaxed. Occasionally slaves were freed or purchased their liberty. Some acquired property and were able to live peaceably side by side with their white neighbors.

But one should not exaggerate even the limited opportunities for blacks, slave or free, to improve their condition in this period. From the 1660s, Virginia began legislating "stringent racial laws" designed to regulate white-black relations and provide planters with greater powers to discipline their slaves. Possibly this development represented an effort by the recently restored royal government to tighten up generally on bound laborers in the colony: to highlight the distinctions between free and unfree and clarify their respective rights and privileges. In this fashion, social position was defined and the preeminence of the elite confirmed. But measures enacted against slaves had no parallel among the white population, and it is certain that conditions for blacks began to deteriorate sharply as a consequence. Mass importation after 1680 and the changing origin of slaves (brought directly from Africa rather than the Caribbean) served only to intensify discriminatory legislation. Chesapeake society took on a new character as planters became irrevocably wedded to slavery and shifted from incoherent racial prejudice to full-blown racism. . . .

In terms of social development, however, the crucial issue was whether the huge numbers of young men and women who ended up laboring in Virginia and Maryland could be absorbed into society once they had completed their period of service.

. . . Like the lotteries that initially helped finance the settlement of Virginia, poor men and women who immigrated under indentures entered a gigantic human lottery themselves. Losers met an early death or lived in poverty for the rest of their lives. Winners secured a comfortable income and independence and in a few cases attained a level of wealth and social standing unthinkable for men and women of humble origins at home. The logic of the lottery, however, dictated that for every ex-servant who made it into the ranks of the middling or upper classes, tens of others, who left barely a trace in the records, died in poverty and obscurity.

Opportunity for all planters was closely attuned to the ebb and flow of the tobacco economy. During the early 1660s the price of leaf dipped below two pennies per pound and then hovered just above one penny for the rest of the decade. There was no improvement in the years that followed; if anything, conditions worsened. English officials were bombarded by a chorus of complaints. Sir William Berkeley wrote in 1662 that prices had fallen so low that tobacco would not "bear the charge of freight and customs, answer the adventure, give encouragement to the traders and subsistence to the inhabitants." A few years later, Thomas Ludwell told Lord Arlington that tobacco was "worth nothing." He elaborated to one of Sir William's kinsmen, Lord John Berkeley, in 1667. "Twelve hundred pounds of tobacco is the medium of men's crops," he wrote, "and half a penny per pound is certainly the full medium of the price given for it, which is fifty shillings out of which when the taxes . . . shall be deducted, is very little to a poor man who hath perhaps a wife and children to cloath and other necessities to buy. Truly so much too little that I can attribute it to nothing but the great mercy of God . . . that keeps them from mutiny and confusion." . . .

. . . Poverty in the Chesapeake had its own distinctive character, expressed by severe material deprivation (poor housing and low standards of living), the inability of many small planters in Virginia after 1660 and Maryland after 1680 to escape from a living of bare subsistence, and the movement out of the region after 1675 of thousands of ex-servants for whom the Chesapeake held no future. As the price of tobacco spiraled downward, the transition from servant to smallholder brought neither the well-being nor economic independence anticipated. At the level of the individual holding, landowners, big and small, had complete freedom to manage their affairs as they felt fit, perhaps limiting the amount of tobacco grown and turning to other products. But economic opportunities for smallholders were considerably limited by the grip of tobacco on the economy and low returns from leaf. The stint placed on Virginia tobacco production in 1668, for example, meant that planters "not able to remove from their ould and over worne grounds, are Kepte by the Limitacon of a certen nomber of plants per poll in Perpetuall poverty." Hedged in by meager profits and dependence on merchants and wealthy planters for credit to buy essentials, the world of the small planter became increasingly constricted as the going got tougher in the last third of the century. . . .

. . . As economic conditions worsened throughout the Chesapeake in the 1670s and opportunities for the poor and middling planters declined, so social divisions and attitudes hardened. It is difficult to avoid the conclusion that many of those at the pinnacle of colonial society viewed the majority of planters as merely a source of revenue to mulct dry. Unable to command the labor of the poor indefinitely, elites devised numerous strategies for siphoning off the small profits of planters into their own coffers. . . . Culpeper, the new governor, wrote from Virginia in 1680 that the "low price of tobacco staggers . . . the continuance of it will be the fatal and speedy ruin of this noble Colony without the application of a remedy." "Our most formidable enemy, poverty," Colonel Nicholas Spencer observed, "is falling violently on us through the low value, or rather no value, of tobacco." A few years later, the colony was described as "a Barbarous and Malancholy part of the world." If rebellion had tempered the worst excesses of government corruption, it did nothing to alleviate the poor planter's problem of making a living. The last two decades of the century were locust years.

Chesapeake society underwent profound changes during the course of the seventeenth century. Evolving from fragile frontier outposts in the early years, the adoption of plantation agriculture and subsequent massive immigration ensured the survival of the Chesapeake Bay colonies and led to the spread of English settlement across thousands of square miles of the tidewater. Gradually the landscape was transformed. The first colonists had envisioned a land of limitless promise where towns and cities would push back the forest, manufactures would thrive, and well-cultivated farms would tap the natural abundance of the earth. The outcome, however, was very different. Plentiful cheap land and plantation agriculture led to the evolution of a form of husbandry excoriated as slovenly and wasteful by English commentators who misunderstood its advantages, the tobacco trade retarded the development of urban centers because marketing and distribution took place in Europe, and no important manufactures took root. These shortcomings were a constant source of frustration and disappointment to colonial officials, who blamed planters' slavish dependence on tobacco for Virginia's and Maryland's failings.

If the Chesapeake did not live up to the expectations of early settlers or projectors, nevertheless during the middle decades of the century the region provided opportunities for poor immigrants who survived the disease environment and the rigors of servitude to earn a modest livelihood and perhaps move a few rungs up the social ladder. With hard work, or perhaps a good marriage, male and female servants might themselves eventually become smallholders and employ their own servants. Potentially, even greater rewards were to be had: a fortunate few enjoyed spectacular success and moved from servitude into the ranks of the local gentry within a few years, a degree of social mobility unthinkable in England. But opportunities for the poor should not be exaggerated. During the 1660s and 1670s, first in Virginia and then in Maryland, opportunities for the poor declined. Ex-servants experienced increasing difficulty in establishing themselves as independent planters, and many smallholders were relentlessly pushed to the brink of poverty by the steady decline in income as the price of tobacco fell. The distinctive features of the Chesapeake's social structure slowly took shape. About half the population was made up of servants, slaves, and recently freed men and women (dependents of established planters): the equivalent of servants in husbandry, day laborers, and domestics in England, although, of course, there was no equivalent of the slave field hand. Small and middling planters, including tenant farmers, who used their own family labor to work their holding or who possessed a few servants, made up about 40 percent of the population, while the rest were wealthy planters, merchants, gentry, and a small group of artisans.

From the 1660s, especially in older-settled regions, the social order became increasingly articulated and social distinctions increasingly visible. Social rank became more predictable and rigid, more like that in England. At the same time, and probably related, settlers' tolerance of nonwhite elements of the population declined. Indian peoples were marginalized, and conditions for blacks rapidly deteriorated. By the turn of the century, the political and economic consolidation of colonial elites in both Maryland and Virginia and the switch from white to slave labor heralded the emergence of the "slave-based, gentry-dominated society" characteristic of the Chesapeake's golden age.

 # F U R T H E R    R E A D I N G

T. H. Breen and Stephen Innes, *"Myne Owne Ground": Race and Freedom on Virginia's Eastern Shore, 1640–1676* (1980).

Kathleen M. Brown, *Good Wives, Nasty Wenches, and Anxious Patriarchs: Gender, Race and Power in Colonial Virginia* (1996).

Lois G. Carr, Russell R. Menard, and Lorena S. Walsh, *Robert Cole's World: Agriculture and Society in Early Maryland* (1991).

Lois Green Carr, Philip D. Morgan, and Jean B. Russo, eds., *Colonial Chesapeake Society* (1988).

David Galenson, *White Servitude in Colonial America: An Economic Analysis* (1981).

Ivor Noël Hume, *The Virginia Adventure, Roanoke to Jamestown: An Archaeological and Historical Odyssey* (1994).

Ann Kussmaul, *Servants in Husbandry in Early Modern England* (1981).

Gloria L. Main, *Tobacco Colony: Life in Early Maryland, 1650–1720* (1982).

Edmund S. Morgan, *American Slavery, American Freedom: The Ordeal of Colonial Virginia* (1975).

James R. Perry, *The Formation of a Society on Virginia's Eastern Shore, 1615–1655* (1990).

Darrett C. Rutman and Anita Rutman, *A Place in Time: Middlesex County, Virginia, 1650–1750* (1984).

Thad W. Tate and David L. Ammerman, eds., *The Chesapeake in the Seventeenth Century: Essays on Anglo-American Society and Politics* (1979).

# New England: The Settlement of Puritan Colonies

*In the early years European colonizers were little interested in the area between Chesapeake Bay and the St. Lawrence. One short-lived attempt to settle a colony in Maine at the same time as Jamestown (1607) had convinced investors that the region was both inhospitable and unlikely to yield products of value. Attention focused on the north—Newfoundland and the great Canadian river—where the rich fishing and furs had attracted hundreds of voyages every year since shortly after the region was discovered. These expeditions came in the spring and left in the autumn; there seemed little reason to build expensive colonies on those cold, rocky shores.*

*New England, then called the North Part of Virginia, became attractive when a new type of colony was planned: transfers of entire communities of English men and women who sought an environment in which they could thrive and worship God as they saw fit. Plymouth was settled in this way in 1620 by a small group of Puritan Separatists who believed the Church of England was so corrupt that they had separated themselves entirely from it. In 1630 a huge exodus of Puritans founded Massachusetts Bay; these considered themselves still loyal members of the church who wished to reform it by example. Thousands left England in the 1630s partly because of the same economic distress that fed emigration to the Chesapeake, but also because Charles I and his archbishop of Canterbury, William Laud, were increasingly pushing the church in directions the Puritans abhorred and requiring conformity.*

*The Puritans chose New England because its environment was conducive to small family farms rather than great plantations; its lack of rich crops would keep out those who might seek to pervert their godly experiment. They found the land depleted of its native population by a disastrous plague that had struck shortly before Plymouth was founded; a second wave of European disease devastated the Indians in the early 1630s. Some Puritans, whose providential outlook caused them to look for God's will in all events, saw this as divine intervention on their behalf, clearing the land for their habitation.*

*Massachusetts Bay began with the kind of organization toward which the earlier colonies had moved slowly and painfully: a relatively large European population of all ages and both genders settled as families on land they owned. By 1630 all English-sponsored colonies had achieved this basic plan, and the North American*

*plantations began to grow rapidly from this point forward. In New England popu-
lation growth resulted in the founding of large numbers of new communities. Although colony leaders celebrated their success, they also lamented what they saw as
movement away from the great unity and dedication of the founding period.*

# D O C U M E N T S

The Pilgrims, who had been forced by their backers to take a large number of skilled
colonists who were not Puritans, quickly sent back reports to their friends in England,
which were published in 1622. Document 1, drawn from a long letter sent by Governor
William Bradford and his closest advisor Edward Winslow, describes the Mayflower
Compact, by which the Pilgrims and the non-Puritan "strangers" among them agreed to
govern themselves. He also describes the first Thanksgiving at Plymouth which took
place in an early spirit of peace with their Wampanoag Indian neighbors.

In the decade following Plymouth's founding in 1620 English Puritans saw increasing signs that their nation was turning away from true religion. In document 2
Thomas Hooker warned that God was preparing to desert England; Hooker and other
leading ministers chose emigration to New England. John Winthrop, governor of Massachusetts Bay, gave a famous sermon on board the *Arbella,* the ship carrying the first
contingent, in which he outlined the distinctive characteristics of his colony bound together by a common purpose. Winthrop's images, related in document 3, vividly outlin-
ing the dedication he expected from the colonists, have stood as the image of America's
founding and have been recalled many times by later leaders. John Pond, a far humbler
member of the *Arbella* fleet, wrote in document 4 to his father for help, as Richard
Frethorne had done from Virginia (in Chapter 3), in facing the rigors of the new plantation. Both New England colonies experienced a high death rate in their first years. In
document 5, minister Thomas Welde wrote to his former parishioners in England certi-
fying that after two years the colony was firmly established. With establishment of a
thriving economy, however, came diversification and competition, which Governor
Winthrop believed violated the principles on which the colony had been founded. In
document 6 he recorded the evidence against Robert Keayne, who was accused of using his position as merchant to take advantage of his neighbors.

## 1. Pilgrim Leaders Create the Mayflower Compact and Describe the First Thanksgiving, 1620, 1621

### *The Mayflower Compact, 1620*

This day before we came to harbor, observing some not well affected to unity and
concord, but gave some appearance of faction, it was thought good there should be
an association and agreement, that we should combine together in one body, and to
submit to such government and governors, as we should by common consent agree
to make and choose, and set our hands to this that follows word for word.

---

Some of the spelling in this document has been modernized.

William Bradford and Edward Winslow, *A Relation or Journall of the beginning and proceedings of the
English Plantation setled at Plimouth in New England* (London, 1622), [Known as *Mourt's Relation*].

In the name of God, Amen. We whose names are underwritten, the loyal Subjects of our dread sovereign Lord King James, by the grace of God of Great Britain, France, and Ireland King, Defender of the Faith, etc.

Having under-taken for the glory of God, and advancement of the Christian Faith, and honor of our King and Country, a Voyage to plant the first Colony in the Northern parts of VIRGINIA, do by these presents solemnly and mutually in the presence of God and one of another, covenant, and combine our selves together into a civil body politic, for our better ordering and preservation, and furtherance of the ends aforesaid: and by virtue hereof to enact, constitute, and frame such just and equal Laws, Ordinances, acts, constitutions, offices from time to time, as shall be thought most meet and convenient for the general good of the Colony; unto which we promise all due submission and obedience. In witness whereof we have here-under subscribed our names. Cape Cod 11 of November, in the year of the reign of our sovereign Lord King James, of England, France, and Ireland 18 and of Scotland 54. Anno Domino 1620.

## The First Thanksgiving, 1621

A Letter Sent from New-England to a friend in these parts . . .

Loving, and old Friend, although I received no Letter from you by this Ship, yet foreasmuch as I know you expect the performance of my promise, which was, to write unto you truly and faithfully of all things, I have therefore at this time sent unto you accordingly. Referring you for further satisfaction to our more large Relations. You shall understand, that in this little time, that a few of us have been there, we have built seven dwelling houses, and four for the use of the Plantation, and have made preparation for divers other. We set the last Spring some twentie Acres of Indian-Corne, and sowed some six Acres of Barley and Peas, and according to the manner of the Indian, we manured our ground with Herrings or rather Shads, which we have in great abundance, and take with great ease at our doors. Our Corne did prove well, and God be praised, we had a good increase of our Indian-Corne, and our Barley indifferent good, but our Peas not worth the gathering, for we feared they were too late sown. They came up very well, and blossomed, but the Sun parched them in the blossom. Our harvest being gotten in, our Governor sent four men on fowling, that so we might after a more special manner rejoice together, after we had gathered the fruit of our labors. They four in one day killed as much fowl, as with a little help beside, served the Company almost a week, at which time amongst other Recreations, we exercised our Arms, many of the Indians coming amongst us, and amongst the rest their greatest King Massasoit, with some ninety men, whom for three days we entertained and feasted, and they went out and killed five Deer, which they brought to the Plantation and bestowed on our Governor, and upon the Captain, and others. And although it be not always so plentiful, as it was at this time with us, yet by the goodness of God, we are so far from want, that we often wish you partakers of our planty. We have found the Indians very faithful in their Covenant of Peace with us; very loving and ready to pleasure us. We often go to them, and they come to us; some of us have been fifty miles by Land in the Country with them; the occasions and Relations whereof you shall understand by our general and more full Declaration of such things as are worth the noting. Yea it hath pleased God so to possess the Indians with a fear of us, and love unto us, that not only the greatest King amongst them called Massasoit, but also all the Princes and people round about us, have either made suit unto us, or been glad of any occasion to make peace with us, so that seven of them at once have sent their messengers to us to that end . . . willingly to be under the protection, and subjects to our sovereign Lord King James, so that there is now great peace amongst the Indians themselves, which was not formerly, neither would have been but for us. And we for our parts walk as peaceably and safely in the wood, as in the highways in England, we entertain them familiarly in our houses, and they as friendly bestowing their Venison on us. They are a people without any Religion, or knowledge of any God, yet very trusty, quick of apprehension, ripe witted, just.

## 2. The Reverend Thomas Hooker Warns of England's Impending Punishment by God, 1631

. . . I will deal plainly with you. As sure of God is God, God is going from England. Shall I tell you what God told me? Nay, I must tell you on pain of my life. Will you give ear and believe me? I am a poor ambassador sent from God to do his message unto you; and, although I be low, yet my message is from above, and he that sent me is great, and from above; and O that he would grant that this my message might be believed (for his sake)!

What if I should tell you what God told me yesternight that he would destroy England and lay it waste? What say you to this, my beloved? It is my message, by meditation in God's word, that he bid me do to you, and he expects an answer from you. I do my message as God commanded me. What sayest thou unto it, England? I must return an answer to my master that sent me, yea, this present night I must return an answer; for the Lord hath appointed a set time, saying, Exodus 9:5, *Tomorrow the Lord will do this thing in the land.* Why speak you not? An answer you must give. Do you think well of it? Will you have England destroyed? Will you put the aged to trouble, and your young men to the sword? Will you have your young women widows, and your virgins defiled? Will you have your dear and tender little ones tossed upon the pikes and dashed against the stones? Or will you have them brought up in Popery, in idolatry, under a necessity of perishing their souls forever, which is worst of all? Will you have these temples wherein we seem to worship God, will you have them and your houses burnt with fire? And will you see England laid waste without inhabitants? Are you well-contented it shall be so? (God bade me ask. Why do you not answer me? I must not stir without it, I must have it.) I am an importunate suitor for Christ. Oh send me not sad away, but speak comfortably and cheerfully! What are you resolved of? Are you willing to enjoy God still, and to have him dwell with you? (You are, are you not?) It is well, I am glad of it if it be so.

But you must not only say so, but you must use the means, and you must plead importunately with your God; for, although his sword be drawn and in his hand, lifted up and ready to strike, yet suffer him not to destroy, but rather to sheath his sword in the blood of his enemies. (God grant it.) I would be glad to have England flourish still. (And so are you, are you not? You are.) But if desolation do come, thank yourselves for it, it is your own fault if you be destroyed, and not God's; for he delights not in the death of any. . . .

---

Thomas Hooker, *The Danger of Desertion* (1641, 1657), reprinted in Alan Heimert and Andrew Delbanco, eds., *The Puritans in America* (Cambridge, MA, 1985) 64–69.

Look to it, for God is going, and if he do go, then our glory goes also. And then we may say with Phineha's wife, I Samuel 4:22, *The glory is departed from Israel.* So glory is departed from England; for England hath seen her best days, and the reward of sin is coming on apace; for God is packing up of his gospel, because none will buy his wares (not come to his price). God begins to ship away his Noahs, which prophesied and foretold that destruction was near; and God makes account that New England shall be a refuge for his Noahs and his Lots, a rock and a shelter for his righteous ones to run unto; and those that were vexed to see the ungodly lives of the people in this wicked land, shall there be safe. Oh, therefore my brethren, lay hold on God, and let him not go out of your coasts. (He is going!) Look about you, I say, and stop him at the town's end, and let not thy God depart! Oh, England, lay siege about him by humble and hearty closing with him, and although he be going, he is not yet gone! Suffer him not to go far, suffer him not to say farewell, or rather fare-ill, England! . . .

## 3. Governor John Winthrop Gives a Model of Christian Charity, 1630

1. For the persons, we are a Company professing ourselves fellow members of Christ. In which respect only though we were absent from each other many miles, and had our employments as far distant, yet we ought to account ourselves knit together by this bond of love, and live in the exercise of it, if we would have comfort of our being in Christ. . . .

2. for the work we have in hand, it is by a mutual consent through a special overruling providence, and a more than an ordinary approbation of the Churches of Christ to seek out a place of Cohabitation and Consortship under a due form of Government both civil and ecclesiastical. In such cases as this the care of the public must oversway all private respects, by which not only conscience, but mere Civil policy doth bind us; for it is a true rule that particular estates cannot subsist in the ruin of the public.

3. The end is to improve our lives to do more service to the Lord the comfort and increase of the body of christ whereof we are members that ourselves and posterity may be the better preserved from the Common corruptions of this evil world to serve the Lord and work out our Salvation under the power and purity of his holy Ordinances.

4. for the means whereby this must be effected, they are 2fold, a Conformity with the work and end we aim at, these we see are extraordinary, therefore we must not content ourselves with usual ordinary means whatsoever we did or ought to have done when we lived in England, the same must we do and more also where we go: That which the most in their Churches maintain as a truth in profession only, we must bring into familiar and constant practice, as in this duty of love we must love brotherly without dissimulation, we must love one another with a pure heart fervently we must bear one another's burdens, we must not look only on our own things, but also on the things of our brethren, neither must we think that the lord will bear with such failings at our hands as he doth from those among whom we have lived. . . .

---

Some of the spelling in this document has been modernized.

John Winthrop, *A Model of Christian Charity,* 1630, in Massachusetts Historical Society's *Collections,* 3rd ser., VII (1838), 33–48; rpt. MHS *Winthrop Papers,* II, 1931, 282–295.

... Thus stands the cause between God and us, we are entered into Covenant with him for his worke, we have taken out a Commission, the Lord hath given us leave to draw our own Articles we have professed to enterprise these Actions upon these and these ends, we have hereupon besought him of favour and blessing: Now if the Lord shall please to hear us, and bring us in peace to the place we desire, then hath he ratified this Covenant and sealed our Commission, [and] will expect a strict performance of the Articles contained in it, but if we shall neglect the observation of these Articles which are the ends we have propounded, and dissembling with our God, shall fall to embrace this present world and prosecute our carnal intentions, seeking great things for ourselves and our posterity, the Lord will surely break out in wrath against us be revenged of such a perjured people and make us know the price of the breach of such a Covenant.

Now the only way to avoid this shipwreck and to provide for our posterity is to follow the Counsel of Micah, to do Justly, to love mercy, to walk humbly with our God, for this end, we must be knit together in this work as one man, we must entertain each other in brotherly Affection, we must be willing to abridge ourselves of our superfluities, for the supply of others' necessities, we must uphold a familiar Commerce together in all meekness, gentleness, patience and liberality, we must delight in each other, make others' Conditions our own, rejoice together, mourn together, labour, and suffer together, always having before our eyes our Commission and Community in the work, our Community as members of the same body, so shall we keep the unity of the spirit in the bond of peace, the Lord will be our God and delight to dwell among us, as his own people and will command a blessing upon us in all our ways, so that we shall see much more of his wisdom power goodness and truth than formerly we have been acquainted with, we shall find that the God of Israel is among us, when ten of us shall be able to resist a thousand of our enemies, when he shall make us a praise and glory, that men shall say of succeeding plantations: the lord make it like that of New England: for we must Consider that we shall be as a City upon a Hill, the eyes of all people are upon us; so that if we shall deal falsely with out god in this work we have undertaken and so cause him to withdraw his present help from us, we shall be made a story and a by-word through the world, we shall open the mouths of enemies to speak evil of the ways of god and all professors for God's sake; we shall shame the faces of many of gods worthy servants, and cause their prayers to be turned into Curses upon us till we be consumed out of the good land whether we are going. . . .

## 4. Colonist John Pond Writes to His Mother and Father for Help, 1631

Most loving and kind Father and Mother:

My humble duty remembered unto you, trusting in God you are in good health, and I pray, remember my love unto my brother Joseife, and thank him for his kind-

---

John Pond, letter to his father and mother, March 15, 1631, in Everett Emerson, ed., *Letters from New England, 1629–1638,* (Amherst: University of Massachusetts Press, 1976), pp. 64–66. Reprinted by permission of Everett Emerson.

ness that I found at his hand at London, which was not the value of a farthing. I know, loving Father, and do confess that I was an undutiful child unto you when I lived with you and by you, for the which I am much sorrowful and grieved for it, trusting in God that He will so guide me that I will never offend you so any more, and I trust in God that you will forgive me for it, and my writing unto you is to let you understand what a country this new Eingland is where we live.

Here are but few eingeines [Indians], and a great sort of them died this winter. It was thought it was of the plague. They are a crafty people and they will cozen and cheat, and they are a subtle people, and whereas we did expect great store of beaver, here is little or none to be had, and their Sackemor John weigheth it, and many of us truck with them and it layeth us many times in eight shillings a pound. They are proper men and clean-jointed men, and many of them go naked with a skin about their loins, but some of them get eingellische menes [Englishmen's] parell [apparel].

And the country is very rocky and hilly and some champion [open] ground, and the soil is very fleet [shallow], and here is some good ground and marsh ground, but here is no Michaelmas [autumnal] spring. Cattle thrive well here, but they give small store of milk. The best cattle for profit is swines, and a good swine is here at five pounds price and a goat is worth three pounds, a gardene [garden?] goat. Here is timber good store and acorns good store, and here is good store of fish, if we had boats to go eight or ten leagues to sea to fish in. Here are good store of wild fowl, but they are hard to come by. It is harder to get a shot than it is in ould eingland. And people here are subject to disease, for here have died of the scurvy and of the burning fever two hundred and odd, besides many layeth lame, and all Sudberey men are dead but three and the women and some children. And provisions are here at a wonderful rate. Wheat meal is fourteen shillings a bushel and peas ten shillings and malt ten shillings and eindey seid [Indian seed] wheat is fifteen shillings and their other wheat is ten shillings, butter twelve pence a pound, and cheese is eight pence a pound, and all kinds of spices very dear and almost none to be got, and if this ship had not come when it did, we had been put to a wonderful straight, but thanks be to God for sending of it in. I received from the ship a hogshead of meal, and the governor telleth me of a hundredweight of cheese, the which I have received part of it. I humbly thank you for it. I did expect two cows, the which I had none nor I do not earnestly desire that you should send me any because the country is not so as we did expect it. Therefore, loving Father, I would entreat you that you would send me a firkin of butter and a hogshead of malt unground, for we drink nothing but water, and a coarse cloth of four-pound price, so it be thick. And for the freight, if you of your love will send them, I will pay the freight, for here is nothing to be got without we had commodities to go into the east parts amongst the eingeines [Indians] to truck, for here where we live is no beaver, and here is no cloth to be had to make no apparel, and shoes are at five shillings a pair for me, and that cloth that is worth two shillings eight pence a yard is worth here five shillings. So I pray, father, send me four or five yards of cloth to make us some apparel, and, loving Father, though I be far distant from you, yet I pray you remember me as your child, and we do not know how long we may subsist, for we cannot live here without provisions from ould eingland. Therefore, I pray, do not put away your shopstuff, for I think that in the end if I live it must be my living, for we do not know how long this plantation will stand, for some of the merchants that did uphold it have turned off their men and have given it over. Besides, God hath taken away the chiefest stud in the land, Mr. Johnson and the lady Arabella his wife, which was the chiefest man of estate in the land and one that would have done most good.

Here came over twenty-five passengers and there come back again four score and odd persons and as many more would have come if they had wherewithal to bring them home, for here are many that came over the last year, which was worth two hundred pounds afore they came out of ould eingland that between this and Michaelmas will be hardly worth thirty pounds, so here we may live if we have supplies every year from ould eingland; otherwise we cannot subsist. I may, as I will work hard, set an ackorne [acre] of eindey [Indian] wheat and if we do not set it with fish and that will cost twenty shillings, and if we set it without fish they shall have but a poor crop.

So, Father, I pray consider of my cause, for here will be but a very poor being and no being without, loving Father, your help with provisions from ould eingland. I had thought to have came home in this ship, for my provisions were almost all spent, but that I humbly thank you for your great love and kindness in sending me some provisions, or else I should and mine have been half famished, but now I will, if it please God that I have my health, I will plant what corn I can, and if provisions be no cheaper between this and Michaelmas and that I do not hear from you what I was best to do, I purpose to come home at Michaelmas.

My wife remembers her humble duty unto you and to my mother and my love to my brother Joseife and to Sarey myler. Thus I leave you to the protection of almighty God.

from Walltur Toune [Watertown] in new eingland [no signature]
the 15 of March 1630[/1]

We were wonderful sick as we came at sea with the smallpox. No man thought that I and my little child would have lived, and my boy is lame and my girl too, and there died in the ship that I came in fourteen persons. To my loving father William Ponde at Etherston in Suffolcke give these.

## 5. The Reverend Thomas Welde Describes the Success of the Massachusetts Bay Colony, 1632

Most dear and well beloved in Tarling [Welde's former parish], even all that love the Lord Jesus Christ's gospel, and myself, rich and poor, weak and strong, young and old, male and female, I [write] unto you all in one letter, wanting time to mention you all in particular, you being all dear unto me, yea, most dear to my heart in Jesus Christ, for whom I bow the knee to the Father of lights, longing to hear of your great welfare and spiritual growth in his dear son. From your presence though I be placed and must see your faces no more, yet I shall after a few weary days ended and all tears wiped away, and though happily never on earth yet in the New Jerusalem. . . .

---

Reprinted from *Letters from New England: The Massachusetts Bay Colony, 1629–1638,* Everett Emerson, ed., (Amherst: University of Massachusetts Press, 1976). Copyright © 1976 by The University of Massachusetts Press.

... Here I find three great blessings, peace, plenty, and health in a comfortable measure. The place well agreeth with our English bodies that they were never so healthy in their native country. Generally all here as never could be rid of the headache, toothache, cough, and the like are now better and freed here, and those that were weak are now well long since, and I can hear of but two weak in all the plantation. God's name be praised. And although there was wanting at the first that provision at the first glut of people that came over two years since, but blessed be God, here is plenty of corn that the poorest have enough. Corn is here at five shillings six pence a bushel. In truth you cannot imagine what comfortable diet the Indian corn doth make and what pleasant and wholesome food it makes. Our cattle of all do thrive and feed exceedingly. I suppose that such as are to come need bring no more or little or no provision except malt (but no more of these things). I would have none aim at outward matters in such an attempt as this, lest the Lord meet him in the way as he met Balaam with a drawn sword, but at things of an higher nature and more spiritual nature.

O how hath my heart been made glad with the comforts of His house and the spiritual days in the same wherein all things are done in the form and pattern showed in the mount, members provided, church officers elected and ordained, sacrament administered, scandals prevented, censured, fast days and holy feast days and all such things by authority commanded and performed according to the precise rule. Mine eyes, blessed be God, do see such administration of justice in civil government, all things so righteously, so religiously and impartially carried. I am already fully paid for my voyage who never had so much in the storms at sea as one repenting thought rested in my heart. Praised and thanked be God who moved my heart to come and made open the way to me. And I profess if I might have my wish in what part of the world to dwell, I know no other place on the whole globe of the earth where I would be rather than here. We say to our friends that doubt this, Come and see and taste. Here the greater part are the better part. . . .

## 6. John Winthrop Laments the Growth of Competitive Economic Practices in New England in the Case of Robert Keayne, 1639

... Mo. 9 (*November*). At a general court holden at Boston, great complaint was made of the oppression used in the country in sale of foreign commodities; and Mr. Robert Keaine, who kept a shop in Boston, was notoriously above others observed and complained of; and, being convented, he was charged with many particulars; in some, for taking above six-pence in the shilling profit; in some above eight-pence; and, in some small things, above two for one; and being hereof convict, (as appears by the records,) he was fined £200, which came thus to pass: The deputies considered, apart, of his fine, and set it at £200; the magistrates agreed but to £100. So, the court being divided, at length it was agreed, that his fine should be £200, but he should pay but £100, and the other should be respited to the further consideration of

John Winthrop, "The Case of Robert Keayne" in James Kendall Hosmer, ed., *Journal* (New York, 1908), pp. 315–318.

the next general court. By this means the magistrates and deputies were brought to an accord, which otherwise had not been likely, and so much trouble might have grown, and the offender escaped censure. For the cry of the country was so great against oppression, and some of the elders and magistrates had declared such detestation of the corrupt practice of this man (which was the more observable, because he was wealthy and sold dearer than most other tradesmen, and for that he was of ill report for the like covetous practice in England, that incensed the deputies very much against him). And sure the course was very evil, especial circumstances considered: 1. He being an ancient professor of the gospel: 2. A man of eminent parts: 3. Wealthy, and having but one child: 4. Having come over for conscience' sake, and for the advancement of the gospel here: 5. Having been formerly dealt with and admonished, both by private friends and also by some of the magistrates and elders, and having promised reformation; being a member of a church and commonwealth now in their infancy, and under the curious observation of all churches and civil states in the world. These added much aggravation to his sin in the judgment of all men of understanding. Yet most of the magistrates (though they discerned of the offence clothed with all these circumstances) would have been more moderate in their censure: 1. Because there was no law in force to limit or direct men in point of profit in their trade. 2. Because it is the common practice, in all countries, for men to make use of advantages for raising the prices of their commodities. 3. Because (though he were chiefly aimed at, yet) he was not alone in this fault. 4. Because all men through the country, in sale of cattle, corn, labor, etc., were guilty of the like excess in prices. 5. Because a certain rule could not be found out for an equal rate between buyer and seller, though much labor had been bestowed in it, and divers laws had been made, which, upon experience, were repealed, as being neither safe nor equal. Lastly, and especially, because the law of God appoints no other punishment but double restitution; and, in some cases, as where the offender freely confesseth, and brings his offering, only half added to the principal. After the court had censured him, the church of Boston called him also in question, where (as before he had done in the court) he did, with tears, acknowledge and bewail his covetous and corrupt heart, yet making some excuse for many of the particulars, which were charged upon him, as partly by pretence of ignorance of the true price of some wares, and chiefly by being misled by some false principles, as 1. That, if a man lost in one commodity, he might help himself in the price of another. 2. That if, through want of skill or other occasion, his commodity cost him more than the price of the market in England, he might then sell it for more than the price of the market in New England, etc. These things gave occasion to Mr. Cotton, in his public exercise the next lecture day, to lay open the error of such false principles, and to give some rules of direction in the case.

Some false principles were these:—

1. That a man might sell as dear as he can, and buy as cheap as he can.
2. If a man lose by casualty of sea, etc., in some of his commodities, he may raise the price of the rest.
3. That he may sell as he bought, though he paid too dear, etc., and though the commodity be fallen, etc.

4. That, as a man may take the advantage of his own skill or ability, so he may of another's ignorance or necessity.
5. Where one gives time for payment, he is to take like recompense of one as of another.

The rules for trading were these:—

1. A man may not sell above the current price, i. e., such a price as is usual in the time and place, and as another (who knows the worth of the commodity) would give for it, if he had occasion to use it; as that is called current money, which every man will take, etc.
2. When a man loseth in his commodity for want of skill, etc., he must look at it as his own fault or cross, and therefore must not lay it upon another.
3. Where a man loseth by casualty of sea, or, etc., it is a loss cast upon himself by providence, and he may not ease himself of it by casting it upon another; for so a man should seem to provide against all providences, etc., that he should never lose; but where there is a scarcity of the commodity, there men may raise their price; for now it is a hand of God upon the commodity, and not the person.
4. A man may not ask any more for his commodity than his selling price, as Ephron to Abraham, the land is worth thus much.

The cause being debated by the church, some were earnest to have him excommunicated; but the most thought an admonition would be sufficient. Mr. Cotton opened the causes, which required excommunication, out of that in 1 Cor. 5. 11. The point now in question was, whether these actions did declare him to be such a covetous person, etc. Upon which he showed, that it is neither the habit of covetousness, (which is in every man in some degree,) nor simply the act, that declares a man to be such, but when it appears, that a man sins against his conscience, or the very light of nature, and when it appears in a man's whole conversation. But Mr. Keaine did not appear to be such, but rather upon an error in his judgment, being led by false principles; and, besides, he is otherwise liberal, as in his hospitality, and in church communion, etc. So, in the end, the church consented to an admonition. . . .

 # E S S A Y S

The colonization of New England differed dramatically from that of the southern plantation colonies. Whereas the Chesapeake immigrant stream was composed largely of single young men, with few women, New England was settled by families, who comprised a wide variety of ages. Except for the very wealthy and the very poor, its society resembled the parent country. Moreover a very large number, more than 10,000, came during the single decade of the 1630s, creating the preconditions for success from the beginning. Virginia Anderson, of the University of Colorado, confronts the issue of these immigrants' motivation in the first essay. The problem stems from the fact that, although the New England migrants were Puritan, most Puritans chose not to emigrate. Therefore we must explain what drove this particular group. Some historians have argued it was primarily economic distress that caused them to leave at that particular time. Using extant passenger lists, Anderson re-creates the lives of migrants, their circumstances and aspirations, and concludes that religion was the primary motivating factor in their decision.

In the second essay Mark Peterson of the University of Iowa examines both the development of the society and religious life of those migrants and their descendants in seventeenth-century New England and the way that historians have interpreted that development. He argues that the original generation of Puritan leaders created a framework for discussing their own history, and they cast it in terms of decline (or declension) from the great fervor, dedication, and piety that motivated the first generation as the settlements became established and comfortable. This model has continued to frame the writing of modern historians, and Peterson both explains and questions the persistence of the declension paradigm. Should we see vitality, growth, and development where historians have seen decline?

# Religion, the Common Thread of Motivation

### VIRGINIA DEJOHN ANDERSON

No man, perhaps, would seem to have been an unlikelier candidate for transatlantic migration than John Bent. He had never shown any particular interest in moving; indeed, in 1638, at the age of forty-one, Bent still lived in Weyhill, Hampshire, where both he and his father before him had been born. Having prospered in the village of his birth, John Bent held enough land to distinguish himself as one of Weyhill's wealthiest inhabitants. One might reasonably expect that Bent's substantial economic stake, combined with his growing familial responsibilities—which by 1638 included a wife and five children—would have provided him with ample incentive to stay put. By embarking on a transatlantic voyage—moving for the first time in his life and over a vast distance—Bent would exchange an economically secure present for a highly uncertain future and venture his family's lives and fortunes no less than his own. Yet in the spring of 1638, Bent returned his Weyhill land to the lord of the manor, gathered his family and possessions, and traveled twenty-five miles to the port of Southampton. There, he and his family boarded the *Confidence,* bound for Massachusetts Bay.

In doing so, the Bent family joined thousands of other men, women, and children who left for New England between 1630 and 1642. We know more about John Bent than about the vast majority of these other emigrants because certain information has fortuitously survived. Bent's name appears on one of the few extant ship passenger lists of the Great Migration, and genealogists and local historians have compiled enough additional data to sketch in the outlines of his life in Old and New England. Yet despite this rare abundance of information, John Bent's reasons for moving to Massachusetts remain obscure. In fact, the surviving biographical details render the question of motivation all the more tantalizing because they provide no identifiable economic reason for leaving but rather depict a man firmly rooted in his English homeland.

Virginia DeJohn Anderson, "Migrants and Motives: Religion and the Settlement of New England," *New England Quarterly,* LVIII (1985), 339–383. Reprinted by permission of the author and the publisher. Includes 1992 updates.

Most accounts of early New England include a general discussion of the emigrants' motivations, but none has dealt with the issue systematically. If we are ever to comprehend the nature and significance of the Great Migration, however, we must understand why men like John Bent left their homes. The Great Migration to New England, unlike the simultaneous outpouring of Englishmen to other New World colonies, was a voluntary exodus of families and included relatively few indentured servants. The movement, which began around 1630, effectively ceased a dozen years later with the outbreak of the English Civil War, further distinguishing it from the more extended period of emigration to other colonies.

These two factors—the emigrants' voluntary departure and the movement's short duration—suggest that the Great Migration resulted from a common, reasoned response to a highly specific set of circumstances. Such circumstances must have been compelling indeed to dislodge a man like John Bent from a comfortable niche in his community. And while Bent and his fellows could not have known it, their reasons for embarking for New England would not only change their own lives but also powerfully shape the society they would create in their new home.

# I

Although modern commentators have disagreed over why New England's settlers left the mother country, none of the original chroniclers ever suggested that motivation was an open question. Edward Johnson, for example, knew exactly why the Great Migration occurred. The author of *The Wonder-Working Providence of Sion's Saviour in New England* ... announced that he and his fellow emigrants left England to escape the evils generated by "the multitude of irreligious lascivious and popish affected persons" who had spread "like Grashoppers" throughout the land. As England strayed from the paths of righteousness, the Lord had sought to preserve a saving remnant of His church by transferring it to an untainted refuge. Johnson adopted a military metaphor to describe the process: the decision to emigrate constituted a voluntary enlistment in Christ's Army, the instrument with which He would "create a new Heaven, and a new Earth in, new Churches, and a new Common-wealth together." Other writers concurred with Johnson's providentialist interpretation. Nathaniel Morton and William Hubbard, both of whom emigrated as children, likewise believed the founding of Massachusetts to be the centerpiece of a divine plan to preserve the Gospel and proper forms of worship. The most emphatic explication of the settlers' religious motivation, however, came not from a participant in the Great Migration but from a descendant of emigrants. Cotton Mather never doubted that the Lord "carried some Thousands of *Reformers* into the Retirements of an *American Desert,* on purpose," that "He might there, *To* them first, and then *By* them, give a *Specimen* of many Good Things, which He would have His Churches elsewhere aspire and arise unto."

Few modern scholars have shared the steadfast conviction of Mather and his predecessors. . . . They have instead reminded us that deciding to emigrate was a complicated and highly individualistic affair. But their conclusions are, in the end, disappointing, for they suggest that we must accept the notion that the motives for emigration were so complex as to be irrecoverable. If we examine more closely the lives of the emigrants themselves, we may yet find clues that reveal a common incentive underlying the Great Migration.

In seeking to identify emigrants and explore their motives for moving, historians have received invaluable assistance from none other than Charles I. Not long after the exodus to Massachusetts began, the king and his archbishop of Canterbury became increasingly concerned about the departure of so many English folk for wilderness homes across the seas. On 21 July 1635, in an attempt to keep track of the movement, Charles I issued a proclamation requiring all those who wished to leave the realm to obtain a special license from the Privy Council. Customs officers were instructed to obtain certain information from prospective emigrants aboard each ship, including name, residence, occupation, age, and destination. Although the royal edict was loosely enforced and the passage of more than three centuries has inevitably reduced the amount of extant information, several of these ship passenger lists do survive, and they provide a unique opportunity to examine the lives of ordinary emigrants.

Seven ship passenger lists, which together include the names of 693 colonists, provide the information upon which this essay is based. These appear to be the only lists that have been published in their entirety from surviving documents. All the lists contain the names of emigrants; most also include occupation (for adult males), residence, age, and evidence of family structure. In other words, each list provides sufficiently specific information to permit accurate tracing of individual passengers in the New World. The lists themselves, of course, can only tell us about the emigrants at one moment in time, the date of registration for the voyage, but an astonishingly large amount of additional information can be found in genealogies and local histories. Using these materials, it has been possible to reconstruct the New England careers of 578 emigrants, or 83.4 percent of those included on the lists. . . .

Evidence from these lists suggests that although few emigrants left explicit records of their reasons for moving, the motives of the majority need not remain a mystery. Analyzing the lists in light of supporting genealogical materials enables us to construct a social profile of the emigrants, which can then be compared with that of the English population at large. This comparison in turn suggests that once we know who the emigrants were, we can begin to understand why they came.

## II

The New England settlers more closely resembled the nonmigrating English population than they did other English colonists in the New World. The implications of this fact for the development of colonial societies can scarcely be overstated. While the composition of the emigrant populations in the Chesapeake and the Caribbean hindered the successful transfer of familiar patterns of social relationships, the character of the New England colonial population ensured it. The prospect of colonizing distant lands stirred the imaginations of young people all over England but most of these young adults made their way to the tobacco and sugar plantations of the South. Nearly half of a sample of Virginia residents in 1625 were between the ages of twenty and twenty-nine, and groups of emigrants to the Chesapeake in the seventeenth century consistently included a majority of people in their twenties. In contrast, only a quarter of the New England settlers belonged to this age group.

The age structure of New England's emigrant population virtually mirrored that of the country they had left. Both infancy and old age were represented: the *Rose* of Great Yarmouth carried one-year-old Thomas Baker as well as Katherine Rabey, a widow of sixty-eight. The proportion of people over the age of sixty was, not surprisingly, somewhat higher in the general English population than among the emigrants. Although Thomas Welde reported in 1632 that he traveled with "very aged" passengers, "twelve persons being all able to make well nigh one thousand years," a transatlantic voyage of three months' duration was an ordeal not easily undertaken, and the hardships involved in settling the wilderness surely daunted prospective emigrants of advanced years. On the whole, however, New England attracted people of all ages and thus preserved a normal pattern of intergenerational contact.

Similarly, the sex ratio of the New England emigrant group resembled that of England's population. If women were as scarce in the Chesapeake as good English beer, they were comparatively abundant in the northern colonies. In the second decade of Virginia's settlement, there were four or five men for each woman; by the end of the century, there were still about three men for every two women. Among the emigrants studied here, however, nearly half were women and girls. Such a high proportion of females in the population assured the young men of New England greater success than their southern counterparts in finding spouses.

These demographic characteristics derive directly from the fact that the migration to New England was primarily a transplantation of families. Fully 87.8 percent (597 out of 680) of the emigrants traveled with relatives of one sort or another. Nearly three-quarters (498 out of 680) came in nuclear family units, with or without children. Occasionally, single spouses migrated with their children, either to meet a partner already in the New World or to wait for his or her arrival on a later ship. Grandparents comprised a relatively inconspicuous part of the migration, but a few hardy elders did make the trip. In 1637, Margaret Neave sailed to Massachusetts with her granddaughter Rachel Dixson, who was probably an orphan. In the following year, Alice Stephens joined her sons William and John and their families for the voyage to New England. More frequently, emigrant family structure extended horizontally, within a generation, rather than vertically, across three generations. Several groups of brothers made the trip together, and when the three Goodenow brothers decided to leave the West Country, they convinced their unmarried sister Ursula to come with them as well.

Thus, for the majority of these New England settlers, transatlantic migration did not lead to permanent separation from close relatives. Some unscrupulous men and women apparently migrated in order to flee unhappy marriages, but most nuclear family units arrived intact. When close kin were left behind, they usually joined their families within a year or so. Samuel Lincoln, for instance, who traveled abroad the *Rose* in 1637, soon joined his brother Thomas, who had settled in Hingham in 1633. Another brother, Stephen, arrived in the following year with both his family and his mother. Edward Johnson, who had first crossed the ocean with the Winthrop fleet in 1630, returned to England in 1637 to fetch his wife and seven children. For Thomas Starr, who left Sandwich in 1637, migration meant a reunion with his older brother Comfort, a passenger on the *Hercules* two years earlier. Although some disruption of kin ties was unavoidable, it was by no means the rule. . . .

Further exploration of demographic patterns reveals . . . subtle but significant differences between the migrating population and that of England. These differences illustrate the important fact that migration was a selective process; not all people were equally suited to or interested in the rigors of New World settlement. Since the movement to New England was a voluntary, self-selective affair, most of this winnowing-out process occurred before the hearths of English homes, as individuals and families discussed whether or not to leave.

Although family groups predominated within the emigrant population, many individuals came to New England on their own. The vast majority of these solitary travelers were male—men outnumbered women by a factor of ten to one—and together they constituted 38 percent of the emigrant households. This figure stands in sharp contrast to England's population, where only about 5 percent of all households were composed of one individual. About one in six emigrants aged twenty-one to thirty sailed independently, perhaps drawn to New England by hopes of employment or freeholdership. These men were hardly freewheeling adventurers; instead, they provided the new settlements with skilled labor. The unaccompanied travelers included shoemakers, a carpenter, butcher, tanner, hempdresser, weaver, cutler, physician, fuller, tailor, mercer, and skinner. Some were already married at the time of the voyage, and those who were single seldom remained so for more than a couple of years after their arrival. Through marriage, the men became members of family networks within their communities. Within a few years of his arrival in 1635, for instance, Henry Ewell, a young shoemaker from Sandwich in Kent, joined the church in Scituate and married the daughter of a prominent local family. William Paddy, a London skinner, managed to obtain land, find a wife, and get elected to Plymouth's first general court of deputies within four years of his voyage. . . .

Yet it is important to remember that New England primarily attracted families—and families of a special sort. . . . The westward-bound ships carried couples who were mature, who had probably been married for nearly a decade, and who had established themselves firmly within their communities. The typical migrating family was complete—composed of husband, wife, and three or four children—but was not yet completed. They were families in process, with parents who were at most halfway through their reproductive cycle and who would continue to produce children in New England. They would be responsible for the rapid population growth that New England experienced in its first decades of settlement. Moreover, the numerous children who emigrated with their parents contributed their efforts to a primitive economy sorely lacking in labor.

The task of transforming wilderness into farmland, however, demanded more labor than parents and their children alone could supply, and more than half of the emigrating families responded to this challenge by bringing servants with them to the New World. Perhaps some had read William Wood's advice in *New England's Prospect* and learned that "men of good estates may do well there, always provided that they go well accommodated with servants." In any case, servants formed an integral part, just over 17 percent, of the colonizing population and in fact were at first somewhat more commonplace in New England than in England. Most were males (80 of 114) and labored alongside their masters, clearing land, planting corn, and building houses and barns. Their presence substantially increased the ratio of producers to consumers in the newly settled towns. . . .

Before departing for New England, the emigrants had called a wide variety of English towns and villages their homes. Most lived in the lowland area of England . . . and within this expanse of territory . . . had known many different forms of social organization, agricultural practice, industrial development, and local government. At one end of the spectrum, Parnell Harris, William Paddy, and Edmund Hawes all left the burgeoning metropolis of London, which was about to overtake Paris as the largest city in Europe; at the other, the widow Emme Mason left the tiny Kentish parish of Eastwell, which was "not more than a mile across each way" and whose church in 1640 counted just 55 communicants.

A relatively large proportion of the New England settlers dwelled in urban areas prior to their emigration. . . . Among other things, town life . . . equipped future emigrants with complex and regionally distinctive experiences of local government. Most incorporated boroughs were run by an annually elected mayor, but the numbers and duties of subsidiary officeholders varied widely. . . . In addition, seventeenth-century English towns, especially the larger ones, often encompassed a multiplicity of civil and ecclesiastical jurisdictions. . . . Provincial centers such as Canterbury and Norwich were divided into several parishes; the Kentish city had at least eight in 1640, while the East Anglian capital boasted thirty-four parishes. Moreover, town-dwellers lived in the midst of a more heterogeneous population than did persons who resided in the countryside. Major textile manufacturing centers received an influx of foreign artisans in the late sixteenth and early seventeenth centuries. The newcomers, mainly Dutch and Walloon tradesmen, settled primarily in Kent and East Anglia and helped to revitalize the depressed cloth industry in those areas. . . .

In the countryside, although the contrasts were perhaps less striking, villages also differed significantly from one another. Much of seventeenth-century England was an intricate patchwork of parishes with particular local customs dating from time out of mind. Ancient practice often dictated the shape of the landscape, patterns of settlement, modes of landholding, and rituals of agrarian activity. Even within a single county, substantial variation was evident. . . . In the migration to New England, then, not only would villagers and townsfolk intermingle but farmers would also encounter other countrymen with very different experiences of rural life.

The diversity of the emigrants' English backgrounds—and their urban origins in particular—influenced the distribution of their occupations. . . . Artisans, both in the cloth trades and in other pursuits, formed a greater proportion of the emigrant population than tradesmen did in the English population as a whole. In 1696, Gregory King estimated that "freeholders" and "farmers" outnumbered "artizans and handicrafts" by a factor of more than seven to one; among the emigrants to New England, however, artisans predominated by a ratio of nearly two to one.

The occupational spectrum of future New Englanders placed them at the more prosperous end of English society. . . . Yet in striking contrast to Virginia, where, at least initially, the population included "about six times as large a proportion of gentlemen as England had," New England attracted very few members of the upper class. Sir Henry Vane and Sir Richard Saltonstall were unique among the leaders of the migration, and for the most part even they submitted to government by such gentle but untitled figures as John Winthrop and Thomas Dudley. On the whole, emigrants were neither very high nor very low in social and economic status. Husbandmen predominated among the farmers who came to Massachusetts; thirty of them emigrated compared to just five yeomen. By the seventeenth century, the legal distinctions between the status of yeoman and that of husbandman had largely eroded and evidence indicates that the labels generally denoted relative position on the economic and social ladder. Both groups primarily made their livings from the land, but yeomen were generally better off. New England, however, was peopled by less affluent—but not necessarily poor—husbandmen.

Emigrant clothworkers practiced trades that also placed them on the middle rungs of the economic ladder. . . . Among the non-clothworking artisans, shoemakers and carpenters predominated, and they too worked in trades that would bring comfort, if not riches. All in all, the New England–bound ships transported a population characterized by a greater degree of social homogeneity than existed in the mother country. Despite Winthrop's reminder to his fellow passengers on the *Arbella* that "some must be rich some poor, some highe and eminent in power and dignitie; others meane and in subieccion," New Englanders would discover that the process of migration effectively reduced the distance between the top and the bottom of their social hierarchy.

## III

In a letter to England written in 1632, Richard Saltonstall commented on the social origins of New England's inhabitants. "It is strange," he wrote, "the meaner sort of people should be so backward [in migrating], having assurance that they may live plentifully by their neighbors." At the same time, he expressed the hope that more "gentlemen of ability would transplant themselves," for they too might prosper both spiritually and materially in the new land. For young Richard, the twenty-one-year-old son of Sir Richard Saltonstall, New England promised much but as yet lacked the proper balance of social groups within its population that would ensure its success. The migration of the "meaner sort" would help lower the cost of labor, while richer emigrants would "supply the want we labor under of men fitted by their estates to bear common burdens." Such wealthy men would invest in the colony's future even as they enhanced their own spiritual welfare by becoming "worthy instruments of propagating the Gospel" to New England's natives.

Saltonstall wrote early in the migration decade, but the succeeding years did little to redress the social imbalance he perceived in Massachusetts. Two years later, William Wood could still write that "none of such great estate went over yet." Throughout the decade of the 1630s, New England continued to attract colonists who were overwhelmingly ordinary. Demographically they presented a mirror image of the society they had left behind, and socially and economically they fairly represented England's relatively prosperous middle class. The question is inescapable: why did so many average English men and women pass beyond the seas to Massachusetts' shores?

Whether or not they have assigned it primary importance, most historians of the period have noted that economic distress in England in the early seventeenth century must have been causally related to the Great Migration. These were years of agricultural and industrial depression, the farmers and weavers were conspicuous passengers on the transatlantic voyages. A closer examination of the connections between economic crisis and the movement to New England, however, indicates that the links were not as close as they have been assumed to be.

Agriculture—especially in the early modern period—was a notoriously risky business. Success depended heavily upon variables beyond human control. A dry summer or an unusually wet season rendered futile the labor of even the most diligent husbandman, and English farmers in the early seventeenth century had to endure more than their share of adversity. While the decade of the 1620s began propitiously, with excellent harvests in 1619 and 1620, the farmers' luck did not hold. The next three years brought one disastrous harvest after another; improvement in 1624 was followed by dearth in 1625. The beginning of the 1630s, especially in the eastern counties, was marked by further distress; in 1630, the mayor of Norwich complained that "scarcity and dearth of corn and other victuals have so increased the number and misery of the poor in this city" that civic taxes had to be boosted to unprecedented heights and the city's stock of grain dwindled dangerously. In 1637, a severe drought spawned further hardship.

Although this period of agricultural depression undoubtedly touched the lives of many English families, it did not necessarily compel them to emigrate. The worst sustained period of scarcity occurred in the early 1620s, a decade or so before the Great Migration began; if agrarian distress was a "push" factor, it produced a curiously delayed reaction. Furthermore, annual fluctuations were endemic in early modern agriculture. Englishmen knew from experience that times would eventually improve, even if that day were unpleasantly distant; moreover, they had no reason to suppose that farmers in New England would somehow lead charmed lives, exempt from similar variations in the weather. In addition, dearth was not an unmitigated disaster for families engaged in husbandry; as supplies of grain and other products shrank, prices rose. In 1630, a year with one of the worst harvests in the first half of the seventeenth century, the price of grain was twice what it had been in the more plentiful years of 1619 and 1620. Thus for farmers involved in market agriculture, a bad year, with half the yield of a good one, could still bring the same income. As the Norwich mayor's lament amply demonstrates, the people really hurt in times of scarcity were city-dwellers dependent on the countryside for their food. That urban dwellers left for New England to assure themselves of a steady food supply, however, is highly unlikely. Emigrants would surely have anticipated the primitive state of the region's agriculture; reports of scarcity at Plymouth and the early Massachusetts Bay settlements had quickly filtered back to England. Moreover, emigrating urban artisans certainly understood that, in the New World, responsibility for feeding their families would lie in their own hands—hands more accustomed to the loom or the last than the plow.

The slump in England's textile industry has also been accounted an incentive for emigration. The industry was indeed mired in a severe depression in the early seventeenth century; it is true as well that a quarter of the adult male emigrants were employed in a trade related to cloth manufacture. . . .

Yet even if evidence did suggest that emigrant weavers were compelled by economic adversity to leave their homeland, Massachusetts would not have been a wise choice of destination if they hoped to continue in their trade. Flight to the

Netherlands, a place with a well-developed textile industry, would have been a more rational choice for artisans worried about the fate of their trade in England and anxious to persist in its practice. Massachusetts lacked both the wool supply and the intricate network of auxiliary tradesmen—such as combers, carders, calenderers, fullers, dyers, etc.—upon which England's weavers depended. Several of the emigrants packed up their looms along with their other belongings, but there is little evidence that they were able to earn their livings in Massachusetts solely by weaving.

Arguments linking the Great Migration to economic hardship in England all share an important weakness. Although historians have discovered that many *places* from which emigrants came suffered from agricultural or industrial depression, they have had little success in connecting those unfavorable economic circumstances to the fortunes of individual emigrants. On the contrary, it appears that the families that went to New England had largely avoided the serious setbacks that afflicted many of their countrymen during those years. . . .

. . . If migration to New England was not a sensible economic decision for farmers or weavers hurt by hard times in England, it was even less sensible for people doing well. Most emigrants exchanged an economically viable present for a very uncertain future. . . . The emigrant groups studied here all left England five or more years after the Great Migration had begun and a decade and a half after the landing at Plymouth; they surely heard from earlier arrivals that New England was no land of milk and honey. If any had a chance to read Edward Winslow's *Good Newes from New England,* published in 1624, he or she would have learned that the "vain expectation of present profit" was the "overthrow and bane" of plantations. People might prosper through "good labor and diligence," but in the absence of a cash crop, great wealth was not to be expected. The message of William Wood's *New England's Prospect,* published a decade later, was similar. Some colonists were lured westward by descriptions of plenty, Wood acknowledged, but they soon fell to criticizing the new society, "saying a man cannot live without labor." . . . Letters as well as published reports informed would-be settlers that New England was not a particularly fertile field for profit. In 1631, one young colonist wrote to his father in Suffolk, England, that "the cuntrey is not so as we ded expecte it." Far from bringing riches, New England could not even provide essentials; the disillusioned settler begged his father to send provisions, for "we do not know how longe we may subeseiste" without supplies from home.

If prospective emigrants were not hearing that New England offered ample opportunities for economic betterment, they *were* informed that life in Massachusetts could bring betterment of another sort. When Governor Thomas Dudley provided the countess of Lincoln with an account of his first nine months in New England, he announced that "if any come hether to plant for worldly ends that canne live well at home hee comits an errour of which he will soon repent him. But if for spirtuall [ends] and that noe particular obstacle hinder his removeall, he may finde here what may well content him." Dudley worried that some might be drawn to Massachusetts by exaggerations of the land's bounty and wanted to make clear who would benefit most from emigration. "If any godly men out of religious ends will come over to helpe vs in the good worke wee are about," the governor wrote, "I think they cannot dispose of themselves nor of their estates more to God's glory and the furtherance of their owne reckoninge." New England promised its settlers *spiritual* advantages only; men merely in search of wealth could go elsewhere. Emmanuel Downing, in a letter to Sir John Coke, clarified the important difference between New England and other colonial ventures. "This plantation and that of Virginia went not forth upon the same reasons nor for the same end. Those of Virginia," he explained, "went forth for profit. . . . These went upon two other designs, some to satisfy their own curiosity in point of conscience, others . . . to transport the Gospel to those heathen that never heard thereof." . . .

Prospective emigrants, then, could hardly have been unaware of the peculiar religious character of New England society. Accounts of the region's commitment to Puritanism were too numerous to be overlooked; those who made the voyage had to know what they were getting into. Adherence to Puritan principles, therefore, became the common thread that stitched individual emigrants together into a larger movement. As Rev. John White declared, "Necessitie may presse some; Noveltie draw on others; hopes of gaine in time to come may prevaile with a third sort: but that the most and most sincere and godly part have the advancement of the *Gospel* for their maine scope I am co[n]fident."

White's confidence was by no means misplaced. The roster of passengers to New England contains the names of scores of otherwise ordinary English men and women whose lives were distinguished by their steadfast commitment to nonconformity, even in the face of official harassment. . . .

. . . Those few men who recorded their own reasons for removal likewise stressed the role of religion. Roger Clap, who sailed in 1630, recalled in his memoirs that "I never so much as heard of *New-England* until I heard of many godly Persons that were going there" and firmly believed that "God put it into my Heart to incline to Live abroad" in Massachusetts. John Dane, who seems to have spent most of his youth fighting off his evil inclinations, "bent myself to cum to nu ingland, thinking that I should be more fre here then thare from temptations." Arriving in Roxbury in the mid-1630s, Dane soon discovered that relocation would not end his struggle with sinfulness; the devil sought him out as readily in the New World as in the Old.

To declare that most emigrants were prompted by radical religious sentiment to sail to the New World, however, does not mean that these settlers resembled Hawthorne's memorable "stern and black-browed Puritans" in single-minded pursuit of salvation. The decision to cross the seas indelibly marked the lives of those who made it. Even the most pious wrestled with the implications of removal from family, friends, and familiar surroundings. Parents often objected to the departure of their children; a son following the dictates of his conscience might risk the estrangement of a disappointed father. Although religious motivation is the only factor with sufficient power to explain the departure of so many otherwise ordinary families, the New England Puritans should not be seen as utopians caught up in a movement whose purpose totally transcended the concerns of daily life.

Solitary ascetics can afford to reject the things of this world in order to contemplate the glories of the next; family men cannot. Even as prospective settlers discussed the spiritual benefits that might accompany a move to New England, they worried about what they would eat, where they would sleep, and how they would make a living. In the spring of 1631, Emmanuel Downing wrote with considerable relief to John Winthrop that the governor's encouraging letters "haue much refreshed my hart and the myndes of manie others" for "yt was the Iudgement of most men here, that your Colonye would be dissolved partly by death through want of Food, howsing and rayment, and the rest to retorne or to flee for refuge to other plantacions." Other leaders and publicists of the migration continued both to recognize and to sympathize with the concerns of families struggling with the decision of whether or not to move, and they sought to reassure prospective settlers that a decision in favor of emigration would not doom their families to cold and starvation in the wilderness. At the same time, the way in which these writers composed their comforting messages to would-be emigrants underscored the settlers' understanding of the larger meaning of their mission.

Although several of the tracts and letters publicizing the migration contained favorable descriptions of the new land, they were never intended to be advertisements designed to capture the interest of profit-seekers. When John White, Thomas Dudley, and others wrote about the blessings of New England's climate, topography, and flora and fauna, they simply hoped to assure godly English men and women that a move to the New World would not engender poverty as well as piety. . . . John White repeatedly assured his readers that "all Gods directions"—including the divine imperative to settle New England—"have a double scope, mans good and Gods honour." "That this commandement of God is directed unto mans good *temporall and spirituall,*" he went on, "is as cleere as the light." The Lord, in other words, would take care of His own.

To providentialists steeped in the conviction that God intervened directly in human lives, that divine pleasure or disapproval could be perceived in the progress of daily events, White's statement made eminent sense. If emigrant families embarked on their voyages with the purpose of abandoning England's corruption in order to worship God according to biblical precepts in their new homes, and if they adhered to this purpose, they might expect as a sign of divine favor to achieve a competency, if not riches. Thus John Winthrop could assert that "such thinges as we stand in neede of are vsually supplied by Gods blessing vpon the wisdome and industry of man." The governor's firm belief in the connection between divine favor and human well-being explains why in his "Particular Considerations" concerning his own removal out of England, he admitted that "my meanes heere [in England] are so shortned (now my 3 eldest sonnes are come to age) as I shall not be able to continue in this place and imployment where I now am." If he went to Massachusetts, Winthrop anticipated an improvement in his fortunes, noting that "I [can] live with 7. or 8: servants in that place and condition where for many years I have spent 3: or 400 *li.* per an[num]." Winthrop, despite these musings on his worldly estate, did not emigrate in order to better his economic condition. Rather, he removed in order to undertake the "publike service" that God had "bestowed" on him and hoped that God might reward him if his efforts were successful. In similar fashion, thousands of other emigrants could justify their decisions to move to New England. They believed that, by emigrating, they followed the will of God and that their obedience would not escape divine notice. In return for their submission to His will, the emigrants sincerely hoped that God might allow them—through their own labor— to enjoy a competency of this world's goods.

Historians have generally agreed that early New England displayed a distinctive social character. The first colonists, after all, succeeded in creating a remarkably stable society on the edge of a vast wilderness. But stability alone does not sum up the New Englanders' achievement, for colonists who went to other parts of North America also established lasting settlements. What set New England society apart was its Puritan heritage. Religious and social ideals became inextricably intertwined as settlers applied the Puritan concept of the covenantal relationship between God and man to their temporal as well as religious affairs. When New Englanders pledged themselves to God in their churches and to each other in their towns, they imbued their society with a deeply spiritual significance. Other British colonists would also strive to create social harmony, but none would do so with the same intensity of religious purpose as New England's founding generation. . . .

At the heart of the colonists' achievement lies an apparent paradox. Settlers in Massachusetts, Plymouth, and Connecticut created a remarkably unified culture and a homogeneous society in a setting where the power of central authorities was exceedingly weak. Preachers and magistrates could have expended every effort extolling the virtues of communal and spiritual harmony and yet failed miserably had not their audience shared in their aspirations. But since the majority of emigrants responded to a common spiritual impulse in moving to New England, they readily accepted the idea of the covenant as the proper model for their social as well as spiritual relationships. Indeed, covenants, because of their voluntary nature, provided the only truly effective means of maintaining social cohesion where coercive power was limited. The social homogeneity of the emigrant population—the absence of both rich and poor folk—unintentionally reinforced covenantal ideals by reducing the differences in status among partners. In this way, social fact joined with communal ideals to create a society of comparative equals pledged to one another's support. At the same time, social and religious covenants helped settlers from diverse geographical and occupational backgrounds to come to terms with their new common enterprise. Emigrants concerned solely with their own material improvement would scarcely have acceded so readily to an ideal of mutual cooperation. It is only because most colonists (at least initially) placed the good of their souls above all else and trusted in the Lord to provide for them that the story of New England's origins occupies a unique place in American history.

## The Mythical Opposition Between Piety and Prosperity in Colonial New England

MARK A. PETERSON

. . . Beginning with the first colonists themselves, and continuing through to the present, the dominant narrative of the history of New England Puritanism has maintained that piety and prosperity were enemies, that the rise of commerce delivered a mortal blow to the fervor of the founders, and that later generations of Puritans fell away from their religious heritage as they moved out across the New England landscape. For nearly four centuries, this story line, the myth of declension, has been

Excerpted from *The Price of Redemption: The Spiritual Economy of Puritan New England,* by Mark A. Peterson with the permission of the publishers, Stanford University Press. © 1997 by the Board of Trustees of the Leland Stanford Junior University.

repeated so frequently and told with such force and literary grace that it has become deeply ingrained in the American historical imagination. To offer a viable alternative to a narrative that has endured for so long and assumed such a mythic status, it may be useful to account for the declension narrative's power and tenacity, and perhaps to locate within its foundations a new way of seeing the Puritan past.

The myth-making impulse that produced the declension narrative began with the founding generation, for whom this particular story line served a vital purpose. William Bradford, governor of the Plymouth colony and author of New England's first Puritan history, consciously borrowed Old Testament metaphors to lend a sense of cosmic significance to the Pilgrims' experience of persecution. The opening chapters of his history of Plymouth Plantation provide a clear and powerful narrative of his community's origins in England, exile in the Netherlands, and escape to the freedom of the New World. Yet once his people had arrived in their promised land, his story lost its direction and Bradford was reduced to a mere keeper of annals, bewildered by a flood of events that lacked the meaning, clarity, and promise he had once seen for the future of his colony. Gradually, Bradford began to associate the material gains his fellow colonist made with his growing sense that the spiritual fervor he had once enjoyed as part of a latter-day apostolic community had seriously declined. In the end, he lamented the dispersal of the population through the countryside in search of richer pasture lands, a movement which left the "poor church" of Plymouth "like an ancient mother grown old and forsaken of her children."

Bradford's disappointment with the progress of a colony begun with such great hopes was a natural perspective for the founding generation to assume. Bradford and his fellow colonists frequently likened themselves to God's chosen people, the ancient Israelites. Worldliness and decay, the worship of false idols, the dispersal of the population, captivity, exile, and destruction—such was the fate of the children of Israel after they had reached their promised land, and such were the available metaphorical constructs that shaped New England Puritans' historical vision of themselves. Given Bradford's intense identification with Moses and the Exodus mythos in his description of the Pilgrims' escape from European bondage, it would have been remarkable if his account of the latter days of their New English Canaan had not taken on an elegiac tone. The part of the prophet lamenting the decline of his people was, in effect, scripted for Bradford already. But this rhetorical strategy served an important function for Bradford, reminding later generations of their religious heritage and encouraging continued commitment to the founders' faith.

The image of a New England soul lost in the colony's material progress created a compelling framework for understanding the region's early history. Bradford's successors among the Puritan clergy did their work thoroughly; their jeremiads made a lasting impression on the way their congregations understood themselves and their own experience. This peculiar form of historical thinking entered the consciousness of ordinary people and framed how they thought about themselves. In this sense, declension can be said to be neither right nor wrong as a way to understand New England's history. It is simply there, an artifact of the conceptual lives of early New Englanders, no more nor less important than the form of their town governments or the average size of their families. Yet more than most artifacts of the past, this Puritan tendency to see history as declension has led subsequent scholars to look for similar patterns in constructing a story, to follow Bradford's Puritan script. Even historians unsympathetic to the souls of the Puritans, who decry Puritan "theocracy" as an oppressive evil happily overcome by the free spirit of commerce, tend to make the same assumptions and tell the same story, if only to celebrate what Bradford lamented.

Like any powerful narrative, the declension model creates meaning by privileging some aspects of past experience while concealing others. William Bradford's viewpoint has encouraged later historians to ask whether the number of communicants in a particular Puritan church decreased over time, but has steered historians away from considering the remarkable numerical proliferation of churches across the countryside, the enduring popular devotion to the unusual form of church polity that Bradford helped to create. Most other European colonists of North America had great difficulty in maintaining any level of commitment to churches as institutions, and failed to create them in numbers sufficient to replicate European patterns. In this light, it becomes difficult to see how New Englanders could manage this singular achievement if the dispersal of New England's population really led, as Bradford insisted, to "the ruin . . . of the churches of God there." . . .

For historians of colonial New England, the question of where to begin the story has typically posed few problems. The tendency has always been to begin at the "beginning," with Plymouth Colony in 1620, with Massachusetts Bay in 1630, and with sufficient backward glances at English history to set a context for New World developments. Yet by commencing this story with the triumphs of the founding generation, set against the background of the Puritan revolution in England, a powerful mythology of New England's origins shapes the way in which all subsequent events are understood. The migration to the New World and the early establishment of New England's religious and social institutions have become definitive standards for the meaning of American Puritanism, against which all changes in New England's religious culture after the Cambridge Platform of 1648 are measured, judged, and usually condemned as decline. Given the Puritans' obsession with "primitive" models of ecclesiastical purity, the tendency of succeeding generations to revere their ancestors' original accomplishments should come as no surprise. But there are excellent reasons to challenge the assumption that the first generation's churches were a normative standard for evaluating the subsequent history of orthodoxy in New England.

First, the evolution of the Puritan movement over many decades in England and America defies the possibility of defining a single normative moment. English Puritanism before the Great Migration went through many phases, shaped by its internal logic of development and by the influence of external conditions. In the early seventeenth century, the more militant political aspects of Puritan reform temporarily subsided; the movement went "underground" and because more of a cultural "persuasion" than a drive for ecclesiastical reform. Yet by the 1630s, the policies of Charles I and Archbishop Laud had forced conforming Puritans into political opposition again. The timing of the migration to New England with these mounting political pressures served to "radicalize" many members of the founding generation and profoundly altered their understanding of religious belief and its institutional underpinnings. . . .

The self-selecting nature of the migrating group created an unusual population in New England's first generation, providing yet another reason not to think of this period as normative. The great mass of ungodly people, with whom English Puritans had been engaged in ongoing cultural warfare in England, were left behind. The godly in New England were further distinguished by the fervor they shared in their common enterprise, for the migration experience aroused utopian hopes along with daunting anxieties over the tasks of building a new society, lest they "be made a story and a by-word through the world, . . . and shame the faces of many of gods worthy servants, and cause theire prayers to be turned into Cursses upon us till wee be consumed out of the good land whether we are goeing." The heightened hopes and fears of this period shaped the emotional lives of the first generation in distinctive ways, but these were not definitive characteristics of the Puritan movement as a whole, nor were they experiences that subsequent generations could possibly have shared.

. . . First-generation colonists enjoyed the freedom to develop their Bible Commonwealths without fear of opposition and formed a strong sense of themselves as a distinct and independent people, a development that would have been impossible under closer imperial supervision.

The direct consequence of these unusual circumstances was a radicalization of the Puritan movement in its transplanted form. . . .

If the notion of early New England as a "laboratory" for the development of a Puritan society has any value, it is in this sense that the conditions offered to New England's settlers were ideally suited to the flourishing of the Puritan movement's most utopian impulses, a rarefied atmosphere where many of the harsh conditions of the "real world" of English society were filtered out. . . . In moving to a new world, they expected to find new feelings of closeness to God and to enjoy his ordinances in a pure form unattainable in the corrupted Church of England. As Thomas Shepard said to his Cambridge, Massachusetts, congregation in the 1630s, "there is no place in all the world where there is such expectation to find the Lord as here."

However, the Puritan movement encompassed much more than a desire to enjoy God's ordinances in pristine purity. The staunch insistence of the Massachusetts founders that they were not separatists and had no intention of abandoning the Church of England points to the abiding sense of responsibility to the world that was part of the Puritan reforming impulse. In a later sermon, Thomas Shepard warned his Cambridge congregation not to "fall a-dreaming" here in New England, and to oppose the utopian "delusion of men's brains" and "swarm of strange opinions" that were the product of a society where "we have ordinances to the full, sermons too long, and lectures too many, and private meetings too frequent." Shepard was not opposed to New England's pure ordinances and overabundant "means," but he realized that "golden dreams of grace" were as dangerous to the course of salvation as "drunken dreams of the world." In Shepard's eyes, the unique circumstances of the first decade of settlement made utopian delusions a greater temptation than worldly corruptions.

A full generation of experience was necessary before the most fervent Puritan colonists would awaken from their golden dreams to realize that the New World was as much a spiritual wilderness as the England they had left behind. What caused this awakening were developments that made New England into a mature society and brought an end to the "hothouse" environment that nurtured the first generation's radical florescence. First and foremost, the Restoration of the Stuart monarchy in 1660 threatened the basic terms of the colonies' existence, as earlier neglect of colonial matters gave way to increasing crown supervision of the nascent empire. New Englanders were aware of the implications of this development from the very start. The founders, lacking significant opposition from the English government, were free to mold their colonies according to their religious and cultural objectives. The real test of New England's ability to sustain these objectives came only when the orthodox colonies had to survive against the compromising power of the Restoration monarchy, with its opposition to Puritan religion and its hostility to decentralized self-rule anywhere within the crown's domain. The Anglican merchants and officials who began to appear in Boston reminded Puritans of their differences from mainstream English society and forced New Englanders to make accommodations to the world's demands—demands that had been easy to forget in the rarefied atmosphere of the first thirty years of settlement.

In addition, after a generation of experimentation, New England society had developed institutions and practices that would persist for the next century. In the migration period, colonists had relied upon assistance from the native American population and had looked to the fur trade for income to pay for their import needs, but these transitory patterns had given way to agricultural production and the fishing and trading enterprises that became the enduring staples of New England economic life. By the 1660s, the orthodox New England colonies had formed stable governments, had joined together in an alliance for mutual defense, and had created judicial systems connecting local affairs to colonial power centers. The pattern of settlement for new towns in the interior of New England had been established, and a population growing rapidly through natural increase began to fill up newly acquired lands. A system of schools was taking hold throughout the towns of Massachusetts, and Harvard College, while still a fledgling enterprise, was beginning to train homegrown ministers to replace the immigrant clergy of the first generation.

Finally, the Cambridge Platform of 1648, a written standard of ecclesiastical structure and discipline for the churches of Massachusetts, signalled the institutional maturation of orthodox religious culture. Although the platform stopped short of resolving the problems of baptism and membership of future generations, it pointed toward the Synod of 1662's "Halfway Covenant" as the next logical step in the development of the Puritan church as an institution that could persist through time. In effect, the Halfway Covenant acknowledged that New England's population could not forever be a self-selected body of saints already prepared to be incorporated in churches, as the majority of the migrants had been. Future American generations also had to be prepared for conversion, had to be kept within the "garden" of the churches and protected from the dangers of the "wilderness" without diminishing the purity of the church itself. By broadening the eligibility standards for baptism while reserving communion and full membership for those who had experienced saving grace, this is exactly what the Halfway Covenant did.

The challenges faced by the second and subsequent generations in New England were the challenges of a mature society, not an immigrant company. These challenges, while different from those of the first generation, were met with

responses no less "Puritan" than the actions of the founders. But in looking for simple continuity or repetition of first-generation events in later years, historians writing within the declension framework have overlooked growth and change that were
part of the Puritan tradition. In the 1630s, Thomas Shepard had warned his congregation not to be deluded by "golden dreams of grace." Shepard's sermon can be
read as a valuable corrective for modern scholars as well. Just as the purity and
plenitude of worship in early New England churches pushed the first generation toward radical delusions of God's kingdom appearing on earth, so historians have
been captivated by the remarkable success of New England as a utopian experiment
and have taken the events and circumstances of the first generation as a normative
standard for American Puritanism. Modern historians did not invent this tendency;
the original myth-makers were those like John Davenport who became rigidly committed to the first forms of church polity. To these founders and their immediate descendants, any change from the radical forms of the early New England Way
constituted declension from the true church, and they encouraged an almost slavish
ancestor worship among subsequent generations. It is their rhetorical emphasis on
loss and lamentation that subsequent historians have singled out as the dominant
pattern of New England's religious development after the first generation. Yet their
myth of origin obscures an equally important counter-narrative. If the Halfway
Covenant signalled an end to the "golden dreams of grace," it also marked the
emergence of this religious culture's sense of responsibility to the world, a development which paralleled the growing stability of New England society as a whole. By
beginning a new narrative of New England Puritanism in 1660, when the "real
world' returned to New England with a vengeance, we can remind ourselves that
the Puritan movement was not a form of ascetic monasticism, a withdrawal from
the world, but rather an attempt to change it, and we can begin to see the efforts of
later Puritans in a new light, as an ongoing reformation.

The Puritan notion of the exemplary life, a way of understanding the self and
historical development that complements the mythology of origins, has also contributed to the power and tenacity of the declension model. Puritans constantly
modelled themselves and interpreted their personal experiences through comparisons to the lives of others. The imitation of Christ, of course, was central to Christian piety, but all Biblical figures, saintly or wicked, were available models against
which Puritans could measure their own behavior and beliefs. . . .

To model one's life on these exemplary figures . . . was to embrace declension
as an organizing framework for one's own personal experience. It meant accepting
a vision of contemporary history in which the pious individual was always engaged
in a valiant but ultimately losing battle against a vain and wicked world. To inter-
nalize this biographical genre therefore made it easy to conflate the life of the individual with the imagined evolution of society as a whole. . . .

. . . But there are risks in conflating the fate of individuals with the development of societies or accepting a single family's perspective as the most valid view
of an era. To return again to William Bradford, his personal interpretation of the
dispersal of the Plymouth population was quite idiosyncratic. To him it meant the
dissipation of the particular community of exiles that had been at the center of his
own experience, but dispersal did not, in fact, lead to the "ruin of the churches of

God" in New England, as Bradford had imagined it would. The economic resources that the settlers sought were eventually responsible for strengthening and expanding the Puritan churches of Plymouth Colony. Yet virtually every history of Plymouth ever written has taken Bradford's emotional reaction as a definitive statement of the character of Plymouth's development. The problem, in brief, is that Puritan biographies projected history as declension, Puritan histories tended to be biographical, and modern scholars have (perhaps unconsciously) relied on these sources for their plot structures when writing both biographies and general histories. . . .

The assumption that commercial capitalism is antithetical to Puritan piety and destructive of its communal ideals pervades the town studies of the "new social history" and reinforces the declension narrative. The common tendency of New England town studies has been to assume that Puritan churches were best suited to the social conditions found in villages cut off from the world of the market, where subsistence agriculture was practiced and communal values associated with premodern economic forms predominated. Perhaps the most influential study to advance this position argues that New England's early Puritan towns were intended to be "closed corporate utopian peasant communities," covenanted to the task of mutual cooperation, resistant to change, and anti-commercial. In this formulation, the "peasant" mentality fosters both Puritan piety and economic backwardness, as though these were the religious and economic sides of the same cultural coin. Competition, conflict, and migration away from the original town center for economic gain are taken to be destructive of community and therefore indicators of Puritan declension, a historical analysis that repeats the pattern originally described by William Bradford. . . .

Like the other major elements of the declension paradigm, the origins of these ideas about community can be found in the Puritans' own rhetoric and in the inner workings of the Puritan mind. John Winthrop's "Modell of Christian Charity" declared the importance of communal solidarity and denounced the evils of a selfishly acquisitive spirit. The clergy frequently warned their congregations against the dangers of worldliness, and Puritans took to heart the parable of the rich fool, who "layeth up treasure for himself, and is not rich toward God" (Luke 12:21). But to assume, as many historians have done, that Puritanism therefore required pre-modern anti-capitalist village communalism in order to thrive is to miss a subtle but vital distinction. Worldliness was not merely the "laying up" of treasure, but the failure to spend it to sow the seeds of grace. Ideals of communal charity and freedom from worldliness were not prerequisite conditions for the existence of Puritanism, but challenges that the godly gladly took on, challenges that were in many ways made easier by the "treasure" that a thriving market economy produced. . . .

Later generations of New England's historians celebrated their ancestors' communal cohesion and unworldly asceticism, but these qualities were not choices made by the founders, and they were not dictated by an opposition to money or markets. Communal cohesion, where it did exist in the first generation, was often a by-product of the experience of migration; in many cases, self-selecting communities organized by charismatic leaders were bound together by their common backgrounds and experiences. The homogeneity of these immigrant companies offers the illusion of aboriginal communal harmony in New England, hiding the fact that many of these Puritans were contentious troublemakers whose beliefs had created turmoil in the Old England of their birth. Similarly first-generation asceticism was not a choice dictated by Puritan religious belief. English Puritans did, of course, abhor the decorative artwork and elaborate priestly vestments that the Church of England still retained. But what they hated was the idolatry, not the wealth and finery, that these Roman Catholic vestiges stood for. John Cotton did not forsake St. Botolph's, the largest non-cathedral church in England, for a log meetinghouse in Boston because he opposed grand buildings and preferred to shiver in the cold, but because he could no longer safely practice his brand of Puritan ministry without molestation from ecclesiastical authorities. John Davenport did not instruct his congregation of pious merchants in London's commercial district to renounce their riches; nor did he leave them for New Haven because he preferred rustic simplicity. The asceticism of early Massachusetts Puritans was not a conscious program of the colonists, but an artifact of the experience of all English colonizing enterprises, the unavoidable "stripping down" of European culture caused by transplantation. The first colonists were ascetics because they had no choice in the matter, and they were communitarians by default, but the mythology of origins and the privileging of the first generation has transformed early necessities into retrospective virtues.

The biographical genre of the exemplary Puritan life also reinforces the tendency to see the passage of time as a triumph of worldliness over piety. Demographic studies of church records have shown that conversion typically occurred at the time in life when people were leaving the protections of adolescence and assuming the responsibilities of adulthood. For women, conversion often coincided roughly with the age of marriage or first childbearing; for men, formal economic responsibilities and the assumption of public office were as important as changes in family status. In either case, the most fervent spiritual experiences of a lifetime were associated with the moment when youth was left behind and engagement with the demands of the world commenced. It is no wonder, then, that at the end of a successful life in which property was accumulated, families were provided for, and civic duties were performed, the publicly active men who most commonly wrote autobiographies should look back and see their spiritual evolution as an early moment of grace followed by a life-long losing battle against worldliness. For highly educated men, the college experience contributed to this tendency as well, for in retrospect, college was a time to cultivate the mind and soul in communal cooperation, while later life's spiritual pilgrimage was more isolated and subject to greater worldly constraints, even for the many graduates who went on to become ministers. The conventions of Puritan autobiography make the belief that prosperity and piety were enemies all the more difficult to shake.

. . . For several decades, critics of the declension model have been subtly suggesting the possibility that commercial development may have been beneficial to Puritan religion, and that later generations may well have retained the theological rigor and spiritual fervor of the founders. The time has come to begin by assuming the truth of these notions and asking not *whether* this was the case, but *how* this process worked. When John Cotton preached that "Christ cannot be had for money, yet sometimes without expense of money he cannot be had," he may have been attempting to explicate the contrary demands for striving and passivity implicit in the conversion process, but he was also describing an obvious truth about the social reality of Puritan religious culture. . . .

*F U R T H E R    R E A D I N G*

David Grayson Allen, *In English Ways: The Movement of Societies and the Transferal of English Local Law and Custom to Massachusetts Bay in the Seventeenth Century* (1982).

David Cressy, *Coming Over: Migration and Communication Between England and New England in the Seventeenth Century* (1987).

Stephen Foster, *The Long Argument: English Puritanism and the Shaping of New England Culture, 1570–1700* (1991).

Stephen Innes, *Creating the Commonwealth: The Economic Culture of Puritan New England* (1995).

Janice Knight, *Orthodoxies in Massachusetts: Rereading American Puritanism* (1994).

John Frederick Martin, *Profits in the Wilderness: Entrepreneurship and the Founding of New England Towns in the Seventeenth Century* (1992).

Edmund S. Morgan, *The Puritan Dilemma: The Story of John Winthrop* (1958).

Daniel Vickers, *Farmers and Fishermen: Two Centuries of Work in Essex County, Massachusetts, 1630–1830* (1994).

# C H A P T E R
## 5

# New England:
# Growth and Conflict

*○*

*Puritanism was a highly individualistic creed. People took the enormous step of leaving their families and friends and the society they knew in England because they were so committed to the project of creating a society that operated along the lines they chose. They came because they knew they were right when everyone else was wrong. The problem for New England's communities was containing such strong personalities within the framework their leaders had designed. The Puritans held learning in the highest regard, and many of the leaders in the New England towns were university-educated men. These scholars were consulted for guidance and inspiration. But there could be no abdication of responsibility; each member of the community was expected to read the Bible and understand God's message. Each went through the same process of self-examination to find the sparks of God's grace within. As the colony grew and continued to diversify, tensions grew in towns and villages across the countryside. Both men and women challenged their ministers and political leaders, and some were forcibly expelled from Massachusetts; others left voluntarily when they decided that the colony had taken the wrong path. But most stayed and tried to make their own choices stick. Women, denied the opportunity to take active roles in determining the direction of the congregations and towns, seem to have been particularly troublesome. Their outspokenness in challenging authority transgressed prescribed gender roles and led male leaders to foresee the breakdown of society in their actions. As discord grew, many were prepared to believe that it was the work of the devil through the influence of witches who chose to ally themselves with him. Everything that happened reflected divine will; if God allowed the devil to be active, then Puritans must both rid their society of his agents and redouble examination of their own conduct to see what had brought God's wrath.*

*One part of the agenda in the founding of Massachusetts was conversion of the Indians. Early promoters had justified the whole project by pointing to the necessity of bringing the word of God to people who had been denied access to it. Although Europeans thought of Christianity as a universal religion, they also believed that "civility," adoption of a European style of life, was a necessary pre-*

*requisite to conversion. Because reading the Bible was essential to receiving God's message, Puritans also felt that converts had to be able to read. Thus the project of converting the New England Algonquians was a long-term one. Most colonists, even ministers, thought of converting the Indians as something for the future, but some, especially the Reverend John Eliot, took on the immense job of learning Massachusett, creating a written form of the language, and, with his Indian associates, translating the Bible and classic devotional works. Relations with the southern New England Algonquians were always complex, whether the Indians concerned were Indian converts who lived in the separate "praying towns" Eliot sponsored or those who steadfastly maintained their own cultural standards. Indians resisted the colonists' attempts to determine the terms of life in New England. Ultimately the relationship exploded in King Philip's War in 1676. King Philip, or Metacom, was, ironically, the son of Massasoit, the Wampanoag chief who participated in the first Thanksgiving.*

## D O C U M E N T S

On the eve of the outbreak of King Philip's War, John Easton, the attorney general of Rhode Island, met with King Philip or Metacom to try to negotiate a settlement. In document 1 he recorded the Indians' grievances as presented by Philip, including the loss of their land, the depredations of unfenced English animals on their crops, and manipulation of native leadership. Document 2 is an excerpt of Cotton Mather's biography of John Eliot, who was called the Apostle to the Indians. Although Eliot devoted much of his life to working with converts and prospective converts, Mather's dismissive and contemptuous attitude toward the American natives in this book written after the war shows the climate of opinion in which Indians were forced to live by the end of the seventeenth century. Document 3 is from Mary Rowlandson's narrative of her captivity. She was captured in the frontier village of Lancaster, Massachusetts, by a mixed group of Narragansetts, Nipmucs, and Wampanoags and spent several weeks with her captors before being ransomed. Despite her hostility, she made it clear that many of the natives around her tried to make her as comfortable as possible. She met King Philip and used her needlework skills for him as well as for other Indians. Speaking through biblical texts, she wrote in an acceptable manner for Puritan women and her book was the first of the popular captivity narratives and became a best-seller. How does her interview with Philip compare with Easton's?

Accusations of witchcraft were endemic in New England as in England, and scattered prosecutions of individual witches happened throughout the colonies from as early as 1647. Increase Mather, one of the greatest intellectuals of the time, collected instances of bewitching in his book *Remarkable Providences* in document 4 published in 1684. Fear of witches as agents of the devil culminated in the massive accusations at Salem in 1692. The trial testimonies have been preserved. The genuine puzzlement and dismay both of one of the accused, Rebecca Nurse, and of her neighbors comes through in the testimony presented in document 5.

## 1. John Easton Tries to Avert the War by Hearing King Philip's Grievances, 1675

... The English were afraid and Philip was afraid and both increased in arms but for 40 years time reports and jealousies of war had been very frequent that we did not think that now a war was breaking forth, but abut a week before it did we had case to think it would, then to endeavor to prevent it, we sent a man to Philip that if he would come to the ferry we would come over to speak with him. About 4 miles we had to come thither. Our messenger came to them, they not aware of it behaved themselves as furious but suddenly appeased when they understood who he was and what he came for. He called his council and agreed to come to us, came himself unarmed and about 40 of his men armed. Then 5 of us went over. 3 were magistrates. We sat very friendly together. We told him our business was to endeavor that they might not receive or do wrong. They said that was well, they had done no wrong, the English wronged them. We said we knew the English said the Indians wronged them and the Indians said the English wronged them but our desire was the quarrel might rightly be decided in the best way, and not as dogs decided their quarrels. The Indians owned that fighting was the worst way, then they propounded how right might take place, we said by arbitration. They said all English agreed against them, and so by arbitration they had had much wrong, many square miles of land so taken from them for English would have English arbitrators, and once they were persuaded to give in their arms would not deliver them as they had promised, until they consented to pay £100, and now they had not so much land or money, that they were as good be killed as leave all their livelihood.

... they had a great fear to have [lest] any of their Indians should be called or forced to be Christian Indians. They said that such were in every thing more mischievous, only dissemblers, and then the English made them not subject to their kings, and by their lying to wrong their kings. We knew it to be true, and we promising them that how ever in government to Indians all should be so alike and that we knew it was our king's will it should be so, that although we were weaker than other Colonies, they having submitted to our king to protect them others dared not otherwise to molest them, so they expressed they took that to be well, that we had little Case to doubt but that to us under the king they would have yielded to our determinations in what any should have complained to us against them, but Philip charged it to be dishonesty in us to put off the hearing the complaints. Therefore we Consented to hear them. They said they had been the first in doing good to the English, and the English the first in doing wrong. Said when the English first came, their king's father [Massasoit] was as a great man and the English as a little child, he constrained other Indians from wronging the English and gave them Corn and showed them how to plant and was free to do them any good and had let them have a 100 times more land, than now the king had for his own people, but their king's brother when he was king came miserably to die by being forced to Court as they judged poisoned, and another grievance was if 20 of their honest Indians testified that an Englishman had done them wrong, it was as nothing,

Some of the spelling and punctuation in this document has been modernized.

John Easton, "A Relacion of the Indyan Warre, by Mr. Easton, of Rhode Isld., 1675," in Charles H. Lincoln, ed., *Narritives of the Indian Wars* (New York, 1913), 7–17.

and if but one of their worst Indians testified against any Indian or their king when it pleased the English that was sufficient. Another grievance was when their kings sold land the English would say it was more than they agreed to and a writing must be proof against all them, and some of their kings had done wrong to sell so much he left his people none and some being given to drunkenness the English made them drunk and then cheated them in bargains, but now their kings were forewarned not for to part with land for nothing in comparison to the value thereof. Now whom the English had owned for king or queen they would disinherit, and make another king that would give or sell them their land, that now they had no hopes left to keep any land. Another grievance: the English cattle and horses still increased [so] that when they removed 30 miles from where [the] English [had] anything to do, they could not keep their corn from being spoiled, they never being used to fence, and thought when the English bought land of them that they would have kept their cattle upon their own land. Another grievance: the English were so eager to sell the Indians liquors that most the Indians spent all in drunkenness and then ravened upon the sober Indians they did believe often did hurt the English cattle, and their kings could not prevent it. We knew before these were their grand Complaints, but then we only endeavored to persuade that all complaints might be righted without war.

## 2. Cotton Mather Describes the Indians of Massachusetts and John Eliot's Mission to Them, 1702

The Natives of the Country now Possessed by the *New-Englanders,* had been forlorn and wretched *Heathen* ever since their first herding here; and tho' we know not *When* or *How* those *Indians* first became Inhabitants of this mighty Continent, yet we may guess that probably the Devil decoy'd those miserable Salvages hither, in hopes that the Gospel of the Lord Jesus Christ would never come here to destroy or disturb his *Absolute Empire* over them. But our *Eliot* was in such ill Terms with the Devil, as to alarm him with sounding the *Silver Trumpets* of Heaven in his Territories, and make some Noble and Zealous Attempts towards outing him of his Ancient Possessions here. There were, I think, Twenty-several *Nations* (if I may call them so) of *Indians* upon that spot of Ground, which fell under the Influence of our *Three United Colonies;* and our *Eliot* was willing to rescue as many of them as he could, from that old usurping *Landlord* of *America,* who is *by the Wrath of God, the Prince of this World.*

I cannot find that any besides the Holy Spirit of God, first moved him to the blessed Work of *Evangelizing* these perishing *Indians;* 'twas that Holy Spirit which laid before his Mind the Idea of that which was on the *Seal* of the Massachuset Colony; *A poor Indian having a Label going from his Mouth, with a,* Come over and Help Us. It was the Spirit of our Lord Jesus Christ, which enkindled in him a *Pitty* for the dark Souls of these Natives, whom the *God of this World had blinded,* through all the By-past Ages. He was none of those that make, *The Salvation of the*

Cotton Mather, *Magnalia Christi Americana* (London, 1702), Book III.

*Heathen,* an Article of their *Creed;* but (setting aside the unrevealed and extraordinary Steps which the *Holy one of Israel* may take out of his *usual Paths*) he thought men to be *lost* if our *Gospel* be hidden from them; and he was of the same Opinion with one of the Ancients, who said, *Some have endeavoured to prove* Plato *a Christian, till they prove themselves little better than Heathens.* It is indeed a Principle in the Turkish *Alcoran,* That *Let a Man's Religion be what it will, he shall be saved, if he conscientiously live up to the Rules of it:* But our *Eliot* was no *Mahometan.* He could most heartily subscribe to that Passage in the Articles of the Church of *England.* "They are to be held accursed, who presume to say, that every Man shall be saved by the Law or Sect which he professeth, so that he be diligent to frame his Life according to that Law, and Light of Nature; for Holy Scripture doth set out unto us, only the Name of Jesus Christ, whereby Men must be saved." . . .

The exemplary *Charity* of this excellent Person in this important Affair, will not be seen in its due Lustres, unless we make some Reflections upon several Circumstances which he beheld these forlorn *Indians* in. Know then, that these doleful Creatures are the veriest *Ruines of Mankind,* which are to be found any where upon the Face of the Earth. No such *Estates* are to be expected among them, as have been the *Baits* which the pretended *Converters* in other Countries have snapped at. One might see among them, what an *hard Master* the Devil is, to the most devoted of his *Vassals!* These abject Creatures, live in a Country full of *Mines;* we have already made entrance upon our *Iron;* and in the very Surface of the Ground among us, 'tis thought there lies *Copper* enough to supply all this World; besides other Mines hereafter to be exposed; but our shiftless *Indians* were never Owners of so much as a *Knife,* till we come among them; their Name for an *English-man* was a *Knife-man;* Stone was instead of Metal for their *Tools;* and for their *Coins,* they have only little *Beads* with Holes in them to string them upon a *Bracelet,* whereof some are *white;* and of these there go six for a Penny; some are *black* or *blew;* and of these, *go three* for a Penny; this *Wampam,* as they call it, is made of the *Shell-fish,* which lies upon the Sea Coast continually.

The[y] live in a Country, where *we* now have all the Conveniencies of human Life: But as for *them,* their *housing* is nothing but a few *Mats* ty'd about *Poles* fastened in the Earth, where a good *Fire* is their *Bed Clothes* in the coldest Seasons; their *Clothing* is but a Skin of a Beast, covering their *Hind-parts,* their *Fore-parts* having but a little Apron, where Nature calls for Secrecy; their *Diet* has not a greater Dainty than their *Nokehick,* that is a spoonful of their *parch'd meal,* with a spoonful of *Water,* which will strengthen them to travel a Day together; except we should mention the Flesh of *Deers, Bears, Mose, Rackoons,* and the like, which they have when they can *catch* them; as also a little *Fish,* which if they would preserve, 'twas by *drying,* not by *salting;* for they had not a grain of *Salt* in the World, I think, till we bestow'd it on them. Their *Physick* is, excepting a few odd *Specificks,* which some of them Encounter certain Cases with, nothing hardly, but an *Hot-House,* or a *Powaw;* their *Hot-House* is a little *Cave* about eight foot over, where after they have terribly heated it, a Crew of them go sit and sweat and smoke for an Hour together, and then immediately run into some very cold adjacent Brook, without the least Mischief to them; 'tis this way they recover themselves from some Diseases, particularly from the *French;* but in most of their dangerous Distempers, 'tis a *Powaw* that must be sent for; that is, a *Priest,* who has more Familiarity with Satan than his Neighbours; this Conjurer comes and Roars, and Howls, and uses

Magical Ceremonies over the Sick Man, and will be well paid for it, when he has done; if this don't effect the Cure, the *Man's Time is come, and there's an end.*

They live in a Country full of the best *Ship-Timber* under Heaven: But never saw a *Ship,* till some came from *Europe* hither; and then they were scar'd out of their Wits, to see the *Monster* come sailing in, and spitting Fire with a mighty noise, out of her floating side; they cross the Water in *Canoo's,* made sometimes of *Trees,* which they burn and hew, till they have hollow'd them; and sometimes of *Barks,* which they stitch into a light sort of a Vessel, to be easily carried over Land; if they overset, it is but a little paddling like a Dog, and they are soon where they were.

Their way of living, is infinitely Barbarous: The Men are most abominably *slothful;* making their poor *Squaws,* or Wives, to plant and dress, and barn, and beat their Corn, and build their *Wigwams* for them; which perhaps may be the reason of their extraordinary Ease in Childbirth. In the mean time, their chief Employment, when they'll *condescend* unto any, is that of *Hunting;* wherein they'll go out some scores, if not Hundreds of them in a Company, driving all before them. . . .

This was the miserable People, which our *Eliot* propounded unto himself, to teach and save! And he had a double Work incumbent on him; he was to make Men of them, e'er he could hope to see them *Saints;* they must be *civilized* e'er they could be *Christianized;* he could not, as *Gregory* once of our Nation, see any thing *Angelical* to bespeak his Labours for their Eternal Welfare, all among them was *Diabolical.* To think on raising a Number of these hideous Creatures, unto the *Elevations* of our Holy Religion, must argue more than common or little Sentiments in the Undertaker; but the Faith of an *Eliot* could encounter it! . . .

The *First Step* which he judg'd necessary now to be taken by him, was to learn the *Indian* Language; for he saw them so stupid and senseless, that they would never do so much as enquire after the Religion of the Strangers now come into their Country, much less would they so far imitate us, as to leave off their beastly way of living, that they might be Partakers of any Spiritual Advantage by us: Unless we could first address them in a *Language* of their own. Behold, new Difficulties to be surmounted by our indefatigable *Eliot!* He hires a Native to teach him this exotick Language, and with a laborious Care and Skill, reduces it into a *Grammar* which afterwards he published. . . . Nor do we find in all this Language the least Affinity to, or Derivation from any *European* Speech that we are acquainted with. I know not what Thoughts it will produce in my Reader, when I inform him, that once finding that the *Dæmons* in a possessed young Woman, understood the *Latin* and *Greek* and *Hebrew* Languages, my Curiosity led me to make Trial of this *Indian* Language, and the *Dæmons* did seem as if they did not understand it. This tedious Language our *Eliot* (the Anagram of whose Name was Toile) quickly became a Master of; he employ'd a pregnant and witty *Indian,* who also spoke *English* well, for his Assistance in it; . . . And being by his *Prayers* and *Pains* thus furnished, he set himself in the Year 1646. to preach the Gospel of our Lord Jesus Christ, among these Desolate Outcasts. . . .

**Mr. Eliott's Way of Opening the Mysteries of the Gospel, to Our Indians**

'Twas in the Year 1646, that Mr. *Eliot,* accompany'd by three more, gave a Visit unto an Assembly of *Indians,* of whom he desired a Meeting at such a Time and Place, that he might lay before them the Things of their Eternal Peace. After a serious *Prayer,* he gave them a *Sermon* which continued about a Quarter above an Hour, and contained the principal Articles of the Christian Religion, applying all to the Condition of the *Indians* present. Having done, he asked of them, Whether *they understood?* And with a General Reply they answered, *They understood all.* He then began what was his usual Method afterwards in treating with them; that is, he caused them to propound such *Questions* as they pleas'd unto himself; and he gave wise and good *Answers* to them all. Their *Questions* would often, tho' not always, refer to what he had newly preached; and he this way not only made a *Proof* of their profiting by his Ministry, but also gave an Edge to what he delivered unto them. Some of their *Questions* would be a little *Philosophical,* and required a good Measure of Learning in the Minister concerned with them; but for this our *Eliot* wanted not. He would also put proper *Questions* unto them, and at one of his first Exercises with them, he made the Young Ones capable of regarding those three Questions,

Q. 1.   *Who made you and all the World?*
Q. 2.   *Who do you look should save you from Sin and Hell?*
Q. 3.   *How many Commandments has the Lord given you to keep?*

It was his Wisdom that he began with them upon such Principles as they themselves had already some Notions of; such as that of an *Heaven* for good, and *Hell* for bad People, when they dy'd. It broke his gracious Heart within him to see, what Floods of Tears fell from the Eyes of several among those degenerate Salvages, at the first Addresses which he made unto them; yea, from the very worst of them all. He was very inquisitive to learn who were the *Powawes,* that is, the *Sorcerers,* and *Seducers,* that maintained the Worship of the Devil in any of their Societies. . . .

## 3. Mary Rowlandson Interprets Her Captivity During King Philip's War, 1676

### The Eight Remove

. . . On the morrow morning we must go over the River, *i. e.* Connecticot, to meet with King Philip; two Cannoos full, they had carried over, the next Turn I my self was to go; but as my foot was upon the Cannoo to step in, there was a sudden outcry among them, and I must step back; and instead of going over the River, I must go four or five miles up the River farther Northward. Some of the Indians ran one way, and some another. The cause of this rout was, as I thought, their espying some English Scouts, who were thereabout. In this travel up the River, about noon the Company made a stop, and sate down; some to eat, and others to rest them. As I sate amongst them, musing of things past, my Son Joseph unexpectedly came to me: we asked of each others welfare, bemoaning our dolefull condition, and the change that had come upon uss. We had Husband and Father, and Children, and Sisters, and Friends, and Relations, and House, and Home, and many Comforts of this Life: but now we may say, as Job, *Naked came I out of my Mothers Womb, and*

---

Mary Rowlandson, *A Narritive of the Captivity and Restauration of Mrs. Mary Rowlandson* (Boston, 1682). Reprinted in Charles H. Lincoln, ed., *Narritives of the Indian Wars* (New York, 1913), 133–136.

*naked shall I return: The Lord gave, and the Lord hath taken away, Blessed be the Name of the Lord.* I asked him whither he would read; he told me, he earnestly desired it, I gave him my Bible, and he lighted upon that comfortable Scripture, Psal. 118. 17, 18. *I shall not dy but live, and declare the works of the Lord: the Lord hath chastened me sore, yet he hath not given me over to death.* Look here, Mother (says he) did you read this? And here I may take occasion to mention one principall ground of my setting forth these Lines: even as the Psalmist sayes, To declare the Works of the Lord, and his wonderfull Power in carrying us along, preserving us in the Wilderness, while under the Enemies hand, and returning of us in safety again, And His goodness in bringing to my hand so many comfortable and suitable Scriptures in my distress. But to Return, We travelled on till night; and in the morning, we must go over the River to Philip's Crew. When I was in the Cannoo, I could not but be amazed at the numerous crew of Pagans that were on the Bank on the other side. When I came ashore, they gathered all about me, I sitting alone in the midst: I observed they asked one another questions, and laughed, and rejoyced over their Gains and Victories. Then my heart began to fail: and I fell a weeping which was the first time to my remembrance, that I wept before them. Although I had met with so much Affliction, and my heart was many times ready to break, yet could I not shed one tear in their sight: but rather had been all this while in a maze, and like one astonished: but now I may say as, Psal. 137. 1. *By the Rivers of Babylon, there we sate down: yea, we wept when we remembered Zion.* There one of them asked me, why I wept, I could hardly tell what to say: yet I answered, they would kill me: No, said he, none will hurt you. Then came one of them and gave me two spoonfulls of Meal to comfort me, and another gave me half a pint of Pease; which was more worth than many Bushels at another time. Then I went to see King Philip, he bade me come in and sit down, and asked me whether I woold smoke it (a usual Complement nowadayes amongst Saints and Sinners) but this no way suited me. For though I had formerly used Tobacco, yet I had left it ever since I was first taken. It seems to be a Bait, the Devil layes to make men loose their precious time: I remember with shame, how formerly, when I had taken two or three pipes, I was presently ready for another, such a bewitching thing it is: But I thank God, he has now given me power over it; surely there are many who may be better imployed than to ly sucking a stinking Tobacco-pipe.

Now the Indians gather their Forces to go against North-Hampton: over-night one went about yelling and hooting to give notice of the design. Whereupon they fell to boyling of Ground-nuts, and parching of Corn (as many as had it) for their Provision: and in the morning away they went. During my abode in this place, Philip spake to me to make a shirt for his boy, which I did, for which he gave me a shilling: I offered the mony to my master, but he bade me keep it: and with it I bought a piece of Horse flesh. Afterwards he asked me to make a Cap for his boy, for which he invited me to Dinner. I went, and he gave me a Pancake, about as big as two fingers; it was made of parched wheat, beaten, and fryed in Bears grease, but I thought I never tasted pleasanter meat in my life. There was a Squaw who spake to me to make a shirt for her *Sannup,* for which she gave me a piece of Bear. Another asked me to knit a pair of Stockins, for which she gave me a quart of Pease: I boyled my Pease and Bear together, and invited my master and mistriss to dinner, but the proud Gossip, because I served them both in one Dish, would eat nothing, except one bit that he gave her upon the point of his knife. Hearing that my son was come to this place, I went to see him, and found him lying flat upon the ground: I asked him how he could sleep so? he answered me, That he was not asleep, but at Prayer; and lay so, that they might not observe what he was doing. I pray God he may remember these things now he is returned in safety. At this Place (the Sun now getting higher) what with the beams and heat of the Sun, and the smoak of the Wigwams, I thought I should have been blind. I could scarce discern one Wigwam from another. There was here one Mary Thurston of Medfield, who seeing how it was with me, lent me a Hat to wear: but as soon as I was gone, the Squaw (who owned that Mary Thurston) came running after me, and got it away again. Here was the Squaw that gave me one spoonfull of Meal. I put it in my Pocket to keep it safe: yet notwithstanding some body stole it, but put five Indian Corns in the room of it: which Corns were the greatest Provisions I had in my travel for one day.

The Indians returning from North-Hampton, brought with them some Horses, and Sheep, and other things which they had taken: I desired them, that they would carry me to Albany, upon one of those Horses, and sell me for Powder: for so they had sometimes discoursed. I was utterly hopless of getting home on foot, the way that I came. I could hardly bear to think of the many weary steps I had taken, to come to this place.

### The Ninth Remove

But in stead of going either to Albany or homeward, we must go five miles up the River, and then go over it. Here we abode a while. Here lived a sorry Indian, who spoke to me to make him a shirt. When I had done it, he would pay me nothing. But he living by the River side, where I often went to fetch water, I would often be putting of him in mind, and calling for my pay: at last he told me if I would make another shirt, for a Papoos not yet born, he would give me a knife, which he did when I had done it. I carried the knife in, and my master asked me to give it him, and I was not a little glad that I had any thing that they would accept of, and be pleased with. When we were at this place, my Masters maid came home, she had been gone three weeks into the Narrhaganset Country, to fetch Corn, where they had stored up some in the ground: she brought home about a peck and half of Corn. This was about the time that their great Captain, Naananto, was killed in the Narrhaganset Countrey. My Son being now about a mile from me, I asked liberty to go and see him, they bade me go, and away I went: but quickly lost my self, travelling over Hills and thorough Swamps, and could not find the way to him. And I cannot but admire at the wonderfull power and goodness of God to me, in that, though I was gone from home, and met with all sorts of Indians, and those I had no knowledge of, and there being no Christian soul near me; yet not one of them offered the least imaginable miscarriage to me. I turned homeward again, and met with my master, he shewed me the way to my Son: When I came to him I found him not well: and withall he had a boyl on his side, which much troubled him: We bemoaned one another awhile, as the Lord helped us, and then I returned again. When I was returned, I found my self as unsatisfied as I was before. I went up and down mourning and lamenting: and my spirit was ready to sink, with the thoughts of my poor Children: my Son was ill, and I could not but think of his mournfull looks, and no Christian Friend was near him, to do any office of love for him, either for Soul or Body. And my poor Girl, I knew not where she was, nor whither she was sick, or well, or alive, or dead. I repaired under these thoughts to my Bible (my great comfort in that time) and that Scripture came to my hand, *Cast thy burden upon the Lord, and He shall sustain thee,* Psal. 55. 22.

But I was fain to go and look after something to satisfie my hunger, and going among the Wigwams, I went into one, and there found a Squaw who shewed her self very kind to me, and gave me a piece of Bear. I put it into my pocket, and came home, but could not find an opportunity to broil it, for fear they would get it from me, and there it lay all that day and night in my stinking pocket. In the morning I went to the same Squaw, who had a Kettle of Ground nuts boyling; I asked her to let me boyle my piece of Bear in her Kettle, which she did, and gave me some Ground-nuts to eat with it: and I cannot but think how pleasant it was to me. I have sometime seen Bear baked very handsomly among the English, and some like it, but the thoughts that it was Bear, made me tremble: but now that was savoury to me that one would think was enough to turn the stomach of a bruit Creature.

One bitter cold day, I could find no room to sit down before the fire: I went out, and could not tell what to do, but I went in to another Wigwam, where they were also sitting round the fire, but the Squaw laid a skin for me, and bid me sit down, and gave me some Ground-nuts, and bade me come again: and told me they would buy me, if they were able, and yet these were strangers to me that I never saw before.

## 4. Increase Mather Describes the Proofs of Witchcraft, 1684

Inasmuch as things which are preternatural, and not accomplished without diabolical operation, do more rarely happen, it is pity but that they should be observed. Several accidents of that kind have hapned in New England, which I shall here faithfully relate, so far as I have been able to come unto the knowledge of them.

Very remarkable was that Providence wherein Ann Cole of Hartford in New England was concerned. She was, and is accounted, a person of real piety and integrity; nevertheless, in the year 1662, then living in her fathers house (who has likewise been esteemed a godly man), she was taken with very strange fits, wherein her tongue was improved by a dæmon to express things which she herself knew nothing of; sometimes the discourse would hold for a considerable time; the general purpose of which was, that such and such persons (who were named in the discourse which passed from her) were consulting how they might carry on mischievous designs against her and several others, mentioning sundry wayes they should take for that end, particularly that they would afflict her body, spoil her name, &c. The general answer made amongst the dæmons was, "She runs to the rock." This having continued some hours, the dæmons said, "Let us confound her language, that she may tell no more tales." She uttered matters unintelligible. And then the discourse passed into a Dutch tone (a Dutch family then lived in the town), and therein an account was given of some afflictions that had befallen divers; amongst others, what had befallen a woman that lived next neighbour to the Dutch family, whose arms had been strangely pinched in the night, declaring by whom and for what cause that course had been taken with her. The Reverend Mr. Stone (then teacher of the church in Hartford) being by, when the

Increase Mather, *An Essay for the Recording of Remarkable Providences* (Boston, 1684), 135–167, 168–185.

discourse hapned, declared, that he thought it impossible for one not familiarly acquainted with the Dutch (which Ann Cole had not in the least been) should so exactly imitate the Dutch tone in the pronunciation of English. Several worthy persons (viz., Mr. John Whiting, Mr. Samuel Hooker, and Mr. Joseph Hains) wrote the intelligible sayings expressed by Ann Cole, whilest she was thus amazingly handled. The event was, that one of the persons (whose name was Greensmith, being a lewd and ignorant woman, and then in prison on suspicion for witchcraft) mentioned in the discourse as active in the mischief done and designed, was by the magistrate sent for; Mr. Whiting and Mr. Haines read what they had written, and the woman being astonished thereat, confessed those things to be true, and that she and other persons named in this preternatural discourse, had had familiarity with the devil. Being asked whether she had made an express covenant with him, she answered, she had not, only as she promised to go with him when he called, which accordingly she had sundry times done, and that the devil told her that at Christmass they would have a merry meeting, and then the covenant between them should be subscribed. The next day she was more particularly enquired of concerning her guilt respecting the crime she was accused with. She then acknowledged, that though when Mr. Haines began to read what he had taken down in writing, her rage was such that she could have torn him in pieces, and was as resolved as might be to deny her guilt (as she had done before), yet after he had read awhile, she was (to use her own expression) as if her flesh had been pulled from her bones, and so could not deny any longer: she likewise declared, that the devil first appeared to her in the form of a deer or fawn, skipping about her, wherewith she was not much affrighted, and that by degrees he became very familiar, and at last would talk with her; moreover, she said that the devil had frequently the carnal knowledge of her body; and that the witches had meetings at a place not far from her house; and that some appeared in one shape, and others in another; and one came flying amongst them in the shape of a crow. Upon this confession, with other concurrent evidence, the woman was executed; so likewise was her husband, though he did not acknowledge himself guilty. Other persons accused in the discourse made their escape. Thus doth the devil use to serve his clients. After the suspected witches were either executed or fled, Ann Cole was restored to health, and has continued well for many years, approving herself a serious Christian.

There were some that had a mind to try whether the stories of witches not being able to sink under water were true; and accordingly a man and woman, mentioned in Ann Cole's Dutch-toned discourse, had their hands and feet tyed, and so were cast into the water, and they both apparently swam after the manner of a buoy, part under, part above the water. A by-stander, imagining that any person bound in that posture would be so born up, offered himself for trial; but being in the like matter gently laid on the water, he immediately sunk right down. This was no legal evidence against the suspected persons, nor were they proceeded against on any such account; however, doubting that an halter would choak them, though the waters would not, they very fairly took their flight, not having been seen in that part of the world since. Whether this experiment were lawful, or rather superstitious and magical, we shall enquire afterwards.

Another thing which caused a noise in the countrey, and wherein Satan had undoubtedly a great influence, was that which hapned at Groton. There was a maid in that town (one Elizabeth Knap) who in the moneth of October, anno 1671, was taken after a very strange manner, sometimes weeping, sometimes laughing, sometimes roaring hideously, with violent motions and agitations of her body, crying out "Money, money," &c. In November following, her tongue for many hours together was drawn like a semicircle up to the roof of her mouth, not to be removed, though some tried with their fingers to do it. Six men were scarce able to hold her in some of her fits, but she would skip about the house yelling and looking with a most frightful aspect. December 17: Her tongue was drawn out of her mouth to an extraordinary length; and now a dæmon began manifestly to speak in her. Many words were uttered wherein are the labial letters, without any motion of her lips, which was a clear demonstration that the voice was not her own. Sometimes words were spoken seeming to proceed out of her throat, when her mouth was shut; sometimes with her mouth wide open, without the use of any of the organs of speech. The things then uttered by the devil were chiefly railings and revilings of Mr. Willard (who was at that time a worthy and faithful pastor to the church in Groton). Also the dæmon belched forth most horrid and nefandous blasphemies, exalting himself above the Most High. After this she was taken speechless for some time. One thing more is worthy of remark concerning this miserable creature. She cried out in some of her fits, that a woman (one of her neighbours) appeared to her, and was the cause of her affliction. The person thus accused was a very sincere, holy woman, who did hereupon, with the advice of friends, visit the poor wretch: and though she was in one of her fits, having her eyes shut, when the innocent person impeached by her came in, yet could she (so powerful were Satans operations upon her) declare who was there, and could tell the touch of that woman from any ones else. But the gracious party, thus accused and abused by a malicious devil, prayed earnestly with and for the possessed creature; after which she confessed that Satan had deluded her, making her believe evil of her good neighbour without any cause. Nor did she after that complain of any apparition or disturbance from such an one. Yea, she said, that the devil had himself, in the likeness and shape of divers, tormented her, and then told her it was not he but they that did it. . . .

## 5. The Court Examines Rebecca Nurse and Takes Testimony from Her and Her Friends, Salem, 1692

### Testimony of Ann Putnam, Junior

The deposition of Ann Putnam, junior, who testifieth and saith that on the 13th March, 1691/92, I saw the apparition of Goody Nurse, and she did immediately afflict me, but I did not know what her name was then, though I knew where she used to sit in our meetinghouse. But since that, she hath grievously afflicted by biting,

"Testimony of Ann Putnam, Senior and Ann Putnam, Junior Against Rebecca Nurse, May 31, 1692;" "Testimony of Israel and Elizabeth Porter, Daniel Andrew, and Peter Cloyse;" and "Examination of Rebecca Nurse," in Paul Boyer and Stephen Nissenbaum, eds., *Salem-Village Witchcraft: A Documentary Record of Local Conflict in Colonial New England* (Belmont, California: Wadsworth, 1972), 18–19, 21–22, 23–25. Reprinted by permission of Stephen Nissenbaum.

pinching, and pricking me, [and] urging me to write in her book. And, also, on the 24th of March, being the day of her examination, I was grievously tortured by her during the time for her examination, and also several times since. And, also, during the time of her examination, I saw the apparition of Rebekah Nurs go and hurt the bodies of Mercy Lewis, Mary Wolcott, Elizabeth Hubbard, and Abigail Williams.

Ann Putnam, Junr, did own the oath which she hath taken: this her evidence to be truth, before us, and Jurors for Inquest, this 4 day of June, 1692.

### Testimony of Ann Putnam, Senior, and Ann Putnam, Junior

The deposition of Ann Putnam, the wife of Thomas Putnam, aged about 30 years, who testifieth and saith that on the 18th March 1692, I being wearied out in helping to tend my poor afflicted child and maid, about the middle of the afternoon I lay me down on the bed to take a little rest; and immediately I was almost pressed and choked to death, that, had it not been for the mercy of a gracious God and the help of those that were with me, I could not have lived many moments; and presently I saw the apparition of Martha Corey, who did torture me so as I cannot express, ready to tear me all to pieces, and then departed from me a little while; but before I could recover strength or well take breath, the apparition of Martha Corey fell upon me again with dreadful tortures, and hellish temptations to go along with her. And she also brought to me a little red book in her hand and a black pen, urging me vehemently to write in her book; and several times that day she did grievously torture me, almost ready to kill me.

And on the 19th March, Martha Corey again appeared to me; and also Rebecca Nurse, the wife of Francis Nurse, Sr.; and they both did torture me a great many times this day with such tortures as no tongue can express, because I would not yield to their hellish temptations, that, had I not been upheld by an Almighty arm, I could not have lived [the] night. The 20th March being sabbath-day, I had a great deal of respite between my fits. 21st March being the day of the examination of Martha Corey I had not many fits, though I was very weak, my strength being, as I thought, almost gone.

But on the 22nd March, 1692, the apparition of Rebecca Nurse did again set upon me in a most dreadful manner, very early in the morning, as soon as it was well light. And now she appeared to me only in her shift, and brought a little red book in her hand, urging me vehemently to write in her book; and because I would not yield to her hellish temptations, she threatened to tear my soul out of my body, blasphemously denying the blessed God and the power of the Lord Jesus Christ to save my soul, and denying several places of Scripture which I told her of, to repel her hellish temptations. And for near two hours together, at this time, the apparition of Rebecca Nurse did tempt and torture me, and also the greater part of this day with but very little respite. 23d March, am again afflicted by the apparitions of Rebecca Nurse and Martha Corey, but chiefly by Rebecca Nurse. 24th March being the day of the examination of Rebecca Nurse, I was several times in the morning afflicted by the apparition of Rebecca Nurse, but most dreadfully tortured by her in the time of her examination, insomuch that the honored magistrates gave my husband leave to carry me out of the meetinghouse; and as soon as I was carried out of the meetinghouse doors, it pleased Almighty God, for his free grace and mercy's sake, to deliver me out of the paws of those roaring lions, and jaws of those tearing bears [so] that ever since that time they have not had power so to afflict me, until this 31st May 1692. At the same moment that I was hearing my evidence read by the honored magistrates, to take my oath, I was again re-assaulted and tortured by my before-mentioned tormentor, Rebecca Nurse.

> Sworn Salem Villiage, May the 31st, 1692
> Before us   John Hathorne   ⎫
>                Jonathan Corwin ⎬ Assistants

    Ann Putnam, Senior, appeared before us, the Jurors of Inquest, and owned this her evidence this 3rd day of June, 1692.

    The testimony of Ann Putnam, Jr., witnesseth and saith that being in the room when her mother was afflicted, she saw Martha Corey, Sarah Cloyse and Rebecca Nurse, or their apparition, upon her mother.

> Testified to the truth thereof by
> Ann Putnam, Salem, May 31st, 1692
> Before us   John Hathorne   ⎫
>                Jonathan Corwin ⎬ Assistants

## Testimony of Israel and Elizabeth Porter, Daniel Andrew, and Peter Cloyse

We whose names are underwritten, being desired to go to Goodman Nurse's house to speak with his wife and to tell her that several of the afflicted persons mentioned her; and accordingly we went, and we found her in a weak and low condition in body as she told us, and had been sick almost a week.

    And we asked her how it was, otherwise, with her. And she said she blessed God for it, she had more of his presence in this sickness than sometime she have had, but not so much as she desired. But she would, with the apostle, press forward to the mark, and many other places of Scripture to the like purpose.

    And then, of her own accord, she began to speak of the affliction that was amongst them, and in particular of Mr. Parris's family, and how she was grieved for them, though she had not been to see them by reason of fits that she formerly used to have, for people said it was awful to behold. But she pitied them with all her heart, and went to God for them. But she said she heard that there was persons spoke of that were as innocent as she was, she believed.

    And after much to this purpose, we told her we heard that she was spoken of also. Well, she said, if it be so, the will of the Lord be done. She sat still a while, being as it were amazed, and then she said, Well, as to this thing, I am as innocent as the child un-born. But surely, she said, what sin hath God found out in me unrepented of, that he should lay such an affliction upon me in my old age? And, according to our best ob-servation, we could not discern that she knew what we come for before we told her.

> Israel Porter
> Elizabeth Porter

    To the substance of what is above we, if called thereto, are ready to testify on oath.

> Daniel Andrew
> Peter Cloyse

### Examination of Rebecca Nurse

The examination of Rebeckah Nurse at Salen Village, 24 Mar., 1691/92.

Mr. Harthorn. What do you say (speaking to one afflicted), have you seen this woman hurt you?

Yes, she beat me this morning.

Abigail, have you been hurt by this woman?

Yes.

Ann Putnam, in a grievous fit, cried out that she hurt her.

Goody Nurse, here are two—Ann Putnam the child and Abigail Williams—complains of your hurting them. What do you say to it?

N. I can say before my Eternal Father, I am innocent, and God will clear my innocency.

Here is never a one in the assembly but desires it. But if you be guilty, pray God discover you.

Then Hen: Kenney rose up to speak.

Goodman Kenney, what do you say?

Then he entered his complaint and farther said that since this Nurse came into the house he was seized twice with an amazed condition.

Here are not only these, but here is the wife of Mr. Tho Putnam who accuseth you by creditable information, and that both of tempting her to iniquity and of greatly hurting her.

N. I am innocent and clear, and have not been able to get out of doors these 8 or 9 days.

Mr. Putman, give in what you have to say.

Then Mr. Edward Putnam gave in his relate.

Is this true, Goody Nurse?

I never afflicted no child, never in my life.

You see these accuse you. Is it true?

No.

Are you an innocent person, relating to this witchcraft?

Here Tho: Putnam's wife cried out: Did you not bring the Black man with you? Did you not bid me tempt God and die? How oft have you eat and drunk your own damnation? What do you say to them?

Oh Lord, help me, and spread out her hands, and the afflicted were grievously vexed.

Do you see what a solemn condition these are in? When your hands are loose, the persons are afflicted.

Then Mary Walcott (who often heretofore said she had seen her, but never could say, or did say, that she either bit or pinched her, or hurt her) and also Elis. Hubbard, under the like circumstances, both openly accused her of hurting them.

Here are these 2 grown persons now accuse you. What say you? Do not you see these afflicted persons, and hear them accuse you?

The Lord knows. I have not hurt them. I am an innocent person.

It is very awful for all to see these agonies, and you, an old professor, thus charged with contracting with the devil by the effects of it, and yet to see you stand with dry eyes when there are so many wet.

You do not know my heart.

You would do well, if you are guilty, to confess. Give Glory to God.

I am as clear as the child unborn.

What uncertainty there may be in apparitions I know not, yet this with me strikes hard upon you, that you are, at this very present, charged with familiar spirits. This is your bodily person they speak to. They say now they see these familiar spirits come to your bodily person. Now what do you say to that?

I have none, sir.

If you have confessed, and give Glory to God, I pray God clear you, if you be innocent. And if you be guilty, discover you. And therefore give me an upright answer: have you any familiarity with these spirits?

No. I have none but with God alone.

How came you sick, for there is an odd discourse of that in the mouths of many.

I am sick at my stomach.

Have you no wounds?

I have not but old age.

You do know whether you are guilty, and have familiarity with the devil, and now when you are here present, to see such a thing as these testify: a black man whispering in your ear and birds about you. What do you say to it?

It is all false. I am clear.

Possibly you may apprehend you are no witch, but have you not been led aside by temptations that way?

I have not.

What a sad thing it is that a church member here, and now another of Salem, should be thus accused and charged.

Mrs. Pope fell into a grievous fit and cried out: a sad thing sure enough. And then many more fell into lamentable fits.

Tell us, have you had visible appearances more than what is common in nature?

I have none, nor never had in my life.

Do you think these suffer voluntary or involuntary?

I cannot tell.

That is strange: everyone can judge.

I must be silent.

They accuse you of hurting them, and if you think it is not unwilling but by design, you must look upon them as murderers.

I cannot tell what to think of it. Afterwards, when this was somewhat insisted on, she said: I do not think so. She did not understand aright what was said.

Well then, give an answer now, do you think these suffer against their wills or not?

I do not think these suffer against their wills.

Why did you never visit these afflicted persons?

Because I was afraid I should have fits, too.

Note: Upon the motion of her body, fits followed upon the complainants, abundantly and very frequently.

Is it not an unaccountable case that when you are examined these persons are afflicted?

I have got nobody to look to but God.

Again, upon stirring her hands, the afflicted persons were seized with violent fits of torture.

Do you believe these afflicted persons are bewitched?

I do think they are.

When this witchcraft came upon the stage, there was no suspicion of Tituba (Mr. Parris's Indian woman). She professed much love to that child, Betty Parris. But it was her apparition did the mischief, and why should not you also be guilty, for your apparition doth hurt also?

Would you have me belie myself?

She held her neck on one side, and accordingly so were the afflicted taken.

Then, authority requiring it, Sam: Parris read what he had in characters taken from Mr. Tho: Putman's wife in her fits.

What do you think of this?

I cannot help it, the Devil may appear in my shape.

This is a true account of the sum of her examination, but by reason of great noise, by the afflicted and many speakers, many things are pretermitted.

Memorandum

Nurse held her neck on one side and Eliz. Hubbard (one of the sufferers) had her neck set in that posture. Whereupon another patient, Abigail Williams, cried out: Set up Goody Nurse's head, the maid's neck will be broke. And when some set up Nurse's head, Aaron Wey observed that Betty Hubbard's was immediately righted. . . .

 *E S S A Y S*

Mary Rowlandson recorded many conversations with her captors and her narrative showed that even hostile New England Algonquians knew a great deal about English culture after more than half a century of colonization, just as some English understood much of Indian cultures. In the first essay historian Jill Lepore of Boston University explores the experience of native people who, through choice or necessity, became involved in English life in the early colonies. Through the experience of John Sassamon who had been educated from childhood by colonial leaders and was literate in both English and in Eliot's written form of Massachusett, Lepore gauges the mental dividedness converts endured, and the choices they faced constantly. Looking at the life of Sassamon also allows her to assess the place of Indians within the new order settlers were creating in New England.

The subject of the second essay, by historian Jane Kamensky of Brandeis University, is characterizations of women who refused to express themselves within the limits endorsed by the male Puritan leadership. Women who disagreed with the standing order chose to resist and refused to be silenced, just as Puritans had done in England before they emigrated. Often such critics voiced their opinions over the course of many years, making their communities increasingly uncomfortable. Ultimately some outspoken women were castigated as witches, when their presence had become so threatening that neighbors and leaders believed their speech must have been inspired by the devil rather than the pursuit of true religion. Witchcraft beliefs allowed early modern men and women to explain mysterious occurrences and to understand and account for evil and disorder.

## John Sassamon Between Two Cultures

JILL LEPORE

Dead men tell no tales, or so the saying goes. It makes a wonderful threat, a line Humphrey Bogart might use on a sniveling Peter Lorre as he holds a gun to his head: "Keep your mouth shut, weasel, or your number's up—you know what they say, dead men tell no tales, at least not in this two-bit gin-joint." Yes, it makes a very effective threat, especially in a *film noir* setting. But "dead men tell no tales" is also a piece of folk wisdom, morbid and somewhat fatalistic, which means just what it says: the stories of the dead die with them. With this, most historians would disagree. After all, we have a great deal invested in the idea that the dead do tell tales. It is our task, and our passion, to listen to those tales, or rather to *read* and interpret them, hoping to make sense of the surviving written fragments of a day, a life, a nation-state.

No doubt but that this is tricky work, especially when we are trying to read the tales of those whom some historians have labeled "inarticulate," people who left few written documents, if any, that might tell us about their lives. Trickier still is telling the tales of dead people who, when alive, spoke a language now dead—dead not in the sense that Greek and Latin are dead languages but dead in the sense that almost no one living today can understand them. These are among the problems involved in writing the history of Native Americans of Southeastern New England whose languages—Massachusett, Narragansett, and Mohegan-Pequot—have become extinct. . . .

In seventeenth-century New England, many Indians were literate, yet none of them wrote an account of perhaps the most devastating conflict in their history, King Philip's War, which nearly destroyed the native population in Southeastern New England and set in motion the extinction of the Massachusett language. The English colonists suffered dramatic wartime losses as well: twenty-five of their towns burned to the ground and more than one in ten colonists died. Puritan minister Increase Mather was not alone in calling the war "the saddest time with New England that ever was known." (In proportion to population, King Philip's War has the distinction of being the most fatal war in American history.) Unlike their Indian neighbors, however, literate English colonists were quick to pick up their pens to write about the war; their letters, news reports, sermons, and histories all survive in startling abundance. Many of these writings were brief, personal notes, but a significant number of lengthier accounts, including Mary Rowlandson's famous captivity narrative, was published and widely distributed. In all, nineteen different English stories about King Philip's War were printed in London, Boston, and Cambridge, many in more than one edition, for a total of no fewer than thirty

Jill Leopre, "John Sassamon Between Two Cultures." *American Quarterly,* vol. 46, no. 4, December 1994: pp. 479–503. © 1994. The American Studies Association. Reprinted by permission of the Johns Hopkins University Press.

separate printings. Even with a conservative estimate of press-run size, a minimum of fifteen thousand copies of books about King Philip's War descended on the very small Anglo-American book market in the span of seven years.

Yet none of these books was written by any of the many literate Indians in New England, several of whom were ministers and at least one of whom even worked as a printer at the press in Cambridge. Clearly, literacy is not an uncomplicated tool, like a pen or a printing press. Instead, literacy is bound, as it was for New England's Indians, by the conditions under which it is acquired—in this case, at great cost. In order to become literate, seventeenth-century Indians had first to make a graduated succession of cultural concessions—adopting English ways and English dress, living in towns, learning to speak English, converting to Christianity. But these very concessions made them vulnerable. Neither English nor Indian, assimilated Indians were scorned by both groups, and they were even subject to attack. Because the acquisition of literacy, and especially English-language literacy, was one of the last steps on the road to assimilation, Indians who could read and write placed themselves in a particularly perilous, if at the same time a powerful, position, caught between two worlds but fully accepted by neither. . . .

. . . There is perhaps no better example of an assimilated seventeenth-century Indian than John Sassamon. As one Puritan minister reported, Sassamon "was observed to conform more to the English Manners than any other Indian." Sassamon may also have been the most educated Indian in all of New England; he was probably the most hated. As a scribe, translator, and interpreter, Sassamon provided valuable services to English and Indian leaders, many of whom probably resented their dependence on him. Someone hated Sassamon enough to murder him, and it was his death that most immediately led to King Philip's War, in which thousands of Indians, both literate and nonliterate, were killed or sold into slavery. . . .

. . . In December 1674, Sassamon, a Christianized or "praying" Indian, traveled to Plymouth to confide to Governor Josiah Winslow that Philip, leader of the Pokanokets, was plotting a war against the English. Sassamon confessed to Winslow his fear that Philip would surely murder him if his betrayal were discovered. Winslow, however, neither heeded Sassamon's warnings nor assuaged his fears; instead, the injudicious governor dismissed Sassamon's information "because there was but this one testimony of an Indian, and therefore of a *suspected* original." As Cotton Mather would later lament, "before the truth of the matter could be inquired into, poor John was barbarously murdered."

Within a week of his meeting with Winslow, Sassamon mysteriously disappeared. Solicitous neighbors soon found his bloated body under the ice of Assawampsett Pond and buried it without delay. Meanwhile, rumors abounded. In Rhode Island, one observer noted that "sum English suposed him throne in [while] sum indians . . . did think he fell in and was so drouned." The dispute was conveniently resolved when a praying Indian named Patuckson appeared on the scene claiming to have witnessed three of Philip's men violently murder Sassamon and then conceal their crime by casting the body through a hole in the ice. In March 1675, these three Indians—Wampapaquan, Tobias, and Mattashunnamo—were formally accused of the crime. Nonetheless, many English "believed that [Philip] was the Author of [the] murther" and the accused merely "the Actors." Three months later, the Plymouth court (including a jury of twelve Englishmen and six praying Indians) tried and convicted the alleged murderers. The execution took place on June 8. In just three days, on June 11, Pokanokets were reported arming outside Plymouth; by June 29, Philip's men attacked and nearly destroyed the town of Swansey in the first battle of King Philip's War.

And so it is that the unfortunate Sassamon, . . . is better remembered for his death than for his life. Before that fateful day in the winter of 1674 when he sat uncomfortably in the governor's house and nervously whispered that "Philip was undoubtedly indeavouring to Raise new troubles; and was Indeavouring to engage all the Sachems round about in a warr," John Sassamon had entered the historical record only a handful of times—and most of these were brief appearances indeed. The abundance of contemporary and historical accounts of John Sassamon's death stand in stark contrast to the scarcity of references to his life; this makes any reconstruction of his biography necessarily speculative.

Yet only in the reconstruction of his biography can we hope to find the answer to the key question in this mystery: Why was John Sassamon killed? At first blush, the answer seems clear: dead men tell no tales. In other words, Philip had Sassamon killed either as punishment for his betrayal or to prevent further leaks of information to the English. Boston merchant Nathaniel Saltonstall wrote to a friend in London that, "King Philip suspecting he either would divulge or had already made known this Secret to the English, took Councel to kill this Sosoman." Increase Mather said of Philip's men that "the main ground why they murthered him seems to be, because he discovered their subtle and malicious designs, which they were complotting against the English." In Rhode Island, John Easton remarked, "it was reported Sausimum before his death had informed of the Indian Plot, and that if the Indians knew it they wold kill him."

This motive seems simple enough, yet each of these three observers—Saltonstall, Mather, and Easton—suggested other, broader reasons behind the murder. First among these was Sassamon's religion. According to Mather, "no doubt but one reason why the Indians murthered John Sausaman, was out of hatred against him for his Religion." Before he revised his story, Saltonstall claimed that Wampapaquan, Tobias, and Mattashunnamo killed Sassamon because they were annoyed at his preaching: "not liking his Discourse, [they] immediately Murthered him after a most Barbarous Manner." Others claimed Philip had Sassamon killed because he himself was tired of Sassamon's proselytizing. And Sassamon's death was also attributed to his greed. In Rhode Island, the Pokanokets John Easton interviewed said Sassamon had cheated Philip: "king Philop got [Sassamon] to write his will and he made the writing for a gret part of the land to be his but read as if it had bine as Philop wold."

Was Sassamon killed because he betrayed Philip, because he cheated him, or because he tried to convert him? The surviving reports conflict so greatly that it is impossible to determine with any certainty the exact motive for Sassamon's murder. But the exact motive may not matter. Although the shape and size of the possible motives vary, they cast an identical shadow; behind each of them lies the spectre of John Sassamon's position as a cultural mediator. For Sassamon, the ability to act as a mediator was predicated on his bilingualism and his literacy—his skill at speaking, reading, and writing English was intricately intertwined with his loyalty to the colonists, his conversion to Christianity, his betrayal of Philip, and even his ability to cheat Philip in the writing of his will. To fully understand the shades and shadows of cultural conversion, and of literacy's role within it, we must start at the very beginning of the story of John Sassamon's life.

When the first English settlers arrived in Massachusetts Bay in 1630, John Sassamon's parents might have welcomed the newcomers warmly. Among the few survivors of the epidemics that plagued the coastal Indians between 1616 and 1618, Sassamon's family perhaps looked to the English for protection against hostile inland neighbors. Sassamon's parents saw fit, at any rate, to remain among the English in Dorchester and to convert to Christianity. While later chroniclers, such as Cotton Mather, would casually note that Sassamon "was the son of Christian Indians," earlier observers—such as Cotton's father, Increase—specified that Sassamon's "father and mother liv[ed] in Dorchester, and they both *died Christians.*" This may seem a minor distinction, but it provides an important clue, for the elder Mather implies that Sassamon's parents converted *only at the time of their deaths* and, thereby, suggests that they were among the numerous Indian victims of a 1633 smallpox epidemic, many of whom converted to Christianity on their deathbeds. Interpreting the epidemic as supernatural evidence of the power of the Puritans' God, many Indians in Massachusetts Bay were thus dramatically and hastily converted.

At their deaths, many of these converts left their orphaned children in the care of English families. . . . Although only a few of these adopted children survived into adulthood, John Sassamon may well have been among them. If so, he would have learned to speak English at a relatively young age, for he was probably in his early teens when his parents died. At that point, Sassamon would have entered the ranks of a very small group of seventeenth-century New England bilingualists, the vast majority of whom were Indian.

By 1637, Sassamon had evidently demonstrated his command of English and his loyalty to the Puritans well enough to serve as an interpreter and to fight on the colonists' side during the war against the Pequot Indians. "Sosoman, the Indian" served with Richard Callicott of Dorchester and was very likely to have been the Indian interpreter mentioned by John Underhill in his account of the war. . . .

. . . Throughout his life, Sassamon, ambivalent about Puritan society, alternately embraced and rejected it. It is tempting to imagine that he was the Indian boy mentioned in one early Puritan tract "who for some misdemeanour that laid him open to publique punishment, ran away; and being gone, God so followed him, that of his owne accord he returned home, rendred himselfe to Justice, and was willing to submit himselfe, though he might have escaped." If so, it may well have been Eliot who received the errant Christian back into the fold, for William Hubbard, minister of Ipswich, noted that Sassamon was subject to "the frequent Sollicitations of Mr. Eliot, that had known him from a Child, and instructed him in the Principles of our Religion, who was often laying before him the heinous Sin of his Apostacy."

Eliot himself probably taught Sassamon to read. It is also possible, of course, that Sassamon learned from a member of the English family with whom he lived or that he attended an Indian School in Dorchester. In any case, Sassamon was very likely taught with methods similar to those Eliot would later describe:

When I taught our Indians first to lay out a word into syllables, and then according to the sound of every syllable to make it up with the right letters, viz. if it were a simple sound, then one vocall made the syllable; if it were such a sound as required some of the consonants to make it up, then the adding of the right consonants either before the vocall, or after it, or both. They quickly apprehended and understood this Epitomie of the art of spelling, and could soon learn to read. The men, women, and up-grown youth do thus rationally learn to read. . . .

In future years, Indian students learning to read would have benefitted from the Indian catechisms and primers that Eliot and his assistants (including Sassamon) would soon translate, but Sassamon's acquisition of literacy preceded their publication. At about the same time that Sassamon was learning to read and write English, Eliot was himself learning the Massachusett language. . . .

At this point, then, in the early 1640s, Eliot and Sassamon were engaged in similar projects. Syllable by syllable and word by word, both were mastering new languages, pulling letters apart and pushing them back together again, making familiar meanings out of unfamiliar sounds. If Eliot did in fact teach Sassamon, then Sassamon also taught Eliot—their relationship would have been in some important ways reciprocal. But once Eliot's linguistic apprenticeship ended, the power would have shifted dramatically in the Englishman's favor. Eliot's mission, after all, was to eradicate native cultural practices and replace them with Puritan ones.

Beginning in 1647, Eliot was involved in the publication of a set of promotional tracts designed to solicit funds for the propagation of the Gospel in New England; from this time on, Eliot's reigning passion was the conversion of the Indians to Christianity; for this reason, and this reason above all, he had painstakingly learned the Massachusett language. His missionary work was cultural as well as religious. As one historian has recently noted, "in teaching Indians how to live a full Christian life, they were actually teaching them to act like Englishmen."

It was for the twin purposes of converting and anglicizing Indians that Eliot established the first "praying town" in nearby Natick in 1650. Before his death forty years later, Eliot would have aided in the establishment of fourteen praying towns and the conversion of some 3,600 Indians. Praying towns were to provide settings in which Christian Indians could live and worship like Englishmen, free of the cultural influences of their non-Christian peers. Like Eliot, Sassamon was engaged in this project from the start; he literally helped build the town where he would soon become a schoolmaster. In his accounts for the year 1651, Eliot recorded distributing tools to several Indian and English assistants, including two axes to "John Sosoman." . . .

In describing the Indian schools at Natick during the time when Sassamon was either becoming a schoolteacher or already teaching (1651), Eliot wrote:

> we have two men in some measure able to teach the youth with my guidance, and inspection. And thus we order the school: The master daily prayeth among his scholars, and instructeth them in catechism, for which purpose I have compiled a short catechism, and wrote it in the master book, which he can read, and teach them; and also all the copies he setteth his scholars when he teacheth them to write, are the questions and answers of the catechism, that so the children may be the more prompt and ready therein: we aspire to no higher learning yet, but to spell, read, and write.

Eliot's careful attention to the techniques used to teach reading and writing merits further investigation—here the question necessarily arises as to why the missionary placed so much emphasis on literacy. If he simply wanted to convert Indians, why did he pursue the laborious task of teaching them to read? The answer lies in part in the fact that the Puritans were Protestants for whom becoming a Christian meant first acquiring the ability to read the Bible. . . .

John Sassamon—who could speak, read, and write both English and Massachusett—was surely among the elite of praying Indians, especially in the 1650s, ten years before this survey was taken when there were fewer literate Indians. Evidently, Sassamon was, at this time, one of Eliot's favorite students because by 1653 Eliot had arranged for the Natick schoolmaster to attend Harvard College. . . . As Eliot had written in 1649, "there be sundry prompt, pregnant witted youths, not viciously inclined, but well disposed, which I desire may be wholly sequestred to learning and put to school for that purpose." Although Sassamon was in fact "put to school," we have no information on what he studied there and for how long. Still, we do know that, for at least one semester in 1653, John Sassamon was a classmate of the fortunate sons of Massachusetts Bay, among them John Eliot, Jr., Samuel Bradstreet, Thomas Shepard, Samuel Hooker, and a very young Increase Mather. (Soon after Sassamon left Cambridge, a special Indian College was opened at Harvard. Although a college specifically for Indians had been proposed as early as 1635, no concrete arrangements were made until 1651, when Harvard President Henry Dunster began soliciting funds for the Indian College to be built. It was finally erected in 1655.)

Whatever his successes or failures at Harvard, it seems Sassamon may have fallen from Eliot's favor in 1654. As part of his plan for praying Indians' full participation in the Puritan religious community, Eliot had scheduled a day of examination for members of the Natick church. Unhappily for Eliot, about ten days before the examination, three Natick Indians became obnoxiously drunk and, to make matters worse, forced liquor on the young son of a more pious Natick resident. . . . Although there is no unequivocal proof that this sinning interpreter was Sassamon, he is clearly the most likely convert to have committed the shameful sins and acts of apostasy that so disappointed Eliot.

Nonetheless, Sassamon was still in Natick in 1656. After that time, whether because of a gradual or sudden falling out with Eliot, Sassamon disappears from the historical record until 1662. That year, the Pokanoket sachem Massasoit died and his eldest son, Alexander, succeeded him. Sassamon's presence at a treaty signing between Alexander and Rhode Island authorities suggests that Sassamon had switched sides and was now working for Alexander as a scribe and translator. Soon after the treaty signing, Alexander died under suspicious circumstances and Philip, Alexander's younger brother, assumed the sachemship. Later that same year, Sassamon set his signature down as witness to Philip's oath of loyalty to the English. William Hubbard claimed that Sassamon had "upon some Misdemeanour fled from his Place [at Natick] to Philip, by whom he was entertained in the Room and Office of Secretary, and Chief Councellor." Whether as scribe, interpreter, secretary, counselor, or some combination thereof, Sassamon assumed a role of considerable influence and importance to Philip because, in 1664, 1665, and 1666, Sassamon's name appeared again and again as a witness to Philip's land transactions. Cotton Mather would later report that Sassamon "apostatiz[ed] from the profession of Christianity, [and] lived like an heathen in the quality of a Secretary to King Philip; for he could write, though the King his master could not so much as read."

The same skills that had made Sassamon valuable to Eliot now made him almost indispensable to Philip: the ability to speak, read, and write both English and Massachusett. There can be no doubt that Sassamon used his literacy skills as a tool in acquiring status and prestige in the Indian community. And, in gaining a position of intimacy with Philip, Sassamon certainly exploited the "power of print" the way the Puritan missionaries could and did not. Still, it is difficult to know if Sassamon's work for Philip at this time represents a genuine change of heart in relation to the English or whether, essentially acting as a spy for Eliot, he infiltrated Philip's council in order to convert him. That Eliot wanted passionately to convert Philip is clear. Most missionaries believed that "When a sachem or sagamore is converted to the faith, and yields himself up to embrace the gospel, it hath a great influence upon his subjects." Philip, however, apparently had no desire to be converted. An anecdote recorded by Cotton Mather told of how

> Eliot made a tender of the everlasting salvation to that king [Philip]; but the monster entertained it with contempt and anger, and after the Indian mode of joining signs with words, he took a button upon the coat of the reverend man, adding, That he cared for his gospel, just as much as he cared for that button.

Nonetheless, Eliot, at one point, rejoiced with an indication that Philip was finally succumbing. In 1664, at the very time when Sassamon was working closely with Philip as a scribe and witness to treaties, Eliot asked the Commissioners of Plymouth Colony "to give incouragmt to John Sosaman, who teacheth Phillip and his men to read." Eliot claimed that Philip, "did this winter past, upon solicitations and means used, send to me for books to learne to read, in order to praying unto God, wch I did send unto him, and prsents with all." Sassamon, Eliot believed, was "a means to put life into the work."

Apparently neither Sassamon's work nor the books Eliot sent were successful in converting Philip because Eliot, making the same attempt all over again, sent even more Indian missionaries to visit Philip seven years later. In formal instructions dated August 1, 1671, the Natick church declared, "we do send these our two brethren, Anthony and William [Nahaton] . . . and we request John Sausiman to join them" to go and preach to the Indians at Plymouth. But still Philip was not converted, and Eliot may well have blamed Sassamon for this failure. Later in 1671, Eliot published a tract called *Indian Dialogues,* a set of conversion conversations, which he claimed were "partly historical, of some things that were done and said, and partly instructive, to show what might or should have been said, or that may be (by the Lord's assistance) hereafter done and said." In one lengthy, imaginary dialogue, two barely fictionalized praying Indians, "Anthony" and "William Abahton," speak with "Philip Keitasscot," sachem of "Paganoehket." That Eliot left Sassamon out of his *Indian Dialogues* suggests either that Sassamon left the company of Anthony and William Nahaton and never made it to Plymouth to preach to Philip or that Eliot considered Sassamon's contributions unworthy.

*Indian Dialogues,* however, remains interesting, if only for how much it reveals about Eliot's frantic desire to convert Philip. In one scene, "Philip" expresses his "serious thoughts of accepting the offer, and turning to God, to become a praying Indian" but is concerned about whether his conversion would mean a diminishment of his authority as a sachem. The eloquent and persuasive Indian missionaries assuage his every fear and soon a very humbled "Philip" confesses, "I am drowned and overwhelmed with the weight of your reasonings." Much of the dialogue concerns the goodness of the Bible, to which "Philip" meekly and gratefully responds, "Your discourse doth breed in my heart an admiration at that excellent book." Again and again, "Philip's" objections to conversion are defeated by the wisdom of Anthony and William: "Who can oppose or gainsay the mountainous weight of these arguments?" a helpless "Philip" asks. Finally deferring to the missionaries' superior knowledge he proclaims, "I am more than satisfied. I am ashamed of my ignorance, and I abhor myself that ever I doubted."

Yet, in spite of the shipment of books, the visits by William and Anthony Nahaton, and Eliot's richly detailed fantasies, neither Sassamon, Eliot, nor any other missionary ever converted Philip to Christianity. But the missionary work continued. . . . During this time, Sassamon apparently left Philip's employ to return to the Christian fold (or was told by Eliot to give up trying to convert Philip) and became minister in the praying town of Namasket (present-day Middleboro) sometime in the early 1670s. In 1673, he was given a tract of land to induce him to stay, and, the same year, he deeded this land to his daughter Betty and her husband Felix. The next year, Sassamon was either working for Philip or spying on him when he found out about Philip's plans to attack the English and passed them on to the governor of Plymouth. Just four years after Eliot published his fictional dialogues, Philip, instead of peaceably and humbly converting to Christianity, waged war against the English settlers.

We have come full circle and arrived once more at Sassamon's death. Here we must ask yet again, why was John Sassamon murdered? Was he killed simply because he betrayed Philip's plans to the English? Remember, Increase Mather was convinced that

> No doubt but one reason why the Indians murthered John Sausaman, was out of hatred against him for his Religion, for he was Christianized, and baptiz'd, and was a Preacher amongst the Indians, being of very excellent parts, he translated some part of the bible into the Indian language, and was wont to curb those Indians that knew not God on the account of their debaucheryes.

Eliot's colleague Daniel Gookin agreed and claimed that "this John Sasamand was the first Christian martyr of the Indians; for it is evident he suffered death upon the account of his Christian profession, and fidelity to the English." . . .

. . . To the Pokanokets, at least, Sassamon's literacy was mysterious, potent, and dangerous. It marked him as a man who could not be trusted.

But it was not his literacy that made Sassamon untrustworthy; it was how he got that way in the first place. Learning to read and write—and especially learning to read and write English—were among the very last steps on the path to cultural conversion. Steps taken earlier along this same path were considered not nearly as corrupting. Many New England Indians were bilingual; speaking English was useful for trading, among other things, and did not necessarily signify any particular loyalty to the English. Dressing as an Englishman and worshipping the Christian God were of course much less ambiguous; those practices clearly marked an Indian as having a compromised relationship with the English. Still, many Indians lived and attended church in praying towns simply because they needed the food and shelter, and then only temporarily; they took off English clothes as easily as they had put them on. Literacy, however, was a special kind of marker, one that branded its possessor, perhaps most especially in his own eyes, as an Indian who had spent years and years with the English; his very "Indianness" was thus called into question. . . .

If the native community considered a literate, Christian Indian too English, the English probably considered him too educated and, ultimately, still too Indian. Josiah Winslow, after all, paid no attention to John Sassamon's warning about Philip's plans for war. Even though Winslow knew Sassamon was a minister in Namasket, his word was still only "the testimony of an Indian and therefore of a suspected original." Just how little the English trusted praying Indians can be seen in how badly they treated them when the war broke out. Unconvinced of the converts' loyalty, the colonists quickly shipped hundreds of praying Indians to Deer Island in Boston Harbor, where they were interred for the war's duration and left with neither food, shelter, nor adequate means to obtain them. During the bitter winter, many of these Indians died from starvation or exposure. Joseph Tachuppouillan, an Indian minister in the praying town of Hassanomessit, managed to escape from Deer Island to John Eliot's house, where he spoke of his impossible position, as a man hated by Indians and English alike.

> Oh Sir [said Tachuppouillan] I am greatly distressed this day on every side, the English have taken away some of my estate, my corn . . . my plough, cart, chaine, & other goods. The enemy Indians have also taken a part of what I had, & the richest Indians mock & scoff at me, saying now what has become of your praying to God. The English also censure me, & say I am a hypocrite. In this distress, I have no where to look, but up to God in Heaven, to help me.

. . . Although Sassamon "was observed to conform more to the English Manners than any other Indian," the facts of his life are by no means clear on the question of whether his primary attachment was to one people or the other. He may well have been a devout Christian and servant of Eliot's cause who experienced brief and minor crises of faith. If this were so, he probably was acting more or less as a spy for Eliot when he worked for Philip and therefore was, in many ways, a traitor to his own people. But who were his own people? Sassamon had apparently been raised by an English family from a relatively young age. No doubt this caused him significant confusion. Rather than being unequivocally loyal to the English, it seems most likely that Sassamon remained troubled and confused about to whom he most owed his allegiance. Serving as secretary to Alexander and Philip may have been a genuine embracing of the native community from which he recoiled only as rumors of war began. Or, as the most cynical interpreter might read the facts, Sassamon switched sides according to the potential for personal and pecuniary gain.

Whatever their motivations in doing so, Sassamon and others like him were able to switch sides with such facility because of their linguistic abilities. Sassamon had skills to offer both Eliot and Philip. As a child, he learned to read and write in a religious context; whoever taught him meant to convert him. Sometimes, he used his linguistic skills to further Eliot's missionary program: he helped Eliot translate religious works into English, became a teacher at Natick, and proselytized to Philip. At other times, Sassamon used his linguistic skills to help Philip: he served as scribe, witness, translator, interpreter, and clerk. Sassamon also used his skills and position to acquire land for himself and his family and, possibly, to steal from Philip.

But these same skills, and the untenable cultural position they put him in, would eventually lead Sassamon to his death, a death that signaled the failure of the English and native cultures to live together peaceably, the gradual loss of native political autonomy, and the eventual extinction of the Massachusett language. Immediately after King Philip's War, thousands of captured Indians were sold out of the country as slaves; this ensured the impossibility of another large-scale insurrection and further restricted the political power of the remaining, unconverted Indians. And converted Indians, left to suffer and starve on an isolated island, were no less immune to the war's devastations. By the time the war ended in 1676, the Christian and non-Christian native population of southeastern New England had been dramatically reduced. King Philip's War, often referred [to] today as "Metacom's Rebellion," was the last concerted effort of a federation of New England tribes to oust the English settlers; Philip's defeat ushered in a new era of accommodation with the colonists, one that interspersed with more limited warfare.

But the war also marked the decline of English attempts to convert and educate the Indians; in some ways, Eliot's missionary program died with Sassamon. As Neal Salisbury has remarked, "the war brought not only the defeat of the hostile Indians but the end of the missionary program as conceived by Eliot." At Harvard, the building erected as an Indian College was soon put to other purposes. By 1677, two years after the war ended, its only use, ironically, was to house the Cambridge Press, where the colonists' many accounts of their version of the story of King Philip's War were printed. Few praying towns survived King Philip's War, and most of the Indian Bibles that Sassamon helped translate and Eliot printed were destroyed during the fighting, some maliciously, no doubt. . . .

Despite the new printing, the Society for the Propagation of the Gospel became more and more reluctant to publish any more works in the Indian language; instead, they urged missionaries to teach the Indians English. While a handful of praying towns, including Natick, survived into the eighteenth century, they soon lost first their religious zeal, then their political autonomy, and finally their ability to preserve their native language. . . .

. . . It was not until 1836 that a New England Indian writer, Pequot William Apess, emerged to write the history of King Philip's War. If Sassamon had survived the consequences of literacy, he might have written such a history a century and a half earlier.

. . . Murder may have silenced John Sassamon but something else silenced John Eliot. In his diary at the end of 1675, Eliot looked back at the year's devastations, "the history whereof," he wrote helplessly, "I cannot, I may not relate." Much later, after the war had ended, Eliot recalled, "I desisted fro[m] this work of recording p'ticular matters," partly because "I thought not my selfe so fitting." Moreover, "knowing that it was comited to othrs" (including powerful Puritan divines like Increase Mather and William Hubbard), Eliot explained, "I declined it." . . .

# Outspoken Women and Witchcraft Accusations

JANE KAMENSKY

*"I will take heed . . . that I sin not with my Tongue; I will keep my Mouth with a Bridle."* Thus Cotton Mather reminded women: feminine virtue meant careful speech. Drawing on a long tradition that linked women's voices with disorder, Mather cautioned the "daughters of Zion" that their *"Tongues* are frequently not so Governed by the *Fear of God,* as they ought to be." To avoid this womanly vice, the pious matron needed to cultivate what Mather called a "silver tongue": speech rare and pure, free of boastful "dross." He urged: "Be careful that you don't *Speak too soon. . . .* And be careful that you don't *Speak too much. . . .* 'tis the *Whore,* that is *Clamorous."*

He might easily have said it was the *witch* that was clamorous. For in 1692, the same year Mather told Zion's daughters to mind their tongues, cataclysmic witch trials shook Massachusetts. Many observers measured the real women on trial in Salem against an ideal of modest female speech much like the one Mather invoked in his sermon. . . .

Hectoring, threatening, scolding, muttering, mocking, cursing, railing, slandering: the list reads like a handbook of verbal etiquette for witches. How far from the judicious, infrequent, and well-placed words of the silver-tongued woman! To a society that was deeply concerned with governing the verbal exchanges that constituted and enforced social hierarchy, the witch's speech revealed the full destructive potential of the female voice. The witch's cursing, the demoniac's roaring: these were the ultimate ravages of women's words left unchecked. Careful speech was one of the comeliest "ornaments" for the "daughters of Zion." The threat of disorderly speech—particularly *female* speech—played a pivotal role in New England witchcraft beliefs. The need to control women's voices was one element that united elite and popular conceptions of witchcraft. Ministers, magistrates, and common folk would have agreed that the witch's crime was often, at root, a crime of female speech. Witchcraft offered all levels of society a rubric under which certain elements of female discourse could be classified, prosecuted, and held in check.

To understand early New England's intense preoccupation with disorderly speech, particularly women's speech, it is necessary to realize that speaking meant something different to Anglo-Americans in the seventeenth century than it does to us in the twentieth. We tend to regard speech—talking—as a natural part of human interaction, and therefore as something that exists outside history. But a growing body of scholarship asks us to consider spoken exchange as an aspect of daily life that—like gender, race, or class—only *appears* to be "natural" but is in fact "cultural." Drawing on the work of sociolinguists who study the ways people in different societies create distinct kinds of "speech communities," historians have begun to explore the ways in which the meaning of speech varies historically, across time. Early New England is a case in point. The spoken word in colonial Massachusetts had a kind of power that we can scarcely imagine. Speech functioned as a central arena for the definition of self. People measured their own worth by the way their neighbors, servants, trading partners, and families talked to and about them. . . .

Ordinary people, along with their ministers and magistrates, recognized that speech falling outside the parameters of "Christian-like conversation" could wreak havoc. People of all social ranks in seventeenth-century New England had a heightened awareness of the damage the tongue could inflict. While many of us grew up hearing that "sticks and stones can break our bones, but names can never hurt us," early New Englanders were taught just the opposite. The "tongue breaketh the bone" was the equivalent in seventeenth-century folk wisdom. Puritan ideology saw "heated" speech as a threat to the social order. Traditional beliefs cast words as potent sources of literal, physical harm. Both perspectives invested speech with dramatic and fearful *power*.

One of the most literal manifestations of the power of speech in Puritan Massachusetts was the language of witches, a genre of verbal aggression that has largely escaped scholarly attention. Words were at their most dangerous in the theater of New England witchcraft. Recent scholarship is suggestive in this regard. We know about the importance of local gossip—what John Demos has called a "thick trail of *talk*"—in defining and prosecuting witches. . . .

Cotton Mather once referred to himself and his fellow ministers as "Earwitnesses" to witchcraft. Like Mather, many people in seventeenth-century New England believed they could *hear* the Devil's presence in the speech of a local woman before their other senses offered corroborating evidence. Their detailed recollections of the ways witches spoke allow us, at more than three hundred years' remove, to be earwitnesses of a sort. Ministers' observations of the ravages witches inflicted upon their possessed victims, taken together with court papers documenting the verbal "crimes" witches committed in their local communities, offer rich evidence of what women said that made them be perceived as witches by their neighbors and their leaders in early New England.

Although Europeans had persecuted witches for centuries before the Reformation, Protestant theologians added a new "wrinkle" to elite conceptions of the witch. Among her neighbors, the witch remained what she had always been: a source of harm, a "criminal who worked in supernatural ways." But to the Protestant minister or magistrate, she became first and foremost a heretic, in league with Satan to undermine the godly society on earth. Concern with the witch's speech bridged these two levels of belief. But regardless of whether she was feared and hated for her harmfulness or her heresy—whether, that is, her audience was "popular" or "elite"—the witch announced herself and often damned herself through her disorderly tongue. . . .

. . . Where the demoniac "roared" and "screamed," yelled, bleated, and barked, the penitent girl demonstrated a more appropriate (and earthly) range of verbal skills: "sighings, sobbings," "bitter tears," "earnest profession" and "methodical declarations." The witch or her victim might also be gripped by unpredictable, implacable *silences*. Witches and those under their influence were "seized with dumbness," their "mouths were stopped," devils "confound[ed]" their language, rendered them "uncapable of saying anything," and so on. And even this was not the greatest disruption of speech witches might effect.

The bodily process of speaking—that defining human faculty—was perverted and distorted in the most literal, material sense in the ravings of possessed girls. Dramatic physical symptoms revealed that the Devil had invaded the victim's speech. One victim's tongue clung to the roof of her mouth, "not to be removed" though "some tried with their fingers to do it." Others suffered as their tongues were "drawn down their Throats . . . pull'd out upon their Chins. their Mouths [forced] opened to such Wideness, that their Jaws went out of joint." Empowered by the Devil or his human emissaries, young women could rage with their mouths shut or hanging wide open, belching forth horrifying words "without the use of any of the Organs of speech." The voice of the witch sounded recognizably unfeminine—even *inhuman*—to her ministerial audience.

But verbal *style* did not alone brand a witch: the "where" and "what" of her speech combined to transform a "heated" exchange into a diabolic one. The physical setting of many such "conversations" was significant. An element of public spectacle often gave a witch's heated words broader scope and amplified their danger to established authority. Witches and their victims dared to spout verbal poison at elevated male targets in public settings.

Ministers victimized by these stinging words reacted with hurt and surprise. Samuel Willard noted somewhat defensively that Elizabeth Knapp had "always been observed to speak respectfully concerning" him before the Devil took control of her tongue. Martha Godwin, Cotton Mather recalled, addressed him with "a Sauciness that I had not been us'd to." Secular authorities were no less sensitive to witches' abuse of prominent audiences. The magistrates of Salem's Court of Oyer and Terminer often chided a suspect for her lack of deference. And the records suggest that accused witches had raised their voices against civil authorities long before Salem. John Winthrop noted in 1648, during one of the first formal witch-hunting proceedings in Massachusetts, that Margaret Jones's "behavior at her trial was very intemperate, lying notoriously, and railing upon the jury and witnesses." A woman's verbal tone often signaled the presence of witchcraft. *Where* and *to whom* the suspect spoke made such strident speech impossible to overlook.

Finally, we must look at the "what" of the witch's words, for the *content* of her speech was arguably the most important component of its disorderly potential in the minds of the Puritan elite. Through her heated words to prominent men, the witch effectively positioned herself as a dark mirror of male authority. Like a minister, she selected and interpreted texts. One afflicted girl challenged Increase Mather in open assembly to " 'stand up, and Name your Text': And after it was read, she said, 'it is a long Text.' " She went on mocking him, saying " 'I know no Doctrine you had, If you did name one, I have forgot it.' " Others claimed a similar power of choice and interpretation, refusing to say what they should, too easily able to say what they should not. Cotton Mather recalled one victim who "in the Bible could . . . read [not] a word," yet when he "brought her a Quakers Book . . . That she could quietly read whole pages of." She read aloud from "a Jest-book . . . without any Disturbance. . . . A popish Book also she could endure very well." But, Mather commented (and here we glimpse her authority clashing openly with his): "it would kill her" to read from "any Book that (in my Opinion) . . . might have bin profitable and edifying for her." Speaking out, stridently and publicly, challenging the sole right of male authorities (magistrates, ministers, and husbands) to speak for them:

this was the essence of the witch's challenge to the elite. Witches and their possessed victims personified the danger of female verbal authority, much like Quaker
women preachers, themselves often subject to prosecution as witches, and much
like Anne Hutchinson, who had conducted herself as a preacher and interpreter, and
wound up under the shadow of witchcraft.

Elite reactions to witches' speech reveal the boundaries of feminine discourse
in Puritan New England. Certainly "vertuous women" were granted a degree of
authority by their ministers. Preachers exhorted their increasingly "feminized"
congregations to read, to converse, and even to write on pious subjects. But if pious
matrons knew that it were their right—even their duty—to reflect and expound
on sacred texts, they would also have been aware (and been *kept* aware by the
persecution of witches, slanderers, and other misspeakers) that certain implicit
limits bounded their discourse. The witch's speech made those implicit limits
manifest.

In one sense, the witch linguistically outperformed the virtuous woman. The
virtuous woman was fluent in the language of the Bible, but the witch spoke in
tongues—foreign and learned languages of which she was expected to know nothing. The virtuous woman read, but the witch read backwards. The virtuous woman
read, but the witch read backwards. The virtuous woman knew her scripture, but the
witch could cite chapter and verse of Biblical texts with facility ministers found distinctly unsettling. Mercy Short, for example, uttered "innumerable Things . . .
which would have been more Agreeable to One of a greater Elevation in Christianity," finding scriptural support for her arguments with a speed that "no man living
ever" could have matched. Mather found her "Discourses . . . *incredibly beyond*
what might have been expected, from one of her small education." Another young
woman demonstrated her bewitchment through "strains of Expression and Argument" that were "truly Extraordinary; A person of the best Education and Experience and . . . Attainments much beyond hers could not have exceeded them." Any
seventeenth-century listener would have recognized the implicit message: one of
"small education," the recipient of the kind of learning that better suited a hearer
than a preacher, was more than likely to be female. Conversely, a "person of the
best Education and Experience," one who had attained significant "elevation in
Christianity," was invariably male. And the woman who breached these implied
gender boundaries was, as likely as not, a witch.

And yet, at other moments, the witch also fell far short of the virtuous woman
in her capacity for elevated Christian speech. For all her diabolic skill when acting
the part of the minister, the witch could also fail to equal the verbal proficiency of
even a well-catechized child. This accounted for her often-demonstrated inability to
recite the Lord's prayer, and her mute rage at words like "God," and "Love," and
"Good." Such grand "failures" of speech were considered just as damning as the
witch's equally florid "successes," for both claimed a linguistic authority that was
inappropriate. The witch decided what she would read and what would be read to
her. She chose when and what to hear, whether and how to speak, and—most dramatically—what to say. She was, in the fullest seventeenth-century sense, an *author,* an inventor and teller of her own story, a creator and founder of others'
misery. If the New England clergy was beginning to advance a version of feminin-

ity that included some verbal authority—the right to read and discourse modestly on Biblical texts—the witch showed the need to limit that authority.

To elite ears, the witch's speech posed a grand threat, challenging nothing less than the hierarchical framework of Puritan society. For common folk—her neighbors and victims—her voice held a different sort of menace. The witch's words struck at the very foundation of local life: the dominion of men over their wives and farmers over their crops and livestock, the ability of parents to protect and nurture their children. But if the theater of her malice was smaller, the impact of her words in the community setting was more literal and immediate. Babies and animals dropped dead. Inanimate objects moved at will. Luck ran out.

As was true for the Puritan elite, the witch's power in the neighborhood was embodied by her fiery tongue and her effect upon the speech of others. Heated words both by and against witches were a vital part of the local matrix of witch-hunting. As a subject of slander, and as the issuer of curses and other verbal "injuries," the witch was defined and prosecuted by the spoken word.

That the witch's speech to her neighbors was what some scholars have called "assaultive" is the stuff of drama and legend. Images of the witch-as-scold resonated in England and in New England. One English dramatist put the question poetically: "She on whose tongue a whirlwind sits. . . . Is not that scold a witch?" Was she? Evidence of witches' "scolding" is impressionistic, but suggestive. It is important to note that the witch's words were *interpreted* by her neighbors as contentious and aggressive, not necessarily that they *were* so in any objective sense. But bearing this caveat in mind, the connection between being accused of witchcraft and having a reputation for scolding appears strong in quantitative and qualitative terms. We know, for example, that accused witches exceeded the general population (and especially the population of women) in rates of "assaultive speech," lying, and speech against authority. And the testimony of neighbors in numerous cases shows that the malicious acts of a suspected witch and her heated words were often inseparable in the minds of local accusers.

Witnesses against accused witches often pointed to a contentious verbal exchange with the suspect as the incident that first tipped them off to diabolic goings-on. The neighbors of Elizabeth Garlick in East Hampton, Long Island, described her as a "duble tongued woman" who made herself suspect by having "jeered" and "laughed" at them on numerous occasions. Sarah Good, executed at Salem, had spoken "in a very wicked, spitfull manner . . . with base and abusive words. . . . mutring & scolding extreamly." Sarah Bibber, accused Salem witch and self-described possessed victim, was also called "double-tongued": "a woman of an unruly turbulent spirit. . . . much given to tatling & tale Bareing . . . amongst her neighbors . . . very much given to speak bad words and would call her husband bad names." Another neighbor recalled that Goody Bibber "wood be very often spekeking againts won and [a]nother very obsa[n]ely . . . and *wichshing very bad wichchis*" [emphasis added].

This "wishing of bad wishes" was one aspect of the speech of suspected witches that stood out in neighbors' ears from the deafening array of contentious speech that was a constant presence in their "face-to-face" communities. Only a tiny fraction of those formally accused of speech crimes in early Massachusetts were ever prosecuted as witches. But unlike the insults hurled by common slanderers and railers, the witch's words had a very literal *power*—power of a sort not common to women in other areas of colonial life. As "cursing" or "foretelling," a witch's words broke free of the boundaries of speech and took harmful, physical form. One woman told a neighbor that he "should Repent of" his words to her "afore Seven years Came to an End," saying that she would "hold [his] noss so Closs to the grindstone as Ever it was held." Some curses were more specific: that a cow would die or a child would be taken ill. Most bespoke a generic malice on the part of the "witch": that "shee would be even with" a neighbor, or that her victim might "Rue it hereafter." No matter how mundane the particular threat, the witch's cursing held out the danger of words made real. As several of her Ipswich neighbors recalled about Goody Batchelor's threats against their cattle, "as she sayde so it came to pass."

And there was one final quality of the witch's speech as interpreted by common folk. If her words, as curses and threats, could be too trustworthy, too literal, they might also be slippery and falsely seductive. Pretended kindness or unduly "smooth words"—followed in many cases by preternatural "harm"—were as distrusted as threats. One witness found the "fauneing & flattering manner" of Salem merchant Phillip English highly suspect. Mary Parker had "fauned upon" a deponent's wife "w'th very Smooth words," after which his child fell sick. Elizabeth Howell feared, after a heated exchange with suspected witch Elizabeth Garlick, that Garlick would "cum fauninge" to her in the morning. Here we glimpse the very essence of the "double-tongued" woman: muttering and menacing at one turn, flattering and fawning at the next. Her verbal challenge came not only from the "heat" of her speech, but also from its unpredictability. . . .

. . . The quality of a woman's "conversation" went a long way toward marking her as either a good Christian neighbor or a witch.

The connection between disorderly speech and the construction of womanhood figured into both elite and popular conceptions of the witch. This is not to say that speech is the "key" to witchcraft, for we know that many other factors—social, economic, and psychological—combined to make certain women in certain places and at certain historical moments into witches. Nor is it my claim that witchcraft is the "key" to the Puritans' preoccupation with speech, for "governing the tongue" meant listening for all misspeaking, not only to the witch's curse. . . .

. . . But the witch's evil speech meant something different to the Puritan minister than it did to the fearful neighbor. The minister heard a version of female authorship that threatened social hierarchy and Puritan male rule. The neighbor heard words made real—words that promised not only social disruption, but physical harm. Like medieval "charms," the witch's words literally embodied danger to those around her.

Being able to hear a witch—to distinguish her by her manner of speaking—was a vital step on the road to disempowering her. Regulating this particular sort of women's disorderly speech was a project of central importance for both the Puritan rulers and the common folk in early New England. . . . Denouncing the disorderly speech of the witch was one way to demonstrate that the Puritan elite and their subjects did, in effect, speak the same language, and that a serious break with that language would not be tolerated. . . .

In seventeenth-century New England, the proposition that words were capable of inflicting real damage would not have aroused debate. The ruling elite and common folk alike recognized that speech was a source of power and of danger, and that the boundaries between speaking and doing were fuzzy ones. A woman who crossed the boundaries her culture set for socially "correct" speech might be counted a witch by the minister whose role she usurped, or the neighbors who believed themselves harmed by her words. And the price she might pay for disrupting the social order with her speech might be as high as life itself.

## F U R T H E R     R E A D I N G

Russell Bourne, *The Red King's Rebellion: Racial Politics in New England, 1675–1678* (1990).

Alfred A. Cave, *The Pequot War* (1996).

Colin G. Calloway, ed., *After King Philip's War: Presence and Persistence in New England* (1997).

Cornelia Hughes Dayton, *Women Before the Bar: Gender, Law, and Society in Connecticut, 1639–1789* (1995).

John Putnam Demos, *Entertaining Satan: Witchcraft and the Culture of Early New England* (1982).

———, *The Unredeemed Captive: A Family Story from Early America* (1994).

Philip L. Gura, *A Glimpse of Sion's Glory: Puritan Radicalism in New England, 1620–1660* (1984).

Carol F. Karlsen, *The Devil in the Shape of a Woman: Witchcraft in Colonial New England* (1987).

Douglas Edward Leach, *Flintlock and Tomahawk: New England in King Philip's War* (1958).

Jill Lepore, *The Name of War: King Philip's War and the Origins of American Identity* (1998).

Richard I. Melvoin, *New England Outpost: War and Society in Colonial Deerfield* (1989).

Mary Beth Norton, *Founding Mothers and Fathers: Gendered Power and the Forming of American Society* (1996).

Elizabeth Reis, *Damned Women: Sinners and Witches in Puritan New England* (1997).

Robert Blair St. George, *Conversing by Signs: The Poetics of Implication in Colonial New England Culture* (1998).

# CHAPTER
## 6

# *Spanish Policy and Native Response in New Mexico*

*Ｏ*

*Spanish colonization differed from English colonization in many ways. One important difference lay in the separate religious organizations that operated within Spain's American empire. These organizations, such as the Jesuits and the Franciscans, were part of the Spanish program, yet they were ultimately responsible to the papacy in Rome. They often moved beyond the frontier of settlement and formed their own relationships with the natives among whom they settled. Whereas the Protestants, as they did in New England, argued that the Indians must learn to read the Bible for themselves and rejected paintings and music, the Roman Catholic missionaries taught their message in visual and dramatic forms, through pictures, statues, and plays.*

*In New Mexico, from the foundation of Santa Fé in 1610, Franciscan friars began their mission to the Pueblos. From about 1630, the same time as the Chesapeake colonies and New England began to grow rapidly, larger numbers of Spanish colonists began to come into New Mexico, and a larger group of priests went out as individuals or in pairs to live in the pueblos. In these circumstances they necessarily presented their message in ways that the natives would accept; they were in no position to force conversion. They were welcomed in part because they brought new crops, some from indigenous sources in Mexico, and new agricultural technologies that made the life of the Pueblos easier and more productive.*

*The welcome given by Native Americans misled both priests and political leaders who anxiously sought any indication that the Indians would willingly and easily give up their own culture and traditions for a European style of life. In reality the natives were interested in choosing from European culture the elements that would enhance their traditional lives, making them fuller or more efficient. They had no desire to give up a satisfying way of life and, if pushed too hard, would resist in ways that Europeans saw as treachery.*

*A further misperception concerned tribal organization. Europeans tended to perceive complex hierarchical structures headed by powerful leaders, whereas modern scholars are more apt to see decentralized organization, with village or band-level leaders operating on a consensual basis. The Pueblos did not have an overarching tribal organization, and the Apaches and Navajos were just beginning to coalesce into groups at this time. Often such groupings emerged out of the experience of dealing with the Europeans and tribal names reflected Spanish perceptions of similarities. However, the Spanish themselves were not unified. Within the Spanish empire, religious leaders argued with civil officials and military officers about the paths to follow and these arguments were often bitter. Native Americans, with often long-standing rivalries, also fought each other and vied for power in the changed situation.*

 D O C U M E N T S

The Tewa creation myth, recounted in document 1, accounts for the character of the land these Pueblos occupy, the people living on it, and also explains the presence of evil in the world. These Native Americans' first experience of Europeans came early. In the early 1540s Spanish explorer Francisco Vásquez de Coronado, lured by reports of golden cities to the north, led a two-year expedition through the American Southwest as far as central Kansas. Pedro de Castañeda, a member of the company, wrote the report in document 2. It was to be many decades before the Spanish again attempted to move into that area.

Document 3 is from the reports of Fray Alonso de Benavides, the leader of a group of priests who went to New Mexico in the 1630s. He was convinced of good prospects for many conversions among the Pueblo and Apache Indians and urged the Spanish authorities to concentrate efforts on the New Mexico territory. The Pueblo Revolt of 1680, coming after the missions seemed so successful, shocked the Spanish authorities and they collected testimony, seen in document 4, about its extent and causes. The reports include Indians' affirmations that it was the overconfident priests' forbidding them to practice their own religion that drove them to rebel, as well as statements by missionaries about their suffering during the revolt. Document 5, the testimony of Pedro Naranjo, describes the leadership and vision of Popé.

## 1. In the Beginning: Tewa Creation Story, Oral Tradition from Pre-Contact Times

The Tewa were living in *Sipofene* beneath Sandy Place Lake far to the north. The world under the lake was like this one, but it was dark. Supernaturals, men, and animals lived together at this time, and death was unknown. Among the supernaturals were the first mothers of all the Tewa, known as "Blue Corn Woman, near to summer," or the Summer mother, and "White Corn Maiden, near to ice," the Winter mother.

These mothers asked one of the men present to go forth and explore the way by which the people might leave the lake. Three times the man refused, but on the fourth request he agreed. He went out first to the north, but saw only mist and haze; then he went successively to the west, south, and east, but again saw only mist and haze. After each of these four ventures he reported to the corn mothers and the people that he had seen nothing, that the world above was still *ochu,* "green" or "unripe."

---

Tewa creation story in Alfonso Ortiz, *The Tewa World: Space, Time, Being and Becoming in a Pueblo Society* (Chicago, 1969), 13–16.

Next the mothers told him to go to the above. On his way he came upon an open place and saw all the *tsiwi* (predatory mammals and carrion-eating birds) gathered there. There were mountain lions and other species of cat; wolves, coyotes, and foxes; and vultures and crows. On seeing the man these animals rushed him, knocked him down, and scratched him badly. Then they spoke, telling him: "Get up! We are your friends." His wounds vanished immediately. The animals gave him a bow and arrows and a quiver, dressed him in buckskin, painted his face black, and tied the feathers of the carrion-eaters on his hair. Finally they told him: "You have been accepted. These things we have given you are what you shall use henceforth. Now you are ready to go."

When he returned to the people he came as Mountain Lion, or the Hunt chief. This is how the first Made person came into being. On approaching the place where the people awaited, he announced his arrival by calling out like a fox (*de*). This is his call. The people rejoiced, saying, "We have been accepted."

The Hunt chief then took an ear of white corn, handed it to one of the other men, and said, "You are to lead and care for all of the people during the summer." To another man he handed another ear of white corn and told him, "You shall lead and care for the people during the winter." This is how, according to the myth, the Summer and Winter chiefs were instituted. They joined the Hunt chief as Made People.

Among the people were also six pairs of brothers called *Towa é*, literally "persons." To the first pair, who were *blue*, the newly appointed chiefs said: "Now you shall go forth to the north and tell us what you see." They went with the older one in the lead, but could not walk very far because the earth was soft. All they saw was a mountain to the north. They returned and reported their observations to the people. Next the *yellow* pair were sent out to the west, followed by the *red* ones who went south, the *white* ones who went east, and the *dark* (*nuxu in*) ones who went to the zenith. Each successive pair returned and reported that the earth was still soft. The yellow, red and white brothers reported seeing mountains in each direction, while the dark pair who went above reported seeing *agoyo nuxu,* a large star in the eastern sky. The first four pairs each picked up some mud and slung it toward each of the cardinal directions, thereby creating four *tsin,* or flat-topped hills.

Finally, the last pair of *Towa é,* the *all-colored* (*tsege in*) ones of the nadir, were sent out. They found that the ground had hardened somewhat, and they saw a rainbow in the distance. When they returned and reported this, the people made preparations to leave the lake. The Summer chief led the way, but as he stepped on the earth it was still soft and he sank to his ankles in the mud. Then the Winter chief came forth, and as he stepped on the ground there was hoarfrost. The ground became hard, and the rest of the people followed. The original corn mothers and other supernaturals, the predatory mammals, and the carrion-eaters remained beneath the lake. The *Towa é,* or brothers, went to the mountains of the directions to stand watch over the people.

As the people started southward many began to fall ill. The Winter and Summer chiefs decided that they were not yet complete; something else was needed. All returned once again to the home under the lake, and there the Hunt chief opened up Summer chief's corn mother. He discovered that the hollow core was filled with pebbles, ashes, and cactus spines. The Hunt chief replaced these with seeds and declared that one among the people was "of a different breath," or a witch, for the items discovered in the corn mother were recognized as items of witchcraft. This, then, marked the beginning of witchcraft and other forms of evil. In order to combat these and to make the people well, the *Ke* (medicine man) was created as the fourth Made person. The people then started out once again.

Before they proceeded very far south, they all had to return to the lake three times more, because the chiefs felt they were still not complete. At each subsequent return the *Kossa* and *Kwirana* (clown), the Scalp chief, and the *Kwiyoh* (Women's society) were instituted, in that order. The *Kossa* and *Kwirana* were created to entertain the people when they grew tired and unhappy, the Scalp chief to insure success in warfare, and the Women's society to care for the scalps and to assist the Scalp chief. The people at last felt they were complete, and prepared to proceed southward once again.

Before doing so, the Hunt chief divided the people between the Summer chief and the Winter chief. Those who were to follow the Summer chief would proceed south along the mountains on the west side of the Rio Grande. The Winter chief and his group would proceed along the mountains on the east side of the river. The Summer People, as the former group came to be called, subsisted by agriculture and by gathering wild plant foods, while the Winter People subsisted by hunting. Each group "took twelve steps" (made twelve stops) on this journey, and after each step they built a village and stayed for a day. "In that time one day was one year." Those who died along the way—for death was now known—were buried near the village and stones piled over the graves.

At the twelfth step the two groups rejoined and founded a village called *Posi,* near present day Ojo Caliente. The village grew and prospered, and the people remained there for a long while. In time, however, an epidemic struck and the elders decided to abandon the village. Six different groups left and founded the six Tewa villages we know today. San Juan was founded first, so it became the "mother pueblo" for the other five. Each of the six departing groups included both Winter and Summer people, so the chiefs and other Made People were replicated in each village. . . .

## 2. Coronado Explores the Southwest, 1540–1542

Cibola* is seven villages. The largest is called Maçaque. The houses are ordinarily three or four stories high, but in Maçaque there are houses with four and seven stories. These people are very intelligent. They cover their privy parts and all the immodest parts with cloths made like a sort of table napkin, with fringed edges and a tassel at each corner, which they tie over the hips. They wear long robes of feathers and of the skins of hares, and cotton blankets. The women wear blankets, which they tie or knot over the left shoulder, leaving the right arm out. These serve to cover the body. They wear a neat well-shaped outer garment of skin. They gather

---

*Coronado's Cibola is Háwikuh Pueblo.

Pedro de Castañeda, "Account of the Expedition to Cíbola which took place in the year 1540." In George Parker Winship, ed., *The Coronado Expedition, 1540–1542* (Chicago: Rio Grande Press, 1964), 254–274.

their hair over the two ears, making a frame which looks like an old-fashioned headdress.

This country is a valley between rocky mountains. They cultivate corn, which does not grow very high. The ears start at the very foot, and each large fat stalk bears about 800 grains, something not seen before in these parts. There are large numbers of bears in this province, and lions, wild-cats, deer, and otter. There are very fine turquoises, although not so many as was reported. They collect the pine nuts each year, and store them up in advance. A man does not have more than one wife. There are estufas or hot rooms in the villages, which are the courtyards or places where they gather for consultation. They do not have chiefs as in New Spain, but are ruled by a council of the oldest men. They have priests who preach to them, whom they call papas. These are the elders. They go up on the highest roof of the village and preach to the village from there, like public criers, in the morning while the sun is rising, the whole village being silent and sitting in the galleries to listen. They tell them how they are to live, and I believe that they give certain command-ments for them to keep, for there is no drunkenness among them nor sodomy nor sacrifices, neither do they eat human flesh nor steal, but they are usually at work. The estufas belong to the whole village. It is a sacrilege for the women to go into the estufas to sleep. They make the cross as a sign of peace. They burn their dead, and throw the implements used in their work into the fire with the bodies. . . .

Tiguex is a province with twelve villages on the banks of a large, mighty river; some villages on one side and some on the other. . . .

. . . [The villages] are governed by the opinions of the elders. They all work to-gether to build the villages, the women being engaged in making the mixture and the walls, while the men bring the wood and put it in place. They have no lime, but they make a mixture of ashes, coals, and dirt which is almost as good as mortar, for when the house is to have four stories, they do not make the walls more than half a yard thick. They gather a great pile of twigs of thyme and sedge grass and set it afire, and when it is half coals and ashes they throw a quantity of dirt and water on it and mix it all together. They make round balls of this, which they use instead of stones after they are dry, fixing them with the same mixture, which comes to be like a stiff clay. Before they are married the young men serve the whole village in gen-eral, and fetch the wood that is needed for use, putting it in a pile in the courtyard of the villages, from which the women take it to carry to their houses.

The young men live in the estufas, which are in the yards of the village. . . . When any man wishes to marry, it has to be arranged by those who govern. The man has to spin and weave a blanket and place it before the woman, who covers herself with it and becomes his wife. The houses belong to the women, the estufas to the men. If a man repudiates his woman, he has to go to the estufa. It is forbidden for women to sleep in the estufas, or to enter these for any purpose except to give their husbands or sons something to eat. The men spin and weave. The women bring up the children and pre-pare the food. The country is so fertile that they do not have to break up the ground the year round, but only have to sow the seed, which is presently covered by the fall of snow, and the ears come up under the snow. In one year they gather enough for seven. A very large number of cranes and wild geese and crows and starlings live on what is sown, and for all this, when they come to sow for another year, the fields are covered with corn which they have not been able to finish gathering. . . .

. . . They keep the separate houses where they prepare the food for eating and where they grind the meal, very clean. This is a separate room or closet, where they have a trough with three stones fixed in stiff clay. Three women go in here, each one having a stone, with which one of them breaks the corn, the next grinds it, and the third grinds it again. They take off their shoes, do up their hair, shake their clothes, and cover their heads before they enter the door. A man sits at the door playing on a fife while they grind, moving the stones to the music and singing together. They grind a large quantity at one time, because they make all their bread of meal soaked in warm water, like wafers. They gather a great quantity of brushwood and dry it to use for cooking all through the year. There are no fruits good to eat in the country, except the pine nuts. They have their preachers. . . .

Cicuye* is a village of nearly five hundred warriors, who are feared throughout that country. It is square, situated on a rock, with a large court or yard in the middle, containing the estufas. The houses are all alike, four stories high. One can go over the top of the whole village without there being a street to hinder. There are corridors going all around it at the first two stories, by which one can go around the whole village. These are like outside balconies, and they are able to protect themselves under these. The houses do not have doors below, but they use ladders, which can be lifted up like a drawbridge, and so go up to the corridors which are on the inside of the village. As the doors of the houses open on the corridor of that story, the corridor serves as a street. The houses that open on the plain are right back of those that open on the court, and in time of war they go through those behind them. The village is inclosed by a low wall of stone. There is a spring of water inside which they are able to divert. The people of this village boast that no one has been able to conquer them and that they conquer whatever villages they wish. The people and their customs are like those of the other villages. . . .

## 3. Fray Alonso de Benavides Reports New Mexico Indians Eager for Conversion, 1634

On February 27 of the same year, 1632, Father Fray Martin de Arvide, who had spent many years in preaching the divine word in New Mexico [suffered martyrdom]. The great pueblo of Picuries had fallen to his lot. Here he converted more than two hundred Indians, suffering great hardships and personal dangers, as these people are the most indomitable of that kingdom. He founded a church and convent large enough to minister to all the baptized. Among the newly converted, there was a young man, a son of one of the principal sorcerers. On a certain occasion, the latter undertook to pervert his son and dissuade him from what the padre taught. When the father was informed of it, he left the convent with a crucifix in his hands and, filled with apostolic spirit, he went to the place where the infernal minister was perverting that soul and began to remonstrate with him, saying, "Is it not sufficient that you yourself want to go to hell without desiring to take your son also?" Addressing the young man, he said, "Son, I am

---

*Cicuye is modern Pecos Indians.

Frederick Webb Hodge, George P. Hammond, and Agapito Rey, eds., *Fray Alonso de Benavides' Revised Memorial of 1634* (Albuquerque: University of New Mexico Press, 1945), 42–44, 82–83, 89–91, 216–221.

more your father and I love you more than he, for he wants to take you with him to the suffering of hell, while I wish you to enjoy the blessings of being a Christian." With divine zeal, he advanced these and other arguments. The old sorcerer arose, grasped a large club near by, and struck the blessed father such a blow on the head that he felled him and then he and others dragged him around the plaza and ill-treated him cruelly. Miraculously he escaped from their hands; although very eager to offer his life to its Giver, God preserved him for a later occasion.

As a result of this the Indians rebelled, so that for several years that pueblo refused to receive a friar who might preach our holy Catholic faith to them. This situation continued until the year 1628 when I stationed there Father Andrés de Zea, who converted many people. . . .

. . . All the Indians are now converted, baptized, and very well ministered to, with thirty-three convents and churches in the principal pueblos and more than one hundred and fifty churches throughout the other pueblos; here, where scarcely thirty years earlier all was idolatry and worship of the devil, without any vestige of civilization, today they all worship our true God and Lord. The whole land is dotted with churches, convents, and crosses along the roads. The people are so well taught that they now live like perfect Christians. They are skilled in all the refinements of life, especially in the singing of organ chants, with which they enhance the solemnity of the divine service.

All these nations settled in this most northerly region in order to escape the intolerable cold and to find there a milder climate, but they met with opposition and resistance from the native inhabitants of this whole land, that is, from the huge Apache nation. In fact, the Apaches surround the above-mentioned nations on all sides and have continuous wars with them.

Thus, since we had converted all these nations, we endeavored to convert the Apaches, who alone are more numerous than all the others together, and even more numerous than the people of New Spain. These Indians are very spirited and belligerent. They are a people of a clearer and more subtle understanding, and as such they laugh at the other nations because they worship idols of wood and stone. The Apaches worship only the sun and the moon. They wear clothing, and although their chief sustenance is derived from hunting, they also plant much corn. Their houses are modest, but adequate for protection against the cold spells of that region. In this nation only, the husband often has as many wives as he can support. This also depends on rank, for it is a mark of prestige to have numerous wives. They cut off the nose and ears of the woman taken in adultery. They pride themselves on never lying but on always speaking the truth. The people of this nation are countless, for they occupy the whole of New Mexico. Thus, armies of more than thirty thousand have been seen on the way to war against each other, the fields swarming with them. They have no one king who governs them, in general, but in each district or province they allow themselves to be ruled by one who is famous for some brave deed. The neighboring provinces, however, always heed and have respect for someone from a larger province. . . .

Starting, then, with that portion of this nation nearest to the Pira [Piro] nation, which is the first we meet on reaching New Mexico, there is, on the opposite bank of the Rio del Norte to the west, the province and tribe of the Xila Apaches. It is fourteen leagues from the pueblo of San Antonio Senecú, where their chief captain, called Sanaba, oftentimes comes to gamble. After he had heard me preach to the Piros several times, he became inclined to our holy Catholic faith and confided his thoughts to me; and when I had satisfied him in regard to certain difficulties that he had encountered, he determined to become a Christian and said that he wanted to go and tell his people in order that they too should become Christians. This he did, and within a few days he returned to see me, with some of his people already converted by what he had told them. Confirming them in their good intentions, I persuaded them, since they were the chief lords, that, as a good beginning to their Christianity, they should at once erect a cross in the center of the plaza of their pueblo so that I could find and worship it when I came to visit them. They promised me to do this and departed very happy. And, although I, because of the demands of my office and the lack of friars, could not go there that year, withal I learned that Captain Sanaba was an apostolic preacher and desired that all of his tribe should be converted, and he had already prepared them for it.

After the lapse of a few days, I returned there to ascertain the state of that conversion. When Captain Sanaba heard that I had arrived at San Antonio Senecú, he came those fourteen leagues to see me, accompanied by many of his people. After I had welcomed him with honor in the presence of all, he presented me with a folded chamois, which is a dressed deerskin. It is customary among these people, when going to visit someone, to bring a gift. I accepted it to gratify him, although I told him that I did not want anything from him except that he and all his people should become Christians. He asked me to unfold the chamois and see what was painted on it. This I did and saw that it had been decorated with the sun and the moon, and above each a cross, and although the symbolism was apparent to me, I asked him about it. He responded in these formal words: "Father, until now we have not known any benefactors as great as the sun and the moon, because the sun lights us by day, warms us, and makes our plants grow; the moon lights us by night. Thus we worship them as our gods. But, now that you have taught us who God, the creator of all things is, and that the sun and the moon are His creatures, in order that you might know that we now worship only God, I had these crosses, which are the emblem of God, painted above the sun and the moon. We have also erected one in the plaza, as you commanded."

Only one who has worked in these conversions can appreciate the joy that such happenings bring to a friar when he sees the results of his preaching. Recognizing this gift as the fruit of the divine word, I took the chamois and placed it on the high altar as a banner won from the enemy and as evidence of the high intelligence of this nation, for I do not know what more any of the ancient philosophers could have done. With this I bade farewell to him and his people, who were very happy. Within a few days he came more than sixty leagues to see me, rejoicing that all of his people had decided to become Christians. In his own name and in behalf of all of them he rendered obedience to me in the name of our holy mother, the church. With this good start, I founded that conversion in their pueblo of Xila, placing it in charge of Father Fray Martín del Espíritu Santo, who administered it with great courage during the year 1628.

## 4. New Mexico's Indians Rebel Against Suppression of Their Native Religion, 1680: Four Accounts

### *Alonso García to Fray Francisco de Ayeta*

The señor governor tells me to advise your reverence of the state in which he finds himself, which must certainly arouse great pity in every one, at seeing so many children and women on foot, naked, and dying of hunger, according to reports that have reached us, they not having been able to escape with even a shirt.

The señor governor informs me that all the rest are coming in the same plight. Let your reverence reflect upon the afflictions that the señor governor and all those of us who are present will have experienced. I am going out to meet the señor governor and to ascertain his lordship's decision, leaving all the families in this place, guarded by most of the men.

It is said that nothing remains of the temples and sacred vestments—that they have burned everything. From your reverence's report and from the necessary slowness of the señor governor, I judge that he will arrive here at about the same time as the wagons with the supplies. That which the señor governor urges me most strongly is to advise your reverence as quickly as possible, for the relief of such great suffering.

Meanwhile, may our Lord keep your reverence for the protection of so many poor people, who desire to see you with the spiritual increase which your reverence merits. In this place of Fray Cristóbal, to-day, September 4, 1680. Your reverence's humblest servant, who kisses your feet.

Alonso García

### *Fray Antonio de Sierra to Fray Francisco de Ayeta*

. . . My escape from [La Isleta] was a divine dispensation, through circumstances which I will tell personally, or of which your reverence will learn from many persons. All the rest have perished. The Indians who have done the greatest harm are those who have been most favored by the religious and who are most intelligent. Many of them have already paid with their lives in the fighting in the villa, where the entire battery was, as well as a large number of Indians. The latter, terrified by the conflict, gave the Spaniards an opportunity to retire from the villa with small loss, although that of Sargento Mayor Andrés Gómez Parra and other soldiers was a great one. According to reports, few were wounded, among them the señor governor. . . .

### *Statement of One of the Rebellious Christian Indians*

. . . Having been asked his name and of what place he is a native, his condition, and age, he said that his name is Don Pedro Nanboa, that he is a native of the pueblo of Alameda, a widower, and somewhat more than eighty years of age. Asked for what reason the Indians of this kingdom have rebelled, forsaking their obedience to his

Documents on the revolt of the Pueblo Indians, 1680. "Letter of the lieutenant general, Alonso García, to the Father Visitador," "Letter of Father Fray Antonio de Sierra to Father Visitador," "Statement of one of the rebellious Christian Indians," and "Statement of Pedro García." In Charles W. Hackett ed., *Revolt of the Pueblo Indians of New Mexico and Otermin's Attempted Reconquest, 1680–1682* (Albuquerque: University of New Mexico Press, 1942), I, 56–62.

Majesty and failing in their obligation as Christians, he said that for a long time, because the Spaniards punished sorcerers and idolaters, the nations of the Teguas, Taos, Pecuríes, Pecos, and Jemez had been plotting to rebel and kill the Spaniards and the religious, and that they had been planning constantly to carry it out, down to the present occasion. Asked what he learned, saw and heard in the juntas and parleys that the Indians have held, what they have plotted among themselves, and why the Indians have burned the church and profaned the images of the pueblo of Sandia, he said that he has not taken part in any junta, nor has he harmed any one; that what he has heard is that the Indians do not want religious or Spaniards. Because he is so old, he was in the cornfield when he learned from the Indian rebels who came from the sierra that they had killed the Spaniards of the jurisdiction and robbed all their haciendas, sacking their houses. Asked whether he knows about the Spaniards and religious who were gathered in the pueblo of La Isleta, he said that it is true that some days ago there assembled in the said pueblo of La Isleta the religious of Sandia, Jemez, and Zia, and that they set out to leave the kingdom with those of the said pueblo of La Isleta and the Spaniards—not one of whom remained—taking along their property. The Indians did not fight with them because all the men had gone with the other nations to fight at the villa and destroy the governor and captain-general and all the people who were with him. He declared that the resentment which all the Indians have in their hearts has been so strong, from the time this kingdom was discovered, because the religious and the Spaniards took away their idols and forbade their sorceries and idolatries; that they have inherited successively from their old men the things pertaining to their ancient customs; and that he has heard this resentment spoken of since he was of an age to understand. What he has said is the truth and what he knows, under the oath taken, and he signs and ratifies it, it being read and explained to him in his language through the interpretation of Captain Sebastián Montaño, who signed it with his lordship, as the said Indian does not know how, before me, the present secretary.

Antonio de Otermín

## Statement of Pedro García

... [T]here appeared before his lordship an Indian named Pedro García, a sworn witness in these *autos,* and he stated under oath that he remembers distinctly that the captains of the Tagnos told him before the revolt that they had desired and discussed it in these parts for more than twelve years; that the said Indians wished to rebel because they resented it greatly that the religious and the Spaniards should deprive them of their idols, their dances, and their superstitions. ....

# 5. Pedro Naranjo Describes
# Popé's Vision and Leadership, 1681

In the said plaza de armas on the said day, month, and year, for the prosecution of the judicial proceedings of this case his lordship caused to appear before him an Indian prisoner named Pedro Naranjo, a native of the pueblo of San Felipe, of the

---

"Statement of Pedro Naranjo," in Charles W. Hackett, ed. *Revolt of the Pueblo Indians of New Mexico and Otermin's Attempted Reconquest, 1680–1682* (Albuquerque: University of New Mexico Press, 1942) 56–62.

Queres nation, who was captured in the advance and attack upon the pueblo of La Isleta. He makes himself understood very well in the Castilian language and speaks his mother tongue and the Tegua. He took the oath in due legal form in the name of God, our Lord, and a sign of the cross, under charge of which he promised to tell the truth concerning what he knows and as he might be questioned, and having understood the seriousness of the oath and so signified through the interpreters, he spoke as indicated by the contents of the *autos*.

Asked whether he knows the reason or motives which the Indians of this kingdom had for rebelling, forsaking the law of God and obedience to his Majesty, and committing such grave and atrocious crimes, and who were the leaders and principal movers, and by whom and how it was ordered; and why they burned the images, temples, crosses, rosaries, and things of divine worship, committing such atrocities as killing priests, Spaniards, women, and children, and the rest that he might know touching the question, he said that since the government of Señor General Hernando Ugarte y la Concha they have planned to rebel on various occasions through conspiracies of the Indian sorcerers, and that although in some pueblos the messages were accepted, in other parts they would not agree to it; and that it is true that during the government of the said señor general seven or eight Indians were hanged for this same cause, whereupon the unrest subsided. Some time thereafter they [the conspirators] sent from the pueblo of Los Taos through the pueblos of the custodia two deerskins with some pictures on them signifying conspiracy after their manner, in order to convoke the people to a new rebellion, and the said deerskins passed to the province of Moqui, where they refused to accept them. The pact which they had been forming ceased for the time being, but they always kept in their hearts the desire to carry it out, so as to live as they are living to-day. Finally, in the past years, at the summons of an Indian named Popé who is said to have communication with the devil, it happened that in an estufa of the pueblo of Los Taos there appeared to the said Popé three figures of Indians who never came out of the estufa. They gave the said Popé to understand that they were going underground to the lake of Copala. He saw these figures emit fire from all the extremities of their bodies, and that one of them was called Caudi, another Tilini, and the other Tleume; and these three beings spoke to the said Popé, who was in hiding from the secretary, Francisco Xavier, who wished to punish him as a sorcerer. They told him to make a cord of maguey fiber and tie some knots in it which would signify the number of days that they must wait before the rebellion. He said that the cord was passed through all the pueblos of the kingdom so that the ones which agreed to it [the rebellion] might untie one knot in sign of obedience, and by the other knots they would know the days which were lacking; and this was to be done on pain of death to those who refused to agree to it. As a sign of agreement and notice of having concurred in the treason and perfidy they were to send up smoke signals to that effect in each one of the pueblos singly. The said cord was taken from pueblo to pueblo by the swiftest youths under the penalty of death if they revealed the secret. Everything being thus arranged, two days before the time set for its execution, because his lordship had learned of it and had imprisoned two Indian accomplices from the pueblo of Tesuque, it was carried out prematurely that night, because it seemed to them that they were now discovered; and they killed religious, Spaniards, women, and children. This being done, it was proclaimed in all the pueblos that everyone in common should obey the commands of their father whom they did not know, which would be given through El Caydi or El Popé. This was heard by Alonso Catití, who came to the pueblo of this declarant to say that everyone must unite to go to the villa to kill the governor and the Spaniards who had remained with him, and that he who did not obey would, on their return, be beheaded; and in fear of this they agreed to it. Finally the señor governor and those who were with him escaped from the siege, and later this declarant saw that as soon as the Spaniards had left the kingdom an order came from the said Indian, Popé, in which he commanded all the Indians to break the lands and enlarge their cultivated fields, saying that now they were as they had been in ancient times, free from the labor they had performed for the religious and the Spaniards, who could not now be alive. He said that this is the legitimate cause and the reason they had for rebelling, because they had always desired to live as they had when they came out of the lake of Copala. Thus he replies to the question.

Asked for what reason they so blindly burned the images, temples, crosses, and other things of divine worship, he stated that the said Indian, Popé, came down in person, and with him El Saca and El Chato from the pueblo of Los Taos, and other captains and leaders and many people who were in his train, and he ordered in all the pueblos through which he passed that they instantly break up and burn the images of the holy Christ, the Virgin Mary and the other saints, the crosses, and everything pertaining to Christianity, and that they burn the temples, break up the bells, and separate from the wives whom God had given them in marriage and take those whom they desired. In order to take away their baptismal names, the water, and the holy oils, they were to plunge into the rivers and wash themselves with amole, which is a root native to the country, washing even their clothing, with the understanding that there would thus be taken from them the character of the holy sacraments. They did this, and also many other things which he does not recall, given to understand that this mandate had come from the Caydi and the other two who emitted fire from their extremities in the said estufa of Taos, and that they thereby returned to the state of their antiquity, as when they came from the lake of Copala; that this was the better life and the one they desired, because the God of the Spaniards was worth nothing and theirs was very strong, the Spaniard's God being rotten wood. These things were observed and obeyed by all except some who, moved by the zeal of Christians, opposed it, and such persons the said Popé caused to be killed immediately. He saw to it that they at once erected and rebuilt their houses of idolatry which they call estufas, and made very ugly masks in imitation of the devil in order to dance the dance of the cacina; and he said likewise that the devil had given them to understand that living thus in accordance with the law of their ancestors, they would harvest a great deal of maize, many beans, a great abundance of cotton, calabashes, and very large watermelons and cantaloupes; and that they could erect their houses and enjoy abundant health and leisure. As he has said, the people were very much pleased, living at their ease in this life of their antiquity, which was the chief cause of their falling into such laxity. Following what has already been stated, in order to terrorize them further and cause them to observe the diabolical commands, there came to them a pronouncement from the three demons already described, and from El Popé, to the effect that he who might still keep in his heart a regard for the priests, the governor, and the Spaniards would be known from his unclean face and clothes, and would be punished. And he stated that the said four persons stopped at nothing to have their commands obeyed. Thus he replies to the question.

Asked what arrangements and plans they had made for the contingency of the Spaniards' return, he said that what he knows concerning the question is that they were always saying they would have to fight to the death, for they do not wish to live in any other way than they are living at present; and the demons in the estufa of Taos had given them to understand that as soon as the Spaniards began to move toward this kingdom they would warn them so that they might unite, and none of them would be caught. He having been questioned further and repeatedly touching the case, he said that he has nothing more to say except that they should be always on the alert, because the said Indians were continually planning to follow the Spaniards and fight with them by night, in order to drive off the horses and catch them afoot, although they might have to follow them for many leagues. What he has said is the truth, and what happened, on the word of a Christian who confesses his guilt. He said that he has come to the pueblos through fear to lead in idolatrous dances, in which he greatly fears in his heart that he may have offended God, and that now having been absolved and returned to the fold of the church, he has spoken the truth in everything he has been asked. His declaration being read to him, he affirmed and ratified all of it. He declared himself to be eighty years of age, and he signed it with his lordship and the interpreters and assisting witnesses, before me, the secretary. ANTONIO DE OTERMÍN (rubric); PEDRO NARANJO; NICOLÁS RODRÍGUEZ REY (rubric); JUAN LUCERO DE GODOY (rubric); JUAN RUIZ DE CASARES (rubric); PEDRO DE LEIVA (rubric); SEBASTÍAN DE HERRERA (rubric); JUAN DE NORIEGA GARCÍA (rubric); LUIS DE GRANILLO (rubric); JUAN DE LUNA Y PADILLA (rubric). Before me, FRANCISCO XAVIER, secretary of government and war (rubric). . . .

# E S S A Y S

In the first essay Ramón A. Gutiérrez of the University of California at San Diego discusses how the Franciscan priests presented themselves to the Pueblo Indians of New Mexico. They emulated the priests of the natives' own religion by acting as healers and offering, through miracles and through the animals and technology they brought with them, enhanced agricultural productivity. As peaceful repositories of wisdom who controlled the natural world through supernatural means, they presented an attractive face to their American hosts.

In the second essay David J. Weber of Southern Methodist University analyzes the relationship between the civil and military government of New Mexico and the Franciscans who ran the missions in the seventeenth century. Both authorities vied for the loyalty of the Indians and each group accused the other of greedily exploiting Indian labor. Such internal controversy made life difficult for the natives but also gave them room to maneuver between the various competing Spanish groups. By the middle of the century the Spanish began to think that they were so well established that they could begin to force out native religious practices and bring the natives more firmly under Spanish control. This drive to control Indian life coincided with a period of extreme drought, conditions that showed the Franciscans' religious practices did not control the natural world as effectively as the natives had thought. The Indians felt an intense need to revive their own worship and reconcile themselves to their gods who supported their way of life. In 1680, led by the priest Popé, they rose up to eradicate the Spanish. A debate among themselves then ensued over whether to relinquish all the items, particularly agricultural technology and animals, that the Spanish had brought. Once the Spanish were evicted, the pan-pueblo organization that conducted the revolt dissolved and the Spanish were back by the end of the century. Why did the Pueblos not keep a strong organization able to resist reconquest?

## Franciscan Conversion Techniques in New Mexico

### RAMÓN A. GUTIÉRREZ

. . . When the friars entered New Mexico they attempted to portray themselves to the Indians as supermen who controlled the forces of nature—a portrayal that worked, attested Fray Gerónimo de Mendieta. So simple-minded had the Indians proven, wrote Mendieta in 1596, that they thought "we were gods or men from the sky . . . whom they received like angels without the least suspicion." The Spanish conquest was a cataclysm of unprecedented proportions for the Puebloans. Amid the chaos and excitement created by the arrival of the "Children of the Sun," accompanied by fire-brandishing katsina (soldiers) with animals at their command, stood the friars who were prepared to show the Indians through thespian acts that they were men of enormous magical power. The Indians were understandably awestruck. All the magic of the native chiefs had not halted the Christians' advance, and indeed seemed impotent against them. These Christian chiefs (friars) combined in one person what it took five native chiefs to accomplish.

One of the first functions the friars assumed was that of potent rain chiefs. Because the Pueblo cosmology was not very different from that of the Indians of central Mexico, the friars were well aware of the symbolic power of rain in the Pueblo belief system. Thus the friars tried to time their arrival in New Mexico to coincide with the rainy season. No sooner had they set foot on the Rio Grande Valley in 1598 than a terrible tempest arose. It seemed as if the natural forces at Satan's command resisted the Christians' advance, wrote Gaspar Pérez de Villagrá, chronicler of the kingdom's settlement. "The sky darkened with heavy black clouds and the entire earth shook and trembled with the force of a mighty earthquake." The friars exorcized the clouds with their crosses and to the great "amazement of the Indians as well as the Spaniards," the storm immediately subsided. Later, when the friars entered San Juan Pueblo, they found the earth parched and the crops wilted for lack of rain. The friars constructed a cross, prayed for rain, and ordered the Indians to do likewise. Then, "while the sky was as clear as a diamond, exactly twenty-four hours after the outcry had gone up, it rained . . . so abundantly that the crops recovered." San Juan's inhabitants rejoiced and presented many feathers, corn meal, and other gifts to the crucifix and to the friars.

The padres who aped rain chiefs also impersonated medicine men. Fray Gerónimo de Pedraza, a surgeon of some renown, took it upon himself to cure Quinía, a widely feared war chief who had been shot in the chest with an arrow by his own

Excerpted from W*hen Jesus Came, The Corn Mothers Went Away* by Ramón A. Gutiérrez with the permission of the publishers, Stanford University Press. © 1991 by the Board of Trustees of the Leland Stanford Junior University.

warriors because of his friendliness towards the Franciscans. Fra Gerónimo examined Quinía's infected wound, took a large copper medal with the images of the blessed Virgin Mary and Saint Francis, placed it over the wound and bound it tightly with a cord. The friar returned the next day and found that the medal had penetrated the wound and attached itself to the arrowhead. He untied the cord and out popped the medal and arrowhead in a stream of pus. Quinía speedily recovered and eventually sought baptism in 1627.

But perhaps the most impressive medical "miracle" occurred in 1632 at Awatobi. The medicine men there were irritated by Fray Francisco de Porras' successes in curing minor ailments and decided to test his medicine magic. They presented to him a thirteen-year-old who had been blind since birth saying, "You go about deceiving us and disturbing the people with what you call a cross. If what you say about it is true, place it on the eyes of this boy; if he regains his sight, we shall believe everything you tell us; but if not, we will kill you or cast you out in shame." Fra Francisco fell to his knees, prayed for a miracle "for the confusion of all these infidels," and placed a cross over the boy's eyes. He took dirt, made a little mud with his own spittle, rubbed the mud on the boy's eyes and said *epheta*. Suddenly the boy saw! The Hopi proclaimed the friar a powerful healer. The medicine men retreated, muttering and promising revenge; a promise they made good on June 28, 1633, when they poisoned Fra Francisco.

Equally daunting was the friars' animal magic, which far exceeded anything hunt chiefs could conjure. The only animals the Pueblos had domesticated were the turkey, for its feathers rather than for its meat, and the dog, as a beast of burden. The appearance of friars shepherding enormous flocks of docile animals, their escorts riding atop horses that were stronger, faster, and more obedient than any animal they had ever seen before, was quite astounding. The rapid reproduction of the European herds, which, according to a 1634 account by Fray Alonso de Benavides, nearly doubled every fifteen months, and the introduction of beef, pork, and mutton into the native diet marginalized the role of the hunt chiefs. Here was a permanent, year-round meat supply that, at least for the moment, was not the object of intense competition between neighboring villages and Athapaskan bands, or subject to the vicissitudes of the hunt chiefs' magic.

The spatial organization of force that the friars and Spanish soldiers presented to the Indians meshed well with its indigenous counterpart. Force in the Indian world was exercised by the Outside Chiefs and their warriors, who protected the village from external enemies. Within the pueblo, force was culturally prohibited. There the Inside Chief, the symbol of cosmic order, ruled. To the Pueblo Indians force was young and outside society; the sacred was old and at the very center. Whenever the Franciscans established a parish to indoctrinate the natives, they tried to reproduce this spatial relationship between force and the sacred. The friars always insisted on keeping the soldier-settlers outside the Indian villages to minimize their corrupting influences, but not too far away should the friar require their assistance imposing mission discipline or extirpating idolatry.

From the Indians' perspective the Spanish governor and his young soldiers resembled an Outside Chief and warriors whom the friars could mobilize at a moment's notice. The soldiers repeatedly warned the Puebloans "that if they attempted to injure [the friars] . . . the governor would bring his army against them and burn their pueblos and lay waste their fields," said Fray Estevan de Perea. After all, the soldiers carried the forces of nature that gave warriors their power—lightning, thunder, and fire in the form of guns. A poignant example of how the Franciscans communicated the embodiment and spatial location of force under colonial rule comes from 1582 when the Rodríguez expedition entered New Mexico. One day three horses were stolen from the party and slaughtered by the Indians at Pueblo Malpartida (San Lázaro). The soldiers quickly apprehended the culprits and sentenced them to death. Fearing that the executions might spark rebellion, the friars devised a theatrical ploy to rescue the guilty from the chopping block. At a preordained moment, the friars would free the Indians and assail the soldiers, making the Indians believe that the friars had saved their lives. All went as planned. Just as the executioner's ax was to sever an Indian's head, "the friars came out in flowing robes and removed the Indians from the block. As we pretended that we were going to take them, the Indians who were watching immediately took hold of the said friars and Indians and carried them away to their houses. . . . Due to what had been done and attempted the natives became so terrified of us [*sic*]." In 1599 Don Juan de Oñate made explicit the intent of such rescues: "They [the Indians] will recognize the friars as their benefactors and protectors and come to love and esteem them, and to fear us." Indeed, from surface appearances it seemed that the Franciscans commanded a legion of ruthless and invincible warriors.

The Franciscans also aggressively asserted their dominance over village affairs as Inside Chiefs. The Inside Chief embodied the sacred in Pueblo society, coordinating the various chieftaincies that promoted fertility, mobilizing force, and keeping sacred time. The Franciscans masterfully asserted their control over fertility and force, and by presenting themselves as ritual specialists before whom mortals had to kneel, the unmistakable conclusion was that the friars were Inside Chiefs who controlled the sacred. For after all, the Christian fetishes invested with power—be they crucifixes, statues, relics, or other sacred objects—were in the hands of the friars, as was the Holy Eucharist, the living presence of Christ in the community. To elucidate how the sacred was structured and conceived in colonial New Mexico, let us examine the structure of the Christian cosmology before returning to our narrative thread.

Space, objects, and time were the three dimensions that structured both the Pueblo and the Christian cosmologies. When Christians gathered together to ritualize their relations, it was on ground sanctified by the presence of sacred objects, at times that commemorated the life of Christ or those of his saints. The landscape the Pueblos inhabited was profane space by Christian standards. Certainly the physical geography was the handiwork of the Almighty, but before the land could be claimed for God and king, the false spirits that inhabited it had to be exorcised by Christ's redemptive matrix. Thus when Fray Marcos de Niza gazed on Hawikuh in 1539, he immediately christened the area and marked its possession with a cross. Don Juan de Oñate did likewise on reaching the Gulf of California while en route to New Mexico in 1597. He plunged into the ocean with sword in hand, cutting a cross into the water and proclaiming it "Christian territory." The ease with which New Mexico's topography was transformed into Christian space prompted Fray Juan de Prada to wonder whether the conquest was prophetic, for the Indians, almost as if by divine design, had located their villages in "the shape . . . of a cross."

Since reverential objects were the most potent loci of the holy in Christianity, it was primarily through enclosure, through the construction of a church or an oratory, that space received its power. Placement of a church was not particularly important, except when its superimposition atop a native shrine or kiva served an instructional end. The things of greatest importance enclosed in a church were "the things of divine worship," noted Fray Lucas Maldonado. The Eucharist, tabernacle, altar stone, and images of Christ, Mary, and the saints were all objects essential for efficacious ritual. The friars brought these sacred objects to New Mexico to serve as the focus for the celebration of community. The mobile quality of these items allowed them to be moved to and fro, to be processed solemnly through town and countryside, and to be stolen and profaned. New Mexican churches, unlike their European counterparts, were rarely consecrated. Consequently, as soon as a church's *sacra* were removed, the edifice became but a hollow memory of its past.

The mission church was a physical symbol of the celestial community in which humanity participated and by which it was sustained. The church was a ritual field for the experience of community when the faithful gathered as one to revere the sacred objects that embodied supernatural power. Logically, the edifice that represented this union was an architectural bulwark; its walls were massive, 3 to 4 feet thick and 25 to 30 feet high. Church interiors were spacious and unobstructed, and their parapets served a military function, offering its defenders cover against enemy fire. In times of war, the Christian community huddled together inside the church with their sacred objects. In times of festivity or natural disaster they sanctified the space in their village by processing outdoors with these objects.

The hierarchy of power New Mexico's friars attributed to their holy objects is best studied by examining the spatial organization of the reredos, those ornamental screens that stood as backdrops for the main altar, as well as the division of space within the church. The main altar on which the Mass was celebrated was the center of Christian ritual. Through the miracle of the Mass, God was made man and bread and wine were transformed into the body and blood of Jesus Christ. This conjunction of the divine and the human, of the triune godhead and the community that filled the church, was visually represented in the union of the reredos and the altar. The reredos, divided horizontally into three ascending sections rising up behind the altar, was an image of the heavenly order and a visual representation of Christian theology and history. Reigning over the top was the Trinity, portrayed either as three persons each wearing the papal tiara, as a triangle surrounded by rays of light, or as the triangular eye of God in a sunburst. The reredos section below this was vertically subdivided into three niches (sometimes into two). The tier of Santa Fe's main altar in 1776 had in the center niche a statue of St. Francis, the church's patron saint, in the right niche St. Joseph, and in the left niche St. Didacus, a Franciscan saint. The lowest section of the screen, a physical extension of the altar, duplicated the spatial organization of the section above it. In the center niche of Santa Fe's altar was a statue of Our Lady of the Pillar of Saragossa, flanked by St. Dominic, founder of the Dominican Order, and by the theologian St. John Capistran "with a crucifix in his hand and a heretic at his feet." Below the center niche was the tabernacle, "as is customary on altar screens," said Fray Francisco Atanasio Domínguez, and over the tabernacle a crucifix. Here at a glance were the historic pillars of the Church—its theologians, founders of religious orders, saints, and members of the Holy Family, all hierarchically juxtaposed to the Trinity in a triangular space.

The altar on which the redemptive sacrifice of the crucifixion was celebrated stood on a step known as the *predella,* which was "all adorned with relics," the physical fragments or clothing of holy dead. The reredos, the altar, and the predella formed the sanctuary. This concentration of holy objects was separated from the rest of the church by a communion rail beyond which only the priest and assistants could pass.

The space that extended from the communion rail back through the church proper and out into its courtyard and cemetery was organized hierarchically according to worldly inequalities. One's proximity to the main altar and the Eucharistic table was a sign of one's standing in the terrestrial community. Closest to the altar sat the provincial governor. Throughout the seventeenth and eighteenth centuries, his seat was located on a dais outside the sanctuary in the left transept of Santa Fe's church. After the governor came the men of honor and might who bickered over where they would kneel in the church and squabbled over their proximity to the holy. Don Bernardino Bustamante y Tagle's family secured a place of prominence in church in the early 1700s by purchasing two small altars in Mexico City—one to Our Lady of Guadalupe and the other to St. Anthony of Padua—and having them installed in the transept of Santa Fe's Church. Behind the settlers came the Indian children; boys on the Epistle side of the nave, girls on the Gospel side. Next were their parents, standing as couples. And finally, widowers and widows formed another row in the church careful always to leave "the passage free for the entrance of settlers."

In death as in life, one's honor in the community determined where one's bones would rest in relation to the sacred objects. Close to the altar, at the foot of the predella in San Francisco de Sandía Church, were buried the bones of New Mexico's first martyrs, Fray Francisco López and Fray Agustín Rodríguez. When Fray Estevan de Perea died in 1639, he too was buried here beside his brothers. Citizens of wealth and power buried their dead as close to the altar as possible. Those of lesser means were buried farther back in the nave, and impecunious souls found rest outside in the cemetery. Fray Andrés García made this schema explicit in his 1768 chart listing interment prices in Santa Cruz Church. A transept burial close to the altar cost 19 pesos, nave burials cost 8, one at the back of the church cost 4, and burial in the cemetery cost 2 pesos. A church burial insured participation in the communion of saints and everlasting life. Only infidels and excommunicates were denied sacred resting ground. For New Mexico's colonists, whose common identity was shaped by their religion, to be denied burial near the sacred objects of the community was to relegate one's soul and memory to obscurity.

Time was also thoroughly imbued with the holy. Much as a kiva's shipapu, altars, and fetishes recreated the time of Pueblo emergence from the underworld, so too the reredos that rose up behind the church's main altar brought as witnesses to Christ's sacrifice the saints who over the centuries had toiled to build Christianity. The cycle of Christ's life was the measure of time, marking the days and years. Don Juan de Oñate so reckoned time, noting in his journal that April 30, 1598, was the "day of the ascension of our Lord," that May 10 was the feast of the Pentecost, that May 17 was the "day of the Holy Trinity," that May 21 was the "day of the Most

Holy Sacrament," and so on. This concept of time inspired numerous toponyms. The Indian pueblo Oñate visited on June 24, 1598, was named San Juan Bautista because it was the feast of St. John the Baptist. Zía Pueblo was called St. Peter and St. Paul for a similar reason. When, as in 1599, conflict arose among the settlers as to the identity of the mounted soldier that had assisted the Christians during their infamous siege of Acoma, the Christian calendar became their final authority. Though the men who fought at Acoma were convinced that they had seen St. James, Fray Alonso de Benavides insisted that it could not have been. The battle occurred on January 25, the feast of the Conversion of St. Paul. Thus, Benavides argued, it was St. Paul and not St. James who had appeared to them.

At no moment were space, objects, and time more perfectly conjoined than during the celebration of Mass. Then the high altar became a cosmic stage for the violent sacrifice of the crucifixion whereby Jesus, the son of God, was mocked and put to death at the behest of his Almighty Father. Through this sacrifice Christ atoned for humanity's sins, thereby restoring the covenant between God and mankind. Lest the congregation lose sight of the centrality of the Mass, churches were always illuminated to draw the eye to the sacrificial table. Naves were dimly lit, shadowy tunnels that stood in stark contrast to the luminescent altar and its brightly painted reredos. The directional force of the lighting immediately drew one's attention to the altar "as in a theatre."

The Mass New Mexico's friars celebrated was a rite that promoted communal peace and social accord. Organized into three parts—introduction, canon, communion—the drama of the Mass unfolded as follows. The introduction began with a psalm on humanity's sinfulness; a general confession and absolution of sin followed. In the *Gloria* God's redemptive plan was announced, and the community responded by singing glory to Him on high and praying for peace on earth. The epistles, gospel, and Nicene Creed acclaimed the congregation's faith. The offertory followed and here began the canon proper and the sacrifice of the Mass.

The offertory brought together the community's various parts, and in unison they presented the priest gifts of wine and bread. Spaniards and Indians, slave and free, male and female, the living and the dead, stood as one, suspending the earth's inequalities for union as one body in Christ. Together with the priest they prayed for a successful sacrifice: a sacrifice that represented the discord of mutual murder, its preclusion, and the peace that ritual murder made possible. Before a kneeling congregation, in magical formulas whispered over the bread and wine, the offerings were transformed into Jesus Christ. The priest elevated Christ's body first and then his blood for everyone to see.

Before the consecration there had been prayers for the living; now there were prayers for the dead. The congregation affirmed its unity, praying the *Paternoster,* bidding each other reconciliation—avoidance of temptation and deliverance from evil. Next the priest performed the *Fractio panis,* the breaking of the bread by which the body of the crucified Christ embossed on the host's surface was shattered and torn apart. Uttering words evocative of sacrifice—"Grant peace in our days, that we may be helped by thy merciful assistance, always free from sin, and secure from all disturbance"—the celebrant split the host vertically in half, and then one of the halves again in half. Because the host as the body of Christ represented both the church and Christian society, the fraction symbolized the way in which the *corpus mysticum,* the mystical body of Christ as an image of society, could be torn asunder. To preclude this possibility and to neutralize latent hostilities, the tearing of the host was followed immediately by the Pax, the Kiss of Peace. The friars were hesitant to offer women the Kiss of Peace, or for that matter to allow husbands to give it to their wives. So a pax-board (called *portapaz* or simply pax on church inventories) bearing the words "My peace I give to you," was passed among the faithful for everyone to kiss. Through this sacrificial rite the congregation as a whole was put, in the words of Godfrey Lienhardt, "at peace with itself." Amity among the faithful was reinforced by reciting the *Agnus dei,* thrice praying that the sacrificial Lamb of God grant the assemblage peace. Now the celebrant consumed the consecrated host, and if it was one of those rare occasions when the laity also received the Eucharist, they knelt at the communion rail to consume the body and blood of Christ. Finally, with a communal blessing, the Mass ended.

Much in the same way that the town chief conjoined a pueblo's various clans during Pueblo ceremonials, and by recreating the primordial time of creation promoted peace in the community, so too the friars sought to preclude societal discord and unrest by celebrating the union made possible through the sacrifice of the Mass. Before marching into New Mexico, and always before marching into battle, Don Juan de Oñate instructed his soldiers to "make their peace with God" at Mass. If nothing else, Oñate continued, Mass and Communion would bring them good luck.

For the Pueblos who saw how the friars controlled the sacred, mobilized force, conjured rain, healed the sick, and provided the community with meat, there was little doubt that the padres resembled mighty Inside Chiefs. Equally significant was the Franciscans' vow of perpetual chastity, a mark of immense spiritual strength to the Indians. "Continence . . . [was] essential to being *teshkwi,* sacred," writes Elsie C. Parsons. Pueblo men temporarily abstained from sex while practicing their ritual magic, but the idea that men would willingly pledge themselves to life-long chastity was truly astounding. Understandably some of the Indians responded to the presence of these new caciques by offering them gifts of food, labor, and respect to obtain their ritual blessings and gifts, as they previously had done with their own native chiefs. Others probably took a wait-and-see attitude toward the friars, and still others wanted nothing to do with these witches.

The forceful conquest of the Pueblos by the Spaniards and the imposition of their Christian deities and leaders was a familiar process to the Indians. As a result of the warfare that had plagued their world, they understood very well the habits of victors: how they imposed their tribal gods, their chiefs, and their rituals. . . . the Pueblo female rituals, which celebrated the transformation of outsiders into insiders, of virile warriors into native chiefs, be it through fertility or scalp dances, attested to this. Ever since Franz Fanon wrote on African colonialism we have come to see as axiomatic the tendency for certain colonized adults to ally themselves with the colonizers. They do so at certain times but not at others, and in certain spaces but not in others.

It was thus to be expected that some of the native chiefs rapidly allied themselves with the Franciscans, subordinating their pantheon of gods to that which the Europeans brought. We see this poignantly in the words Sanaba, a native chief, allegedly uttered to Fray Alonso de Benavides in 1626 on presenting him with a gift of a soft deerskin decorated "with the sun and the moon, and above each a cross." "What did the picture mean?" asked Benavides. Sanaba explained:

Father, until now we have not known any benefactors as great as the sun and the moon, because the sun lights us by day, warms us, and makes our plants grow; the moon lights us by night. Thus we worship them as our gods. But, now that you have taught us who God, the creator of all things is, and that the sun and moon are His creatures, in order that you might know that we now worship only God, I had these crosses, which are the emblems of God, painted above the sun and the moon. We have also erected one in the plaza, as you commanded.

Benavides was deeply moved by the gift and "placed it on the high altar as a banner from the enemy as evidence of their high intelligence."

Fray Estevan de Perea reported with great glee that in 1629 the chiefs of the Zuñi Pueblos presented themselves to Fray Roque de Figueredo asking "to be purified by the sacred ceremony of baptism." On the appointed day, before a specially constructed altar, Father Roque christened their "highest chief" with the name Agustín (it being the feastday of Saint Augustine). Agustín then turned to his people, exhorting them "to accept such a good law and such a good God . . . he had been baptized and had not died from it, but, on the contrary, that he felt such great rejoicing and courage in his heart that he considered himself to be much braver than before." On hearing this, Augustín's tribesmen were said to have also clamored for baptism.

But such windfalls were rare. More common, said Fray Estevan de Perea in 1633, was for the Indians to receive the friars "with some coolness, because the devil was trying in all possible ways to impede and obstruct the promulgation of the divine law." Perea's work in the Hopi Pueblos had been particularly difficult because an Indian apostate from a Christian pueblo preceded him, announcing that "some Spaniards, whom they would meet shortly . . . with the tonsures and vestments were nothing but impostors and that they should not allow them to sprinkle water on their heads because they would be certain to die from it."

This explained why, when Fray Roque de Figueredo arrived in Hawikuh in 1628, the town chief explained that neither he nor his people wished to become "wet-heads" (the Indian name for baptized Christians) "because with the water of baptism they would have to die." The Puebloans probably had death from diseases and labor drafts in mind. But Figueredo gave their words little thought and brazenly concluded that "the words of the demon are equivocal, he really wanted to say that they had to die for their guilt and sin, and for his domination." The cacique urged his people "to throw that foreign priest out," but as the friar's presence deeply divided the community, he was not expelled. . . .

## Conflict Within the Spanish Regime and the Pueblo Revolt

### DAVID J. WEBER

Throughout the Spanish empire the sacred and the profane contended for Indian labor, but in remote areas that lacked powerful mediators and had no other sources of wealth, the struggle became especially intense. New Mexico, more isolated than

Florida and less able to depend upon outside resources for support, seems to have been the scene of especially bitter contention over Indian labor. . . .

Franciscans defended their use of Indian labor with the classic rationalization of colonialists, arguing that it improved the natives' naturally indolent character. Conversely, the friars accused settlers, soldiers, and government officials of exploiting natives in ways that were not only illegal but that also weakened the mission Indians' ability to provide for their own livelihood and that obstructed the padres' efforts to evangelize. Excessive demands for labor and tribute from Christian Indians, the friars argued, made pagans wary of missionaries. Perhaps most abhorrent to the priests, some government officials sought to curry favor with the mission neophytes by refusing to enforce strict discipline and undermining the missionaries' work. Governors such as Juan de Eulate (1618–25) and Bernardo López de Mendizábal (1559–61) of New Mexico, and Diego de Rebolledo (1654–58) of Florida took the Indians' side in the Franciscans' war against the natives' "idolatry," ceremonial dances, polygamy, and concubinage. López de Mendizábal, for example, professed to see no religious significance in Pueblo ceremonies. When he attended a dance at Isleta, one of his companions noted, the Pueblos "sang something which sounded like 'Hu-hu-hu.'" "Look there," the governor said, "this dance contains nothing more than this 'hu-hu-hu,' and these thieving friars say that it is superstitious."

Outraged and determined to exert authority over the neophytes, the padres fought back. Ignoring the exhortation of their order's founder to "neither quarrel nor contend in words," Franciscans marshalled the power of church and state. Over the heads of local governors, Franciscans in Florida appealed directly to the king; friars in New Mexico appealed directly to the viceroy. The men of the cloth usually emerged victorious. As the only religious order in Florida or New Mexico, Franciscans generally spoke with one voice. Because they represented the most sacred values of their culture, at least in theory if not always in practice, they made a persuasive case against local officials. Complaints lodged by Franciscans, for example, led to the arrest and conviction of Gov. Juan de Eulate for exporting slaves from New Mexico. . . .

In addition to enlisting the aid of outside authorities, Franciscans in New Mexico wielded fearsome spiritual weapons to win their way. In remote New Mexico, where they operated independently of episcopal authority and where Indian labor was the only source of wealth (New Mexico had no garrison to receive an annual stipend, or *situado*), Franciscans used their ecclesiastical arsenal with less restraint and greater fervor than they did in Florida. Friars in New Mexico excommunicated so many of their political opponents that the town council of Santa Fe complained to the viceroy in 1639 that "on the doors of the church are posted more excommunications than bulls." Among the excommunicated were the province's first three governors following Oñate—Pedro de Peralta (1609–14), Bernardino de Ceballos (1614–18), and Juan de Eulate (1618–25). Friars excommunicated Governor Peralta twice! If they needed heavier artillery, the friars sent their enemies before the Inquisition (established in New Mexico in 1626)—as they did governors López de Mendizábal and Diego de Peñalosa (1661–64). Tactical weapons, called upon to achieve more limited objectives, included the withholding of spiritual services to an individual or an entire community. Indeed, the friars discovered that the mere threat of deploying any of these weapons often forced their opponents to surrender.

Reliance upon force instead of diplomacy brought mixed results for the Franciscans. In the short run, victory often came their way. . . . In the long run, however, the Franciscans lost respect. They alienated government officials and settlers alike, just as they alienated Indian neophytes, with unrestrained displays of power over what were often petty issues.

Contention over Indian labor was not the only issue that caused Franciscans to take aim at their secular rivals, but it often lay behind their fusillades. For their part, officials, settlers, and soldiers defended their own use of native labor and attacked the friars for exploiting the natives. Unlike the friars, the secular community spoke with many voices, for its members contended with one another as well as with the priests for native workers. Missionaries, however, who usually controlled the best land and whose neophytes constituted nearly all tributary Indians, were the easiest target. The most outspoken of the governors assailed the friars for failing to pay Indians for their work, for overworking Indians so that they fled the missions, and for enriching themselves at the expense of Indians. Settlers and soldiers coveted the mission lands and labor and criticized the friars. The town council of Santa Fe, for example, contrasted the poverty of New Mexico's settlers with the "all-powerful" Franciscans, who "enjoy rich profits from the labor of the natives." The council members complained to the viceroy in 1639 that the friars received a sufficient subsidy from the Crown and should not be allowed to use native labor to produce surpluses. Instead, their herds should be divided among the poor. . . .

Not content to limit their charges and countercharges to appeals to higher officials, Spaniards fought openly with one another. In New Mexico, where the struggle over Indian labor was most bitter, insults and blows were exchanged, mail opened, and documents forged. One governor interrupted Mass to call a priest a liar, and friars hurled the pew of another governor into the street in front of the church. Friars used the authority of the Inquisition to arrest and imprison governors, and governors arrested friars. At their most bitter, these conflicts between church and state amounted to civil war. Gov. Luis de Rosas was assassinated by his enemies—Franciscans among them, although the friars did not bloody their own hands. In Florida as well as New Mexico, all sides engaged in character assassination, accusing one another of sexual improprieties and greed—often with good reason.

Natives could not remain blind to these contretemps, and at times they were caught in the middle. In Apalachee, for example, women neophytes who failed to spend their days in the woods gathering nuts to make oil received fifty lashes from one priest. Capt. Francisco de Fuentes, who objected to the missionaries' demands on these women, threatened them with one hundred lashes if they *did* obey the priest. Both the friars and the governors enlisted or coerced natives to testify against the other side.

Through such behavior, Spaniards must have demeaned themselves in the eyes of natives and diminished their own prestige and authority. One priest in New Mexico suggested as much during a period of especially acrimonious feuding between friars and Gov. López de Mendizábal over the question of unpaid Indian labor: "The Indians are totally lost, without faith, without law, and without devotion to the Church; they neither respect nor obey their ministers." Certainly among the Pueblos, where one sign of an effective religious leader was an ability to maintain harmony in the community, the contentious Franciscans must have lost face. At the very least, the Spaniards' failures to cooperate among themselves in Florida and New Mexico weakened the administration of the two colonies and left them more vulnerable in time of crisis. . . .

By squandering their moral authority and dissipating their energies through internal quarrels, Spaniards weakened their hold over their Indian subjects. At the same time, native societies grew increasingly volatile, aggrieved by religious persecution and oppressive demands on their labor and resources. When the natives' resentment reached the boiling point, it shattered the fragile colonial structures of Florida and New Mexico. . . .

Occasionally rebellions brought lasting independence for natives. Isolated groups, such as Hopis and Apalachicolas, revolted and retained their liberty through Spanish inadvertence; Pueblos from Taos, who killed two priests and burned the church down in 1639, retained their freedom by fleeing to western Kansas and remaining for over twenty years at an Apache settlement the Spaniards called El Cuartelejo. In the main, however, rebels won only temporary reprieves from Spanish domination. Although vastly outnumbered, Spaniards crushed most of these rebellions primarily because the linguistically and culturally diverse native communities could not unite. On a few occasions, as in New Mexico in 1650 and 1667, several Indian villages joined in rebellion, but they lacked sufficient strength to prevail. Spaniards hanged their leaders and sold suspected participants into slavery.

Not until 1680 did Pueblos launch a highly unified, full-scale offensive against Spanish intruders. . . .

Pueblo society in New Mexico grew increasingly restive during two decades of low rainfall and higher-than-average temperatures, which began in 1660 and lasted until the Pueblo Revolt of 1680. During the worst of it, one priest reported, "a great many Indians perished of hunger, lying dead along the roads, in the ravines, and in their huts."

Pueblos lost herds and crops not only to bad weather, but to raids by Navajos, Apaches, and others. Traditional trade between Pueblos and nomads had probably deteriorated in the seventeenth century as Spanish demands for labor crippled the Pueblos' ability to produce surplus crops for trade. Plains Indians apparently responded by taking by force what they could no longer obtain through commerce. Then, in the 1660s and 1670s the nomads intensified their raids on the Pueblos' fields, flocks, and storehouses. Recently imposed Spanish prohibitions against trade with the Pueblos gave them little choice, and shortages brought on by the great drought must have increased their desperation. Some of the eastern Pueblos on the marginal farming lands on the edge of the high plains could not survive the years of scanty rainfall, much less raids by nomads. Pueblo communities such as Abó, with its great red stone mission complex, were abandoned in the 1670s and refugees moved into the Rio Grande pueblos where they put additional strain on the meager resources of those drought-stricken communities.

To the Pueblos, these years of starvation, disease, and death offered grim testimony to the Christians' inability to intercede with supernatural forces. In search of more efficacious prayers, Pueblos turned to traditional religious leaders and ceremonies. Anxious to halt this Pueblo religious revival and to maintain orthodoxy,

Spaniards harshly suppressed native ceremonies and persecuted native priests. In the most notorious case, Spanish officials in 1675 hanged three Pueblo priests (a fourth committed suicide in jail) and lashed forty-three others at the whipping post for crimes of sorcery and sedition.

The escalation of Spanish oppression at a time of unusual stress galvanized Pueblo leaders. They worked out a strategy to regain their religious freedom and, perhaps of equal importance, to free themselves from obligations of labor and tribute. Rather than settle for halfway measures that had failed in the past, they planned to rid New Mexico entirely of Spaniards. In 1680 Pueblo leaders united most of their communities against the European intruders.

It required careful planning to coordinate an offensive involving some 17,000 Pueblos living in more than two dozen independent towns spread out over several hundred miles and further separated by at least six different languages and countless dialects, many of them mutually unintelligible. The magnet that drew these disparate people together seems to have been Popé. A resolute religious leader from San Juan Pueblo, Popé had been among those accused of sorcery and whipped in the witch hunt of 1675. Five years later, concealing himself in a sacred room, or kiva, at Taos, the most northerly and remote pueblo in the province, Popé directed a rebellion against his oppressors. Popé failed to unify all of the Pueblos, however, for mutual suspicions ran deep. Some communities were not invited to join; others refused to join. Within rebel Pueblo communities, some individuals remained staunchly loyal to the Spaniards (dissent created severe rifts within pueblos if the civil strife that swept Pecos may be taken as typical). Nonetheless, Popé did unite most of the Pueblos. Moreover, some neighboring Apaches, who had their own score to settle with Spanish slavers, also joined his cause.

From Popé's headquarters at Taos, runners secretly carried calendars in the form of knotted cords to participating pueblos. Each knot marked a day until the Pueblos would take up arms. The last knot was to be untied on August 11, but rebellion erupted a day early. Tipped off by sympathetic Pueblos, Spaniards had captured two of the rebel messengers on August 9. When Pueblo leaders learned that their plans had been betrayed, they moved the attack up a day. Although the Spaniards had received some warning, they could not have imagined the magnitude of this unprecedented plan. The revolt caught them off guard. Scattered in farms and ranches along the Rio Grande and its tributaries, Spaniards were easy prey.

Spaniards who survived the initial attacks fled to Santa Fe and to Isleta Pueblo, one of the few pueblos that did not follow Popé. Believing themselves the only survivors, 1,500 refugees at Isleta abandoned the Pueblo on September 14 and fled down the Rio Grande toward El Paso. Meanwhile, in Santa Fe, Gov. Antonio de Otermín found himself under siege by Pueblos who were armed not only with bows and arrows, but also with guns, lances, swords, and leather armor that they had seized from unfortunate victims. At the height of the siege, nearly 2,000 Pueblos surrounded Santa Fe. Inside the city, Spaniards numbered about 1,000, but only 100 or so were men capable of bearing arms.

Despite the odds, the Spaniards put up a game struggle. According to their own reports, they inflicted heavy casualties on the Pueblos. Slowly, however, they lost ground, crowding into a few government buildings as the Pueblos sacked and burned their homes. Governor Otermín, who suffered two arrow wounds in the face and a gunshot wound in the chest, finally concluded that they had to flee or be slaughtered. Pueblos had cut off the villa's water supply, and the Spaniards had no prospects for reinforcements. Caught up in the momentum of the revolt, even once-friendly Pueblo leaders had turned against them. On September 21, the Spaniards abandoned the charred remains of Santa Fe. The Pueblo rebels allowed their adversaries, including several hundred Christian Pueblos, to retreat down the Rio Grande some three hundred miles to El Paso.

In a matter of weeks, the Pueblos had eliminated Spaniards from New Mexico above El Paso. The natives had killed over 400 of the province's 2,500 foreigners (nearly all in the initial days of the rebellion), destroyed or sacked every Spanish building, and laid waste to the Spaniards' fields. There could be no mistaking the deep animosity that some natives, men as well as their influential wives and mothers, held toward their former oppressors. "The heathen," wrote one Spanish officer in New Mexico, "have conceived a mortal hatred for our holy faith and enmity for the Spanish nation." Some Pueblo leaders, including Popé, urged an end to all things Spanish as well as Christian. After the fighting subsided, they counselled against speaking Castilian or planting crops introduced by the Europeans. This nativistic resurgence succeeded only partially in reversing the cultural transformation that Spaniards had set in motion. Some reminders of Spanish rule, such as forms and motifs in pottery, seem to have disappeared, but Pueblos continued to raise Spanish-introduced crops and livestock and to make woolen textiles. Just as they had been selective in adapting aspects of Hispanic culture, so too were they selective in rejecting them.

The Pueblos' repudiation of the symbols of Christianity suggested the strong religious impulse behind the rebellion. The natives desecrated churches and sacred objects. They killed twenty-one of the province's thirty-three missionaries, often humiliating, tormenting, and beating them before taking their lives. Under questioning, one Pueblo captive later explained how Popé traveled from pueblo to pueblo ordering that

> they instantly break up and burn the images of the holy Christ, the Virgin Mary and the other saints, the crosses, and everything pertaining to Christianity, and that they burn the temples, break up the bells, and separate from the wives whom God has given them in marriage and take those whom they desired. In order to take away their baptismal names, the water, and the holy oils, they were to plunge into the rivers and wash themselves . . . there would thus be taken from them the character of the holy sacraments.

Spaniards clearly understood the Pueblo Rebellion as a rejection of Christianity. As Governor Otermín watched the church in Santa Fe burn, he listened to "the scoffing and ridicule which the wretched and miserable Indian rebels made of the sacred things, intoning . . . prayers of the church with jeers." Far to the south in Querétaro, witnesses reported that on the day of the revolt, between 1:00 and 3:00 P.M. an ancient and sacred stone cross shook thirty-three times (once for every year that Christians believe Christ walked on the earth).

Spanish survivors of the tragedy, however, were unwilling or unable to acknowledge that they themselves had goaded the natives into rebelling either through religious persecution or through excessive demands on native labor. "This ruin did not originate because either of the repartimientos or of other drudgery which might have aggrieved these Indians," Governor Otermín explained to the viceroy. Instead, Spaniards imagined the revolt as divine retribution for their sins or as the work of the devil—explanations that had helped them understand earlier native rebellions. More on target, a royal attorney in Mexico City who examined the testimony in the case concluded that the Spaniards' "many oppressions . . . have been the chief reason for the rebellion."

The Pueblos had conducted one of the most successful Indian rebellions against Spanish colonizers anywhere in the hemisphere, but they could not maintain their independence. Buffered from the nearest Spaniards at El Paso by three hundred miles of rugged terrain, much of it controlled by Apaches, Pueblos repelled initial Spanish efforts to return. As the Pueblos' unity fractured, however, internal divisions made them increasingly susceptible to the Spanish invaders' tactics of divide and conquer. . . .

Thirteen years passed before Spaniards reestablished a base in the Pueblo country. Meanwhile, many remained in or near El Paso, then located on what is today the Mexican side of the Rio Grande at Ciudad Juárez. . . .

The struggle for independence had cost the Pueblos dearly. Their population declined sharply, from about 17,000 in 1680 to 14,000 in 1700. A disproportionate number of Pueblo males had died, and entire families had fled their communities. Many, for example, joined the apostate Hopis, and some Pueblos from Picurís fled to the Apache settlements at El Cuartelejo in western Kansas, just as Pueblos from Taos had done in a time of trouble a few generations earlier. A shrinking population forced Pueblos to abandon some of their smaller communities, never to rebuild them. Zunis, who occupied six villages when Coronado encountered them, consolidated their reduced population into the single village of Halona—still today the principal Zuni community.

Exhausted from war, their property and population diminished, Pueblos did not launch another major rebellion while under Spanish rule. Nor did the Spaniards, fearful of another rebellion, offer as much provocation. After the 1696 revolt the Spaniards lowered the level of exploitation. In the eighteenth century, pragmatic Franciscans displayed less zeal in attempting to stamp out Pueblo religious practices, and colonists and officials eased (but did not cease) their demands on Pueblo laborers. The encomienda system, destroyed by the Pueblos, was never reestablished in New Mexico. The diminution of Spanish provocation, then, diminished tensions and opened the way for an era of peaceful coexistence between Pueblos and Hispanics—an accommodation cemented by their common need for defense against unrelenting attacks by Utes, Apaches, and Navajos. . . .

 *F U R T H E R    R E A D I N G*

Donald E. Chipman, *Spanish Texas, 1519–1821* (1992).
Jack D. Forbes, *Apache, Navajo, and Spaniard* (1960).
Elizabeth A. H. John, *Storms Brewed in Other Men's Worlds: The Confrontation of Indians, Spanish, and French in the Southwest, 1540–1795,* 2nd ed. (1996).

John L. Kessell, *Kiva, Cross, and Crown: The Pecos Indians and New Mexico, 1540–1840* (1979).

Andrew L. Knaut, *The Pueblo Revolt of 1680: Conquest and Resistance in Seventeenth-Century New Mexico* (1995).

Carroll L. Riley, *Rio del Norte: People of the Upper Rio Grande from Earliest Times to the Pueblo Revolt* (1995).

Edward H. Spicer, *Cycles of Conquest: The Impact of Spain, Mexico, and the United States on the Indians of the Southwest, 1533–1960* (1962).

David J. Weber, *The Spanish Frontier in North America* (1992).

————, *What Caused the Pueblo Revolt of 1680?* (1999).

# The Ethnic Diversity of the Middle Colonies: Benefits and Consequences

*The Middle Colonies—Delaware, New Jersey, Pennsylvania, and New York—dif-*
*fered radically from the Chesapeake and New England from the beginning. Whereas*
*the latter regions were settled by English companies, and continued predominantly*
*English in their free populations, the Middle Colonies were the true melting pot, eth-*
*nically and religiously mixed from their foundation. New York was founded as New*
*Netherland in 1624; Delaware was settled as New Sweden with a mixed population*
*of Swedes and Finns in 1638. Both colonies held a mixture of people from all over*
*Europe; New Sweden was incorporated into New Netherland in 1655.*

*New Netherland and New Sweden both plunged immediately into the complex*
*trade activity along the coast. Delaware Bay and the Hudson River were major trade*
*centers; the Susquehannocks and the Iroquois League were powerful and highly or-*
*ganized Indian entities anxious for trade and prepared to link the colonies with the*
*resources of the interior. These trade opportunities, when combined with the region's*
*rich farmland, poised the Middle Colonies for economic success.*

*England and the Netherlands fought a series of wars in the later seventeenth*
*century, which brought the conquest of New Netherland, renamed New York, in*
*1664. Settlers of continental European origin were now brought under alien English*
*institutional structures and they responded in various ways to the now-dominant*
*English system. Pennsylvania was settled in the early 1680s as a proprietary colony*
*of Quaker leader William Penn. Because of the falling off of English interest in emi-*
*gration, promoters of the Middle Colonies sought colonists among both the economi-*
*cally deprived within Britain, such as the Scots-Irish, and those suffering religious*
*persecution in Europe, particularly French Huguenots and German pietists, who,*
*like Quakers, stressed the inner experience of religion. Thus the tradition of ethnic*
*and religious mixture continued. Historians debate whether these colonies saw a*
*melting pot or a series of islands of self-isolated ethnic enclaves.*

D O C U M E N T S

Daniel Denton described the newly acquired port of New York in document 1, and related its appearance and possibilities for English life. But many travelers commented on the persistence of Dutch culture in New York and New Jersey, demonstrating the success with which colonists of Dutch descent protected their heritage. In document 2 Jasper Dankaerts recorded his 1680 visit with Maria van Rensselaer who ran her plantation, Rensselaerswyck on the Hudson River, after the death of her husband. Bostonian Sarah Kemble Knight kept a journal of her business trip to New York in 1704, which is excerpted in document 3; in it she recorded the diversity of cultures she found. In the mid-eighteenth century Swedish scientist Per Kalm found settlers of Dutch descent living in a recognizably Dutch way, and keeping separate from their neighbors. He describes this in document 4 and also transmits some of the prejudice against them.

William Penn issued an invitation, document 5, to merchants to settle in Pennsylvania, in which he described the advantages they would have there. In document 6 Francis Daniel Pastorius recorded his founding of the settlement of Germantown in 1685 in Pennsylvania "situated in the Farthest Limits of America, in the Western World." In document 7 Gabriel Thomas, who was in the colony from the beginning, described the high wages labor commanded and the opportunities for both men and women. But Gottlieb Mittelberger, while agreeing that opportunities for good wages existed, wrote an exposé of the organized trade of colonists in document 8.

## 1. Daniel Denton Describes the Recently Acquired Colony of New York, 1670

That Tract of Land formerly called The New Netherland, doth Contain all that Land which lieth in the North-parts of America, betwixt New-England and Mary-Land in Virginia, the length of which Northward into the Countrey, as it hath not been fully discovered, so it is not certainly known. The breadth of it is about two hundred miles. The principal Rivers within this Tract are Hudsons River, Raritan River, and Delawarebay River. The chief Islands are the Manahatans Island, Long-Island, and Staten-Island.

And first to begin with the Manahatans Island, so called by the Indians, it lieth within land betwixt the degrees of 41. and 42. of North-latitude, and is about 14 miles long, and two broad. It is bounded with Long-Island on the South, with Staten-Island on the West, on the North with the Main Land. And with Conecticut Colony on the East-side of it; only a part of the Main Land belonging to New-York Colony where several Towns and Villages are settled, being about thirty miles in breadth, doth intercept the Manahatans Island, and the Colony of Conecticut before mentioned.

New York is settled upon the West-end of the aforesaid Island, having that small arm of the Sea, which divides it from Long-Island on the South side of it, which runs away Eastward to New-England, and is Navigable, though dangerous.

Some of the punctuation and spelling in this passage has been modernized.

Daniel Denton, *A Brief Description of New York* (London, 1670), 1–3.

For about ten miles from New York is a place called Hell-Gate, which being a narrow passage, there runneth a violent stream both upon flood and ebb, and in the middle lieth some Island of Rocks, which the Current sets so violently upon, that it threatens present Shipwreck; and upon the Flood is a large Whirlpool, which continually sends forth a hideous roaring, enough to affright any stranger from passing further, and to wait for some Charon to conduct him through; yet to those that are well acquainted little or no danger; yet a place of great defence against any enemy coming in that way, which a small Fortification would absolutely prevent, and necessitate them to come in at the West-end of Long Island by Sandy Hook, where Nutten-Island doth force them within Command of the Fort at New York which is one of the best Pieces of Defence in the North-parts of America.

New York is built most of Brick and Stone, and covered with red and black Tile, and the Land being high, it gives at a distance a pleasing Aspect to the Spectators. The Inhabitants consist most of English and Dutch, and have a considerable Trade with the Indians, for Beavers, Otter, Raccoon Skins, with other Furs; As also for Bear, Deer, and Elk Skins; and are supplied with Venison and Fowl in the Winter, and Fish in the Summer by the Indians, which they buy at an easy rate. And having the Country round about them, they are continually furnished with all such provisions as is needful for the life of man; not only by the English and Dutch within their own, but likewise by the Adjacent Colonies.

The Commodities vented [sold] from thence is Furs and Skins beforementioned; As likewise Tobacco made within the Colony, as good as is usually made in Mary-land. Also Horses, Beef, Pork Oil, Peas, Wheat, and the like.

Long-Island, the West-end of which lies Southward of New-York, runs Eastward above one hundred miles, and is in some places eight, in some twelve, in some fourteen miles broad; it is inhabited from one end to the other. On the West end is four or five Dutch Towns, the rest being all English to the number of twelve, besides Villages and Farm houses. The Island is most of it of a very good soyle, and very natural for all sorts of English Grain; which they sow and have very good increase of, besides all other Fruits and Herbs common in England and also Tobacco, Hemp, Flax, Pumpkins, Melons, etc.

## 2. Traveler Jasper Dankaerts Calls on New York Planter Maria van Rensselaer, 1680

*27th, Saturday.* We went to call upon a certain Madam Rentselaer, widow of the Heer Rentselaer, son of the Heer Rentselaer of the colony named the colony of Rentselaerswyck, comprising twelve miles square from Fort Orange, that is, twenty-four miles square in all. She is still in possession of the place, and still administers it as *patroonesse,* until one Richard van Rentselaer, residing at Amsterdam, shall arrive in the country, whom she expected in the summer, when he would assume the management of it himself. This lady was polite, quite well informed, and of good life and disposition. She had experienced several proofs of the Lord.

---

Bartlett Burleigh James and J. Franklin Jameson, eds., *Journal of Jasper Danckaerts, 1679–1680,* (New York: Charles Scribner's Sons, 1913; copyright renewed Barnes and Noble, 1941), 214–215.

The breaking up of the ice had once carried away her entire mansion, and every thing connected with it, of which place she had made too much account. Also, in some visitations of her husband, death, and others before. In her last child-bed, she became lame or weak in both of her sides, so that she had to walk with two canes or crutches. In all these trials, she had borne herself well, and God left not Himself without witness in her. She treated us kindly, and we ate here exceedingly good pike, perch, and other fish, which now began to come and be caught in great numbers. We had several conversations with her about the truth, and practical religion, mutually satisfactory. We went to look at several of her mills at work, which she had there on an ever-running stream, grist-mills, saw-mills, and others. One of the grist-mills can grind 120 schepels [90 bushels] of meal in twenty-four hours, that is, five an hour. Returning to the house, we politely took our leave. Her residence is about a quarter of an hour from Albany up the river. . . .

## 3. Sarah Kemble Knight Encounters Dutch and English in New York, 1704

The City of New York is a pleasant, well compacted place, situated on a Commodious River which is a fine harbour for shipping. The Buildings Brick Generally, very stately and high, though not altogether like ours in Boston. The Bricks in some of the Houses are of divers Colours and laid in Checkers, being glazed look very agreeable. The inside of them are neat to admiration, the wooden work, for only the walls are plastered, and the Sumers [main beam] and Girt [girder] are planed and kept very white scourr'd as so is all the partitions if made of Boards. The fire places have no Jambs (as ours have). But the Backs run flush with the walls, and the Hearth is of Tiles and is as far out into the Room at the Ends as before the fire, which is Generally Five foot in the Low'r rooms, and the piece over where the mantle tree should be is made as ours with Joiners' work, and as I suppose is fasten'd to iron rods inside. The House where the Vendue was, had Chimney Corners like ours, and they and the hearths were laid with the finest tile that I ever see, and the stair cases laid all with white tile which is ever clean, and so are the walls of the Kitchen which had a Brick floor. They were making Great preparations to Receive their Governor, Lord Cornbury from the Jerseys, and for that End raised the militia to Guard him on shore to the fort.

They are Generally of the Church of England and have a New England Gentleman for their minister, and a very fine church set out with all Customary requisites. There are also a Dutch and Divers Conventicles as they call them, viz. Baptist, Quakers, &c. They are not strict in keeping the Sabbath as in Boston and other places where I had been, But seem to deal with great exactness as far as I see or Deal with. They are sociable to one another and Courteous and Civil to strangers and fare well in their houses. The English go very fashionable in their dress. But the Dutch, especially the

———————
Some of the spelling in this document has been modernized.

*The Journal of Madam Knight* [Sarah Kemble Knight], ed. Malcolm Freidberg (Boston, 1972), 28–34.

middling sort, differ from our women, in their habit go loose, wear French muches which are like a Cap and a head band in one, leaving their ears bare, which are set out with Jewels of a large size and many in number. And their fingers hoop't with Rings, some with large stones in them of many Colours as were their pendants in their ears, which You should see very old women wear as well as Young.

They have Vendues very frequently and make their Earnings very well by them, for they treat with good Liquor Liberally, and the Customers Drink as Liberally and Generally pay for't as well, by paying for that which they Bid up Briskly for, after the sack has gone plentifully about, tho' sometimes good penny worths are got there. Their Diversions in the Winter is Riding Sleighs about three or four Miles out of Town, where they have Houses of entertainment at a place called the Bowery, and some go to friends' Houses who handsomely treat them. . . .

. . . [A]fter about a fortnight's stay there I left New-York with no Little regret, and Thursday, Dec. 21, set out for New Haven with my Kinsman Trowbridge, and the man that waited on me about one afternoon, and about three come to half-way house about ten miles out of town, where we Baited and went forward, and about 5 come to Spitting Devil, Else Kings bridge, where they pay three pence for passing over with a horse, which the man that keeps the Gate set up at the end of the Bridge receives.

We hoped to reach the french town and Lodge there that night, but unhappily lost our way about four miles short, and being overtaken by a great storm of wind and snow which set full in our faces about dark, we were very uneasy. But meeting one Gardner who lived in a Cottage thereabout, offered us his fire to set by, having but one poor Bed, and his wife not well, &c. or he would go to a House with us, where he thought we might be better accommodated—thither we went, But a surly old she Creature, not worthy the name of woman, who would hardly let us go into her Door, though the weather was so stormy none but she would have turned out a Dog. But her son whose name was gallop, who lived Just by Invited us to his house and shewed me two pair of stairs, viz. one up the loft and the other up the Bed, which was as hard as it was high, and warmed it with a hot stone at the feet. I lay very uncomfortably, insomuch that I was so very cold and sick I was forced to call them up to give me something to warm me. They had nothing but milk in the house, which they Boiled, and to make it better sweetened with molasses, which I not knowing or thinking oft till it was down and coming up again which it did in so plentiful a manner that my host was soon paid double for his portion, and that in specie. But I believe it did me service in Clearing my stomach. So after this sick and weary night at East Chester, (a very miserable poor place,) the weather being now fair, Friday the 22d Dec. we set out for New Rochell, where being come we had good Entertainment and Recruited ourselves very well. This is a very pretty place well compact, and good handsome houses, Clean, good and passable Roads, and situated on a Navigable River, abundance of land well fined and Cleared all along as we passed, which caused in me a Love to the place, which I could have been content to live in it. Here we Rid over a Bridge made of one entire stone of such a Breadth that a cart might pass with safety, and to spare— it lay over a passage cut through a Rock to convey water to a mill not far off. Here are three fine Taverns within call of each other, very good provision for Travelers. . . .

# 4. Per Kalm Offers Impressions
# of New Jersey and New York, 1750

## [New Jersey]

*Trenton* is a long narrow town, situated at some distance from the Delaware River, on a sandy plain; it belongs to New Jersey, and they reckon it thirty miles from Philadelphia. . . . [F]rom Trenton to New Brunswick, the travellers go in wagons which set out every day for that place. Several of the inhabitants however subsist on the transportation of all sorts of goods, which are sent every day in great quantities, either from Philadelphia to New York, or from there to the former place. Between Philadelphia and Trenton all goods are transported by water, but between Trenton and New Brunswick they are carried by land, and both these means of transportation belong to people of this town. . . .

We continued our journey in the morning; the country through which we passed was for the greatest part level, though sometimes there were some long hills; some parts were covered with trees, but by far the greater part of the country was without woods; on the other hand I never saw any place in America, the city excepted, so well peopled. An old man, who lived in the neighborhood and accompanied us a short distance, assured me however that he could well remember the time when between Trenton and New Brunswick there were not above three farms, and he reckoned it was about fifty and some odd years ago. During the greater part of the day we saw very extensive cultivated fields on both sides of the road, and we observed that the country generally had a noticeable declivity towards the south. Near almost every farm was a spacious orchard full of peaches and apple trees, and in some of them the fruit had fallen from the trees in such quantities as to cover nearly the whole surface of the ground. Part of it they left to rot, since they could not take care of it all or consume it. Wherever we passed by we were welcome to go into the fine orchards and gather our hats and pockets full of the choicest fruit, without the owner so much as looking at us. Cherry trees were planted near the farms, on the roads, etc.

The *barns* had a peculiar kind of construction in this locality, of which I shall give a concise description. The main building was very large almost the size of a small church; the roof was high, covered with wooden shingles, sloping on both sides, but not steep. The walls which supported it were not much higher than a full grown man; but on the other hand the breadth of the building was all the greater. In the middle was the threshing floor and above it, or in the loft or garret, they put the unthrashed grain, the straw, or anything else, according to the season. On one side were stables for the horses, and on the other for the cows. The young stock had also their particular stables or stalls, and in both ends of the building were large doors, so that one could drive in with a cart and horses through one of them, and go out at the other. Here under one roof therefore were the thrashing floor, the barn, the

Adolph B. Benson, ed., *Peter Kalm's Travels in North America: The English Version of 1770,* (New York: Wilson-Erickson Inc., 1937), I, 117–119, 121, 129–130, 141–143, 342–345, 602–603.

stables, the hay loft, the coach house, etc. This kind of building is used chiefly by the Dutch and Germans, for it is to be observed that the country between Trenton and New York is not inhabited by many Englishmen, but mostly by Germans or Dutch, the latter of which are especially numerous.

*Indians.* Before I proceed I must mention one thing about the Indians or old Americans; for this account may find readers, who, like many people of my acquaintance, have the opinion that North America is almost wholly inhabited by savage or heathen nations; and they may be astonished that I do not mention them more frequently in my account. Others may perhaps imagine that when I state in my journal that the country is widely cultivated, that in several places houses of stone or wood are built, round which are grain fields, gardens and orchards, that I am speaking of the property of the Indians. To undeceive them I shall here give the following explanation. The country, especially that along the coasts in the English colonies, is inhabited by Europeans, who in some places are already so numerous that few parts of Europe are more populous. The Indians have sold the land to the Europeans, and have retired further inland. In most parts you may travel twenty Swedish miles, or about a hundred and twenty English miles, from the coast, before you reach the first habitation of the Indians. And it is very possible for a person to have been at Philadelphia and other towns on the seashore for half a year without so much as seeing an Indian. . . .

About noon we arrived at *New Brunswick,* (situated about thirty miles from Trenton and sixty from Philadelphia), a pretty little town in the province of New Jersey, in a valley on the west side of the river Raritan. On account of its low location, it cannot be seen (coming from Pennsylvania) before you get to the top of the hill, which is quite close to it. The town extends north and south along the river. The German inhabitants have two churches, one of stone and the other of wood. The English church is likewise of the latter material, but the Presbyterians are building one of stone. The Town Hall makes a good appearance. Some of the other houses are built of brick, but most of them are made either wholly of wood, or of brick and wood. The wooden buildings are not made of strong timber, but merely of boards or planks, which are within joined by laths. Houses built of both wood and brick have only the wall towards the street made of the latter, all the other sides being boards. This peculiar kind of ostentation would easily lead a traveller who passes through the town in haste to believe that most of the houses are built of brick. The houses are covered with shingles. Before each door is a veranda to which you ascend by steps from the street; it resembles a small balcony, and has benches on both sides on which the people sit in the evening to enjoy the fresh air and to watch the passersby. The town has only one street lengthways, and at its northern extremity there is a cross street: both of these are of a considerable length.

The river Raritan passes close by the town, and is deep enough for large sailing vessels. Its breadth near the town is about the distance of a common gun shot. The tide comes up several miles beyond the town, which contributes not a little to the ease and convenience of securing vessels which dock along the bridge. The river has generally very high and steep banks on both sides, but near the town there are no such banks, because it is situated in a low valley. One of the streets is almost entirely inhabited by Dutchmen who came hither from Albany, and for that reason it is called Albany Street. These Dutch people keep company only with themselves, and seldom or never go amongst the other inhabitants, living as it were quite separate from them. . . .

**[New York]**

*The Jews.* Besides the different sects of Christians, many Jews have settled in New York, who possess great privileges. They have a synagogue, own their dwelling-houses, possess large country-seats and are allowed to keep shops in town. They have likewise several ships, which they load and send out with their own goods. In fine, they enjoy all the privileges common to the other inhabitants of this town and province. . . .

During my residence in New York, both at this time and for the next two years, I was frequently in company with Jews. I was informed among other things that these people never boiled any meat for themselves on Saturday, but that they always did it the day before, and that in winter they kept a fire during the whole Saturday. They commonly eat no pork; yet I have been told by several trustworthy men that many of them (especially the young Jews) when travelling, did not hesitate the least about eating this or any other meat that was put before them, even though they were in company with Christians. I was in their synagogue last evening for the first time, and to-day at noon I visited it again, and each time I was put in a special seat which was set apart for strangers or Christians. A young rabbi read the divine service, which was partly in Hebrew and partly in the Rabbinical dialect. Both men and women were dressed entirely in the English fashion; the former had their hats on, and did not once take them off during the service. The galleries, I observed, were reserved for the ladies, while the men sat below. During prayers the men spread a white cloth over their heads, which perhaps is to represent sackcloth. But I observed that the wealthier sort of people had a much richer cloth than the poorer ones. Many of the men had Hebrew books, in which they sang and read alternately. The rabbi stood in the middle of the synagogue and read with his face turned towards the east; he spoke however so fast as to make it almost impossible for any one to understand what he said. . . .

The *first colonists* in New York were Dutchmen. When the town and its territories were taken by the English and left to them by the next peace in exchange for Surinam, the old inhabitants were allowed either to remain at New York, and enjoy all the privileges and immunities which they were possessed of before, or to leave the place with all their goods. Most of them chose the former; and therefore the inhabitants both of the town and of the province belonging to it are still for the greatest part Dutch, who still, and especially the old people, speak their mother tongue.

They were beginning however by degrees to change their manners and opinions, chiefly indeed in the town and in its neighborhood; for most of the young people now speak principally English, go only to the English church, and would even take it amiss if they were called Dutchmen and not Englishmen. . . .

*The Dutch Settlers.* But the lack of people in this province may likewise be accounted for in a different manner. As the Dutch, who first cultivated this section, obtained the liberty of staying here by the treaty with England, and of enjoying all their privileges and advantages without the least limitation, each of them took a very large piece of ground for himself, and many of the more powerful heads of families made themselves the possessors and masters of a country of as great territory as would be sufficient to form one of our moderately-sized, and even one of our large, parishes. Most of them being very rich, their envy of the English led them not to sell them any land, but at an excessive rate, a practice which is still punctually observed among their descendants. The English therefore, as well as people of other nations, have but little encouragement to settle here. On the other hand, they have sufficient opportunity in the other provinces to purchase land at a more moderate price, and with more security to themselves. It is not to be wondered then, that so many parts of New York are still uncultivated, and that it has entirely the appearance of a frontier-land. This instance may teach us how much a small mistake in a government can hamper the settling of a country. . . .

*Trade.* . . . Albany carries on a considerable commerce with New York, chiefly in furs, boards, wheat, flour, peas, several kinds of timber, etc. There is not a place in all the British colonies, the Hudson's Bay settlements excepted, where such quantities of furs and skins are bought of the Indians as at Albany. Most of the merchants in this town send a clerk or agent to Oswego, an English trading town on Lake Ontario, to which the Indians come with their furs. I intend to give a more minute account of this place in my Journal for the year 1750. The merchants from Albany spend the whole summer at Oswego, and trade with many tribes of Indians who come with their goods. Many people have assured me that the Indians are frequently cheated in disposing of their goods, especially when they are drunk, and that sometimes they do not get one half or even one tenth of the value of their goods. I have been a witness to several transactions of this kind. The merchants of Albany glory in these tricks, and are highly pleased when they have given a poor Indian, a greater portion of brandy than he can stand, and when they can, after that, get all his goods for mere trifles. The Indians often find when they are sober again, that they have for once drunk as much as they are able of a liquor which they value beyond anything else in the whole world, and they are quite insensible to their loss if they again get a draught of this nectar. Besides this trade at Oswego, a number of Indians come to Albany from several places especially from Canada; but from this latter place, they hardly bring anything but beaver skins. . . .

*The Dutch in Albany.* The inhabitants of Albany and its environs are almost all Dutchmen. They speak Dutch, have Dutch preachers, and the divine service is performed in that language. Their manners are likewise quite Dutch; their dress is however like that of the English. It is well known that the first Europeans who settled in the province of New York were Dutchmen. During the time that they were the masters of this province, they seized New Sweden of which they were jealous. However, the pleasure of possessing this conquered land and their own was but of short duration, for towards the end of 1664 Sir Robert Carr, by order of King Charles the second, went to New York, then New Amsterdam, and took it. Soon after Colonel Nicolls went to Albany, which then bore the name of Fort Orange, and upon taking it, named it Albany, from the Duke of York's Scotch title. The Dutch inhabitants were allowed either to continue where they were, and under the protection of the English to enjoy all their former privileges, or to leave the country. The greater part of them chose to stay and from them the Dutchmen are descended who now live in the province of New York, and who possess the greatest and best estates in that province.

The avarice, selfishness and immeasurable love of money of the inhabitants of Albany are very well known throughout all North America, by the French and even by the Dutch, in the lower part of New York province. If anyone ever intends to go to Albany it is said in jest that he is about to go to the land of Canaan, since Canaan and the land of the Jews mean one and the same thing, and that Albany is a fatherland and proper home for arch-Jews, since the inhabitants of Albany are even worse. If a real Jew, who understands the art of getting forward perfectly well, should settle amongst them, they would not fail to ruin him. For this reason nobody comes to this place without the most pressing necessity; and therefore I was asked in several places, both this and the following year, what induced me to make the pilgrimage to this New Canaan. I likewise found that the judgment which people formed of them was not without foundation. For though they seldom see any strangers, (except those who go from the British colonies to Canada and back again) and one might therefore expect to find victuals and accommodation for travellers cheaper than in places where they always resort, yet I experienced the contrary. I was here obliged to pay for everything twice, thrice and four times as much as in any part of North America which I have passed through. If I wanted their assistance, I was obliged to pay them very well for it, and when I wanted to purchase anything or be helped in some case or other, I could at once see what kind of blood ran in their veins, for they either fixed exorbitant prices for their services or were very reluctant to assist me. Such was this people in general. However, there were some among them who equalled any in North America or anywhere else, in politeness, equity, goodness, and readiness to serve and to oblige; but their number fell far short of that of the former. If I may be allowed to declare my conjectures, the origin of the inhabitants of Albany and its neighborhood seems to me to be as follows. While the Dutch possessed this country, and intended to people it, the government sent a pack of vagabonds of which they intended to clear their native country, and sent them along with a number of other settlers to this province. The vagabonds were sent far from the other colonists, upon the borders towards the Indians and other enemies, and a few honest families were persuaded to go with them, in order to keep them in bounds. I cannot in any other way account for the difference between the inhabitants of Albany and the other descendants of so respectable a nation as the Dutch, who are settled in the lower part of New York province. The latter are civil, obliging, just in prices, and sincere; and though they are not ceremonious, yet they are well meaning and honest and their promises may be relied on. . . .

*Dutch Food.* The whole region about the Hudson River above Albany is inhabited by the Dutch: this is true of Saratoga as well as other places. During my stay with them I had an opportunity of observing their way of living, so far as food is concerned, and wherein they differ from other Europeans. Their breakfast here in the country was as follows: they drank tea in the customary way by putting brown sugar into the cup of tea. With the tea they ate bread and butter and radishes; they would take a bite of the bread and butter and would cut off a piece of the radish as they ate. They spread the butter upon the bread and it was each one's duty to do this for himself. They sometimes had small round cheeses (not especially fine tasting) on the table, which they cut into thin slices and spread upon the buttered bread. At noon they had a regular meal and I observed nothing unusual about it. In the evening they made a porridge of corn, poured it as customary into a dish, made a large hole in the center into which they poured fresh milk, but more often buttermilk. They ate it taking half a spoonful of porridge and half of milk. As they ordinarily took more milk than porridge, the milk in the dish was soon consumed. Then more milk was poured in. This was their supper nearly every evening. After that they would eat some meat left over from the noonday meal, or bread and butter with cheese. If any of the porridge remained from the evening, it was boiled with butter-milk in the morning so that it became almost like a gruel. In order to make the butter-milk more tasty, they added either syrup or sugar, after it had been poured into the dish. Then they stirred it so that all of it should be equally sweet. Pudding or pie, the Englishman's perpetual dish, one seldom saw among the Dutch, neither here nor in Albany. But they were indeed fond of meat. . . .

## 5. William Penn Offers A Prospectus for Merchants, 1683

. . . Your Provincial Settlements both within and without the Town, for Scituation and Soil, are without Exception; Your City-Lot is an whole Street, and one side of a Street, from River to River, containing near one hundred Acers, not easily valued, which is besides your four hundred Acers in the City Liberties, part of your twenty thousand Acers in the Countery. Your Tannery hath such plenty of Bark, the Saw-Mill for Timber, the place of the Glass-house so conveniently posted for Water-carriage, the City-Lot for a Dock, and the Whalery for a sound and fruitful Bank, and the Town Lewis by it to help your People, that by Gods blessing the Affairs of the Society will naturally grow in their Reputation and Profit. I am sure I have not turned my back upon any Offer that tended to its Prosperity; and though I am ill at Projects, I have sometimes put in for a Share with her Officers, to countenance and advance her Interest. You are already informed what is fit for you further to do, whatsoever tends to the Promotion of Wine, and to the Manufacture of Linnen in these parts, I cannot but wish you to promote it; and the French People are most likely in both respects to answer that design: To that end, I would advise you to send for some Thousands of Plants out of France, with some able Vinerons, and People of the other Vocation: But because I believe you have been entertained with this and some other profitable Subjects by your President, I shall add no more, but to assure you, that I am heartily inclined to advance your just Interest, and that you will always find me

Your Kind Cordial Friend,<br>WILLIAM PENN.

Philadelphia, the 16th of the 6th Moneth, call'd August, 1683.

### *A Short Advertisement upon the Scituation and Extent of the City of Philadelphia and the Ensuing Plat-form thereof, by the Surveyor General.*

The City of Philadelphia, now extends in Length, from River to River, two Miles, and in Breadth near a Mile; and the Governour, as a further manifestation of his Kindness to the Purchasers, hath freely given them their respective Lots in the City, without defalcation of any their Quantities of purchased Lands; and as its now placed and modelled between two Navigable Rivers upon a Neck of Land, and that Ships may ride in good Anchorage, in six or eight Fathom Water in both Rivers,

---

Albert Cook Myers, ed., *Narratives of Early Pennsylvania, West New Jersey, and Delaware* (New York: Charles Scribner's Sons, 1912; copyright renewed Barnes and Noble, 1940), 240–244.

close to the City, and the Land of the City level, dry and wholsom: such a Scituation is scarce to be parallel'd.

The Model of the City appears by a small Draught now made, and may hereafter, when time permits, be augmented; and because there is not room to express the Purchasers Names in the Draught, I have therefore drawn Directions of Reference, by way of Numbers, whereby may be known each mans Lot and Place in the City.

The City is so ordered now, by the Governour's Care and Prudence, that it hath a Front to each River, one half at Delaware, the other at Skulkill; and though all this cannot make way for small Purchasers to be in the Fronts, yet they are placed in the next Streets, contiguous to each Front, *viz.* all Purchasers of One Thousand Acres, and upwards, have the Fronts, (and the High-street) and to every five Thousand Acres Purchase, in the Front about an Acre, and the smaller Purchasers about half an Acre in the backward Streets; by which means the least hath room enough for House, Garden and small Orchard, to the great Content and Satisfaction of all here concerned.

The City, (as the Model shews) consists of a large Front-street to each River, and a High-street (near the middle) from Front (or River) to Front, of one hundred Foot broad, and a Broad-street in the middle of the City, from side to side, of the like breadth. In the Center of the City is a Square of ten Acres; at each Angle are to be Houses for publick Affairs, as a Meeting-House, Assembly or State-House, Market-House, School-House, and several other Buildings for Publick Concerns. There are also in each Quarter of the City a Square of eight Acres, to be for the like Uses, as the Moore-fields in London; and eight Streets, (besides the High-street), that run from Front to Front, and twenty Streets, (besides the Broad-street) that run cross the City, from side to side; all these Streets are of fifty Foot breadth.

In each Number in the Draught, in the Fronts and High-street, are placed the Purchasers of One Thousand Acres, and upwards, to make up five Thousand Acres Lot, (both in the said Fronts and High-street) and the Numbers direct to each Lot, and where in the City; so that thereby they may know where their Concerns are therein.

The Front Lots begin at the South-ends of the Fronts, by the Numbers, and so reach to the North-ends, and end at Number 43.

The High-street Lots begin towards the Fronts; at Number 44, and so reach to the Center.

The lesser Purchasers begin at Number 1, in the second Streets, and so proceed by the Numbers, as in the Draught; the biggest of them being first placed, nearest to the Fronts.

## 6. Francis Daniel Pastorius Recalls the Founding of Germantown, 1685

On October 24, 1683, I, Francis Daniel Pastorius, with the good will of the governor, laid out another new city, of the name of Germanton, or Germanopolis, at a distance of two hours' walk from Philadelphia, where there are a good black fertile

Francis Daniel Pastorius, "Circumstantial Geographical Description of Pennsylvania, 1700," in Albert Cook Myers, ed., *Narratives of Early Pennsylvania, West New Jersey, and Delaware* (New York: Charles Scribner's Sons, 1912; copyright renewed by Barnes and Noble, 1940), 380–386.

soil, and many fresh wholesome springs of water, many oak, walnut, and chestnut trees, and also good pasturage for cattle. The first settlement consisted of only twelve families of forty-one persons, the greater part High German mechanics and weavers, because I had ascertained that linen cloth would be indispensable.

I made the main street of this city sixty feet wide, and the side streets forty; the space, or ground-plot, for each house and garden was as much as three acres of land, but for my own dwelling twice as much. Before this, I had also built a little house in Philadelphia, thirty feet long and fifteen wide. Because of the scarcity of glass the windows were of oiled paper. Over the house-door I had written: *Parva Domus, sed amica Bonis, procul este profani* [A little house, but a friend to the good; remain at a distance, ye profane.], Whereat our Governor, when he visited me, burst into laughter, and encouraged me to keep on building.

I have also acquired for my High-German Company fifteen thousand acres of land in one piece, upon the condition that, within a year, they shall actually place thirty households thereon; and for this reason, that we High-Germans may maintain a separate little province, and thus feel more secure from all oppression.

It would, therefore, be a very good thing if the European associates should at once send more persons over here, for the common advantage of the Company; for only the day before yesterday, the Governor said to me that the zeal of the High-Germans in building pleased him very much, and that he preferred them to the English, and would grant them special privileges. . . .

### Concerning the Inhabitants of this Province

Of these, three sorts may be found: 1. The natives, the so-called savages. 2. The Christians who have come here from Europe, the so-called Old Settlers. 3. The newly-arrived Associations and Companies.

So far as concerns the first, the savages, they are, in general, strong, agile, and supple people, with blackish bodies; they went about naked at first and wore only a cloth about the loins. Now they are beginning to wear shirts. They have, usually, coal-black hair, shave the head, smear the same with grease, and allow a long lock to grow on the right side. They also besmear the children with grease, and let them creep about in the heat of the sun, so that they become the color of a nut, although they were at first white enough by Nature.

They strive after a sincere honesty, hold strictly to their promises, cheat and injure no one. They willingly give shelter to others, and are both useful and loyal to their guests.

Their huts are made of young trees, twined, or bent, together, which they know how to roof over with bark. They use neither table nor bench, nor any other household stuff, unless perchance a single pot in which they boil their food.

I once saw four of them take a meal together in hearty contentment, and eat a pumpkin cooked in clear water, without butter and spice. Their table and bench was the bare earth, their spoons were mussel-shells, with which they dipped up the warm water, their plates were the leaves of the nearest tree, which they do not need to wash with painstaking after the meal, nor to keep with care for future use. I thought to myself, these savages have never in their lives heard the teaching of Jesus concerning temperance and contentment, yet they far excel the Christians in carrying it out.

They are, furthermore, serious and of few words, and are amazed when they perceive so much unnecessary chatter, as well as other foolish behavior, on the part of the Christians.

Each man has his own wife, and they detest harlotry, kissing, and lying. They know of no idols, but they worship a single all-powerful and merciful God, who limits the power of the Devil. They also believe in the immortality of the soul, which, after the course of life is finished, has a suitable recompense from the all-powerful hand of God awaiting it.

They accompany their own worship of God with songs, during which they make strange gestures and motions with the hands and feet, and when they recall the death of their parents and friends, they begin to wail and weep most pitifully.

They listen very willingly, and not without perceptible emotion, to discourse concerning the Creator of Heaven and earth, and His divine Light, which enlightens all men who have come into the world, and who are yet to be born, and concerning the wisdom and love of God, because of which he gave his only-begotten and most dearly-beloved Son to die for us. It is only to be regretted that we can not yet speak their language readily, and therefore cannot set forth to them the thoughts and intent of our own hearts, namely, how great a power and salvation lies concealed in Christ Jesus. They are very quiet and thoughtful in our gatherings, so that I fully believe that in the future, at the great day of judgment, they will come forth with those of Tyre and Sidon, and put to shame many thousands of false nominal and canting Christians.

As for their economy and housekeeping, the men attend to their hunting and fishing. The women bring up their children honestly, under careful oversight and dissuade them from sin. They plant Indian corn and beans round about their huts, but they take no thought for any more extensive farming and cattle-raising; they are rather astonished that we Christians take so much trouble and thought concerning eating and drinking and also for comfortable clothing and dwellings, as if we doubted that God were able to care for and nourish us.

Their native language is very dignified, and in its pronunciation much resembles the Italian, although the words are entirely different and strange. They are accustomed to paint their faces with colors; both men and women use tobacco with pleasure; they divert themselves with fifes, or trumpets, in unbroken idleness.

### The second sort of inhabitants in the province are the old Christians, who came here from Europe.

These have never had the upright intention to give these needy native creatures instruction in the true living Christianity, but instead they have sought only their own worldly interests, and have cheated the simple inhabitants in trade and intercourse, so that at length those savages who dealt with these Christians, proved themselves to be also for the most part, crafty, lying, and deceitful, so that I can not say much that is creditable of either. These misguided people are wont to exchange the skins and peltry which they obtain for strong drink, and to drink so much that they can neither walk nor stand; also they are wont to commit all sorts of thievery, as the occasion may arise.

Owing to this, their kings and rulers have frequently complained of the sins of falsehood, deceit, thieving, and drunkenness, introduced here by the Christians, and which were formerly entirely unknown in these parts.

If one of these savages allows himself to be persuaded by a Christian to work, he does it with complaining, shame, and fear, as an unaccustomed act; he looks about him all the while on all sides, lest any of his people may find him working, just as if work were a disgrace, and idleness were an especial inborn privilege of the nobility, which should not be soiled by the sweat of toil.

**The third sort of inhabitants of this province are the Christian Societies.**

We, the latest arrivals, being Christians included in honorable associations and companies, after obtaining royal permission from England, in the year 1681, bought certain portions of the country for ourselves from the governor, William Penn, with the intention to erect new cities and colonies, and not only to gain thereby our own temporal advantage and support, but also to make the savages gentle and docile, and to instruct them in the true knowledge of God, insomuch that I live in the hope of being able to announce more good news of their conversion to Christianity within a short time.

## 7. Colonist Gabriel Thomas Promises High Wages and Great Opportunities in Pennsylvania, 1698

. . . I must needs say, even the present Encouragements are very great and inviting, for Poor People (both Men and Women) of all kinds, can here get three times the Wages for their Labour they can in England or Wales.

I shall instance in a few, which may serve; nay, and will hold in all the rest. The first was a Black-Smith (my next Neighbour), who himself and one Negro Man he had, got Fifty Shillings in one Day, by working up a Hundred Pound Weight of Iron, which at Six Pence per Pound (and that is the common Price in that Countrey) amounts to that Summ.

And for Carpenters, both House and Ship, Brick-layers, Masons, either of these Trades-Men, will get between Five and Six Shillings every Day constantly. As to Journey-Men Shooe-Makers, they have Two Shillings per Pair both for Men and Womens Shooes: And Journey-Men Taylors have Twelve Shillings per Week and their Diet. Sawyers get between Six and Seven Shillings the Hundred for Cutting of Pine-Boards. And for Weavers, they have Ten or Twelve Pence the Yard for Weaving of that which is little more than half a Yard in breadth. Wooll-Combers, have for combing Twelve Pence per Pound. Potters have Sixteen Pence for an Earthen Pot which may be bought in England for Four Pence. Tanners may buy their Hides green for Three Half Pence per Pound, and sell their Leather for Twelve Pence per Pound. And Curriers have Three Shillings and Four Pence per Hide for Dressing it; they buy their Oyl at Twenty Pence per Gallon. Brick-Makers have Twenty

Gabriel Thomas, "An Historical and Geographical Account of Pennsilvania and of West-New Jersey, 1698," in Albert Cook Myers, ed., *Narratives of Early Pennsylvania, West New Jersey, and Delaware* (New York: Charles Scribner's Sons, 1912; copyright renewed by Barnes and Noble, 1940), 326–333.

Shillings per Thousand for their Bricks at the Kiln. Felt-Makers will have for their Hats Seven Shillings a piece, such as may be bought in England for Two Shillings a piece; yet they buy their Wooll commonly for Twelve or Fifteen Pence per Pound. And as to the Glaziers, they will have Five Pence a Quarry for their Glass. The Rule for the Coopers I have almost forgot; but this I can affirm of some who went from Bristol (as their Neighbours report), that could hardly get their Livelihoods there, are now reckon'd in Pensilvania, by a modest Computation to be worth some Hundreds (if not Thousands) of Pounds. The Bakers make as White Bread as any in London, and as for their Rule, it is the same in all Parts of the World that I have been in. The Butchers for killing a Beast, have Five Shillings and their Diet; and they may buy a good fat large Cow for Three Pounds, or thereabouts. The Brewers sell such Beer as is equal in Strength to that in London, half Ale and half Stout for Fifteen Shillings per Barrel; and their Beer hath a better Name, that is, is in more esteem than English Beer in Barbadoes, and is sold for a higher Price there. And for Silver-Smiths, they have between Half a Crown and Three Shillings an Ounce for working their Silver, and for Gold equivalent. Plasterers have commonly Eighteen Pence per Yard for Plastering. Last-Makers have Sixteen Shillings per dozen for their Lasts. And Heel-Makers have Two Shillings a dozen for their Heels. Wheel and Mill-Wrights, Joyners, Brasiers, Pewterers, Dyers, Fullers, Comb-Makers, Wyer-Drawers, Cage-Makers, Card-Makers, Painters, Cutlers, Rope-Makers, Carvers, Block-Makers, Turners, Button-Makers, Hair and Wood Sieve-Makers, Bodies-Makers [corset-makers], Gun-Smiths, Lock-Smiths, Nailers, File-Cuters, Skinners, Furriers, Glovers, Patten-Makers, Watch-Makers, Clock-Makers, Sadlers, Coller-Makers, Barbers, Printers, Book-Binders, and all other Trades-Men, their Gains and Wages are about the same proportion as the forementioned Trades in their Advancements, as to what they have in England.

Of Lawyers and Physicians I shall say nothing, because this Countrey is very Peaceable and Healthy; long may it so continue and never have occasion for the Tongue of the one, nor the Pen of the other, both equally destructive to Mens Estates and Lives; besides forsooth, they, Hang-Man like, have a License to Murder and make Mischief. Labouring-Men have commonly here, between 14 and 15 Pounds a Year, and their Meat, Drink, Washing and Lodging; and by the Day their Wages is generally between Eighteen Pence and a Half a Crown, and Diet also; But in Harvest they have usually between Three and Four Shillings each Day, and Diet. The Maid Servants Wages is commonly betwixt Six and Ten Pounds per Annum, with very good Accommodation. And for the Women who get their Livelihood by their own Industry, their Labour is very dear, for I can buy in London a Cheese-Cake for Two Pence, bigger than theirs at that price when at the same time their Milk is as cheap as we can buy it in London, and their Flour cheaper by one half.

Corn and Flesh, and what else serves Man for Drink, Food and Rayment, is much cheaper here than in England, or elsewhere; but the chief reason why Wages of Servants of all sorts is much higher here than there, arises from the great Fertility and Produce of the Place; besides, if these large Stipends were refused them, they would quickly set up for themselves, for they can have Provision very cheap, and Land for a very small matter, or next to nothing in comparison of the Purchase of Lands in England; and the Farmers there, can better afford to give that great Wages than the Farmers in England can, for several Reasons very obvious.

As First, their Land costs them (as I said but just now) little or nothing in comparison, of which the Farmers commonly will get twice the encrease of Corn for every Bushel they sow, that the Farmers in England can from the richest Land they have.

In the Second place, they have constantly good price for their Corn, by reason of the great and quick vent [sale] into Barbadoes and other Islands; through which means Silver is become more plentiful than here in England, considering the Number of People, and that causes a quick Trade for both Corn and Cattle; and that is the reason that Corn differs now from the Price formerly, else it would be at half the Price it was at then; for a Brother of mine (to my own particular knowledge) sold within the compass of one Week, about One Hundred and Twenty fat Beasts, most of them good handsom large Oxen.

Thirdly, They pay no Tithes, and their Taxes are inconsiderable; the Place is free for all Persuasions, in a Sober and Civil way; for the Church of England and the Quakers bear equal Share in the Government. They live Friendly and Well together; there is no Persecution for Religion, nor ever like to be; 'tis this that knocks all Commerce on the Head, together with high Imposts, strict Laws, and cramping Orders. Before I end this Paragraph, I shall add another Reason why Womens Wages are so exorbitant; they are not yet very numerous, which makes them stand upon high Terms for their several Services, in Sempstering, Washing, Spinning, Knitting, Sewing, and in all the other parts of their Imployments; for they have for Spinning either Worsted or Linen, Two Shillings a Pound, and commonly for Knitting a very Course pair of Yarn Stockings, they have half a Crown a pair; moreover they are usually Marry'd before they are Twenty Years of Age, and when once in that Noose, are for the most part a little uneasie, and make their Husbands so too, till they procure them a Maid Servant to bear the burden of the Work, as also in some measure to wait on them too. . . .

Reader, what I have here written, is not a Fiction, Flam, Whim, or any sinister Design, either to impose upon the Ignorant, or Credulous, or to curry Favour with the Rich and Mighty, but in meer Pity and pure Compassion to the Numbers of Poor Labouring Men, Women, and Children in England, half starv'd, visible in their meagre looks, that are continually wandering up and down looking for Employment without finding any, who here need not lie idle a moment, nor want due Encouragement or Reward for their Work, much less Vagabond or Drone it about. Here are no Beggars to be seen (it is a Shame and Disgrace to the State that there are so many in England) nor indeed have any here the least Occasion or Temptation to take up that Scandalous Lazy Life.

Jealousie among Men is here very rare, and Barrenness among Women hardly to be heard of, nor are old Maids to be met with; for all commonly Marry before they are Twenty Years of Age, and seldom any young Married Women but hath a Child in her Belly, or one upon her Lap.

What I have deliver'd concerning this Province, is indisputably true, I was an Eye-Witness to it all, for I went in the first Ship that was bound from England for that Countrey, since it received the Name of Pensilvania, which was in the Year 1681. The Ship's Name was the *John and Sarah* of London, Henry Smith Commander. I have declin'd giving any Account of several things which I have only heard others speak of, because I did not see them my self, for I never held that way infallible, to make Reports from Hear-say. I saw the first Cellar when it was digging for the use of our Governour Will. Penn. . . .

## 8. Gottlieb Mittelberger Describes the System of Recruiting German Colonists, and the Suffering They Endured, 1754

But what really drove me to write this little book was the sad and miserable condition of those traveling from Germany to the New World, and the irresponsible and merciless proceedings of the Dutch traders in human beings and their man-stealing emissaries—I mean the so-called Newlanders. For these at one and the same time steal German people under all sorts of fine pretexts, and deliver them into the hands of the great Dutch traffickers in human souls. From this business the latter make a huge profit, and the Newlanders a smaller one. . . .

So that not only the common people but even princes and lords might be able to hear about what happened to them; and so that innocent souls would no longer leave their native country, persuaded to do so by the Newlanders, and dragged by them into a similar kind of slavery. . . . I vowed to the great God, and promised those people to reveal the entire truth about it to people in Germany, according to the best of my knowledge and ability.

I hope, therefore, that my dear countrymen and indeed all of Germany will be no less concerned to get news and factual information about how far it is to Pennsylvania and how long it takes to get there; about what the journey costs, and what discomforts and dangers one has to undergo in the bargain; about what happens when the people arrive in America well or ill; about how they are sold and scattered around; and, finally, about what conditions in general are like. I conceal neither good nor bad aspects; and thus I hope that the world, liking an honest man, will look on me as impartial and truthful. Once people have read all this I have no doubt that those who might still have some desire to go over there will stay at home and will carefully avoid this long and difficult voyage and the misfortunes connected with it; since such a journey will mean for most who undertake it the loss of all they possess, of freedom and peace, and for some the loss of their very lives and, I can even go so far as to say, of the salvation of their souls.

To travel from Durlach or Württemberg as far as Holland and the open sea one must reckon on a trip of 200 hours. From there across the sea to England as far as Cowes, where all ships drop anchor before they finally begin the great ocean crossing, another 150 hours. From there over 100 hours until one completely loses sight of England. Then across the Atlantic, that is from land to land, as the sailors put it, 1,200 hours. Finally from the first sight of land in Pennsylvania to Philadelphia, over 40 hours. Altogether such a journey adds up to 1,700 hours or 1,700 French miles.

This journey lasts from the beginning of May until the end of October, that it, a whole six months, and involves such hardships that it is really impossible for any description to do justice to them. The reason for this is that the Rhine boats must

---

Gottlieb Mittelberger, *Journey to Pennsylvania*, ed. Oscar Handlin, trans. John Clive (Cambridge, MA, 1960).

pass by thirty-six different customs houses between Heilbronn and Holland. At each of these all the ships must be examined, and these examinations take place at the convenience of the customs officials. Meanwhile, the ships with the people in them are held up for a long time. This involves a great deal of expense for the passengers; and it also means that the trip down the Rhine alone takes from four to six weeks.

When the ships with their passengers arrive in Holland they are there held up once again for from five to six weeks. Because everything is very expensive in Holland the poor people must spend nearly all they own during this period. In addition various sad accidents are likely to occur here. I have, for instance, seen with my own eyes two of the children of a man trying to board ship near Rotterdam meet sudden death by drowning.

In Rotterdam, and to some extent also in Amsterdam, the people are packed into the big boats as closely as herring, so to speak. The bedstead of one person is hardly two feet across and six feet long, since many of the boats carry from four to six hundred passengers, not counting the immense amount of equipment, tools, provisions, barrels of fresh water, and other things that also occupy a great deal of space.

Because of contrary winds it sometimes takes the boats from two to four weeks to make the trip from Holland to Cowes. But, given favorable winds, that voyage can be completed in eight days or less. On arrival everything is examined once more and customs duties paid. It can happen that ships have to ride at anchor there from eight to fourteen days, or until they have taken on full cargoes. During this time everyone has to spend his last remaining money and to consume the provisions that he meant to save for the ocean voyage, so that most people must suffer tremendous hunger and want at sea where they really feel the greatest need. Many thus already begin their sufferings on the voyage between Holland and England.

When the ships have weighed anchor for the last time, usually off Cowes in Old England, then both the long sea voyage and misery begin in earnest. For from there the ships often take eight, nine, ten, or twelve weeks sailing to Philadelphia, if the wind is unfavorable. But even given the most favorable winds, the voyage takes seven weeks.

During the journey the ship is full of pitiful signs of distress—smells, fumes, horrors, vomiting, various kinds of sea sickness, fever, dysentery, headaches, heat, constipation, boils, scurvy, cancer, mouth-rot, and similar afflictions, all of them caused by the age and the highly-salted state of the food, especially of the meat, as well as by the very bad and filthy water, which brings about the miserable destruction and death of many. Add to all that shortage of food, hunger, thirst, frost, heat, dampness, fear, misery, vexation, and lamentation as well as other troubles. Thus, for example, there are so many lice, especially on the sick people, that they have to be scraped off the bodies. All this misery reaches its climax when in addition to everything else one must also suffer through two to three days and nights of storm, with everyone convinced that the ship with all aboard is bound to sink. In such misery all the people on board pray and cry pitifully together.

In the course of such a storm the sea begins to surge and rage so that the waves often seem to rise up like high mountains, sometimes sweeping over the ship; and one thinks that he is going to sink along with the ship. All the while the ship, tossed by storm and waves, moves constantly from one side to the other, so that nobody aboard can either walk, sit, or lie down and the tightly packed people on their cots, the sick as well as the healthy, are thrown every which way. One can easily imagine that these hardships necessarily affect many people so severely that they cannot survive them.

I myself was afflicted by severe illness at sea, and know very well how I felt. These people in their misery are many times very much in want of solace, and I often entertained and comforted them with singing, praying, and encouragement. Also, when possible, and when wind and waves permitted it, I held daily prayer meetings with them on deck, and, since we had no ordained clergyman on board, was forced to administer baptism to five children. I also held services, including a sermon, every Sunday, and when the dead were buried at sea, commended them and our souls to the mercy of God.

Among those who are in good health impatience sometimes grows so great and bitter that one person begins to curse the other, or himself and the day of his birth, and people sometimes come close to murdering one another. Misery and malice are readily associated, so that people begin to cheat and steal from one another. And then one always blames the other for having undertaken the voyage. Often the children cry out against their parents, husbands against wives and wives against husbands, brothers against their sisters, friends and acquaintances against one another.

But most of all they cry out against the thieves of human beings! Many groan and exclaim: "Oh! If only I were back at home, even lying in my pig-sty!" Or they call out: "Ah, dear God, if I only once again had a piece of good bread or a good fresh drop of water." Many people whimper, sigh, and cry out pitifully for home. Most of them become homesick at the thought that many hundreds of people must necessarily perish, die, and be thrown into the ocean in such misery. And this in turn makes their families, or those who were responsible for their undertaking the journey, often-times fall almost into despair—so that it soon becomes practically impossible to rouse them from their depression. In a word, groaning, crying, and lamentation go on aboard day and night; so that even the hearts of the most hardened, hearing all this, begin to bleed.

One can scarcely conceive what happens at sea to women in childbirth and to their innocent offspring. Very few escape with their lives; and mother and child, as soon as they have died, are thrown into the water. On board our ship, on a day on which we had a great storm, a woman about to give birth and unable to deliver under the circumstances, was pushed through one of the portholes into the sea because her corpse was far back in the stern and could not be brought forward to the deck.

Children between the ages of one and seven seldom survive the sea voyage; and parents must often watch their offspring suffer miserably, die, and be thrown into the ocean, from want, hunger, thirst, and the like. I myself, alas, saw such a pitiful fate overtake thirty-two children on board our vessel, all of whom were finally thrown into the sea. Their parents grieve all the more, since their children do not find repose in the earth, but are devoured by the predatory fish of the ocean. It is also worth noting that children who have not had either measles or smallpox usually get them on board the ship and for the most part perish as a result.

On one of these voyages a father often becomes infected by his wife and children, or a mother by her small children, or even both parents by their children, or sometimes whole families one by the other, so that many times numerous corpses lie on the cots next to those who are still alive, especially when contagious diseases rage on board.

Many other accidents also occur on these ships, especially falls in which people become totally crippled and can never be completely made whole again. Many also tumble into the sea.

It is not surprising that many passengers fall ill, because in addition to all the other troubles and miseries, warm food is served only three times a week, and at that is very bad, very small in quantity, and so dirty as to be hardly palatable at all. And the water distributed in these ships is often very black, thick with dirt, and full of worms. Even when very thirsty, one is almost unable to drink it without loathing. It is certainly true that at sea one would often spend a great deal of money just for one good piece of bread, or one good drink of water—not even to speak of a good glass of wine—if one could only obtain them. I have, alas, had to experience that myself. For toward the end of the voyage we had to eat the ship's biscuit, which had already been spoiled for a long time, even though in no single piece was there more than the size of a thaler that was not full of red worms and spiders' nests. True, great hunger and thirst teach one to eat and drink everything—but many must forfeit their lives in the process. It is impossible to drink sea water, since it is salty and bitter as gall. If this were not the case, one could undertake such an ocean voyage with far less expense and without so many hardships.

When at last after the long and difficult voyage the ships finally approach land, when one gets to see the headlands for the sight of which the people on board had longed so passionately, then everyone crawls from below to the deck, in order to look at the land from afar. And people cry for joy, pray, and sing praises and thanks to God. The glimpse of land revives the passengers, especially those who are half-dead of illness. Their spirits, however weak they had become, leap up, triumph, and rejoice within them. Such people are now willing to bear all ills patiently, if only they can disembark soon and step on land. But, alas, alas!

When the ships finally arrive in Philadelphia after the long voyage only those are let off who can pay their sea freight or can give good security. The others, who lack the money to pay, have to remain on board until they are purchased and until their purchasers can thus pry them loose from the ship. In this whole process the sick are the worst off, for the healthy are preferred and are more readily paid for. The miserable people who are ill must often still remain at sea and in sight of the city for another two or three weeks—which in many cases means death. Yet many of them, were they able to pay their debts and to leave the ships at once, might escape with their lives.

Before I begin to describe how this commerce in human beings takes place I must report what the voyage to Philadelphia or Pennsylvania costs. Any one older than ten years has to pay £10, or 60 florins, for the passage from Rotterdam to Philadelphia. Children between five and ten pay half fare, this is to say £5, or 30 florins. All children under the age of five get free passage. In return the passengers are transported across the ocean; and as long as they are at sea, they get their board, however bad it is (as I reported above).

All this covers only the sea voyage; the cost of land transportation from home to Rotterdam, including the Rhine passage, comes to at least 40 florins no matter how economically one tries to live on the way. This does not include the expenses of any extraordinary contingencies. I can assure readers of this much—that many travelers on the journey from their homes to Philadelphia spent 200 florins, even with all possible thrift.

This is how the commerce in human beings on board ship takes place. Every day Englishmen, Dutchmen, and High Germans come from Philadelphia and other places, some of them very far away, sometime twenty or thirty or forty hours' journey, and go on board the newly arrived vessel that has brought people from Europe and offers them for sale. From among the healthy they pick out those suitable for the purposes for which they require them. Then they negotiate with them as to the length of the period for which they will go into service in order to pay off their passage, the whole amount of which they generally still owe. When an agreement has been reached, adult persons by written contract bind themselves to serve for three, four, five, or six years, according to their health and age. The very young, between the ages of ten and fifteen, have to serve until they are twenty-one, however.

Many parents in order to pay their fares in this way and get off the ship must barter and sell their children as if they were cattle. Since the fathers and mothers often do not know where or to what masters their children are to be sent, it frequently happens that after leaving the vessel, parents and children do not see each other for years on end, or even for the rest of their lives.

People who arrive without the funds to pay their way and who have children under the age of five, cannot settle their debts by selling them. They must give away these children for nothing to be brought up by strangers; and in return these children must stay in service until they are twenty-one years old. Children between five and ten who owe half-fare, that is, thirty florins, must also go into service in return until they are twenty-one years old, and can neither set free their parents nor take their debts upon themselves. On the other hand, the sale of children older than ten can help to settle a part of their parents' passage charges.

A wife must be responsible for her sick husband and a husband for his sick wife, and pay his or her fare respectively, and must thus serve five to six years not only for herself or himself, but also for the spouse, as the case may be. If both should be ill on arrival, then such persons are brought directly from the ship into a hospital, but not until it is clear that no purchaser for them is to be found. As soon as they have recovered, they must serve to pay off their fare, unless they have the means immediately to discharge the debt.

It often happens that whole families—husband, wife, and children—being sold to different purchasers, become separated, especially when they cannot pay any part of the passage money. When either the husband or the wife has died at sea, having come more than halfway, then the surviving spouse must pay not only his or her fare, but must also pay for or serve out the fare of the deceased.

When both parents have died at sea, having come more than halfway, then their children, especially when they are still young and have nothing to pawn or cannot pay, must be responsible for their own fares as well as those of their parents, and must serve until they are twenty-one years old. Once free of service, they receive a suit of clothing as a parting gift, and if it has been so stipulated the men get a horse and the women a cow.

When a servant in this country has the opportunity to get married he has to pay £5 to £6, that is, 30 to 36 florins for every year that he would still have had to serve.

But many who must purchase and pay for their brides in this manner come to regret their purchases later. They would just as soon surrender their damnably expensive wares again and lose their money into the bargain.

No one in this country can run away from a master who has treated him harshly and get far. For there are regulations and laws that ensure that runaways are certainly and quickly recaptured. Those who arrest or return a fugitive get a good reward. For every day that someone who runs away is absent from his master he must as a punishment do service an extra week, for every week an extra month, and for every month a half year. But if the master does not want to take back the recaptured runaway, he is entitled to sell him to someone else for the period of as many years as he would still have had to serve.

Occupations vary, but work is strenuous in this new land; and many who have just come into the country at an advanced age must labor hard for their bread until they die. I will not even speak of the young people. Most jobs involve cutting timber, felling oak trees, and levelling, or as one says there, clearing, great tracts of forest, roots and all. Such forest land, having been cleared in this way, is then laid out in fields and meadows. From the best wood that has been felled people construct railings or fences around the new fields. Inside these, all meadows, all lawns, gardens, and orchards, and all arable land are surrounded and enclosed by thickly cut wood planks set in zigzag fashion one above the other. And thus cattle, horses, and sheep are confined to pasture land.

Our Europeans who have been purchased must work hard all the time. For new fields are constantly being laid out; and thus they learn from experience that oak tree stumps are just as hard in America as they are in Germany. In these hot regions there is particularly fulfilled in them that with which the Lord God afflicted man in the first book of Moses, on account of his sin and disobedience, namely: "Thou shalt eat thy bread in the sweat of thy brow." Thus let him who wants to earn his piece of bread honestly and in a Christian manner and who can only do this by manual labor in his native country stay *there* rather than come to America.

For, in the first place, things are no better in Pennsylvania. However hard one may have had to work in his native land, conditions are bound to be equally tough or even tougher in the new country. Furthermore the emigrant has to undertake the arduous voyage, which means not only that he must suffer more misery for half a year than he would have to suffer doing the hardest labor, but also that he must spend approximately two hundred florins which no one will refund to him. If he has that much money, he loses it; if he does not have it, he must work off his debt as a slave or as a miserable servant. So let people stay in their own country and earn their keep honestly for themselves and their families. Furthermore, I want to say that those people who may let themselves be talked into something and seduced into the voyage by the thieves of human beings are the biggest fools if they really believe that in America or Pennsylvania roasted pigeons are going to fly into their mouths without their having to work for them.

How sad and miserable is the fate of so many thousand German families who lost all the money they ever owned in the course of the long and difficult voyage, many of whom perished wretchedly and had to be buried at sea and who, once they have arrived in the new country, saw their old and young separated and sold away into places far removed one from the other! The saddest aspect of all this is that in most instances parents must give away their young children getting nothing in return. For such children are destined never to see or recognize parents, brothers, and sisters again, and, after they have been sold to strangers, are not brought up in any sort of Christian faith. . . .

## E S S A Y S

A. G. Roeber, historian at the Pennsylvania State University, in the first essay looks at Dutch colonists before and after the English conquest, comparing the immigrant stream to the contemporary English migration. He examines efforts to maintain Dutch culture after 1664, and seeks to explain why those efforts varied from region to region as well as why some aspects of culture continued strong in Dutch ways while other, more public, parts of life quickly anglicized. In the second essay Marianne Wokeck of Indiana University-Purdue University at Indianapolis describes the particular organization of the emigration of Germans to America. She emphasizes the role played, both in recruiting new colonists and in financing individual voyages for others from their own region, by people of German origin who had emigrated previously. She points out that many families paid off their passage by indenturing their teenaged sons and daughters and wonders whether selling their children's labor for a specified period was seen as simply a good solution to the problem of financing the family's new beginning in a new land or was it desperately resisted and accepted only as a last resort?

## Dutch Colonists Cope with English Control

### A. G. ROEBER

Migration to New Netherland was an option considered by people on the margins of the spectacular Dutch culture and economy of the seventeenth century. The first colonists were Walloon refugees from the southern part of the Spanish Netherlands, and they mingled with West Frieslanders and others with a minimal stake in the mainstream of Netherlands society. Most came from economically depressed areas such as Utrecht, whose earlier glory had been eclipsed by the rise of Gouda, Delft, and Haarlem. Amsterdam, the cultural center of the Dutch Republic, and its northern environs contributed few settlers to New Netherland.

By 1673, when perhaps six thousand persons inhabited the colony, relatively few were Dutch. Nearly 40 percent came from High Germany—most from Aachen, Cleves, East Friesland, Westphalia, Bremen, Hamburg, and Oldenburg. From an early list of German immigrants to New Amsterdam and New York between 1630 and 1674, 125 of the 180 families can be traced from the Hanseatic cities or extreme northern Germany and not further south than Cologne, Braunschweig, and Berlin. The earliest recorded emigration among the Frieslanders—a cryptic petition cited by the chronicler Peter Sax in 1639–1640—probably refers to the migration via Amsterdam to North America. Danes and Norwegians were attracted to the colony, and European Jews also trickled into the colony's main town. Together, these European arrivals mingled with the dwindling native Americans and growing numbers of African-American slaves in contributing to the heterogeneity of the settlements.

Before the English conquest, but more notably after, Dutch-speakers further diluted their culture by scattering widely. Thus, by 1663, Horekill, a Mennonite colony on the Delaware, numbered only forty-one Dutch Mennonites from Zwaanendael, under Pieter Cornelius Plockhoy's leadership. Jasper Danckaerts and Peter Sluyter, both radical Dutch pietist followers of Jean de Labadie, secured Bohemia Manor on the Delaware from Ephrahim Hermann in 1683, but the experiment in communitarian farming never exceeded one hundred persons and by 1698 faltered, having attracted no migrants from the Netherlands, only displaced Dutch from New York.

The diversity of the original New Netherland population, together with the scattered, isolated locations of later Dutch-speakers, effectively prevented creation of support networks linking the settlements to each other and back to the Netherlands. Settlements were virtual islands, interested only in the territory immediately surrounding them. The New Jersey Dutch or those on the Delaware cared little about Manhattan's life or what went on in Schenectady or Albany. In 1741 the Swedish traveler Peter Kalm pointed out that in New Brunswick, New Jersey, a supposedly Dutch town, immigrants from Albany lived on one lane in utter isolation from the other Dutch "and seldom or never go amongst the other inhabitants."

Leadership was also a long-standing problem among the Dutch. From the beginning of New Netherland, private merchant-traders were at odds with the Dutch West Indies Company. Private, successful merchant-traders, not initially a part of the vision of the West Indies Company for the colony, smuggled, traded in furs, and in 1639 finally got the company to abandon monopoly for regulation. Even as the Schuyler and Cuyler merchant families emerged into prominence in the 1660s, they married on the basis of religious disputes and business alliances brought from the Netherlands that divided rather than united the merchant cadre. Clerical leaders, too, failed to emerge as symbols of unity and concord. In the 1630s Walloons refused to attend the simple services conducted in a mill loft by Jonas Michaëlius. The liberal Amsterdam classis, which favored an episcopal governance, often supplied ministers to a population drawn from more orthodox parts of the United Provinces favoring a presbyterian polity. . . .

In the late 1650s Governor Peter Stuyvesant attempted to cement a social network of patrons and officers for the colony, much like his contemporary in Virginia, Sir William Berkeley. Through this patronage network, the governor apparently intended to crease a self-conscious governing cadre to whom he formally gave *burgerrecht* (city privileges). Composed of clergy, militia officers, and the members of the government appointed by him, the coalition never came together. The wealthier merchants and younger family migrants failed to share a common vision for the scattered Dutch communities stretching along the Hudson to the Delaware.

This failure is nowhere better evident than in the manner of the English conquest. The dominies and merchants, seemingly possessing a large stake in Dutch culture, urged capitulation. Those living closest to the symbol of Dutch authority, Fort Amsterdam, persuaded Stuyvesant to surrender. There is reason to believe that young people of modest means might have resisted, if given a lead by their superiors. Some excoriated "those devilish traders who have so long salted us," and the West Indies Company itself praised those who had not been "moved by the flattering tongues of Preachers and others who were troubled about their private property, without regarding the interest of the State and Company." Nor did a "charter group" of self-conscious leaders emerge after the Dutch recaptured New York in 1673. Anthony Colve, the interim authority in the reconstituted New Netherland, spent much of his time settling conflicts among fractious communities. Poorer Dutch Lutherans in Albany later in the 1670s mocked their new English rulers, the clash between supposed leaders and commoners an inherited fragmentation now intensified by final English conquest.

The rift between merchants and clerics on the one hand and the commonality on the other surfaced even more dramatically during Jacob Leisler's Rebellion. Leisler's Rebellion in 1689 nonetheless seems to undercut a simple story of assimilation of the Dutch by the conquering English. The rebellion occurred within six years of the Naturalization Act of 1683 and the adoption of an English-style Charter of Liberties that underscored the determination of English leaders to complete the political and cultural transformation of New Netherland into New York. The failure of eminent Dutch merchants and clerics to protest these developments completed their estrangement from commoners. Bitter Leislerians complained that "most of the magistrates . . . were also elders and deacons and therefore heads of our church." Following Leisler's execution, his unrepentant followers "began to feel more bitter hatred against those who had instigated this murder," especially clerical leaders like Dominie Henricus Selyns who reciprocated their hostility. Attendance at Dutch Reformed churches plummeted during the 1690s in the aftermath of Leisler's execution. Ministerial salaries went unpaid. Voting no confidence in spiritual and secular leaders with their feet, large numbers of poorer Dutch farmers left the colony for New Jersey.

Orthodox, conservative, liturgical Dutch Reformed leaders had long faced problems in building networks of support for their people. True, the number of people attending the Dutch Reformed church in New York City increased during the last third of the seventeenth century, so that by 1698 the congregation comprised 57 percent of Dutch adults in the city. True, the loyalty of Dutch women to the church was deep; they represented more than 60 percent of the communicants. Yet this was a church of the eminent: the elders and deacons were exclusively merchants or skilled artisans. Wealthy Dutch women married to English men brought their spouses into the Dutch church. Most members were of more than ten years' standing by the 1680s, and newcomers from other towns like Albany, with an occasional newcomer from the Dutch West Indies or the Netherlands, were generally also merchants, silversmiths, or traders. Defections that began with the outmigration to New Jersey in the 1690s afflicted the town congregations in New York by the 1740s. In 1756 William Smith reported that Trinity Church, the seat of New York Anglicanism, was growing from "proselytes from the Dutch churches." In contrast to the defectors of the 1690s who left to preserve their Dutch religion, the eminent who later abandoned the Reformed church were numbered among the economic and social elite of New York.

The thinness of Dutch high culture in North America had other sources. In the highly rural world of seventeenth-century America, the cosmopolitan, urban quality of Dutch culture could not survive transport beyond New Amsterdam. In urban

New York, portraiture, silverware, and finely crafted furniture certainly flourished for a time among wealthy Dutch merchants. But, before long, Dutch high culture became indistinguishable from English. Mannerist portraiture, painted furniture, and mourning rings and seals reflected bonds that William and Mary, one of whom was chief magistrate and captain general in the United Provinces, enjoyed with their wealthy English and Dutch subjects alike. Colonial Dutch paintings reveal no particular Dutch use of color, background, or technique; rather, English mezzotint engravings were their models.

On the other hand, Dutch vernacular culture, particularly evident in the domestic and religious spheres, architectural styles, dietary habits, and testamentary patterns, was quite vibrant until at least the middle of the eighteenth century. "The tie that binds: church and language," in one scholar's words, accurately described the core of surviving Dutch colonial identity. The defense of the Dutch language, particularly by women in the Reformed church, was critical to its maintenance, especially when support for Dutch schooling was curtailed at the conquest. Dutch Bibles were present in many late-seventeenth-century New York homes. As late as 1769, when a catalog of more than seven hundred "mostly German" books was offered for sale in Philadelphia, the seventy-one titles in Dutch consisted mainly of Bibles, hymnals, and pietist tracts. Secular titles were limited to the occasional atlas, a description of the "old and new East Indies," a city directory of Amsterdam. But there was no Dutch press in North America, no newspaper circulating in that language, and by the 1760s only one Dutch almanac still published, by German or English printers. The arrival of the Dutch pietist pastors between the 1690s and the 1730s, however, reinforced the sense that the spoken, formal language was tied to the church. In the 1720s, with the arrival of these preachers, controversialist literature pushed the total of items published in Dutch in British North America to perhaps five a year from 1725 to 1750, as opposed to the normal single issue of the almanac. Indeed, this connection was so pronounced that in the nineteenth century, when one Dutch-American returned to the Netherlands, no one could understand his dialect any longer except an old man who said that it reminded him of the archaic form of "church Dutch" that had fallen out of use since his youth.

The domestic area of Dutch life increasingly became the focus of a separate Dutch culture that in small ways influenced the broader American culture. Foods like beets, endive, spinach, dill, parsley, and chervil were added by Dutch farmers to North American diets. The onion-potato-carrot stew *hutspot* and oil cakes (*olykoek, koekje:* cookies) enriched colonial cuisine. Dutch celebrations of Christmas, particularly the children's figure of Sinter Claes and the practice of putting out the wooden shoe by the door in anticipation of gifts, found imitators in North America from other cultures. The Dutch homes that spread these cultural practices also taught other colonials to speak of "stoops" (*stoep*) on their houses and to appreciate the bulbous Dutch clay pipes exchanged in trade with native Americans from Long Island and Connecticut to the Mohawk Valley and with other Europeans as well.

This domestically oriented culture was unquestionably a hybrid adaptation to North American conditions. If Peter Kalm's observations can be trusted, most rural Dutch were frugal eaters and contented themselves with *sapaan* every night for supper—a porridge of cornmeal in which, Kalm said, "a large hole is made in its center, into which milk is poured, and then one proceeds to help himself." German settlers from Swabia knew the identical dish as *Stöpper* or *brennts Mus;* their descendants would also adapt native American maize to the traditional dish. Like

Dutch barns, so-called Dutch houses, with their gambrel roofs and flared bell eaves, were in fact composite structures, reflecting many influences of Friesian and Danish origin. They were not simple transfers from the Netherlands. From upstate New York, a painting hung in the Van Bergen home details house and barn with hay barracks in 1735, all reflecting this North American rural architecture one would not have found in the Netherlands. Black slaves, visiting Indians, and whites, presumably conversing in the dialect of the upper Hudson (itself an archaic form of Dutch by the mid-eighteenth century), complete the panorama.

The protection of family and hearth among the Dutch took a practical and serious form in property settlements. Dutch-Roman law provided that, unless a marriage contract had been entered into, a common property system prevailed, with the husband acting as the agent for his wife. Yet both partners held common property equally as well as all property acquired during the duration of marriage. Unlike English common law, Roman law provided for the woman's right to make a will jointly with her husband in disposing of both real and chattel property. The right to perpetuate this practice was guaranteed under the Articles of Capitulation of September 1664. Until the eighteenth century, the Dutch in New York continued to write mutual wills, and most gave the widow life use of the *boedel,* or estate. Moreover, Dutch women continued to use their maiden name in these documents until the early eighteenth century. Even when English practices crept in and husbands wrote wills by themselves, Dutch wives through the 1720s continued to receive the same rights of inheritance as women had who jointly prepared wills in the seventeenth century. The widow continued as before to be the administratrix of the property. Until the 1730s, wills generally gave half the estate to the widow, half to the children, in the event of a second marriage.

Unlike the English, who attempted to establish sons on the land and so excluded daughters from realty, Dutch rural testators until about 1770 either gave daughters land or stipulated that they be compensated in cash equaling the value of land given their brothers. The collapse of Dutch tendencies to provide widows with an equal proportion of the estate enjoyed by children occurred by the 1730s in urban New York; rural Dutch continued this practice for another generation. The most obvious question becomes, then, What accounts for the changed status of Dutch women and the rise of the children's interest and their capacity to inherit a larger estate upon the death of the father, and not at the mother's decease or remarriage?

Economic and social developments provide clues to the gradual erosion of distinctive testamentary patterns. If the Dutch area around Acquackanonk and Totowa is any indication, the practice of equal partition began to produce insufficient estate to sustain all heirs by the second decade of the eighteenth century. Concerned fathers naturally shifted control over diminishing resources to children earlier in their lives, even at the expense of widowed wives. Yet the continuation of control over half the estate exercised by rural Dutch women belies a simple economic explanation. Perhaps the rise of Dutch members of the urban bar in New York by the first decade of the eighteenth century is also significant. Dominie Boel's lawyer brother Tobias in New York was but one of a number of eminent Dutchmen to practice at this, one of the colonial bars where technical pleading and correct procedure were increasingly important. Successful Dutch lawyers penetrated the mysteries of the common law to demonstrate sufficiently their prosperous families' adaptation to the public British legal and political world. With Dutch-speaking legal advisers who could intervene to protect at least some of their interests, Dutch urban women may have felt less threatened by the alien legal system than did their rural cousins. Increasingly, prominent Dutch families intermarried with the English and their legal advisers, further accelerating the decline in distinct Dutch testation customs. It is not coincidental that the peculiar testamentary practices in urban New York began to falter in the same decade that the Dutch Reformed church bewailed the collapse of the language among younger people and noticed the first signs of drift away from the Dutch church by the elite in favor of the Anglican. In rural areas, the decline seems tied less to rational, intentional economic planning than to a withering away of a tradition that was also no longer sustained by the perpetuation of either a separate language or a separate religious culture.

This separate religious culture was closely bound up with a radical separatist ideology of Dutch pietism. Not that all Dutch settlements were affected by this new religious sentiment. Rather, the Dutch farmers who fled into New Jersey after 1700 to escape political, social, and religious ostracism at the hands of a prosperous Dutch-English leadership found in separatist Labadist* pietism a congenial religious sentiment and self-concept. This radical pietist tradition had its origins in Dutch Labadist attacks on ungodliness, interpreted to mean the rather laconic, tolerant style of Dutch Christianity that had accompanied the commercial success of the Republic. Such radicalism enjoyed relatively little success in the Netherlands; it had limited appeal in New York; it would characterize the Jersey Dutch.

The arrival of Theodorus Jacobus Frelinghuysen in New Jersey in 1720 signaled a revival in Dutch Reformed Christianity heretofore unknown in North America. Born in 1692 into a Westphalian Calvinist pastor's family, Frelinghuysen studied at Hamm and Lingen. Ordained in 1715, Frelinghuysen arrived from Friesland to accept a call in 1719 from the Raritan Valley Dutch. His arrival was matched by the emergence in the same year in New York of a second pietist leader, the Lutheran tailor Johann Bernhard van Dieren, born in Königsberg, but probably of Dutch or Huguenot ancestry. Removing to Hackensack by 1725, van Dieren preached in Dutch and German to Lutherans and Reformed alike. These two leaders were joined in 1735 by the Swiss-born pietist leader Johan Hendricus Goetschius, who also preached in both continental languages. It was around these popular, charismatic figures that Dutch religious revivals centered for a generation before the English experienced the so-called First Great Awakening of the 1740s.

Pietist groups gathered by these leaders worshiped informally, as had separatist Labadist groups on the Continent. Religious services in this version of Dutch pietism emphasized emotive hymnody in simple meter and a psalmody that eventually gave way to English hymns. The tendency toward spontaneous prayer and a minimum of ritual was intended to unsettle worship in the congregations that pietists found filled with insincerity and rote prayer.

Using a formal liturgy that employed traditional Genevan hymnody in complex meter, the mainstream Dutch Reformed celebrated a high church Dutch liturgy of preaching and sacrament and observed a strict segregation of the sexes in their churches, with preferential seats going to married males, females, and church leaders. A small increase in church attendance occurred in some traditional Reformed

---

*Labadists were followers of the mystical quietistic sect founded by Jean de Labadie (1610–1674).

churches in the 1720s. But the decade was marked more by a mixing of Dutch and English styles in architecture. Typically, the interior furniture, pulpit, altar, pews, and baptismal font of Dutch churches remained largely unchanged in style. But windows and exteriors that connected worshipers with the English world took on eighteenth-century British forms, with more double-hung sash windows. Fewer churches assumed the octagonal shape traceable to the rural Netherlands. The inclusion of English architectural forms in the very institution that had protected Dutch linguistic and religious distinctiveness accompanied the lament that many of the young were abandoning this semianglicized institution and its Dutch language for worship in Anglican churches, where architecture and language both spoke as one for the dominant culture.

Against this genteel, anglicized New World apostasy, Frelinghuysen mounted an assault using the separatist Labadist radicalism of his youth. Upon his own personal and immediate judgment, he claimed, he could recognize "unregenerate" people wanting baptism or access to the Lord's Supper. The public embarrassment visited upon members barred from taking communion earned him their undying enmity. Pietist children were forbidden to learn the Lord's Prayer by heart, since only a "regenerate" and "awakened" person could say these words and mean them. Prosperous Dutch bristled when told that the saved undoubtedly were to be found almost wholly among the poor and outcast of society. Despite fierce assaults directed at him by clergy and laity in North America and the Netherlands, Frelinghuysen's congregants remained fiercely loyal to him. Frelinghuysen, Goetschius, and van Dieren reached for simple values, preached a biblical loyalty to kin and family, viewed the outside world with suspicion and contempt, and enjoyed, as a result, a devoted following. Gilbert Tennent's friendship for Frelinghuysen was matched by George Whitefield's public admiration for the revivals conducted by the Dutch radical.

The appeal of these charismatic figures to Dutch women and the private sphere they defended against English incursions is suggested by the language of their sermons. When Goetschius's sermon "The Unknown God" was reprinted by John Peter Zenger in New York in 1743, the pastor's introduction immediately presented his own image as the embattled son of a persecuted mother: "Woe is me, my mother, that thou hast borne me a man of strife and a man of contention to the whole earth." Goetschius peppered his text with references to the "daughter of my people," the anguish of women in childbirth, and threats to the "daughter of my people," whose children and sucklings begged in vain for corn and wine from their mothers. These harrowing images drawn from Lamentations and Jeremiah could not have failed to touch the beleaguered Dutch, at whose center Dutch women defended both home and altar. Goetschius urged them to be patient, resisting the wealthy and the hypocrite who thinks "he does God a favor when he oppresses the true believers and usurps God's inheritance." The imagery that tied threats to family and meager property was delivered in a fiery Dutch. Observers who found both message and medium harsh and unbending, Frelinghuysen chastised. Dutch was decisively preferable to English, he retorted, the language of the seductive tempter in the garden. Even Frelinghuysen's exclusion of unworthy, unregenerate Dutch worshipers from the Lord's table smacked of the defense of home and religion against those who had cast their lot with the larger worldly, profane society. Such people would only endanger the entire congregation of the saved by their behavior.

Dominie Goetschius's ministry—a Swiss German-speaker finally ordained in Pennsylvania to minister among the Dutch by the German Reformed Peter Dorsius, the Labadist Frelinghuysen, and Presbyterian Gilbert Tennent—personified radical pietism's weakness as a system of cultural support. This was an international movement largely uninterested in ethnic, national, or cultural issues as such. By its very nature it was antagonistic to elaborate institutions and programs, and once the charismatic leadership of the prophetic first generation dissipated, the movement found affinities with English-speaking Presbyterians but failed to perpetuate uniquenesses of a Dutch religious culture.

The preservation of Dutch dialect within the walls of church and home, however, was already in trouble as the Dutch pietist renewal movement got underway, reinforced by the belated English awakening of the 1740s. The Dutch contributed to the common continental legacy of religious renewal that Scots and Irish shared with them, but even the creation of an indigenous North American clerical association dominated by the pietists, the Coetus ("assembly" or "uniting"), did not preserve the separate quality of Dutch culture for long. The classis at Amsterdam finally agreed, after much pietist lobbying from North America, to create this body in 1747. This organization, coming into being when the Dutch language was already disappearing among younger worshipers, provided a clerical network of exchange and cooperation. But by 1753 "the Dutch spoken by ministers educated in the Netherlands could no longer be understood by the Dutch of the Middle Colonies," according to one contemporary observer. The "common barbarous Dutch spoken in our families" was wholly different from the "studied and ornamented Style of the Pulpit." Preaching in the Dutch churches shifted finally to English, precisely a century after the political conquest of New Netherland. Dutch pietism was tamed, finding an institutional home in Queen's College in 1766, where its peculiarly Dutch qualities swiftly vanished. Van Dieren had dropped his ministry to become a prosperous miller by the 1740s; Goetschius also figured in the founding of Queen's and by the time of his death in 1774 was advertising his services as a tutor in the secular press.

The rural, religious, family-centered Dutch culture of the eighteenth century had enjoyed an extension on life partly because Dutch families perpetuated for a time culturally distinct notions about marital property and faith, at least until mid-century. Yet, lacking a systematic, institutionalized support for educating the young, bereft of the charismatic personalities of the pietist revivalists of the 1720s and 1730s, further isolated by more prosperous Dutch families who adapted to English legal ways, this rural culture too began to fade, though still evident in remote hamlets in New Jersey and New York in the early nineteenth century. Despite earlier seventeenth-century differences in agricultural practices, by the mid-1700s no compelling economic or political grounds existed to perpetuate even a separate domestic culture upon a younger generation.

By the 1730s, local Dutchmen in rural New York and New Jersey were functioning as justices of the peace, and their homespun notions of rough justice fitted the domestic-religious sphere they cherished. But whether the Dutch actually understood the laws they were sworn to administer is unclear. Pastor Heinrich Melchior Mühlenberg met Dutch justices of the peace in New York befriended by his father-in-law Conrad Weiser. One of these Dutch justices, Mühlenberg wrote, "had not been very well versed in English law, and . . . lived rather remote from the higher and more learned authorities. Hence, when a quarrel was brought before him, he was not always able to help, and at times he could do nothing but advise both parties to go out in the courtyard and settle the matter with their fists. Whenever this happened, they had to become reconciled and go home in peace. This finally led to his resigning his office." Among the Hackensack Dutch, Mühlenberg reported, the older people were possessed of "a certain natural honesty and artlessness. They did not use documents, seals, signatures, bonds, and other such contracts. A man's word and handshake were his bond. . . . Like all other nationalities, they have a special love for their mother tongue." By 1750, when Mühlenberg wrote, these Dutch in both New York and New Jersey preserved this mother tongue only among themselves at home. Those who had appeared to function in the public arena without comprehending English laws were vanishing from the scene. In their places, Dutch-speakers entered politics or the bar, even from rural New Jersey, working in the public arena in English for their own people and the Germans, who together may have composed one-quarter of New Jersey's population.

The Revolutionary war in the Hackensack Valley proved to be a genuine civil war, pitting poorer Dutch and English settlers against rivals, reflecting bitter religious and cultural quarrels bequeathed to that area by the displaced radical pietist Dutch of the early 1700s. Dominie Goetschius had laid the groundwork for an ethic of resistance that Frelinghuysen also pioneered on the Raritan: both areas became virulently anti-British by the 1760s. The violent response of the Dutch in New Jersey to English political authority seems to have been linked to the intensity of religious renewal that did less to perpetuate an institutionalized form of Dutch life than it did to reawaken and draw upon a heritage of oppression and embattled self-definition that evoked memories of 1664, 1689, and the religious fervor of brave, embattled, charismatic pietist leaders.

Significantly, the Dutch by the 1770s seemed little threatened by Anglo-American political culture. The Dutch had made that culture their own in great measure both at home and in church organizations. They supported the Revolution in proportion to their affinity for separatist religion and a willingness to make their own way, without oversight by or connection to Amsterdam's classis.

That decision, however, worked for Dutch-Americans only when language, a peculiar domestic culture (reflected in property use and inheritance), and religious doctrine and practice watched over from Europe were no longer broadly valued within the Dutch community. The Dutch had long prospered in commerce, politics, and law. By the 1750s their religious and linguistic particularism had waned. Perhaps in rural areas, churches and homes still operated as cultural havens necessary fro emotional sustenance. But the gradual disappearance of the language, the peculiar inheritance customs, and the religious identity provoked little comment from Dutch-American communities. Since more than half the Dutch-speakers on the British North American mainland lived in New York and another fifth in New Jersey's Bergen and Somerset counties, what had occurred there comprehended the experience of most Dutch in British North America. The remaining third—scattered along the Delaware in New Castle County, Delaware, in Pennsylvania, in Virginia, and in small groups from New York to Charleston and Savannah—had anglicized even faster.

# The Dynamics of German-Speaking Immigration to British North America

### MARIANNE WOKECK

In the century from the founding of Germantown in 1683 to the end of the American war for independence in 1783, more than 100,000 German-speaking immigrants streamed into colonial British North America. The vast majority of these newcomers landed at Philadelphia, and many settled in Pennsylvania. Compared with migrations from the British Isles, the influx of German settlers occurred late—after most colonies were founded. It came in response to a variety of official and private settlement schemes that depended on luring foreign Protestants to take up and develop land as far north as Nova Scotia and as far south as Georgia. Colonial governments and private colonizers alike found Germans an attractive source of settlers; in turn, German emigrants responded favorably to several different promises of free land, low taxes, and religious toleration.

In the beginning, only fairly wealthy people could afford the high cost of relocating from Germany to America, since few of the colonizers in America included free transportation among their incentives to settlement. This financial filter kept the numbers of immigrants small until British merchants in Rotterdam devised a system that allowed emigrants with limited means to cross the Atlantic on credit and redeem debts incurred for their passage by a period of servitude in the colonies. This financing feature of the German emigrant trade coupled with favorable reports about opportunity in the colonies and effective recruiting networks in southwestern Germany brought about a mass relocation that transplanted as many as 50,000 Germans in the years around the middle of the eighteenth century. . . .

While the story of the German migration to the American colonies has been told before, some parts of it are much better known than others. Two fundamentally different approaches stand out among the conventional versions. German and Swiss scholars have most often examined aspects of emigration (or Auswanderung), concentrating largely on circumstances in Europe and reasons that pushed migrants to leave their homelands. This focus makes sense in light of the familiarity these particular historians have with the sources that detail the character of regions with substantial outmigration. Conversely, American historians—members of an immigrant society—have focused on immigration (or Einwanderung), putting to use their training in the analysis of records that throw light on the characteristics of European migrants pulled to settle in America and the situation they encountered there. The advantages of telling the story from the perspective one knows best are clear; and many important details come to light only after close scrutiny of local circumstances. Still, the story is not complete unless the views from both sides of the Atlantic are incorporated into an integrated understanding. . . .

First establishing the general features of the transatlantic migration from eighteenth-century Germany is especially important because it makes it possible to relate contributing elements meaningfully to the overall pattern and to each other.

From Ida Altman and James Horn, editors, *To Make America: European Emigration in the Early Modern Period.* pp. 204–43. Copyright © 1991 by the Regents of the University of California. Reprinted by permission of the University of California Press.

Three basic elements determined the nature of German migration to the American colonies: the various conditions in southwestern Germany encouraging emigration; the opportunities that settlement in America offered; and the recruiting and transportation networks that facilitated and channeled the migration flows. Together, these strands interacted in a pattern whose numerical results became a strong surge of migration from the shallow beginning of 1683 until the middle of the eighteenth century, when this wave forcefully crested, and then a relatively rapid decline of German newcomers landing in America through the twelve years leading up to the American Revolution. As the tide of German immigration swelled, peaked, and subsided, its composition altered from a predominance of families often headed by mature men to relatively fewer families of smaller size led by younger males. The makeup of the flow also changed from a majority of migrants who could pay their fare in advance to a large percentage who counted on indentured servitude to finance their relocation. The composition of the migration evolved over time, too, in terms of the areas from which Germans set out for the American colonies. The Palatinate, Württemberg, and Hesse provided a steady supply of settlers throughout the period; but as the flow of migrants increased, most Protestant areas in southwestern Germany, including the Swiss cantons of Basel, Bern, and Zurich as well as Alsace and Lorraine, and also some territories in northwestern Germany contributed to the migration stream. Similarly, the destinations in the colonies varied as the influx of immigrants changed over time. Philadelphia, after the earliest years, was overwhelmingly the most prominent port of arrival, but German immigrants landed in all of the colonies, especially at the height of the immigration wave around 1750. In the end, examination in these terms of how different strands of people were interwoven in successive temporal phases by dynamics of push, pull, and transportation to form a characteristic pattern of historical relocation reveals that the German migration to the American colonies in the eighteenth century evolved to become the prototype of later, nineteenth-century, transatlantic mass migrations. . . .

. . . No simple, clear-cut pattern emerges, however, when testing whether and to what degree emigrants responded to political instability, agricultural crises, economic recessions, religious persecution, raised taxes, harsh conscription laws, or other likely reasons for widespread discontent. Apparently, all such adverse circumstances were contributing factors in the decision to migrate to faraway places, but any one was rarely sufficient cause to leave home. Even the combination of two or more adversities often failed to set the process in motion. Rather, the "push" factors inherent in political oppression and economic instability endemic to the whole region constituted the necessary background against which other dynamics came effectively into play.

Since war hindered long-range migration, and since adverse conditions at home alone did not cause migration streams to swell, the high correlation of the opening of new areas for colonization with peaks in the migration flow suggests that potential emigrants from southwestern Germany were in large part "pulled" to relocate as they perceived a shortfall between their current position and future prospects at home compared with opportunities offered in distant lands. The lure of sufficient land, low taxes, and exemption from pressing obligations like conscription was strong, yet often not strong enough to sway people actually to leave their homes. As many promoters of private and governmental settlement schemes discovered, active recruiting was necessary for a good offer to catch on. . . .

Foreign Protestants first became a source for settlement projects in the American colonies when William Penn invited Quakers in the Rhineland to settle in Pennsylvania in 1682. He published a promotional tract that extolled the virtues of his new colony for continental Europeans and used fellow Quakers—foremost among them Benjamin Furly, merchant in Rotterdam—as agents to attract suitable investors and help organize their move across the Atlantic. Although the number of emigrants from Germany persuaded to settle in Germantown in 1683 was small compared to newcomers from England who made their homes in Pennsylvania, reports of their success in the New World inspired others to devise settlement schemes for foreign Protestants in the American colonies. In the early years of the eighteenth century, several entrepreneurial Europeans, like Francis Louis Michel, Johann Rudolph Ochs, and Christoph von Graffenried, explored possibilities for German settlement in America and negotiated with the British colonial administration and with some proprietory governors to find mutually satisfactory arrangements for relocating Germans to the frontiers of the New World.

The advantages of such settlement schemes seemed compelling to everybody involved. The enterprising colonizer himself obtained often extensive tracts of land at comparatively very low prices, which he could use as an investment for profit, status, and influence in a foreign land or a safe haven for his flock. The British government and most colonial administrations welcomed such suggestions for large-scale settlement, because giving up undeveloped land in America cost little and new settlers promised profits through improvements to the land, better security against hostile Indians and warring Europeans, and increases in revenue and trade. Both the central British administration and colonial governments discouraged undue speculation, however, by stipulating settlement requirements. These usually granted the developer final title only after a specified number of settlers had taken up land within a given time period. The settlers gained from such arrangements between entrepreneurs and foreign governments because they could pursue opportunities in distant lands without having to bear the costs and risks of exploration and of organizing their own relocation. Authorities in the areas of out-migration welcomed and even actively supported such schemes as long as they perceived them as a means of relieving population pressure on the limited resources in their territories or of ridding their lands of troublesome and burdensome citizens.

This was the theory. In practice, the returns on most of these arrangements were much less clear-cut. The risks often outweighed profits; and organizational failure and discontent among settlers brought many endeavors to a halt before yields met expectations. The German immigrant flow to the American colonies and the pattern of its dispersal reflect widely varying levels of success in both private and governmental settlement schemes. William Penn's invitation to continental Protestants to take up residence in Pennsylvania readily produced imitators, who published and distributed their own promotional tracts and thus drew more general attention to settlement opportunities in the American colonies. Distinctive in Pennsylvania's attraction, however, were Penn's connections with coreligionists in Rotterdam. These links with the Anglo-Dutch business community at the mouth of the

Rhine proved critical in establishing a migratory mechanism for German emigrants to cross the Atlantic. Quaker merchants in Rotterdam were instrumental in devising a transportation system that allowed emigrants with limited means to move in large numbers to the American colonies. This market mechanism in the immigrant supply system for Pennsylvania made that flow different from (more successful than) all its American competitors and a precursor of transatlantic mass migration in the modern era.

In the first three decades of the eighteenth century, the majority of German emigrants depended on governmental and charitable aid to finance their relocation. Although Queen Anne and her ministers supported the idea of settlement of foreign Protestants in the colonies, they had anticipated few direct costs. This was based on an assumption that emigrants too poor to finance the move across the Atlantic would not follow the invitation to settle in America. The Palatine mass emigration of 1709 proved them wrong. In the end, it cost the government enormous sums. The semiofficial sponsorship of the German settlement projects in North and South Carolina and Georgia was less costly for the British government because these projects attracted settlers with some capital of their own or the developers could draw on other sources to finance the relocation and first years of settlement.

Although at first numerically less impressive, those emigrants who decided to settle to Pennsylvania in fact paved the way for the steadily rising migration flow to the American colonies in the first half of the eighteenth century. Two factors in particular contributed to that development. Reports about settlement opportunities in the Delaware valley were generally positive, and a moderate climate, religious toleration, and a "quiet" government were added attractions when compared to features known about other colonies. This reputation especially impressed potential emigrants who lived in territories where religious intolerance and political oppression made life difficult. Anabaptists, Baptists, Schwenckfelders, and Moravians were among those who responded favorably to such reports about opportunities in Pennsylvania. They tended to fare well when they relocated because they could rely on networks among coreligionists that enabled them to evaluate opportunities abroad realistically and to plan their move properly and that often afforded them tangible help along the way or on settlement. In turn, they sent favorable reports home and in effect, if not in words, invited others to join them.

The relatively small numbers of Germans who arrived in Pennsylvania before 1727 reflect the difficulties and above all the costs of relocating overseas. Among those drawn to settle in the American colonies, only few could afford to pay the fare for the voyage, especially if all family members were to travel together. Since the ability to move overseas was so closely tied to the wealth of the potential emigrant, it is not surprising that the early immigration flow at first increased only slightly as the information of settlement opportunities in America spread beyond the circles with direct Quaker and Mennonite connections. The large numbers who came in later years, however, suggest that the majority of potential emigrants then ranked among the middling and poorer sorts of southwestern Germany who made their living mostly as farmers and artisans. It took some method of financing to enable this bulk of likely migrants to move across the Atlantic. That was where the role of the Rotterdam merchants was crucial in shaping the history of eighteenth-century German immigration to America.

With the popularity of Pennsylvania on the rise, two developments came together to allow an extraordinary broadening of the base of potential immigrants to the American colonies. Early on, successful immigrants encouraged those who planned to follow in their steps to bring not only their families but also servants. They reported that land was cheap but labor dear and that such sponsorship of emigrants too poor to pay their own way represented a sound investment. Most such arrangements were informal and agreed on in Germany before all members of such an extended household set out on their journey. The other crucial element of change was that some merchants in Rotterdam apparently decided to accept a number of passengers traveling "on credit." The collateral was the emigrant's willingness to serve a master in America for five years in exchange for the price of the voyage. This selling of contracts for indentured servitude in the colonies was common practice in the English and Irish colonial trade. In the 1720s, it was adapted to the German context.

Further, the merchants involved in the German immigrant trade soon developed indentured servitude in a novel form. In the early 1720s, they found that a considerable number of Germans successfully settled in Pennsylvania were willing to redeem the fare costs of poor immigrants, especially when such newcomers were relatives, friends, or former neighbors. At first, the proportion of German immigrants who relied on friends in the Delaware valley to redeem them in this way was relatively small. As the immigration flow began to swell, however, the practice became more widespread, and merchants devised standard procedures for dealing with passengers traveling on credit. On embarkation in Rotterdam, passengers unable to pay their fare signed a contract that stated how much time they had in Philadelphia to get in touch with those whom they expected to defray the cost for the voyage. If they were unable to locate their friends in the time allowed—usually two weeks—the redemption of their outstanding debts was opened to general bidding from anyone willing to invest in their labor. Unlike the practice common since the early seventeenth century in the English and Irish trade, where the length of servitude was a fixed term but the price negotiable, contracts for German redemptioners took the variable amount of outstanding passage debt as their fixed base and adjusted the length and terms of service accordingly. This feature was particularly useful for families whose total fare debts were high but whose teenage children could take on indentures that would defray more than the cost of one passage. Flexible terms of servitude to adjust to variable amounts of outstanding debt on landing and a large number of children who became indentured servants to finance the relocation of their families characterized the German redemptioner system for the rest of the century.

The success of the system depended primarily on two factors: the willingness of the Rotterdam merchants to extend credit to poor emigrants and conditions of the labor market in the American colonies which made investment in bound labor attractive. The merchants found a number of ways to ensure reasonable returns on transporting Germans to the American colonies. Their strategies for making the German passenger trade a profitable business included striving for a high ratio of passengers per ship and a pricing policy that favorably balanced their costs for recruiting passengers, chartering, outfitting, and provisioning ships with the fare payments they could realistically expect to receive. The other side of the equation, the receptiveness of the colonial labor market to German immigrants, especially indentured servants, eluded control, and even gauging it correctly was difficult. As German immigration to the American colonies became regularized and more dependable, however, Pennsylvania gained predominance among all possible destinations and maintained this position throughout the eighteenth century. Its favorable reputation among immigrants accounted for some of this development. Beyond that, the readiness with which newcomers from Germany not only found a way of making a living themselves but succeeded in doing so at a level that allowed them, in turn, to hire other German immigrants distinguished Pennsylvania's immigration still further from that of New York, the Carolinas, Georgia, and other colonies with early German settlements. Although masters without German roots did acquire indentured servants from Germany, the vast majority of redemptioners were bound to former countrymen. . . .

The success of this distinctive interplay of Pennsylvania's good reputation and the willingness of the merchants to extend credit to emigrants unable to pay for the voyage in advance depended, like all settlement ventures, on a recruiting mechanism to advertise these options. In the 1720s and 1730s, most recruiting networks were personal and very informal. Letters and especially visits from earlier migrants to the "new land" (hence the term "newlander") provided powerful incentives for potential emigrants to leave home. . . .

In the early years, migrants returning to visit their homelands had to have compelling reasons to make the arduous and expensive trip. Many went back to settle inheritances. Most seem to have returned only after they had succeeded in the New World—enough so to impress relatives, friends, and neighbors with their accomplishments. Customarily, newlanders carried letters from other immigrants and sometimes also powers of attorney that enabled them to collect inheritances for those settled in America. Acting as go-between in these ways, the newlanders easily expanded the network of their own personal contacts. On their journey back, they were often accompanied by migrants eager to follow their example, taking advantage of making the move in the company of an experienced traveler. In turn, newlanders seem to have thrived on this leadership role. The money they collected for themselves and for others allowed them to invest in goods with high resale value and also to finance, on commission, the passage of poor emigrants whose relatives or friends had offered redemption on arrival in the colonies.

As more newlanders returned and cast an ever wider net of contacts that inspired still further emigration from southwestern Germany, and as groups of migrants traveling down the Rhine and its tributaries became a regular feature of river traffic in late spring and early summer, local authorities in the areas of out-migration showed concern about rising numbers of departures, and the merchants in Rotterdam increasingly realized the recruiting potential of newlanders for their own transport operations. Until 1739, when the United Provinces of the Netherlands required the merchants to post bond for all German migrants bound for the colonies in order to prevent transients from becoming charges of Dutch taxpayers, many emigrants seem to have traveled to Rotterdam before they contracted with a particular shipper for their transatlantic passage. Thereafter many migrants signed contracts for the voyage before they reached the Dutch border, with the boatmen who transported the travelers down the Rhine often acting as recruiters for the Rotterdam merchants.

Competition among the handful of companies seriously involved in the German passenger trade heated up when groups of emigrants collected close to the Netherlands border awaiting permission by the Dutch authorities to proceed. To gain a competitive edge, merchants offered newlanders free passage and other incentives for advising their contingent of emigrants to contract with a particular shipper. Such arrangements between merchants and newlanders proved profitable enough so that, as the migration wave crested around midcentury, each firm involved in the trade had a regular recruiting network in place which relied heavily on newlanders. The effectiveness of newlanders in stimulating emigration, and generally organizing and guiding the transport of emigrants down the Rhine and preparing for the voyage, was curtailed only when local authorities banned newlanders from operating in their territories. . . .

. . . Increasingly, the North American colonies became a familiar place in the imagination of potential emigrants as colonizers of different kinds publicized their schemes and as pioneering groups—often with direct connections to the settlement's entrepreneur or following a chosen leader—had relocated in the New World and communicated their success to those left at home. When such explicit or implicit invitations to settle in America were combined with an immediate stimulus, such as the visit of a newlander, they translated a general readiness to migrate into many particular resolves to relocate to America, especially as the costs and logistics of the move seemed less daunting if one had the assistance and company of an experienced migrant.

Whatever reasons newlanders had for their return to their places of origin, pride of their achievements in the new land and a keen sense for profits that they could realize through the importation of goods as well as labor became driving forces behind their ventures in the old country. Inheritances released to a newlander provided the bulk of both starting and operating capital for these endeavors. Savings of those who decided to emigrate and who entrusted the arrangement of their affairs to a newlander contributed to this investment fund, and commissions newlanders received from merchants for delivering passengers onto their ships were still another source of liquid capital. Since the merchants recouped their recruiting costs through creative pricing of the passage fares they charged, the emigrants themselves in the end bore the costs of recruitment. In exchange, German immigrants to America could take advantage of an increasingly established transportation system that enabled even those with limited cash assets to relocate overseas.

In simplified terms, three characteristics generated the dynamics that distinguished the eighteenth-century migration flow to the American colonies from those destined for Eastern Europe. First, while starting from similar backgrounds of widespread discontent with conditions and prospects at home and promising opportunities in distant lands, the westward migration stream became more *self-generating* as successful immigrants first reported favorably and then invited and helped relatives, friends, and former neighbors to settle in America. Crucially, they became willing to extend their support to strangers of their own language and general cultural background whose passage debts they redeemed in exchange for labor. Further, this feature of assisting (and exploiting) unknown fellow countrymen, which had started in an informal and personal way, was soon developed into a formalized system for funding relocation. The Rotterdam merchants engaging in the German passenger trade initiated this development as they adapted the existing custom of binding English and Irish servants to masters in the colonies to the special family-focused and ethnically distinct characteristics of the swelling German migration by offering passage on flexible credit, redeemable in several possible ways on arrival in America. They profited from this more open fare policy because their returns increased proportionately with the number of passengers each of their ships carried. Third, in their quest for ever greater numbers of emigrants, the merchants systematically exploited the cooperation of those former immigrants who returned to Europe on business and were willing to use their contacts and personal ethnic identity to recruit still more passengers for the merchants and guide them to the right ships at the port of embarkation. The roles, risks, and profits changed for these three groups of active participants in the German passenger trade—the migrants, the merchants, and the newlanders—as the intensity and the composition of the migration flow varied. Conversely, the pattern of the migration over the eighteenth century also reflects the way interaction evolved and changed over time among these participants who shaped and channeled the stream of Germans across the Atlantic. . . .

. . . Since an increasing number of German immigrants financed their relocation with the help of relatives or former neighbors, who redeemed their passage debts on arrival in Philadelphia, fewer were free to follow their own inclination when choosing where to set up farm or shop. Their place and initial mode of adaptation to New World life were governed temporarily by the local market for German help, especially within the social and ethnic network established from Pennsylvania southward by previous German immigrants, not just a general Pennsylvania labor market.

In midcentury, at the height of the immigration, thousands of Germans arrived each fall, and a large proportion of them depended on fellow countrymen to pay for their move across the Atlantic and to employ and subsidize them during the first years in the New World. Many immigrants found that when they indentured their children, much of the family's debt on arrival could be paid off and some of the cost of starting out anew was lowered because the children were taken care of in someone else's household. Although this financing strategy for relocation to America was common among German immigrants, three-fourths of whom traveled in family groups, it is uncertain how much they viewed indentured servitude for themselves or their children as an employment opportunity, as an educational opportunity, or as a last resort. It is clear, however, that the willingness of other Germans already established in the colonies to invest in the future labor of newly arrived immigrants was a crucial element in fueling the migration. Without this incentive, the pool of potential immigrants to a given place in America remained relatively small, and merchants found it unprofitable to offer fares on credit unless they could count on others to assume the risk. Once this mechanism was tried and proven, it remained in place even when the influx of Germans slowed rapidly in the twelve years preceding the American Revolution. Since it was the transaction of shippers to Pennsylvania and the now large existing German community of the Delaware valley which established the effective way to bring in German settlers and place them not only satisfactorily but profitably into New World life, the role of Philadelphia remained central even as the bulk of new settlement moved largely southward out of Pennsylvania. . . .

# F U R T H E R     R E A D I N G

Randall H. Balmer, *A Perfect Babel of Confusion: Dutch Religion and English Culture in the Middle Colonies* (1989).

Richard S. Dunn and Mary Maples Dunn, eds., *The World of William Penn* (1986).

Joyce D. Goodfriend, *Before the Melting Pot: Society and Culture in Colonial New York City, 1664–1730* (1992).

George F. Jones, *The Germans of Colonial Georgia, 1733–1783* (1986).

Ned Landsman, *Scotland and Its First American Colony, 1683–1765* (1985).

Donna Merwick, *Possessing Albany, 1630–1710: The Dutch and English Experiences* (1990).

Oliver A. Rink, *Holland on the Hudson: An Economic and Social History of Dutch New York* (1986).

Robert C. Ritchie, *The Duke's Province: A Study of New York Politics and Society* (1977).

A. G. Roeber, *Palatines, Liberty, and Property: German Lutherans in Colonial British America* (1993).

Sharon V. Salinger, *"To Serve Well and Faithfully": Labor and Indentured Servitude in Pennsylvania, 1682–1800* (1987).

# The Caribbean Connection

From the beginning of colonization, English promoters looked longingly at the Caribbean, universally seen as the richest part of America. Even before sugar was established as the staple crop of the region, the association between hot climates and riches was firm in the minds of English leaders. They knew about the fabulous wealth of the Aztecs and Incas that had rewarded early Spanish efforts at colonization, and they saw that Spain had risen to the level of a superpower on the basis of the treasure they extracted from their American empire. From the time of Sir Walter Raleigh and Queen Elizabeth in the late sixteenth century, English leaders dreamed of an empire in the Caribbean that would allow England to rival the power of the Spanish. This rivalry was not just economic or political. The English believed that God had chosen their nation as the leader of the true, Protestant, religion, and they needed an income to rival Spain's if they were to defend Protestantism in Europe and carry it to new lands. If they allowed the Iberians exclusive control of the richest parts of America, then God might turn his back on them.

Riches were expected from the Caribbean because of early modern environmental beliefs. Heat was expected to produce wealth—not only rich crops, but also minerals, which were thought to be produced in the earth and drawn to the surface through the sun's magnetic power. But even though the English very much wanted a Caribbean empire, their environmental beliefs caused them to fear the effects of life in such great heat. Could true English culture and society survive in such an alien context? Experience in the seventeenth century seemed to bear out both hopes and fears. Mineral wealth was not found, but, once sugar was established in Barbados from the 1640s, England's island colonies became far richer than any on the mainland. However, the society these planters developed seemed to many to have no relationship to the home culture—reports said planters lived lives of abundance and indulgence, but with little cultural value or stability. Slavery very quickly became the labor system of these colonies and the slave population outnumbered the free.

Many of the same hopes and fears attached to the southernmost parts of the mainland. Beginning with Roanoke in the 1580s, English attempts to create colonies south of the Chesapeake had led to failure. But in the second half of the seventeenth century, interest in the region was revived. Carolina, which eventually separated into two colonies, was founded in the 1660s by a group of Lords Proprietors in England. These promoters recruited settlers in part from Barbados; wealthy planters there planned to pass on their plantations to elder sons and were happy to create

*plantations in the southern part of Carolina for their younger sons. These trans-
planted colonists largely replicated the economic system they had known in Barbados, and sought a crop of comparable economic power to the Caribbean's sugar.
Carolina was the first English colony to begin with slavery as the labor system and a
high proportion of Africans in its population.*

 D O C U M E N T S

Document 1 is taken from Richard Hakluyt's manuscript *Discourse of Western Planting,* written to encourage the English government to sponsor the first English-American
plantation: Sir Walter Raleigh's Roanoke in the Outer Banks of North Carolina. One
goal of that colony was to provide a base for attacking the Spanish, and Hakluyt initiated themes that fueled English ventures: the gold, silver, and gems the Caribbean was
thought to have in abundance; the weakness of the Spanish settlements, particularly
their shortage of food; and the readiness of Indians in the region to fight against the
Spanish. The Providence Island colony was founded in 1630 on many of these same assumptions in a slightly more sophisticated form. Sir Hans Sloane wrote, in document 2,
of the way that colony was remembered many years later and the effect it had.

In document 3 Richard Ligon describes the planters' determination in the transition
to sugar cultivation that made Barbados the wealthiest English colony, along with the
English planters' poor adaptation to the climate and environment of the island and their
treatment of servants and slaves in the island. Document 4, a portion of a published letter by Thomas Nairne, continues the environment theme. In it he reassured prospective
settlers in South Carolina about the colony's climate and the kinds of trade they could
expect there. Eliza Lucas Pinckney, left in charge of her soldier-father's South Carolina
plantation at the age of seventeen, worked to develop indigo, the subject of her letter
reprinted in document 5. Indigo was one of the crops that made South Carolina rich. In
document 6 the French writer J. Hector St. John de Crevecoeur describes his impressions of the elaborate culture of Charlestown, South Carolina, in the mid-eighteenth
century and contrasts that with the life of slaves there.

## 1. Richard Hakluyt Lists the Great Riches to Be Had in the Caribbean and the Ease of Toppling the Spanish, 1584

The names of the rich Towns lying along the sea coast on the north side from the
equinoctiall [equator] of the mainland of America under the King of Spain.

1. Over against the island of Margarita there is a Town called Cumina wherein is
great store of pearl. There be divers boats belonging to the Town which only drag
pearls. This Town is the farthest eastward which the king hath on the north side of
India. It is environed with their enemies, viz. the Indians and Caribs. The victuals
come from this Town to Margarita.

---

Spelling and punctuation have been modernized in this document.

Richard Hakluyt, "Discourse of Western Planting," 1584, in E. G. R. Taylor, ed., *The Correspondence
and Writings of the Two Richard Hakluyts,* 2 vols. (London: Hakluyt Society, 1935), 252–7.

2. The next Town westward is Caracas which is very rich of gold. This Town standeth upon the sea and hath some victuals, but not plenty, and is environed likewise with the Indians their mortal enemies.

3. The town Burborowate was destroyed by 50 Frenchmen and the treasure taken away.

4. The next Town to the westward is called Coro which hath great plenty of gold and victuals, this standeth upon the sea. This is a Civil Country, and some of the Indians brought to a civil government.

5. At Rio de Hacha there is Town called Hacha, where is great store of pearl and silver but no gold, and not far from then there is a pearl house. There is plenty of victuals, the Country civil, and some of the Indians at the Spaniards commandment. Mr. John Hawkins told me he won this Town and was master of it three days in his last voyage.

6. Further westward is a town called Santa Maren alias Marta where is great store of gold but little victuals. This is environed with Indians enemies to the Spaniards.

7. The next Town is Cartagena, where is great store of silver, gold, and precious stone. This Town hath a number of Indians and Cimarrons to their enemies, there is also great store of victuals.

8. The next Town thereunto is Nombre de Dios. To this town cometh all the gold, pearl, stone, and Jewels that cometh from Chile, Peru, and Panama out of the south sea. To this town cometh half the fleet which taketh in half their treasure, and goeth to Havana, and so through the Gulf of Bahama unto the Islands of Corvo, Flores, and the Azores and from thence into Spain. This town hath no victuals but such as cometh from Panama and the islands by sea. By this Town is a gulf called Guluata, where the Cimarrons and the Indians have certain Towns and keep wars daily with the Spaniards as well as the Indians. At the south end of the gulf there is not past five leagues over land into the South sea [Pacific Ocean].

9. The next town is called Vraga alias Var, where is much gold and small store of victuals, this is a civil Country near to the Town, the next is Nicaragua.

10. At Nicaragua is much gold that cometh out of the South Sea, and there is a place where they make their frigates. There is little victuals, the people are civil.

11. In the Bay of Honduras is a Town called Honduras alias Tres Islas, where is gold and hides and great store of victuals. This Town standeth upon an hill very strongly, and is but simply manned. This Town hath within a mile great plenty of Indians, which are at war with the Spaniards.

12. Then there is a town called Porto de Cavallos where is store of silver, stones, pearls, and jewels made and set with previous stones and pearls. To this Town come yearly two ships that go from thence to the Havana, and so into Spain with all their riches. The Town is full of victuals. This port of Cavallos adjoineth to the Golfo Dulce.

13. All the Bay of Mexico is full of Indian Towns and full of victuals. There is one Town named Vera Cruz to which Town cometh all their Treasure from the City of Mexico, and from thence to the port of St. John de Ulloa, from thence to Havana, and so into Spain. . . . A brief declaration of the chief Islands in the Bay of Mexico being under the King of Spain with their havens and forts and what commodities they yield.

There is one Island as the fleet cometh into the Bay named Margarita wherein is great store of pearl. A Rich island full of Maize (which is their corn), oxen, sheep, goats, fowl and fish, great store of fruits, grass and woods.

Over against the said Island northward, there is one other Island named St. John de Puerto Rico which hath store of all manner of victuals and sugar.

The next is a fair Island called Hispaniola, in some part well inhabited having one City called Santo Domingo, which hath a fair haven whereunto many of the ships of the king's fleet come and there divide themselves, some go to St. John de Ulua, and come to Nombre de Dios and other ports of the mainland. This is a fruitful Island for all manner of victual, hides, and sugar.

The next Island is called Jamaica and hath in it great store of victuals.

The next is a fair great and long Island called Cuba. This Island hath a fort and haven in it called the Havana, which is the key of all India. It is called the key of India for that the Spaniards cannot well return into Spain, but that they must touch there for victuals, water, wood, and other necessaries. It lieth at the mouth and entrance into the gulf of Bahama. This Island hath great plenty of victuals, but it is not greatly inhabited.

There be divers other Islands rich for victuals, as Aruba, Curaçao, Marie Galante, &c. having not in them some 20 some 10 Spaniards a piece.

Thus you see that in all those infinite Islands in the gulf of Mexico whereof Cuba and Hispaniola are thought to be very near as big as England and Ireland, we read not of past two or three places well fortified, as Santo Domingo in Hispaniola and Havana in Cuba. I may therefore conclude this matter with comparing the Spaniards unto a drum or an empty vessel, which when it is smitten upon yieldeth a great and terrible sound and that afar off, but come near and look into them, there is nothing in them. Or rather like unto the ass which wrapped himself in a lion's skin and marched far off to strike terror into the hearts of the other beasts, but when the fox drew near he perceived his long ears and made him a jest unto all the beasts of the forest. In like manner we (upon peril of my life) shall make the Spaniard ridiculous to all Europe, if with piercing eyes we see into his contemptible weakness in the West Indies, and with true style paint him out *ad vivum* [to the life] unto the world in his faint colors. And if any man would object that if by his weakness he had lost the Treasure of the West Indies, yet the riches of the East Indies would hold up his head, I answer that those Countries being so far off, and such natural malice being between the Portuguese and the Spaniards as greater cannot be, that it is not possible for him to hold those parts no more than the other, wanting the treasure of the West Indies to support his garrisons both there and in Christendom [Europe] against his manifold and mighty enemies.

That the Spaniards have exercised most outragious and more than Turkish cruelties in all the west Indies, whereby they are everywhere there become most odious unto them, who would join with us or any other most willingly to shake off their most intolerable yoke, and have begun to do that already in divers places where they were lords heretofore.

So many and so monstrous have been the Spanish cruelties, such strange slaughters and murders of those peaceable, lowly, mild, and gentle people together with the spoils of Towns, provinces, and kingdoms which have been most ungodly perpetrated in the West Indies, as also divers others no less terrible matters, that to describe the least part of them would require more than one chapter especially where there are whole books extant in print not only of strangers but also even of their own countrymen (as of Bartolomé de Las Casas, a bishop in Nova Spania), yea such and so passing strange and exceeding all humanity and moderation have they been that the very rehearsal of them drove divers of the cruel Spanish which had not been in the West Indies, into a kind of ecstacy and maze. . . .

## 2. Sir Hans Sloane Writes of England's Remembered Relationship to Providence Island and Central America, 1707

For the better understanding of several matters in the *West-Indies,* I think it proper to subjoin some accounts I received from several Credible Persons who had lived, and made Voyages to several parts in the Neighbourhood of *Jamaica.* These follow without any other order than that of the time they were told me, and enter'd in my Journal which was generally when the Persons came upon their first arrival to wait on the Duke of *Albemarle* as Governour of the Island. One King *Jeremy* came from the *Mosquitos* (an *Indian* People near the Provinces of *Nicaragua, Honduras,* and *Costa Rica*) he pretended to be a King there, and came from the others of his Country, to beg of the Duke of *Albemarle,* Governor of *Jamaica,* his Protection, and that he would send a Governour thither, with a power to War on the *Spaniards,* and Pirats. This he alleged to be due to his Country from the Crown of *England,* who had in the Reign of King *Charles* I. submitted itself to him. The Duke of *Albemarle* did nothing in this matter, being afraid it might be a trick of some people to set up a Government for *Bucaniers* or Pirats. This King *Jeremy,* in coming to Town, asking many questions about the Island, and not receiving as he thought, a satisfactory account, he pull'd off his *European* Cloaths his Friends had put on, and climb'd to the top of a Tree, to take a view of the Country. The Memorial, and substance of what he, and the people with him, represented to the Duke of *Albemarle;* was, That in the Reign of King *Charles* I. of ever Blessed Memory, the Earl of *Warwick* (by virtue of Letters of Reprizal granted by his said Majesty for Damages received from the Subjects of his Catholick Majesty) did possess himself of several Islands in the *West-Indies,*particularly that of *Providence,* (since called by the *Spaniards* St. *Catalina,* ) which is situate in 13 *deg.* 10 *m.* N° Lat. lying East from Cape *Gratias de Dios,* (vulgarly known by the name of the *Muskitos*) between Thirty and Forty Leagues; which put the said Earl upon trying all ways and means of future [xxvii] Correspondence with the Natives of the said Cape and neighbouring Country, and in some little time was so successful as to gain that Point, and farther prevail'd with them so far, as to persuade them to send home the King's Son, leaving one of his People as Hostage for him, which was Colonel *Morris,* now living at *New York.* The *Indian* Prince going home with the said Earl, staid in *England* three years, in which time the *Indian* King died, and the said Natives having in that time had intercourse of Friendship and Commerce with those of *Providence,* were soon made sensible of the Grandeur of his Majesty of *Great Britain,* and how necessary his Protection was to them. Upon the return of the said *Indian* Prince, they persuaded him to resign up his Authority and Power over them, and (with them) unanimously declare themselves the Subjects of his said Majesty of *Great Britain,* in which Opinion they

---

Sir Hans Sloane, *A Voyage to the Islands* (London, 1707), I, lxxvi-ixviii.

have ever since persisted, and do own no other Supream Command over them. As to the Fertility of their Soil, 'tis a very great Level, free from any Mountains for several Leagues from the Sea, the Soil black Mold mixt with Sand, where otherwise, the Land is covered with Pine Trees, of the nature of *New England* Fir, well watered with great Rivers and Rivulets. Their chief Commerce being managed in Canoes; for Harbours it hath but two, and they both barr'd, and so not capable of receiving any Vessel that draws above Eleven or Twelve Foot Water, but when within, able to receive Ships of the greatest Burthen, that may lay their Sides to the Shore, and Careen safely. In these Harbours are Banks or rather Rocks of Oisters, from the bigness of Horseshoes, to those of *Colchester,* or less. As to the Nature of the Inhabitants, they are Affable and Courteous, very Hospitable, and ready to relieve all People in Distress, but more especially endear'd to those of the *English* Nation. The Men generally speak broken *English,* there is nothing more hateful to them than breach of Promise, or telling an Untruth, their Words being inviolable. They are always on their Guard for Fear of their neighbouring Enemies, and for the most part get their Living by Fishing. Their most usual Arms are six hand Lances slight ones, and one other very large and strong, with which they nimbly avoid those that are darted from their Enemy, the lesser ones they handle so dextrously, that they dart small Fishes, about the bigness of a Salmon Trout, Thirty Yards, and though their Country have great plenty of Deer, Pecary, and Wild-Fowl; yet they get most of their Provisions out of the Sea. Their manner of living now is Patriarchal, their Families being numerous, they allowing plurality of Wives, of which only the old Women and Children perform the Work of all the rest of the Family, but every individual Person pays great Duty and Respect to the *Paterfamilias,* who is absolute Judge in all Cases, and from [xxviii] whom there is no Appeal. All they produce from the Earth, or Provisions (which they sell to the Men of War, and other Vessels trading on the Coast) is equally divided among the whole Family, only the Chief and his Wife have each two Shares. Were some Persons industrious to settle among them, and encourage them to plant, the richness of the Soil would easily, and advantageously produce any Commodity, especially Indigo, but they will not permit any other Nation to settle among them but the *English;* they have some propensity to the *Dutch,* but the *French* they mortally hate for their wanton behaviour towards their Wives. As to their Number, no sure account can be given, they being settled at such great distance, and uncapable to give a true Estimate of themselves, being wholly unlearned, only some that have been at *Providence,* have learned the Lords Prayer, the Creed and Ten Commandments, which they repeat with great Devotion.

## 3. Richard Ligon Describes the Beginnings of Sugar Cultivation and Planters' Adaptation to the Climate in Barbados, 1654

### The Sugar Revolution

At the time we landed on this Island, which was in the beginning of *September,* 1647. we were informed, partly by those Planters we found there, and partly by our own observations, that the great work of Sugar-making, was but newly practised by

Richard Ligon, *A True and Exact History of the Island of Barbadoes,* 2nd ed. (London, 1673).

the inhabitants there. Some of the most industrious men, having gotten Plants from *Fernambock,* a place in *Brasil,* and made tryal of them at the *Barbadoes;* and finding them to grow, they planted more and more, as they grew and multiplyed on the place, till they had such a considerable number, as they were worth the while to set up a very small Ingenio, and so make tryal what Sugar could be made upon that soyl. But, the secrets of the work being not well understood, the Sugars they made were very inconsiderable, and little worth, for two or three years. But they finding their errours by their daily practice, began a little to mend; and, by new directions from *Brasil,* sometimes by strangers, and now and then by their own people, (who being covetous of the knowledge of a thing, which so much concerned them in their particulars, and for the general good of the whole Island) were content sometimes to make a voyage thither, to improve their knowledge in a thing they so much desired. Being now made much abler to make their queries, of the secrets of that mystery, by how much their often failings, had put them to often stops and nonplusses in the work. And so returning with most Plants, and better Knowledge, they went on upon fresh hopes, but still short, of what they should be more skilful in: for, at our arrival there, we found them ignorant in three main points, that much conduced to the work; *viz.* The manner of Planting, the time of Gathering, and the right placing of their Coppers in their Furnaces; as also, the true way of covering their Rollers, with plates or Bars of Iron: All which being rightly done, advance much in the performance of the main work. At the time of our arrival there, we found many Sugar-works set up, and at work; but yet the Sugars they made, were but bare Muscavadoes, and few of them Merchantable commodities; so moist, and full of molosses, and so ill cur'd, as they were hardly worth the bringing home for *England.* But about the time I left the Island, which was in 1650, they were much better'd; for then they had the skill to know when the Canes were ripe, which was not, till they were fifteen months old; and before, they gathered them at twelve, which was a main disadvantage to the making [86] good Sugar; for, the liquor wanting of the sweetness it ought to have, caused the Sugars to be lean, and unfit to keep. Besides, they were grown greater proficients, both in boyling and curing them, and had learnt the knowledge of making them white, such as you call Lump Sugars here in *England;* but not so excellent as those they make in *Brasil,* nor is there any likelyhood they can ever make such: the land there being better, and lying in a Continent, must needs have constanter and steadier weather, and the Aire much drier and purer, than it can be in so small an Iland, and that of *Barbadoes.* And now, seeing this commodity, Sugar, hath gotten so much the start of all the rest of those, that were held the staple Commodities of the Iland, and so much over-top't them, as they are for the most part slighted and neglected. And, for that few in *England* know the trouble and care of making it, I think it convenient, in the first place, to acquaint you, as far as my memory will serve, with the whole process of the work of Sugar-making, which is now grown the soul of Trade in this Iland. And leaving to trouble you and my self, with relating the errours our Predecessors so long wandred in, I will in brief set down the right and best way they practised, when I left the Island, which, I think, will admit of no greater or farther improvement.

But, before I will begin with that, I will let you see, how much the land there hath been advanc'd in the profit, since the work of Sugar began, to the time of our landing there, which was not above five or six years: For, before the work began, this Plantation of Major *Hilliards,* of five hundred acres, could have been purchased for four hundred pound sterling; and now the halfe this Plantation, with the haste of the Stock upon it, was sold for seven thousand pound sterling. And it is evident, that all the land there, which has been imployed to that work, hath found the like improvement. And I believe, when the small Plantations in poor mens hands, of ten, twenty, or thirty acres, which are too small to lay to that work, be bought up by great men, and put together, into Plantations of five, six, or seven hundred acres, that two thirds of the Iland will be fit for Plantations of Sugar, which will make it one of the richest Spots of earth under the Sun.

### English Adaption in Barbados

Having given you in my Bills of Fare, a particular of such Viands, as this Island afforded, for supportation of life, and somewhat for delight too, as far as concerns the Table; yet, what are you the better for all this, when you must be scorch't up from morning till night with the torrid heat of the Sun; So as in that twelve hours, you hardly can find two, in which you can enjoy your self with contentment. Or how can you expect to find heat, or warmth in your stomack, to digest that meat, when the Sun hath exhausted your heat and spirits so to your outer parts, as you are chill'd and numb'd within? For which reason you are compell'd to take such remedies, as are almost as ill as the disease; liquors so strong, as to take away the breath as it goes down, and red pepper for spice, which wants little of the heat of a fire-coale; and all these will hardly draw in the heat, which the Sun draws out; and part of this deficiency is occasioned by the improvidence, or inconsideration of the Inhabitants, who build their dwellings, rather like stoves then houses; for the most of them are made of timber, low rooft keeping out the wind, letting in the Sun, when they have means to have it otherwise; for I will undertake to contrive a house so, as no one shall have just cause to complain of any excessive heat; and that which gives this great remedy, shall bring with it the greatest beauty that can be look't on. The Palmetoes, which being plac't (as I will give you directions in my plot) in convenient order, shall interpose so between the Sun and house, as to keep it continually in the shade; and to have that shade at such a distance, as very little heat shall be felt in any time of the day: For shades that are made by the highest trees, are undoubtedly the coolest, and freshest, by reason it keeps the heat farthest off. Besides this, there are many advantages to be made, in the contrivance of the house; for I see the Planters there, never consider which way they build their houses, so they get them up; which is the cause that many of them, are so insufferably hot, as neither themselves nor any other can remain in them without sweltring.

And now I have as neer as I can, delivered the sum of all I know of the Island of *Barbadoes,* both for Pleasures and Profits, Commodities and Incommodities, Sicknesses and Healthfulness. So that it may be expected what I can say to perswade or disswade any that have a desire to go and live there. But before I give a full answer to that, I must enquire and be enformed of what disposition the party is that hath this design; If it be such a one as loves the pleasures of *Europe,* (or particularly of *England*) and the great varieties of those, let him never come there, for they are things he shall be sure to miss. But, if he can find in himself a willingness to change the pleasures which he enjoyed in a Temperate, for such as he shall find in a Torrid Zone, he may light upon some that will give him an exchange, with some advantage.

And for the pleasures of *England,* let us consider what they are, that we may be the better able to judge how far they are consistent with the Climate of *Barbadoes,* and what gainers or losers they will be by the exchange, that makes the adventure; and by the knowledge and well weighing of that, invite or deter those, that are the great lovers and admirers of those delights, to come there, or stay away.

## Treatment of Slaves and Servants

The Island is divided into three sorts of men, *viz.* Masters, Servants, and Slaves. The slaves and their posterity, being subject to their Masters for ever, are kept and preserv'd with greater care than the servants, who are theirs but for five years, according to the law of the Island. So that for the time, the servants have the worser lives, for they are put to very hard labour, ill lodging, and their dyet very sleight. When we came first on the Island, some Planters themselves did not eat bone meat, above twice a week: the rest of the seven dayes, Potatoes, Loblolly,and Bonavist. But the servants no bone meat at all, unless an Oxe dyed: and then they were feasted, as long as that lasted. And till they had planted good store of Plantines, the *Negroes* were fed with this kind of food; but most of it Bonavist, and Loblolly, with some ears of Mayes toasted, which food (especially Logblolly,) gave them much discontent: but when they had Plantines enough to serve them, they were heard no more to complain; for 'tis a food they take great delight in, and their manner of dressing, and eating it, is this: 'tis gathered for them (somewhat before it be ripe, for so they desire to have it,) upon *Saturday,* by the keeper of the Plantine grove; who is an able *Negro,* and knowes well the number of those that are to be fed with this fruit; and as he gathers, layes them all together, till they fetch them away, which is about five a clock in the afternoon, for that day they break off work sooner by an hour: partly for this purpose, and partly for that the fire in the furnaces is to be put out, and the Ingenio and the rooms made clean; besides they are to wash, shave and trim themselves against *Sunday.* But 'tis a lovely sight to see a hundred handsom *Negroes,* men and women, with every one a grasse-green bunch of these fruits on their heads, every bunch twice as big as their heads, all coming in a train one after another, the black and green so well becoming one another. Having brought this fruit home to their own houses, and pilling off the skin of so much as they will use, they boyl it in water, making it into balls, and so they eat it. One bunch a week is a *Negroe's* allowance. To this, no bread nor drink, but water. Their lodging at night a board, with nothing under, nor any thing a top of them. They are happy people, whom so little contents. Very good servants, if they be not spoyled by the *English.* But more of them hereafter.

As for the usage of the Servants, it is much as the Master is, merciful or cruel; Those that are merciful, treat their Servants well, both in their meat, drink, and lodging, and give them such work, as is not unfit for Christians to do. But if the Masters be cruel, the Servants have very wearisome and miserable lives. Upon the arrival of any ship, that brings servants to the Island, the Planters go aboard; and having bought such of them as they like, send them with a guid to his Plantation; and being come, commands them instantly to make their Cabins, which they not knowing how to do, are to be advised by other of their servants, that are their Seniors; but, if they be churlish, and will not shew them, or if materials be wanting, to make them Cabins, then they are to lye on the ground that night. These Cabins are to be made of sticks, withs, and Plantine leaves, under some little shade that may keep the rain off; Their suppers being a few Potatoes for meat, and water or Mobbie for drink. The next day they are rung out with a Bell to work, at six a clock in the morning, with a severe Overseer to command them, till the Bell ring again, which is at eleven a clock; and then they return, and are set to dinner, either with a mess of Lob-lolly, Bonavist, or Potatoes. At one a clock, they are rung out again to the field, there to work till six, and then home again, to a supper of the same. And if it chance to rain, and wet them through, they have no shift, but must lye so all night. If they put off their cloaths, the cold of the night will strike into them; and if they be not strong men, this ill lodging will put them into a sickness: if they complain, they are beaten by the Overseer; if they resist, their time is doubled, I have seen an Overseer beat a Servant with a cane about the head, till the blood has followed, for a fault that is not worth the speaking of; and yet he must have patience, or worse will follow. Truly, I have seen such cruelty there done to Servants, as I did not think one Christian could have done to another. But, as discreeter and better natur'd men have come to rule there, the servants lives have been much bettered; for now, most of the servants lie in Hamocks, and in warm rooms, and when they come in wet, have shift of shirts and drawers, which is all the cloths they wear, and are fed with *bone meat* twice or thrice a week. Collonel *Walrond* seeing his servants when they came home, toyled with their labour, and wet through with their sweating, thought that shifting of their linnen not sufficient refreshing, nor warmth for their bodies, their pores being much opened by their sweating; and therefore resolved to send into *England* for rug Gowns, such as poor people wear in Hospitals, that so when they had shifted themselves, they might put on those Gowns, and lye down and rest them in their Hamocks: For the Hamocks being but thin, and they having nothing on but Shirts and Drawers, when they awak'd out of their sleeps, they found themselves very cold; and a cold taken there, is harder to be recovered, than in *England,* by how much the body is infeebled by the great toyl, and the Sun's heat, which cannot but very much exhaust the spirits of bodies unaccustomed to it. But this care and charity of Collonel *Walrond*'s, lost him nothing in the conclusion; for, he got such love of his servants, as they thought all too little they could do for him; and the love of the servants there, is of much concernment to the Masters, not only in their diligent and painful labour, but in fore-seeing and preventing mischiefs that often happen, by the carelessness and slothfulness of retchless servants; sometimes by laying fire so negligently, as whole lands of Canes and Houses too, are burnt down and consumed, to the utter ruine and undoing of their Masters: For, the materials there being all combustible, and apt to take fire, a little oversight, as the fire of a Tobacco-pipe, being knockt out against a dry stump of a tree, has set it on fire, and the wind fanning that fire, if a land of Canes be but near, and they once take fire, all that are down the wind will be burnt up. Water there is none to quench it, or if it were, a hundred *Negroes* with buckets were not able to do it; so violent and spreading a fire this is, and such a noise it makes, as if two Armies, with a thousand shot of either side, were continually giving fire, every knot of every Cane, giving as great a report as a Pistol. So that there is no way to stop the going on of this flame, but by cutting down and removing all the Canes that grow before it, for the breadth of twenty or thirty foot down the wind, and there the *Negroes* to stand and beat out the fire, as it creeps upon the ground, where the Canes are cut down. And I have seen some *Negroes* so earnest to stop this fire, as with their naked feet to tread, and with their naked bodies to tumble, and roll upon it; so little they regard their own smart or safety, in respect of their Masters benefit. . . . [B]efore I came away, there were two eminent Planters in the Island, that with such an accident as this, lost at least 10000 1. sterling, in the value of the Canes that were burnt; the one, Mr. *James Holduppe,* the other, Mr. *Constantine Silvester:* And the latter had not only his Canes, but his house burnt down to the ground. This, and much more mischief has been done, by the negligence and wilfulness of servants. And yet some cruel Masters will provoke their Servants so, by extream ill usage, and often and cruel beating them, as they grow desperate, and so joyn together to revenge themselves upon them.

## 4. Thomas Nairne Reassures Prospective Settlers About the Environment and Trade of South Carolina, 1710

### Air

The Air of *Carolina* is generally very clear and fine, even when the greatest Rains fall, the Weather does not continue long cloudy, for the Sun soon dissipates the Fogs, and restores the Air to its usual Serenity. During the Heat of Summer, the Rains are very refreshing and agreeable, and the Thunder that accompanies them, tho' naturally terrifying, is welcome upon Account of its rarifying the Air. Earthquakes have never yet been known, or heard of in this Country.

### Temperature of the Months

The Heats of *Carolina* are indeed troublesome to Strangers in *June, July,* and *August,* in which Months are smart Claps of Thunder, tho' seldom doing any Prejudice. But the Inconveniency from the Heat during that Time, is made easie by shady Groves, open airy Rooms, Arbours, and Summer-houses; and to make some amends for it, no Country can afford pleasanter Weather, in the Spring, Fall, and greatest Part of Winter. *September, October, November,* are pleasant dry Months, neither hot nor cold. *December* and *January* are moderately cold, sometimes accompanied with sharp cold North-West Winds, and Frost, which seldom last above two or three Days at a Time. There is scarce ever any Snow, or if it does fall, it lies not above one Night. *February* and *March* are pleasant, fair, dry Months, answering in Temperature to *April* and *May* in *England,* which with us are very agreeable Months, the Weather being then clear and fair, refreshed with gentle Showers once in eight or ten Days, but equal in Heat in *June* and *July* in *England.*

Thomas Nairne, *A Letter From South Carolina* (London, 1710). "Trade" in Jack P. Greene, ed., *Selling a New World* (Columbia: University of South Carolina Press, 1989), 42–43.

**Trade**

The Trade between *South Carolina* and *Great Britain,* does, one Year with another, employ 22 Sail of Ships, laden hither with all Sorts of Woollen Cloaths, Stuffs, and Druggets, Linnens, Hollands, printed Linnen and Callicoe, Silks and Muslins, Nails of all sizes, Hoes, Hatchets, and all Kinds of Iron-ware, Bed-ticks, strong Beer, bottled Syder, Raisins, fine Earthen-ware, Pipes, Paper, Rugs, Blankets, Quilts, Hats from 2 *s.* to 12 *s.* Price, Stockings from 1 *s.* to 8 *s.* Price, Gloves, Pewter Dishes and Plates, Brass and Copper Ware, Guns, Powder, Bullets, Flints, Glass Beads, Cordage, Woollen and Cotton Cards, Steel Hand-mills, Grind-stones, Looking and Drinking Glasses, Lace, Thread course and fine, Mohair, and all Kinds of Trimming for Cloaths, Pins, Needles, &c. In return for which are remitted from hence about seventy Thousand Deer-skins a Year, some Furs, Rosin, Tar, Raw Silk, Rice, and formerly Indigo. But since all these don't balance the continual Demand of *European* Goods, and Negro Slaves, sent us by the *English* Merchants, there is likewise sent to *England,* some Cocoa-nuts, Sugar, Tortoise-shell, Money, and other Things, which we have from the *American* Islands, in return for our Provisions. Besides the 22 Sail above-mention'd, there enter and clear annually at the Port of *Charlestown,* about *60* Sail of Ships, Sloops, and Brigantines, all from some Places of *Africa* or *America.*

From *Jamaica, St. Thomas's, Currasso, Barbadoes,* and the *Le[e]ward Islands,* we have Sugar, Rum, Molosses, Cotton, Chocolate made up, Coco-nuts, Negroes, and Mon[e]y. In return whereof we send Beef, Pork, Butter, Candles, Soap, Tallow, Myrtle-wax Candles, Rice, some Pitch and Tar, Cedar and Pineboards, Shingles, Hoop-staves, and Heads for Barrels.

From *New-England, New York,* and *Pen[n]sylvania,* we have Wheat-flower, Bisket, strong Beer, Cyder, salt Fish, Onions, Apples, Hops; and return them ta[n]n'd Hides, small Deerskins, Gloves, Rice, Slaves taken by the *Indians* in War, some Tar and Pitch.

From *Made[i]ra* and the Western Islands, we have Wine, and in return, supply them with Provisions, Staves, and Heads for Barrels, &c. Our Salt comes from the *Bahama Islands.*

From *Guinea,* and other Parts of the Coast of *Africa,* are imported Negroe-Slaves; but the Ships that bring them being sent, with the Effects to purchase them, from *England,* the Returns are sent thither.

## 5. Eliza Lucas Pinckney on the Perfection of Indigo, 1785

My Dear Child

You wish me to inform you what I recollect of the introducing and culture of indigo in this country. You have heard me say I was very early fond of the vegetable world, my father was pleased with it and encouraged it, he told me the turn I

From *The Colonial South Carolina Scene: Contemporary Views, 1697–1774,* ed. H. Roy Merrens, Tricentennial Edition No. 7, 145–146. Reprinted by permission of University of South Carolina Press.

had for those amusements might produce something of real and public utility, if I could bring to perfection the plants of other countries which he would procure me. Accordingly when he went to the West Indies he sent me a variety of seeds, among them the indigo. I was ignorant both of the proper season for sowing it, and the soil best adapted to it. To the best of my recollection I first try'd it in March 1741, or 1742; it was destroyed (I think by a frost). The next time in April, and it was cut down by a worm; I persevered to a third planting and succeeded, and when I informed my father it bore seed and the seed ripened, he sent a man from the Island of Monserat by the name of Cromwell who had been accustomed to making indigo there, and gave him high wages; he made some brick vats on my fathers plantation on Wappo Creek and then made the first indigo; it was very indifferent, and he made a great mistery of it, said he repented coming as he should ruin his own country by it, for my father had engaged him to let me see the whole process. I observed him as carefully as I could and informed Mr. Deveaux an old gentleman a neighbour of ours of the little knowledge I had gain'd and gave him notice when the indigo was to be beat; he saw and afterwards improved upon it, not withstanding the churlishness of Cromwell, who wished to deceive him, and threw in so large a quantity of lime water as to spoil the colour. In the year 1744 I married, and my father made Mr. Pinckney a present of all the indigo then upon the ground as the fruit of my industry. The whole was saved for seed, and your father gave part of it away in small quantities to a great number of people that year, the rest he planted the next year at Ashipo for seed, which he sold, as did some of the gentlemen to whom he had given it the year before; by this means there soon became plenty in the country. Your father gained all the information he could from the French prisoners brought in here, and used every other means of information, which he published in the Gazette for the information of the people at large.

The next year Mr. Cattle sent me a present of a couple of large plants of the wild indigo which he had just discovered. Experiments were afterwards made upon this sort, which proved to be good indigo, but it did not produce so large a quantity as the cultivated sort. I am

> Your truly affectionate mother,
> Eliza Pinckney

## 6. J. Hector St. John Crevecoeur Contrasts the Culture of Charlestown and the Situation of Slaves, 1782

Charles-Town is, in the north, what Lima is in the south; both are Capitals of the richest provinces of their respective hemispheres: you may therefore conjecture, that both cities must exhibit the appearances necessarily resulting from riches. Peru abounding in gold, Lima is filled with inhabitants who enjoy all those gradations of pleasure, refinement, and luxury, which proceed from wealth. Carolina produces commodities, more valuable perhaps than gold, because they are gained by greater industry; it ex-

---

J. Hector St. John Crevecoeur, *Letters From an American Farmer* (London, 1782), Letter IX.

hibits also on our northern stage, a display of riches and luxury, inferior indeed to the former, but far superior to what are to be seen in our northern towns. Its situation is admirable, being built at the confluence of two large rivers, which receive in their course a great number of inferior streams; all navigable in the spring, for flat boats. Here the produce of this extensive territory concentres; here therefore is the seat of the most valuable exportation; their wharfs, their docks, their magazines, are extremely convenient to facilitate this great commercial business. The inhabitants are the gayest in America; it is called the centre of our beau monde, and it always filled with the richest planters of the province, who resort hither in quest of health and pleasure. Here are always to be seen a great number of valetudinarians from the West-Indies, seeking for the renovation of health, exhausted by the debilitating nature of their sun, air, and modes of living. Many of these West-Indians have I seen, at thirty, loaded with the infirmities of old age; for nothing is more common in those countries of wealth, than for persons to lose the abilities of enjoying the comforts of life, at a time when we northern men just begin to taste the fruits of our labour and prudence. The round of pleasure, and the expences of those citizens' tables, are much superior to what you would imagine: indeed the growth of this town and province has been astonishingly rapid. It is pity that the narrowness of the neck on which it stands prevents it from increasing; and which is the reason why houses are so dear. The heat of the climate, which is sometimes very great in the interior parts of the country, is always temperate in Charles-Town; though sometimes when they have no sea breezes the sun is too powerful. The climate renders excesses of all kinds very dangerous, particularly those of the table; and yet, insensible or fearless of danger, they live on, and enjoy a short and a merry life: the rays of their sun seem to urge them irresistably to dissipation and pleasure: on the contrary, the women, from being abstemious, reach to a longer period of life, and seldom die without having had several husbands. An European at his first arrival must be greatly surprised when he sees the elegance of their houses, their sumptuous furniture, as well as the magnificence of their tables can he imagine himself in a country, the establishment of which is so recent? . . .

While all is joy, festivity, and happiness in Charles-Town, would you imagine that scenes of misery overspread in the country? Their ears by habit are become deaf, their hearts are hardened; they neither see, hear, nor feel for the woes of their poor slaves, from whose painful labours all their wealth proceeds. Here the horrors of slavery, the hardship of incessant toils, are unseen; and no one thinks with compassion of those showers of sweat and of tears which from the bodies of Africans, daily drop, and moisten the ground they till. The cracks of the whip urging these miserable beings to excessive labour, are far too distant from the gay Capital to be heard. The chosen race eat, drink, and live happy, while the unfortunate one grubs up the ground, raises indigo, or husks the rice; exposed to a sun full as scorching as their native one; without the support of good food, without the cordials of any chearing liquor. This great contrast has often afforded me subjects of the most afflicting meditation. On the one side, behold a people enjoying all that life affords most bewitching and pleasurable, without labour, without fatigue, hardly subjected to the trouble of wishing. With gold, dug from Peruvian mountains, they order vessels to the coasts of Guinea; by virtue of that gold, wars, murders, and devastations are committed in some harmless, peaceable African neighbourhood, where dwelt innocent people, who even knew not but that all men were black. The daughter torn from her weeping mother, the child from the wretched parents, the wife from the loving husband; whole families swept away and brought through storms and tempests to this rich metropolis! There, arranged like horses at a fair, they are branded like cattle, and then driven to toil, to starve, and to languish for a few years on the different plantations of these citizens. And for whom must they work? For persons they know not, and who have no other power over them than that of violence; no other right than what this accursed metal has given them! Strange order of things! Oh, Nature, where art thou?—Are not these blacks thy children as well as we? On the other side, nothing is to be seen but the most diffusive misery and wretchedness, unrelieved even in thought or wish! Day after day they drudge on without any prospect of ever reaping for themselves; they are obliged to devote their lives, their limbs, their will, and every vital exertion to swell the wealth of masters; who look not upon them with half the kindness and affection with which they consider their dogs and horses. Kindness and affection are not the portion of those who till the earth, who carry the burdens, who convert the logs into useful boards. This reward, simple and natural as one would conceive it, would border on humanity; and planters must have none of it! . . .

 *E S S A Y S*

In 1630 at the same time that a large group of Puritans left England to found the colony of Massachusetts Bay, a smaller group sponsored by the most important lay Puritans in England traveled to settle on Providence Island in the western Caribbean. Karen Ordahl Kupperman of New York University presents in the first essay the goals and problems of the Providence Island colony, and its legacy in spurring Oliver Cromwell's attempt to force the Spanish out of the region. Massachusetts Bay and Providence Island were interconnected ventures, and the backers of the Caribbean colony expected their plantation to become far more successful than New England and hoped that eventually the New Englanders would voluntarily transplant to a future great colony in Central America. The reality was far different, and Providence Island was a failure. But the goal of rich West Indian colonies continued and was realized. Success came in the form of rich crops. The island colonies of Barbados and Jamaica quickly outstripped all other settlements and they created their own particular kind of society. These social and economic forms, in turn, helped to shape the colonies of the lower South founded in the later seventeenth century. Jack P. Greene of Johns Hopkins University, in the second essay, explores Barbadian social and commercial norms and their continuing connection to South Carolina's society and economy.

## England's Dream of Caribbean Empire

### KAREN ORDAHL KUPPERMAN

English puritans of high rank and national prominence were interested in the success of Massachusetts and often helped the colony materially, but they never be-

From Karen Ordahl Kupperman, "Errand to the Indies: Puritan Colonization from Providence Island Through the Western Design," *William and Mary Quarterly,* 3rd ser., XLV pp.70–99. Copyright © 1988. Reprinted by permission.

lieved that New England could ever be anything but the merest sideshow while the real action was carried on elsewhere. During the 1603s, when Stuart pacifism and Arminian advance made constructive work in England itself increasingly difficult, great puritan lords and gentlemen—grandees who would lead the nation in the early years of civil war—sponsored colonization in the West Indies. Only ventures there, they believed, could truly serve England by helping to solve the country's crippling economic problems and, more important, by stemming the flow of gold to Spanish coffers that fueled the great war machine harrying European Protestants back into Roman Catholicism. With England economically strong and independent, and with Spain weakened, true religion would be made secure. Without realization of these goals, any claims to be protecting reformed worship were the merest self-delusion. Puritans who truly cared about God's worship, in the grandees' view, must contemplate colonization of the West Indies.

This vision of empire reached back to the great Elizabethans and pointed forward to enthronement as national policy with Oliver Cromwell's Western Design. Settlement of New England was, from the vantage point of England, a distinctly less important movement of much more limited vision. Cold and rocky New England could never produce the commodities that England needed, and it was too far north to be useful in confronting England's and Protestantism's enemies. In English puritan eyes, the northern colonies' role was to act as a way station, a collecting point for population until a sufficiently large and experienced force could be gathered to allow relatively safe penetration of Spain's empire.

Many in New England, particularly in the economically harsh times of the late 1630s and 1640s when the plantations suffered reverses whose providential meaning was unclear, seem also to have believed that settlement in the north might be a temporary measure. If scholars reinterpreting the errand theme are correct, there was very little consensus on the reasons for the Great Migration among the emigrants other than their conviction that they needed a refuge to protect their faith and an escape from needless suffering. Colonists thus planted would necessarily reflect on their future, and some would be susceptible to calls for remigration, either back to England or to other parts of America. Many, unsure of their destined role in the preservation of true religion, seriously considered bids from English puritan leaders to divert their energies to southern colonies that could better serve the reformed faith and its protector, England.

In 1630, when the Great Migration to Massachusetts Bay began, English puritan grandees, including future national leaders such as the earl of Warwick and his cousin Sir Nathaniel Rich, Lord Brooke, Lord Saye and Sele, Sir Thomas Barrington, Sir Benjamin Rudyerd, Richard Knightley, and John Pym, founded another puritan colony, on an island off the coast of Nicaragua, to which they gave the significant name of Providence. They meant their island to become a great puritan refuge, the germ of a mighty English empire on the Mosquito Coast, which eventually would attract those who had emigrated to New England. . . .

. . . Moreover, the overweening power of Spain aimed to destroy the independence of England in order to extinguish the light of true religion. Grandees such as Brooke, Saye, and the earl of Warwick saw themselves as continuing the policies of the great Elizabethans, enriching themselves, protecting England, and striking at

Spain. They believed that one side must eventually win; Roman Catholic Spain would settle for nothing less than the destruction of Protestantism. Therefore, Spain must be confronted. . . .

The backers, many of whom were veterans of previous colonial foundations, particularly in Virginia and Bermuda, knew the mistakes to avoid. They ensured that men skilled in the crafts necessary to building a community were included in the passenger lists. Since Providence Island was in the heart of the Spanish empire, these included fortifications experts and gunners. Present from the beginning were men of rank who had been in the Indies for some time—men such as Capt. Daniel Elfrith, who had first brought the island to the attention of the earl of Warwick, and his son-in-law Capt. Philip Bell, who left his post as governor of Bermuda to take up the governorship of Providence Island. Once the island became a thriving concern, the company grandees planned that some of their own number would go to live among the planters.

Meanwhile, company members set out to recruit colonists from among their own dependents and clients, hoping to make sure that only the godly were sent to people the island. Many of the ships sent in the early years carried substantial settlers with families, colonists similar to the people who were going to New England, but these mixed uneasily with the experienced Bermudians who had emigrated there with Governor Bell. The company quickly moved to eliminate settlers of bad character, and sent solid puritans such as Henry Halhead, former mayor of the puritan stronghold of Banbury, to join the governor's council.

In 1632, when Halhead and his family arrived at the head of a shipment of substantial godly families, the company ordered that those of "evill disposition" be expelled and prayed that colonists who had considered leaving the island would stay. But, as the adventurers acknowledged in 1634, they never succeeded in attracting enough of the right sort of settlers from England. Masters of company ships were authorized to recruit colonists when they stopped at other West Indian islands, and paid agents were used within England.

Despite the fact that Providence Island Company adventurers had been among the most active in protecting and employing puritan ministers as the Stuart government increasingly restricted their activities, the company was not successful in attracting the best ministers to the island colony. The first clerical recruits were offered £40 per annum, a good ministerial salary in England, but the company quickly resolved to offer as much as £100 in money and commodities to heighten the attractiveness of serving the colony. The first minister, Lewis Morgan, was allowed an extra £20 to buy books for his use while in the West Indies. Much of the company's correspondence and many of its meetings were taken up with recruitment of ministers. Negotiations with the Reverend Henry Roote included an exploratory trip to the island by Roote, and Ezekiel Rogers, founder of Rowley, Massachusetts, seriously considered emigration to Providence Island. Despite everything, the only minister on the island for most of the colony's life was Hope Sherrard, who arrived with Halhead and who, like his predecessor Lewis Morgan, was constantly at odds with the island's other leaders. The company argued that reports of constant dissension put off potential minister-colonists. Sherrard ended up ministering to a small separated congregation, and the other settlers felt themselves bereft.

The Providence Island Company's investors believed that hierarchy was as necessary as godliness to the orderly functioning of society. They ordained a governing council composed of the captains of forts and the substantial civil leaders, such as Halhead, under a governor who was always a captain. These men would be the moral authorities to whom the settlers would look for guidance, and their lives would provide the model. What the adventurers did not understand was that their three goals for the colony were to a very great extent incompatible. If the colony was to confront Spain, as its location dictated, then the military men would rule it. Not only would their point of view predominate, but they would be able to call the settlers from the fields to work on the forts and for military training. Though even the military men were chosen for their godliness, many of them had spent much time in the Indies and were used to a life free from the restrictions of civil society.

Correspondence between the island and the company offers hints of daily grinding hostility between the factions. Company meetings in London often centered on discussions of tensions in the settlement, where the most insignificant event could lead to paralysis. Failure to return a borrowed book on time occasioned the trading of public insults between the first minister, Lewis Morgan, and one of the captains, William Rudyerd, younger brother of the prominent puritan and company investor Sir Benjamin Rudyerd, in 1633. Sir Benjamin protected William in this breach and again when he started a fight at the council table over liturgical practices, arguing that William had been "rudelye and snappishly provoked."

Rudyerd and his assistant, Lt. William Rous, both related to company investors, were constant sources of trouble. They harassed Henry Halhead and brought uproar to the council table. Even when Rudyerd's brutally beaten servant died a lingering death, the company in London was loath to move too harshly against such valuable and well-connected men. Other captains were also sources of dissension, though, as in the case of Captain Rudyerd and the liturgy, often the issues were religious. Capt. William Hooke accused Hope Sherrard of neglect of his duties and argued that his memory was inadequate for his clerical role. In his turn, Sherrard used his only weapon, excommunication, with such frequency that the company begged him to reconsider.

So volatile were relationships on the island that the adventurers in London often found themselves considering questions of precedence or judging conflicts that had grown out of small personal quarrels. As early as 1633 the company warned against this, "nothing being more unwelcome unto us, than complaints arising from private dissensions and secret heartburnings," but nothing could stem the flood. The diary of the colony's last governor, Capt. Nathaniel Butler, the only glimpse of daily life on the island that survives, shows him spending part of almost every day in hearing cases of disputes between colonists. . . .

In 1638, in the face of the continuing turmoil, the company sent Capt. Nathaniel Butler to be the colony's governor. Butler was a skilled administrator; moreover, not only was he an expert in fortifications but he had succeeded in calming the religious conflict that had raged in Bermuda when he was governor there by instituting an order of worship borrowed from the Channel Islands that satisfied everyone. He appeared to have all the qualities that Providence Island needed, but he failed to develop a working relationship with the congregation there: "I never lived amongst men of more spleene nor of less witt to conceale itt." His diary reveals a society hopelessly factionalized, and colonists' complaints against him soon began to roll in.

Partly for personal reasons, Captain Butler left the island in 1640 in the hands of Capt. Andrew Carter, a man much less qualified, both in character and religious convictions, to govern; in his care the situation quickly deteriorated and the island succumbed to a massive Spanish attack. Halhead and Sherrard escaped the devastation only because Carter had acted to stop the dissension by sending them and some of their supporters home to England in chains to face Archbishop Laud.

The adventurers' disappointment, expressed by Sir Benjamin Rudyerd in 1633, lasted as long as their experiment in colonization: "Wee well hoped (according to our Intention) that wee had planted a Relligious Collonye in the Isle of Providence, instead whearof wee fynde the roote of bitterness plentifullye planted amongst you, an industrious supplanting one of another, and not a man theare of Place (a straunge thinge to consider) but hee doth both accuse and is accused; these are uncomfortable fruites of Religion."

Life on Providence Island might have been more harmonious if the venture had been economically successful. Despite their experience, the backers made the universal error of colonizers: they drastically underestimated the time necessary for the colony to become self-sufficient and begin paying its way. Though the experience of West Indian colonies such as Barbados suggests that economic success might have come to Providence Island had it survived, never during the colony's decade of life did it develop a staple commodity of any value. Instead, it was a drain on the investors, growing mainly tobacco of very poor quality and some cotton.

Moreover, the adventurers failed to understand how their plans for the economy would affect social development. The great blunder that should have been avoided, given the experience of Virginia and Bermuda, was the adventurers' requirement that colonists take up their land as tenants, not as freeholders. Company members learned the wrong lessons from earlier failures; wanting to control the plantation's development so it would not go the way of other southern settlements, they created a massive grievance among the middling colonists, who knew that other puritan colonies offered freehold tenure and who had reason to dispute the company's claim that the tropical soil and climate of Providence created an environment so rich that half of one year's proceeds (the amount the original contract allowed settlers to keep) would be more than seven years' labor would produce in England.

The colony's economic goals fed conflict between the civil and military leadership. Unfamiliar crops that required large plantations and large labor forces meant reliance on the expertise of foreigners and on men such as Captain Elfrith who had spent their lives careering around the Indies. Slavery existed in the colony from the beginning, and by the middle of the 1630s slaves probably formed almost half the population; they were part of the society and yet outside the congregations and hierarchy. Both colonists and company were convinced that only by slave labor could they grow even the poor tobacco and cotton produced on the island. . . .

A new chance for prosperity came with defeat of a Spanish attack on the settlement in 1635. Not only did this provide an opening for the privateering ventures so central to the aristocratic anti-Spanish tradition in the Indies, but it gave grounds for renewed hope. Since the colonists had clearly been so completely unprepared to defend themselves, their victory could only mean that they were truly protected by a special providence; repulsion of the attack led to wild punning on the island's name. Even the royal government took an interest in the colony's situation; an investigation was carried out by Secretary of State Sir John Coke. . . .

Providence Island's becoming a base for privateering meant changed priorities in the kinds of ships and supplies sent; it also meant that ships would be sent more often. Through the second half of the colony's short life, colonists' raiding increasingly plagued the Spanish Central American settlements by disrupting the coastal trade and depriving them, especially Cartagena and Portobelo, of much-needed supplies. Because the island therefore lived in greater danger of renewed attack, the military presence was increased, and the voyage to and from the colony became much more dangerous, especially for women and children. It would be wrong to think, though, that the godly grandees of the Providence Island Company now revealed their "true" motive, pursuit of gain through legalized piracy, for which their pretended puritan settlement had never been more than a cover. On the contrary, they clearly believed that privateering would make possible the achievement of all the colony's goals and aid in restoring England to its true path. Privateering would help cripple the Spanish war machine "by annoying the Spaniard and intercepting his treasure whereby he hath troubled and endangered most of the States of Christendom and doth foment the wars against the professors of the reformed Religion." . . .

Privateering did not bring the level of economic return necessary to solve the colony's problems. Though the adventurers recouped some of their losses by it, the intended hundreds of new colonists were never sent. Even so, the adventurers did not give up on the idea that their colony could grow into a great English plantation that would also be a godly community in the Indies. None of the settlement's failures forced them to conclude that the promise of rich commodities from a harmonious society was not realizable—only that too few of the right sort of people had so far emigrated. In May 1640, a combined Portuguese and Spanish fleet of twelve vessels carrying a total of six hundred fighting men set out to wipe the English from Providence. Repulsion of this mighty force, with the help of the reefs and winds, further confirmed both colonists and backers in their conviction of God's special favor.

In 1640 and 1641, despite, or perhaps because of, the rapid political changes in England, Lord Saye and Selle and Lord Brooke renewed their efforts to people the colony. They concentrated on attracting families who had already emigrated to New England, but who, in the looming depression and continuing uncertainty of purpose there, were prepared to look elsewhere. In a famous exchange of letters, Lord Saye and John Winthrop debated whether God clearly intended his people to settle one place or the other. Winthrop was angry because Lord Saye was denigrating New England. Saye accused Winthrop of misapplying Scripture by arrogating to his colony those passages in the Bible in which God chose the land of Canaan for Israel. He suggested that although the Israelites had been commanded to rely on faith alone, perhaps modern-day English people should employ reason as well. He pointed to the artificial nature of New England's economic boom during its first decade and correctly predicted its decline as immigration fell off, leaving colonists with nothing but the cold, barren land, in which "rich men growe pore and poore men if they come over are a burden," in contrast to the rich environment of the Indies. "I pray tell me, be it as it is, is thear any impiety in me to move men to live in a warmer clymate and in a more frutefull soyle when it is fre for them to make theyr choyse, why are you angry with me for this?"

Lord Saye did not deny that emigration to New England had been a work of God; he only questioned whether it was absolutely clear that God had meant all the settlers to stay there. He suggested instead that Massachusetts had been selected as a gathering point to which people would come in small companies, "untill you wear growen unto such a bodye as wear able to doe him service, and sitt downe in safty in such places as may be most fitt for the worke he hath in hande." And, lest there be any confusion over what God's work consisted of, he reminded the governor of the necessity of "the advancement of the gospell and puttinge down the great adversary thearof that man of sinn, whearunto as you are now you neather are able nor are likely to be to putt your handes to the least wheele that is to be turned about in that worke otherwayse then by well wishinge thearunto."

Lord Saye struck a raw nerve, because, as Winthrop wrote, "many men began to inquire after the southern parts." Thomas Gorges, the young puritan governor of his uncle Sir Ferdinando's colony in Maine, visited Boston in 1641 and "found the place in a distracted condition, men unresolved in their mindes what to doe, some for the West Indies, some for Long Iland, some for ould Ingland." Hugh Peter so despaired for the future of New England that he seriously considered emigrating to Providence Island with a large company gathered by Capt. John Humphrey, one of the original patentees of the Massachusetts Bay Company. Edward Johnson, after the fact, was contemptuous of those who considered emigration, portraying them as weak-minded people seeking novelty and license: "they wanted a warmer country, and every Northwest wind that blew, they crept into some odd chimney-corner or other, to discourse of the diversity of Climates in the Southerne parts, but chiefly of a thing very sweet to the pallate of the flesh, called liberty, which they supposed might be very easily attain'd, could they but once come into a place where all men were chosen to the office of a Magistrate, and all were preachers of the Word, and no hearers, then it would be all Summer and no Winter." . . .

What Winthrop could not accomplish, the Spanish enemy did for him. The threatened leaching of settlers from Massachusetts was thwarted by word that the commander of the Plate Fleet, Adm. Don Francisco Díaz Pimienta, incensed by news of "the insult of Santa Catalina," had won the king's approval for a massive assault to avenge the debacle of 1640. In May 1641 the entire force of the Plate Fleet, this time in a very carefully planned attack, overran the English colony on Providence Island.

Winthrop and Johnson both recorded with satisfaction the dramatic events when the vanguard of Humphrey's emigrating band sailed into the harbor of Providence Island's little capital, New Westminster, to find the island taken by the Spaniards and the English settlers dispersed. Returning to Boston, some of the defectors acknowledged "their error . . . in the open congregation, but others were hardened." Even at that date Winthrop emphasized that New England offered a refuge, a place to avoid confrontation with the forces that threatened the reformed religion. He wrote of the foolishness of Humphrey and his band for leaving "a place of rest and safety, to expose themselves, their wives and children, to the danger of a potent enemy, the Spaniard." Winthrop clearly was content to see Massachusetts Bay make its contribution, as Lord Saye had charged, in "well wishinge."

English puritan leaders saw the situation very differently, especially as, with the recall of Parliament in 1640, plans to secure reformed religion could now be put in operation. New England and the other plantations in America, none of which had been very successful, could now serve the great function for which God had intended them. Pym's opening speech to the Short Parliament pointed to the weakness of the Spanish empire and the large numbers of English men and women in America: "There are now in those parts . . . at least Sixty thousand able persons of this Nation, many of them well armed, and their bodies seasoned to that Climate, which with a very small charge might be set downe, in some advantagious parts of these pleasant, rich and fruitfull Countreys, and easily make his Majesty Master of all that treasure, which not onely foments the Warre, but is the great support of Popery in all parts of Christendome." . . .

The puritan colony on Providence Island had failed, but, as puritans assumed national leadership in England, the lessons of that failure were unclear. Many argued that it had failed because of its small size and because the government had treated it as peripheral. Thomas Gage, a former member of the Dominican order who had traveled with the Spanish in Mexico and Central America, wrote in 1648 that Providence Island, "though but little, might have been of a great, nay greater advantage to our Kingdom, than any other of our plantations in America." As Oliver Cromwell moved into leadership, the goals of Providence Island Company investors finally became the goals of the national government. Urged on by English puritan leaders, Cromwell looked to Americans for advice and direction in developing his policies and found that New England clergymen were not indifferent to the need to confront Spain; in fact, they urged such action on the Protector. . . .

But Cromwell saw his policies, not as an anachronistic throwback to the days of Elizabeth, but as the logical culmination of thirty years of development and struggle. The civil wars began in an atmosphere of crisis, in the belief that Laudian policies aimed at reinstating popery in England. This sense of the precariousness of the Calvinist establishment pushed people into open war, and they sought a conclusion that would end threats to it now and in the future. It was given to the Protector to make the reformed religion so secure that no future developments could threaten it. To accomplish that goal, he had to protect England from foreign invasion and from the activities of enemies within. Cromwell and those around him believed that, until Spain was severed from its sources of riches in the Indies, the danger of attacks on England would remain. . . .

. . . After Cromwell's death, Roger Williams wrote to John Winthrop, Jr., of their conversations on this point: "The late renowned Oliver, confessed to me, in close discourse about the Protestants' affairs, &c., that he yet feared great persecutions to the Protestants from the Romanists, before the downfall of the Papacy. The histories of our fathers before us, tell us what huge bowls of the blood of the saints that great whore hath been drunk with, in (now) Protestant dominions." In another letter he reported his telling Cromwell "to which he much inclined," that "the bloody whore is not yet drunk enough with the blood of the saints and witnesses of Jesus." . . .

Now governmental leaders lamented the parsimonious short-sightedness of Charles I and pointed to the advantage England might have reaped from keeping control of Providence Island. Veterans of that colony joined the force attacking

Spanish possessions. Cromwell, in a letter to Maj. Gen. Richard Fortescue at Jamaica, announced that his government would "strive with the Spaniard for the mastery of all those seas" and went on, "therefore we could heartily wish that the Island of Providence were in our hands again" because its location made it perfect for attacking the mainland and for "the hindrance of the Peru trade and Cartagena."

Justification for the Protectorate's aggressively anti-Spanish policy rested ultimately on the assumption that peace between the two nations was not possible. Cromwell alleged that the Spanish had driven the English into war through repeated acts of hostility. Moreover, because Spain had denied access to English traders, the Western Design would give English trade a fair chance to thrive. Much of the rhetoric focused on the legendary cruelty of the Spanish, the English portraying themselves as saviors of the brutally mistreated Indians and slaves of the Indies. Edward Winslow, for example, argued that the expedition was an instrument in God's right hand "to execute his determined vengeance upon that tyrannous and idolatrous and bloudy nation that hath inflicted so many cruelties upon the nations of the earth." As part of this campaign, John Phillips published his translation of Bartolomé de Las Casa's indictment of the Spanish record in America under the title *The Tears of the Indians; Being an Historical and True Account of the Cruel Massacres and Slaughters . . . Committed by the Spaniards in the Ilands of Hispaniola, Cuba, Jamaica, &c. As also, in the Continent of Mexico, Peru, and Other Places of the West-Indies to the Total Destruction of Those Countries.* He dedicated the book to Cromwell, lauding the Protector for using his "vast Power and Dignity onely to the advancement of [God's] glory." Phillips warned "all true English-men" that the Spanish were "a Proud, Deceitful, Cruel, and Treacherous Nation, whose chiefest Aim hath been the Conquest of this Land, and to enslave the People of this Nation." Rhetoric portraying the Spaniards as a cruel people who abused the Indians and aimed to conquer England itself reiterated a favorite theme of Sir Walter Ralegh. . . .

For men who saw divine purpose in all events, the sailing of the expedition was a heady experience. Cromwell wrote to Adm. William Penn, commander of the fleet, that if it was, as they thought, God's business, then all would see his hand in it. Roger Williams was ecstatic, writing that the sailing of the ships was the beginning of "greater & greater Revolutions approaching" and that thousands in England now wished to crown the Protector with gold. . . .

Cromwell was as convinced as the earlier Providence Island investors that New England had no future, that God had gathered upright English citizens there so that, when the time came, they could answer the call to do his work elsewhere. According to Roger Williams, John Cotton's "interpreting of Euphrates to be the West Indies" was all the Protector needed. Together with that interpretation of prophecy, "the supply of gold, (to take of taxes), & the provision of a warmer Diverticulum & Receptaculum then N. England is, will make a footing into those parts very precious & if it shall please God to vouchsafe successe to this fleete, I looke to heare of an invitation at least to these parts for remooval from his Highnes, who lookes on N.E. only with an eye of pitie, as poore, cold & useles." Thomas Gage, trading on his presumed experience of America, had told the Council that New England and Virginia "are even worn out" and would provide many colonists for Panama and elsewhere. . . .

The Massachusetts Bay leadership was right to want to avoid Jamaica. The great expedition of the Western Design, after failing miserably in an attempt to conquer Hispaniola, limped on to take Jamaica, where disease, exacerbated by inadequate and inappropriate supplies, mowed the forces down. Edward Winslow died on the voyage from Hispaniola to Jamaica, some said of a broken heart, and one by one the other leaders either died or gave up. As letters from Massachusetts Bay made clear, the news of the reproof God had given England, laying it "low in the dust," was soon known all over the Atlantic world. Letters home described the sadly depleted army as distracted skeletons who could not or would not grow food for their own sustenance, though many still affirmed that Jamaica itself was a good land, even better for English purposes than Hispaniola would have been.

Moreover, the newly wise commanders now informed Cromwell that it was not so easy to encounter the Spanish treasure fleet at sea or to besiege a mainland city like Cartagena. In fact, English planters on Barbados had tried to dissuade the fleet even from attempting Hispaniola before that disastrous attack.

The New Englander Robert Sedgwick knew what the problem was: "God is angry." As he wrote to John Winthrop, Jr., "What God will do with this designe I know not. I was willing some time to beleive God was in it, but hee yet seemes to disowne us." In a long letter to the Protector, Sedgwick wrote that unless God stayed his hand the entire army would die "and shall be as water spilt upon the grass, that cannot be gathered up again." He concluded that "this generation" might simply be destined to "die in the wilderness."

Sedgwick contended that the army sent in the Western Design had not been of the godly and upright stamp necessary to such a great work, but he perceived a more fundamental problem that reached right down to the basic conception of the enterprise. As in Providence Island, preying on the fortunes of others, however unworthily gained, could not be the foundation of a godly society. Analyzing the problems of Jamaica, Sedgwick made his case to Cromwell: it was not "honourable, that your highnes's fleet should follow this old trade of West-India cruisers and privateers, to ruin and plunder poor towns, and so leave them." He reiterated this judgment in a later letter to Secretary John Thurloe, saying that the practice gave the English a bad name among the very Indians and slaves they said they were coming to protect, making them seem to be spoilers only, and ruining the grand design for which they embarked. . . .

Those who take providence for their guide must also, in the final analysis, listen to its judgments. Oliver Cromwell was forced to acknowledge what the Providence Island Company had already learned: a godly settlement could not be erected by a military expedition, and it could not pay its own way in the short run. Cromwell was shattered by the defeat at Hispaniola; his confidence that he and the English nation were the agents of God never fully recovered from the blow. There were many who were prepared to point to England's sins, and even to the Protector's usurpation, as the reason for God's wrath. Cromwell repeatedly called for days of fasting and humiliation so that the nation could determine in what ways it had sinned, but no clear answer came. He never accepted that the failure of the Western Design signaled God's endorsement of Spain, but he was forced to see it as a rebuke of England. The goals advocated over thirty years by the puritan grandees were not God's goals after all. . . .

Probably the greatest success of the Western Design lay in the area least considered by Cromwell, that of trade. Jamaica, which seemed to be second best in the 1650s, became, with the other sugar islands, the foundation of a great commercial empire. Moreover, the puritan grandees were right in thinking that the English textile industry would thrive on fibers and dyes from colonies in hot regions, though the regions turned out to be other than the West Indies. And New Englanders did have a great role to play in the new trade networks, but it was a very different one from that envisioned by the grandees. . . .

# The Continuing Connection Between Barbados and South Carolina

## JACK P. GREENE

Within the leavings of the Hispanic and Portuguese American Empires during the first half of the seventeenth century, English adventurers established viable settlements in four separate areas: the Chesapeake, Bermuda, New England, and Barbados. Notwithstanding the fact that they all shared a common English heritage, no two of the new societies that emerged out of these settlements were alike, and three of them—those in the Chesapeake, New England, and Barbados—became what some cultural geographers refer to as culture hearths. That is, they became sites for the creation of powerful local cultures, including social institutions and ways of manipulating a particular kind of environment, that proved to be remarkably capable of recreation and, with appropriate modifications, transferable to other areas in the Anglo-American world.

Historians have long been familiar with the processes by which the tobacco and mixed farming culture of Virginia spread north into Maryland, Delaware, and parts of Pennsylvania and south into North Carolina and by which the mixed-farming and fishing culture of Puritan Massachusetts Bay extended itself into offshoot societies in Connecticut, Rhode Island, New Haven, New Hampshire, Long Island, New Jersey, and Maine. Until recently, they have paid far less attention to the equally fecund staple agricultural culture of Barbados.

During the last half of the seventeenth century, the culture first articulated in Barbados slowly spread to the nearby Leeward Islands in the eastern Caribbean and, after its capture from the Spaniards in 1655, to the large island of Jamaica in the central Caribbean. After 1750, a variant strain of that culture, developed—within the English-world, in the Leeward Island colonies of St. Kitts, Antigua, Nevis, and Montserrat—found a congenial setting in the new British West Indian island colonies of the Virgin Islands, Grenada, St. Vincent, Dominica, and Tobago.

As most South Carolinians familiar with their early history will know, however, the extension of Barbadian culture went beyond the West Indies to the North American mainland. Established in 1670 with some small settlements near the confluence of the Ashley and Cooper Rivers, South Carolina and the Lower South

Jack P. Greene. "Colonial South Carolina and the Caribbean Connection," *South Carolina Historical Magazine, 88,* 1987, pp. 192–210. Reprinted by permission.

culture that developed out of those small beginnings and gradually spread north to the Cape Fear region of North Carolina and south into Georgia and East and West Florida, was as much the offspring of Barbados as was Jamaica or the other English Caribbean colonies.

Although scholars have long appreciated the role of Barbados in the origins of the Lower South, the sudden and artificial separation of the North American continental colonies from the West Indian colonies as a result of the American Revolution and the simultaneous incorporation of South Carolina and Georgia into the larger American culture of the United States have tended to focus attention away from the continuing vibrancy of South Carolina's Caribbean connection throughout the colonial period. The same developments have also tended to obscure the related fact that, for much of its colonial existence, South Carolina exhibited socio-economic and cultural patterns that, in many important respects, corresponded more closely to those in the Caribbean colonies than to those in the mainland colonies to the north. Though it is still far from complete, new work over the past fifteen years on the social history of Britain's early modern colonies now makes it more possible than ever before to analyze the developmental parallels and contrasts among the several colonies that trace their origins in some major part to the Barbados culture hearth.

This essay will explore three themes: first, South Carolina's Caribbean roots; second, its continuing connection with the Caribbean colonies during the colonial period; and third, the developmental parallels between it and the other colonies—the Leeward Islands and Jamaica—that emerged out of the Barbadian culture hearth during the seventeenth and early eighteenth centuries.

Why Barbados became a base and a prototype for the establishment of so many other colonies in the Caribbean and in the Lower South can only be explained by an examination of its early history. For ten years after its initial settlement in 1627, Barbados, like earlier English colonies in Virginia and Bermuda, concentrated very largely on tobacco culture, though it also began producing considerable quantities of cotton and indigo during the late 1630s. From the beginning, Barbados was a reasonably successful producer of staples for the English market, and this success drew large numbers of English immigrants to it and set off a feverish rush for land that, within a decade, had resulted in the occupation of virtually all of the arable land both in Barbados, which covered an area of only 166 square miles and in the nearby Leeward Islands, all four of which covered an area of only 251 square miles.

As had been the case in early Virginia, the entire society was organized for profit. A few people from English gentry and commercial families, mostly younger sons, came to make their fortunes, but most immigrants were single male dependent indentured servants imported to labor in the cultivation and processing of tobacco, cotton, and indigo. Every bit as competitive, exploitative, and materialistic as early Virginia, Barbados experienced a rapid concentration of wealth, as the society polarized into small groups of proprietors and a mass of dependent indentured servants or mobile free laborers. Paying but scant attention to religion or other social and cultural institutions, Barbados and the Leeward Islands were notorious for their riotous and abandoned styles of life, while high mortality among new immigrants and the imbalance of women in the population contributed to the slow process of family development.

Most of these early tendencies were even further enhanced by the gradual substitution of sugar for minor staple cultivation beginning in Barbados in the mid-1640s and gradually extending to the Leeward Islands and Jamaica in subsequent decades. This capital and labor intensive crop led to the further concentration of property into the hands of the few people who could command the capital to purchase the labor and equipment necessary to produce sugar competitively. At the same time they were amassing larger and larger estates for themselves, these plantation owners were replacing white servants and free white laborers with African slaves, who seem to have been both a more economical and a more reliable source of labor. Like their counterparts in Virginia, Barbadian planters had, from the beginning of settlement, shown no reluctance to treat white servant labor as a disposable commodity, and the wholesale importation of African slaves into Barbados and the Leeward Islands represented both a logical extension of that impulse and the first large-scale use of slavery and non-European labor in any of the English colonies.

By the early 1650s, as a result of the sugar revolution, Barbados had achieved a population density greater than any comparable area in the English-speaking world, except London. But the introduction of black slaves into Barbados contributed to a rapid decline of white population, as many whites migrated to other colonies where there were greater opportunities to acquire land or returned to England. From a high of about 30,000 in 1650, the number of whites fell to about 20,000 in 1680 and 15,500 in 1700. Despite the fall in numbers of white settlers, Barbados, in 1670, was certainly, as Richard S. Dunn has written, "the richest, most highly developed, most populous, and most congested English colony in America, with a thriving sugar industry and 50,000 inhabitants, including 30,000 Negroes."

As Barbados and its neighboring colonies in the Leeward Islands became more black and the concentration on sugar production became ever more intensive, profits soared and wealth accumulation among the possessing classes was phenomenal. By 1660, the wealth of Barbados, the earliest and best developed of the island colonies, exceeded that of any other contemporary English overseas possession. But the rapid rise of a wealthy and conspicuous elite did not immediately give either much cohesion or stability to Barbadian society. Indeed, many of those wealthy few proprietors who could afford it began to flee the tropical sugar factories they had established for the more settled and, especially after 1680, healthier world of England.

That the socio-economic model first successfully articulated in Barbados with its exploitative and materialistic orientation, concentration on sugar production, a slave-powered plantation system, a highly stratified social structure, great disparities in wealth and styles of life, a high ratio of blacks to whites, little attention to the development of family life and other traditional social institutions and cultural amenities, high levels of absenteeism among the wealthy, a rapid turnover among the elite, and heavy mortality. . . .

. . . Barbadian model . . . proved capable of transfer beyond the Lesser Antilles in the eastern Caribbean to much larger physical entities in Jamaica and South Carolina. Settled by the English in the second half of the seventeenth century, these two colonies, like the Leeward Islands, . . . developed far more slowly than Barbados. But they eventually became highly successful plantation colonies on the Barbadian model. Indeed, by the mid-eighteenth century, they had become two of the three wealthiest and economically most important British-American colonies, with only Virginia—and not even Barbados—approaching them in this regard.

Continuously occupied by Spaniards since the early sixteenth century, Jamaica, prior to the English conquest in 1655, had been primarily a producer of livestock and minor staples, especially cocoa, and had never been an important part of the Hispanic American empire. With 4,411 square miles of territory, more than twenty-six and a half times that of Barbados and approximately the same size as the area that would later comprise the South Carolina lowcountry, Jamaica was first settled by disbanded English soldiers and the flow of excess population from England's eastern Caribbean colonies. This flow included many planters who, having made considerable fortunes in Barbados or the Leeward Islands, migrated with their slaves to Jamaica, where they hoped to establish a new, and infinitely more expandable, sugar colony that would have land enough to enable them to provide for their younger sons. This migration began in earnest in 1664 when one of Jamaica's first governors, Sir Thomas Modyford, and some 700 other Barbadian planters arrived in the colony with their slaves.

Jamaica soon rivaled Barbados in riches. But in the early decades its wealth came more from the activities of its freebooting buccaneers, who used its strategic position in the central Caribbean to tap the vast wealth of the Hispanic American empire. Through a combination of trade and raids, they converted their Jamaica base at Port Royal into the richest spot in English America. Primarily because it did not for many decades have access to a plentiful slave supply, however, Jamaica was slow to develop as a sugar-producing staple colony. Following the example of the Spaniards, all of whom had fled the colony within three or four years after the English conquest, leaving their large stocks of cattle behind, many of Jamaica's new proprietors raised cattle and other livestock for food consumption in Jamaica and elsewhere in the Caribbean, while others produced minor staples, including cocoa, indigo, and provisions. Not until the beginning of the eighteenth century did Jamaica export as much sugar as tiny Barbados.

No less than the Leeward Islands and Jamaica, South Carolina also represented a successful extension of the Barbados culture hearth. As more and more of its arable land was converted to sugar and foodstuffs and other supplies had to be imported from elsewhere, Barbadian leaders began to look to the unoccupied portions of the southeastern mainland of North America as a potential site for new settlements that would be able to supply the provisions and other necessities required to sustain the island's sugar economy. With approval of the Lords Proprietors to whom, following his Restoration to the English throne in 1660, Charles II had granted authority to colonize Carolina and the Bahamas, a group of Barbadians, including the same Sir Thomas Modyford who settled in Jamaica in 1664, had unsuccessfully sought to establish settlements at Cape Fear and Port Royal in the mid-1660s.

As several historians have recently emphasized, Barbadians also played an extensive role in the first successful settlement in 1670. Almost half of the whites and considerably more than half of the blacks who came to the new settlement during the first two years were from Barbados, and this distribution continued for at least two decades. The most thorough and authoritative study we have of the origins of the 1,343 white settlers who immigrated to South Carolina between 1670 and 1690 indicates that more than 54 percent were probably from Barbados. They included people from all social classes. The great majority were from the small planter and freeman classes of families, a small planter owning at least ten acres but fewer than twenty slaves and a freeman owning less than ten acres. Some of these simply sold out and used the proceeds to transport themselves and their families and slaves to Carolina, while others came as indentured servants.

But South Carolina's Barbadian immigrants also included a few members of the island's elite. According to Dunn, representatives of eighteen of those 175 big Barbadian sugar planting families which had at least sixty slaves apiece, "held the best land, sold the most sugar, and monopolized the chief offices on the island" obtained land in South Carolina. Not all of these families actually settled in the colony. But a significant number, including, among the earlier immigrants, Edward and Arthur Middleton, James Colleton, and Robert and Thomas Gibbes, did. Further research by Richard Waterhouse has shown that, in addition, "representatives of as many as thirty-three 'middling' [Barbadian] planter families settled in Carolina between 1670 and 1690," middling planters being those who owned between twenty and fifty-nine slaves. Finally, a number of Barbadian merchants acquired land in South Carolina. Although many of them used agents to manage their plantations, several, including John Ladson, Benjamin Quelch, and Bernard Schenckingh, actually moved to the colony.

Not only did these Barbadians bring "energy, experience, and wealth" to South Carolina. They also brought the social and cultural system that had been so fully articulated in the island over the previous four decades. The only mainland English colony that began its existence with a preference for African slave labor and a significant number of African slaves among its original settlers, South Carolina early revealed that strong commercial, materialistic, and exploitative mentality that had found such a ready field for action in the Caribbean. For at least a generation, the colony functioned effectively as its West Indian proponents had initially intended, as an adjunct to the Barbadian economy. South Carolina developed a vigorous grazing economy that in size rivaled that of Jamaica, and, in return for sugar products and black slaves, it sent large quantities of beef, pork, corn, lumber, naval stores, and Indian slaves to Barbados, the Leeward Islands, and Jamaica.

Even in its earliest days, however, the South Carolina economy was never wholly dependent on trade to the Caribbean. Provisioning privateers and pirates and, even more important, trading with the large number of Indians residing in the southeastern part of the North American continent for great quantities of deerskins for export to England were also lucrative activities. No less than early Barbadians, however, early South Carolinians were avid in their search for a profitable agricultural staple that would do for their colony what sugar had done for Barbados. Early experiments with tobacco and indigo were reasonably successful, but it was not until the successful experimentation with rice in the 1690s that the colony's planters found a staple that was sufficiently profitable to provide the basis for a viable plantation system on the Barbadian model. Over the next three decades, rice, naval stores, provisions, and deerskins brought in the capital necessary to acquire the almost wholly African slave labor force that helped to give South Carolina such a close resemblance to its West Indian progenitors. Already by 1710 there were more blacks than whites in South Carolina. By 1720, blacks outnumbered whites by almost two to one, a far higher ratio than would ever be exhibited by any other English mainland colony.

If, especially in recent decades, historians have tended to emphasize the extent to which, "more than any mainland colony," South Carolina's "roots and early commercial ties stretched toward Barbados and other islands of the English Caribbean," they have paid far less attention to the continuing vitality of that connection. Within the early modern British Empire, such connections were maintained through flows of people, goods, and ideas along the major arteries of trade. Of these various flows, that of people probably dropped to quite low levels during the eighteenth century. A small number of wealthy planters and merchants fled the island colonies throughout the eighteenth century. Though most of them went to Britain or to one of the more northerly colonies, especially Rhode Island and New York, a few came to South Carolina. The families of Rawlins Lowndes, which came from St. Kitts in 1730, and Eliza Lucas Pinckney, which came from Antigua in 1738, are conspicuous examples.

But the fact was that few of the island colonies had an exportable population in the eighteenth century. . . .

Although the stream of immigrants from the West Indies to South Carolina all but dried up in the eighteenth century, the flow of goods remained strong. In addition to small quantities of wine, limes, lime juice, cocoa, coffee, and sugar, South Carolina imported directly from the West Indies between 70 percent and 85 percent of the roughly 1,000 hogsheads each of sugar and molasses and 4,000 hogsheads of rum it consumed each year. Down through the 1730s, Barbados was the primary source of these sugar products, but both the Leeward Islands and Jamaica surpassed Barbados in the 1750s and 1760s.

In return, South Carolina shipped a variety of products to all of the West Indian colonies. Exports of naval stores were high early in the century but diminished over time; beef and pork, corn and peas, and leather remained fairly steady over the whole period, with Jamaica, Barbados, and the Leeward Islands continuing to be the leading importers of each down into the 1760s. Exports of lumber, barrel staves, and shingles increased dramatically after 1750, with Jamaica usually taking the largest quantities followed by Barbados, Antigua, and St. Kitts. To the West Indies, as to Europe, South Carolina's leading export was rice. The island colonies took about 10 percent of South Carolina's total rice exports in 1717–20 and around 20 percent in the 1760s. Barbados was the largest market through the 1730s, but it had fallen to third place behind Jamaica and the Leeward Islands by the late 1750s.

Altogether, in most years during the eighteenth century, about a fourth to a third of the total tonnage entering Charleston came from or via the West Indies, while between 15 percent to 25 percent of the ships cleared from Charleston traded to the West Indies. This disparity can be partly explained by contemporary shipping routes. Prevailing wind patterns dictated that many vessels from Britain came via the West Indies, while return voyages usually proceeded directly back to Britain. Although more ships entered Charleston from the West Indies than returned, by the 1760s, nearly forty ships based in the West Indies annually cleared the port of Charleston with return cargoes of rice and other commodities for Jamaica, Barbados, the Leeward Islands, and the Bahamas.

This steady flow of goods back and forth between South Carolina and the West Indies brought news, ideas, even architectural innovations. The published business correspondence of Robert Pringle and Henry Laurens contain frequent correspondence with trading partners in Bridgetown, Barbados, and elsewhere in the West Indies, and the *South Carolina Gazette* often reprinted items from island newspapers, and vice versa. Especially interesting to South Carolina readers was news of the frequent slave uprisings in Jamaica and other sugar islands. As a recent architectural historian has shown, the verandah or front porch, first developed in the West Indies, appeared almost simultaneously about 1735 in most of the North American colonies engaged in the West Indian trade, including South Carolina. . . .

Unlike the Leeward Islands but like Barbados, Jamaica managed, despite some absenteeism, to sustain a "self-conscious, articulate, cohesive social class of proprietor-administrators" well into the later eighteenth century. Like the large estate owners in Barbados, there were "committed settlers" who, especially after 1750, constructed grand houses in an emergent Jamaican vernacular style; supported an active press; built churches, schools, and hospitals; and exerted political and social control through dynamic and self-conscious local political institutions.

In many ways, South Carolina's eighteenth-century development paralleled that of Jamaica. Its economic welfare was also closely tied to the fortunes of an external market for its principal staple. What sugar was for the West Indian colonies, rice became for South Carolina. Following its emergence in the 1690s, rice production as measured by exports grew steadily during the first three decades of the eighteenth century from 1.5 million pounds in 1710 to nearly 20 million by 1730. By the 1720s, it had become South Carolina's most valuable export, a position it held throughout the colonial period. Between 1730 and 1750, the rice market was erratic, and exports increased slowly, except for a brief period in the late 1730s. But starting in the early 1750s exports once again began to surge steadily upward. In terms of total value, rice, by the early 1770s, ranked fourth among exports from Britain's American colonies behind sugar, tobacco, and wheat.

Like Jamaica, South Carolina never became monocultural, however. Throughout the colonial period, it continued to export most of its earliest products: deerskins, naval stores, lumber and barrel staves, grains, and meat. Beginning in the 1740s, the reintroduction of indigo by Eliza Lucas Pinckney and others and its successful production provided South Carolina with a second highly profitable staple, albeit one whose quality was not sufficiently high to sustain it following the withdrawal of a British bounty after the American Revolution. Around 1770, rice accounted for about 55 percent of the value of all exports, indigo for 20 percent, deerskins, naval stores and lumber products each for between 5 percent and 7 percent, and grain and meat products each for about 2 percent. The diversity of the South Carolina economy is illustrated by Robert M. Weir's calculation that the record rice crop of 1770 was grown by less than 50% of the slave population on no more than 3 percent of the land in private hands, while the largest harvest of indigo was grown by only about 13% of the slaves on less than 0.5 percent of such land.

Also like Jamaica, staple agriculture brought South Carolina masses of black slaves, a precarious racial balance in the population, and enormous wealth. The black population rose dramatically from about 2,500 in 1700 to 5,000 in 1710, 39,000 in 1730, and 75,000 in 1770. Before 1720, South Carolina's black population seems to have been able to generate a natural increase. But with the intensification of staple agriculture in the 1720s and 1730s and, probably much more important, the importation of large numbers of new slaves from Africa, it began, like its counterparts in the West Indian colonies, to experience a net annual decrease. Though the slave population seems to have again become self-sustaining after 1750, most of the enormous increase in slaves was, throughout the colonial period, the result of large imports, which, except for the decade of the 1740s, remained high.

Though it was greater by far than any other contemporary British continental colony, the ratio of blacks to whites for South Carolina as a whole never approached that in the Caribbean colonies. For most of the period after 1720, it seems to have remained roughly at 2 to 2.5 to 1. But these figures are deceptive. In some lowcountry parishes, the importation of blacks and the emigration of whites had, by the 1750s, raised the ratio as high as nine to one, a figure well beyond that found in Barbados and only slightly below that found in Jamaica. Such a racial distribution indeed made those parts of the lowcountry seem, in the words of one contemporary, "more like a Negro country" than a settlement of people of European descent.

Because of the proximity of the Spanish in Florida, the French in Louisiana, and many powerful Indian tribes, South Carolina, like the Caribbean colonies, already lived in persistent danger of external attack, and the large disproportion of blacks in the rural rice-growing areas gave the colony, again like those in the Caribbean, a potentially powerful domestic enemy. Based on that of Barbados, South Carolina's slave code was the most draconian on the continent, though some of the harshness that characterized Jamaican slavery may have been mitigated in South Carolina by the task system. Most South Carolina slaves worked not in gangs, like the sugar slaves of the Caribbean or the tobacco slaves of the Chesapeake, but by tasks, an arrangement that permitted the more industrious to grow their own produce and raise their own animals for sale to whites in a domestic marketing system that in its extent and economic importance probably approached that of Jamaica. For whatever reasons, South Carolina, in contrast to seventeenth-century Barbados and to Jamaica throughout the colonial period, both of which were riven by slave revolts, had only one major slave uprising, the Stono Rebellion of 1739. But the specter of slave revolt always lurked in the background. Also like the situation in the Caribbean colonies, South Carolina seems to have had a higher incidence of interracial sexual unions than any other colony on the continent.

If staple agriculture and slavery brought South Carolina danger for whites and degradation for blacks, it also, by the middle of the eighteenth century brought whites wealth that, while considerably less than that enjoyed by their counterparts in Jamaica, far exceeded that of any other settler population in British North America. Per capita wealth in the Charleston district of South Carolina in 1774 was an astonishing £2,337.7, more than four times that of people living in the tobacco areas of the Chesapeake and nearly six times greater than that of people living in the towns of New York and Philadelphia.

This wealth enabled South Carolina's richest planters and merchants to live a luxurious life comparable to that of similar groups in seventeenth-century Barbados and eighteenth-century Jamaica. Beginning in the 1740s, members of this group built, usually in the English style but sometimes with some West Indian modifications, several expensive public buildings and many sumptuous private houses. Most wealthy rice planters chose Charleston as the site for their most elegant residence, and, with this large absentee planter class resident for much of the year, Charleston, a city of 11,000 by the 1770s, was a lively cultural center with a library company, concerts, theatre, horse races, and a variety of benevolent organizations, fraternal groups, and social clubs. By the 1770s, some South Carolina families had become sufficiently wealthy that they were even following the example of the West Indians and abandoning the colony altogether. In the early 1770s, as many as fifty absentee South Carolina proprietors were living in London.

An important reason why England appealed to both West Indians and South Carolinians was the appalling health conditions that obtained in their home colonies. Life expectancy in South Carolina seems to have been slightly better than that in either Jamaica or the Leeward Islands, both of which were notorious for their high mortality among both whites and blacks. But both Charleston and lowcountry South Carolina suffered from a disease environment that was far more malignant than that of any other British continental colony. Crude death rates recently calculated for Charleston in the 1720s show that they were almost twice as high as those in contemporary Philadelphia or England and Wales. . . .

South Carolina had begun in the late seventeenth century as an offshoot of the prolific Barbadian culture hearth; although it lagged somewhat behind, in its subsequent demographic, socio-economic, and cultural development it thus closely paralleled that of Jamaica, Barbados's other principal seventeenth-century colony. Both South Carolina and Jamaica were heavily involved in the production of agricultural staples and both imported extraordinarily high numbers of African slaves that resulted in a population in which the numerical preponderance of blacks was overwhelming. As a result, both had a harsh system of labor discipline and lived in fear of slave revolt. Elites in both colonies enjoyed phenomenal wealth that enabled them to live splendidly in the English manner and to build elaborate public buildings, private houses, and showy cultural institutions, while at least the wealthiest among them even managed altogether to escape the unhealthy disease environment that characterized both colonies. . . .

## F U R T H E R   R E A D I N G

Hilary McD. Beckles, *White Servitude and Black Slavery in Barbados, 1627–1715* (1989).

Hilary McD. Beckles, ed., *Inside Slavery: Process and Legacy in the Caribbean* (1996).

Carl and Roberta Bridenbaugh, *No Peace Beyond the Line: The English in the Caribbean, 1624–1690* (1972).

Joyce E. Chaplin, *An Anxious Pursuit: Agricultural Innovation and Modernity in the Lower South, 1730–1815* (1993).

David Leroy Coon, "Eliza Lucas Pinckney and the Reintroduction of Indigo Culture in South Carolina, *Journal of Southern History,* 42 (1976), 61–76.

Richard S. Dunn, *Sugar and Slaves: The Rise of the Planter Class in the English West Indies, 1624–1713* (1972).

Rachel N. Klein, *Unification of a Slave State: The Lives of the Planters in the South Carolina Backcountry, 1760–1808* (1990).

Daniel C. Littlefield, *Rice and Slaves: Ethnicity and the Slave Trade in Colonial South Carolina* (1981).

Roderick A. McDonald, ed., *West Indies Accounts: Essays on the History of the British Caribbean and the Atlantic Economy in Honour of Richard Sheridan* (1996).

Richard B. Sheridan, *Sugar and Slavery: An Economic History of the British West Indies, 1623–1775* (1994).

Peter H. Wood, *Black Majority: Negroes in Colonial South Carolina from 1670 Through the Stono Rebellion* (1974).

Richard Waterhouse, *A New World Gentry: The Making of a Merchant and Planter Class in South Carolina, 1670–1770* (1989).

# CHAPTER
# 9

# Expansion in the South:
# Hopes and Realities

*In the later seventeenth century the character of colonization changed. The immi-grant stream ceased to draw primarily on England and instead was composed of people from other parts of the British Isles, particularly Scotland and Ulster [north-ern Ireland], and continental Europe. Like the contemporaneous migration to the Middle Colonies, the settlement of the region south of the Chesapeake was carried out by an ethnically mixed population, and many of these people came for religious rea-sons. Like the Puritans in Massachusetts and the Roman Catholics in Maryland in the 1630s, they sought the chance to build societies according to their own standards and to live with like-minded people. These planters came in groups, building com-munities designed to sustain their own heritage in the new environment. Although the backcountry was within the colonial patents of the established colonies, in many ways it was a region with a unity of its own. Settlers who arrived at the port of Philadelphia flowed southward along the foothills, adding to populations moving directly west, and built chains of settlements.*

*The experience of the Lower South colonies differed from earlier English colonies because they were located in an international arena. St. Augustine in Florida had been established as an outpost of the Spanish empire by 1560 and French, Spanish, and English traders had long been active throughout the Southeast. Large and pow-erful Indian confederations, including Cherokees, Creeks, and Tuscaroras, partici-pated in the trade. This multifaceted and shifting international scene gave Indians and Africans room to maneuver. Some Africans were able to escape from slavery throughout the whole colonial period and gain a degree of freedom in Spanish terri-tory. On the other hand, English traders armed Indians who acted for them and made the trade, particularly in deerskins, more exploitive than formerly. The deerskin trade led to slavery for many Indians. Because of its proximity to well-es-tablished French and Spanish interests, the Lower South was vulnerable to the ef-fects of the long series of wars between France and England which began in 1689 with the conflict known in America as King William's War and continued through the American Revolution. Fears for the rich colony of South Carolina led the English government to detach a portion of its territory, forming Georgia in 1730, to serve as a buffer between South Carolina and Spanish Florida.*

## D O C U M E N T S

Indian trader John Lawson wrote of the natives and the land in his journal of his thousand-mile journey through the Southeast published under the title of *A New Voyage to Carolina* (1709). Lawson clearly showed the close relationships of traders and Indians in document 1, as well as the devastating effect of colonization on native life. Edward Randolph, sent by the Board of Trade to inspect the colonies, reported in document 2 on the South Carolinians' fear of depredations from Spanish St. Augustine; rice and indigo, the two great cash crops, were not yet established when he wrote in 1699. Newly arrived Governor William Tryon wrote home to his uncle, Sewallis Shirley, about his estimate of the people and the land of North Carolina, particularly the hard life of the frontier illustrated in document 3, July 26, 1765.

Many documents survive from communities that came to the lower south from all over Europe. An anonymous letter from the new Swiss settlement led by Christoph Von Graffenried near New Bern in North Carolina in document 4, 1711, expresses both the great promise of the land and the colonists' intense homesickness. The backcountry was attractive to groups such as the Moravians, a pietistic sect organized in Germany in the 1720s under the leadership and patronage of Count Nicholas Zinzendorf. The Moravians had previously settled in Pennsylvania and Georgia, and in 1752 Bishop August Gottlieb Spangenberg traveled from Bethlehem in Pennsylvania to survey the prospective site in North Carolina. His entry, document 5, shows the potential conflict between paternalistic plans developed in Europe and experience in the field.

James Oglethorpe presented the original benevolent picture of the founding of Georgia as a refuge for the English laboring poor in document 6, while also suggesting that they would be useful against the French and Spanish. In document 7 William Byrd of Virginia wrote Lord Egmont, one of the Georgia Trustees, of the harm done in Virginia by large-scale reliance on slaves and praised Georgia's plan of prohibiting slavery and rum.

## 1. Indian Trader John Lawson's Journal of Carolina, 1709

Next Morning very early, we waded thro' the Savanna, the Path lying there; and about ten a Clock came to a hunting Quarter, of a great many *Santees;* they made us all welcome; shewing a great deal of Joy at our coming, giving us barbacu'd Turkeys, Bear's Oil, and Venison.

Here we hir'd *Santee Jack* (a good Hunter, and a well-humour'd Fellow) to be our Pilot to the *Congeree Indians;* we gave him a Stroud-water-Blew, to make his Wife an *Indian* Petticoat, who went with her Husband. After two Hours Refreshment, we went on, and got that Day about twenty Miles. . . . The Weather was very cold, the Winds holding *Northerly.* We made our selves as merry as we could, having a good Supper with the Scraps of the Venison we had given us by the *Indians,* having kill'd 3 Teal and a Possum, which Medly all together made a curious Ragoo.

This Day all of us had a Mind to have rested, but the *Indian* was much against it, alledging, That the Place we lay at, was not good to hunt in; telling us, if we would go on, by Noon, he would bring us to a more convenient Place; so we mov'd forwards, and about twelve a Clock came to the most amazing Prospect I had seen

Lawson, John. *A New Voyage to Carolina.* (London, 1709), 25–28.

since I had been in *Carolina;* we travell'd by a Swamp-side, which Swamp I believe to be no less than twenty Miles over, the other Side being as far as I could well discern, there appearing great Ridges of Mountains, bearing from us *W.N.W.* One Alp with a Top like a Sugar-loaf, advanc'd its Head above all the rest very considerably; the Day was very serene, which gave us the Advantage of seeing a long Way; these Mountains were cloth'd all over with Trees, which seem'd to us to be very large Timbers.

At the Sight of this fair Prospect, we stay'd all Night; our *Indian* going about half an Hour before us, had provided three fat Turkeys e'er we got up to him.

The Swamp I now spoke of, is not a miry Bog, as others generally are, but you go down to it thro' a steep Bank, at the Foot of which, begins this Valley, where you may go dry for perhaps 200 Yards, then you meet with a small Brook or Run of Water, about 2 or 3 Foot deep, then dry Land for such another Space, so another Brook, thus continuing. The Land in this Percoarson, or Valley, being extraordinary rich, and the Runs of Water well stor'd with Fowl. It is the Head of one of the Branches of *Santee*-River; but a farther Discovery Time would not permit; only one Thing is very remarkable, there growing all over this Swamp, a tall, lofty Bay-tree, but is not the same as in *England,* these being in their Verdure all the Winter long; which appears here, when you stand on the Ridge, (where our Path lay) as if it were one pleasant, green Field, and as even as a Bowling-green to the Eye of the Beholder; being hemm'd in on one Side with these Ledges of vast high Mountains.

Viewing the Land here, we found an extraordinary rich, black Mould, and some of a Copper-colour, both Sorts very good; the Land in some Places is much burthen'd with Iron, Stone, here being great Store of it, seemingly very good: . . . When we were all asleep, in the Beginning of the Night, we were awaken'd with the dismall'st and most hideous Noise that ever pierc'd my Ears: This sudden Surprizal incapacitated us of guessing what this threatning Noise might proceed from; but our *Indian* Pilot (who knew these Parts very well) acquainted us, that it was customary to hear such Musick along that Swamp-side, there being endless Numbers of Panthers, Tygers, Wolves, and other Beasts of Prey, which take this Swamp for their Abode in the Day, coming in whole Droves to hunt the Deer in the Night, making this frightful Ditty 'till Day appears, then all is still as in other Places.

The next Day it prov'd a small drisly Rain, which is rare, there happening not the tenth Part of Foggy falling Weather towards these Mountains, as visits those Parts. Near the Sea-board, the *Indian* kill'd 15 Turkeys this Day; there coming out of the Swamp, (about Sun-rising) Flocks of these Fowl, containing several hundreds in a Gang, who feed upon the Acorns, it being most Oak that grow in these Woods. These are but very few Pines in those Quarters.

Early the next Morning, we set forward for the *Congeree-Indians,* parting with that delicious Prospect. By the Way, our Guide kill'd more Turkeys, and two Polcats, which he eat, esteeming them before fat Turkeys. Some of the Turkeys which we eat, whilst we stay'd there, I believe, weigh'd no less than 40 pounds.

The Land we pass'd over this Day, was most of it good, and the worst passable. At Night we kill'd a Possum, being cloy'd with Turkeys, made a Dish of that, which tasted much between young Pork and Veal; their Fat being as white as any I ever saw.

Our *Indian* having this Day kill'd good Store of Provision with his Gun, he always shot with a single Ball, missing but two Shoots in above forty; they being curious Artists in managing a Gun, to make it carry either Ball, or Shot, true. When they have bought a Piece, and find it to shoot any Ways crooked, they take the Barrel out of the Stock, cutting a Notch in a Tree, wherein they set it streight, sometimes shooting away above 100 Loads of Ammunition, before they bring the Gun to shoot according to their Mind. We took up our Quarters by a Fish-pond-side; the Pits in the Woods that stand full of Water, naturally breed Fish in them, in great Quantities. We cook'd our Supper, but having neither Bread, or Salt, our fat Turkeys began to be loathsome to us, altho' we were never wanting of a good Appetite, yet a Continuance of one Diet, made us weary.

The next Morning, *Santee Jack* told us, we should reach the *Indian* Settlement betimes that Day; about Noon, we pass'd by several fair Savanna's, very rich and dry; seeing great Copses of many Acres that bore nothing but Bushes, about the Bigness of Box-trees; which (in the Season) afford great Quantities of small Black-berries, very pleasant Fruit, and much like to our Blues, or Huckle-berries, that grow on Heaths in *England.* Hard by the Savanna's we found the Town, where we halted; there was not above one Man left with the Women, the rest being gone a Hunting for a Feast. The Women were very busily engag'd in Gaming: The Name or Grounds of it, I could not learn, tho' I look'd on above two Hours. Their Arithmetick was kept with a Heap of *Indian* Grain. When their Play was ended, the King, or *Cassetta's* Wife, invited us into her Cabin. The *Indian* Kings always entertaining Travellers, either *English,* or *Indian;* taking it as a great Affront, if they pass by their Cabins, and take up their Quarters at any other *Indian's* House. The Queen set Victuals before us, which good Compliment they use generally as soon as you come under their Roof.

The Town consists not of above a dozen Houses, they having other stragling Plantations up and down the Country, and are seated upon a small Branch of *Santee* River. Their Place hath curious dry Marshes, and Savanna's adjoining to it, and would prove an exceeding thriving Range for Cattle, and Hogs, provided the *English* were seated thereon. Besides, the Land is good for Plantations.

These *Indians* are a small People, having lost much of their former Numbers, by intestine Broils; but most by the Small-pox, which hath often visited them, sweeping away whole Towns; occasion'd by the immoderate Government of themselves in their Sickness; . . . treating of the *Sewees.* Neither do I know any Savages that have traded with the *English,* but what have been great Losers by this Distemper. . . .

# 2. English Official Edward Randolph
## Reports to the Board of Trade on Economic
## Prospects and the Spanish Threat, 1699

*May it please your Lordships,*

After a dangerous voyage at Sea, I landed at Charles Town, in the Province of So. Carolina. . . .

---

Some of the spelling in this document has been modernized.

Edward Randolph to the Board of Trade, March, 1699, in Alexander S. Sally, ed., *Narratives of Early Carolina, 1650–1708* (New York: Charles Scribner's Sons, 1911), 204–210.

There are but few settled Inhabitants in this Province, the Lords have taken up vast tracts of land for their own use, as in Colleton County and other places, where the land is most commodious for settlement, which prevents peopling the place, and makes them less capable to preserve themselves. As to their civil Governt., 'tis different from what I have met with in the other Proprieties. Their Militia is not above 1500 Soldiers White men, but have thro' the Province generally 4 Negroes to 1 White man, and not above 1100 families, English and French.

Their Chief Town is Charles Town, and the seat of Govt. in this Province, where the Governor, Council and Triennial Parliamt. set, and their Courts are holden, being above a league distance from the entrance to their harbour mouth, which is barred, and not above 17 foot water at the highest tide, but very difficult to come in. The Harbour is called by the Spaniards, St. George; it lies 75 leagues to the Northward of St. Augustine, belonging to the Spaniards. . . . In the year 1686, one hundred Spaniards, with Negroes and Indians, landed at Edistoe, (50 miles to the southward of Charles Town,) and broke open the house of Mr. Joseph Moreton, then Governor of the Province, and carried away Mr. Bowell, his Brother-in-law, prisoner, who was found murdered 2 or 3 days after; they carried away all his money and plate, and 13 slaves, to the value of £1500 sterling, and their plunder to St. Augustine. Two of the Slaves made their escape from thence, and returned to their master. Some time after, Govr. Moreton sent to demand his slaves, but the Govr. of St. Augustine answered it was done without his orders, but to this day keeps them, and says he can't deliver them up without an order from the King of Spain. About the same time they robbed Mr. Grimball's House, the Sec. of the Province, whilst he attended the Council at Charles Town, and carried away to the value of over £1500 sterling. They also fell upon a settlement of Scotchmen at Port Royal, where there was not above 25 men in health to oppose them. The Spaniards burnt down their houses, destroyed and carried away all that they had, because (as the Spaniards pretended) they were settled upon their land, and had they at any time a superior force, they would also destroy this town built upon Ashley and Cooper Rivers. . . .

I find the Inhabitants greatly alarmed upon the news that the French continue their resolution to make a settling at Messasipi River, from [whence] they may come over land to the head of Ashley River without opposition, 'tis not yet known what care the Lords Proprietors intend to take for their preservation. . . . I heard one of the Council (a great Indian Trader, and has been 600 miles up in the Country west from Charles Town) discourse that the only way to discover the Meschasipi is from this Province by land. He is willing to undertake it if His Majesty will please to pay the charge which will not be above £400 or £500 at most; he intends to take with him 50 white men of this Province and 100 Indians, who live 2 days journey east from the Meschasipi, and questions not but in 5 or 6 months time after he has His Majesty's commands and instructions to find out the mouth of it and the true latitude thereof.

The great improvement made in this Province is wholly owing to the industry and labour of the Inhabitants. They have applied themselves to make such commodities as might increase the revenue of the Crown, as Cotton, Wool, Ginger, Indigo, etc. But finding them not to answer the end, they are set upon making Pitch, Tar and Turpentine, and planting rice, and can send over great quantities yearly, if they had encouragement from England to make it, having about 5,000 Slaves to be employed in that service, upon occasion, but they have lost most of their vessels, which were but small, last war by the French, and some lately by the Spaniards, so that they are not able to send those Commodities to England for a market, neither are sailors here to be had to man their vessels.

I humbly propose that if His Majesty will for a time suspend the Duties upon Commodities, and that upon rice also, it will encourage the Planter to fall vigilantly upon making Pitch and Tar, etc., which the Lords Proprietors ought to make their principal care to obtain from His Majesty, being the only way to draw people to settle in their Province, a place of greatest encouragement to the English Navy in these parts of the world. Charles Town Bay is the safest port for all vessels coming thro' the gulf of Florida in distress, bound from the West Indies to the Northern Plantations; . . .

I have by the extreme of cold last Winter in Maryland and Pennsylvania, and by my tedious passage in the Winter time from New York to this place, got a great numbness in my right leg and foot. I am in hopes this warm climate will restore me to my health. I have formerly wrote to your Board and the Commissioners of H. M. Customs, the necessity of having a Vessel to transport me from one Plantation to another.

I humbly pray Your Lordships favour to direct that the little residence I am to make in these parts of the World, may be in this Province, and that a Vessel well manned may be sent me hither, which may answer all occasion, my intentions being not to lie idle, for when the Hurricane times come in these parts of the World, I can go securely to Virginia, Maryland and Pennsylvania and New England, without fear of being driven from those Plantations by North West Winds, and when they come I can pass from one Plantation to another without difficulty.

## 3. Governor William Tryon Assesses the Prospects for Life in the North Carolina Backcountry, 1765

The Calculation of the Inhabitants in this Province is one hundred and twenty Thousand White & Black, of which there is a great Majority of White People. The Negroes are very numerous I suppose five to one White Person in the Maritime Counties, but as you penetrate into the Country few Blacks are employed, merely for this Simple reason, that the poorer Settlers coming from the Northward Colonies sat themselves down in the back Counties where the land is the best but who have not more than a sufficiency to erect a Log House for their families and procure a few Tools to get a little Corn into the ground. This Poverty prevents their purchasing of Slaves, and before they can get into Sufficient affluence to buy Negroes their own Children are often grown to an age to work in the Field. not but numbers of families in the back Counties have Slaves from three to ten, Whereas in the Counties on the Sea Coast Planters have from fifty to 250 Slaves. A Plantation with Seventy Slaves on it, is esteemed a good property. When a man marries his Daughters he never talks of the fortune in Money but 20 30 or 40 Slaves is her Portion and

Governor William Tryon to his uncle, Sewallis Shirley, July 26, 1765, in William S. Powell, ed., "Tryon's 'Book' on North Carolina," *North Carolina Historical Review,* 34 (1957), 411. Reprinted with permission of North Carolina Division of Archives and History, Raleigh.

possibly an agreement to deliver at stated Periods, a Certain Number of Tarr or Turpentine Barrels, which serves towards exonerating the charges of the Wedding which are not grievous here. . . .

## 4. An Anonymous Letter Evokes the Swiss Settlement Near New Bern, North Carolina, 1711

With a thousandfold greeting, I wish all true friends, neighbors, and acquaintances God's grace and blessing. I an my wife, two children, and my old father have, the Lord be praised, arrived safe and sound in Carolina, and live twenty English miles from New Bern. I hope to plant corn enough this year. The land is good, but the beginning is hard, the journey dangerous. My two children, Maria and Hansli died at Rotterdam in Holland and were buried in the common burial place.

This country is praised too lightly in Europe and condemned too much. I hope also in a few years to have cows and swine as much as I desire. Mr. Graffenried is our landgrave. Of vermin, snakes, and such like, there is not so much as they tell of in Europe. I have seen crocodiles by the water, but they soon fled. One should not trust to supporting himself with game, for there are no wild oxen or swine. Stags and deer, ducks and geese and turkeys are numerous.

I wish that I had my child with me, which I left with my father-in-law, together with forty-five pounds which I left behind me in the parish of Tofen. And if my father-in-law wishes to come to me I will give to him from my land. One can have as much swine and cattle as he wants without labor and expense. I am very sorry that Christian Balsiger took away his Uhli from me again at Bern.

## 5. Bishop August Gottlieb Spangenberg Reports on Moravian Plans for the Settlement of Wachovia, 1752

*. . . Nov. 11. From camp on the Catawba River, about forty miles above Andreas Lambert's place, according to the judgment of our hunters.* [This sheet is marked "dem Jünger," that is, for the special consideration of Count Zinzendorf.] I am sitting in the tent thinking about your Patriarchal Plan for the settlement in North Carolina, and considering it in view of the local circumstances. First, there are the Indians. Our land lies in a region much frequented by the Catawbas and Cherokees, especially for hunting. The Senecas, too, come here almost every year, especially when they are at war with the Catawbas. The Indians in North Carolina behave quite differently from those in Pennsylvania. There no one fears an Indian, unless indeed he is drunk. Here the whites must needs fear them. If they come to a house and find the man away they are insolent, and the settler's wife must do whatever they bid. Sometimes they come in such large companies that a man who meets them

*Christoph Von Graffenreid's Account of the Founding of New Bern,* ed. Vincent H. Todd (Raleigh: NC Hist. Commission, 1920), 312–313.

Bishop A. G. Spagenburg diary, Entry for November 11, 1752. *Records of Moravians in North Carolina,* ed. Vincent H. Todd (Raleigh: NC Hist. Commission, 1920), I, 48–49.

is in real danger. Now and then a man can do as Andreas Lambert did:—A company of Senecas came on his land, injured his corn, killed his cattle, etc. Lambert called in his bear hounds, of which he has eight or nine, and with his dogs and his loaded gun drove the Indians from his place.

Every man living alone is in this danger, here in the forest. North Carolina has been at war with the Indians, and they have been defeated and have lost their lands. So not only the tribes that were directly concerned, but all the Indians are resentful and take every opportunity to show it. Indeed they have not only killed the cattle of the whites, but have murdered the settlers themselves when they had a chance.

There are other things to make life hard for those living *alone* and *for themselves.* For instance a woman is ill, has a high fever,—where is the nurse, medicine, proper food? The wife of the nearest neighbor lives half a mile, perhaps several miles away, and she has her children, her cattle, her own household, to care for, and can give her only a couple of hours, or at most only one day or one night.

Another thing.—By the Patriarchal Plan I understand that each family would live alone, and work for its own support. What will happen to those who have not the necessary talents? How will it go with men and women brought up in our congregations, who I fear have little conception of the difficulties they will have to face? What will they do in circumstances where each must help himself as best he can? How bear the hard work necessary to success, when each must say with Jacob, "In the day the drought consumed me and the frost by night"?

To speak plainly:—Among fifty members brought up in our congregation, or who have lived with us some years, there is probably not one who could maintain himself alone in the forest. They have had no experience, and even those who have the intelligence do not know how.

I do not say this to throw difficulties in the way of your whole plan, on the contrary I consider it important, and believe the Lord through it will achieve His own ends, but I suggest consideration of the best method of attaining that end.

Perhaps it would be wise to settle six to ten families together, each in its own house, all working under a capable overseer; and after a time, if any wishes to settle on his own farm, as in Pennsylvania, then to try to arrange it for him.

But I desist. I know I may not have found the right solution of the problem; the Lord will show us how it may best be done. . . .

# 6. James Oglethorpe, "Persons Reduc'd to Poverty May Be Happy in Georgia," 1732

. . . Let us . . . cast our Eyes on the Multitude of unfortunate People in the Kingdom of reputable Families, and of liberal, or at least, easy Education: Some undone by Guardians, some by Law-Suits, some by Accidents in Commerce, some by Stocks and Bubbles, and some by Suretyship. But all agree in this one Circumstance, that

---

Oglethorpe, James. *A New and Accurate Account of the Provinces of South-Carolina and Georgia* (London, 1732; facs. rpt. Savannah, GA: Beehive Press, 1972)

they must either be Burthensome to their Relations, or betake themselves to little Shifts for Sustenance, which ('tis ten to one) do not answer their Purposes, and to which a well-educated Mind descends with the utmost Constraint. What various Misfortunes may reduce the Rich, the Industrious, to the Danger of a Prison, to a moral Certainty of Starving! These are the Poeple that may relieve themselves and strengthen *Georgia,* by resorting thither, and Great *Britain* by their Departure. . . .

Having thus described (I fear, too truly) the pityable Condition of the better Sort of the Indigent, an Objection rises against their Removal upon what is stated of their Imbecility for Drudgery. It may be asked, if they can't get Bread here for their Labour, how will their Condition be mended in *Georgia?* The Answer is easy; Part of it is well attested, and Part self-evident. They have Land there for nothing, and that Land is so fertile that . . . they receive an Hundred Fold increase for taking very little Pains. Give here in *England* Ten Acres of good Land to One of these helpless Persons, and I doubt not his Ability to make it sustain him, and this by his own Culture, without letting it to another: But the Difference between no Rent, and Rack-Rent, is the Difference between eating and starving. If I make but Twenty Pound of the Produce of a Field, and am to pay Twenty Pound Rent for it; 'tis plain I must perish if I have not another Fund to support me: But if I pay no Rent, the Produce of that Field will supply the mere Necessities of Life.

With a View to the Relief of People in the Condition I have described, His Majesty has this present Year incorporated a considerable Number of Persons of Quality and Distinction, and vested a large Tract of *South-Carolina* in them, by the Name of *Georgia,* in Trust to be distributed among the Necessitous. These Trustees not only give Land to the Unhappy who go thither, but are also impower'd to receive the voluntary Contributions of charitable Persons to enable them to furnish the poor Adventurers with all Necessaries for the Expence of the Voyage, occupying the Land, and supporting them 'till they find themselves comfortably settled. So that now the Unfortunate will not be obliged to bind themselves to a long Servitude, to pay for their Passage, for they may be carried *gratis* into a Land of Liberty and Plenty; where they immediately find themselves in Possession of a competent Estate, in an happier Climate than they knew before, and they are Unfortunate indeed if here they can't forget their Sorrows. . . .

It is also highly for the Honour and Advancement of our holy Religion to assign a new Country to the poor *Germans,* who have left their own for the Sake of Truth. It will be a powerful Encouragement to Martyrs and Confessors of this Kind to hold fast their Integrity, when they know their Case not to be desperate in this World. Nor need we fear that the King of *Prussia* will be able to engross them all, we shall have a Share of them if we contribute chearfully to their Removal. The Society for the Propagation of the Gospel in foreign Parts have gloriously exerted themselves on this Occasion: They have resolv'd to advance such a Sum of Money to the Trustees for the Colony of *Georgia,* as will enable them to provide for Seven Hundred poor *Salzburghers.* This is laying a Foundation for the Conversion of the Heathen, at the same Time, that they snatch a great Number of poor Christians out of the Danger of Apostacy. 'Tis to be hoped this laudable Example will be followed by private Persons, who may thus at once do much for the Glory of God, and for the Wealth and Trade of *Great Britain.* Subjects thus acquir'd by the impolitick

Persecutions, by the superstitious Barbarities of neighbouring Princes, are a noble Addition to the capital Stock of the *British* Empire. . . .

The Encrease of our People, on this fruitful Continent, will probably, in due Time, have a good Effect on the Natives, if we do not shamefully neglect their Conversion: If we were moderately attentive to our Duty on this Head, we have no Reason to doubt of Success. The *Spaniard* has at this Day as many Christians, as he has Subjects in *America,* Negroes excepted. We may more reasonably hope to make Converts and good Subjects of the *Indians* in Amity with us, by using them well, when we grown numerous in their Neighbourhood, than the *Spaniards* could have expected to have done by their inexpressible Cruelties, which raised the utmost Aversion in the Minds of the poor *Indians* against them and their Religion together. One of their own Friers who had not relinquish'd his Humanity, tells us of an *Indian* Prince, who just as the *Spaniards* were about to murder him, was importuned by one of their Religious to become a Christian; the Priest told him much of Heaven and Hell, of Joy and Misery eternal; the Prince desired to be informed which of the two Places was allotted for the *Spaniards?* Heaven, quoth the Priest; says the Prince, I'm resolved not to go there. How different from this was the Reflection of an *Indian* Chief in *Pensilvania: What is the Matter, says he, with us that we are thus sick in our own Air, and these Strangers well? 'Tis as if they were sent hither to inherit our Land in our steads; but the Reason is plain, they love the Great God and we do not.* Was not this *Indian* almost become a Christian? *New-England* has many Convert-*Indians,* who are very good Subjects, tho' no other Colony has such long and cruel Wars with its *Indian* Neighbours. . . .

But this is not all, that Sum which settles one poor Family in the Colony does not end there; it in Truth purchases an Estate to be applied to like Uses, in all future Times. The Author of these Pages is credibly inform'd that the Trustees will reserve to themselves square Lots of Ground interspers'd at proper Distances among the Lands, which shall be given away: As the Country fills with People, these Lots will become valuable, and at moderate Rents will be a growing Fund to provide for those whose melancholy Cases may require Assistance hereafter: Thus the Settlement of Five Hundred Persons will open the Way to settle a Thousand more afterwards with equal Facility. Nor is this Advance of the Value of these Lots of Land a chimerical Notion; it will happen certainly and suddenly. All the Lands within Fifty Miles of *Charlestown* have within these Seven Years encreas'd near Four-Fold in their Value, so that you must pay Three or Four Hundred Pounds for a Plantation, which Seven Years ago you could have bought for a Hundred Pounds, and 'tis certain that Fifty Years ago you might have purchas'd at *Charlestown* for Five Shillings a Spot of Land which the Owner would not sell at this Day for Two Hundred Pounds Sterling.

The Legislature is only able to take a proper Course for the Transportation of small Offenders, if it shall seem best, when the Wisdom of the Nation is assembled; I mean only those who are but Novices in Iniquity. Prevention is better than the Punishment of Crimes, it may reform such to make them Servants to such Planters were reduc'd from a good Condition. The Manners and Habits of very young Offenders would meliorate in a Country not populous enough to encourage a profligate Course of Life, but a Country where Discipline will easily be preserv'd. These might supply the Place of Negroes, and yet (because their Servitude is only to be temporary) they might upon Occasion be found useful against the *French,* or *Spaniards;* indeed, as the Proportion of Negroes now stands, that Country would be in great Danger of being lost, in Case of a War with either of those Powers. The present Wealth of the Planters in their Slaves too probably threatens their future Ruin, if proper Measures be not taken to strengthen their Neighbourhood with large Supplies of Free-men. I would not here be understood to advance that our common Run of *Old-Baily* Transports wou'd be a proper Beginning in the Infancy of *Georgia.* No, they would be too hard for our young Planters, they ought never to be sent any where but to the Sugar Islands, unless we had Mines to employ them. . . .

## 7. William Byrd Praises the Plan for Georgia, 1736

. . . Your Lordship's opinion concerning Rum & negroes is certainly very just & your excluding both of them from your colony of Georgia will be very Happy: tho' with Respect to Rum, the Saints of New England, I fear will find out some trick, to evade your Act of Parliament. They have a great dexterity at palliating a perjury so well, as to leave no tast of it in the mouth, nor can any People like them slip through a Penal Statute. They will give some other name to their Rum which they may safely do, because it gos by that of Kill Devil in this Country, from its baneful qualitys. A watchfull eye, must be kept on these foul Traders, or all the precautions of the Trustees will be vain. I wish we could be blessed with the same Prohibition. They import so many negro's hither, that I fear this Colony will sometime or other be confounded by the name of New Guinea. I am sensible of many bad consequences of multiplying these Ethiopians amongst us. They blow up the pride, & ruin the Industry of our White People, who Seeing a Rank of poor Creatures below them, detest work for fear it should make them look like Slaves. Then that poverty which will ever attend upon Idleness, disposed them, as much to pilfer as it dos the Portuguise, who account it much more like a gentleman to steal, than to dirty their hands with Labour of any kind. Another unhappy Effect of many Negroes is, the necessity of being severe. Numbers make them insolent & then foul Means must do what fair will not. We have however nothing like the Inhumanity here, that is practiced in the Islands & God forbid we ever shou'd. But these base Tempers require to be rid with a tort rein, or they will be apt to throw their Rider. Yet even this is terrible to a good natured Man, who must submit to be either a Fool or a Fury. And this will be more our unhappy case, the more the Negros are increast amongst us. But these private mischeifs are nothing, if compared to the publick danger. We have already at least 10,000 men of these descendants of Ham, fit to bear Arms, & these numbers increase every day, as well by birth, as by Importation. And in case there should arise a Man of desperate courage amongst us, exasperated by a desperate fortune, he might with more advantage than Cataline kindle a Servile War. Such a man might be dreadfully mischeivous before any opposition coud be formed against him, & tinge our Rivers as wide as they are with blood, besides the Calamitys which wou'd be brought upon us by such an attempt, it wou'd cost our Mother

William Byrd to Lord Egmont, 12 July 1736, *Virginia Magazine of History and Biography,* XXXVI (1928), 219–222.

Country many a fair Million, to make us as profitable, as we are at present. It were there-fore, worth the consideration, of a British Parliament, My Lord, to put an end, to this unchristian Traffick, of makeing Merchandise of our Fellow Creatures. At Least, the farther importation of them, into our Colonys, should be prohibited, lest they prove as troublesome, & dangerous every where, as they have been lately in Jamaica, where besides a vast expence of money, they have cost the lives of many of his Majesty's Subjects. We have mountains in Virginia too, to which they may retire, as Safely, & do as much mischief, as they do in Jamaica. All these matters, duly considered, I wonder the Legislature will Indulge a few ravenous Traders, to the danger of the Publick safety, & such Traders as woud freely sell their Fathers, their Elder Brothers, & even the Wives of their bosomes if they cou'd black their Faces & get anything for them. In intirely agree with your Lordship in the Detestation you seem to feel for that Diabolical Liquor Rum, which dos more mischief to Peoples Industry & morals, than any thing except Gin & the Pope. And if it were not a little too Poetical, I should fancy, as the Gods of old are said to quaff Nector, so the Devils are fobb'd off with Rumm. Tho my Dear Country-men, woud think this unsavory Spirit, much too good for Devils, because they are fonder of it, than Wives or Children, for they often sell the Bread, out of their mouths, to buy Rumm to put in their own. Thrice happy Georgia, if it be in the power of any Law to keep out so great an enimy to Health, Industry & Virtue! The new Settlers there had much better plant vinyards like Noah & get drunk with their own wine. I wish Mr. Oglethorp after he has put his generous Scheme in Execution in that favourite Colony, would make the Tour of the Continent & then I should hope for the pleasure of seeing Him in some of his Planetary motions, I was acquainted with Him formerly, when I cou'd see he had the Seeds of Virtue in Him, which have since grown up into Fruit. Heaven give both your Lordship & him-self success in your disinterested endeavours, for making Georgia, a very flourishing & happy place: . . .

## E S S A Y S

Daniel B. Thorpe of Virginia Polytechnic Institute and State University examines the settlements created by Moravians at Wachovia in Piedmont North Carolina in the first essay. Thorpe finds that the planters came with well-defined idealistic plans for community structure and modes of agriculture, but that these were modified without losing their core in order to adapt to circumstances in the region. In the process the planters discovered that agricultural and settlement practices that looked "slovenly" to the outsider were chosen because they seemed to make the best sense in that environment.

Georgia, founded as a buffer between Florida and South Carolina, was originally built on a philanthropic scheme in which deserving poor families would emigrate with the promise of fifty-acre freehold estates. Planters were forbidden to sell their land without permission, and slaves and rum were prohibited. The colonists were to be citizen-soldiers spread over the country and ready to defend their own colony and their neighbors. This original plan was amended within a few years and Georgia came under the sway of Carolina planters. In the second essay historian Alan Gallay of Western Washington University shows through examination of the career of Jonathan Bryan how immense plantations and great power were acquired in Georgia.

# Moravian Ideals and North Carolina Backcountry Realities

### DANIEL B. THORP

In the United States the story of cultural contact and assimilation has largely been the story of a white, English, Protestant culture established during the seventeenth century affecting and being affected by subsequent waves of African, European, and Asian immigrants and their cultural impedimenta. Some of these non-English groups have entered the Anglo-American mainstream quickly and unobtrusively, while others have done so reluctantly and incompletely. It is to the latter group that historians and sociologists have generally assigned those members of the Moravian Church (Unity of the Brethren) who migrated from eastern Germany to America during the middle years of the eighteenth century and arrived in central North Carolina during the final years of the colonial period to establish a cluster of settlements known as Wachovia.

For two centuries historians have described these Moravian pioneers as xenophobes who regarded any change in their community, however minor or remote from Wachovia's theological underpinnings, as declension from the colony's initial perfection. In the 1760s Charles Woodmason labeled the Moravians "a Set of *Recabites* among the People of *Israel*—Forming a Distinc[t] Body, different in all things from All People". . . .

But such descriptions seriously distort the true nature of Moravian colonization and of the church's response to Anglo-American culture in North Carolina. Certainly the men who planned and supervised Wachovia's establishment wanted the colony to remain Moravian, but they also wanted it to survive. Consequently the Brethren distinguished between those ideas and practices that were fundamental to their Moravian identity and those that merely contributed to their worldly success. The former they guarded like zealots, but the latter they valued only as long as their usage contributed to the colony's success. The Moravians were quite willing to replace Old World ways with Anglo-American practices when the latter seemed better suited to Moravian goals. Woodmason . . . and the others not-withstanding, Wachovia's early history provides a clear example not of cultural protectionism but of what Terry G. Jordan describes as "partial assimilation." . . . Shortly after arriving in Carolina they [Moravians] demonstrated a willingness to abandon many external characteristics of their German heritage, but they jealously guarded their Moravian identity until the second quarter of the nineteenth century.

Two aspects of Wachovia's development that indicate the process of partial assimilation—village morphology and farming techniques—will be described here. The Moravians who established Wachovia arrived in North Carolina with the intention of setting up compact, German-style, agricultural villages because their leaders believed that such villages would contribute to the colony's success. Within a dozen years, however, many of those same leaders had decided that with slight modifications the settlement pattern of their Anglo-American neighbors would meet Moravian needs better and adopted it. Moreover, they realized that the often denigrated

From Daniel B. Thorp, "Assimiliation in North Carolina's Moravian Community," *Journal of Southern History,* LII, February 1986. pp. 19–42 (text abridged and footnotes deleted). Copyright by the Southern Historical Association. Reprinted by permission of the Managing Editor.

practices of Carolina farmers were actually much better suited to that colony's environment and demography than the improved methods emerging in Europe and gave up the latter for their neighbors' backward techniques. This partial assimilation of Anglo-American norms was not the result of any unconscious change in the Moravians' ultimate goal, as others have suggested; rather, it was a conscious change in the means by which they sought to achieve that goal.

The region of North Carolina into which the Moravians moved in 1753 was dominated by small family farms. This situation had long disturbed the English government, and the North Carolina assembly had tried to rectify it by legislating towns into existence. But the effort was something of a disappointment; a Moravian visitor, August Gottlieb Spangenberg, said of these communities in 1752, "they have neither houses nor inhabitants, are towns only by Act of Assembly." Europeans had been arriving in the Piedmont for two decades by the early 1750s, but the only towns in the region, Hillsboro and Salisbury, barely deserved the name. Hillsboro was established in the early 1750s and by 1764 had become, as William Few, one of its residents, recalled, "a small village, which contained thirty or forty inhabitants, with two or three small stores and two or three ordinary taverns. . . ." The legislature called Salisbury into being in 1753, though construction did not actually begin until 1755. Later that year, when Governor Arthur Dobbs passed through, Salisbury consisted of a courthouse and seven or eight log houses.

The role of these settlements was, of course, much greater than their physical dimensions; they were central places performing important administrative, commercial, and social functions for the rapidly growing population around them. But the settlement pattern was predominantly rural. . . . Families on these farms lived quite distant from their neighbors and were often miles from the church or meeting house that was the only center the settlement had.

The Moravians, however, had no intention of living like their neighbors-to-be in Carolina. When in 1753 they purchased nearly 100,000 acres of land from John Carteret, Earl Granville and proprietor of the northern half of North Carolina, their plans for the tract demonstrated a clear determination to resist whatever it was in the southern environment that had continually frustrated English expectations of significant urban development in the region. The Brethren planned to resell two-thirds of the land to wealthy members or friends of the church to help cover the cost of settling the tract and on the remaining 30,000 acres to establish a refuge in which church members could live and worship in peace, free from the accusations and persecution they had encountered elsewhere during the preceding twenty years. At the center of the colony they intended to build an impressive octagonal city. In fact, if built as planned it would have been the largest city in eighteenth-century North Carolina. From this central location church elders would administer the society and economy of the entire Moravian colony. Plans for Wachovia also included the establishment of family farms, several communal farms operated by the church, and thirty-five "villages of the Lord"—compact agricultural villages scattered across the colony and occupied by members or friends of the church.

Moravian leaders seem to have had two major reasons for settling many of Wachovia's residents in villages. First, Wachovia was to be a *Moravian* colony. Not every resident of the colony had to be a member of the church, but Wachovia was to be a theocracy administered by the Moravian Church for the temporal benefit of the church and the spiritual benefit of its members. The accomplishment of that goal depended, in part, on the establishment of a colony in which compact settlement predominated, because the Unity was somewhat pessimistic about its members' ability to maintain their faith in the face of worldly temptation. Congregational elders, therefore, were supposed to watch their flocks carefully, and every member of the church was expected to keep an eye on his or her neighbors in an effort to prevent backsliding. If Wachovia's settlers scattered across the colony, it would be much more difficult to provide that sort of brotherly oversight. So the Unity wanted most of Wachovia's residents in either the central city or the "villages of the Lord." Moreover, compact settlement facilitated communal worship, an essential element in the eighteenth-century Moravian Church and the preferred forum in which to praise and thank the Lord for his role in salvation. While such worship was not impossible in a region of dispersed settlement, it was easier when members of the congregation lived close together.

Second, Wachovia's planners wanted the colony to succeed. By the 1750s most Europeans knew quite well that America was no Eden. It was an environment that was at best challenging and at worst fatal to newcomers. Among the elders who planned Wachovia there were certainly some, like the church's leader Nicholas Ludwig, Count von Zinzendorf, who underestimated the demands of colonization. But the founders also included Bishop August Spangenberg, who as a veteran of both the Moravians' abortive effort to settle in Georgia and their successful settlement in Pennsylvania, understood very well what was necessary for Wachovia's success. Thus, when Zinzendorf suggested early in the planning for Wachovia that some of its residents live on family farms, Spangenberg quickly pointed out the physical dangers inherent in that scheme—the chance of Indian attack and the inability of widely scattered settlers to help one another in emergencies. "What will happen," he asked,

> to those who have not the necessary talents? How will it go with men and women brought up in our congregations, who I fear have little conception of the difficulties they will have to face? What will they do in circumstances where each must help himself as best he can? How bear the hard work necessary to success, when each must say with Jacob, 'In the day the drought consumed me and the frost by night.'?
>
> To speak plainly:—Among fifty members brought up in our congregation, or who have lived with us some years, there is probably not one who could maintain himself alone in the forest. They have had no experience, and even those who have the intelligence do not know how.

Spangenberg argued in favor of settling the colonists, at least initially, in groups of six to ten families so they could look after one another. Only after they had learned to cope with the unfamiliar environment would some be free to move out to family farms if they wanted.

In addition to these declared motives for establishing towns and villages in Wachovia, Moravian leaders were probably influenced by a powerful psychological motive as well—the hope of recreating many, if not all, aspects of the Old World societies from which they came. Cut off from the familiar environment, culture, and political and economic institutions of home, in strange and often hostile surroundings, colonists seized upon anything resembling their Old World as a reaffirmation of their membership in the core culture, proof that they were not slipping into the maw of savagery. This mimetic urge, no doubt, contributed to the Moravians' determination to avoid the dispersed pattern of settlement common in North Carolina. Most of the brothers and sisters in the Unity, and their leaders, came from a society in which nearly everyone lived in towns and villages. The need to demonstrate that they were still civilized undoubtedly inspired in them a determination to establish a similar pattern of settlement in North Carolina.

The result of these spiritual, temporal, and psychological factors was more than a simple desire to establish villages and a city in the Carolina backcountry. The Moravians also intended to model most of their new settlements on traditional plans found in their native Germany. The only exception was Wachovia's central city, later called Salem. Church leaders did not originally design that city according to any known German precedent. Instead, they chose a strikingly different plan adapted from the work of Vitruvius, the ancient Roman architect whose rediscovered writings were influential in seventeenth- and eighteenth-century Europe. But in building the "villages of the Lord," which were to occupy most of Wachovia's land, the elders did intend to follow German precedents. . . .

The Moravians . . . came from a region in which there was a long tradition of compact linear villages and open-field agriculture. One would therefore expect them to favor a similar pattern when they settled in North Carolina because it would offer them a familiar enclave in an unfamiliar environment. As Bishop Peter Böhler wrote in 1754, Unity officials hoped that the colonists would settle together "and have their woods and fences in common as it is in many villages in Europe."

The Moravians' first settlement in North Carolina, Bethabara, was not, however, the sort of community that church leaders envisioned for Wachovia, but only because it was unplanned and was supposed to last no more than a few years. Bethabara was begun in 1753 as a temporary settlement from which the Brethren would carry on construction of Wachovia's central city. Thus no one seems to have given any thought to its layout until it had grown into a flourishing village that refused to be temporary. Nor was the pattern of fields around Bethabara typical of that anticipated for villages in Wachovia. During Bethabara's early years the Unity established a communal economy. Orchards, gardens, and fields were all undivided tracts that the residents farmed together for the Unity in return for food, housing, clothing, and medical care for themselves and their children.

Not until 1759, when the church began its second settlement in Wachovia, did the Moravians consciously plan the sort of village with which they intended to dot the colony's landscape. By then a consensus had emerged that it was time to start building the thirty-five "villages of the Lord," and in May of that year the Provincial Synod for the United Brethren in America met in Lancaster, Pennsylvania, and directed August Spangenberg to go to North Carolina and establish "the first little village intended for Wachovia." The synod even supplied a name for the village, Bethania, which European leaders had sent to America via Bishop Peter Böhler—an indication that Count von Zinzendorf himself had probably authorized establishment of the village as a prototype for Wachovia's other "villages of the Lord." By June of that year Spangenberg was in Wachovia, and later that summer, as Bethania took shape, Spangenberg wrote an unknown correspondent describing what was becoming an almost perfect German street village. It already contained two rows of houses lining the main road and surrounded by orchard lots assigned to specific house lots. "All the remaining fields," the bishop explained, "will come later beyond these orchards and perhaps will be arranged in layers as is normal in Germany." . . .

The resulting pattern of landholding was quite like that found in eastern Germany and very unlike patterns found elsewhere in colonial North Carolina. First, the size of the holdings was extraordinarily small by North Carolina standards. . . . The median landholding among Bethania's residents was slightly over 22 acres, and no one held more than 33. In Germany such diminutive holdings were quite common. . . . But throughout backcountry North Carolina, the median estate was about 250 acres—more than ten times the median in Bethania.

Second, the disposition of the tracts in Bethania was radically different from the pattern usually found in North Carolina but was very similar to that common in eastern Germany. In colonial North Carolina, and the southern colonies in general, the great majority of farmers worked a single large piece of land. In Bethania, however, an individual's farm was invariably divided into a half-dozen tracts that were often widely separated from one another. . . . Moreover, residents of Bethania enjoyed communal rights to pasture land and a wood lot, as was common in the openfield systems of Germany. In Bethania, Wachovia's first planned village, the Moravians recreated the patterns of settlement and land distribution they had known in Germany.

The Brethren did not, however, replicate Bethania and fill their colony with German farming villages, in spite of their original intention to do so. In fact, when the church next established a settlement in Wachovia, Friedland in 1770, it forsook the compact German model altogether in favor of a more dispersed pattern similar to that common among Wachovia's Anglo-American neighbors. . . . The reason behind this shift from Bethania's compact settlement to the dispersed pattern of settlement in Friedland and from Bethania's agriculture on small tracts of land to Friedland's individual 200-acre holdings seems to have been the increasing difficulty the Unity faced in attracting settlers to Wachovia.

The Moravians had established Wachovia to provide a refuge in which church members would be able to live "without interfering with others & without being disturbed by them." Obviously, the accomplishment of that goal demanded that settlers be of acceptable quality; if not actually members of the Moravian Church, they had to be its friends and willing to live under its supervision in order to insure that the colony's Moravian population remained free from improper influences. But Wachovia's success also depended on the church's ability to provide an adequate number of colonists; there had to be enough settlers to make Wachovia as self-sufficient as possible and, thus, free it from the possibility that enemies of the church could undermine the colony by withholding supplies.

Throughout the colony's history the peopling of Wachovia demanded that the church pay close attention to both the quality and the number of its settlers. At first, there was no shortage of acceptable candidates for settlement in Wachovia because the Unity itself had the human and financial resources to provide them. By the late 1750s, however, the church could no longer afford to transport faithful but impoverished members from Europe to North Carolina. By 1764 migration to Wachovia had slowed to the point that Unity officials were afraid that unless they found an alternative source of colonists "this great Tract will not be settled . . . in fifty years." One such source was the general population of Britain's mainland colonies. That meant competing with other large landowners for the relatively small number of available tenants, and in that contest the Moravians quickly learned that replicas of European villages or estates seldom overcame the lure of individual farm ownership. This realization led the church to modify its settlement policy in ways that doomed the compact German village plan with which Wachovia's colonization had begun. This did not represent a change in basic Moravian goals or values, though; the Brethren still intended Wachovia to be a refuge for the benefit of the Moravian Church.

To attract additional settlers to Wachovia, the church began to issue advertisements describing the Moravian colony in glowing terms. "The land is very good," they declared, "has moderate water, pasture, arable land and woods." And they assured potential settlers that tracts were available near "mills, smiths, a store and craftsmen which one cannot do without in agriculture." The Moravians knew that land prices in colonies north of Carolina had risen in recent years and hoped that the lure of good land would increase the number of families interested in settling Wachovia. With an enlarged pool of applicants, the Unity would have a better chance of finding enough acceptable tenants to insure Wachovia's success. Those judged unfit to settle near the Brethren could be offered church-owned land outside Wachovia.

The Unity's campaign to attract new settlers was not confined to heralding the quality of Wachovia's land. It also included an increased willingness on the Moravians' part to sell rather than to rent their land and to convey it in larger parcels. . . . The decision to sell more church land was almost certainly the Unity's response to a preference among would-be settlers to own rather than rent their land. Frederic William Marschall, Wachovia's administrator, reported to his superiors that only the least enterprising people were willing to rent land, and the Moravians' financial records show that relatively few people moved to Wachovia as long as land there could only be leased. Evidently the church had realized by 1765 that the chance to own rather than rent land might attract to Wachovia the settlers it needed. When it became possible to buy Moravian land, there was a marked increase in the number of people from North Carolina, Maryland, Pennsylvania, and elsewhere seeking to settle in Wachovia.

The Moravians also decided during the early 1760s that they would have to offer larger tracts. . . .

The opportunity to buy individual lots large enough to farm profitably seems to have lured a sufficient number of settlers to Wachovia to warrant establishment of its next settlement, Friedland, which was begun in 1770. Friedland's first residents had originally emigrated from the Palatinate region of Germany to Broadbay (now Waldoboro), Maine, sometime before 1762. The Broadbay settlers had known Moravians in Germany, and in 1762 they welcomed the arrival of George Soelle, a Moravian missionary from Bethlehem, Pennsylvania. Soelle soon organized the community into a society, an association of Christians affiliated with the Moravian Church and served by a Moravian minister but whose members were not communicants of the church. Seven years later, in 1769, members of the Broadbay Society began moving to Wachovia at the invitation of the Reverend John Ettwein, formerly the acting executive in Wachovia and in 1769 a prominent leader of the Moravian community in Bethlehem.

From the Unity's point of view the Broadbay settlers were ideal candidates for admission to Wachovia. As members of a Moravian Society they had already shown their willingness to live in accordance with the rules of the Moravian Church, but as members of a society rather than a congregation they had no right to expect financial help from that church and would have to pay their own way to North Carolina. To the Broadbay families, Wachovia was inviting because the Unity could provide the land society members wanted with clear title to it. In Maine they had discovered that land they bought on arriving from Germany did not belong to the man from whom they bought it, and in searching for a place to move they wanted to be certain they could obtain clear title to whatever land they purchased. They had considered moving to an area near the Kennebec River in Maine but chose Wachovia instead, believing that in Wachovia they would be more likely to acquire both land and a legal deed. One year after the Broadbay families began arriving in Wachovia, nine 200-acre lots were laid out, and in early 1771 each family was allowed either to purchase a lot outright or to rent one with the option to buy it at any time during the next seven years. By mid-1771 at least seven families had purchased lots.

Those seven families were the nucleus of a community that soon expanded to include fourteen families, a meeting house, and a name—Friedland. It did not, however, resemble the compact German villages that had inspired plans for Bethania. Rather, Friedland's design was an amalgamation of those villages and the looser settlements that Moravian colonists had found in North Carolina. . . .

. . . After the mid-1770s colonists arriving in Wachovia were free to settle on family farms unattached to any village. Bethania, therefore, remained an isolated example of the compact German pattern the Moravians had originally intended to use in settling Wachovia. But this shift from a compact village to a dispersed village to no village was not, as others have maintained, the result of a decline in the Moravians' commitment to their goals. Rather, it is an example of the church's willingness to adopt new methods in order to accomplish those goals. Wachovia required not only a population that accepted Moravian control but also one large enough to be self-sufficient. Success depended on maintaining a proper balance between the two. Church leaders quickly discovered that adherence to their original plan for the colony's villages might help to maintain the quality they wanted among settlers, but it would not attract them in numbers sufficient to guarantee Wachovia's success. The original plan was adequate only as long as Wachovia did not have to *attract* settlers, that is, as long as the Unity simply sent to North Carolina those people it deemed fit for the colony. When that became impossible and Wachovia had to compete with other settlements to attract colonists, the Unity then had to modify its plans. If the more popular, dispersed pattern of settlement denied the church one means of supervising Wachovia's residents, it had a variety of other mechanisms for controlling the population. An array of spiritual and secular authorities kept their eyes on every resident, and the power of those authorities to grant or withhold both religious and material comfort gave them a strong hold over the brothers and sisters. Moreover, by the mid-1770s the practical necessity for compact settlement declined. The Indian threat had been eliminated, and the decision to concentrate on attracting settlers experienced with American frontier life meant that close mutual support was less necessary than when the colony first began. So the elders felt it was safe to adopt different settlement patterns in order to make Wachovia more attractive.

The Moravians' assimilation of Anglo-American practices was not limited to village morphology, though. In addition to changing the way they settled their land, Moravian colonists in Wachovia also changed the way they farmed it. Earlier writers have described the Moravians as "advanced" agriculturalists who worked their land "intensively . . . and exhibited attitudes we should now characterize as 'conservationist,'" while their neighbors employed extensive farming practices and raped the land with no concern for the needs of future generations. The surviving records indicate, however, that Moravian settlers abandoned some of their "advanced" practices in favor of their neighbors' "backward" techniques as soon as they discovered that the latter were better suited to the environment of Wachovia. Here again the Brethren demonstrated partial assimilation; they took from their neighbors those practices that made it easier to establish a successful Moravian colony and left the rest.

This is not to say that the Brethren were particularly advanced farmers when they came to North Carolina. In fact, few of them were farmers at all. Most members of the eighteenth-century Moravian Church were craftsmen or professionals. . . .

Moreover, those Brethren who were raised on farms had generally learned their craft in an agriculturally conservative region. During the eighteenth century English farmers led their European counterparts into an era of rapid change; new crops, new tools, and new techniques resulted in greatly increased yields on many English farms. Few of these improvements reached Germany, however, before the nineteenth century. Many Germans of the mid-eighteenth century still relied solely on the application of manure, the rotation of crops, and regular periods of fallow to maintain the fertility of their fields. Though the more innovative among them had begun cultivating clover, turnips, beans, and other crops on fallow land to revive the soil, there seem to have been few efforts to improve the quality of seed or crops in Germany. Throughout the region grain was still broadcast, then covered by harrowing, and harvested with a sickle. In the mid-eighteenth century German farming had changed remarkably little since the Middle Ages. . . .

There is little evidence that Moravian farmers were more aware than other Germans of advances in agricultural practices, though it does appear that August Spangenberg had learned something of the new scientific agriculture. He urged the Wachovia colonists to use oxen rather than horses as draft animals, on the grounds that "nearly all sensible economists are unanimous in maintaining that it is very thrifty to use carts drawn by oxen." Furthermore, when the colonists began raising grapes to produce wine, he directed them to use local rather than French vines because the former were better suited to the climate of North Carolina. The Brethren continued, however, to rely on regular periods of fallow, crop rotation, and manure application to maintain their fields, and there is no indication that they considered planting clover or applying lime. They continued to scatter their seed over lightly plowed fields, which they then harrowed, and to employ sickles in harvesting their grain crops.

Despite the lack of innovation in their own agricultural practices, the Moravians initially regarded North Carolina farmers as backward. In 1752 August Spangenberg led a party across North Carolina in search of land on which to establish the colony that became Wachovia. In a diary he kept during the journey Spangenberg noted with disdain the "farms of a North Carolina kind" on which "with the exception of corn ... and hogs ... the work is poorly done." Unfortunately, the peripatetic bishop seldom criticized specific practices of Carolina farmers. He was, however, particularly appalled by the treatment of cattle in North Carolina, and his diary contains several passages sharply critical of the many farmers who left their cows and horses to fend for themselves through the winter months. According to Spangenberg, these owners provided neither food nor shelter for their animals and demonstrated remarkable indifference to their fate. The prevailing attitude was, "if they live, they live," the bishop wrote. Spangenberg also criticized North Carolinians' animal husbandry on the grounds that it deprived them of manure, an indication that he disapproved of their reliance on the fertility of virgin soil to maintain crop yields.

It was essential to Wachovia's success that its settlers employ productive agricultural practices, and to Spangenberg, at least, that meant German rather than North Carolina techniques. Once the Moravians themselves began to farm Wachovia, however, they quickly adopted many of the same techniques that had so dismayed Spangenberg when he toured the province in 1752. The most fundamental change in Moravian farming was the nearly complete abandonment of efforts to preserve soil fertility. Like many others who settled on the southern frontier, the Brethren soon found that land there was so rich and labor so scarce that even rudimentary efforts at soil conservation were counterproductive. There are no indications that Moravian farmers in Wachovia made any attempt to manure their fields in the years before the American Revolution. Collecting and spreading manure required so much labor that with the same amount of work brothers could contribute more to the colony's productivity by clearing new fields. The age-old practice of letting fields lay fallow at regular intervals, which the Moravians seem to have used elsewhere, was equally unsuited to conditions in western Carolina. . . .

The Brethren also discovered that, in the Carolina climate, what Spangenberg had regarded as careless animal husbandry was actually a much more efficient allocation of resources than the labor-intensive methods common in northern Europe. The apparently limitless supply of fertile land in Wachovia removed the necessity of gathering manure to fertilize fields, which eliminated one of the principal reasons for penning livestock. Furthermore, except during especially harsh winters, the weather in North Carolina was mild enough to permit cattle and horses to winter safely in the bush. They seldom needed the weathertight German barns that required weeks of precious labor to erect. So, first impressions notwithstanding, Moravian farmers in Wachovia quickly followed their neighbors' example. They penned and fattened steers picked for slaughter and stabled their milch cows during the winter, but they left most of their livestock free to roam.

Moravian settlers brought with them to Wachovia a knowledge of traditional German agricultural practices, just as they brought a familiarity with traditional German village plans. And just as they modified their opinion of the settlement pattern most likely to produce a successful Moravian colony in North Carolina, they changed their opinion of the farming techniques best suited to the southern frontier. Moravian farmers had no particular interest in preserving German practices simply because they were German; they attached no spiritual or social significance to any particular agricultural techniques. Their priority was to find the particular allocation of resources that would best permit them "to clear land, plant corn, clear meadows, raise a good stock of cattle, build a mill, erect a smith shop, and [provide] the other essentials one needs" for successful colonization. They quickly discovered that in a region of abundant fertile land, mild winters, and a perennial shortage of labor the extensive farming of their Anglo-American neighbors was far more suitable to their circumstances than the more intensive techniques they had known in Germany. So almost immediately they began to accept some of their neighbors' practices. The Brethren did not, however, adopt North Carolina agricultural customs completely. Moravian assimilation was both partial and selective; they refused, for example, to raise as much corn as their neighbors did because they preferred the taste of wheat and realized greater profits from it. The Brethren adopted only those elements of Carolina farming that were more likely than their German equivalents to help them establish a successful Moravian colony.

In contrast to the historiographic tradition surrounding them, the Moravian founders of Wachovia did not object to every change that tended toward assimilation of Anglo-American patterns. Nor did they regard all such changes as detrimental. Members and leaders of the Unity recognized a distinction between the spiritual ends they sought, which were inviolate, and the temporal means they employed to achieve them, which were expendable. From the time they arrived in North Carolina, Moravian settlers demonstrated their willingness to modify many aspects of their heritage, such as village morphology and agricultural practices, if they thought that modifying these superficial characteristics would improve the chances of accomplishing their ultimate goal—the establishment of a successful, autonomous, Moravian community.

## Jonathan Bryan's Plantation Empire in Georgia

### ALAN GALLAY

From 1736 until his death in 1788 Jonathan Bryan acquired lands by grant and purchase in Georgia and South Carolina in excess of 32,000 acres, on which he employed, at one time or another, over 250 slaves. These possessions placed him at the very top of the small group of men who ruled Georgia during the quarter century before the American Revolution. Bryan became one of the colony's richest and most powerful men because he understood every aspect of landownership, from accumulation to development and sale. Aggressive and astute, he built an estate that can truly be termed a plantation empire. This essay shows how Bryan used political influence and economic calculation to create that empire. His example illustrates the process by which the ruling class of colonial Georgia was formed.

Bryan was born in the vicinity of Port Royal, South Carolina, in 1708. The few whites who inhabited this frontier region engaged in trade with the neighboring Yamassee. On several occasions Bryan's father, Joseph, a trader, was rebuked by the South Carolina government for abusing the Indians and illegally settling on their land, which the colony's governor described as "the best part of this province." In 1715 Port Royal traders provoked the Yamassee to a war that left the region virtu-

Alan Gallay, "Jonathan Bryan's Plantation Empire: Land Politics and the Formation of a Ruling Class in Colonial Georgia," *William and Mary Quarterly,* 3rd ser. XLV (1988), 253–279. Reprinted with permission of Alan Gallay.

ally stripped of people of all races for fifteen years. Only a few traders and their families, including the Bryans, remained on the southern frontier, awaiting the day when the government would permit them to take possession of the Yamassees' land. In the meantime, they engaged in a variety of economic enterprises: farming, soldiering, and filling government contracts. In the late 1720s Jonathan Bryan reached adulthood and found employment as a scout. This gave him opportunities to explore the territory between South Carolina and Spanish Florida. From this experience he gained direct knowledge of the topography and ecology of the southeast, which he later applied in the management of his vast estate.

Bryan's elder brother Hugh played an active role in preparing for white settlement the so-called "Indian Land," in what became first St. Helena's and later Prince William's Parish. After this land was opened to public sale in 1731, Hugh surveyed approximately half of the tracts. His expertise, coupled with the family's political connections, provided the Bryan clan with choice parcels along the Pocotaligo River and Stoney Creek. As did many of their neighbors, the Bryans thus became wealthy in less than a decade. Using slave labor, they transformed the region from a frontier to a commercial economy. The multitalented Hugh accumulated great riches by investing in numerous capitalistic enterprises: rice production, cattle ranching, manufacture of shingles for the West Indian market, shipping, buying and selling of land, and fulfillment of government contracts for defense and internal improvements. Jonathan followed in his brother's footsteps. Hugh sold him a prime piece of land in 1736, and Jonathan began building his plantation estate. Like Hugh, Jonathan diversified investments and cultivated government contacts. Within five years, he became one of St. Helena's most prominent citizens.

The Bryans' elevated social status was reflected in their selection to ecclesiastical and political offices. Joseph Bryan was elected to the South Carolina House of Commons in 1728, and Hugh served from 1733 to 1736; Jonathan became church warden for St. Helena's Parish in 1738, while Hugh served as vestryman from 1738 to 1740. In addition, the brothers received appointments to the local militia, Hugh as major and Jonathan as lieutenant. Related by marriage to many of the leading families of their parish, the Bryans enjoyed a secure position among the social, economic, and political elite of southern South Carolina.

Concern for their region's defense led the Bryans to take an active interest in the establishment of Georgia. Quite possibly, Jonathan or his elder brother Joseph led James Oglethorpe to the site that was chosen for Savannah. All three Bryan brothers devoted time and effort to helping the new colony. They provided advice, laborers, goods, arms, and soldiers—sometimes for profit and sometimes gratis— over a twenty-year period. Although the Bryans established strong ties to the new colony, they remained in South Carolina through the 1730s and 1740s. They had no economic motive for moving south of the Savannah River, for the Georgia Trustees, intending to create a society of small landowners, sought to prevent the rise of a wealthy aristocratic class by prohibiting slavery and limiting landownership. These measures effectively deterred the Bryans and other South Carolina slaveholders from migrating to Georgia.

In the mid-1740s the prosperity of the Bryans and their neighbors began to wane. Economic depression struck South Carolina and proved especially severe in the southern parishes. . . .

. . . French privateering, rising freight and insurance rates, and declining rice prices forced many planters to sell or mortgage their lands and to contract heavy debts. . . .

Southern parish representatives submitted petitions to the assembly from their constituents begging for debtor relief. The petitioners claimed that currency was short in South Carolina "in Proportion to the Trade and Number of Inhabitants" and that "many industrious and well disposed Persons and their Families are and must be reduced to extream Poverty and Want." . . . Alienated by the government's failure to provide substantial aid, a number of planters moved their operations to Georgia when the Trustees legalized slavery in 1750. One of them was Jonathan Bryan.

The promise of free land in Georgia attracted slaveowners from South Carolina and the West Indies, who immigrated with their laborers. The influx of slaves, the lifting of restrictions on land tenure and accumulation, and the privatization of public lands resulted in a new class system in Georgia. The smallholders' utopia was replaced by a slave society modeled in important ways upon that of South Carolina. Free white men were entitled to parcels from the public domain, but their tracts were from market or unsuitable for cash crops. These men usually became subsistence farmers or laborers. A minority of Georgians had both capital and land that could be used to produce modest surpluses. Their standard of living placed them above the colony's majority but far below the much smaller group of men who possessed the very best land and the largest amounts of capital.

The great planters towered above the rest of society not only by the size of their estates but also by their prominence in politics. Wealthy slaveholders filled almost all official positions. In 1754, after acquiring the colony from the Trustees, the king selected from the ranks of the new slaveholding immigrants a few rich men who joined a handful of the Trustees' former assistants and several royal administrators to form the colony's Executive Council. Officially empowered in 1755, the council served as the organizational basis of Georgia's ruling class until the American Revolution.

Jonathan Bryan was an original appointee to the council. Twenty years of social, business, and political connections with important Georgia figures had earned him a reputation as a man of great skill, and his ownership of a large labor force—he moved to Georgia with forty to fifty slaves—entitled him to extensive tracts of land, social prestige, and consideration for membership among the colony's political elite. When he petitioned for 500 acres of "Marsh and Swamp Land" in 1750, Georgia magistrates "readily granted" his request because "this piece of Land cannot be cultivated without great Strength, which they know He is capable of performing." Bryan's talents were especially valued because politically experienced men were few in the young province. Legal skills were in great demand—Georgia had no lawyers in 1755—so councillors filled multiple positions. In addition to his council seat, Bryan served on the General Court and the Court of Oyer and Terminer, as justice of the peace, and as the colony's treasurer. . . .

Bryan served on the council from 1755 until 1770, when he was expelled for patriot activities. Turnover during that period was slight: governors were replaced more frequently than councillors. Power rested in the hands of an active core of just eleven men. Bryan, James Habersham, Noble Jones, Francis Harris, James McKay, James Edward Powell, William Clifton, and Patrick Houston were appointed in the 1750s and were joined by William Knox, Grey Elliot, and John Graham in the early

1760s. All eleven were men of substance, though three—Jones, Harris, and Haber-sham—had arrived in Georgia nearly penniless. Composing the council's inner cir-cle, this entrenched group formed a ring of prestige and power around the office of the governor.

Bryan pursued his interests on the council and in the upper house in many ways. He served as commissioner for an array of public works projects such as re-pairing and refurbishing the lighthouse of Tybee Island, constructing and maintain-ing roads in the northwest district, and erecting of sundry forts, magazines, and blockhouses. These appointments enhanced his prestige while providing numerous opportunities to dispense patronage. The activity that most attracted his attention was the distributing of the public lands.

Control over the public lands was the major source of the council's economic and political power. Although the rules governing the land-granting system ap-peared to be equitable (all free white males were entitled to receive a portion of the public domain), the formal entitlement to land was of negligible importance in ob-taining a valuable parcel. The council held final say over who got which tracts. Since the Trustees had severely restricted landownership and little land had been ceded by the Indians, much of Georgia's chartered domain had yet to be granted when royal government was established. Thus it fell to the council to distribute most of the land that came under cultivation in the late colonial period.

Under the system established by royal officials, each head of household was en-titled to one hundred acres for himself and fifty acres for every member of his house-hold, including slaves. Among the slaveholders themselves, those who possessed influence on the council were most likely to receive the best land—freshwater swamp located along transportation routes and cultivatable by the tidal-flow method. Although rice could be produced inland, planters who obtained land affected by the Atlantic tides, whereby fields could be easily flooded and drained, enjoyed a dis-tinct advantage. This land lay above the saltwater line in an area ten to twenty miles wide along the coast. Eighteenth-century maps reveal the result of the colony's land-granting system: a small group of land barons monopolized Georgia's premier rice lands, while the rest of the population became dispersed throughout the colony.

Before examining how Bryan used his political offices and his varied skills in build-ing his estate, we should trace the development of his plantation empire. We have seen that he began by petitioning the Trustees for 500 rice land acres in 1750. He settled the tract on New Year's Day, 1751, with forty to fifty slaves and moved his family there in August 1752. The plantation, Walnut Hill, was located on the Sa-vannah River, several miles below the capital. Almost immediately after he re-ceived this grant, Bryan began selling parcels of his land in Prince William's Parish, though he retained the most valuable portion until 1757. Although he valued Wal-nut Hill, he considered establishing his base plantation in several other areas. In 1752 he received from the Trustees 500 acres on the Little Ogeechee River, several miles south of Savannah. He named this plantation Dean Forrest. An additional 500 were granted contiguous to this land in 1754.

In 1755 Bryan began petitioning for land on the Great Ogeechee, a freshwater river that many Georgians believed would replace the Savannah as the colony's major waterway. When the town of Hardwicke was laid out by Georgia's first royal governor, who tried unsuccessfully to make it the capital, Bryan petitioned for and received 500 acres and a town lot. But his gaze continued to drift southward. In August 1755 he petitioned the council: "having Seventy eight Persons in Family, he was desirous of improving another Tract; and therefore pray[ed] for eighteen hundred Acres of Land on the Fort Swamp at the Head of Sapola [Sapelo] River." Thus by 1755 Bryan had become engaged in establishing rice plantations on four Georgia rivers.

Bryan's tracts were too distant from one another for him to maintain effective control over them. Roads were few and rough: transportation from one plantation to another by water meant travel along the sometimes difficult coastal waterways. When it became apparent that the Atlantic trade would continue to flow through Savannah, Bryan began selling off or resigning lands that were not along the Savannah River. . . . Bryan determined to concentrate his holdings along the Savannah. In 1757 he began requesting land adjacent to his Walnut Hill plantation, which he supplemented with numerous tracts of "garden" and "farm" acreage on the east side of Savannah town. He also claimed 1,000 acres on Augustine's Creek, just below the town near Walnut Hill, and he sold his remaining acreage in Prince William's Parish. It was probably at this time that Bryan increased his purchases and development of tracts on the South Carolina side of the Savannah River. He had begun settling land in 1752 at Monmouth Point in the township of Purrysburg, about seventeen miles northwest of Savannah. By the mid-1760s he owned from four to seven thousand acres on the South Carolina side of the river. The £864 he made from selling land in 1756–1757 may have provided some of the capital for the purchase of those acres. . . .

. . . All together, his holdings in South Carolina probably amounted to between six and seven thousand acres, all selected because of their riverfront location. They were convenient to Savannah town and to each other, and their crops could be shipped downriver. Not all land along the Savannah was of good quality or easily reached. Much of it was worthless swamp. But Bryan selected parcels with good harbors and ones that his large labor force could turn to rice, indigo, and corn. . . .

Why Bryan established a plantation between the North Newport and South Newport rivers in 1758 is unknown. It may have been experimental, for he raised a variety of crops and animals there. In an advertisement for the plantation's sale in 1763, he described it as good for corn, rice, and indigo, and able to maintain horses, cattle, and other stock. He had built there "a good new framed barn, overseer's house, and negro houses." One hundred acres had been cleared and fenced, and he stated that the marsh land for the animals could be easily enclosed. Apparently, however, the local planters had difficulty attracting oceangoing vessels, with the result that the cost of transporting goods to market was raised. Bryan, at any rate, gave up: the result of his five-year development of land along the Newport rivers was a determination to leave the region to others.

Bryan continued to develop Walnut Hill during the 1750s and 1760s. By grant he added 600 acres of rice land and 300 acres of garden and farm lots in 1758 and 1762. He referred to himself in legal documents as Jonathan Bryan of Walnut Hill, and he used the plantation as headquarters for his other operations. In 1758 he added to his holdings Cockspur Island, east of Walnut Hill, in the Savannah River. He also requested and received a wharf in Savannah and 300 acres above the town at Pipemaker's Creek. . . .

After fifteen years in the colony Bryan finally had arranged his plantations to allow easy access from one to another. In 1762 he began to consolidate his holdings by selling all of his land below the capital on the Savannah River. He resigned his tract at Augustine's Creek and in 1763 sold his Walnut Hill plantation. Bryan determined to build a new homestead west of the city at Brampton, where Pipemaker's Creek flowed into the Savannah. This locale was considered one of the best rice-producing areas of the colony. Fields were easily flooded by both the creek and the river, and goods could be readily conveyed downriver for export abroad. Bryan's original grant on the creek was 600 acres in 1759. He added 250 acres in 1765 and 350 more in 1770. Brampton's location was excellent for both business and politics. It enabled Bryan to attend to his affairs in Savannah and gave him easy access to his Carolina holdings along the Savannah. He need travel only a few miles by piragua to reach the road to his Union and Little Yemassee plantations; both were also approachable by water. (Reaching these same plantations from Walnut Hill meant an additional ten miles of travel upstream.) Furthermore, Brampton lay close to the terminus of the Newmarket road at Pipemaker's Creek. Cattle could be run directly there from his cowpen, whereas they could not have been run to Walnut Hill. Though Bryan continued to consider establishing plantations in other areas of the colony, for the remainder of his life Brampton and his plantations along the Savannah formed the central component of his economic empire.

The sources of Bryan's extraordinary land hunger are obscure, but an important motivation may well have been a desire to leave each of his many children an estate large enough to secure a place among the ruling elite. If this was his goal, he achieved it remarkably well. His son James became a member of Georgia's Executive Council, filling Jonathan's seat when the latter retired from politics at the end of the Revolution. Bryan's daughter Hannah married John Houstoun, the son of a baronet and an original member of the council. Houstoun held many important political offices in Georgia, including the governorship in 1778 and 1784. Two other sons, Hugh and William, served in the state's Revolutionary government; daughter Mary twice married leading Georgia patriots; grandson Joseph became a United States congressman.

Bryan was able to build his empire largely because of his position on the Executive Council, which regulated Georgia's land system through legislation and control of the distribution of land in the public domain. Bryan took an active part in this advantageous business. For instance, he sponsored legislation against absentee owners who showed no intention of cultivating their land. He also initiated an act for the "quieting of men's estates." This law stipulated that those who retained twenty years' "quiet possession" of a parcel of land had legal right over past and future claimants to purchase that land from the crown. These measures probably pleased Georgia landowners of all classes who opposed outside speculators and also helped bring order to the land-granting system by resolving the problem of multiple grants made under the Trustees' careless practices. Georgia's slaveowners required order in the land system if they were going to build large estates.

The most important aspect of council control over the public domain was the consideration of petitions for land. Anyone wishing a grant presented his or her petition in person to the governor and council. This gave the council direct contact with virtually every landowner in Georgia and provided occasions for it to display its "apartness" and majesty to the populace. . . .

Over the whole colonial period perhaps one million acres were handed out by the council. The percentage of petitions granted was high. In the most competitive period, 1755–1760, 1,406 of 1,785 petitions, or 79 percent, were accepted at least in part. From 1761 to 1769 the yearly figure was over 80 percent. These statistics appear to illustrate the ease with which Georgians acquired land, but they can be misleading. What they do not show is that sponsors often were needed for the granting of land and that many who hoped to obtain a portion, particularly of valuable low-country swamp or marsh, had little chance of success without a friend on the council. The case of Mark Noble illustrates the importance of council patronage.

Noble's case does not enter our statistics because his petition was never officially adjudged by the council in session. He was the overseer of Henry Lauren's Broughton Island plantation. Laurens became furious when Noble, without his approval and "under the sanction of Jonathan Bryan, Esquire . . . petitioned for a Warrant to Survey a parcel of that Marsh Land adjoining to the College Land and pretending that he had eight or ten Negroes." Laurens made his displeasure known to James Habersham and other council members. In behind-the-scenes maneuvering Laurens was able to prevent his overseer from receiving the desired land. From the particulars of the case it is evident that Noble and Laurens realized that council patronage was necessary for the overseer to receive the desired land and that politicking members of the council could promote or hinder a claim. . . .

Bryan followed the granting of land with great interest. His attendance on land days was below 75 percent only one year during the period 1755–1764, and in six of those nine years was above 85 percent. One reason for this regularity was the steady stream of petitions he submitted on his own behalf, thirty-eight in all, over two-thirds of which were submitted between 1755 and 1764. The thirty-eight were for over 18,000 acres plus wharfage and town and garden lots. Only two of his petitions were postponed; only one was rejected. His completed grants totaled upwards of 10,000 acres. This land formed the basis for several of his plantations, though he used a substantial portion for speculative purposes.

Bryan's council seat enabled him to obtain not only land of best quality but more than he was entitled to by freehold. Some Georgians were permitted to obtain public land by purchase. This allowed a privileged few to receive such land at minimal cost, once their freehold was completed. To purchase public land, planters had to swear that tracts would be developed and not used for speculation. The council was the final arbiter of who could buy and who could not; thus Bryan was in an excellent position to have his purchase requests approved. . . .

Bryan had made intermittent purchases from private individuals in the 1750s, but it was not until 1764 that he began buying large tracts in Georgia. Extant evidence indicates that he bought approximately 22,000 acres in both Georgia and South Carolina. . . .

Bryan's selection of land was based upon familiarity with Georgia topography acquired through years of travel and experience. He was expert in the native plants of the southeast and an excellent assessor of soil for crop production. James Habersham recommended Bryan to naturalist John Ellis as one who possessed "a general knowledge of this Province and South Carolina, and of its many unnoticed, tho' usefull Plants—both medicinal, and ornamental." The naturalist William Bartram also testified to Bryan's horticultural talents. Bartram visited Bryan at his Brampton plantation in 1776, where he found a beautiful "villa" in "a very delightful situation." He was impressed by Bryan's "spacious gardens, furnished with a variety of fruit trees and flowering shrubs." Benjamin Franklin learned of Bryan's talents and from England sent to him for experimentation some "Upland Rice, brought from Cochin China." This experiment failed but another succeeded: Franklin sent seeds of the Chinese tallow tree, which Bryan and a few others germinated so successfully that the tree soon spread through the southeast. . . .

. . . His purchases and grants were often distant from Savannah and required travel over difficult terrain. But Bryan was among the most physically fit of men, with the stamina not only to visit the far reaches of Georgia but to develop much of his land into plantations. . . .

Sales of land, both developed and undeveloped, assisted Bryan in capitalizing other enterprises. The thirty-three slaves he received from the sale of Walnut Hill probably were used at his new homestead, Brampton plantation, where he built the villa admired by Bartram. He operated so many plantations that he required constant influxes of new labor. At any given moment in the 1750s, 1760s, and 1770s he had five or more plantations in production. The total number of slaves employed is unknown but may be estimated at about 250 in 1763. In Georgia alone, Bryan held 66 slaves in 1755, 94 in 1760, and 125 in 1763. In South Carolina he possessed numerous plantations, totaling about 7,000 acres in the 1760s and 1770s; Union plantation in particular comprised 2,000 acres, was highly developed, and may have employed 100 or more slaves.

Access to capital was the key factor in obtaining slave labor. Because there were few shortages of black labor in Georgia and South Carolina between 1755 and the Revolution, men who possessed credit or cash could easily buy blacks, especially when, like Bryan, they had close business contacts with Bristol and Charleston merchants. Bryan had no difficulty stocking his plantations with laborers; he was able to provide ten slaves to each of his children when they came of age.

Establishing a plantation took large amounts of capital. The cartographer William Gerhard De Brahm, who immigrated to Georgia in 1751, estimated the cost of creating a rice plantation at £2,476. This sum purchased 200 acres, a barn, slaves, oxen and horses, two carts, tools, provisions for one year, and clothes and medicine for the work force; it also paid an overseer's wages. The greatest single expense De Brahm calculated was £1,800 for the purchase of forty seasoned slaves. He estimated return on the first year of investment at £700. This would pay a quarter of the planter's debt with interest. An overseer or tradesman who earned £50 per year could hardly expect to procure a £2,500 loan. Even a plantation of ten slaves was beyond the means of most men, given the scarcity of capital. Thus most white Georgians did not own slaves. The most recent estimate, by Betty Wood, suggests that "by the early 1760s at least 5 percent of all white Georgians, and probably not less than a quarter of all households, held at least one slave." Most of these were concentrated in the tidewater area.

The value of rice plantations varied greatly. It is noteworthy that when De Brahm calculated the costs of planting he did not mention the 2,000 acres a slaveholder was entitled to by purchase of forty slaves. That was because most of the good rice land was taken by 1760 and De Brahm made his estimate sometime after 1765. He also greatly underestimated the cost of improved rice land. On the Savannah and the fresh-water creeks that fed the river, good land sold for much more than the ten shillings per acre he calculated. On Hutchinson Island in the Savannah, Bryan bought and sold land in 1773 valued from £2 10s. to £6 per acre, or 500 to 1,200 percent higher than De Brahm had figured. The value of acreage on the island rose greatly in the next decade. Across from Hutchinson Island Bryan added a 250-acre tract to his holdings at Pipemaker's Creek. He paid close to £1 5s. per acre for this land. In 1768 he sold the 450-acre Little Yemassee plantation on the South Carolina side of the Savannah for £450. Only 50 acres were cleared for rice, while on another 50–60 were knolls of corn; the plantation also had an overseer's house. The Little Yemassee was not a major plantation, at least not to Bryan. He had purchased the tract five years earlier for about £150. But the few improvements he made and the value of the rice land, which was ex-cellently located, increased the plantation's value by 200 percent, despite the fact that 300 acres of the tract were uncleared. De Brahm, though expert in topography, was not a great planter and did not understand how to use slavery and land to gain riches as Bryan did. Thus we must revise his estimate of the cost for establishing a plantation of forty slaves from £2,476 to between £3,000 and £3,600, with the latter the closer fig-ure when prime rice land was purchased.

There are few records of how Bryan operated his plantations. We do not know whether he used his sons, slave drivers, or overseers to direct his work force. He recognized the family unit among his slaves, twice directing in his will that, if at all possible, families should not be broken up in the settlement of his estate. John Mar-tin Boltzius asserted that Bryan's plantations were run in an orderly manner. Boltz-ius reported in 1742 that the slaves were well treated and, as a result, were contented and worked efficiently. Unlike most slaveholders, who denied their bondsmen the privilege of reading and of practicing Christianity, Bryan actively promoted the education and Christianization of his slaves in both South Carolina and Georgia. Cornelius Winter, an evangelical who attempted to instruct Georgia blacks in the precepts of Christianity, testified in 1771 that many of Bryan's labor-ers knew Christian prayers by heart. Later in the decade Bryan took the unusual step of permitting one of his slaves, Andrew Bryan, to preach. His treatment of slaves with a respect ordinarily denied them may have contributed to the great success of his plantations.

Bryan's laborers performed a variety of tasks. They were cowboys, field hands, carpenters, sawyers, and house servants. Those skilled in woodwork produced lum-ber and shingles for market and built barns and slave quarters. Thus with great speed Bryan cleared tracts and erected the buildings necessary to begin plantation operations; he then developed the land or sold it as a fully functioning plantation. It appears that the latter was his intention or at least the result of his efforts in the sale of Little Yemassee, Dean Forrest, his plantation on the North Newport River, and possibly those on Wereat Island and Camber's Island in the Altamaha River.

Bryan's plantations were largely self-sufficient. Not only did they produce their own food, but the skills of his laborers made him less dependent upon hired labor than most planters, thus minimizing cash expenditures. When cash was needed, he could sell slaves, plantations, or undeveloped land, but his credit was always good and we may conclude that his notes were taken everywhere. . . . By the mid-1760s he had built no less than a plantation empire.

The building of that empire illustrates the sophisticated way in which a wealthy southern planter used political office, scientific knowledge, and business acumen in the conduct of his affairs. Bryan's ability to adapt his financial interests to the environment in which he lived displays a logic that was highly rational and practical. In combining his political and personal interests, Bryan was typical of Georgia's slaveholding elite. They were men of talent who understood the importance of patronage, political preferment, and public works projects, as well as the marketing of crops and the intricacies of English law. . . .

On the eve of the Revolution, Jonathan Bryan's plantation empire contained some 10,000 acres and 300 slaves. Fueled by his aggressive quest for power, prestige, and affluence—for himself and for his offspring—it had grown over the years into a network of prosperous estates that complemented one another, and Bryan himself had grown so great, as a planter, that he could stand for Independence almost alone among the colony's ruling elite. He can thus be said to exemplify the possessive individualism of his class—a class of planter-capitalists who mastered the economic and political arts of creating, on the southern frontier, a society shaped in their image and geared to their interest.

# FURTHER  READING

Harold E. Davis, *The Fledgling Province: Social and Cultural Life in Colonial Georgia, 1733–1776* (1976).

A. Roger Ekirch, *"Poor Carolina": Politics and Society in Colonial North Carolina, 1729–1762* (1981).

James H. Merrell, *The Indians' New World: Catawbas and Their Neighbors from European Contact Through the Era of Removal* (1989).

Clarence L. Ver Steeg, *Origins of a Southern Mosaic: Studies of Early Carolina and Georgia* (1975).

Betty Wood, *Slavery in Colonial Georgia, 1730–1775* (1984).

Peter H. Wood, Gregory A. Waselkov, and M. Thomas Hatley, eds., *Powhatan's Mantle: Indians in the Colonial Southeast* (1989).

CHAPTER
10

# Slave Life and Culture

When Americans think of slavery, they visualize the plantation system of the early nineteenth century, slavery in its "mature" American form. That system comprised African Americans, American-born Creoles who were the sons and daughters of earlier generations of Africans who had been forceably brought to America. Both owners and slaves operated within a context into which they had been born, and whose forms they knew well.

Slavery in the colonial period was far more varied. Seventeenth-century colonists on the mainland moved slowly toward slavery. The English colonies began with indentured servitude, in which colonists from Europe agreed to serve for a specified period in return for their passage over and a grant of land when their servitude was up. This concept seems to have been extended to the first Africans in the English Chesapeake colonies; the expense of acquiring an African servant was high, so their term of servitude was longer. But some Africans did serve out their terms, and, like their European counterparts, acquired their freedom dues of land. After the middle of the seventeenth century, however, the pattern began to change, and the Chesapeake colonies began to import ever larger numbers of Africans. From the 1660s on, the law specified that Africans were to serve for their entire lives and their children inherited their status: the legal condition of slavery was fully set. Carolina colony was founded at this time and, partly because of its ties to the Caribbean, began with the assumption that slavery was the norm. From the end of the seventeenth century, slavery was the labor system of the southern colonies.

Even though the legal definition of slavery was established in the 1660s, internal development within the institution across the colonies saw great variation. Although increasingly some people were born into slavery, Africans continued to be imported throughout the period and they brought the customs and assumptions of many African peoples to the consciousness of American-born slaves. Depending on the particular situation and mix of peoples, slaves responded in many ways and on a variety of levels in creating their own social and cultural forms and in interacting with those who owned and ran southern plantations. In some locations in the North slaves were also a substantial presence who built a different kind of cultural niche for themselves. In the colonial period we can see slavery coming into its mature form through a variety of routes.

⌀  *D O C U M E N T S*

In 1708 the Board of Trade, the part of the British government responsible for the colonies, wrote to the governors asking them about the importation of slaves. Document 1 is this letter and replies sent by Governors Samuel Cranston of Rhode Island, John Seymour of Maryland, and Edmund Jennings of Virginia. They describe the arrival of slaves, their prices, and the circuitous route by which they came.

Olaudah Equiano wrote a classic narrative, document 2, describing the experience of being enslaved in Africa and transported for sale and slavery in America in the mid-eighteenth century. He vividly recounts his feelings as a young boy, coming to Virginia in 1757 at the age of twelve, as he began to understand the full meaning of his enslavement. From the other side, the Reverend Hugh Jones in document 3 wrote a description of Virginia in 1724 in which he described the slaves' lives, and blamed the turn to slavery on the unwillingness of Europeans to come as indentured servants. His title page carried a quotation from the book of Genesis in the Bible: "God shall enlarge Japtheth, and he shall dwell in the Tents of Shem, and Canaan shall be his Servant." In the 1750s, Johann Martin Bolzius sent answers to a questionnaire from Germany, including, in document 4, answers about slavery, which had recently been allowed in the colony of Georgia.

## 1. The Board of Trade Seeks Information on the Slave Trade, 1708

Sir: Some time since, the Queen was pleased to refer to us a petition relating to the trade of Africa, upon which we have heard what the Royal African Company, and the separate traders had to offer; and having otherwise informed ourselves, in the best manner we could, of the present state of that trade, we laid the same before Her Majesty. The consideration of that trade came afterwards into the house of commons, and a copy of our report was laid before the house; but the session being then too far spent to enter upon a matter of so great weight, and other business intervening, no progress was made therein. However, it being absolutely necessary that a trade so beneficial to the kingdom should be carried on to the greatest advantage, there is no doubt but the consideration thereof will come early before the Parliament at their next meeting; and as the well supplying of the plantations and colonies with sufficient number of negroes at reasonable prices, is in our opinion the chief point to be considered in regard to that trade, and as hitherto we have not been able to know how they have been supplied by the company, or by separate traders, otherwise than according to the respective accounts given by them, which for the most part are founded upon calculations made from their exports on one side and the other, and do differ so very much, that no certain judgment can be made upon those accounts.

Wherefore, that we may be able at the next meeting of the Parliament to lay before both houses when required, an exact and authentic state of that trade, particularly in regard to the several plantations and colonies; we do hereby desire and

---

John Russell Bartlett, ed., *Records of the Colony of Rhode Island and Providence Plantations* (Providence, 1859), Vol. 4, pp. 1707–1740 (letter from the Board of Trade and Cranston's reply). Elizabeth Donnan, ed., *Documents Illustrative of the History of the Slave Trade to America* (Washington, DC: Carnegie Institution, 1930–1935), pp. 21–23, 88–90 (Seymour's and Jennings's replies).

strictly require you, that upon the receipt hereof, you do inform yourself from the proper officers or otherwise, in the best manner you can, what number of negroes have been yearly imported directly from Africa into Jamaica, since the 24th of June, 1698, to the 25th of December, 1707, and at what rate per head they have been sold each year, one with another, distinguishing the numbers that have been imported on account of the Royal African Company, and those which have been imported by separate traders; as likewise the rates at which such negroes have been sold by the company and by separate traders. We must recommend it to your care to be as exact and diligent therein as possibly you can, and with the first opportunity to transmit to us such accounts as aforesaid, that they may arrive here in due time, as also duplicates by the first conveyance.

And that we may be the better able to make a true judgment of the present settlement of that trade, we must further recommend it to you to confer with some of the principal planters and inhabitants within your government touching that matter, and to let us know how the negro trade was carried on, and the island of Jamaica supplied with negroes till the year 1698, when that trade was laid open by act of Parliament; how it has been carried on, and negroes supplied since that time, or in what manner they think the said trade may best be managed for the benefit of the plantations.

We further desire you will inform us what number of ships, if any, are employed from Jamaica to the coast of Africa in the negro trade, and how many separate traders are concerned therein.

Lastly, whatever accounts you shall from time to time send us touching these matters of the negro trade, we desire that the same may be distinct, and not intermixed with other matters; and that for the time to come, you do transmit to us the like half yearly accounts of negroes, by whom imported and at what rates sold; the first of such subsequent accounts, to begin from Christmas, 1707, to which time those now demanded, are to be given. So we bid you heartily farewell.

Your very loving friends,

STAMFORD,<br>HERBERT,<br>PH. MEADOWS,<br>I. PULTENEY,<br>R. MONCKTON,

P. S. We expect the best account you can give us, with that expedition, which the shortness of the time requires.

Memorandum. This letter, mutatis mutandis, was writ to the Governors of Barbadoes, the Leeward Islands, Bermuda, New York, New Jersey, Maryland, the President of the Council of Virginia, the Governor of New Hampshire and the Massachusetts Bay, the Deputy Governor of Pennsylvania, the Lords proprietors of Carolina, the Governors and Companies of Connecticut and Rhode Island.

### Reply from Rhode Island Governor Samuel Cranston

May it please your Lordships: In obedience to your Lordships' commands of the 15th of April last, to the trade of Africa.

We, having inspected into the books of Her Majesty's custom, and informed ourselves from the proper officers thereof, by strict inquiry, can lay before your Lordships no other account of that trade than the following, viz.:

1. That from the 24th of June, 1698, to the 25th of December, 1707, we have not had any negroes imported into this colony from the coast of Africa, neither on the account of the Royal African Company, or by any of the separate traders.
2. That on the 30th day of May, 1696, arrived at this port from the coast of Africa, the brigantine Seaflower, Thomas Windsor, master, having on board her forty-seven negroes, fourteen of which he disposed of in this colony, for betwixt £30 and £35 per head; the rest he transported by land for Boston, where his owners lived.
3. That on the 10th of August, the 19th and 28th of October, in the year 1700, sailed from this port three vessels, directly for the coast of Africa; the two former were sloops, the one commanded by Nicho's Hillgroue, the other by Jacob Bill; the last a ship, commanded by Edwin Carter, who was part owner of the said three vessels, in company with Thomas Bruster, and John Bates, merchants, of Barbadoes, and separate traders from thence to the coast of Africa; the said three vessels arriving safe to Barbadoes from the coast of Africa, where they made the disposition of their negroes.
4. That we have never had any vessels from the coast of Africa to this colony, nor any trade there, the brigantine above mentioned, excepted.
5. That the whole and only supply of negroes to this colony, is from the island of Barbadoes; from whence is imported one year with another, betwixt twenty and thirty; and if those arrive well and sound, the general price is from £30 to £40 per head.

According to your Lordships' desire, we have advised with the chiefest of our planters, and find but small encouragement for that trade to this colony; since by the best computation we can make, there would not be disposed in this colony above twenty or thirty at the most, annually; the reasons of which are chiefly to be attributed to the general dislike our planters have for them, by reason of their turbulent and unruly tempers.

And that most of our planters that are able and willing to purchase any of them, are supplied by the offspring of those they have already, which increase daily; and that the inclination of our people in general, is to employ white servants before negroes.

Thus we have given your Lordships a true and faithful account of what hath occurred, relating to the trade of Africa from this colony; and if, for the future, our trade should be extended to those parts, we shall not fail transmitting accounts thereof according to your Lordships' orders, and that at all times be ready to show ourselves,

Your Lordships' obedient servant,
SAMUEL CRANSTON, Governor.

Newport, on Rhode Island, December 5, 1708.

## Reply from Maryland Governor John Seymour

*May it please your Lordships:* I have your Commands of the 15th of Aprill, which came to hand by a Chance Sloope from Barbadoes; but not untill the 13th of Octob., by which your Lordships may perceive how tedious and uncertain that Conveyance is; And therefore have not the least apprehensions your Lordships Justice will impute any neglect to me; since in Obedience thereto I immediately made the best

Inquiry I could, what numbers of Negros have been supplyd to this her Ma'tys Province by the Royall Affrican Company, or by the Seperate Traders who pay the tenn per ct., Since the 24th of June 1698. And by the List here inclosed, which is as exact as the speedy dispatch of this Answer would admitt, Your Lordships will find the Royall Affrican Company have not supplyd one Negro to this province during that tyme; Nor can I, on Enquiry of above twenty years last past heare of any ship belonging to the Company that has come hither; but Wee have been wholy supply'd by the seperate Traders, as your Lordships may perceive (tho by the Death and Removeall of severall Officers of the Customes here, I cannot learne the Owners or Importers, further than the Names of the severall shipps and Commanders[)]; yet am satisfied they were exclusive of the Royall Affrican Company.

And these Negroes have been sold for Bills of Excha. payable in London, generally men at £30 sterl., per head and Women at five and six and twenty pounds.

I have pursuant to your Lordships' directions discurst many of the principall planters here, by whom I am inform'd that before the year 1698, this province has been supplyd by some small Quantitys of Negro's from Barbados and other her Ma'tys Islands and Plantations, as Jamaica and New England Seaven, eight, nine or ten in a Sloope, and sometymes larger Quantitys, and sometymes, tho very seldom, whole ship Loads of Slaves have been brought here directly from Affrica by Interlopers, or such as have had Lycenses, or otherwise traded there. At present the Trade seems to run high, there having been between six and seaven hundred Negro's imported hither this yeare 1708. And the Planters owne themselves obliged to the seperate Traders for these supplys having never had any from the Company, and now the price of Negro's begins to abate, as Wee suppose by reason of the plentifull Importation by the seperate Traders, so that 'tis the Opinion of most here, should the seperate Traders be totally excluded, the Company would take no better care to supply them with slaves, than they have formerly done, which would not only be a great Detriment to the planters, but also to her Ma'tys Revenue of so valuable Customes on tob'o.

As to shipping belonging to this Country and imployed to the Coast of Affrica at present I cannot learne of any, nor above two or three persons concern'd therein with the Merchts. in London.

I humbly begg your Lordships pardon that the Account of what number of Negro's the province has been yearly supplyd with, and at what Rates has not been transmitted, which being interwoven with the Encouragement. and Protection I am enjoyned to give the Royall Affrican Company, made me mistake to be intended of those to be supplyd by them only. And to convince your Lordships of my future exact Complyance with Commands, I esteeme so sacred, have sent you a list of those imported this present year 1708. And shall in all other Matters punctually observe and obey your Commands on all Occasions . . .

MARYLAND, November 18th, 1708.

### Reply from Edmund Jennings of Virginia

Virginia November the 27th, 1708.

*May it please yr Lordships,* It was the 11th of last moneth and the Fleet then sailed, before I had the honr to receive yor Lordships of the 15th of April concerning the Negro Trade Since which I have endeavoured by the means of the proper Officers, and the informations of the ancient Inhabitants, to answer Yo'r Lordps Commands, and in Order thereto have herewith sent yo'r Lordships an account of all the Negros imported into this Colony from the 24th of June 1699 to the 12th of October last past distinguishing those imported by the Royal African Company (679), and those by Seperate Traders (5928), wherein yo'r Lordships will perceive the latter have had much the greater Share. As to the particular Rates at which those Negros have been sold, they have been variable according to the Different times of their coming in and the quality and ages of the Slaves, but the medium for men and women may be reckoned from 20 to 30 pounds a head for those sold by the Company and from 20 to 35 £ a head for the like kinds sold by the Seperate Traders, who in gen'll have sold theirs at a higher rate than the Company.

How the Country was supplyed with Negros before the Trade to Affrica was laid open in the year 1698, I have endeavoured to Inform my Self from some ancient Inhabitants conversant in that Trade as well as by recollecting what hath happened in my own knowledge, and find that before the year 1680 what negros were brought to Virginia were imported generally from Barbados for it was very rare to have a Negro ship come to this Country directly from Africa since that time, and before the year 1698, the Trade of Negros became more frequent, tho not in any proportion to what it hath been of late, during which the Affrican Company sent several Ships and others by their Licence (as I have been informed) having bought their Slaves of the Company brought them in hither for Sale, Among which I remember the late Alderman Jeffrys and Sr Jeffry Jeffrys were principally concerned, but all this time the price of the Negros was currant from £18 to 25 per head for men and women and never exceeded that Rate. Whether the opening the Trade to Africa having created an Emulation between the Company and the Seperate Traders which should outbid the other in the purchase of their Slaves there, or whether the dexterity of their Factors there in taking advantage of the prevailing humour of our Inhabitants for some years past of buying Negros even beyond their abilities, or the Concurrence of both, hath raised the Rates of Negros so extravagantly I shall not pretend to determine but this I may venture to say that it will be much harder to lower the price again now 'tis raised unless there be the same Freedome of Trade continued as formerly for tho the Inhabitants of this Country in gen'll will not be so fond of purchasing Negros as of late being sensibly convinced of their Error which has in a manner ruined the Credit of the Country yet there will still be some that must, and others that will at any rate Venture to buy them, and if the Company alone have the Management of the Trade, they'l find pretences enough to keep up the price if not to impose what higher rate they please, which the buyer must submit to, knowing he cannot be supplyed by any other hand. As for Vessells trading directly from this place to the Coast of Africa I never knew of any nor is the same practicable this Country not being provided with Comoditys suitable for carrying on such a Trade. This is the best account I am able to give in answer to yor Lordships Commands wherein if I have failed or mistaken in any point I beg yo'r Lordships favourable Construction thereof Since I can with truth assure yo'r Lordships that no man hath a greater Desire to serve yo'r Lordships. . . .

P. S. The Instructions to our late Governour were sealed up at his death, and were not opened till I had the hon'r of being intrusted with the Government by her

Majesty's late Instruction, else I should not have failed in sending yr Lordships the amount of Negros required therein.

## 2. Olaudah Equiano Recalls His Enslavement, 1750s

. . . I have already acquainted the reader with the time and place of my birth. My father, besides many slaves, had a numerous family, of which seven lived to grow up, including myself and sister, who was the only daughter. As I was the youngest of the sons, I became, of course, the greatest favorite with my mother, and was always with her; and she used to take particular pains to form my mind. I was trained up from my earliest years in the art of war: my daily exercise was shooting and throwing javelins, and my mother adorned me with emblems, after the manner of our greatest warriors. In this way I grew up till I had turned the age of eleven, when an end was put to my happiness in the following manner: Generally, when the grown people in the neighborhood were gone far in the fields to labor, the children assembled together in some of the neighboring premises to play; and commonly some of us used to get up a tree to look out for any assailant, or kidnapper, that might come upon us—for they sometimes took those opportunities of our parents' absence, to attack and carry off as many as they could seize. One day as I was watching at the top of a tree in our yard, I saw one of those people come into the yard of our next neighbor but one, to kidnap, there being many stout young people in it. Immediately on this I gave the alarm of the rogue, and he was surrounded by the stoutest of them, who entangled him with cords, so that he could not escape, till some of the grown people came and secured him. But, alas! ere long it was my fate to be thus attacked, and to be carried off, when none of the grown people were nigh. One day, when all our people were gone out to their works as usual, and only I and my dear sister were left to mind the house, two men and a woman got over our walls, and in a moment seized us both, and, without giving us time to cry out, or make resistance, they stopped our mouths, and ran off with us into the nearest wood. Here they tied our hands, and continued to carry us as far as they could, till night came on, when we reached a small house, where the robbers halted for refreshment, and spent the night. We were then unbound, but were unable to take any food; and, being quite overpowered by fatigue and grief, our only relief was some sleep, which allayed our misfortune for a short time. The next morning we left the house, and continued travelling all the day. For a long time we had kept the woods, but at last we came into a road which I believed I knew. I had now some hopes of being delivered; for we had advanced but a little way before I discovered some people at a distance, on which I began to cry out for their assistance; but my cries had no other effect than to make them tie me faster and stop my mouth, and then they put me into a large sack. They also stopped my sister's mouth, and tied her hands; and in this manner we proceeded till we were out of sight of these people. When we went to rest the following night, they offered us some victuals, but we refused it; and the only comfort we had was in being in one another's arms all that night, and bathing each other with our tears. But alas! we were soon deprived of even the small comfort of weeping to-

Olaudah Equiano, *The Life of Olaudah Equiano, or Gustavus Vassa, the African* (London, 1789).

gether. The next day proved a day of greater sorrow than I had yet experienced; for my sister and I were then separated, while we lay clasped in each other's arms. It was in vain that we besought them not to part us; she was torn from me, and immediately carried away, while I was left in a state of distraction not to be described. I cried and grieved continually; and for several days did not eat anything but what they forced into my mouth. . . .

. . . Thus I continued to travel, sometimes by land, sometimes by water, through different countries and various nations, till, at the end of six or seven months after I had been kidnapped, I arrived at the sea coast. It would be tedious and uninteresting to relate all the incidents which befell me during this journey, and which I have not yet forgotten; of the various hands I passed through, and the manners and customs of all the different people among whom I lived—I shall therefore only observe, that in all the places where I was, the soil was exceedingly rich; the pumpkins, eadas, plantains, yams, &c. &c., were in great abundance, and of incredible size. There were also vast quantities of different gums, though not used for any purpose, and everywhere a great deal of tobacco. The cotton even grew quite wild, and there was plenty of red-wood. I saw no mechanics whatever in all the way . . . The chief employment in all these countries was agriculture, and both the males and females, as with us, were brought up to it, and trained in the arts of war.

The first object which saluted my eyes when I arrived on the coast, was the sea, and a slave ship, which was then riding at anchor, and waiting for its cargo. These filled me with astonishment, which was soon converted into terror, when I was carried on board. I was immediately handled, and tossed up to see if I were sound, by some of the crew; and I was now persuaded that I had gotten into a world of bad spirits, and that they were going to kill me. Their complexions, too, differing so much from ours, their long hair, and the language they spoke (which was very different from any I had ever heard), united to confirm me in this belief. Indeed, such were the horrors of my views and fears at the moment, that, if ten thousand worlds had been my own, I would have freely parted with them all to have exchanged my condition with that of the meanest slave in my own country. When I looked round the ship too, and saw a large furnace of copper boiling, and a multitude of black people of every description chained together, every one of their countenances expressing dejection and sorrow, I no longer doubted of my fate; and, quite overpowered with horror and anguish, I fell motionless on the deck and fainted. When I recovered a little, I found some black people about me, who I believed were some of those who had brought me on board, and had been receiving their pay; they talked to me in order to cheer me, but all in vain. I asked them if we were not to be eaten by those white men with horrible looks, red faces, and long hair. They told me I was not, and one of the crew brought me a small portion of spirituous liquor in a wine glass; but, being afraid of him, I would not take it out of his hand. One of the blacks, therefore, took it from him and gave it to me, and I took a little down my palate, which, instead of reviving me, as they thought it would, threw me into the greatest consternation at the strange feeling it produced, having never tasted any such liquor before. Soon after this, the blacks who brought me on board went off, and left me abandoned to despair. . . .

At last, when the ship we were in, had got in all her cargo, they made ready with many fearful noises, and we were all put under deck, so that we could not see how they managed the vessel. But this disappointment was the least of my sorrow. The stench of the hold while we were on the coast was so intolerably loathsome, that it was dangerous to remain there for any time, and some of us had been permitted to stay on the deck for the fresh air; but now that the whole ship's cargo were confined together, it became absolutely pestilential. The closeness of the place, and the heat of the climate, added to the number in the ship, which was so crowded that each had scarcely room to turn himself, almost suffocated us. This produced copious perspirations, so that the air soon became unfit for respiration, from a variety of loathsome smells, and brought on a sickness among the slaves, of which many died—thus falling victims to the improvident avarice, as I may call it, of their purchasers. This wretched situation was again aggravated by the galling of the chains, now became insupportable, and the filth of the necessary tubs, into which the children often fell, and were almost suffocated. The shrieks of the women, and the groans of the dying, rendered the whole a scene of horror almost inconceivable. Happily perhaps, for myself, I was soon reduced so low here that it was thought necessary to keep me almost always on deck; and from my extreme youth I was not put in fetters. In this situation I expected every hour to share the fate of my companions, some of whom were almost daily brought upon deck at the point of death, which I began to hope would soon put an end to my miseries. Often did I think many of the inhabitants of the deep much more happy than myself. I envied them in the freedom they enjoyed, and as often wished I could change my condition for theirs. Every circumstance I met with, served only to render my state more painful, and heightened my apprehensions, and my opinion of the cruelty of the whites.

One day they had taken a number of fishes; and when they had killed and satisfied themselves with as many as they thought fit, to our astonishment who were on deck, rather than give any of them to us to eat, as we expected, they tossed the remaining fish into the sea again, although we begged and prayed for some as well as we could, but in vain; and some of my countrymen, being pressed by hunger, took an opportunity, when they thought no one saw them, of trying to get a little privately; but they were discovered, and the attempt procured them some very severe floggings. One day, when we had a smooth sea and moderate wind, two of my wearied countrymen who were chained together (I was near them at the time), preferring death to such a life of misery, somehow made through the nettings and jumped into the sea; immediately, another quite dejected fellow, who, on account of his illness, was suffered to be out of irons, also followed their example; and I believe many more would very soon have done the same, if they had not been prevented by the ship's crew, who were instantly alarmed. Those of us that were the most active, were in a moment put down under the deck; and there was such a noise and confusion amongst the people of the ship as I never heard before, to stop her, and get the boat out to go after the slaves. However, two of the wretches were drowned, but they got the other, and afterwards flogged him unmercifully, for thus attempting to prefer death to slavery. In this manner we continued to undergo more hardships than I can now relate, hardships which are inseparable from this accursed trade. Many a time we were near suffocation from the want of fresh air, which we were often without for whole days together. This, and the stench of the necessary tubs, carried off many. . . .

. . . At last, we came in sight of the island of Barbadoes, at which the whites on board gave a great shout, and made many signs of joy to us. We did not know what to think of this; but as the vessel drew nearer, we plainly saw the harbor, and other ships of different kinds and sizes. . . .

We were not many days in the merchant's custody, before we were sold after their usual manner, which is this: On a signal given (as the beat of a drum), the buyers rush at once into the yard where the slaves are confined, and make choice of that parcel they like best. The noise and clamor with which this is attended, and the eagerness visible in the countenances of the buyers, serve not a little to increase the apprehension of terrified Africans, who may well be supposed to consider them as the ministers of that destruction to which they think themselves devoted. In this manner, without scruple, are relations and friends separated, most of them never to see each other again. I remember, in the vessel in which I was brought over, in the men's apartment, there were several brothers, who, in the sale, were sold in different lots; and it was very moving on this occasion, to see and hear their cries at parting. O, ye nominal Christians! might not an African ask you—Learned you this from your God, who says unto you, Do unto all men as you would men should do unto you? It is not enough that we are torn from our country and friends, to toil for your luxury and lust of gain? Must every tender feeling be likewise sacrificed to your avarice? Are the dearest friends and relations, now rendered more dear by their separation from their kindred, still to be parted from each other, and thus prevented from cheering the gloom of slavery, with the small comfort of being together, and mingling their sufferings and sorrows? Why are parents to lose their children, brothers their sisters, or husbands their wives? Surely, this is a new refinement in cruelty, which, while it has no advantage to atone for it, thus aggravates distress, and adds fresh horrors even to the wretchedness of slavery.

. . . I now totally lost the small remains of comfort I had enjoyed in conversing with my countrymen; the women too, who used to wash and take care of me were all gone different ways, and I never saw one of them afterwards.

I stayed in this island for a few days, I believe it could not be above a fortnight, when I, and some few more slaves, that were not saleable amongst the rest, from very much fretting, were shipped off in a sloop for North America. On the passage we were better treated than when we were coming from Africa, and we had plenty of rice and fat pork. We were landed up a river a good way from the sea, about Virginia county, where we saw few or none of our native Africans, and not one soul who could talk to me. I was a few weeks weeding grass and gathering stones in a plantation; and at last all my companions were distributed different ways, and only myself was left. I was now exceedingly miserable, and thought myself worse off than any of the rest of my companions, for they could talk to each other, but I had no person to speak to that I could understand. In this state, I was constantly grieving and pining, and wishing for death rather than anything else. While I was in this plantation, the gentleman, to whom I suppose the estate belonged, being unwell, I was one day sent for to his dwelling-house to fan him; when I came into the room where he was I was very much affrighted at some things I saw, and the more so as I had seen a black woman slave as I came through the house, who was cooking the dinner, and the poor creature was cruelly loaded with various kinds of iron machines; she had one particularly on her head, which locked her mouth so fast that she could scarcely speak; and could not eat or drink. I was much astonished and shocked at this contrivance, which I afterwards learned was called the iron muzzle. Soon after I had a fan put in my hand, to fan the gentleman while he slept; and so I did indeed with great fear. While he was fast asleep I indulged myself a great deal in looking about the room, which to me appeared very fine and curious. The first object that engaged my attention was a watch which hung on the chimney, and was going. I was quite surprised at the noise it made, and was afraid it would tell the gentleman anything I might do amiss; and when I immediately after observed a picture hanging in the room, which appeared constantly to look at me, I was still more affrighted, having never seen such things as these before. At one time I thought it was something relative to magic; and not seeing it move, I thought it might be some way the whites had to keep their great men when they died, and offer them libations as we used to do our friendly spirits. In this state of anxiety I remained till my master awoke, when I was dismissed out of the room, to my no small satisfaction and relief; for I thought that these people were all made up of wonders. In this place I was called Jacob; but on board the *African Snow,* I was called Michael. I had been some time in this miserable, forlorn, and much dejected state, without having anyone to talk to, which made my life a burden, when the kind and unknown hand of the Creator (who in very deed leads the blind in a way they know not) now began to appear, to my comfort; for one day the captain of a merchant ship, called the *Industrious Bee,* came on some business to my master's house. This gentleman, whose name was Michael Henry Pascal, was a lieutenant in the royal navy, but now commanded this trading ship, which was somewhere in the confines of the county many miles off. While he was at my master's house, it happened that he saw me, and liked me so well that he made a purchase of me. I think I have often heard him say he gave thirty or forty pounds sterling for me; but I do not remember which. However, he meant me for a present to some of his friends in England: and as I was sent accordingly from the house of my then master (one Mr. Campbell) to the place where the ship lay. . . .

## 3. The Reverend Hugh Jones Describes Virginia Slavery in 1724

The Negroes live in small cottages called quarters, in about six in a gang, under the direction of an overseer or bailiff; who takes care that they tend such land as the owner allots and orders, upon which they raise hogs and cattle, and plant Indian corn (or maize) and tobacco for the use of their master; out of which the overseer has a dividend (or share) in proportion to the number of hands including himself; this with several privileges is his salary, and is an ample recompence for his pains, and encouragement of his industrious care, as to the labour, health, and provision of the Negroes.

Hugh Jones. *The Present State of Virginia* (London, 1724), 75–6, 130.

The Negroes are very numerous, some gentlemen having hundreds of them of all sorts, to whom they bring great profit; for the sake of which they are obliged to keep them well, and not overwork, starve, or famish them, besides other inducements to favour them; which is done in a great degree, to such especially that are laborious, careful, and honest; though indeed some masters, careless of their own interest or reputation, are too cruel and negligent.

The Negroes are not only encreased by fresh supplies from Africa and the West India Islands, but also are very prolifick among themselves; and they that are born there talk good English, and affect our language, habits, and customs; and though they be naturally of a barbarous and cruel temper, yet are they kept under by severe discipline upon occasion, and by good laws are prevented from running away, injuring the English, or neglecting their business.

Their work (or chimerical hard slavery) is not very laborious; their greatest hardship consisting in that they and their posterity are not at their own liberty or disposal, but are the property of their owners; and when they are free, they know not how to provide so well for themselves generally; neither did they live so plentifully nor (many of them) so easily in their own country, where they are made slaves to one another, or taken captive by their enemies.

The children belong to the master of the woman that bears them; and such as are born of a Negroe and an European are called Molattoes; but such as are born of an Indian and Negroe are called Mustees.

Their work is to take care of the stock, and plant corn, tobacco, fruits, etc. which is not harder than thrashing, hedging, or ditching; besides, though they are out in the violent heat, wherein they delight, yet in wet or cold weather there is little occasion for their working in the fields, in which few will let them be abroad, lest by this means they might get sick or die, which would prove a great loss to their owners, a good Negroe being sometimes worth three (nay four) score pounds sterling, if he be a tradesman; so that upon this (if upon no other account) they are obliged not to overwork them, but to cloath and feed them sufficiently, and take care of their health.

Several of them are taught to be sawyers, carpenters, smiths, coopers, etc. and though for the most part they be none of the aptest or nicest; yet they are by nature cut out for hard labour and fatigue, and will perform tolerably well; though they fall much short of an Indian, that has learned and seen the same things; and those Negroes make the best servants, that have been slaves in their own country; for they that have been kings and great men there are generally lazy, haughty, and obstinate; whereas the others are sharper, better humoured, and more laborious.

The languages of the new Negroes are various harsh jargons, and their religions and customs such as are best described by Mr. Bosman in his book intitled (I think) *A Description of the Coasts of Africa.*

The Virginia planters readily learn to become good mechanicks in building, wherein most are capable of directing their servants and slaves. . . .

It is a monkish opinion too prevalent with many still, that there is no good living without the bounds of their own cloyster. An abundance of English entertain the Chinese notion, that they are all fools and beggars that live in any country but theirs. This home fondness has been very prejudicial to the common sort of English, and has in a great measure retarded the plantations from being stocked with such inhabitants as are skilful, industrious, and laborious.

For these reasons, such persons of sense and resolution as have entered into projects for improvements in the plantations (who have evinced us, that all schemes are not bubbles) have been obliged for the generality to make use of the worst and vilest of mankind, for the execution of the noblest and most useful undertakings; though indeed continually several people of sense, virtue, and fortune, entertaining tolerable good notions of these affairs, have embarked themselves and families in such laudable and useful designs: But for the generality, the servants and inferior sort of people, who have either been sent over to Virginia, or have transported themselves thither, have been, and are, the poorest, idlest, and worst of mankind, the refuse of Great Britain and Ireland, and the outcast of the people.

These servants are but an insignificant number, when compared with the vast shoals of Negroes who are imployed as slaves there to do the hardest and most part of the work; the most laborious of which is the felling of trees and the like, to which kind of slavery (if it must be so called) our wood-cutters in England are exposed; only with this difference, that the Negroes eat wholesomer bread and better pork with more plenty and ease; and when they are sick, their owners interest and purse are deeply engaged in their recovery, who likewise are obliged to take all the care imaginable of the children of their slaves for their own great profit; so that the Negroes, though they work moderately, yet live plentifully, have no families to provide for, no danger of beggary, no care for the morrow.

## 4. Johann Martin Bolzius Describes the Slaves' Lives in Georgia, 1750s

9th Question. About how costly is a Negro man, and a Negro woman?

Answer. There is a large difference between those Negroes who are born in Carolina or have at least lived there several years and those who have just been brought over from Africa. Today a good Negro man costs between £30 and £40, a price for which newly arrived Negroes also have recently been sold. A good Negro woman is not bought under £30 (N.B., £1 I figure at 9 fl.). . . .

10th Question. Whether these people are as false, malicious, and terrible as they are described.

Answer. A faithful and sincere Negro is a very rare thing, but they do exist, particularly with masters who know how to treat them reasonably and in a Christian way. Foolish masters sometimes make disloyal and malicious Negroes. Nearly all like to lie and steal, and if they gain the upper hand in a rebellion they give no mercy, but treat the whites very cruelly. Eternal slavery to them as to all people is an unbearable yoke, and very harsh treatment as regards food and work exasperates them greatly. New Negroes therefore must be treated very carefully, for they frequently take their own lives out of desperation, with the hope of resurrection in their homeland, and of rejoining their people.

11th Question. How many Negroes are necessary for the cultivation of a well-appointed plantation of about 1,000 acres?

From Klaus G. Loewald, Beverly Starika, and Paul S. Taylor, eds. "Johann Martin Bolzius Answers a Questionnaire on Carolina and Georgia," *William and Mary Quarterly,* 3rd ser., XIV (1957), pp. 232–237.

Answer. There is a difference among plantations, or cultivated fields. Some are being, and have been, cleared first of trees and bushes, and must be fenced (for not a single field must be without a good 6-foot-high fence, because of horses, cattle, and pigs, which walk about freely in the woods without herdsmen). Others, however, have already been fenced and cultivated for several years. Some [Negroes] can do the former work more easily than the latter, for in the third and following years a grass grows on the old plantations which is so harmful that in humid weather it grows again on the same day on which it was removed, and covers the earth like a fur. On new land a Negro can work 6 to 10 acres, and plant Indian corn, beans, pumpkins, rice, and potatoes on it. On old land, however, he has his hands full with 6 acres. From this one can easily compute how many Negroes are required for 1,000 acres. But it is not advisable to start with many at a time. Those who tried to take, as it were, overly big steps in Carolina have fallen and have ruined themselves and others. The fewer Negroes at the start, the better.

12th Question. How many white servants or people are necessary to keep the blacks in order, or, more exactly, what is the ratio of whites to the black servants in a household?

Answer. In Carolina a law was made that every planter shall keep a white man as an overseer for 10 Negroes, but this law, like many others, is *quasi Campana sine Pistillo,* for quite a few have perhaps 100 and more Negroes and no white person except their own family, but install the most loyal Negroes as Negro drivers *(Treiber)* and beaters *(Schläger).* That is how it comes about that in Carolina the Negroes outnumber the white inhabitants possibly 30 times. This dangerous disorder has been prevented in our colony by a beneficent law requiring at all times one white man or servant for 4 Negroes on every plantation, which is all the more necessary because we are situated so close to the Spaniards.

13th Question. Whether there are many instances of Negroes murdering their masters, and whether in this case they have the opportunity to flee inland and to escape punishment with the help of the Indians, and whether for such cases the government has established good regulations.

Answer. To answer this question piecemeal: 1.) In Carolina the instances of Negroes murdering, scorching, and burning their own masters or overseers are not rare; 2.) As long as our colony is not filled with Negroes, the deserters in Carolina, if they want to cross Georgia towards Augustine, cannot easily remain hidden. Generally, however, they escape by water, past Frederica to St. Augustine, where they receive their freedom, be it war or peace. Many just run into the woods, get along miserably, are secretly looked after by the other Negroes and occupy themselves with theft; 3.) The Indians have a natural antipathy toward the Negroes, therefore do not help them, and are likely to report them when meeting them in the woods; 4.) In this regard there are good precautions in Carolina against running away and rebellion. For instance, no Negro may go from one plantation to another unless he has written permission from his master. The land is constantly patrolled, and also on Sundays one goes to church with swords, guns, and pistols, etc. The agitators of rebellion are punished in a very harsh and nearly inhuman way (which is generally not the way of the English), for example, slowly roasted at the fire.

14th Question. Whether one is allowed to give them their liberty because of good behavior, and whether they then enjoy the rights of the whites.

Answer. Those Negroes who have served the country well are bought and freed by the government, receive their own land, and enjoy the English rights. If a private party wants to release a Negro he must have the consent of the governor or get him out of the colony. For the free Negroes abuse their freedom, and it is feared they seduce others.

15th Question. Whether white servants may marry Negresses, & vice versa, white servant girls may marry Negroes, and how the freedom of the children of such marriages is determined.

Answer. Such mixings or marriages are not allowed by the laws; but just as all manner of terrible abominations are rampant in Carolina, I have learned of 2 white women, one French and one German, who have secretly disgraced themselves with Negroes and have borne black children. However, an abomination more common and all too common in Carolina is that white men live in sin with Negresses and father half-black children who walk around in large numbers to the shame of the Christian name. They are perpetual slaves just like their mothers. Up among the Indian nations the merchants and their white servants treat the heathenish women and their daughters in the same way. Their children are half-Indian in color and remain, unfortunately! heathens.

16th Question. Whether everybody may keep as many Negroes as he pleases, or whether the number is limited according to the possession of land.

Answer. In Carolina as well as Georgia everyone may keep as many Negroes as he can, and their number is not limited according to the possession of land.

17th Question. Whether the upkeep of the Negroes is costly, with a request for an estimate of how much it amounts to, adding a little report about their clothing and native way of life, as well as about their marriages among themselves, and yet other things concerning these people.

Answer. The upkeep of the Negroes is cut very sparse. Year in and year out they receive nothing but Indian or Welsh or Turkish corn, which however is much better here than in Europe, healthier and tastier. This corn they must crack themselves in iron mills. Very few receive salt for it, so they cook it in water without salt and lard. Instead of corn they may receive Indian beans, which are planted among the corn, and at certain times also potatoes (almost like potatoes in Germany but sweeter and tastier). They also get to eat the cracked rice, which is not sent to Europe. If they have benevolent masters, or prove themselves loyal, they may receive a little meat a few times a year. They love to eat meat, and sometimes roast mice or steal meat. Some have permission to catch fish on Sundays. But in Carolina many have to plant their own food and also have to earn their few clothes by Sunday work. They plant their tobacco on Sundays, and thus buy something for themselves, their wives, and children. They love their families dearly and none runs away from the other. The separation of families is forbidden in our colony as something unnatural and barbaric; also Sunday work. In winter the Negroes must be kept warm, but in summer they go naked, except that the men cover their shame with a cloth rag which hangs from a strap tied around the body. The women have petticoats; the upper body is bare. The children of both sexes go about in summer just as they left the mother's womb. In winter Negro men and women have shoes, none in summer. One does not give the children any work beyond guarding the rice in the field from the rice birds, and possibly serving at table. They are spared from work so that they may grow big and strong. In winter Negro clothing consists of a woolen blue or white camisole, a pair of long pants of cloth down to the shoes, no shirt, and a woolen cap. At night they lie around the fire, and have woolen blankets. The clothing for each Negro comes to about 10*s.* or 4½ fl. (except for the carpets or woolen blankets). When the masters drive or ride to town with Negroes, they give them better clothes. The skilled Negroes in Charlestown, who are used in the offices and shops or who are mistresses, are very well dressed. Food for a Negro does not come to much over 8*d.* or 16 kr. a week. They have to take as their wives or husbands whomever their master gives them without ceremonies. Most of them live in whoredom.

18th Question. Whether the natives of the land also enter service for wages with the Europeans, whether they are useful also for day-by-day work in the fields, and whether in this case they can be trusted.

Answer. By natives one does not understand the Negroes born in this country (for these remain eternal slaves down to child and grandchild), but the Indians. These do not enter service for any European, consider themselves to be noblemen, and work, slavery. They only go hunting, bring meat and hides to their wives, the former for cooking, and the hides to be prepared for sale. The women also have to plant Indian corn, beans, pumpkins, and potatoes or sweet roots similar to potatoes, and are kept by the men like slaves. Our Indians sometimes sell the captured Spanish Indians to the Europeans as slaves, but with them one cannot accomplish as much as with the Negroes.

19th Question. How is the situation regarding the white servants?

Answer. Poor people from Europe who cannot pay their passage to the ships' captains are sold for 3 or 4 years, and must serve. In Carolina some are treated hardly better than Negroes. In our colony they are treated better. However, they rarely do well, but become lazy and run away if they can. They consider it unjust to serve [even] so few years for their passage money. Boys under 14 years must serve up to the 21st year of their age, and girls up to the 18th year. After that the boys receive 50 acres free.

20th Question. Whether their upkeep in food, wages, and clothing is more costly than in Europe. N.B. At this point an estimate is requested, how much a male white servant and white servant girl cost roughly per year.

Answer. If one wants to keep the white servants in a Christian way and not like Negroes, they will need at least £8 per year for food and clothing, which they do not earn by mere field work; they also fall sick easily through work in summer. Whoever buys them pays the captain £5 or £6 or 45 to 54 fl. Sensible housefathers employ their servants in lumbering and silk manufacturing because they can stand it better [than field work] and earn more. All this refers to purchased servants. But if one wants to hire male and female servants, like in Germany, they are very hard to get unless one pays these servants £12 to £14 a year with moderate work and good treatment regarding food, which by mere work in the field they do not earn. They prefer to start their own household, or go into day labor, by which they earn 1*s.* and 6*d.* or 36 kr. a day. They can get free land everywhere; therefore they do not like to serve, but marry soon. Never yet have male servants and servant girls such as one has in Germany come into this country except a very few 4 months ago, who are getting on well among us. . . .

## E S S A Y S

In the first essay historian Ira Berlin of the University of Maryland analyzes the development of distinctive slave regimes in three regions: the North, the Chesapeake, and the Lower South. Paying attention to the internal history of slavery and the timing and circumstances of the arrival of new slaves into the regions, he delineates similarities and differences in the slave regimes and between slaves direct from Africa and Creoles who were acculturated and used to working within the owners' regime. He rejects blanket characterizations and instead looks for the variety and complexity within these systems. In the second essay Philip D. Morgan, of the Omohundro Institute of Early American History and Culture, argues in the second essay that early eighteenth-century Virginia piedmont plantations replicated the pattern of the contemporary tidewater, with large slave forces in which Africans were incorporated into Creole cultures. Thus slaves had the same ability to form kin and neighborhood networks as those on the longer settled eastern plantations and also suffered the same problems of life on overseer-run plantations with absentee landlords.

## Time, Space, and the Evolution of Afro-American Society . . .

### IRA BERLIN

. . . Recent interest in the beginnings of slavery on the mainland of British North America, however, has revealed a striking diversity in Afro-American life. During the seventeenth and eighteenth centuries, three distinct slave systems evolved: a Northern nonplantation system and two Southern plantation systems, one around Chesapeake Bay and the other in the Carolina and Georgia lowcountry. Slavery took shape differently in each with important consequences for the growth of black culture and society. The development of these slave societies depended upon the nature of the slave trade and the demographic configurations of blacks and whites as well as upon the diverse character of colonial economy. Thus, while cultural differences between newly arrived Africans and second and third generation Afro-Americans or creoles everywhere provided the basis for social stratification within black society, African-creole differences emerged at different times with different force and even different meaning in the North, the Chesapeake region, and the lowcountry. A careful examination of the diverse development of Afro-American culture in the colonial era yields important clues for an understanding of the full complexity of black society in the centuries that followed.

The nature of slavery and the demographic balance of whites and blacks during the seventeenth and first decades of the eighteenth centuries tended to incorporate Northern blacks into the emerging Euro-American culture, even as whites denied them a place in Northern society. But changes in the character of the slave trade during the middle third of the eighteenth century gave new impetus to African culture and institutions in the Northern colonies. By the American Revolution, Afro-American culture had been integrated into the larger Euro-American one, but black

From Ira Berlin, "Time, Space, and the Evolution of Afro-American Society on British Mainland North America," *American Historical Review, 85,* pp. 44–78. Copyright © 1980. Reprinted by permission of the author.

people remained acutely conscious of their African inheritance and freely drew on it in shaping their lives.

Throughout the colonial years, blacks composed a small fraction of the population of New England and the Middle Colonies. . . . But these colony-wide enumerations dilute the presence of blacks and underestimate the importance of slave labor. In some of the most productive agricultural regions and in the cities, blacks composed a larger share of the population, sometimes constituting as much as one-third of the whole and perhaps one-half of the work force. Although many Northern whites never saw a black slave, others had daily, intimate contact with them. And, although some blacks found it difficult to join together with their former country-men, others lived in close contact. . . .

The vast majority of Northern blacks lived and worked in the countryside. A few labored in highly capitalized rural industries—tanneries, salt works, and iron furnaces—where they often composed the bulk of the work force, skilled and un-skilled. Iron masters, the largest employers of industrial slaves, also were often the largest slaveholders in the North. . . . But in an overwhelmingly agrarian society only a small proportion of the slave population engaged in industrial labor.

Like most rural whites, most rural blacks toiled as agricultural workers. In southern New England, on Long Island, and in northern New Jersey, which con-tained the North's densest black populations, slaves tended stock and raised crops for export to the sugar islands. Farmers engaged in provisioning the West Indies with draft animals and foodstuffs were familiar with slavery and had easy access to slaves. Some, like the Barbadian émigrés in northern New Jersey, had migrated from the sugar islands. Others, particularly those around Narragansett Bay, styled themselves planters in the West Indian manner. They built great houses, bred race horses, and accumulated slaves, sometimes holding twenty or more bondsmen. But, whatever the aspirations of this commercial gentry, the provisioning trade could not support a plantation regime. Most slaves lived on farms (not plantations), worked at a variety of tasks, and never labored in large gangs. No one in the North suggested that agricultural labor could be done only by black people, a common assertion in the sugar islands and the Carolina lowcountry. In northern New England, the Hud-son Valley, and Pennsylvania, the seasonal demands of cereal farming undermined the viability of slavery. . . . While slaves labored in the fields part of the year, as did nearly everyone, they also spent a large portion of their time working in and around their masters' houses as domestic servants, stable keepers, and gardeners. Signifi-cantly, the wills and inventories of Northern slaveholders listed their slaves with other high status objects like clocks and carriages rather than with land or agricul-tural implements.

The distinct demands of Northern agriculture shaped black life in the country-side. Where the provisioning trade predominated, black men worked as stock mind-ers and herdsmen while black women labored as dairy maids as well as domestics of various kinds. The large number of slaves demanded by the provisioning trade and the ready access to horses and mules it allowed placed black companionship within easy reach of most bondsmen. Such was not always true in the cereal region. Living scattered throughout the countryside on the largest farms and working in the house as often as in the field, blacks enjoyed neither the mobility nor the autonomy of slaves employed in the provisioning trade. But, if the demands of Northern agriculture affected black life in different ways, almost all rural blacks lived and worked in close proximity to whites. Slaves quickly learned the rudiments of the English language, the Christian religion, the white man's ways. In the North, few rural blacks remained untouched by the larger forces of Euro-American life. . . .

Northern slaves were also disproportionately urban. . . .

Urban slaves generally worked as house servants—cooking, cleaning, tending gardens and stables, and running errands. They lived in back rooms, lofts, closets, and, occasionally, makeshift alley shacks. Under these cramped conditions, few masters held more than one or two slaves. However they might cherish a large retinue of retainers, urban slaveholders rarely had the room to lodge them. Because of the general shortage of space, masters discouraged their slaves from establishing families in the cities. Women with reputations for fecundity found few buyers, and some slaveholders sold their domestics at the first sign of pregnancy. . . . The inability or unwillingness of urban masters to support large households placed a severe strain on black family life. But it also encouraged masters to allow their slaves to live out, hire their own time, and thereby gain a measure of independence and freedom. . . .

. . . Generally, the importance of these slaves to the growth of Northern cities increased during the eighteenth century. Urban slavery moved steadily away from the household to the docks, warehouses, and shops, as demonstrated by the growing disproportion of slave men in the urban North. Aside from those skills associated with the maritime trades, however, few slaves entered artisan work. Only a handful could be found in the carriage trades that enjoyed higher status and that offered greater opportunity for an independent livelihood and perhaps the chance to buy freedom.

In the cities as in the countryside, blacks tended to live and work in close proximity to whites. Northern slaves not only gained first-hand knowledge of their masters' world, but they also rubbed elbows with lower-class whites in taverns, cock fights, and fairs where poor people of varying status mingled. If urban life allowed slaves to meet more frequently and enjoy a larger degree of social autonomy than did slavery in the countryside, the cosmopolitan nature of cities speeded the transformation of Africans to Afro-Americans. Acculturation in the cities of the North was a matter of years, not generations.

For many blacks, the process of cultural transformation was well under way before they stepped off the boat. During the first century of American settlement, few blacks arrived in the North directly from Africa. Although American slavers generally originated in the North, few gave priority to Northern ports. The markets to the south were simply too large and too lucrative. Slaves dribbled into the Northern colonies from the West Indies or the mainland South singly, in twos and threes, or by the score but rarely by the boatload. . . . The absence of direct importation during the early years and the slow, random, haphazard entry of West Indian creoles shaped the development of black culture in the Northern colonies. While the nature of the slave trade prevented the survival of tribal or even shipboard ties that figured so prominently in Afro-American life in the West Indies and the Lower South, it better prepared blacks to take advantage of the special circumstances of their captivity.

Newly arrived blacks, most already experienced in the New World and familiar with their proscribed status, turned Northern bondage to their advantage where they could. They quickly established a stable family life and, unlike newly imported Africans elsewhere on the continent, increased their numbers by natural means during the first generation. . . . The transplanted creoles also seized the opportunities provided by the complex Northern economy, the relatively close ties of master and slave, and, for many, the independence afforded by urban life. In New Amsterdam, for example, the diverse needs of the Dutch mercantile economy induced the West India Company, the largest slaveholder in the colony, to allow its slaves to live out and work on their own in return for a stipulated amount of labor and an annual tribute. "Half-freedom," as this system came to be called, enlarged black opportunities and allowed for the development of a strong black community. When the West India Company refused to make these privileges hereditary, "half-free" slaves organized and protested, demanding that they be allowed to pass their rights to their children. Failing that, New Amsterdam slaves pressed their masters in other ways to elevate their children's status. Some, hearing rumors that baptism meant freedom, tried to gain church membership. A Dutch prelate complained that these blacks "wanted nothing else than to deliver their children from bodily slavery, without striving for piety and Christian virtues." Even after the conquering English abolished "half-freedom" and instituted a more rigorous system of racial servitude, blacks continued to use the leverage gained by their prominent role in the city's economy to set standards of treatment well above those in the plantation colonies. Into the eighteenth century, New York slaves informally enjoyed the rights of an earlier era, including the right to hold property of their own. "The Custome of this Country," bristled a frustrated New York master to a West Indian friend, "will not allow us to use our Negroes as you doe in Barbados." . . .

During the middle decades of the eighteenth century, the nature of Northern slavery changed dramatically. Growing demand for labor, especially when European wars limited the supply of white indentured servants and when depression sent free workers west in search of new opportunities, increased the importance of slaves in the work force. Between 1732 and 1754, blacks composed fully a third of the immigrants (forced and voluntary) arriving in New York. The new importance of slave labor changed the nature of the slave trade. Merchants who previously took black slaves only on consignment now began to import them directly from Africa, often in large numbers. . . . Slaves increasingly replaced white indentured servants as the chief source of unfree labor not only in the areas that had produced for the provisioning trade, where their pre-eminence had been established earlier in the century, but in the cities as well. In the 1760s, when slave importation into Pennsylvania peaked, blacks composed more than three-quarters of Philadelphia's servant population.

Northern whites generally viewed this new wave of slaves as substitutes for indentured labor. White indentured servants had come as young men without families, and slaves were now imported in much the same way. . . . Such sexual imbalance and the proscription of interracial marriage made it increasingly difficult for blacks to enjoy normal family lives. As the birth rate slipped, mortality rates soared, especially in the cities where newly arrived blacks appeared to be concentrated. Since most slaves came without any previous exposure to New World diseases, the harsh Northern winters took an ever higher toll. Blacks died by the score;

the crude death rate of Philadelphia and Boston blacks in the 1750s and 1760s was well over sixty per thousand, almost double that of whites. In its demographic outline, Northern slavery at mid-century often bore a closer resemblance to the horrors of the West Indies during the height of a sugar boom than to the relatively benign bondage of the earlier years.

Whites easily recovered from this demographic disaster by again switching to European indentured servants and then to free labor as supplies became available, and, as the influx of slaves subsided, black life also regained its balance. But the transformation of Northern slavery had a lasting influence on the development of Afro-American culture. Although the Northern black population remained predominantly Afro-American after nearly a century of slow importation from the West Indies and steady natural increase, the direct entry of Africans into Northern society reoriented black culture. . . .

Newly arrived Africans reawakened Afro-Americans to their African past by providing direct knowledge of West African society. Creole blacks began to combine their African inheritance into their own evolving culture. In some measure, the easy confidence of Northern whites in their own dominance speeded the syncretization of African and creole culture by allowing blacks to act far more openly than slaves in the plantation colonies. Northern blacks incorporated African culture into their own Afro-American culture not only in the common-place and unconscious way that generally characterizes the transit of culture but also with a high degree of consciousness and deliberateness. They designated their churches "African," and they called themselves "Sons of Africa." They adopted African forms to maximize their freedom, to choose their leaders, and, in general, to give shape to their lives. This new African influence was manifested most fully in Negro election day, a ritual festival of role reversal common throughout West Africa and celebrated openly by blacks in New England and a scattering of places in the Middle Colonies. . . .

African acculturation in the Northern colonies at once incorporated blacks into American society and sharpened the memory of their African past and their desire to preserve it. While small numbers and close proximity to whites forced blacks to conform to the forms of the dominant Euro-American culture, the confidence of whites in their own hegemony allowed black slaves a good measure of autonomy. In this context it is not surprising that a black New England sea captain established the first back-to-Africa movement in mainland North America.

Unlike African acculturation in the Northern colonies, the transformation of Africans into Afro-Americans in the Carolina and Georgia lowcountry was a slow, halting process whose effects resonated differently within black society. While creolization created a unified Afro-American population in the North, it left lowcountry blacks deeply divided. A minority lived and worked in close proximity to whites in the cities that lined the rice coast, fully conversant with the most cosmopolitan sector of lowland society. A portion of this urban elite, increasingly light-skinned, pressed for further incorporation into white society, confident they could compete as equals. The mass of black people, however, remained physically separated and psychologically estranged from the Anglo-American world and culturally closer to Africa than any other blacks on continental North America.

The sharp division was not immediately apparent. At first it seemed that African acculturation in the Lower South would follow the Northern pattern. The first blacks arrived in the lowcountry in small groups from the West Indies. Often they accompanied their owners and, like them, frequently immigrated in small family groups. Many had already spent considerable time on the sugar islands, and some had doubtless been born there. Most spoke English, understood European customs and manners, and, as their language skills and family ties suggest, had made the difficult adjustment to the conditions of black life in the New World. . . .

The unsettled conditions that made the lowcountry vulnerable to external enemies strengthened the slave's hand in other ways. Confronted by an overbearing master or a particularly onerous assignment, many blacks took to the woods. Truancy was an easy alternative in the thinly settled, heavily forested lowcountry. Forest dangers generally sent truant slaves back to their owners, but the possibility of another flight induced slaveholders to accept them with few questions asked. Some bondsmen, however, took advantage of these circumstances to escape permanently. Maroon colonies existed throughout the lowland swamps and into the backcountry. Maroons lived a hard life, perhaps more difficult than slaves, and few blacks chose to join these outlaw bands. But the ease of escape and the existence of a maroon alternative made masters chary about abusing their slaves.

The transplanted African's intimate knowledge of the subtropical lowland environment—especially when compared to the Englishman's dense ignorance—magnified white dependence on blacks and enlarged black opportunities within the slave regime. Since the geography, climate, and topography of the lowcountry more closely resembled the West African than the English countryside, African not European technology and agronomy often guided lowland development. From the first, whites depended on blacks to identify useful flora and fauna and to define the appropriate methods of production. Blacks, adapting African techniques to the circumstances of the Carolina wilderness, shaped the lowland cattle industry and played a central role in the introduction and development of the region's leading staple. In short, transplanted Englishmen learned as much or more from transplanted Africans as did the former Africans from them. . . .

. . . The autonomy of the isolated cowpen and the freedom of movement stock raising allowed made a mockery of the total dominance that chattel bondage implied. Slaves set the pace of work, defined standards of workmanship, and divided labor among themselves, doubtless leaving a good measure of time for their own use. . . .

Such independence burdened whites. They complained bitterly and frequently about blacks traveling unsupervised through the countryside, congregating in the woods, and visiting Charles Town to carouse, conspire, or worse. Yet knowledge of the countryside and a willingness to take the initiative in hunting down cattle or standing up to Spaniards were precisely the characteristics that whites valued in their slaves. They complained but they accepted. . . .

Thus, during the first years of settlement, black life in the lowcountry, like black life in the North, evolved toward a unified Afro-American culture. Although their numbers combined with other circumstances to allow Carolina blacks a larger role in shaping their culture than that enjoyed by blacks in the North, there remained striking similarities in the early development of Afro-American life in both regions. During the last few years of the seventeenth century, however, changes in economy and society undermined these commonalities and set the development of lowcountry Afro-American life on a distinctive course.

The discovery of exportable staples, first naval stores and then rice and indigo, transformed the lowcountry as surely as the sugar revolution transformed the West Indies. Under the pressure of the riches that staple production provided, planters banished the white yeomanry to the hinterland, consolidated small farms into large plantations, and carved new plantations out of the malaria-ridden swamps. Before long, black slaves began pouring into the region and, sometime during the first decade of the eighteenth century, white numerical superiority gave way to the lowcountry's distinguishing demographic characteristic: the black majority.

Black numerical dominance grew rapidly during the eighteenth century. By the 1720s, blacks outnumbered whites by more than two to one in South Carolina. In the heavily settled plantation parishes surrounding Charles Town, blacks enjoyed a three to one majority. . . .

Direct importation of slaves from Africa provided the impetus to the growth of the black majority. . . . As African importation increased, Charles Town took its place as the largest mainland slave mart and the center of the lowland slave trade. Almost all of the slaves in Carolina and later in Georgia—indeed, fully 40 percent of all pre-Revolutionary black arrivals in mainland North America—entered at Charles Town. The enormous number of slaves allowed slave masters a wide range of choices. Lowcountry planters developed preferences far beyond the usual demands for healthy adult and adolescent males and concerned themselves with the regional and tribal origins of their purchases. . . .

Whatever their origins, rice cultivation shaped the destiny of African people arriving at Charles Town. Although the production of pitch and tar played a pivotal role in the early development of the staple-based economy in South Carolina, rice quickly became the dominant plantation crop. . . . By the beginning of the nineteenth century, the rice coast stretched from Cape Fear in North Carolina to the Satilla River in Georgia. Throughout the lowcountry, rice was king.

The relatively mild slave regime of the pioneer years disappeared as rice cultivation expanded. Slaves increasingly lived in large units, and they worked in field gangs rather than at a variety of tasks. The strict requirements of rice production set the course of their work. And rice was a hard master. For a large portion of the year, slaves labored knee deep in brackish muck under the hot tropical sun; and, even after the fields were drained, the crops laid-by, and the grain threshed, there were canals to clear and dams to repair. By mid-century planters had also begun to grow indigo on the upland sections of their estates. Indigo complemented rice in its seasonal requirements, and it made even heavier labor demands. The ready availability of African imports compounded the new harsh realities of plantation slavery by cheapening black life in the eyes of many masters. As long as the slave trade remained open, they skimped on food, clothing, and medical attention for their slaves, knowing full well that substitutes could be easily had. With the planters' reliance on male African imports, slaves found it increasingly difficult to establish and maintain a normal family life. Brutal working conditions, the disease-ridden, lowland environment, and the open slave trade made for a deadly combination. Slave birth rates fell steadily during the middle years of the eighteenth century and mortality rates rose sharply. Between 1730 and 1760, deaths outnumbered births among blacks and only African importation allowed for continued population growth. Not until the eve of the Revolution did the black population begin again to reproduce naturally.

As the lowcountry plantation system took shape, the great slave masters retreated to the cities of the region; their evacuation of the countryside was but another manifestation of the growing social and cultural distance between them and their slaves. The streets of Charles Town, and, later, of Beaufort, Georgetown, Savannah, Darien, and Wilmington sprouted great new mansions as planters fled the malarial lowlands and the black majority. By the 1740s, urban life in the lowcountry had become attractive enough that men who made their fortunes in rice and slaves no longer returned home to England in the West Indian tradition. Instead, through intermarriage and business connections, they began to weave their disparate social relations into a close-knit ruling class, whose self-consciousness and pride of place became legendary. Charles Town, as the capital of this new elite, grew rapidly. Between 1720 and 1740 its population doubled, and it nearly doubled again by the eve of the Revolution to stand at about twelve thousand. With its many fine houses, its great churches, its shops packed with luxury goods, Charles Town's prosperity bespoke the maturation of the lowland plantation system and the rise of the planter class.

Planters, ensconced in their new urban mansions, their pockets lined with the riches rice produced, ruled their lowcountry domains through a long chain of command: stewards located in the smaller rice ports, overseers stationed near or on their plantations, and plantation-based black drivers. But their removal from the plantation did not breed the callous indifference of West Indian absenteeism. For one thing, they were no more than a day's boat ride away from their estates. Generally, they resided on their plantations during the non-malarial season. Their physical removal from the direct supervision of slave labor and the leisure their urban residences afforded appear to have sharpened their concern for "their people" and bred a paternalist ideology that at once legitimated their rule and informed all social relations.

The lowcountry plantation system with its urban centers, its black majority, its dependence on "salt-water" slaves transformed black culture and society just as it reshaped the white world. The unified Afro-American culture and society that had evolved during the pioneer years disappeared as rice cultivation spread. In its place a sharp division developed between an increasingly urban creole and a plantation-based African population. The growth of plantation slavery not only set blacks further apart from whites, it also sharply divided blacks.

One branch of black society took shape within the bounds of the region's cities and towns. If planters lived removed from most slaves, they maintained close, intimate relations with some. The masters' great wealth, transient life, and seasonal urban residence placed them in close contact with house servants who kept their estates, boatmen who carried messages and supplies back and forth to their plantations, and urban artisans who made city life not only possible but comfortable. . . . Black artisans also played a large role in urban life. Master craftsmen employed them in every variety of work. . . . Although most black artisans labored along the waterfront as shipwrights, ropemakers, and coopers, lowcountry blacks—unlike blacks in Northern cities—also entered the higher trades, working as gold beaters, silversmiths, and cabinetmakers. In addition, black women gained control over much of the marketing in the lowcountry ports, mediating between slave-grown produce in the countryside and urban consumption. . . .

Mobile, often skilled, and occasionally literate, urban slaves understood the white world. They used their knowledge to improve their position within lowcountry society even while the condition of the mass of black people deteriorated in the wake of the rice revolution. Many urban creoles not only retained the independence of the earlier years but enlarged upon it. They hired their own time, earned wages from "overwork," kept market stalls, and sometimes even opened shops. Some lived apart from their masters and rented houses of their own, paying their owners a portion of their earnings in return for *de facto* freedom. Such liberty enabled a few black people to keep their families intact and perhaps even accumulate property for themselves. The small black communities that developed below the Bluff in Savannah and in Charles Town's Neck confirm the growing independence of urban creoles.

The incongruous prosperity of urban bondsmen jarred whites. By hiring their own time, living apart from their masters, and controlling their own family life, these blacks forcibly and visibly claimed the white man's privileges. Perhaps no aspect of their behavior was as obvious and, hence, as galling as their elaborate dress. While plantation slaves—men and women—worked stripped to the waist wearing no more than loin cloths (thereby confirming the white man's image of savagery), urban slaves appropriated their masters' taste for fine clothes and often the clothes themselves. . . .

Increasingly during the eighteenth century, blacks gained privileged positions within lowcountry society as a result of intimate, usually sexual, relations with white slave masters. Like slaveholders everywhere, lowland planters assumed that sexual access to slave women was simply another of the master's prerogatives. Perhaps because their origin was West Indian or perhaps because their dual residence separated them from their white wives part of the year, white men established sexual liaisons with black women frequently and openly. Some white men and black women formed stable, long-lasting unions, legitimate in everything but law. More often than other slaveholders on continental British North America, lowcountry planters recognized and provided for their mulatto offspring, and, occasionally, extended legal freedom. . . .

While one branch of black society stood so close to whites that its members sometimes disappeared into the white population, most plantation slaves remained alienated from the world of their masters, physically and culturally. Living in large units often numbering in the hundreds on plantations that they had carved out of the malarial swamps and working under the direction of black drivers, the black majority gained only fleeting knowledge of Anglo-American culture. What they knew did not encourage them to learn more. Instead, they strove to widen the distance between themselves and their captors. In doing so, they too built upon the large degree of autonomy black people had earlier enjoyed.

In the pioneer period, many masters required slaves to raise their own provisions. Slaves regularly kept small gardens and tended barnyard fowl to maintain themselves, and they often marketed their surplus. Blacks kept these prerogatives with the development of the plantation system. In fact, the growth of lowcountry towns, the increasing specialization in staple production, and the comparative absence of nonslaveholding whites enlarged the market for slave-grown produce. Planters, of course, disliked the independence truck gardening afforded plantation blacks and the tendency of slaves to confuse their owners' produce with their own, but the ease of water transportation and the absence of white supervision made it difficult to prevent. . . .

. . . For the most part, slave propertyholding remained small during the eighteenth century. But it helped insulate plantation blacks from the harsh conditions of primitive rice production and provided social distance from their masters' domination.

The task system, a mode of work organization peculiar to the lowcountry, further strengthened black autonomy. Under the task system, a slave's daily routine was sharply defined: so many rows of rice to be sowed, so much grain to be threshed, or so many lines of canal to be cleared. Such a precise definition of work suggests that city-bound planters found it almost impossible to keep their slaves in the fields from sunup to sundown. With little direct white supervision, slaves and their black foremen conspired to preserve a large portion of the day for their own use, while meeting their masters' minimum work requirements. . . . Like participation in the lowcountry's internal economy, the task system provided slaves with a large measure of control over their own lives.

The autonomy generated by both the task system and truck gardening provided the material basis for lowland black culture. Within the confines of the overwhelmingly black countryside, African culture survived well. The continual arrival of Africans into the lowcountry renewed and refreshed slave knowledge of West African life. In such a setting blacks could hardly lose their past. . . .

Even where blacks enjoyed numerical superiority and a considerable degree of autonomy, they could no more transport their culture unchanged than could their masters. But lowcountry blacks incorporated more of West African culture—as reflected in their language, religion, work patterns, and much else—into their new lives than did other black Americans. Throughout the eighteenth century and into the nineteenth, lowcountry blacks continued to work the land, name their children, and communicate through word and song in a manner that openly combined African traditions with the circumstances of plantation life.

The new pattern of creolization that developed following the rice revolution smashed the emerging homogeneity of black life in the first years of settlement and left lowcountry blacks deeply divided. One branch of black culture evolved in close proximity to whites. Urban, often skilled, well-traveled, and increasingly American-born, creoles knew white society well, and they used their knowledge to better themselves. Some, clearly a well-connected minority, pressed for incorporation into the white world. . . . Plantation slaves shared few of the assimilationist aspirations of urban creoles. By their dress, language, and work routine, they lived in a world apart. Rather than demand incorporation into white society, they yearned only to be left alone. Within the quarter, aided by their numerical dominance, their plantation-based social hierarchy, and their continued contact with Africa, they developed their own distinctive culture, different not only from that of whites but also from the cosmopolitan world of their Afro-American brethren. . . . [B]y the eve of the Revolution, deep cultural differences separated those blacks who sought to improve their lives through incorporation into the white world and those who determined to disregard the white man's ways. If the movement from African to creole obliterated cultural differences among Northern blacks, creolization fractured black society in the lowcountry.

Cultural distinctions between Africans and Afro-Americans developed in the Chesapeake as well, although the dimension of differences between African and creole tended to be time rather than space. Unlike in the lowcountry, white planters did not promote the creation of a distinctive group whose origins, function, and physical appearance distinguished them from the mass of plantation slaves and offered them hope, however faint, of eventual incorporation into white society. And, compared to the North, African immigration into the Chesapeake came relatively early in the process of cultural transformation. As a result, African-creole differences disappeared with time and a single, unified Afro-American culture slowly emerged in the Chesapeake.

As in the lowcountry, little distinguished black and white laborers during the early years of settlement. Most of the first blacks brought into the Chesapeake region were West Indian creoles who bore English or Spanish surnames and carried records of baptism. Along the James, as along the Cooper, the demands of pioneer life at times operated to strengthen the slaves' bargaining position. Some blacks set the condition of their labor, secured their family life, participated in the region's internal economy, and occasionally bartered for their liberty. . . .

Many did well. During the seventeenth century, black freemen could be found throughout the region owning land, holding servants, and occasionally attaining minor offices. Like whites, they accumulated property, sued their neighbors, and passed their estates to their children. . . .

By the middle of the seventeenth century, Negro freemen sharing and fulfilling the same ideals and aspirations that whites held were no anomaly in the Chesapeake region. An Eastern Shore tax list of 1668 counted nearly a third of black tithables free. If most blacks did not escape the tightening noose of enslavement, they continued to live and work under conditions not much different from white servants. Throughout the seventeenth and into the first decades of the eighteenth century, black and white servants ran away together, slept together, and, upon occasion, stood shoulder to shoulder against the weighty champions of established authority. Thus viewed from the first years of settlement—the relatively small number of blacks, their creole origins, and the initial success of some in establishing a place in society—black acculturation in the Chesapeake appeared to be following the non-plantation pattern of the Northern colonies and the pioneer lowcountry.

The emergence of a planter class and its consolidation of power during a series of political crises in the middle years of the seventeenth century transformed black life in the Chesapeake and threatened this pattern of cultural change. Following the legalization of slavery in the 1660s, black slaves slowly but steadily replaced white indentured servants as the main source of plantation labor. By 1700, blacks made up more than half the agricultural work force in Virginia and, since the great planters could best afford to purchase slaves, blacks composed an even larger share of the workers on the largest estates. Increased reliance on slave labor quickly outstripped

West Indian supplies. Beginning in the 1680s, Africans entered the region in increasingly large numbers. The proportion of blacks born in Africa grew steadily throughout the waning years of the seventeenth century, so that by the first decade of the eighteenth century, Africans composed some three-quarters of the region's blacks. Unlike the lowcountry, African imports never threatened the Chesapeake's overall white numerical superiority, but by the beginning of the eighteenth century they dominated black society. Some eighty years after the first blacks arrived at Jamestown and some forty years after the legalization of slavery, African importation profoundly transformed black life.

Slave conditions deteriorated as their numbers increased. With an eye for a quick profit, planters in the Chesapeake imported males disproportionately. Generally men outnumbered women more than two to one on Chesapeake slavers. Wildly imbalanced sex ratios undermined black family life. Physically spent and emotionally drained by the rigors of the Middle Passage, African women had few children. Thus, as in the North and the Carolina lowlands, the black birth rate fell and mortality rate surged upward with the commencement of direct African importation.

The hard facts of life and death in the Chesapeake region distinguished creoles and Africans at the beginning of the eighteenth century. The demands of the tobacco economy enlarged these differences in several ways. Generally, planters placed little trust in newly arrived Africans with their strange tongues and alien customs. While they assigned creoles to artisanal duties on their plantations and to service within their households, they sent Africans to the distant, upland quarters where the slaves did the dull, backbreaking work of clearing the land and tending tobacco. The small size of these specialized upcountry units, their isolation from the mainstream of Chesapeake life, and their rude frontier conditions made these largely male compounds lonely, unhealthy places that narrowed men's vision. The dynamics of creole life, however, broadened black understanding of life in the New World. Traveling freely through the countryside as artisans, watermen, and domestic servants, creoles gained in confidence as they mastered the terrain, perfected their English, and learned about Christianity and other cultural modes that whites equated with civilization. Knowledge of the white world enabled black creoles to manipulate their masters to their own advantage. If Afro-Americans became increasingly knowledgeable about their circumstances and confident of their ability to deal with them, Africans remained provincials, limited by the narrow alternatives of plantation life.

As in the lowcountry and the Northern colonies, Africans in the Chesapeake strove to escape whites, while creoles used their knowledge of white society for their own benefit. These cultural differences, which were reflected in all aspects of black life, can be seen most clearly in the diverse patterns of resistance. Africans ran away toward the back country and isolated swamps. They generally moved in groups that included women and children, despite the hazards such groups entailed for a successful escape. Their purpose was to recreate the only society they knew free from white domination. . . . But Afro-Americans ran away alone, usually with the hope of escaping into American society. Moving toward the areas of heaviest settlement, they found refuge in the thick network of black kinship that covered the countryside and sold their labor to white yeomen with few questions asked. While the possibility of passing as free remained small in the years before the Revolution, the creoles' obvious confidence in their ability to integrate themselves into American society stands in stark contrast to that of Africans, who sought first to flee it.

As reflected in the mode of resistance, place of residence, occupation, and much else, Africans and creoles developed distinctive patterns of behavior and belief. To a degree, whites recognized these differences. They stigmatized Africans as "outlandish" and noted how creoles "affect our language, habits, and customs." They played on African-creole differences to divide blacks from each other, and they utilized creole skills to maximize the benefits of slave labor. But this recognition did not elevate creoles over Africans in any lasting way. Over the course of the century following legal enslavement, it had precisely the opposite effect. Chesapeake planters consolidated their class position by asserting white racial unity. In this context, the entry of large numbers of African—as opposed to creole—blacks into the region enlarged racial differences and helped secure planter domination. Thus, as reliance on black labor increased, the opportunities for any black—no matter how fluent in English or conversant with the countryside—to escape bondage and join the scramble for land, servants, and status diminished steadily.

By the middle of the eighteenth century, the size and character of the free Negro population had been significantly altered. Instead of a large minority of the black population, Negro freemen now composed just a small proportion of all blacks, probably not more than 5 percent. Many were cripples and old folks whom planters discarded when they could no longer wring a profit from their labor. . . .

During the middle years of the eighteenth century, changes in the Chesapeake economy and society further diminished differences within black society and created a unified Afro-American culture. The success of the tobacco economy enlarged the area of settlement and allowed planters to increase their holdings. The most successful planters, anxious to protect themselves from the rigors of the world marketplace, strove for plantation self-sufficiency. The great estates of the Chesapeake became self-contained enterprises with slaves taking positions as artisans, tradesmen, wagoners, and, sometimes, managers. . . . Bondsmen increasingly lived in large groups, and those who did not could generally find black companionship within a few miles' walk. Finally, better food, clothing, and shelter and, perhaps, the development of immunities to New World diseases enabled blacks to live longer, healthier lives.

As part of their drive for self-sufficiency, Chesapeake slaveholders encouraged the development of an indigenous slave population. Spurred by the proven ability of Africans to survive and reproduce and pressed in the international slave market by the superior resources of West Indian sugar magnates and lowland rice growers, Chesapeake planters strove to correct the sexual imbalance within the black population, perhaps by importing a large proportion of women or lessening the burden of female slaves. Blacks quickly took advantage of this new circumstance and placed their family life on a firmer footing. . . . Under these circumstances, the black population increased rapidly. Planters relied less and less on African importation and, by the 1740s, most of the growth of the black population came from natural increase. Within a generation, African importation was, for all practical purposes, no longer a significant source of slave labor. . . .

The establishment of the black family marked the re-emergence of Afro-American culture in the Chesapeake. Although Africans continued to enter the region, albeit at a slower pace, the nature of the slave trade minimized their impact on the development of black society in the region. Unlike those in the lowcountry, newly arrived Africans could rarely hope to remain together. . . . The resulting fragmentation sent newly arrived Africans in all directions and prevented the maintenance of tribal or shipboard ties. Chesapeake slaveholders cared little about the origins of their slaves. . . .

Over the long term, however, economic changes sped the integration of Africans into Afro-American society. Under the pressure of a world-wide food shortage, Chesapeake planters turned from the production of tobacco to that of foodstuff, especially wheat. The demands of wheat cultivation transformed the nature of labor in the region. . . . Economic changes encouraged masters to teach their slaves skills and to hire them out during the slack season. . . . Africans became Afro-Americans with increasing rapidity as the century wore on, eliminating the differences within black society that African importation had created.

Chesapeake blacks enjoyed considerably less autonomy than their lowcountry counterparts. Resident planters, small units of production, and the presence of large numbers of whites meant that most blacks lived and worked in close proximity to whites. While lowcountry planters fled to coastal cities for a large part of the year, the resident planter was a fixture of Chesapeake life. Small freeholders labored alongside slaves, and great planters prided themselves on regulating all aspects of their far-flung estates through a combination of direct personal supervision and plantation-based overseers. The latter were usually white, drawn from the region's white majority. . . . Afro-American culture in the Chesapeake evolved parallel with Anglo-American culture and with a considerable measure of congruence.

The diverse development of Afro-American culture during the seventeenth and eighteenth centuries reveals the importance of time and place in the study of American slavery. Black people in colonial America shared many things: a common African lineage, a common racial oppressor, a common desire to create the richest life possible for themselves and their posterity in the most difficult of circumstances. But these commonalities took different shape and meaning within the diverse circumstances of the North American mainland. The nature of the slave trade, the various demographic configurations of whites and blacks, and the demands of particular staples—to name some of the factors influencing the development of slave society—created at least three distinctive patterns of Afro-American life. . . .

## Slave Life in Virginia's Piedmont

### PHILIP D. MORGAN

Slavery first expanded into the Virginia piedmont in the 1720s. The institution took root rapidly. By the middle of the eighteenth century—just about a generation after its introduction—forty thousand slaves, one-third of the colony's total, resided in the piedmont's rolling hills. Within a further generation, a remarkable transformation

Philip Morgan, "Slave Life in Piedmont Virginia, 1720–1800," in Lois Green Carr, Philip Morgan, and Jean Russo, eds., *Colonial Chesapeake Society*, 433–484. Published for the Institute of Early American History and Culture, Williamsburg, Virginia.© 1989 The University of North Carolina Press.

took place. The piedmont slave population almost trebled in size; Virginia emerged from the Revolutionary War with more slaves living beyond, than within, the fall line. The center of black life had shifted extraordinarily rapidly from tidewater to piedmont. . . .

Turning from the technicalities of population growth to its implications, we need to investigate the changing balance of Africans and creoles among the piedmont slave population. Two contrasting facts immediately command attention. First, although African immigration was not central to slave population growth in the piedmont, more Africans resided beyond the fall line than in tidewater in the late colonial era. In terms of the relative proportions of Africans and creoles, in other words, the late colonial piedmont did replicate to some degree an earlier tidewater experience. Even more notable, however, was the speed at which the piedmont slave population approximated the contemporary, rather than an earlier, tidewater pattern. Native-born slaves soon came to dominate the piedmont slave population, much as they did in contemporary tidewater. Once again, extension rather than replication seems the dominant story.

Still, in certain piedmont counties at particular times the adult population was heavily African. In Amelia County, which probably received more Africans than any other Chesapeake county in the forty years before Independence, about 60 percent of the adult slaves in 1755 were Africans. In 1782, although the proportion had dropped considerably, it still stood at around one-fifth. Even by the late 1760s and early 1770s, the demand for Africans was relatively brisk in certain piedmont counties. In July 1769 Richard Adams considered himself fortunate to have eighty slaves to sell on the upper James. Two years later, another James River merchant informed a correspondent who had proposed an "African Scheme" that "Negroes will always sell well here." As if to prove the point, in 1772 Paul Carrington bought fifty slaves at Bermuda Hundred in order to sell them to eager southside purchasers.

Once Africans reached the plantations, their presence was not always documented. An occasional name or ethnic designation in an inventory, as in Angola Jack, Ebo Sam, Malagawyou Bess, and Gambia James, often provides the only clue to an African identity. Somewhat more exceptional were the quarters of Mrs. Mayo and those of Philip Mayo of Goochland County. On the former estate, seven of seventeen tithables had African names (Jolloff, Quaw, Fatima, Congo, Cudjo, Shantee, and Cudjee), as did four of thirteen on the latter (Bussee, Jallapa, Jubah, and Abanah). Or it might take an unusual event for Africans to come to our notice. The deaths of "two new Negroes" in Goochland County in 1762 prompted the county court to order an inquest. In Prince Edward County, an African influence might explain the extraordinary action of Jacob, who when cornered by six whites, defended himself with "sharp pointed darts of a sufficient length and size to kill a man at a great distance." Or, even more indirectly, we might infer an African presence from place-names. Eighteenth-century Cumberland County, for instance, had its Angola and Guinea roads, its Little Guinea Neck, and its Great Guinea and Angola creeks.

The prominence of Africans among the piedmont runaway population, particularly in the earliest years, provides the most direct evidence of their widespread presence. The residences of two slave runaways captured in Louisa County in the mid-1740s could not be determined because neither spoke English. Presumably, it was the slave himself who gave his name to a capturer in Spotsylvania County in

1744: he called himself "Angola Tom." In the following year Sambo, Aaron, and Berwick ran away from their quarter in Orange County eight months after their arrival in the colony; two slaves imported from Senegambia ran away within a month of being brought to Hanover County; and in 1751 David ran from his quarter on Willis Creek in Albemarle County less than a month after arriving on the ship *Williamsburg* with 294 other Africans. These aliens in the piedmont, like their compatriots throughout the New World, took to flight to express their detestation of their new surroundings and situation.

Also typical of Africans throughout the New World, these piedmont immigrants formed strong attachments to fellow shipmates. The snow *Yanimarew* imported 240 Africans in the summer of 1770. One month after being purchased and taken to Amherst County, Charles ran away. Meanwhile, in Richmond three other African men, imported in the same slaver, fled their master. They apparently sought out the companionship of their former shipmates (perhaps Charles was among them), for their master reported "it is imagined that they were seen some time ago (along with three others of the same cargo) on Chickahominy, and it is supposed they are still lurking about the skirts of that swamp." A similar venture occurred the following year when a twenty-year-old man and a twelve-year-old girl, recently purchased by the same master from an African slaver, "went off with several others, being persuaded that they could find the way back to their own Country."

The presence of restive Africans may help account for the heavy concentration of "poisoning" cases that appeared in piedmont county courts in the second half of the eighteenth century. Of about 180 slaves tried for "poisoning" in colonial Virginia county courts, two-thirds resided in the piedmont. Rarely can alleged poisoners be proven to have been Africans, but the high concentrations of such cases in counties where large numbers of Africans lived, together with information such as the African names of some alleged poisoners, make the connection plausible. Furthermore, an offhand remark by Edmund Pendleton, a resident of Caroline County (adjoining the piedmont), suggests such a connection in the contemporary mind. In 1777, when referring to the atrocities perpetrated by the British army, Pendleton exclaimed that they had descended to the "low, mean, petiful, skulking, perfidious, wicked Italian & African business of Poisoning."

Even though an African influence was noticeable in the late-eighteenth-century piedmont, it was a constantly dwindling one. The proportion of Africans in the piedmont slave population quickly assumed a profile similar to that of tidewater. In 1755 perhaps as many as one-third of adult slaves throughout the piedmont were Africans. By 1782, in spite of the importation of around 15,000 Africans, almost all of whom went to various piedmont counties, the proportion had dropped to about one in ten. Moreover, by the late colonial period, many Africans were longtime residents of the piedmont region and no longer easily distinguished from creoles. In 1777, Aberdeen, a thirty-five-year-old blacksmith, resided on the Falls Plantation in Chesterfield County. He "came into the country young," his master noted, and therefore spoke "very good English." In the same year, a Fauquier County African was described as "affect[ing] to pronounce the English language very fine, or rather to clip it." He could also read and write.

An African named Bacchus best personifies the speed with which these immigrants adjusted to their new surroundings. In the space of about three years in the early 1770s, Bacchus left a dizzying trail of crime across both tidewater and pied-mont. In that time, he ran away at least four times, faced four separate criminal charges, was branded in the hand, heard himself pronounced guilty and sentenced to hang in two county courts, but evaded the hangman's noose on both occasions. In 1771 this "thick set, and well made," seventeen-year-old lad spoke "broken Eng-lish," but two years later his proficiency had improved so that his master described his speech as only "somewhat broken." His assimilation was never total, however, for he retained his African name, Juba, while also employing the English names Jemmy and James. Nevertheless, he was sufficiently conversant with white ways to pass as a free black in Chesterfield County. In that capacity, it seems, Bacchus got wind of the Somerset Case (a famous legal decision of 1772 that was widely but er-roneously perceived to outlaw slavery in England) and imagined he would be free if only he could get to that country. This was, according to his master, "a Notion now too prevalent among the Negroes." Indeed, Bacchus was thought to be in the com-pany of another of his master's fugitives, a twenty-seven-year-old "very black" woman who had since passed herself as free, using the name Sukey Jones. That news of the Somerset Case had reached the ears of a humble African like Bacchus in piedmont Virginia, some three thousand miles away, speaks well of his initiative and resolve, but more particularly of his political education.

Piedmont Africans creolized quickly, one might conjecture, precisely because they came into contact with large numbers of accomplished and assimilated slaves. By the late colonial era, the African newcomer could regularly encounter slaves like painter Peter Brown, raised in Petersburg, who was "fond of Singing," or thirty-year-old Jacob from Louisa County, who could read and write, spoke "in the Scotch-Irish dialect, and in conversation frequently use[d] the words moreover and likewise," or twenty-eight-year-old Sam from Amelia County, a carpenter and cooper, who could "read print, pretends to a deal of religion, has been a good fid-dler, and is acquainted with many parts of Virginia." If an African ran away in a group after midcentury, he usually accompanied creoles, not fellow Africans. Three men ran away from Archibald Cary's forge in Chesterfield County in 1766. One was a Virginia-born carpenter, another a Virginia-born foreman, and the third a Gold Coast native, now a fireman. Nine years later, two Africans who spoke only a rudimentary English ran away with a Jamaica-born black and a Virginian mulatto from their Prince Edward County quarter.

Masters must have been reduced to hoping that their African slaves would fail to emulate the examples set by their creoles. An incident involving a highly assimi-lated slave belonging to Peter Nunnery of Goochland County illustrates the prob-lems with which masters had to contend. In 1747, Nunnery's runaway slave was thought to have stolen a horse's bell. He was pursued and eventually overtaken in Henrico County by three whites. When confronted, the slave at first denied the charge, then under some duress confessed to the theft, and finally promised to re-veal the bell's hiding place. He first took the group to a pile of logs, pretended to search for the missing item, then "s[ai]d with a Laughter that he made [a] fool of them and that the Bell was not there." Not surprisingly, this charade angered his captors, who proceeded to beat him, whereupon the slave promised to reveal the true whereabouts of the bell. But he repeated the performance at a fodder stack. By now the whites were livid with rage and began cutting switches in order to whip the impudent black, but the slave attempted to convince them to follow him one more time to a hollow tree stump by the river's edge where all would be revealed. At this point, one of his captors declared that "he would . . . follow [the] son of a bitch no more for he could make a bell sooner," but the slave won his reprieve from the other two. On their way to the river, the bondman managed to slip away, get ahead of his captors, and jump into the river. When urged to come out, he began "laughing at [them and] Sunk in their sight & they saw him no more." If, as seems likely, this self-assured slave went to his death making a fool of whites, no doubt he would have wanted it no other way.

Creoles soon dominated slave life in the piedmont. Although almost all Africans who reached Virginia from midcentury onward made their home in the piedmont, their numbers were never large enough to put much of an African stamp on the emerging slave society. Piedmont Africans certainly resisted slavery in characteristic ways and seem to have been at the heart of the widespread resort to magic. More noticeable, however, is the speed at which they creolized, evident in everything from their acquisition of English language skills to their running away with native-born slaves. Creoles set the standard and tone of this regional society remarkably quickly.

Since the piedmont received many immigrants in the colonial era, the region's slaves did not find it easy to establish a measure of family life. In this sense, black life in the piedmont replicated an earlier phase of the tidewater slave experience. At the same time, there were important differences between the two experiences. Piedmont immigrants were primarily creoles, not Africans. Not surprisingly, therefore, the adult sex ratios among piedmont slaves rapidly approached equality. Taking the region as a whole, adult male slaves outnumbered females heavily during the first decade or so of piedmont settlement. But these imbalanced sex ratios were relatively short-lived. By the late 1730s and early 1740s, there were fewer than 120 men for every 100 slave women in the piedmont. More-skewed imbalances periodically reoccurred as waves of immigrants moved into the region, but the overall trend was a rapid downward one. By the late 1760s and 1770s there were almost as many women as men.

Even more striking is the proportion of children to be found in the piedmont slave population. In part this can be attributed to the composition of both migration streams, since young slaves predominated among creole and African newcomers. In any case, from the first years of piedmont settlement, and for much of the colonial period, children outnumbered women by at least two to one. . . . In sum, the youthfulness of the piedmont slave population was striking.

The available measures of the fecundity of female slaves—such indicators as age at first birth, length of intervals between births, and completed family size—support and help account for this youthfulness. Some piedmont slave women were remarkably young when they conceived their first child. Lilly, a Jerdone slave, was not even fifteen when she first conceived. The average age of conception in the late colonial period was 18.2 years, dropping slightly to 17.7 years in the late eighteenth century. Piedmont slave mothers bore children regularly and rapidly—one every twenty-eight months on average, not taking into account early infant mortality. Finally, piedmont slave women probably lived longer than their tidewater counterparts. Robert Rose thought the death of his slave woman Judith sufficiently noteworthy to put in his diary because she was "the first Slave of Mine that has died in Albemarle." This was almost a decade after Rose first set up quarters there. Not surprisingly, therefore, completed family sizes were generally larger for piedmont, than for tidewater, slaves.

Truncated family structures inevitably characterized such a youthful immigrant population. In the late 1750s Peyton Randolph, like many another tidewater planter, established a new plantation in the piedmont. He transferred a number of his young slaves to a quarter in what became Charlotte County, over a hundred miles away from his home plantation. No doubt these teenagers and young adults left kin behind when they moved west. Moreover, the imbalance between men and women meant that large age differentials (of about ten years) separated spouses, when they were fortunate enough to marry. Just over twenty years later, however, some of the children of the original immigrants had reached maturity and established families of their own. Nanny, for instance, certainly left kin behind when she came to the piedmont as a twenty-five-year-old mother of four children. But by 1784, at least two of her three daughters had given birth themselves and Nanny was a grandmother to four children, one of whom bore her name. Sarah, another Randolph slave, was about twenty years of age when she was moved to the piedmont and already the mother of three children, including twins; she gave birth to at least three more children in her new home. By 1784 two of her daughters had married and each had one child apiece. Nanny and Sarah were therefore matriarchs of rapidly growing slave clans.

Struggling to re-create a semblance of an ordered family life, Nanny, Sarah, and their fellow Randolph slaves were at least more fortunate than the slaves of Francis Willis, a planter who made his home in Gloucester County, but who had quarters in the piedmont. In 1766 Willis died and the majority of his slaves in Cumberland and Hanover counties were sold. Few piedmont planters could afford to purchase large lots of slaves. Indeed, most could buy no more than a single slave, so the sale scattered 101 slaves among sixty-one purchasers. Only occasionally can we be certain that families were separated (the couple Butcher Will and his wife Venus were sold with their "sucking child," also named Venus, but their two sons Sam and Lewis were sold separately). However, since three-quarters of the men were sold singly, while almost half of the women were sold with at least one child, it seems a fair assumption that these sales broke many husband-wife, not to mention parent-child, relationships.

A firsthand description of one slave sale is sufficiently interesting to be explored in depth. It took place in the winter of 1787 in Powhatan County, the very heart of the piedmont. Mr. Gay, a Powhatan resident, was apparently in deep debt, particularly to Robert Hare of Philadelphia, who employed the local planter Benjamin Harrison to look after his interests. Gay was forced to put up every one of his slaves, fifty-seven in all, for public auction at the Powatan County Courthouse. Six slaves who were already mortgaged were immediately claimed. Of those remaining, twelve were not even "set up," owing to their advanced ages and generally unsuitability. Their fate is unknown. The sale itself went slowly; as night fell, only twelve slaves had been purchased. In order to protect Mr. Hare's interest, Harrison bought the remaining twenty-seven slaves at £40 apiece. Harrison showed a measure of compassion by allowing his acquisitions to return to Gay that night in order to "collect their little effects together." However, within a few days, Harrison had sold six at £70 each, making a tidy profit. He then advertised his willingness to sell the others privately and set another date for a second public auction. Noting that his purchases had not been clothed that year, he proposed remedying the omission so that they might "sell better." He explained to Hare that "the plan of carrying them from Court to Court will not do at this season of the year for so many [are] small negroes." No mention was made of keeping families together; rather, business decisions ruled this, and presumably many another, slave sale.

The arbitrariness with which slave family members could be dispersed is revealed in a number of cases concerning a father's verbal gift of a slave to one of his children. In the early 1750s George Thompson of Goochland County gave a slave to his daughter Joyce "as soon as the said [slave] Girl was born." He told Joyce "to take care of her for that he had no more to do with the said Girl." In 1769 a lodger in the Cumberland County household of William Angela, Sr., remembered a conversation between Angela and his daughter Betty some fifteen years previous. The father promised to give his daughter a slave infant named Biddy, provided Betty take care of the child. His action was largely a response to the "grumblings" of his son Benjamin, who as overseer on his father's plantation objected to Biddy's mother "coming in to tend the negro child." In this way, Betty acquired her own slave, and a slave mother was deprived of the care of her own daughter.

Small holdings, constant sales and mortgages, and distribution of property among large numbers of heirs, not to mention the heartlessness displayed by men like Angela, must have exacerbated the chances of separation facing many piedmont slave families. An elderly couple, Tony and his wife, Phillis, were perhaps typical. Both had been born in Lancaster County around the 1720s, but were sold to a Culpeper master, who in turn sold them to an adjacent Fauquier County planter. With each sale, Tony and Phillis had been separated from progressively more of their "several children," so that almost a half-century later they had children "dispersed through Culpeper, Frederick and Augusta Counties." When they ran away in 1770, their master had trouble predicting their whereabouts, in part because they might be harbored by any one of their many progeny. Later in the century, when riding the Hanover circuit, the Methodist minister James Meacham was distraught to see a black couple's children torn from them because they were "legacy'd" to widely scattered heirs. "The crys of the poor Captive Woman . . . on her Taking leave of her children," were, in Meacham's opinion, "enough to move the heart of the most obdurate."

Yet many slaves like Tony and Phillis struggled to maintain kin ties; some, particularly those belonging to the larger planters, managed to create a remarkably robust family life. . . .

Larger planters could more readily afford to be respectful of slave kin ties. In 1776, when John Blair offered to exchange his slaves in Hanover County for Thomas Adams's land in Albemarle County, he acknowledged that the predominantly youthful character of his slaves "might not suit," but stressed that he "could not think of separating them from their mothers." Thirteen years later, in an action that must have been repeated on many a piedmont plantation, a slave named Frank "asked leave" of his master, Col. Francis Taylor of Orange County, to "have Miss M. Conway's Pat for a Wife." Taylor employed Frank as his messenger and errand runner, a valuable slave whose wishes ought to be respected if possible and who already traveled off the plantation. Thus Taylor "did not object," particularly when Frank told him that he "had the necessary consent." Frank must have anticipated his master's approval, because he had already set the time of the wedding for the following evening.

Some slaves—those who became Baptists in the late eighteenth century—were exposed most directly to white views on family morality. Indeed, the most common disciplinary offense brought against black Baptist church members involved a transgression of family norms—whether adultery, fornication, attempted rape, even in one case "attempting to bead with a white woman." At the same time, white Baptists at least recognized slave marriages. . . .

Slave families also took the initiative in naming their children. Two patterns are particularly noticeable. Naming after extended kin was perhaps the most common. . . . Only one slave family in many piedmont slave lists named a daughter after a mother.

Just as naming patterns indicate the emergence of strong nuclear families and extended kin among piedmont slaves, so do the actions of runaway slaves. By the late colonial period, more and more runaway slaves were attempting to reunite with separated spouses and parents; in some cases, kin networks were thought to be supporting the absentee. Sall, a twenty-five-year-old mulatto woman who ran away from an Amherst County quarter in 1774, was said to be "of a numerous Family of Mulattoes, formerly belonging to a Gentleman of the Name of Howard in York County . . . and where probably she may attempt to go again, or perhaps into Cumberland, or Amelia, where . . . many of her kindred live." Abraham, who ran away from his Chesterfield County master in 1777, was said to have "a Wife at a Quarter of the Hon. William Nelson's, Esq. in king William; several Relations at Mr. Claiborne's, in the same county; some at Mr. William Dandridge's and Mr. Sherwood Tinsley's, in Hanover County, at some of which Places," his master conjectured, "he is haboured." Cuthie from Mecklenburg County was supposed to have gone toward York County, where she had "several relations"; Sye from Chesterfield County was thought to be "lurking" in Gloucester County, where he had "many Relations." A wide range of "connections," as contemporary masters termed them, supported some piedmont runaways in the late colonial period.

By the end of the eighteenth century, the building and rebuilding of kin ties had produced dense social networks for some piedmont slaves, in both town and countryside. . . . In deepest Bedford County, in the southwestern part of the piedmont, an old couple belonging to Thomas Jefferson was surrounded by a bevy of grown children, in-laws, and grandchildren. The quarter was almost one extended family.

Although the obstacles placed in the way of family formation and maintenance were formidable, many piedmont slaves overcame them. It is impossible to say how many of the region's slaves enjoyed a measure of family life, but the surviving evidence, overrepresentative as it may be of the larger plantations, suggests a surprisingly high number, at least after midcentury. . . .

The development of a robust family life went hand in hand with the emergence of an Afro-American society in the piedmont. In part, this was a function of demographic and economic forces. . . . The increasing size of plantation units also created greater opportunities for piedmont slaves to develop a social life of their own. Generally speaking, within one or two decades after the formation of a piedmont county, a majority of its slaves resided on plantations with more than ten slaves. Indeed, by the early 1780s about 40 percent of slaves in most piedmont counties resided on plantations of more than twenty slaves. The rapidity with which plantation sizes in the piedmont caught up with—and, in some cases, surpassed—those in the tidewater is remarkable. Finally, by the 1780s at least, the density of the slave population in many piedmont counties approached tidewater levels, thereby facilitating contacts and communication among slaves.

Black actions, not just impersonal forces, made vital contributions to the development of an Afro-American society in the piedmont. A prime example of the black community ministering to its own needs is the widespread resort to magic, something that contemporary whites pejoratively labeled a propensity for poisoning. At any rate, the dispenser of medicines, charms, or poisons clearly was a person of influence within the slave community. Indeed, even whites recognized the power of such slaves. . . .

On the other hand, a large number of alleged poisonings appear to have been little more than one slave administering roots, powders, or charms to others. Court judgments reflect the harmlessness of many "poisoning" cases. . . . Some slaves used "poisons" as charms to influence their masters. Peg of Louisa County administered a substance procured from a slave man in the neighborhood "to keep peace in the family, and to make her Master kind to her." Sarah of Prince Edward County put black seeds "resembling Jaucestor seeds" into the peas she prepared for her white family "for the purpose of making her mistress love her."

Although the widespread resort to magic bound piedmont slaves together, the practice also reflected serious internal tensions within the slave community. In fact, many poisoning incidents that came before piedmont county courts were as much inwardly directed at blacks as outwardly targeted against whites. Intrablack conflict, perhaps stemming from frictions between different African ethnic groups or between Africans and creoles, or from the natural stresses to which all slave communities were subject, lay at the heart of many of these cases. . . .

Exciting much less controversy, slaves turned to black doctors, as well as black conjurers, though they may have made less of this distinction than did their masters. In 1752, William Dabney of Goochland County paid 11s. 3d. to John Bates "for the use of his negroe Doctor" among his slaves. Over two decades later, Charles Yates bought a slave in Culpeper County only to find that he had been long "distempered" and under the hands of "Negro Doctors" for years. Benjamin Harrison employed a slave doctor on his plantation, while a Chesterfield County master disapproved of his slave Sambo's doctoring. Black midwives often delivered slave women. Francis Taylor noted that "Granny Venus" attended at the delivery of his slave woman Milly. Blacks turned to other blacks for physical as well as psychological support.

The growth of intercounty and cooperative networks in the actions of slave runaways also provides evidence of an emergent cohesiveness within the black community. As the century proceeded, slaves ran away over greater distances and often remained at large for extensive periods. . . .

Cooperative actions were common in the committing of crimes. Just over 40 percent of the four hundred or more slaves prosecuted in a number of piedmont county courts committed their alleged crimes in groups of two or more persons. . . . [A] large proportion of the group crimes involved slaves belonging to separate masters. Indeed, this was true of 60 percent of the crimes committed by groups. Cross-plantation alliances were the norm. . . .

Whites also encouraged blacks to turn on one another. An unwritten but consistently pursued policy of divide and rule put considerable pressure on black cohesiveness. Sometimes slaves served as prosecution witnesses against other bondmen. In cooperative crimes, one slave might be induced to secure his freedom by incriminating his comrades. In Cumberland County in 1765, Toby was found guilty of hog stealing when his partner in crime, Charles, turned King's evidence. It later transpired that Charles had been "a false witness"; for his pains, he was nailed to a pillory for an hour by his ears, which were then cut off. Though the white community encouraged slaves to act as turncoats, they had to be reliable ones. Pecuniary incentives also induced divisiveness, as when slaves or free blacks secured rewards for capturing runaways or conveying them back to their masters. In these and other ways, whites encouraged divisions among slaves.

Another division among blacks arose from the simple fact that not all blacks were slaves. Apart from all the obvious and distinguishing advantages of freedom, skin color usually demarcated free blacks from slaves. Unlike the vast majority of slaves, most pre-Revolutionary free blacks were mulattoes. . . .

However, whatever their complexion, most free blacks were not far removed from slaves—either in station or residence. Most lived for a large part of their lives as bound servants, presumably alongside slaves. . . .

A small Afro-Indian community also emerged in the piedmont. Like the free black community, it lived in a twilight zone between slavery and freedom. Thus, a Cumberland County slave, a "Mulatto" named Jim, ran away from his master in 1772 seeking the "Right to his Freedom," as his master put it. His father "was an Indian of the Name of Cheshire," so his master guessed he would "call himself JAMES Cheshire or Chink." Another mulatto runaway slave, from Dinwiddie County, was thought to be joining his brother, who had been "several Times brought from among the Indians on Pamunkey River." A third mulatto slave, also from Dinwiddie, was said to be "of the Indian breed"; he sought his freedom from the General Court in 1773. Again, like free blacks, Afro-Indians lived in close proximity to slaves. In 1762 two quarters in Chesterfield County contained thirty "Negroes," fourteen mulattoes, and four Indians. Indians and blacks inevitably married one another. Patrick Rose of Amherst County assumed that his runaway slave Ben had joined his Indian wife, because "she sold off, and moved from her late Dwelling Place in Albermarle, a few Days before the Fellow ran away."

In sum, although serious divisions existed within the Afro-American community of the piedmont, a voluntary cohesiveness, not to mention the cohesion forced on blacks by white hostility, developed quickly. From the actions of runaways and rebels to the more mundane activities of black conjurers and doctors, the black community attempted to stand together. Not always successful, the black community appeared resilient in the face of formidable odds. There were always casualties, ranging from a slave like Ralph who, piqued at being given a mule to ride rather than a horse, beat "the poor Jack without mercy" until it died, to "old Caesar," who was charged with the attempted rape and buggery of a four-year-old white girl. Nobody escaped the effects of slavery no matter where they lived. But the pathology of slavery does not seem to have been any more developed in the piedmont than in the tidewater.

Black-white relations assumed a special character in the piedmont. Generally speaking, as plantation units increased in size throughout tidewater, more Afro-Americans lived on quarters beyond their masters' direct supervision. In the piedmont, however, a reverse trend was evident—at least in the short run. In the earliest years of a piedmont county, large numbers of slaves resided on quarters with overseers. In Amelia in 1740 at least a third of the county's slaves lived on units where masters were absent. In 1760 just over half of the slaves in recently created Loudoun County lived on quarters supervised by overseers. As more piedmont whites became slaveholders and as some tidewater masters transferred their residences into the piedmont, the proportion of slaves under the direct purview of a master increased. By the late 1770s, the vast majority of slaves in Amelia County, and other piedmont counties, resided on plantations with a resident master, although a significant minority occupied satellite quarters some distance from the home estate.

The more-distanced relationship with a master, which was a prominent feature of the slave experience particularly in the early piedmont, had obvious advantages. Some piedmont slaves no doubt enjoyed the relative autonomy inherent in absentee estates. Others may have valued the opportunities for traveling back and forth between piedmont quarter and tidewater home plantation, driving livestock, or taking crops to market. . . .

Yet from the perspective of the slaves' material well-being, the drawbacks of a more-distanced relationship with masters probably outweighed the advantages. Many piedmont slaves depended on distant tidewater owners for supplies. . . .

The poor opinion in which piedmont overseers were generally held was undoubtedly small compensation to the slaves for the cruelties they suffered, but at least it provided them with opportunities to redress grievances. . . .

Piedmont slaves could . . . occasionally exploit the tenuous position occupied by many a white overseer. Most piedmont overseers averaged only a year or two in the employ of a single planter. A particularly revealing incident occurred on one of Edward Ambler's piedmont quarters in 1770, with the hiring of a new overseer, John Smith. He immediately incurred the opposition of the fourteen adult slaves put under him. According to the plantation steward, the problem lay in the attitude of Smith's predecessor, Thomas Wingfield, who "was so good natured to the Negroes under him that he suffered them to Impose on him very much." In the last year of Wingfield's incumbency, the steward continued, "the Negroes were almost free." As a result, they were "very unwilling to give up the privileges they [had been] allowed." Indeed, "they seem," noted the steward, "to be determined to Maintain them" and tried to get Smith "turned off." The slaves prevailed on George, the oldest bondman on the plantation, to visit their master, thinking that "a complaint from him wou'd be listened to." Although Smith apparently had the backing of his superiors at this time, he was replaced the following year.

The example of Thomas Wingfield suggests that some overseers, only too well aware of the precariousness of their position, took the line of least resistance and sided with the slaves. . . .

By the late colonial era, many more piedmont slaves resided on plantations headed by masters and, particularly on the larger estates, became subject to a more patriarchal planter style. . . .

Patriarchs prided themselves on their responsiveness to the human, as well as the material, needs of their slaves. Erasmus Gill of Stirling Castle in Dinwiddie County allowed his slave Aggy and her youngest children to go to Petersburg because Aggy was "desirous of living with her Husband." Gill arranged for her eldest child, Page, to be "brought up by some genteel Lady to learn how to soe, and attend to other domestic duties" in a three-year apprenticeship "for good Cloaths &c. provided she is treated with tenderness." A Fredericksburg master permitted his "old & faithful family slave" Charles to "see for the last time" his "other old acquaintances" in Stafford County. Patriarchal benevolence was not confined to the tidewater gentry.

Indeed, as the eighteenth century proceeded, the rough edges of life in the interior were gradually smoothed away. Harsh sentences for slaves seem to have become less common over time. A good indication of the changing temper of the times comes from an anonymous letter to the *Virginia Gazette* in 1773. In it, a man known by the initials R. M. (almost undoubtedly Robert Munford of Amelia County) is said to have practiced barbaric cruelties upon his slaves, including the slaughter of at least fifty and the castration and dismemberment of a captured runaway. Presumably, the claims were exaggerated, but most notable is that one piedmonter would criticize the inhumanity of another. Whatever the reality, slavery was not *meant* to be barbaric any longer.

Smaller planters were, of course, less able to afford the liberality of their more prosperous neighbors. . . . And it is they who invariably stood in the dock when masters were accused of either killing or wounding one of their own slaves. In most of these cases, the gentlemen justices discharged their less affluent neighbors without further trial—confirming the gentry's magnanimity toward fellow whites. Humble yeomen, however, were often incorrigible. When Daniel McPherson, a veteran of the Royal Highland Company Regiment that had fought in Quebec, confronted a slave suspected of theft, he acted in the classic small slaveholder manner. Rather than resorting to the courts, he whipped the man. Later, the same slave was incautious enough to jeer at McPherson, using "scurrilous language" to boot. McPherson was on his schooner at the time, but waded into the water intent on beating the slave a second time. The two men fought in the river, oblivious to the larger dangers they faced, were swept away, and drowned. This sort of confrontation was a far cry from the patriarchal ideal.

Not all small planters were devoid of benevolent feelings. In July 1773 Toby, a slave belonging to James Wimbish of Halifax County, disappeared for over twelve years. When Wimbish discovered his bondman, he found that Toby had fought for his country in the Revolutionary War by enlisting in the 14th Virginia Regiment under a fictitious name. Upon his retirement, he had married a white woman, by whom he had several children. Wimbish, in his words, felt "compassion" toward his slave and "subscribed a considerable sum toward obtaining his freedom, which was effected by several Gentlemen who bore part of the loss." Even here, then, gentlemen aided a small planter. . . .

. . . [T]he piedmont was the center of the evangelical revival that swept Virginia in the late colonial era. In this respect, the piedmont was hardly replicating or extending a tidewater experience; it was leading the way. . . . However, the first sustained proselytization of slaves took place in neighboring Hanover County at midcentury, under the inspired leadership of the charismatic Presbyterian Samuel Davies. In 1751 Davies reported that one hundred slaves attended his services and that forty had been baptized in the previous three years. Four years later, the numbers had increased to three hundred and one hundred, respectively. His efforts then gained momentum, for in 1757 he claimed to have baptized one hundred and fifty black adults in the previous eighteen months and to have sixty black communicants in attendance. The influence of this revival radiated outward to other piedmont counties. Slaves who had been converted by Davies but transferred to Charlotte County proselytized other slaves in their new home.

What is perhaps most surprising about this Presbyterian success was its conservative and bookish nature. Davies and his disciples thought it part of their mission to teach the slaves to read. In the middle of the nineteenth century, one Virginian recalled seeing African slaves clasping the books given to them by their eminent preacher. Davies was also demanding of his converts. He acknowledged that he was "affraid of discouraging them . . . by imposing high Forms of Admission to Baptism," but equally he underlined his caution at not "swelling the number of proselites with only nominal Christians." He excluded many blacks from baptism because they thought it either a fashionable communal rite or, more ominously, a means to "be upon an Equality with their Masters." Davies strenuously opposed these misinterpretations of his message. Indeed, he reported that planters were impressed "by the visible Reformation wrought by his preaching among the Slaves, whose Sobriety and diligence excited their Curiosity."

Evangelical successes among the slaves gained impetus as less conservative groups—first the New Light Baptists and then the Methodists—began to make their influence felt. The New Lights established their first beachhead in Virginia in the southside. The earlier Baptist church records report small black memberships. In 1759 the Lunenburg County Anglican minister spoke of the "spectre of dissenters" hovering around him. He singled out for particular notice their opening up of the ministry to all, "whether he be a slave or a free Person." Piedmont slaves were certainly preaching. . . .

Indeed, Baptist slaves had to be independent, for masters openly scorned their slaves' religious sincerity. In 1767 a Buckingham County master referred to his slave woman "pretend[ing] much to the religion the Negroes of late have practised." Ten years later a Prince Edward County master described his mulatto runaway as "pretend[ing] to know something of religious matters, and misses no opportunity of holding forth on that subject." Slaves faced more than derision for their beliefs. In 1769 James Ireland noted that the "poor negroes have been stripped and subjected to stripes" in Culpeper County for listening to the Baptists. Nine years later, Cumberland County masters petitioned the governor to put a halt to their slaves' attendance at night meetings. They cited two reasons: first, the "fruits of disobedience and insolence to Masters," but even more significant, the slaves' "glorying in what they are taught to believe to be the persecution for Conscience's Sake."

In the 1770s the Methodists too began to make inroads in the piedmont, particularly in the southside. In June 1776, at a chapel near Petersburg, Methodist circuit rider Thomas Rankin had "a powerful meeting" with a large number of whites and blacks. "What was peculiarly affecting to him," he noted, were the blacks in the gallery, "almost everyone of them upon their knees; some for themselves, and others for their distressed companions." In the following month, Rankin, now joined by Francis Asbury, attended a number of extremely emotional meetings in this area. On one occasion, Asbury had to stop a meeting "again and again, and beg of the people to compose themselves." In the congregation were "Hundreds of Negroes . . . with tears streaming down their faces." . . .

Why were the Baptists, Methodists, and to a lesser extent, Presbyterians so successful among piedmont slaves? Part of the reason lay in the evangelicals' emphasis on an untutored, spontaneous religious response. . . .

The musical and emotional responsiveness of slaves encouraged and impressed evangelical preachers. Samuel Davies spoke of the "torrent of sacred harmony" of which blacks were capable. "The Negroes above all the human species that ever I knew," he declared, "have an ear for Music, and a Kind of extatic delight in Psalmody." One evening in Mecklenburg County, the singing of blacks in a nearby cottage inspired James Meacham to pray with them. He was so moved as to feel that "Heaven was just then at hand." A month later, at another home, Meacham "awaked in raptures of Heaven by the sweet Echo of Singing in the Kitchen among the dear Black people (who my Soul loves)." Scarcely had he "ever heard anything to equal it upon earth." The "hollering" of slaves impressed John Kobler when on the Bedford circuit, while Thomas Morrell observed at Lanes Chapel near Petersburg that "the people in Virginia are fond of noisy meetings particularly the blacks." If the "noise" made by blacks appeared "too mechanical" to Morrell, he was nevertheless impressed by its "power." By mechanical, Morrell may have been suggesting a choreographed response, a characteristic feature of the Afro-American religious tradition.

The evangelicals' success among slaves also owed much to their initial willingness to adopt a radical stance toward the white opponents of black conversion. Until the 1700s many Baptist and Methodist preachers actively opposed slavery. . . .

Another indication of the radical stance of evangelicalism—at least in the context of late-eighteenth-century Chesapeake society—was the implicit or even explicit egalitarianism that characterized their disciplinary proceedings. Although evangelical church discipline certainly served to buttress the master's authority over his slave, disciplinary meetings rarely served to rubber-stamp a master's whim. In 1786 Tussekiah Baptist Church in Lunenburg County resolved to "deal" with black members just as with whites. At the Boar Swamp Baptist Church in Hanover County, five years later, a disciplinary action followed precisely this procedure: two women, one a slave and the other a free white, were together brought before the church, accused of adultery, and excommunicated. The Meherrin Baptist Church of Lunenburg County disciplined whites for their transgressions against slaves. Brother Charles Cook "acknowledged his sin in unlawfully burning one of his negroes." In another case, two blacks accused a white woman of "the sin of anger & unchristian language."

Who among the slaves responded to the evangelical message? Creoles were probably the most likely converts, but Africans were not to be discounted. Samuel Davies described his efforts to teach a forty-year-old African, "a very stupid lubberly Fellow in appearance and but [in]differently acquainted with our Language." Despairing of his own abilities, Davies was later amazed to find the slave succeeding on his own. Simply passing on further books to him, Davies discovered that his former pupil could "read English almost as intelligibly as he can speak it." . . .

Most significant of all, perhaps, is the occasional suggestion of a distinctive black religiosity, owing something no doubt to these African roots. . . .

Perhaps no better testimonial exists to some of the dominant themes of slave life in the piedmont than the prayer said to have been written by a slave in "the lower part of Virginia" in the year 1790 and recorded by the Quaker Joshua Evans. It speaks to the formidable odds slaves faced; to their resilience of spirit; to their familiarity with white ways; to their religious faith; and, above all, to their desire and hopes for freedom.

Lord, if thou dost with equal eye.
See all the sons of Adam rise,
Why dost thou hide thy face from slaves,
Confin'd by fate to serve such knaves?
Stolen and sold in Africa,
Transported to America,
Like hogs and sheep in market sold,
To stand the heat, and bear the cold,

When will Jehovah hear our cries?
When will the sun of freedom rise?
When will a Moses for us stand,
And free us all from Pharoah's hand?
What tho' our skin be black as jet,
Our hair be curl'd our noses flat,
Must we for this, no freedom have
until we find it in the grave?
Contentment, Lord, on me bestow,
While I remain a slave below,
And whilst I suffer grief and wrong;
May thy Salvation be my song.

 # FURTHER READING

Ira Berlin, *Many Thousands Gone: The First Two Centuries of Slavery in North America* (1998).

*Constructing Race,* special issue of *William and Mary Quarterly,* 3rd ser., LIV (1997).

Michael A. Gomez, *Exchanging our Country Marks: The Transformation of African Identities in the Colonial and Antebellum South* (1998).

Philip D. Morgan, *Slave Counterpoint: Black Culture in the Eighteenth-Century Chesapeake and Low Country* (1998).

Michael Mullin, *Africa in America: Slave Acculturation and Resistance in the American South and the British Caribbean, 1736–1831* (1992).

Gary B. Nash, *Forging Freedom: The Formation of Philadelphia's Black Community, 1720–1840* (1988).

Robert Olwell, *Masters, Slaves, and Subjects: The Culture of Power in the South Carolina Low Country, 1740–1790* (1998).

Jon A. Sensbach, *A Separate Canaan: The Making of an Afro-Moravian World in North Carolina, 1763–1840* (1998).

John A. Thornton, *Africa and Africans in the Making of the Atlantic World, 1400–1800,* 2nd ed. (1998).

CHAPTER

11

# Religious Awakenings

The Great Awakening was a series of religious revivals that affected every part of English America in the first half of the eighteenth century. Although some historians have argued that the experience was too diffuse and spread over too long a time to be considered a movement, others point out that the revivals, wherever and however they happened, had many aspects in common.

The revivals all stressed interior experience of salvation, emphasizing emotional knowledge rather than great learning. Many caught up in the experience character- ized themselves as having been spiritually dead, merely going through the motions of worship, before being touched by the hand of God. Although the theology of the Awakeners stressed the Calvinist doctrine of human depravity, maintaining that sin- ful men and women could do nothing to lift themselves out of sin without divine help, their effect was energizing. Congregations left meetings feeling that salvation was available to them if only they reached out and wanted badly enough to achieve it.

In some cases the awakenings began with small local revivals; others were spread by itinerants' preachers like the famous George Whitefield who traveled all over the colonies carrying their message. Ministers initially welcomed the itinerants and the enthusiasm they generated, but many also felt threatened. Local ministers suffered by comparison with the dramatic and gifted itinerants, and some feared that the emotional conversions were surface phenomena that would not last. They dis- liked the denigration of learning and the implication that the experience of the low- born and unlearned might be more genuine than theirs. Many ministers sought to welcome the new enthusiasm for religion the itinerants brought while at the same time bringing their activities within a recognized order. Ultimately the movement split many communities into Old Light or Side and New Light and some congrega- tions split permanently.

## DOCUMENTS

Benjamin Franklin was a friend and supporter of George Whitefield, but was not con- verted by him. Franklin listened to Whitefield preach with an analytical ear. Although he demonstrated his analytical stance in document 1, it did not prevent him from being affected by Whitefield's words. Connecticut farmer Nathan Cole wrote in document 2 of his excitement at hearing that Whitefield would preach in his neighborhood; he dropped his tools and went off with his wife immediately, as did a huge throng that were all attracted by word of mouth advertisement. Gilbert Tennent, leader of the Awakening in the Middle Colonies, preached a famous sermon, document 3, on the danger to congregations led by ministers who were merely "natural," that is, not having experienced a true spiritual rebirth. He argued that such ministers could never be good guides to their flocks.

Many became critical of the revivals and their effects. Reverend Joseph Fish of Connecticut described in document 4 the illiterate native preacher he found among the Narragansett Indians of Rhode Island and recommended that the authorities send help. Eventually he became a part-time preacher to the Narragansetts. An anonymous opponent, who signed himself Anti-Enthusiasticus, wrote a letter, document 5, to the *Boston Weekly News-Letter* describing the trial and expulsion of Connecticut New Light activist James Davenport in 1742 under the newly passed laws against itineracy. Davenport was famous for the extreme actions of himself and his followers. The Anglican minister Charles Woodmason traveled as a missionary through the Carolina backcountry in the 1760s. His influential journal, document 6, provided the definitive picture of the poor quality of life and religious decadence seen on the frontier; he believed the New Light preachers in particular had done harm in the region.

## 1. Benjamin Franklin Listens to His Friend George Whitefield, 1739

In 1739 arrived among us from Ireland the Reverend Mr. Whitefield, who had made himself remarkable there as an itinerant preacher. He was at first permitted to preach in some of our churches; but the clergy, taking a dislike to him, soon refused him their pulpits, and he was obliged to preach in the fields. The multitudes of all sects and denominations that attended his sermons were enormous, and it was a matter of speculation to me, who was one of the number, to observe the extraordinary influence of his oratory on his hearers, and how much they admired and respected him, notwithstanding his common abuse of them, by assuring them, they were naturally *half beasts and half devils.* It was wonderful to see the change soon made in the manners of our inhabitants. From being thoughtless or indifferent about religion, it seemed as if all the world were growing religious, so that one could not walk through the town in an evening without hearing psalms sung in different families of every street.

And it being found inconvenient to assemble in the open air, subject to its inclemencies, the building of a house to meet in was no sooner proposed, and persons appointed to receive contributions, than sufficient sums were soon received to procure the ground, and erect the building, which was one hundred feet long and seventy broad; and the work was carried on with such spirit as to be finished in a much shorter time than could have been expected. Both house and ground were vested in trustees, expressly for the use of *any preacher of any religious persuasion* who

---

Benjamin Franklin. *Autobiography* (London: Hutchinson & Co., 1903), 121–126.

might desire to say something to the people at Philadelphia; the design in building being not to accommodate any particular sect, but the inhabitants in general; so that even if the Mufti of Constantinople were to send a missionary to preach Mahometanism to us, he would find a pulpit at his service.

Mr. Whitefield, on leaving us, went preaching all the way through the colonies to Georgia. The settlement of that province had been lately begun, but, instead of being made with hardy, industrious husbandmen, accustomed to labour, the only people fit for such an enterprise, it was with families of broken shopkeepers and other insolvent debtors; many of indolent and idle habits, taken out of the jails, who, being set down in the woods, unqualified for clearing land, and unable to endure the hardships of a new settlement, perished in numbers, leaving many helpless children unprovided for. The sight of their miserable situation inspired the benevolent heart of Mr. Whitefield with the idea of building an Orphan House there, in which they might be supported and educated. Returning northward, he preached up this charity, and made large collections; for his eloquence had a wonderful power over the hearts and purses of his hearers, of which I myself was an instance.

I did not disapprove of the design, but, as Georgia was then destitute of materials and workmen, and it was proposed to send them from Philadelphia at a great expense, I thought it would have been better to have built the house at Philadelphia, and brought the children to it. This I advised; but he was resolute in his first project, rejected my counsel, and I therefore refused to contribute. I happened soon after to attend one of his sermons, in the course of which I perceived he intended to finish with a collection, and I silently resolved he should get nothing from me. I had in my pocket a handful of copper money, three or four silver dollars, and five pistoles in gold. As he proceeded I began to soften, and concluded to give the copper. Another stroke of his oratory made me ashamed of that, and determined me to give the silver; and he finished so admirably that I emptied my pocket wholly into the collector's dish, gold and all. At this sermon there was also one of our club, who, being of my sentiments respecting the building in Georgia, and suspecting a collection might be intended, had by precaution emptied his pockets before he came from home. Towards the conclusion of the discourse, however, he felt a strong inclination to give, and applied to a neighbour, who stood near him, to lend him some money for the purpose. The request was fortunately made to perhaps the only man in the company who had the firmness not to be affected by the preacher. His answer was, "At any other time, friend Hopkinson, I would lend to thee freely; but not now; for thee seems to be out of thy right senses."

Some of Mr. Whitefield's enemies affected to suppose that he would apply these collections to his own private emolument; but I, who was intimately acquainted with him, being employed in printing his Sermons and Journals, never had the least suspicion of his integrity; but am to this day decidedly of opinion that he was in all his conduct a perfectly *honest man;* and methinks my testimony in his favour ought to have the more weight, as we had no religious connexion. He used, indeed, sometimes, to pray for my conversion, but never had the satisfaction of believing that his prayers were heard. Ours was a mere civil friendship, sincere on both sides, and lasted to his death.

The following instance will show the terms on which we stood. Upon one of his arrivals from England at Boston, he wrote to me that he should come soon to

Philadelphia, but knew not where he could lodge when there, as he understood his old friend and host, Mr. Benezet, was removed to Germantown. My answer was, "You know my house; if you can make shift with its scanty accommodations, you will be most heartily welcome." He replied, that if I made that kind offer for *Christ's* sake, I should not miss of a reward. And I returned, "Don't let me be mistaken; it was not for *Christ's* sake, but for *your* sake." One of our common acquaintance jocosely remarked that, knowing it to be the custom of the saints, when they received any favour, to shift the burden of the obligation from off their own shoulders, and place it in heaven, I had contrived to fix it on earth.

The last time I saw Mr. Whitefield was in London, when he consulted me about his Orphan-House concern, and his purpose of appropriating it to the establishment of a college.

He had a loud and clear voice, and articulated his words so perfectly that he might be heard and understood at a great distance; especially as his auditors observed the most perfect silence. He preached one evening from the top of the Court-House steps, which are in the middle of Market Street, and on the west side of Second Street, which crosses it at right angles. Both streets were filled with his hearers to a considerable distance. Being among the hindmost in Market Street, I had the curiosity to learn how far he could be heard, by retiring backwards down the street towards the river; and I found his voice distinct till I came near Front Street, when some noise in that street obscured it. Imagining then a semicircle, of which my distance should be the radius, and that it was filled with auditors, to each of whom I allowed two square feet, I computed that he might well be heard by more than thirty thousand. This reconciled me to the newspaper accounts of his having preached to twenty-five thousand people in the fields, and to the history of generals haranguing whole armies, of which I had sometimes doubted.

By hearing him often, I came to distinguish easily between sermons newly composed, and those which he had often preached in the course of his travels. His delivery of the latter was so improved by frequent repetition that every accent, every emphasis, every modulation of voice, was so perfectly well turned and well placed that, without being interested in the subject, one could not help being pleased with the discourse; a pleasure of much the same kind with that received from an excellent piece of music. This is an advantage itinerant preachers have over those who are stationary, as the latter cannot well improve their delivery of a sermon by so many rehearsals. . . .

## 2. Nathan Cole Describes the Crowds Going to Hear Whitefield at Middletown, 1740

Now it pleased God to send Mr. Whitefield into this land; and my hearing of his preaching at Philadelphia, like one of the old apostles, and many thousands flocking to hear him preach the Gospel, and great numbers were converted to Christ, I felt the Spirit of God drawing me by conviction; I longed to see and hear him and wished he

Alan Heimert and Perry Miller, eds., *The Great Awakening* (Indianapolis: Bobbs-Merrill, 1967), pp. 184–186.

would come this way. I heard he was come to New York and the Jerseys and great multitudes flocking after him under great concern for their souls which brought on my concern more and more, hoping soon to see him; but next I heard he was at Long Island, then at Boston, and next at Northampton. Then on a sudden, in the morning about 8 or 9 of the clock there came a messenger and said Mr. Whitefield preached at Hartford and Wethersfield yesterday and is to preach at Middletown this morning at ten of the clock. I was in my field at work. I dropped my tool that I had in my hand and ran home to my wife, telling her to make ready quickly to go and hear Mr. Whitefield preach at Middletown, then ran to my pasture for my horse with all my might, fearing that I should be too late. Having my horse, I with my wife soon mounted the horse and went forward as fast as I thought the horse could bear; and when my horse got much out of breath, I would get down and put my wife on the saddle and bid her ride as fast as she could and not stop or slack for me except I bade her, and so I would run until I was much out of breath and then mount my horse again, and so I did several times to favour my horse. We improved every moment to get along as if we were fleeing for our lives, all the while fearing we should be too late to hear the sermon, for we had twelve miles to ride double in little more than an hour and we went round by the upper housen parish. And when we came within about half a mile or a mile of the road that comes down from Hartford, Wethersfield, and Stepney to Middletown, on high land I saw before me a cloud of fog arising. I first thought it came from the great river, but as I came nearer the road I heard a noise of horses' feet coming down the road, and this cloud was a cloud of dust made by the horses' feet. It arose some rods into the air over the tops of hills and trees; and when I came within about 20 rods of the road, I could see men and horses slipping along in the cloud like shadows, and as I drew nearer it seemed like a steady stream of horses and their riders, scarcely a horse more than his length behind another, all of a lather and foam with sweat, their breath rolling out of their nostrils every jump. Every horse seemed to go with all his might to carry his rider to hear news from heaven for the saving of souls. It made me tremble to see the sight, how the world was in a struggle. I found a vacancy between two horses to slip in mine and my wife said "Law, our clothes will be all spoiled, see how they look," for they were so covered with dust that they looked almost all of a colour, coats, hats, shirts, and horse. We went down in the stream but heard no man speak a word all the way for 3 miles but every one pressing forward in great haste; and when we got to Middletown old meeting house, there was a great multitude, it was said to be 3 or 4,000 of people, assembled together. We dismounted and shook off our dust, and the ministers were then coming to the meeting house. I turned and looked towards the Great River and saw the ferry boats running swift backward and forward bringing over loads of people, and the oars rowed nimble and quick. Everything, men, horses, and boats seemed to be struggling for life. The land and banks over the river looked black with people and horses; all along the 12 miles I saw no man at work in his field, but all seemed to be gone. When I saw Mr. Whitefield come upon the scaffold, he looked almost angelical; a young, slim, slender youth, before some thousands of people with a bold undaunted countenance. And my hearing how God was with him everywhere as he came along, it solemnized my mind and put me into a trembling fear before he began to preach; for he looked as if he was clothed with authority from the Great God, and a sweet solemn solemnity sat upon his brow, and my hearing him preach gave me a heart wound. By God's blessing, my old foundation was broken up, and I saw that my righteousness would not save me.

## 3. Gilbert Tennent Presents the Danger of an Unconverted Ministry, 1740

... And Pharisee-Teachers, having no Experience of a special Work of the Holy Ghost, upon their own Souls, are therefore neither inclined to, nor fitted for, Discoursing, frequently, clearly, and pathetically, upon such important Subjects. The Application of their Discourses, is either short, or indistinct and general. They difference not the Precious from the Vile, and divide not to every Man his Portion, according to the Apostolical Direction to *Timothy.* No! they carelessly offer a common Mess to their People, and leave it to them, to divide it among themselves, as they see fit. This is indeed their general Practice, which is bad enough: But sometimes they do worse, by misapplying the Word, through Ignorance, or Anger. They often strengthen the Hands of the Wicked, by promising him Life. They comfort People, before they convince them; sow before they plow; and are busy in raising a Fabrick, before they lay a Foundation. These fooling Builders do but strengthen Men's carnal Security, by their soft, selfish, cowardly Discourses. They have not the Courage, or Honesty, to thrust the Nail of Terror into sleeping Souls; nay, sometimes they strive with all their Might, to fasten Terror into the Hearts of the Righteous, and so to make those sad, whom GOD would not have made sad! And this happens, when pious People begin to suspect their Hypocrisy, for which they have good Reason. I may add, That inasmuch as Pharisee-Teachers seek after Righteousness as it were by the Works of the Law themselves, they therefore do not distinguish, as they ought, between *Law* and *Gospel* in their Discourses to others. They keep Driving, Driving, to Duty, Duty, under this Notion, That it will recommend natural Men to the Favour of GOD, or entitle them to the Promises of Grace and Salvation: And thus those blind Guides fix a deluded World upon the false Foundation of their own Righteousness; and so exclude them from the dear Redeemer. All the Doings of unconverted Men, not proceeding from the Principles of Faith, Love, and a new Nature, nor being directed to the divine Glory as their highest End, but flowing from, and tending to Self, as their Principle and End; are doubtless damnably Wicked in their Manner of Performance, and do deserve the Wrath and Curse of a Sin-avenging GOD; neither can any other Encouragement be justly given them, but this, That in the Way of Duty, there is a Peradventure or Probability of obtaining Mercy. . . .

I may add, that sad Experience verifies what has been now observed, concerning the Unprofitableness of the Ministry of unconverted Men. Look into the Congregations of unconverted Ministers, and see what a sad Security reigns there; not a Soul convinced that can be heard of, for many Years together; and yet the Ministers are easy; for they say they do their Duty! Ay, a small Matter will satisfy us in the Want of that, which we have no great Desire after. But when Persons have their

---

Gilbert Tennent, "The Danger of an Unconverted Ministry, Considered in a Sermon on Mark VI.34" in Alan Heimert and Perry Miller, eds., *The Great Awakening: Documents Illustrating the Crisis and Its Consequences* (Indianapolis and New York: Bobbs-Merrill, 1967), 76–83.

Eyes opened, and their Hearts set upon the Work of God; they are not so soon satisfied with their Doings, and with Want of Success for a Time. . . .

Third general Head was to shew, *How Pity should be expressed upon this mournful Occasion?*

*My Brethren,* We should mourn over those, that are destitute of faithful Ministers, and sympathize with them. Our Bowels should be moved with the most compassionate Tenderness, over those dear fainting Souls, that are *as Sheep having no Shepherd;* and that after the Example of our blessed LORD.

Dear Sirs! We should also most *earnestly pray* for them, that the compassionate Saviour may preserve them, by his *mighty* Power, thro' Faith unto Salvation; support their sinking Spirits, under the *melancholy Uneasinesses of a dead Ministry;* sanctify and sweeten to them the *dry* Morsels they get under such blind Men, when they have none better to repair to.

And more especially, *my Brethren,* we should pray to the LORD of the Harvest, to send forth faithful Labourers into his Harvest; seeing that the Harvest truly is plenteous, but the Labourers are few. And O Sirs! how humble, believing, and importunate should we be in this Petition! O! let us follow the LORD, Day and Night, with Cries, Tears, Pleadings and Groanings upon this Account! For GOD knows there is great *Necessity* of it. *O! thou Fountain of Mercy, and Father of Pity, pour forth upon thy poor Children a Spirit of Prayer, for the Obtaining this important Mercy! Help, help, O Eternal GOD and Father, for Christ's sake!*

And indeed, *my Brethren,* we should join our Endeavours to our *Prayers.* The most likely Method to stock the Church with a faithful *Ministry,* in the present Situation of Things, the publick Academies being so much corrupted and abused generally, is, to encourage private Schools, or Seminaries of Learning, which are under the Care of skilful and experienced Christians; in which those only should be admitted, who upon strict Examination, have in the Judgment of a reasonable *Charity,* the plain Evidences of experimental Religion. Pious and experienced Youths, who have a good natural Capacity, and great Desires after the Ministerial Work, from good Motives, might be sought for, and found up and down in the *Country,* and put to Private Schools of the Prophets; especially in such Places, where the Publick ones are not. This Method, in my Opinion, has a *noble Tendency,* to build up the Church of God. And those who have any Love to Christ, or Desire after the Coming of his Kingdom, should be *ready,* according to their Ability, to give somewhat, from time to time, for the Support of such poor Youths, who have nothing of their own. . . .

## 4. Joseph Fish Reveals the Activities of Samuel Niles, Narragansett New Light Preacher, 1765

. . . Some of the Indian Brethren (as Im informd) not in any Office, took and ordaind one Samel. *Niles* their Pastor, And he has been their Minister ever Since, for a Number of years: preaching, Administing the Supper, Baptism, and Marriage.

Reverand Joseph Fish to Dr. Joseph Sewall, September 1765, *Old Light on Separate Ways: The Narragansett Diary of Joseph Fish, 1765–1776,* eds. William S. Simmons and Cheryl L. Simmons (Hanover, NH: University Press of New England, 1982): 3–7.

This Niles, (Who I have known Some Years,) is a Sober Religious Man, of Good Sense and great Fluency of Speech; and know not but a very honest Man. Has a good deal of the Scriptures by heart, and professes a Regard for the Bible. But his unhappiness is this, He *cannot read a Word,* and So is wholly dependant Upon the (too Seldom) Reading of others: Which exposes him, (doubtless) to a great deal of Inacuracy in using Texts of Scripture, if not to gross Mistakes in the Application of them. And as hereby, (I conclude,) very Much upon the *Spirit* to teach him *Doctrine* and *Conduct,* he is in imminent danger of leaving *The Word,* for the Guidance of *Feelings, Impressions, Visions, Appearances* and *Directions* of Angels and of Christ himself in a Visionary Way. An Instance, of which I have heard of in his ordaining one Indian.

I dont learn that They Are visited and Instructed by Any english Ministers; Unless it be now and then *One* of the Seperate Stamp. I have not heard of any One of our regular Standing Ministers, being among them for Many Years: which perhaps is a Faulty omission, if they Woud be Willing to *hear* us. Which Indeed I thought they would *not,* till their Freedom to hear *Me* the Other Day, Attended with Expressions of Approbation, and Requests from Some that I'd Visit and *preach* to them Again, Convincd Me that the Door is open, much Wider than I imagind.

Im inclind to think that they are within the reach of Instruction and capable of being corrected in their religious notions, and Set right (at least greatly Mended,) in their Gospel Order, if due pains were usd, and proper Measures taken.

This woud doubtless be the most easily and effectually done, by a faithfull and prudent Missionary Sent among them, Who Should be to their liking. But I apprehend the present Times wont admit of any Such Attempt: as it might look like, (at least be taken for,) a Superceding of their Minister *Niles,* or Some way Lessening his Influence and authority—which, I Suppose Neither *He* nor *They* would relish the Thought of.

Another Method to help them, might hopefully be, by Some Neighbouring Minister, or Ministers (who Shoud be to their good Acceptance, if Such coud be found, Visiting of them and preaching to them, frequently, Taking a little time and pains by Way of free Conversation, on Religious Matters.

Or if the Honourable Commissioners Shoud think proper to Desire their Teacher *Niles,* to come and make them a Visit at Boston, They Might, by free Conversation, hopefully, assist him greatly, in Religious Matters.

The *Report* of the Indian Committee, Who Went down with a Petition for a Schoolmaster, (containing accounts of the favourable Acceptance and kind Treatment they met with,) has raisd the Commissioners So high in the Esteem of the Indians that their Influence over them must needs be Very Considerable; and, I imagine, that They have now in hand a Singular Advantage, in Some Way that their Wisdom may direct, to Serve their best Intrest to good purpose.

The poor people are not fit to be left alone, Not being Equal to the Important affair of Conducting their Religious and ecclesiastical Matters, agreable to Gospel Order. They Want Instruction, Guidance, Counsell. But the most difficult Undertaking to administer it.

I apprehend they cant bear to be told their Errors, and Mistakes in Any *direct* way of Speech. Father Sam, (as they Call him—Their Teacher Niles,) I suppose cant endure to be told, off hand, that his Ordination twas not According to Gospel Order, though ordaind, not by the Church, (for I dont learn there was Any Formed), nor by the Presbytery, As the Gospel Directs, But only by a few Individual Professing Christian

Indians. Nor will Any of them, (I imagine,) bear to be told, that the Spirit (which They think they have,) is a Safe and Sufficient Guide, Without the Scriptures, And So of *many* Enthusiastic Notions which I Suppose they have. They cant bear to be told, *Directly* that These are *Errors.* This would be too Strong meat. I apprehend They must be told, What is *Truth*—*Truth* opposite to their Errors, not mentioning *them. Be shown the right Way;* passing by the *wrong* at least for a While,) Unnoticd. So that Turning their *Eyes,* and keeping them fixd for a While, Upon *Right Objects,* they May, of themselves take up a good liking to them; and either lose Sight of the *False,* or Gradually See that they were forreign to Truth. And So with respect to all their Errors, Say little or nothing about their wrong ways, but take them by the Hand, put them into and lead them in Right *paths,* till they get a good liking to *these,* and they'll of Course leave the old, and by and by See the Danger of them. These Candi[d] Sentiments I submit to your Correction. The Indians will know that Ive writ you. And they may likely be Jealous (Jealousy being deeply rooted in their Nature,) Jealous, that I've writ Something to their Disadvantage, though I mean Nothing but their best good. If you See it needfull to tell them any thing of the Contents of Mine to you, tell them (as you may truly,) that I have writ you with the highest Friendship to their best Intrest.

## 5. A Newspaper Account of the Expulsion of James Davenport, 1742

*Extract of a Letter from* Hartford, *dated* June 15th 1742.

Sir,

*Inclos'd is a faithful Account of the Trial of Mr.* Davenport, *which I have been desired to transmit to some Friend in order to make it publick in the News-Papers: The Gentleman that drew it up, has, I believe, been desired to do it by the most considerable in the Government. Yours, etc.*

*Hartford, June* 10, 1742.

. . . And now *Sir,* As the matters complain'd of and the grounds of these proceedings are in but general terms exprest, and to gratify your curiosity as to the circumstances, etc. of the above affair, I shall proceed to give you in substance from minutes taken at the time; 1. The *principal* and more *particular things* either evidenced or conceded to. And, 2 His *behaviour* and treatment during, and sundry *circumstances* attending, the agitation of these things.

I. The *particular and principal things* either evidenced or conceded to, were,

1. That speaking of his, and his adherents *conduct* and *doctrines* and the effects thereof in the land, and under the general character of, This good work; and speaking also of the *laws of the government* made, or about to be made, to regulate or restrain the same, he declared and insisted, that *all such laws ought to be disregarded,* and were *against the laws of GOD.*

Anti-Enthusiasticus [pseud.] to *Boston Weekly Newsletter,* Boston, 1 July 1742, *The Great Awakening: Documents on the Revival of Religion, 1740–1745,* ed. Richard L. Bushman (New York, 1970): 47–49.

2. That he earnestly inculcated it upon the minds of children and youth, that this work was the work of God, which they also were engaged in carrying on; and that all *prohibitions* and *commands* of *parents and masters* not to adhere to them, and attend their religious exercises, meetings, etc. were in *no wise to be obeyed.*

3. That he declared that *people ought not to regard or attend the preaching of unconverted ministers;* and that *he was well-assured the greater part of the ministers in the country* were such.

And 4. That he endeavoured by *unwarrantable means* to *terrify* and *affect* his hearers. And that,

(1.) By pretending some *extraordinary discovery and assurance* of the very near approach of the *end of the world;* and that tho' he didn't assign the *very day,* yet that he then lately had it *clearly open'd to him,* and *strongly imprest upon his mind,* that in a very *short time* all these things will be involv'd in devouring flames. And also that on supposition and pretence of *extraordinary intercourse with heaven,* he frequently pray'd for direction and acted in his undertakings.

(2.) By an *indecent and affected imitation* of the agony and passion of our blessed SAVIOUR; and also, by *voice* and *gesture,* of the surprize, horror and amazement of persons suppos'd to be sentenc'd to eternal misery. And,

(3.) By a *too peremptory and unconditioned* denouncing damnation against such of his auditory he look'd upon as opposers; vehemently crying out, That *he saw hell-flames slashing in their faces;* and that *they were now! now! dropping down to hell;* and also added, *Lord! Thou knowest that there are many in that gallery and in these seats, that are now dropping down to Hell!* etc.

5. It appeared also, That sundry of these things happened *unseasonably* and *late at night.*

II. Touching his *behaviour* and *treatment* during, and the *circumstances* attending, the agitation of these things, take as follows, *viz*—On notice first given him by the sheriff of the will of the assembly, he shew'd himself thereto resign'd, tho' just before, it seems had been determined to a different course by the special guidance of a superior authority.

On his arrival at *Hartford,* by the indulgence of the sheriff (who from first to last, treated and entertain'd at his own house, him and Mr. *Pomroy,* with unexceptionable tenderness and civility) he spent the first night, and the greater part of the next day, among his special friends [and] followers, uninterrupted in religious Devotions; in his way: by no means therein forgetting to vent the most virulent invectives against both ministers and magistrates, especially the general assembly, representing them as opposers of the work of God, and doing the work of the devil, etc.

Nextly, view him at the barr of the asembly: his approach to which, his air and posture there; that inflexibility of body, that affectatious oblique reclining of the head, that elevation, or rather inversion of the eyes, that forced negligence and retirement of soul, and that uncouth shew, that motly mixture of pride and gravity wrought up to sullenness, is not easily to be described. . . . With vehement stentorian voice, and wild distortions of body, said *Davenport* began an exhortation; on which the sheriff, by speaking and gently taking him by the sleeve, endeavouring to silence and remove him, he instantly fell a praying, crying out, *Lord! thou knowest somebody's got hold of my sleeve, strike them! Lord, strike them*—which said *Pomroy* also observing cry'd out to the sheriff and his assistants, *take heed how you do that heaven daring action! 'tis heaven-daring presumption, to take him away! and the God of Heaven will assuredly avenge it on you! strike them, Lord, strike them!* many of the concourse beginning to sigh, groan, beat their breasts, cry out, and to be put into strange agitations of body. Others of their adherents rushing in violently interposed to prevent and resist the sheriff; while others refused their assistance when commanded, saying, *they were serving the devil,* etc. . . .

In the mean time, almost all night, in other parts of the town, were such shocking scenes of horror and confusion, under the name and pretext of religious devotion, as language can't describe. Which wild ungovernable efforts of enthusiastic zeal and fury, being regarded as a bold and threatening insult upon the whole legislative body of the government, then on the spot; orders were forthwith given out to one of the commanding officers of the town, with about forty men in arms the next morning to wait upon the assembly; and so 'til the conclusion of these affairs: to prevent further insolencies, which seem'd to be threatening. Which orders were accordingly observed 'til the rising of the assembly.

But to return: Next morning being again bro't before the assembly, and seeming more on a level with his fellow-mortals, and to act something in resemblance of a man, being put on his defence, he on motion, had the witnesses which the night before had given in their evidence, interrogated anew: The import of which interrogation was, Whether when they had heard him express himself as abovesaid, touching obedience to laws, etc. and the end of the world, etc. he didn't thereto annex some qualifying words from whence different construction might be put upon what he delivered? To which they all answer'd in the negative. Nextly, His own witnesses being sworn and interrogated, and especially touching such qualifications, answered generally, affirmatively, that he did so qualify such of said expressions as they heard, full to their satisfaction and understanding; but on more particular inquiry what any of those qualifying expressions were, were not able to tell one word.

Then on his defence proceeding with a demeanour wholly his own, insisted, That the apparent effects of his ministry might well authenticate his conduct—That the greater part of the ministers in the land were undoubtedly unconverted; and that four or five of them had lately own'd to him *they* were such—That he had lately had clear discoveries and strong impressions made on his mind touching these things, etc.—And in a word, in the face of the assembly spake and acted so like himself, as to render in a measure useless all other evidence of his extravagancies. . . .

I am Sir, Yours, etc.
Anti-Enthusiasticus.

# 6. The Reverend Charles Woodmason
## Views the Backcountry in the 1760s

. . . Saturday September 3) Rode down the Country on the West Side the Wateree River into the Fork between that and the Congaree River—This is out of my

---

Reprinted, by permission of the editor and the publisher, from *The Carolina Backcountry on the Eve of the Revolution: The Journal and Other Writings of Charles Woodmason, Anglican Itinerant,* edited by Richard J. Hooker. Published for the Institute of Early American History and Culture, Williamsburg, Virginia. © 1969 The University of North Carolina Press.

Bounds—But their having no Minister, and their falling (therefrom) continually from the Church to Anabaptism, inclin'd me to it—The People received me gladly and very kindly. Had on Sunday 4—a Company of about 150—Most of them of the Low Class—the principal Planters living on the Margin of these Rivers.

Baptiz'd 1 Negroe Man—2 Negroe Children—and 9 White Infants and married 1 Couple—The People thanked me in the most kind Manner for my Services—I had very pleasant Riding but my Horse suffered Greatly. The Mornings and Evenings now begin to be somewhat Cool, but the Mid day heat is almost intolerable—Many of these People walk 10 or 12 Miles with their Children in the burning Sun—Ought such to be without the Word of God, when so earnest, so desirous of hearing it and becoming Good Christians, and good Subjects! How lamentable to think, that the Legislature of this Province will make no Provision—so rich, so luxurious, polite a People! Yet they are deaf to all Solicitations, and look on the poor White People in a Meaner Light than their Black Slaves, and care less for them. Withal there is such a Republican Spirit still left, so much of the Old Leaven of Lord Shaftsbury and other the 1st principal Settlers still remains, that they seem not at all disposed to promote the Interest of the Church of England—Hence it is that above 30,000£ Sterling have lately been expended to bring over 5 or 6000 Ignorant, mean, worthless, beggarly Irish Presbyterians, the Scum of the Earth, and Refuse of Mankind, and this, solely to ballance the Emigrations of People from Virginia, who are all of the Established Church.—50 [miles]; [total] Miles 2846

It will require much Time and Pains to New Model and form the Carriage and Manners, as well as Morals of these wild Peoples—Among this Congregation not one had a Bible or Common Prayer—or could join a Person or hardly repeat the Creed or Lords Prayer—Yet all of 'em had been educated in the Principles of our Church. So that I am obliged to read the Whole Service, omitting such Parts, as are Repetitious, and retaining those that will make the different Services somewhat Uniform—Hence it is, that I can but seldom use the Litany, because they know not the Responses.

It would be (as I once observ'd before) a Great Novelty to a Londoner to see one of these Congregations—The Men with only a thin Shirt and pair of Breeches or Trousers on—barelegged and barefooted—The Women bare-headed, barelegged and barefoot with only a thin Shift and under Petticoat—Yet I cannot break [them?] of this—for the heat of the Weather admits not of any [but] thin Cloathing—I can hardly bear the Weight of my Whig and Gown, during Service. The Young Women have a most uncommon Practise, which I cannot break them off. They draw their Shift as tight as possible to the Body, and pin it close, to shew the roundness of their Breasts, and slender Waists (for they are generally finely shaped) and draw their Petticoat close to their Hips to shew the fineness of their Limbs—so that they might as well be in Puri Naturalibus—Indeed Nakedness is not censurable or indecent here, and they expose themselves often quite Naked, without Ceremony— Rubbing themselves and their Hair with Bears Oil and tying it up behind in a Bunch like the Indians—being hardly one degree removed from them—In few Years, I hope to bring about a Reformation, as I already have done in several Parts of the Country.— . . .

Received Letters from England—One acquaints me with death of the Reverend Mr. Crallan, 10 days after his Embarking. This is the 13th or 14th of the Clergy dead or gone here within these 2 Years—This Gentleman grew insane before his departure. He was a Saint—An Angel in his Life and Manners— A most pious and devout Young Man, and yet he could not escape the Censure of these flighty, Proud, Illprincipled Carolin[i]ans. They are enough to make any Person run Mad—And they crack'd the Brain of one Young Man Mr. Amory the Year before. We have two now in the same Condition—And others, whose Situation is so uneasy, that Life is a Burden to them—I would not wish my worst Enemy to come to this Country (at least to this) Part of it to combat perpetually with Papists, Sectaries, Atheists and Infidels—who would rather see the Poor People remain Heathens and Ignorants, than to be brought over to the Church. Such Enemies to Christ and his Cross, are these vile Presbyterians. . . .

But let us go on, and examine if in the General Corruption of Manners these New Lights have made any Reform in the Vice of Drunkenness? Truly, I wot not. There is not one Hogshead of Liquor less consum'd since their visiting us, or any Tavern shut up—So far from it, that there has been Great Increase of Both. Go to any Common Muster or Vendue, Will you not see the same Fighting, Brawling Gouging, Quarreling as ever? And this too among the Holy ones of our New Israel? Are Riots, Frolics, Races, Games, Cards, Dice, Dances, less frequent now than formerly? Are fewer persons to be seen in Taverns? or reeling or drunk on the Roads? And have any of the Godly Storekeepers given up their Licences, or refus'd to retail Poison? If this can be made appear, I will yield the Point. But if [it] can be made apparent that a much greater Quantity of Rum is now expended in private families than heretofore—That the greater Part of these religious Assemblies are calculated for private Entertainments, where each brings his Quota and which often terminates in Intemperance and Intoxication and both Sexes, Young and Old: That one half of those who resort to these Assemblies Go more for sake of Liquor, than Instruction, or Devotion. That if it be proven that Liquor has been top'd about even in their very Meeting Houses, and the Preachers refreshed with Good Things, and after the Farce ended Stuff'd and Cramm'd almost to bursting, then it must be granted that little or no Reform has been made among the Vulgar in Point of Intemperance save only among some few Persons in some Places where the Mode only is chang'd, and drinking in Public wav'd for the Indulgence of double the Consumption in Private.

The horrid Vice of Swearing has long been a reproach to the Back Inhabitants, and very justly—for few Countries on Earth can equal these Parts as to this greivous Sin. But has it ceas'd since the Admission of rambling Fanatics among us? I grant that it has with and among many, whom they have gain'd to their Sect. Yet still it too much prevails. But the Enormity of this Vice, when at the Highest, produc'd no Evils, Jarrs, disturbances Strifes, Contentions, Variance, Dissimulations, Envyings, Slanders, Backbitings and a thousand other Evils that now disturb both the Public Places and repose of Individuals. So that where they have cast out one Devil, Seven, and twice Seven others have enter'd In and possess the Man. For never was so much Lying, Calumny, Defamation, and all hellish Evils and vexations of this Sort that can spring from the Devil and his Angels, so brief so prevalent, so abounding as since the Arrival of these villanous Teachers, Who blast, blacken, Ruin, and destroy the Characters, Reputations, Credit and Fame of all Persons not linked with them to the Ruin of Society, the Peace of families, and the Settlement of the Country.

We will further enquire, if Lascivousness, or Wantoness, Adultery or Fornication [are] less common than formerly, before the arrival of these *Holy* Persons? Are there fewer Bastards born? Are more Girls with their Virginity about them, Married, than were heretofore? The Parish Register will prove the Contrary: There are rather more Bastards, more Mullatoes born than before. Nor out of 100 Young Women that I marry in a Year have I seen, or is there seen, Six but what are with Child? And this as Common with the Germans on other Side the River, as among You on this Side: So that a Minister is accounted as a Scandalous Person for even coming here to marry such People, and for baptizing their Bastard Children as the Law obliges Me to register All Parties who are Married, and all Children Born. This occasions such Numbers (especially of the Saints) to fly into the next Province, and up to the German Ministers and any where to get Married, to prevent their being register'd, as therefrom the Birth of their Children would be trac'd: And as for Adulteries, the present State of most Persons around 9/10 of whom now labour under a fifthy Distemper (as is well known to all) puts that Matter out of all Dispute and shews that the Saints however outwardly Precise and Reserved are not one Whit more Chaste than formerly, and possibly are more privately Vicious.

And nothing more leads to this Than what they call their Love Feasts and Kiss of Charity. To which Feasts, celebrated at Night, much Liquor is privately carried, and deposited on the Roads, and in Bye Paths and Places. The Assignations made on Sundays at the Singing Clubs, are here realized. And it is no wonder that Things are as they are, when many Young Persons have 3. 4. 5. 6 Miles to walk home in the dark Night, with Convoy, thro' the Woods? Or staying perhaps all Night at some Cabbin (as on Sunday Nights) and sleeping together either doubly or promiscuously? Or a Girl being mounted behind a Person to be carried home, or any wheres. All this indeed contributes to multiply Subjects for the King in this frontier Country, and so is wink'd at by the Magistracy and Parochial Officers but at some time, gives great Occasion to the Enemies of Virtue, to triumph, for Religion to be scandalized and brought into Contempt; For all Devotion to be Ridicul'd, and in the Sequel, will prove the Entire banishment and End of all Religion—Confusion—Anarchy and ev'ry Evil Work will be the Consequence of such Lewdness and Immorality.

But certainly these Reformers have put some Stop to the many Thefts and Depradations so openly committed of late Years?—To answer this Question recourse must be had to the Magistrates and Courts of Justice, who are ready to declare, that since the Appearance of these New Lights, more Enormities of all Kinds have been committed—More Robberies Thefts, Murders, Plunderings, Burglaries and Villanies of ev'ry Kind, than ever before. And the Reason hereof, Is, That most of these Preaching fellows were most notorious Thieves, Jockeys, Gamblers, and what not in the Northern Provinces, and since their Reception and Success here have drawn Crowds of their old Acquaintances after them; so that the Country never was so full as at present of Gamesters Prostitutes, Filchers, Racers, Fidlers and all the refuse of Mankind. All which follow these Teachers, and under the Mask of Religion carry on many detestable Practises. In short, they have filled the Country with Idle and Vagrant Persons, who live by their Criminalities. For it is a Maxim with these

Vermin of Religion, That a Person must first be a Sinner e're He can be a Saint. And I am bold to say, That the Commonality around, do not now make half the Crops nor are $\frac{1}{4}$ so Industrious, as 3 Years ago. Because half their Time is wasted in traveling about to this and that Lecture—and to hear this and that fine Man, So that they are often a Month absent from their families. . . .

For only draw a Comparison between them and Us, and let an Impartial Judge determine where *Offence* may chiefly be taken, At our Solemn, Grave, and Serious Sett Forms, or their Wild Extempore Jargon, nauseaus to any Chaste or refin'd Ear. There are so many Absurdities committed by them, as wou'd shock one of our *Cherokee* Savages; And was a Sensible Turk or Indian to view some of their Extravagancies it would quickly determine them against Christianity. Had any such been in their Assembly as last Sunday when they communicated, the Honest Heathens would have imagin'd themselves rather amidst a Gang of frantic Lunatics broke out of Bedlam, rather than among a Society of religious Christians, met to celebrate the most sacred and Solemn Ordinance of their Religion. Here, one Fellow mounted on a Bench with the Bread, and bawling, *See the Body of Christ,* Another with the Cup running around, and bellowing—*Who cleanses his Soul with the Blood of Christ,* and a thousand other Extravagancies—One on his knees in a Posture of Prayer—Others singing—some howling—These Ranting—Those Crying—Others dancing, Skipping, Laughing and rejoycing. Here two or 3 Women falling on their Backs, kicking up their Heels, exposing their Nakedness to all Bystanders and others sitting Pensive, in deep Melancholy lost in Abstraction, like Statues, quite insensible—and when rous'd by the Spectators from their pretended Reveries Transports, and indecent Postures and Actions declaring they knew nought of the Matter. That their Souls had taken flight to Heav'n, and they knew nothing of what they said or did. Spect[at]ors were highly shocked at such vile Abuse of sacred Ordinances! And indeed such a Scene was sufficient to make the vilest Sinner shudder. Their Teacher, so far from condemning, or reproving, them, call'd it, the Work of God, and returned Thanks for Actions deserving of the Pillory and Whipping Post. But that would not have been *New* to some of them. And if they can thus transgress all bounds of Decency Modesty, and Morality, in such an Open Public Manner, it is not hard to conceive what may pass at their Nocturnal Meetings, and Private Assemblies. Is there any thing like this in the Church of England to give Offence?

But another vile Matter that does and must give Offence to all Sober Minds Is, what they call their *Experiences;* It seems, that before a Person be dipp'd, He must give an Account of his Secret Calls, Conviction, Conversion, Repentance &c &c. Some of these Experiences have been so ludicrous and ridiculous that *Democritus* in Spite of himself must have burst with Laughter. Others, altogether as blasphemous Such as their Visions, Dreams, Revelations—and the like; Too many, and too horrid to be mention'd. Nothing in the *Alcoran* Nothing that can be found in all the Miracles of the Church of Rome, and all the Reveries of her Saints can be so absurd, or so Enthusiastic, as what has gravely been recited in that *Tabernacle* Yonder—To the Scandal of Religion and Insult of Common Sense. And to heighten the Farce, To see two or three fellows with fix'd Countenances and grave Looks, hearing all this Nonsense for Hours together, and making particular Enquiries, when, How, Where, in what Manner, these Miraculous Events happen'd—To see, I say, a

Sett of Mongrels under Pretext of Religion, Sit, and hear for Hours together a String of Vile, cook'd up, Silly and Senseless Lyes, What they know to be Such, What they are Sensible has not the least foundation in Truth or Reason, and to encourage Persons in such Gross Inventions must grieve, must give great Offence to ev'ry one that has the Honour of Christianity at Heart.

Then again to see them Divide and Sub divide, Split into Parties—Rail at and excommunicate one another—Turn out of Meeting, and receive into another—And a Gang of them getting together and gabbing one after the other (and sometimes disputing against each other) on Abstruse Theological Question—Speculative Points—Abstracted Notions, and Scholastic Subtelties, such as the greatest Metaph[ys]icians and Learned Scholars never yet could define, or agree on—To hear Ignorant Wretches, who can not write—Who never read ten Pages in any Book, and can hardly read the Alphabett discussing such Knotty Points for the Edification of their Auditors, is a Scene so farcical, so highly humoursome as excels any Exhibition of Folly that has ever yet appear'd in the World, and consequently must give High offence to all Inteligent and rational Minds.

If any Thing offensive beyond all This to greive the Hearts and Minds of serious Christians presents it Self to view among them, it is their Mode of Baptism, to which Lascivous Persons of both Sexes resort, as to a Public Bath. I know not whether it would not be less offensive to Modesty for them to strip wholly into Buff at once, than to be dipp'd with those very thin Linen Drawers they are equipp'd in—Which when wet, so closely adheres to the Limbs, as exposes the Nudities equally as if none at All. If this be not Offensive and a greivous Insult on all Modesty and Decency among Civiliz'd People I know not what can be term'd so. Certainly a few chosen Witnesses of the Sex of the Party, and performance of the Ceremony in a Tent, or Cover'd Place, would be equally as *Editying,* as Persons being stript and their Privities expos'd before a gaping Multitude who resort to these Big Meetings (as they are term'd) as they would to a Bear or Bullbaiting.

It must give Great Scandal and Offence to all Serious Minds thus to see the Solemn Ordinances of God become the Sport, Pastime and Derision of Men. . . .

# E S S A Y S

In the first essay Timothy D. Hall of Central Michigan University examines the impact of itineracy, the practice of ministers moving from place to place to preach, on the religious life of Americans in the early decades of the eighteenth century. He attributes the revivals that swept the colonies to the activities of the itinerants and to writings about them, and shows how they broke down local boundaries and gave Americans access to a transatlantic world of experience. Many ministers welcomed the itinerants and tried to shape the way in which their message would be experienced by the congregations.

In the second essay Frank Lambert analyzes the role of the greatest of the itinerants, George Whitefield, whose tours of the colonies from Georgia to New England spurred waves of awakenings. Lambert traces Whitefield's huge success to his adoption of the mass merchandising techniques of the burgeoning transatlantic marketplace that he used to create a demand for spiritual access by people from all walks of life.

# Itinerancy and the Awakenings

### TIMOTHY D. HALL

. . . Revivalists united in the belief that a "great and general awakening" had issued directly from the "special Labours" of George Whitefield, Gilbert Tennent, and "other itinerant Preachers, animated by their good Example." . . .

This willingness to identify itinerancy so thoroughly with the "great revival" imposed an enormous interpretive burden on the revivalist ministers who employed printed literature to represent the movement to a reading public. It required that they develop an alternative reading of the language of going into other men's parishes— one that countered Old Light images of disorder with visions of a newfound openness to receive the Spirit of God wherever and however the Spirit willed to appear. The task also challenged revivalist ministers to explore the new possibilities for human action and identity which itinerancy represented. The freedom with which itinerants traversed the empire, drawing throngs wherever they appeared; the appeal of their message across boundaries of race, class, and gender; the readiness of large numbers everywhere to forsake the parish ministry and hang on a stranger's every word—these novel attitudes and behaviors had afforded a glimpse of possibilities that barely existed in the bounded, deferential, face-to-face world of the parish. Revivalist ministers produced the vast majority of published material in defense of the Awakening. To them fell the task of construing itinerancy and its attendant phenomena as manifestations of God's blessing rather than judgment. . . .

. . . Itinerancy made possible a world radically open to the free operation of God's Spirit, which could operate unhindered by human boundaries of space, time, custom, class, race, or gender through those who disseminated the gospel freely to all in every place. The defenders of itinerancy proclaimed themselves the true guardians of vital Christianity in this expansive world.

Throughout this process of interpretation, defenders of itinerancy implicitly criticized the Old Lights' strict parochialism while generating a tacit model of the dynamic, expansive world in which itinerancy throve. . . .

Revivalists attempted to turn the criticism of itinerancy on its head by casting the practice, despite its attendant disorders, as part of the solution to a much deeper problem of religious decline. Revivalists throughout the empire claimed that the outbreak of revival had arrested the irreligion that was "rushing in, even upon the Protestant world like a flood," prompting pious men to doubt of "the Continuance of Christianity among us." . . .

Itinerants had reversed the course of this decline by reviving the "searching and awakening preaching" which too many parish ministers had forsaken. God had given George Whitefield a "wonderful *Manner of Entrance*" in every place he visited, drawing "Old and Young, Parents and Children, Masters and Servants, high and low, rich and poor together, gathering and passing as *Clouds* in the *Streets.*" Gilbert Tennent encountered the same response as he traveled in the Middle Colonies and New England, "delivering his Message with Vehemence, Importunity

Timothy D. Hall, "Itinerancy and the Evangelical Imagination," *Contested Boundaries: Itinerancy and the Reshaping of the Colonial American Religious World,* pp. 71–99. Copyright 1994, Duke University Press. All rights reserved. Reprinted with permission.

& Thunder." God's Spirit had used the work of these and others who followed their example to catch "Multitudes in the Gospel Net," prompting New Light bards to "honour those (altho' Itinerants) / who have herein been happy Instruments."

In the context of this vast outbreak of revival, the refusal of many parish clergy to admit its "happy Instruments" into their parishes revealed to New Lights the glaring inadequacies in the Old Light conception of the parochial system. Revivalists argued that by claiming such absolute authority over what transpired within their parish bounds, Old Lights not only obstructed the work of "faithful servants of Christ" but also attempted to seal their parish bounds against the Holy Spirit himself. Such naked arrogation of power flaunted the will of God and the laws of man. . . .

Although many revivalist ministers expressed concerns about the disorder caused by itinerants like James Davenport, they recognized that a new world was taking shape in which ministers could no longer hope to maintain their moral and spiritual authority simply by defending parish boundaries. In earlier times orthodox ministers could draw on the localistic sentiments of their parishioners when they asserted their spiritual leadership against figures such as traveling Quaker prophets. Yet now, Davenport's ability to win a following by denouncing parish ministers demonstrated how readily people would abandon local loyalties to entertain a "stranger" within their parish bounds or leave their home parish to hear him elsewhere. Revivalist pastors who permitted the "preaching of the Word of God by Strangers" found that an alliance with itinerants enhanced their status among parishioners. A message from a stranger could now carry more weight than one from the parish clergy. God's Spirit seemed to them to be blessing this novel social reality by using itinerancy to spread revival despite its potential for disorder.

Recognition of this reality led defenders to see the problem posed by itinerancy as one of regulation rather than repression. . . .

The defense began, therefore, with a definition of itinerancy that minimized its inconsistencies with the Puritan tradition of ministry. Defenders commonly argued that itinerancy should only be practiced, in the Reverend William Hobby's words, by men who "being ordained minister[s] of Christ, and yet not having any particular pastoral Charge of [their] own, make it [their] business to go from Place to Place preaching the Gospel of Jesus Christ." This definition excluded lay exhorters, reserving itinerancy for those who possessed the qualifications for ministry most important in the Puritan tradition: conversion, adequate education, preparation, and calling for ministry certified by ordination. The assumption that the practice of itinerancy belonged exclusively to ordained ministers was present in most discussions of the concept. Apart from James Davenport and Andrew Croswell, few revivalist ministers approved the intrusion of "*illiterate* and *half-learnt*" persons into the gospel ministry. . . .

Having restricted the practice of itinerancy to men who were educated and ordained, revivalists set out to defend it as a legitimate means of bringing the Puritan tradition forward into the eighteenth-century world. . . .

For revivalists as well as opposers the loosening of boundaries formed a central theme of discourse about itinerancy and the Awakening, but the literary defenders of itinerancy celebrated rather than lamented the new openness. Itinerancy had enabled Whitefield and others to break through conventional bounds of space, time, denomination, class, even gender and race in response to the Spirit's leading. An empirewide revival had resulted in "circumstances so wonderful" that William Cooper believed "there has not been the like since the extraordinary pouring out of the Spirit immediately after our Lord's ascension." . . . These dramatic results justified continued use of itinerancy despite any disorder that might attend it.

For revivalists, the glorious extent of the work more than compensated for the tendency of itinerancy to weaken traditional patterns of deference and decorum within the localities. Where Old Lights fought to preserve the "station" of each person within a bounded, hierarchical network of face-to-face relationships, revivalists yielded to and often celebrated the erosion of such boundaries as the Spirit's work. . . .

. . . Accounts in newspapers, pamphlets, and periodicals of the 1740s reveal that awakening usually came to communities of the British North Atlantic in the wake of an itinerant's visit. . . . Some ministers, to be sure, attempted to avoid allegations of disorder or to stress the supernatural work of the Spirit by minimizing outside influences and insisting on the spontaneous nature of a local revival. Yet very few were truly spontaneous. From 1734 on, revival generally spread as people heard of revivals elsewhere by printed matter, word of mouth, or firsthand from an itinerant minister. . . .

Among the varied forces that were eroding local boundaries, itinerancy and print were by far the most visible. Long-distance ties of trade, credit, and consumption also contributed to the opening of local bounds through increased participation in the world beyond the parish. Colonial merchants and planters conducted business and received lines of credit from unseen contacts an ocean away. Ordinary colonists avidly sought an increasing range of imported goods. Yet these links by themselves played at the edge of most people's consciousness, exciting sustained reflection primarily among debt-laden merchants, eighteenth-century political economists, and social theorists. Print, on the other hand, drew readers out of their provincial horizons into conscious participation in a reading, thinking British public that spanned the Atlantic. Itinerancy cut across boundaries to challenge directly the deferential, face-to-face relationships which had traditionally fixed the members of the community in clearly defined roles. For critics itinerancy functioned both as a powerful symbol of a general loosening of eighteenth-century boundaries and as an instrument by which they were further loosened. For converts it modeled an alternative way of situating the self in this open world, a model which the *Christian History* and other prorevival publications encouraged by self-consciously striving to foster the sense of participation in a movement of empirewide scope. . . .

. . . Participation in the Awakening demanded that the parish minister gladly accept a diminished role in the religious and social life of the community. He must no longer expect to act as the primary anchor of the parish's moral and spiritual life, or expect to play the role of a spiritual broker mediating unity among the parishes. Instead, revivalist pamphleteers urged him to relinquish a significant measure of his spiritual and moral authority to strangers, and to permit his own conduct and character to be judged by his willingness to cooperate with the movement. It cannot "grieve an holy faithful Pastor." . . . "If other Workmen drive his Nails yet faster."

Friends of revival also argued that participation in this potentially boundless movement required a willingness to recognize the priority of the New Birth and faith over denominational differences. George Whitefield's itinerancy dramatized this as the Anglican cleric rejected captivity to any single denomination, preached from dissenting pulpits across the empire, held "sweet conversations" with Quakers, and shared the Lord's Supper with Baptist, Presbyterian, and Congregationalist alike. American revivalists followed Whitefield's example with their own evangelical ecumenism. . . .

Most significant, however, was the effect that participation in this empirewide movement of God exerted on the way in which individual colonists, parishioners and ministers alike, shaped their social identities as the horizons of their world expanded. "Strangers" with little stake in the local community were displacing parish ministers as the "happy instruments of conversion" for an increasing number of people. Itinerants worked primarily to draw these converts into a transatlantic work of God. Some, like Whitefield and Tennent, allied with local ministers and left to them the problem of integrating converts into the bounded, deferential moral world of the parish. Some went much further, denouncing that world and urging converts to reject it. . . . Conversion was beginning to draw people into a worldwide community of imagined strangers bound together by a power transcending local church covenants: a common experience of new birth supplemented by a vast network of itinerancy and print.

The doctrine of inward assurance complemented this reorientation of the self within a long-distance, anonymous community by weakening the networks of deference and obligation which bound persons exclusively to specific local stations within local parishes. The direct "witness of God's Spirit" with the convert's spirit diminished the need to submit one's experience of grace to the approval of one's neighbors or parish minister. . . .

Revivalist ministers further encouraged this reorientation of the self in their eagerness to open their parishes to the Spirit's vast outpouring. They not only entertained itinerants from afar but relaxed or inverted traditional patterns of deference in the quest for souls. . . . Compassion for tender young souls prompted George Whitefield to bypass ordinary familial deference by urging, "Little children, if your parents will not come to Christ, do you come, and go to Heaven without them!" Several revival accounts described how the Spirit had used to "saving effect" the words of children who threw off customary deference to exhort adults and words of slaves who dared to exhort masters. . . .

Revival narratives composed during the Awakening likewise reflect the reorientation of the newborn self within a wider, more open setting than the immediate environment of the local parish. The locus of God's dealings with the individual remained in the heart and soul, and the pastor's ministrations continued to play a role for most. Yet the Spirit brought the light of grace to the hearts of increasing numbers by the mouths of strangers who traveled long distances "like . . . the old apostles." The narrative of the Connecticut farmer Nathan Cole, for example, reveals a poignant awareness that its author's experience was part of a movement of God's Spirit which had already drawn "many thousands" in England, Pennsylvania, New York, and the Jerseys. The mere report of "great numbers converted to Christ" in these places prompted Cole to feel "the Spirit of God drawing me by conviction." The Spirit chose the moment when Cole first saw Whitefield in Middletown, Connecticut to inflict the "heart wound" that would eventuate in his conversion. The youthful David Brainerd, though not converted under the preaching of George

Whitefield, declared the news of the Grand Itinerant's passage "through the land" a "great comfort to him" in his spiritual travails. . . .

Prorevival correspondence and publications began flooding across the parishes of the empire, further enhancing the sense of a dynamic movement that knew no bounds. George Whitefield's *Journals* appeared at regular intervals throughout his first American tour, permitting readers to trace the Spirit's path throughout southern England, across the Atlantic, and along the colonial coastline. Newspaper accounts, often submitted by revivalists, reminded all readers that the Spirit was at work simultaneously in the colonies and in places as distant as Edinburgh and Rotterdam. The *Christian History,* which had counterparts in London and Glasgow, labored to expand these conceptual horizons even further by collecting in one publication accounts of revival wherever it occurred. Within its pages a reader could learn that revival had not only swept across New England but had reached Philadelphia, the Jerseys, Charleston, Wales, England, Scotland, and even Egypt. . . .

While eighteenth-century evangelistic itinerancy promised revival on an unprecedented scale, it also posed an intellectual challenge for the historically conscious religious leaders who advocated it. . . . This preoccupation with history represented more than mere nostalgia for the primitive piety of a bygone age. It also represented more than an attempt to retreat into that age from the commercial transformations of the eighteenth century, much as revivalists deplored their age's preoccupation with "increase Cent per Cent." On the contrary, this New Light interpretative enterprise formed a vital element of a larger effort to bring that older piety forward into a new mobile world of commerce and communication, to adapt the message of New Birth to that world, and to take advantage of new means made available by the commercial revolution for maintaining genuine piety in places already Christianized as well as for proclaiming the message more widely than ever before. . . .

. . . Revivalists compared the "dead formalism" of eighteenth-century religious leaders to the New Testament accounts of first-century Pharisees who had abused their authority to maintain their place within a corrupt social order. It was only natural that such persons should regard a dramatic revival of genuine piety as a threat to their position, especially when it seemed to parallel so closely the apostolic era's spread of the gospel to the farthest reaches of a vast empire.

These elaborate comparisons enabled revivalists to see the openness and dynamism of the New Testament world reflected in their own eighteenth-century context. They also found their new liberty to preach where they wished fully reflected in New Testament practice. The choices which their mobile world had opened to them had also been available to their first-century predecessors. Thomas Prince of Boston declared to the consternation of critics that "our Blessed Saviour was an Itinerant Preacher; and that he preach'd in no other Way." . . .

Prorevival pamphlets sought to delegitimate Old Light opposition to itinerancy by casting it as a resurgence of first-century persecution of Jesus and his disciples. . . .

. . . Defenders of itinerancy followed up by casting it as a revival of the apostles' method for flouting such man-made barriers to the "Work." No "precedent Practice" in either Scripture or English law gave ministers the power to prohibit itinerancy, observed a writer to the *Boston Gazette.* Jesus did not "ask Leave of the

Jewish Doctors and Teachers to preach and teach in their Temple & Synagogues, much less in the Streets and private Houses." Neither did he direct his apostles to "ask Leave of the Rulers either of Church or State, and to forbear preaching where such Leave could not be obtained." Indeed, their example authorized "every true Minister of Christ to preach in any Place where God shall give him Opportunity." Nowhere in Scripture had either Christ or his apostles "restrictive Bounds defin'd / of Time or Place to preach or hear [God's] Mind."

The revivalist reading of Scripture presented the hopeful vision of a world radically open to the free movement of the Spirit of God through men equipped and poised to go anywhere to preach his gospel at any time. In this vision the Old Lights' "Bounds of time and place" and "Rules and good Order" took on the character of oppressive, illusory structures that secured stability by squeezing the life out of religion, obscuring the light of the Gospel and shutting the meetinghouse door and parish line against the Spirit's visitation. . . .

Testimonies of contributors and extracts from the writings of English divines confirmed that since the dawn of the English Reformation, zeal for the message of the New Birth had often prompted English Protestant itinerants to flout church order in pursuit of souls. In the days of Elizabeth, it had spurred Richard Rothwell to undertake a traveling ministry that earned him the title "Apostle of the North." Godly English preachers ever since had been ready when necessary to ignore parish bounds and church order to disseminate the message of the New Birth. . . .

Although these historical examples were chosen to demonstrate that revivalists, not their opponents, held legitimate title to the Reformation tradition, their significance extended far beyond that. The examples showed how God's "Free Spirit" often led faithful ministers to break out of man-made ecclesiastical structures in order to deal with people's souls. Godly people had paid "due respect" to ecclesiastical order whenever possible, but had regarded no boundary of time or place as absolute and no form so inflexible as to hinder proclamation of the New Birth. Biblical and ecclesiastical history consistently supported Samuel Finley's contention that God always did something extraordinary to reform his Church. Itinerancy provided an appropriate—indeed almost literal—model of the Spirit's activity in the expansive eighteenth-century world.

While revivalist ministers worked to expand the conceptual horizons of their congregations and their reading public, few wished to abolish the parish and none to abandon converts to antinomian license. Revivalists detected in the practice of James Davenport, Andrew Croswell, and their unruly followers the echo of the seventeenth-century visionary Anne Hutchinson, whose belief in inward assurance was thought to have led her followers to forsake moral, orderly behavior as mere "works-righteousness." Ministerial friends of the revival responded by employing print media to dissociate themselves from the extremism of Davenport and Croswell. They reaffirmed their regard for the concept of the "settled ministry." They continued to profess esteem for proper training and dismay at the "invasion of the ministerial office" by "illiterate and half-learnt" lay exhorters. Most important, they represented the "essential part" of the transatlantic revival as productive of the enduring peace, order, and harmony which came through the New Birth. . . .

Gilbert Tennent made one of the earliest attempts to renegotiate the boundaries of parochial deference in a newspaper essay responding to published criticism of his

1741 tour through New England. Tennent's critic had charged him with abandoning his own flock for months on end to intrude uninvited into New England ministers' parishes in the vain conceit that he could "do more Good" than they. The itinerant's response was a model of humility and cooperation whose themes would be echoed and developed for several years. Tennent assured his readers that he had not left his own flock without a shepherd. Ministers "of whose integrity I have good Assurance" had voluntarily supplied his people. His decision to travel had not been made out of vain conceit but in response to "importunate" invitations from New England ministers and then only after much soul searching and prayer. Through these he overcame reluctance to tax his "mean Qualification of Mind and cold Constitution of Body" and set out to "promote God's kingdom by traveling." . . .

Defenders of itinerancy also labored to accommodate the behavior of the awakened while preserving order within assemblies and communities. The method's penchant for breaking down social constraints, releasing people to express terrors and joys with unchecked emotion, not only provoked the outrage of foes but also caused discomfort among friends. James Davenport had fueled the fires of controversy by throwing off all restraints, whipping the emotions of his hearers to a fever pitch, leading followers in disorderly procession through the streets of towns with loud singing, even seeming to base the authenticity of conversion on the intensity of emotional release. He had urged people to separate from unconverted ministers, even to shape their conduct exclusively by private impressions and convictions informed by a personal reading of Scripture. Revivalist ministers shared Old Light concerns that such persons were cutting themselves entirely adrift from traditional networks of behavioral constraints.

Revivalist leaders responded by fashioning bounds of decorum which could prevent disruption of communal harmony without denying the validity of emotional religious experience. Jonathan Edwards and Jonathan Dickinson led the way by developing a theology of the Spirit's work in revival that placed strong affections at the very core of true religion. At the same time they reaffirmed the spiritual value of decorous social conduct. Both Edwards and Dickinson rejected the notion that emotional outbursts were necessary features of conversion. Some they acknowledged to be genuine results of the work of God's Spirit on souls. Other outbursts, however, might be mere human emotion aroused in the supercharged atmosphere of a revival meeting. Others might even arise from the prompting of the Devil. The only sure way to determine whether or not the outburst signified the work of God was to measure the convert's subsequent manner of life against scriptural guidelines: love for God and his Word, holiness of life, and humility and charity in conduct toward others. . . .

Revivalist ministers crowned their efforts to fashion a model of itinerancy within an open, yet orderly world by securing James Davenport's *Confessions and Retractions*. The repentance of the firebrand who had become the symbol of "enthusiasm" for all parties symbolized for most revival ministers the orderly adaptation of itinerancy to its eighteenth-century environment. They ensured that the document received as much publicity as had Davenport's antics. Davenport's *Confessions* was published as a pamphlet and widely advertised in the newspapers. Several news weeklies reprinted the document in full. It also appeared in the pages of the *Christian History*. . . .

By the time George Whitefield returned for his second tour of the colonies late in 1744, revivalist ministers had defined a set of guidelines for the orderly integration of itinerancy and the settled ministry. . . .

Whitefield's second tour provided revivalists an opportunity to demonstrate that orderly coordination of itinerancy and a settled ministry was possible. Since 1741 Old Light controversial literature had been tracing the "Errors & Disorders that have prevailed in the Land" to itinerancy and had been portraying Whitefield as the fountainhead of them all. His return in November of 1744 offered a chance to demonstrate that disorders erupting after he took his leave of America had been "no just Consequences from Mr. Whitefield's Principles." Consequently, the Grand Itinerant and evangelical clergy collaborated in a publicity campaign that was much more self-conscious concerning matters of conduct and decorum than publicity surrounding the first tour had been. . . .

. . . Wherever he traveled, he avoided arousing unnecessary emotional fervor by "applying himself first to the Understandings of his Hearers, and then to the Affections." By 1746 his exemplary conduct was winning him cordial receptions even from former opponents.

Whitefield's model second tour provided revivalists with evidence that itinerancy could be harnessed into coexistence with a parochial ministry. Old divisions persisted long after 1745, but the relative lack of significant new ruptures satisfied moderate revivalists that no inevitable link existed between itinerancy and disorder. . . .

. . . Moreover, its capacity to penetrate boundaries and to provide long-distance links between people sharing a common inner experience made itinerancy subversive despite its inventors' best efforts to control it. Revivalists had indeed taught their people to "love Strangers," just as William Worthington had warned, and the people were now prepared to "go after" itinerant preachers. The colonial American religious world would never be the same.

## George Whitefield, the Grand Itinerant

### FRANK LAMBERT

When the Anglican evangelist George Whitefield arrived at Lewis Town, Pennsylvania, on October 30, 1739, he brought with him more than his zeal to declare the necessity of a spiritual new birth. His cargo in the hold of the *Elizabeth* contained boxes of evangelical books and pamphlets, including Benjamin Jenks's *Prayers and Offices of Devotion for Families,* John Flavel's *Husbandry Spiritualised,* Isaac Watts's *Divine Songs,* William Law's *A Practical Treatise Upon Christian Perfection,* John Norris's *A Treatise Concerning Christian Prudence,* 200 copies of the *Country-parson's advice to his parishioners,* and 150 volumes of the *Book of Common Prayer.* He also transported cartons of his own printed sermons, journals, letters, and prayers. These items represented just part of the apparatus he employed to

Frank Lambert, "'Pedlar in Divinity': George Whitefield and the Great Awakening, 1737–1745," *Journal of American History* 77(3) December 1990, pp. 812–837. Copyright © 1990 by the Organization of American Historians. Reprinted by permission.

generate religious enthusiasm in the intercolonial revivals known as the Great Awakening.

Whitefield's shipload of consumer merchandise symbolizes his immersion in a thoroughly commercialized society, one that provided him with the means of constructing a new religious discourse—modern revivalism. . . .

. . . However, by applying means from the world of commerce to publicize his meetings, Whitefield generated large, enthusiastic crowds. Like the rest of us, the evangelist constructed his social reality with the elements at hand, and in the mid-eighteenth century, commercial language and techniques abounded, affording him a new way of organizing, promoting, and explaining his evangelical mission. Thus, the spreading market enabled him to conceive of organizing a revival spanning the Atlantic, making "the whole world his parish." Improvements in marketing organization and practices provided the means of relieving the suffering of "strangers at a distance," transforming mere awareness of distant needs in to a moral imperative to deliver spiritual and material aid. In Whitefield's case, that meant preaching the gospel to the "uttermost parts of the earth," including the wilderness of Georgia. Drawing upon the experience of enterprising merchants selling their wares at great distances, Whitefield prepared remote auditors to receive the spoken word through advance publicity, especially that of newspaper advertising. And he employed a commercial vocabulary to convey the necessity of the New Birth to his listeners who themselves thought in categories of market exchange.

An argument that advance publicity and self-promotion alone explain the Grand Itinerant's attraction of unprecedented crowds is unfounded and reductionist. However, an examination of his promotional strategies does provide a new understanding not only of Whitefield's success but also of the diffusion of commercialism throughout mid-eighteenth-century society. It indicates a need to view the Great Awakening in a larger context, as part of an evangelical stirring that occurred throughout the Atlantic world. And such a study points toward a reexamination of the relation between commerce and religion, challenging the interpretation that the two were antithetical, suggesting instead a creative tension whereby evangelists such as Whitefield, while preaching against a selfish preoccupation with the pursuit of wealth, employed the tools of trade to promote the gospel.

Contemporaries observed and commented on the extent and importance of Whitefield's advance publicity. Opponents and supporters alike remarked on the evangelist's use of print to promote his work. . . .

. . . First Whitefield mailed copies of his journals and printed sermons to prominent ministers such as Benjamin Colman and Jonathan Edwards. Then Boston newspapers furnished New Englanders accounts of the preacher's successes in the middle and southern colonies—self-promoting reports written by Whitefield himself or his traveling companion William Seward, a London stockjobber, and transmitted through Benjamin Franklin's intercolonial newspaper network. Then supporters such as the Reverend Josiah Smith, heeding Whitefield's plea to "take up [their] pen[s]" on behalf of the revival, published glowing testimonials extolling Whitefield's evangelism and humanitarianism—works that recommended the itinerant to New Englanders. Thus when Whitefield began his services, Bostonians, indeed, "were prepared to embrace him."

By 1739 Whitefield had discovered that "the meanest instruments," especially the press, promoted the gospel by "excit[ing] people's curiosity, and serv[ing] to raise their attention." He explained to Colman his motives for publishing accounts of the revivals, expressing his confidence that "our Lord's cause might be promoted thereby." Whitefield believed that his mission was so great that his publicity should exceed that of "the world." . . .

Although the London clergy had long employed newspapers to publicize charity sermons, under Seward's guidance Whitefield transformed mere notices into advertisements rivaling those promoting the latest consumer goods. Typical ecclesiastical entries in the *London Daily Advertiser* announced sermons by presenting the bare essentials: who was to preach, for what charity, in which church, and at what time. And rarely did the ministers provide the press with a report of the services, such as the number attending and the amount collected. By contrast, Seward "sold" Whitefield to the readers, complete with advertising "puffs," appealing details designed to pique interest. Seward's paid advertisements appeared on the front page in the form of news articles written by a third party. The former recounted recent successes and announced upcoming events. In describing Whitefield's performance at St. Swithin's church in September 1737, Seward reported that the evangelist preached an "*excellent*" charity sermon before a "*crowded*" congregation whose contributions were "*remarkable.*" He noted that Whitefield's sermon on the "*greatness* of the charity of the poor-widow's mites" inspired the auditors to contribute over five pounds including "no less than 800 halfpence." He concluded by announcing Whitefield's next sermon as a continuation of the evangelist's "*truly pious*" undertaking to promote the "*good effects* [charity schools] have on the lower ranks of the people." . . .

Whitefield also benefited from the extensive advertising of his printed works, which both contributed to his growing popularity and resulted from his spreading fame. Booksellers recognized Whitefield as an author who had "made sermons, once a drug, a vendible commodity." Consequently, enterprising publishers vied with each other to exploit the lucrative demand for the evangelist's writings. In one issue of the *Daily Advertiser,* for instance, a printseller advertised a portrait of Whitefield, "neatly engrav'd from a drawing taken by an excellent painter," and on the same page, a bookseller advertised two of the evangelist's sermons plus a collection of prayers "recommended by George Whitefield." In the summer of 1738, competition between publishers over which had the right to publish Whitefield's first journal resulted in a windfall of publicity. The rivals, Thomas Cooper and James Hutton, advertised their editions on the same pages of the *Daily Advertiser* for a full week. They also engaged in a front-page debate over whose edition offered the more faithful rendering of Whitefield's manuscript. . . .

By the beginning of 1738, colonial newspapers reprinted Whitefield's advertisements, almost two years before his preaching tour that triggered the Great Awakening. . . .

Upon arriving in America in October 1739, Whitefield continued to promote his revivals through vigorous newspaper coverage. Though Whitefield's associates, John Syms and James Habersham, handled "press relations" while traveling with the itinerant, Seward proved the most aggressive and effective agent. In his own journal, published in 1740 in England and America, the zealous businessman recorded his role in newspaper reporting and press relations. Successive entries during 1740 reveal the nature and extent of his activities. "April 27. Wrote paragraph for the News, of our Brother's Preaching, etc., particularly the following to be published in New York. April 29. Wrote and examined sundry things for the Press; Particularly Mr. Whitefield's Letter. . . . May 2. Call'd at Mr. Franklin's the Printer."

While advance men and merchants performed the role of press agents, Whitefield himself exercised direct control over press coverage. After he dispatched Seward to England in April 1740 to raise money, the itinerant reported his own performances and successes, producing third-person accounts of his latest preaching tour in the middle colonies, complete with puffs. He opened a typical report with a statistical account of his activities, indicating he was on shore thirty-three days, traveled "hundreds" of miles, preached fifty-eight sermons, attracted crowds of up to twenty thousand, and collected "near 500 pounds sterling." Then, assessing the power of the revival, he wrote, "Great and visible effects followed his preaching. There was never such a general awakening, and concern for the things of God known in America before." He closed by announcing his intention to visit New England in the fall and return to Philadelphia afterwards. Thus, Whitefield advertised his revivals under the guise of a newspaper article—just the kind of "objective" third-party report Josiah Wedgwood instructed his associates to secure to promote pottery sales because he considered it the most powerful of advertisements.

Although print runs remained small for mid-eighteenth-century newspapers, seldom numbering more than a few hundred, improvements in marketing and distribution meant that Whitefield could reach a wide audience. . . . But the number of subscribers does not indicate the readership of newspapers and books. Coffeehouses, which sprang up throughout England in the half century before Whitefield's revivals, operated as circulating libraries where gentlemen gathered to read the latest newspapers and books. And entrepreneurial booksellers offered books for loan as well as for sale, enabling those who could not afford the purchase price to read the latest works. In Whitefield's evangelical circles, religious societies and itinerant preachers served a similar function, widening the readership of evangelical papers and books. . . .

Most of the fourteen colonial newspaper publishers played important roles in promoting Whitefield's revivals, advertising his writings, and soliciting contributions. As the major intercolonial event in 1740–1741, Whitefield's revival enjoyed extensive coverage. For example, 60 percent of the *Pennsylvania Gazette's* issues of that period devoted space to Whitefield, often including reports of his successes and itineraries, reprints of his publications, and advertisements for his writings. And though Whitefield conducted most of his preaching tours in northern cities, the *Virginia Gazette* carried stories of the evangelist in a third of its issues. But, more than frequency, the space allotted Whitefield within single editions attested to the widespread interest he generated. For instance, during 1740, Andrew Bradford often devoted the entire front page of the *American Weekly Mercury* to the evangelist's letters, journals, endorsements, and testimonials. In seventeen of fifty-two issues of the *South Carolina Gazette* published between the summers of 1740 and 1741, the lead story was a heated controversy pitting Whitefield and his supporters against his opponents. The disputes centered on whether Whitefield's "enthusiasm" was acceptable behavior for an Anglican minister. Its persistence as a news item suggests revival controversy was good business for the newspaper.

No one was a more aggressive Whitefield promoter than Franklin. Though differing in religious views, Franklin and Whitefield enjoyed a lasting and profitable relationship that satisfied both men—the publisher sold more newspapers and books, and the evangelist reached a wider audience. Franklin sent sermons, pamphlets, and journals through his intercolonial booksellers' network, insuring fast and widespread dissemination. And Franklin's newspaper coverage of the revival was so favorable and extensive he was forced to print a defense against charges of editorial bias in the *Pennsylvania Gazette*. But the printer's support went beyond publishing. He helped Whitefield raise money through an effective subscription by which evangelicals convenanted to make installment payments to underwrite the revival. He also defended the preacher's integrity when opponents accused Whitefield of misappropriating funds donated for the orphan house. However, Whitefield also helped Franklin. From 1739 to 1741, Franklin published 110 titles—as many as he printed during the previous seven years. Almost all the increase came from Whitefield. The itinerant's works sold well. Franklin projected sales of two hundred for an expensive four-volume collection of two volumes each of sermons and journals, but actual sales exceeded the forecast by more than 25 percent. And according to Franklin's ledgers, Whitefield's works generated more revenue in some cities, for example, Charleston, South Carolina, and Newport, Rhode Island, than did his popular *Poor Richard's Almanac*. . . .

Whitefield promoted his revivals through the widespread distribution of sermons and journals. . . . Focusing on the heated controversy the published discourses sparked, Franklin believed the itinerant's sermons gave advantage to his enemies. The printer pointed out that they could not attack "unguarded expressions and erroneous opinions" delivered in oration. But his critics dissected his writings, leading Franklin to conclude, "I am of the opinion if he had never written anything, he would have left behind him a much more numerous and important sect." However, Whitefield did not desire to create another denomination or church nor to swell the ranks of an existing denomination. . . .

To thousands, the printed sermons also had important symbolic significance. They represented the principles of the revival—the primacy of the individual in salvation, renunciation of unconverted ministers, and emotional experience as the basis of religion. Opponents like Charles Chauncy and Timothy Cutler of Boston noted the symbolic nature of the sermons, crediting their ubiquitous presence with perpetuating religious "enthusiasm." Printed sermons in Whitefield's revivals were analogous to consumer goods displayed by the followers of the radical English politician, John Wilkes. Pro-Wilkes potters sold mugs, punch bowls, and other ceramic articles adorned with the candidate's political slogans. Mercers marketed such Wilkite clothing as coats with special buttons, cuffs, and handkerchiefs. Other merchandise symbolizing the radical cause included tobacco pipes, candlesticks, and tankards. All of these goods served as visible means by which supporters identified with and participated in a movement. . . .

Through his publications, Whitefield did more than publicize his revivals. For some people, his writings represented the primary means of receiving his message. While traveling through the southern colonies in 1739, the evangelist noted the difficulty of holding revivals among a sparse and scattered population. Though he conducted services, the absence of sizable towns and difficulty of travel limited the crowds. While in Virginia, the evangelist preached in Williamsburg, unaware of a small group of evangelicals just sixty miles away in Hanover County who were unable to come to hear him preach. The lay leader of the group, Samuel Morris, observed that Whitefield's "fame was much spread abroad, as a very warm and alarming Preacher, which made such of us in Hanover as had been awakened, very eager to see and hear him." Despite Morris's eloquent statement of the efficacy of Whitefield's promotional campaign, the group did not hear him. They procured, however, from a Scottish traveler a "book of his sermons preached in Glasgow and taken from his mouth in short Hand." Thus Whitefield's publications circulated through unexpected routes and with surprising consequences.

Through reading Whitefield's sermons, the Virginians spread the revival. Acting as a surrogate preacher, Morris began to read the sermons aloud at meetings attended by ten to twelve faithful souls. While the writings of reformers like Martin Luther had introduced the members to "the Way of Justification," the "Concern was not very extensive." But when Morris read Whitefield's works, "many were convinced to seek deliverance with the greatest solicitude." As the readings continued, the group grew too large to meet in homes and built its first meetinghouse. Unable to find a suitable pastor—that is, one who was evangelical and Calvinist—these dissenting evangelicals continued to rely on Whitefield's printed sermons. "When the report of these Sermons and the Effects occasioned by reading them was spread Abroad," Morris reported, he was invited to several places to read them, and "by this Means the concern was propagated." Through the aid of Whitefield's printed sermons, the group survived and evolved into the first Presbyterian church in Virginia. . . .

. . . In the weeks before the first Boston preaching tour, lengthy journal extracts in the newspapers traced the revival's northward progress.

Whitefield disseminated his journals in various forms and through several media. The evangelist and his assistants circulated his latest journals through the letterwriting network. Often he mailed extracts from the version in process to give his supporters a current account of the revival. And on occasion the evangelist even read from his journals to religious societies. He also sent copies to newspapers where they sometimes appeared in successive issues on the front page. Eager to print anything with Whitefield's name on it, book publishers facilitated the dispersion of the journals. Though all sixteen printed versions emanated from Boston and Philadelphia presses, they radiated through an intercolonial bookseller network. Franklin published the seven journals in a two-volume set and distributed it to other printers and booksellers in Massachusetts, Connecticut, Rhode Island, Pennsylvania, Delaware, Maryland, Virginia, and South Carolina. He also issued an eighth volume for a regional audience, covering only Whitefield's travels in the environs of Philadelphia. Franklin's colonywide network was a new scheme in America, just as Whitefield's open-air preaching was novel. These two innovators naturally joined their intercolonial interests to serve each other.

Not only did Whitefield exploit a wide variety of printed forms, he also employed several merchandising techniques to promote his evangelical activities. One marketing strategy Whitefield favored was serial publication of his sermons and journals. Introduced by imaginative publishers earlier in the eighteenth century, "this method of weekly publication allure[d] multitudes to peruse books, into which they would otherwise never have looked." Through serialization, Whitefield increased demand two ways. First, the low price for each segment made it affordable for a larger group of people than could purchase the two-volume collection. Second, the serialized journals created a heightened sense of anticipation as readers followed the evangelist's progress toward their own communities. . . . About every six months, the itinerant sent new editions to his publishers on both sides of the Atlantic.

Whitefield increased publication sales through a variety of creative pricing schemes. Seeking widespread distribution in a mass market, Whitefield instructed his publisher to "print so as to sell cheap." In the preface to his hymnal, he made explicit the connection between price and purchaser, "As the generality of those who receive the Gospel are commonly the poor of the flock, I have studied cheapness, as well as conciseness." . . . Through his London printer, Lewis, Whitefield offered a cash discount to encourage early payment on subscription sales. Through flexible pricing Whitefield expanded the market for his publications, facilitating widespread publicity. . . .

Whitefield was an innovator in advertising. Merchants who viewed markets as restricted to a fixed number of customers did not advertise to create consumer demand. Instead, they merely provided information about the availability of their goods and the terms of sale. However, English capitalists in the eighteenth century expanded both domestic and foreign markets and advertised in order to exploit what they considered to be an elastic consumer demand. With a similar view, Whitefield sought to generate interest in his revivals through aggressive advertising. Opponents protested "the various methods taken up by Mr. Whitefield and his adherents, for trumpeting abroad his fame, and magnifying his person and performance."

Whitefield recognized that negative as well as positive publicity could generate interest in his revivals. Especially during his first three American trips, the evangelist engaged in polemics to differentiate his message of the new birth from what he considered to be the "stirrings of dry bones," rattling from unconverted ministers. In a published letter to the students at Harvard and Yale, he charged both colleges with allowing their "light [to] become darkness." That incendiary tract attacking cherished institutions sparked a heated exchange of supporting and opposing publications. Whitefield wrote of the debate, "A few mistaken, misinformed good old men are publishing halfpenny testimonials against me." However, Whitefield agreed with Colman that such opponents had done him "a real service" by giving the evangelist's friends an opportunity "to publish testimonials in [his] favour." Whitefield recorded in his journal that opponents' charges served in the end to benefit him and the revival because they kept readers' attention focused on him. . . .

How Whitefield managed the revival's funds illustrates a final important commercial influence on his ministry. After announcing his intention to evangelize in America, the itinerant preached a series of charity sermons in England, collecting donations of more than a thousand pounds for the orphanage John and Charles Wesley had suggested for Georgia. At the prompting of a merchant, Whitefield bought consumer goods, which he transported on the *Elizabeth,* intending to sell them in America where demand for English merchandise ran high. Upon arriving in Philadelphia, he advertised his wares, conducted an auction, and made a profit sufficient to finance his preaching tour. On a subsequent fund-raising journey, Whitefield purchased a five-hundred-acre plantation in South Carolina with donations he collected in Charleston. Using slave labor, he hoped to generate a surplus to provide working capital for the orphanage. Thus Whitefield the entrepreneur significantly shaped the contours of the ministry of Whitefield the evangelist. . . .

As a tireless fund raiser, Whitefield not only funded his evangelical and humanitarian interests, he amassed an estate in excess of £3,300—exclusive of his lands and buildings in England and America. Such a sum was significant in 1770 when an artisan's house and lot in Savannah cost £250 and a teacher at the Georgia orphan house received an annual stipend of £50.

Whitefield's extensive application of the new merchandising techniques set him apart from his evangelical predecessors and contemporaries. Although the revivalist exploited the power of newspaper publicity to "spread his fame" abroad, even his early colleagues in English pietism, John and Charles Wesley, rejected advertising as a means of promoting their religious enterprises, viewing it as a tasteless "sounding [of] a trumpet." What influenced Whitefield to employ innovations from the marketplace? How and from whom did the evangelist learn the commercial strategies he employed so successfully?

Whitefield's initial inspiration for appropriating commercial means to promote his revivals stemmed from his family's involvement in the market. His father was a wine merchant in Bristol before moving to Gloucester, where he purchased the Bell Inn, whose income placed the elder Whitefield's name near the top of the town's tax rolls. After his father died during George's childhood, the youngster's mother married a man who traded in hardware, who immediately assumed ownership of the tavern. There, George worked as a "common drawer," under both his stepfather and, after the latter's death, his brother Richard, who gained title to the business. Before his departure to begin his studies at Oxford University, Whitefield ran the tavern in his brother's absence for almost a year. In addition to his direct experience in running a local business, Whitefield had at least a glimpse into overseas trade. He spent several months in Bristol with his older brother, James, who was a ship's captain trading in the American and West Indies markets. James sold English manufactured goods, Barbados rum, and muscovado, or raw sugar, at his store on the Charleston, South Carolina, wharf. Indeed, his advertisements appeared in the *South Carolina Gazette* before those of his evangelist brother. James gave financial support to the young minister, but his more important contribution may have been the knowledge he imparted regarding the world of commerce.

Whitefield's childhood friends introduced him to the spreading world of book selling and newspaper publishing. Gabriel Harris, whose father owned Gloucester's most prominent book store, remained a faithful supporter throughout Whitefield's ministry. As a youngster, Whitefield spent considerable time in the Harris home and gained the approbation of the elder Harris, who provided both books and money toward George's studies at Pembroke College at Oxford. . . .

Beyond the influence of family and friends in Gloucester, Whitefield was shaped by the spreading commercialized society itself . . . where "more [people] than ever was known in former years . . . [engaged] in buying and selling." Because of rising incomes and easy credit, consumers on both sides of the Atlantic had the means to purchase the new consumer goods coming on the market. . . .

By the second quarter of the eighteenth century, household producers throughout the English countryside turned out "small consumer goods on an unprecedented scale" to meet the demand of a very large and growing market. Defoe noted in 1722 that 120,000 people were employed in the woolen and silk manufactures of Norwich alone. Most worked out of their country homes, spinning yarn or operating looms. They sold their goods through merchants not only in London and the provinces but throughout the Atlantic world as well. One visitor to Maryland observed that "the quick importation of fashions from the mother country is really astonishing. I am almost inclined to believe that a new fashion is adopted earlier by the polished and affluent American than by many opulent persons in the great metropolis." . . .

Consumer demand spurred enterprising merchants to restructure the marketplace, creating institutions Whitefield found useful in promoting his religious enterprises. The scope and nature of advertising changed. Print capitalists published newspapers throughout provincial England and colonial America and made their readers aware of the latest London fashions. Generic descriptions of products, such as cloth, paper, and ceramics, characterized advertisements in the 1720s, but by the 1750s, New York advertisers publicized the availability of "purple gloves, rough gloves, chamois gloves, buff gloves, 'Maid's Black Silk' gloves, 'Maid's Lamb Gloves,' and even 'Men's Dog Skin Gloves.'" Retailers introduced "bright, glass-fronted and bow-windowed" shops, "enabling English householders to obtain goods from the length and breadth of the country." And Scottish merchants extended the retail network to the sparsely populated Virginia countryside. In 1743 Francis Jerdone, a merchant in Hanover County, observed, "There are 25 stores within 18 miles round me . . . and 4 or 5 more expected next year from some of the [British] outports." Middlemen became more important links in the lengthening distribution chain, as their warehouses and credit smoothed the flow of goods from manufacturers to final consumer. A new breed of wholesalers, traveling merchants, carried with them goods worth upwards of a thousand pounds sterling, supplied country shops with goods in bulk (called "whole pieces"), and gave "large credit" to shopkeepers. And as they had for centuries, itinerant hawkers and peddlers continued to sell their wares directly to consumers in London and beyond. Communications improvements enabled merchants to expand the flow of goods to the widening market. English businessmen raised funds through subscriptions to build the canals and turnpikes necessary to make exchanges easier and to mobilize effective demand.

Consumer demand also prompted businessmen to develop new merchandising techniques that Whitefield applied to the propagation of religion. Prior to the mid-eighteenth century, many manufacturers were content to remain at home and "let the orders come to them." . . .

The new commercialism produced a language of goods that extended to human endeavors beyond the business world. . . . And George Whitefield linked religion and commerce to organize and promote the transatlantic revivals. The young Anglican's message of the necessity of a spiritual new birth was not new. Jonathan Edwards of Northampton, Massachusetts, had sounded a similar theme in the regional awakening he led in 1735. Whitefield's innovation lay in the commercialization of his revivals. Although the eighteenth-century English world underwent significant demographic and economic change, churches clung to tradition. The norm was a settled ministry serving local parishioners who gathered at fixed times for worship.

With a commercialized perspective strengthened by his familiar association with merchants, Whitefield developed a different vision—one informed by patterns of thought gleaned from the expanding market. Like the merchants who generated their own consumer demand by planting colonies and advertising their wares at home and abroad, Whitefield applied the latest marketing strategies to create and exploit a transatlantic audience for evangelicalism.

Whitefield heightened his familiarity with the world of commerce as he immersed himself in the Atlantic market to promote and fund his favorite charity, the Georgia orphan house (which he called Bethesda). Whitefield sharpened his entrepreneurial skills as he sought a commercial enterprise to make the orphanage self-sustaining. Throughout the 1740s, Whitefield's correspondence reflected his preoccupation with such mundane matters as profits from book sales, bills of exchange to settle transatlantic accounts, and the high cost of labor. Whitefield tried to keep track of funds being raised and disbursed on both sides of the Atlantic. While in Charleston in 1745, for instance, he requested his London agent, John Syms, to send "a short sketch of my accompts that I may know how my affairs stand." To balance his books, the evangelist sought to increase his revenue and decrease his expenses. Whitefield wrote Boston supporters concerning his latest publications, expressing his expectation that "some profit will accrue to me from my sermons, etc." But to improve their profitability, Whitefield urged a trusted Bostonian to "make what bargain with [the printers] you think proper" to reduce printing costs. Whitefield also fretted over reducing expenditures, at one point proposing smuggling and illegally introducing slavery into Georgia as a way to lower Bethesda's labor costs. To a South Carolina planter, Whitefield expressed his opinion that although Georgia prohibited slavery, "no notice [was] taken of Negroes at all." Therefore, he suggested if the planter would "give [him] a Negroe, [he would] venture to keep him, and if he should be seized" the itinerant would buy him again. Like merchants of the day, Whitefield relied on credit to operate in overseas trade. He, for example, drew bills on William Seward's brother, Benjamin, a London merchant, to remit funds to Syms to satisfy British suppliers. Thus, Whitefield's own experience in the market influenced his favorable attitude toward merchants and their role in propagating the gospel.

Whitefield deepened his immersion in the commercial culture through consumption—purchases for himself as well as those for Bethesda. Unlike some of the radical revivalists, such as James Davenport of Long Island, who preached against spreading consumerism, Whitefield not only did not condemn consumption, he enjoyed material possessions. After securing the orphan house's financial position in the mid-1750s, the evangelist spent more freely on himself. Concluding that his "one-horse chaise [would] not do for [him]," Whitefield ordered a closed four-wheeled carriage with improved springs to make his trips over England's rough roads more comfortable. It cost "thirty or forty pounds," equivalent to the annual income of some of the lesser clergy. After taking delivery, the itinerant indicated he "like[d] the purchase exceedingly well." And he cherished a handsome watch adorned with a beautiful gold case, though he covered it with leather so the "delicacy [would] not offend." Whitefield also delighted in personal gifts his supporters gave him, including books, horses, and even a slave. One of his most treasured gifts was a slave whom his co-laborer William Hervey purchased for him at a cost of thirty pounds sterling. To remember the donor, Whitefield named the servant Weston, after Hervey's parish, Weston-Flavel. At times, Whitefield even demonstrated great anxiety over his personal goods. While in America in 1746, he wrote successive letters to his mother, brother-in-law, and finally his agent, Syms, requesting that his "padlocked chest... [and] portable furniture" be sent to Charleston. The letters expressed a growing sense of urgency by one attached to his possessions. . . .

Not only did Whitefield view commerce and religion as compatible, he maintained that trade was an essential feature of the divine economy. He argued that God would have deemed creation incomplete if his human creatures lacked company. Therefore, the Almighty made it impossible that "communities be kept up, or commerce carried on, without society." Indeed, "Providence seem[ed] wisely to have assigned a particular product to almost each particular Country, on Purpose, as it were to oblige us to be social." Whitefield concluded that the mutual dependence of commerce and society demonstrated that "the one great end of [human] existence," consisted in individuals' being useful to each other in social life. Toward that end, he determined to share his "particular product"—his evangelical message—with the widest possible audience through the means at hand. . . .

As his ministry progressed in partnership with supporters from the world of commerce, Whitefield inserted commercial language more frequently into his discourses. . . .

. . . What was new about Whitefield was not his appropriation of the language of the market, but his adaptation of marketing techniques. Yet, Whitefield's commercialization of religion need not suggest a secular orientation. Rather it indicates a zeal for propagating the gospel through the most powerful means available. Therefore, he intuitively and self-consciously appropriated merchandising strategies for igniting the transatlantic revivals. . . .

Printers supported Whitefield in part because he was good business. As the revival spread in the colonies, Whitefield and American booksellers profited from the commercial appeal of the evangelist's publications, fostered by his well-publicized successes—huge crowds, numerous conversions, and liberal contributions. Each year from 1739 through 1745, American publishers released more works by Whitefield than by any other writer. The total number of publications printed in the colonies increased by 85 percent from 1738 to 1741, with most of the increase attributable to the Grand Itinerant. In the peak revival year, 1740, Whitefield wrote or inspired thirty-nine titles, or 30 percent of all works published in America. For many printers, Whitefield's writings constituted a significant proportion of their business. For instance, from 1739 to 1742, one of the largest publishers in the colonies, Daniel Henchman of Boston, spent more than 30 percent of his printing budget producing the evangelist's books. Whitefield not only profited from the sale of his works, he also benefited from Henchman's and Franklin's generous contributions to Bethesda. However, the relationship between business and theology was a complicated one with both commerce and religion influencing decisions. Hutton, who had printed most of Whitefield's early works, refused to produce further writings after 1741, when he sided with Wesley's rejection of Whitefield's Calvinism.

Although he had, according to Whitefield, "made hundreds" from the revivalist's publications, Hutton forswore future profits, refusing to print religious matters "except what [he] believed and approved."

Whitefield shared with the new merchants of the consumer revolution both similar strategies and a common view of the market as elastic. Improvements in communications and marketing enabled traders to escape the "cosseted constraints" of local markets and sell their goods to strangers at great distances. And the increased disposable income of urban consumers resulting from falling agricultural prices in the first half of the eighteenth century prompted merchants to consider means of selling consumer goods to the middling and even poorer people, not just the better sort. In a similar way, Whitefield discovered in the new merchandising techniques vehicles for conveying the necessity of a new birth to people far beyond the confines of a single local parish, or the entire Anglican church, or even the very boundaries of Britain itself. Although he subscribed to the Calvinist doctrine of election, Whitefield believed that God used the "meanest instruments" to awaken sinners to his grace. Thus, the evangelist felt compelled to employ every means—even those "the world" used to merchandise its baubles—to deliver the gospel to all people. . . .

 # F U R T H E R    R E A D I N G

Jon Butler, *Awash in a Sea of Faith: Christianizing the American People* (1990).

C. C. Goen, *Revivalism and Separatism in New England, 1740–1800* (1962).

David D. Hall, *Worlds of Wonder, Days of Judgment: Popular Religious Belief in Early New England* (1989).

Alan Heimert, *Religion and the American Mind: From the Great Awakening to the Revolution* (1966).

Rhys Isaac, *The Transformation of Virginia, 1740–1790* (1982).

Frank Lambert, *Pedlar in Divinity George Whitefield and the Transatlantic Revivals, 1737–1770* (1994).

David S. Lovejoy, *Religious Enthusiasm in the New World: Heresy to Revolution* (1985).

Mark A. Peterson, *The Price of Redemption: The Spiritual Economy of Puritan New England* (1997).

Harry S. Stout, *The Divine Dramatist: George Whitefield and the Rise of Modern Evangelism* (1991).

Patricia J. Tracy, *Jonathan Edwards, Pastor: Religion and Society in Eighteenth-Century Northampton* (1979).

Marilyn J. Westerkamp, *Triumph of the Laity: Scots-Irish Piety and the Great Awakening, 1625–1760* (1988).

# *America Within the Empire in the Early Eighteenth Century*

As the eighteenth century opened, the position of the American colonies within the British Empire was changing. Because many early plantations were sponsored by joint-stock companies and these companies designed the governments of their colonies, the seventeenth-century empire looked rather chaotic with its variety of in-stitutions. From the perspective of England, control seemed necessary. The royal gov-ernment took an increasingly stronger role in the government of the colonies; the Board of Trade was set up at the end of the seventeenth century to oversee the ad-ministration of all the colonies and develop common policies. The Board of Trade sought information from a variety of sources including questionnaires such as the circular letter on slavery (see Chapter 10). On the basis of the answers they received, the board formulated policy which was disseminated through the colonial governors and other officials.

One goal of imperial policy was greater control of trade. Colonial producers and merchants had become accustomed to a degree of flexibility in making deals and dis-posing of their crops. In sending over their own officials such as Edward Randolph, whose report is in Chapter 9, the government sought to locate the ways in which colonists might bend or evade the Navigation Acts designed to control all trade within the empire and to find ways to compel compliance. But all the initiatives from London were subject to the realities of colonial societies. No governor sent out, how-ever great his authority on paper, could simply command obedience. They had to lo-cate groups within the colonies with whom they could work and their effectiveness depended on how well they could balance various interests and connections on both sides of the Atlantic.

The position of the colonies within the empire had also changed because Amer-ica was now part of a worldwide struggle between France and England. These coun-tries, with their allies, fought a series of wars from the late seventeenth century through the eighteenth century to the defeat of Napoleon in the early nineteenth cen-tury. At the opening of the eighteenth century that continuing conflict was also pre-sent in America. France was expanding from its bases at Montreal and Quebec in Canada, building forts around the Great Lakes and venturing into the Ohio Valley. The French also settled New Orleans at the mouth of the Mississippi River. Thus France seemed poised to control the center of the continent and keep the English colonies hemmed in behind the mountains on the coast. Powerful native nations, many of which had become numerous through absorption of groups who had been pushed out of their homes by English settlements, occupied the land beyond the *mountains with a determination to prevent expropriation in the future, and English and French emissaries vied for their support. Thus imperial officials in London saw defense of the colonies as part of the great struggle against France and colonists looked to the empire for the protection they required.*

## D O C U M E N T S

Large numbers of letters and affidavits from all the colonies in which members of American interest groups complained to their leaders and counterparts in England about the activities of the colonial governors survive today. One example is a letter, document 1, from James Blair, of the Anglican establishment in Virginia, to the Bishop of London in which he accuses Governor Nicholson of persecuting the ministers the bishop has sent there. Document 2 is a complaint from New Jersey ministers of their treatment. They ask for a bishop to be sent to the colonies to protect them against maladministration. Documents 3 and 4 concern the status of Anglicans in Massachusetts, where the Congregational Church continued to be the established church. In document 3 the Society for the Propagation of the Gospel in Foreign Parts writes from London about reports from Massachusetts that Anglicans were being taxed to support dissenting, that is, Congregational, ministers. Governor Dudley's reply, document 4, makes counter-accusations against the ministers the Society sent.

Document 5, from Governor Bellomont of New York, describes his difficulties in getting the income he needs to do his job and the dishonesty and incompetence of the people he is forced to work with. Much of Bellomont's interest in this document centered on providing for the army and getting it functioning well. The three statements from Governor Spotswood of Virginia in document 6 show a more cooperative mood between the governor and the colonists as they make plans for the settlement and defense of the frontier and for solving problems in the marketing of tobacco early in his administration. By the end of his period as governor in 1720 Spotswood refers to suspicions between the assembly and the governor and the need to do more to encourage the kinds of settlements that would make the frontier safe.

In the 1730s, the Mohegan Indians took their grievances with the Connecticut government directly to the king in document 7; those who identified themselves as the "major part" of the Mohegans asked him to overturn the colony's acceptance of Ben Uncas as sachem and speaker for the entire group. The Mason family, whose activities were central in these disputes, had been selected as the Mohegans' liaison with the English authorities by the original Uncas at the time when Connecticut was settled. The leaders of the "major part" signed with marks, which were witnessed and authenticated by Joseph Tracy and Thomas Grist.

## 1. James Blair Tells the Bishop of London of the Ministers' Persecution in Virginia, 1704

Inductions of Ministers he has totally neglected, not having inducted so much as one Minister during the whole time of his Govt, by which means it comes to pass that the Ministers are kept in miserable precarious circumstances, like domestic Servants, ready to be turned off at pleasure, which makes the better sort leave the country & the rest so obsequious that they are ready to do what he would have them.

---

William Stevens Perry, ed., *Historical Collections Relating to the Anglican Colonial Church: Virginia,* I (Hartford, 1890): 132–133.

As to the Second, he has invaded almost all the other parts of the ecclesiastical Jurisdiction, such as convocating the clergy without taking notice of the Bishop's commissary, appointing who shall preach at those convocations, appearing himself in their meetings, & proposing the subject matter of their consultation, holding separate meetings of the Clergy without the Bishop's commissary, putting those separate meetings upon acts of censure & discipline, getting them to Sign Papers in the name of the Clergy, requiring of some ministers Canonical obedience to himself as their Bishop, taking upon himself to turn out ministers & this without so much as process or trial.

As he has broke thro' all his instructions with relation to the Church, so in other respects he has withheld from the Clergy that necessary countenance & respect which is due to their Function & by his bad example, has contributed very much to increase their contempt among the people. I have heard him say that the Clergy were all a Pack of Scandalous fellows, & that he knew not one man in the country that deserved to be inducted & it is now proved by another affidavit that he said they were all hirelings, and the Quakers were in the right & that when he was told of some of the clergy that were dead, that he said he wished there were 40 more of them dead: which was as much as to wish that there were never a clergyman in the country. Several of them of the most noted good preachers he affronted and abused with the most opprobrious & villifying names of Dog, Rogue, Rascal, Villin, Jesuit. Some of them he has made ride bare headed by him, in the bitter cold of the wind & the scorching head of the Sun, several miles together. Some he has laid violent hands on, whilst they were on Horseback, & pulled off their hat himself. Some he has threatened publicly to tear their Gowns over their ears, has never spared in their presence to Curse & Swear, abundance of the most dreadful oaths, often at the very Church door immediately before or after prayers; & if the minister preached up any duty which the Govr was known to neglect, or against any vice he was known to be guilty of, he seldom escaped without rebukes or threats, & till of late that he had occasion for encomiums from them to support his interest in England, never any Govr used the Clergy so barbarously as he has done.

These addresses he not only barefacedly asks, but uses the way of threats & presents, & threats & insults to obtain, & if their addresses do not come up to what he would have, proposes new draughts & endeavours by making & feeding differences in their Parishes, to make the scrupulous ministers uneasy & to get them laid aside, by which means the basest of the Clergy & the forwardest to flatter are become his greatest favorites & several of the best ministers have been so harrass'd, that they have chosen rather to quit the Country than to endure the fatigues & extorted flatteries, or insults of his Government. . . .

## 2. Several Ministers in New Jersey Attest to Their Suffering and Ask for a Bishop to Protect Them, 1714

The Almighty good and Mercifull God has been graciously pleased to give wonderfull Success to the Pious and Charitable Undertaking of that Religious Society of men, whom his Wisdom was pleased to raise up and make use of as instruments in his hands for effecting the great and glorious work the Salvation of Men. Accord-

Edgar Legare Pennington, *Apostle of New Jersey, John Talbot, 1645–1727* (Philadelphia, 1939), 129–131.

ingly we see many fair Edifices raised for the true and Orthodox Worship of God, and several large Congregations as yet destitute of that convenience supported in Conformity to our pure and Apostolick Church, by the labours of the Missionaries, so that we may justly entertain hopes that the Kingdom of Satan draws nigh to a Period, and that his long and uncontroled Reign will soon give place to that Divinely glorious Faith which the Prince of Peace has promised that the Gates of Hell shall not prevail against: it is known however that the subtle Malicious Fiend the Enemy of God and Religion, the Inveterate Enemy of Man has never been wanting in his Attempts by particular Instruments which he knows where to find and how to choose, to disturb the Peace of the Church and to Obstruct ye progress of the Gospel; Accordingly late years present to our view some disorders in which its sufficiently evident the evil Spirit has acted a great part. . . . Your Excellency knows better than we can tell you, the dismal consequence of such abuses offered to ye Ministers of Religion and as you have the Power, so we are well Assured You have the Will to Screen us from Violence. . . .

But oh! we want Words to represent to Your Excellency the Horror and Indignation we and all good men conceive at ye Execrable Villany lately perpetrated at New York by presumptuous Miscreants who impudently and sacrilegiously broke into the house of God, and most irreligiously prophaned and defiled the Holy Books and Vestments wth Ordue in defiance of God and Religion; a wofull instance how far the Rage and Malice of certain Persons, who dissent from and are irreconcileable Enemys to the Established Church Constitution wou'd transport them, were they not curb'd and restrain'd by the Supreme Civil Authority at home from outrages they have a hearty good will to commit, and we need not tell your Excellency to what these things are owing here. . . .

We have cause to fear that if a Speedy Stop be not put to those grivances the fruit of our Labours here will be destroy'd and the pious aims of the Venble Society for promoting Religion and Piety will be render'd frustrate. The only remedy we can See for preventing of these Calamities is the Speedy Sending a Bishop into these parts to protect us & Stand in the Gap against any Person who may Encourage or countenance any Lawless designs against the Church. . . .

## 3. The Anglican Society for the Propagation of the Gospel in Foreign Parts on Massachusetts Governor Dudley's Treatment of Anglicans, 1713

Hon'd Sir,

I am commanded by the Society for the Propagation of the Gospel in Foreign Parts to inform your Excellency that they have lately received a letter from Mr. Eager lately sent Missionary by them to Braintree in which among other things he takes notice of and complains. That those few who are of the Church of England Communion are rated and taxed most extravagantly to support the dissenting

---

William Stevens Perry, ed., *Historical Collections Relating to the Church in Massachusetts, 1676–1785* (Hartford, 1873): 96–98.

Clergy. The Society conceive this to be a very great hardship and apprehend it is very much in your Excellency's power to do and procure to be done that which is just and equal to such who are so oppressed, and the rather because they observe in a Letter from your Excellency to the late Lord Bishop of London in the 19th December last, you are pleased to say, that as to such Inhabitants who had declared for the Church of England you had at their request exempted them from payment of taxes to any other Ministers but of the Church. The Society therefore entreat you Sir to interpose in the present case of complaint; justice may be done & kindness shewn by your favour and protection. They present their humble service to your Excellency. I am, &c.

## 4. Governor Dudley Presents his Defense and Counter-Accusations, 1714

Sir,

I have the honour of your letter of the 18th December 1713, wherein I have the commands of the Honble Society for Propagation of the Gospel in Foreign Parts wch are most acceptable to me at all times. I very well remember what I last year wrote to my Lord of London referring to giving easement from the taxes for the support of the Ministers in this province to all such as attended the worship after the Church of England, which I have brought to pass at Newbury where there is a chappel and a good number of auditors well establish'd Mr.———their Minister. Upon their first Meeting I wrote to the Magistrates of the Town to direct that nothing should be collected from the Members of that Congregation which has been observ'd ever since, saving that there was an arrear due to the Presbyterian Minister of the Town for some time past before the Chappel was erected, which after some trouble they have agreed among themselves for which arrears nevertheless ye Collectors of Newbury sued some of the Church of England before ye Justices who gave costs to the said Church party & dismist the complaint & all is quiet.

There has been the same trouble at Braintree abt the arrear, wch I hope is over also, but I have a sorrowful account from every body referring to Mr. Eager. I had heard of his rude life in his passage hither being frequently disguised in drink & fighting wth ye Saylors even to wounds & taring his cloaths and during the few months of his stay here he was frequently in quarrels and fighting and sending challenges for duells, that at length the auditory at Brandry were quite ashamed & discouraged, & he is gone to Barbadoes without any direction or order; and the Congregation without any Minister. General Nicholson has been here & seen ye process of the affair as above.

I am sorry for this harsh acct but more is true and the Church is greatly hurt by him as well as ye other people who are almost universally of another perswasion.

I pray you to give my duty and service to the Society wth this account and if there be any thing wherein I can put forward the maintenance of ye Missionarys and

William Stevens Perry, ed., *Historical Collections Relating to the Church in Massachusetts, 1676–1785* (Hartford, 1873): 96–98.

Religion and good manners in all part of these Provinces, I shall be glad to be commanded by ye Society.

I am, Sr, &c.,

J. DUDLEY.

## 5. Governor Bellomont of New York Writes Home of His Money Problems and the Dishonest Ways of the Colonists He Is Forced to Deal With, 1700

. . . There ought be a world of care taken in the choice of the Lieut Colonel, Major, and Captains that are sent over, and I must relie on your favour of that matter, otherwise I shall have a parcel of Tories and perhapps Jacobites put upon me by a certain gentleman who sits one of the Council of Trade, whose custome it is on such occasions to make sale of imployments to any sort of trash as will give him money. That most valuable design of Naval Stores depends in a great measure on the choice of good discreet officers to manage and influence the souldiers in working; therefore it behoves us to be very carefull in that point. . . .

I am under all the uneasinesse in the world at the intollerable folly and mismanagement of Mr Weaver and Mr Champante. Mr Weaver had received a £150 of the King's mony from Sr Wm Ashurst without any direction from me, and Mr Champante has been foolish enough to let him have £425. of the King's mony and still without any direction of mine, and sends me a foolish account of Mr Weaver's, and bill of exchange, wch you will receive wth the other papers, and bids me reimburse my selfe. When the Councill and I came to examine Mr Weaver's account, wch is the foundation of his bill of exchange, we found it so extravagant, that not a man of us (nor I whose interest it is to allow it that I may be reimburs'd) could consent to almost any one article in it. The marchands here getting the wind of this, are not willing to let me have mony on my bills of exchange drawn on Mr Champante; they have such a notion of his unfitnesse for businesse, and thinks he squanders the rest of the King's mony as he has done this to Weaver. So that I, that had begun to pay the Officers and souldiers their subsistence in mony duly every Saturday, am in a fair way of being ruin'd for want of credit to hold on paying the subsistence weekly. But this is not all; Mr Champante has neglected to send the souldiers cloaths; he sent a few suits by the Advice frigat, and he had much better have sent none, for a few souldiers cloath'd gives discontent to the others that are naked. In short the recruits I have sent to Albany are gone away in all the discontent imaginable for want of cloaths, so that I fear I shall hear of some notable mischief this winter at Albany, and now the River is shut up with ice, so that 'tis not in the art of man to send up the cloathing if it were come till the begining of April. One Capt. Wake who arriv'd here above a moneth ago wth a stout marchand ship was to have brought Mr Weaver and the souldiers cloathing, and he and Weaver fell out and arrested one another, and Mr Champante writes me word Mr Weaver told him Capt Wake refus'd to bring the cloathing. Mr Champante should not have taken Weaver's word in that case, who must be suppos'd prejudic'd against Wake, but

E. B. O'Callaghan, ed., *Documents Relative to the Colonial History of the State of New York,* IV (Albany, 1850): 816–817.

should have taken a refusal from Wake himselfe; but I am satisfied Wake never refus'd to bring the cloathing. I sent for him last Wednesday and he offer'd to take his oath that the cloathing was never offer'd him; he own'd that Mr Weaver spoke of bringing the cloathing with him. Mr Champante has writ four or five letters to me, but he is always in such hast that he cannot send me an account of the King's mony, how he lays it out, except that £425. to Mr Weaver. I never intended Mr Champante for Agent for the forces here, but desir'd a friend of mine to whom I sent a letter of Attorney wth a blank for the persons name, to fill it up wth the name of a trading man who I knew understood that sort of businesse, but that friend put in Mr Champante's name. I thought it proper to acquaint you with this whole story, that I might not be accountable for any ill consequence that may happen here from the ill conduct of Mr Weaver and Mr Champante. Every man has his faults and failings, more or less, and 'tis enough for a man to answer for his own faults, and not to be answerable for other men's. Certainly every man that knows the eternall toil of businesse I undergo in this place, and the opposition and trouble given me by an angry party of men here, will judge I have enough to perplex me here, without being so very ill us'd by those I trust in England.

The trouble of this usage makes me very indifferent as to the truth of what's reported here of my being speedily to be call'd home. Tis said the Bp. of London has writ to the Minister of this place Mr Vesey, who herds with the angry party, that by Easter he and his friends will be rid of their grievance. Mr Basse too has writ to several people in the Jersies that I shall speedily be displac'd and he shall be a main instrument in getting it done. As to the good Bishop he has espous'd Fletcher, wth all his corruptions, against me: I have nothing to say to him but that he is as wise as he is learned. Basse is the most a scowndrel that I ever knew; he will bragg and lye with any man living, even with Coll. Fletcher, and is a rank coward, was kick'd on board the Deptford in our voyage from Barbados hither. I sav'd Mr Heathcot and his partners some thousands of pounds that Bradish and his associates ran away with, and they have been such clowns as never to send me a line of thankes. I am, with respect, Sir,

Your most humble and<br>
faithfull Servant<br>
BELLOMONT.

## 6. Virginia Governor Spotswood Addresses the Council and House of Burgesses on Grievances, 1713, 1714, 1720

### Spotswood, 1713

*Gentlemen of the Council and House of Burgesses*

Peace ever comes Attended with innumerable benefits, So that I hope We shall in this Meeting be able happily to lay hold of Some of them, And as We are

---

Some spelling has been modernized.

H. R. McIlwaine, ed., *Journals of the House of Burgesses of Virginia, 1712–14, 1723–26* (Richmond, 1912): 47, 79–80, 250.

in Duty bound to make our thankfull Acknowledgments, both to God for mercifully bestowing this blessing upon us, And to our Sovereign for graciously labouring to procure it; So I think We cannot express our gratefull Sense thereof better than by pursuing the Ends for which it was given us, That is, by heartily Uniting our Selves, and Sincerely endeavouring to Promote Religion, and Cultivate the Arts of Peace.

You Gentlemen of *Virginia* might feel as Early as any of her Majestys Subjects the Advantages of this Peace, if an Assembly would as readily Concurr to prevent pernicious Practices, as a Parlyament has enclined to Redress Grievances in your Tobacco Trade; And without you do your parts in this Colony I fear all means used else where will Scarce make it flourish; for here is certainly an Evil at the very Root of this Trade, which may demonstrably appear to be the present Method the Country is in of Discharging Debts and Levys by tobacco payments, for from hence most evidently proceeds the Exportation of all that Trash which Ruines your Markets abroad, and daily Lessens the Reputation of your Commodity in *Europe.* This gives an unhappy occasion to the breeding up too many persons in a fraudulent way of dealing. Besides the Publick Credit is so Sunk by these payments, that as now no Service is readily performed for them, So I am confident no Money could in any Exigency be borrowed upon the faith of them; In Short there is So much folly and Iniquity in ye Practice, that it can by no means Square either with policy or Justice, And therefore I hope you'l Judge it Worthy of your consideration how to apply Some Remedy to this Evil.

The next Matter I shall Recommend to you is the providing more effectually for the Security of your Frontiers against foreign Indians, who notwithstanding the many partys of Rangers have Since these have been on foot killed and carryed off at least Twenty of our outward Inhabitants and Tributary Indians; I have Attempted by Severall ways to Oppose those Incursions but after Some trouble and expence have only Experienced that our People are not disposed for Warlike undertakings; Whereupon I have begun to try what may be done for their Safety by way of treaty, but do Resolve to conclude it upon no other Terms than Such as I shall find to be entirely agreeable to you; The generality of our Tributarys have of late approved themselves to be very ready and faitfully Allyed, And I am perswaded that the Setling them Along our Frontiers without all our Inhabitants (if it could be done under Such a Regulation as would make them willing to Remove) would be a better and cheaper Safe guard to the Country than the old Method of Rangers. . . .

### Spotswood, 1714

*Gentlemen of the Council and House of Burgesses* [1714]

We now meet under the Authority of another Sovereign, than when We were last Assembled

The Almighty has been pleased to call to his mercy our late most Gracious and most Religious Queen, but has Vouchsafed immediately to Repair that Loss to her Subjects, by fulfilling their Desires in the next Successor and by blessing our Mother Country with Peace and Harmony all on a Sudden, making fears and jealousies to Vanish there, and jarrs to cease at the very name of *King George*

A Prince who can So happily influence the minds of his People even before his Personal Presence among them Seems to be peculiarly cut out by providence for Ruling Remote Colonys: And thereupon We in these parts are particularly Obliged with thankful hearts to congratulate his Majestys Rightful and Lawful Accession to the Crown

It is a most Sensible Pleasure to me that the Representation I have now to make of the State of the Frontiers Differs very much from that I Laid before you last year. No Murther, No Alarms have happened; but on the contrary, Satisfaction has been made for those formerly committed, by Delivering up Some of the Guilty to Justice.

And it is no less pleasing to me, than I conceive it may be to you, that I have been able to Reduce the charge of Guarding the Frontiers to less than a Third of that of the preceding years; besides, I take the Security, I have provided for the Country to be of Such a nature, that if half the pains be used to improve it, which I have taken to Settle it, the Strength of your Barrier may with time be encreasing and the Expence Decreasing

For as, on the one hand, I have begun a Settlement of Protestant Strangers, Several Miles without our Inhabitants, more of their Country folkes might be induced to come over and Joine them if they hear these meet with a favourable Reception (and Sure as they are of the Same Nation with our present Sovereign, they are as fit to be Recommended to your benovolence as the *French* Refugees of the *Manican* Town formerly were)

So on the other hand, our Tributary Indians, whom I am Setling out with a few white men to accompany them in their Ranges, and to observe their Actions or Correspondence with forreign Indians, will need no longer Such a Guard, when by the blessing of God they become Christians, according to a Treaty I have this year made with them, for Educating all their Children in the faith of our Church

This may perhaps to Some appear to be too remote a Consideration but however, Since I judge the undertaking to be practicable, as well as Religious, I cannot but have it very much at heart, and it is a Sufficient encouragement to me, to think Posterity may Reap the benefit thereof

But for a more immediate Advantage to the Colony I Recommend to your Consultations Some Regulation of the Indian Trade: for it is not only almost quite lost, but even proves Pernitious to this Dominion, upon the footing it now is. I have Discovered enough to convince me that the Mischiefs We have of late years Suffered from the Indians are chiefly owing to the Clandestine Trade carryed on by some ill men, And experience Shows that it is not in the Governments power to prevent it, unless other measures be Enacted

I am but too Sensible of the Injury Done by last Summers Drought to the Crops of Corn and Tobacco, and think it Worthy your Consideration how to Relieve the People, under the Streits which many of them must this year be, to Discharge their Levys.

Since your last Session, I have Received a large quantity of Ammunition, with a Number of very good Arms and other necessarys of Warr, given by her late Majesty for the Service of this Country: And your enabling me to take better care of those than formerly has been of Such like Supplys, will not only be the best Return you can make for So generous a Gift, and a full Recompence for the pains I have taken in Solliciting and procuring it, but may also Render it an Estate of Inheritance to your Posterity

In fine Gentlemen

It cannot but be an Advantage to *Virginia,* that the good agreement of its Assembly Should be among the first Impressions Received by our new Sovereign, and if there were any Danger of your being otherwise disposed (of which I have not at present the least Apprehension) I should not doubt but this Single Consideration would be a Sufficient Motive to Harmony.

*November* the 17th: 1714.

*Resolved* That this House will take the Said Speech into Consideration to Morrow Morning

And then the House Adjourned till to Morrow Morning Eleven a Clock. . . .


## Spotswood, 1720

*Gentlemen of the Council and house of Burgesses.* [1720]

After the signal proofs that I have given of my disposition to peace and Union, I may with a good grace recommend to you Moderation and Concord and whoever shall make a just Estimate of what the Colony has gained by the late Contentions, cannot but reckon them Enimies to the Country who shall endeavour to divide us again or will continue to create groundless Jealousies of my administration

If we meet to consult and agree, General Assemblies undoubtedly are a most wholsom part of the Constitution, but if Some Vulgar notions are to prevail as if the body ought to thwart and oppose the head, our Sessions must prove nothing better than a burthen to the People: and that vividious [invidious] distinction of the Countrys and the Governours friends (which I am Sorry to observe Some men have been industrious stil to keep up) must prove a Poison to your proceedings if you Suffer it to take place in your present Consultations.—

To consider the Stake I have among you and the free choice I've made to fix it under this Government You have not Surely any grounds to Suspect me of injurious Designs against the welfare of this Colony, for if a Conscientious discharge of our duty engages us Governours to be Specially mindful of *Great Britains* Interest yet I cannot See why that may not go hand in hand with the prosperity of these plantations and I will frankly declare to you the Political Creed which I profess on this point.

I look upon *Virginia* as a Rib taken from *Britains* Side and believe that while they both proceed as living under the Marriage compact, this *Eve* must thrive so long as her *Adam* flourishes, and I'm perswaded that whatever Serpent shall tempt her to go astray and meddle with forbidden matters will but multiply her Sorrow and quicken her husband to rule more strictly over her.—

If your proceedings be duly tempered with this perswasion, I hardly imagine any thing that can urge us to differ this Session, for (praised be God) this Government is at present under more happy Circumstances than to need my pressing you for Supplies, and as We of the Administration are upon a better Establishment than to become troublesom to you for our Salaries, so my own desires are more bounded than to be Anxious or Solicitous for your Bounties

Besides my purpose is to offer nothing to you at the Opening of this Session but what you may be as forward to enact, as I to pass and therefore I shall no more than barely hint what I think fit to propose assuring you that if the needfulness thereof be not as obvious to you as to me I will acquiesce with all the Indifference that is consistent with my Duty.—

And so I remark to you the naked State both of your harbours and frontiers, the disarmed Condition of your Militia, the Inconvenient length of many Counties, and I leave to your consideration whether the giving Encouragment for Extending your Out Settlements to the high Ridge of Mountains, will not be laying hold of the best Barrier that nature could form, to Secure this Colony from the Incursions of the Indians and more dangerous Incroachments of the *French,* and Lastly I lay before you the Sentiments of the Lords Commissrs for Trade and plantations. with respect to Treaties with the five Nations of Northern Indians.

## 7. Mohegan Indians Petition the King in Their Dispute with the Colonial Government of Connecticut

*The "Major Part" of the Mohegans Protests Connecticut's Recognition of Ben Uncas as Sachem, 1738*

**To His Most Excellent Majesty George The Second King of Great Britain France & Ireland—**

THE HUMBLE PETITION of the Major part of the Tribe of Mohegan Indians in Your Majestys Colony of Connecticut in New England—
   *Most Humbly & Most Submissively Sheweth to Your Majesty—*
   Your Majesty by your princely care of us has been Graciously pleased to grant a Commission of Review in June, 1737, To hold a Court of Commrs in this your Majestys Colony of Connecticut, & thereby Ordered Commrs., by Virtue of a Summons Issued out of sd. Court. We made our Appearance in a Body, & we were denied to be heard, or by our Council, William Shirley & Wm. Bollan, Esqrs., who was denied liberty to plead for us. The Govr. & Comps. of Connecticut set up one Benjamin Uncass, an Impostor, as Sachem, who we denied to be our Lawfull or right Sachem, but one made by sd. Governmt to Answer their End, to evade Justice & Second them in confederacy and Combination to Deprive us of our Lands, Surrepticiously & in an Arbitrary manner detained from us—Which has left us in a Most Deplorable & Miserable scituation of Life & Exposed to the Utmost Limits of Poverty & Want, by being denied Justice, or the benefit of your Majesties Commission. In a particular manner, owing to the death of Captain John Mason, & Mahomet, our lawfull Sachem, whom we sent to England to sollicit your Majesty to Grant us Relief, & restore us to our Rights and Libertys, but death interposed the return of either, and then was left destitute of a Sachem, & Capt. Mason, who was

Mohegan Indians of Connecticut to King George II, 1738, *Collections of the Connecticut Historical Society* V (Bowie, MD: Heritage Books, 1896): 103, 159–63.

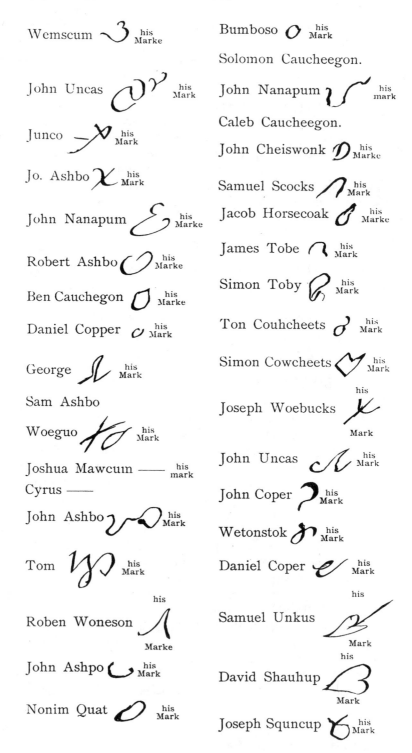

Wemscum   his Marke

John Uncas   his Mark

Junco   his Mark

Jo. Ashbo   his Mark

John Nanapum   his Marke

Robert Ashbo   his Marke

Ben Cauchegon   his Marke

Daniel Copper   his Mark

George   his Mark

Sam Ashbo

Woeguo   his Mark

Joshua Mawcum   his mark

Cyrus ——

John Ashbo   his Mark

Tom   his Mark

Roben Woneson   his Marke

John Ashpo   his Mark

Nonim Quat   his Mark

Bumboso   his Mark

Solomon Caucheegon.

John Nanapum   his mark

Caleb Caucheegon.

John Cheiswonk   his Marke

Samuel Scocks   his Mark

Jacob Horsecoak   his Marke

James Tobe   his Mark

Simon Toby   his Mark

Ton Couhcheets   his Mark

Simon Cowcheets   his Mark

Joseph Woebucks   his Mark

John Uncas   his Mark

John Coper   his Mark

Wetonstok   his Mark

Daniel Coper   his Mark

Samuel Unkus   his Mark

David Shauhup   his Mark

Joseph Squncup   his Mark

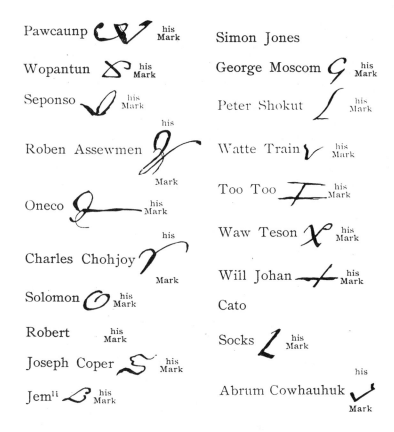

Pawcaunp — his Mark

Wopantun — his Mark

Seponso — his Mark

Roben Assewmen — his Mark

Oneco — his Mark

Charles Chohjoy — his Mark

Solomon — his Mark

Robert — his Mark

Joseph Coper — his Mark

Jem^li — his Mark

Simon Jones

George Moscom — his Mark

Peter Shokut — his Mark

Watte Train — his Mark

Too Too — his Mark

Waw Teson — his Mark

Wiil Johan — his Mark

Cato

Socks — his Mark

Abrum Cowhauhuk — his Mark

unanimously chose by the Tribe to represent us as our Guardian & Trustee, as we had full & evident Demonstration of his Zeal & Family Friendship to discharge the Trust & confidence we reposed in him, being the Grandson of Major John Mason, & Son to Major Saml. Mason. By the Magnanimous Courage & Prudent Managemt. of sd. John Mason as Capt. Genll. of our Tribe destroyed a Great and Numerous Tribe of Indians, called Pucotts [Pequots], that attempted to cutt off the first English that we accommodated with Lands to plant and Improve on, And after his death we chose Majr. Saml. Mason as our Guardian & Trustee, & in consequence, sd. Captn. John Mason, that dyed in England in Decr., 1736, all of wch was faithfull & Just to the Tribe. But sd. Court proceeded to the Merits of the Cause, notwithstanding the York Commissioners dissented from the Arbitrary Proceedings of the Rhode Island Commrs, being in the same Circumstances with Connecticut in wronging the Indians, by selling their Lands they had no Right to. This pretended Sachem, Benjamin Uncass, was bribed by the Governmt. of Connecticut, by giving him the sum of 70£ for his giving them a Quit claim to all the Indian Lands sd. Governmt. dispossest [us?] of as ℔ Deed, bearing date, February 1737/8, Signed Benjamin Uncass, will appear.

MAY it therefore Please your Sovereign Majesty in your great Wisdom & Goodness of Wonted Probity and Justice Illustrated in your Royall Veins to consider the within Premes, and admit your Majesties Petitioning Loyall tribe of

Mohegan Indians, who at present have no Sachem, to Nominate John Mason & Samuel Mason, Gentl., or either of them Surviving, being Sons to Captn. Mason that dyed in England, to be our Trustees & Managers, to Represent us. . . . We being fully satisfyed of their Fidelity, And that your Majesty may be Graciously pleased to receive us under your Protection & relieve us from the Tyranny of Connecticut Governmt., And grant us such Methods as will Conduce to Restore us to our Lands and Libertys, And for Your Majestys Long Life, and Royall Succession, Your Majesties Petrs. as in Duty and Loyalty bound will ever Pray, &ca.

THE TESTIMONY of Captain Joseph Tracy, of Norwich, in the County of New London, aged 56 years, & Mr. Thomas Grist of sd. Norwich, Aged 38 years, Testifyeth & saith, That we being both present when the persons whose names & Marks were annexed on the other side of this paper, & they being all of or belonging to the Tribe of Mohegan Indians, living in his Majesties [Colony of] Connecticut, And that we were both present & see them all make their Marks or set their names to the within Petition.

JOSEPH TRACY.
THOMAS GRIST.
. . . June 30th., 1738.

### Ben Uncas Asks for Recognition of His Status as Sachem, 1739

TO THE KING.

Your Majesties most dutifull Subject, Ben Uncas, Sachem of the Mohegan Indians, in the Colony of Connecticut in New England, begs leave to follow the pompous Trains the English, & sincerely congratulate your Majesty upon the Birth of the 2d son of His Royall Highness, the prince of Wales, as a further addition to your Royal Family to endure to all Generations.

Your Majesty and Royall Ancestors, and by your Influence, your English Subjects, have always Treated ye Mohegans with Great kindness. I have in my hands a Gilt Bible, a Present from his late Majesty, King Charles the Second, to my Grandfather, Uncas. We are in the Quiet possion of our lands, wch are far more than we can Improve, and secured to us by the Laws of the Colony.

And we are Encouraged by our Neighbours to Embrace the Xtian Religion, wch many of us are resolved to do, and tis my daily study to understand & practice according to it.

Almighty God make your Majesty's Reign Long & prosperous, & preserve your Royall family in the peaceable possion of the English Empire as long as the Sun & Moon Endure.

BEN UNCAS.

4th MAY, 1739.

 *E S S A Y S*

In the first essay historian Alison M. Olson of the University of Maryland delineates the challenges faced by colonial governors in the early eighteenth century by looking at the careers of three longtime governors: Joseph Dudley of Massachusetts; Robert Hunter of New York; and Alexander Spotswood of Virginia. The governors faced powerful interest groups—members of the same religious affiliation or people who shared economic goals—that were allied with counterparts in England. Through their allies across the Atlantic the interest groups could circumvent the governors and foil their plans by using their influence with the royal government. Thus the colonial governors could only be effective by courting interest groups and working through them. The second essay, by Warren R. Hofstra of Shenandoah University, examines the British Empire's attempts to secure the western frontiers of the colonies on the eastern seaboard and to ward off French control of the interior of the American continent. Historians have long been aware of the flood of non-English people into the backcountry, but have not recognized that this was the result of imperial policy formulated in London and disseminated through the colonial governors. In his essay, Hofstra presents a picture of the administration of Alexander Spotswood that complements the portrait drawn by Olson.

## Transatlantic Interest Groups and the Colonial Governors

### ALISON M. OLSON

Beginning in the quarter-century after 1690, the world in which the colonial governors worked was shaped in vitally important ways by the influence of London interests. Colonial groups which supported particular governors could pass on their approval to their counterparts in London, which would in turn pass it on to the British government. Those that disapproved of a governor's policies could do the same thing, and the Londoners would bring pressure on the imperial government to make the governor change his ways. The interests worked on governors indirectly, suggesting councillors to the Board of Trade, advising the Board on the wording of instructions, or urging the acceptance or disallowance of colonial laws, and directly, calling on the governors before they left London, seeing that they were greeted once they arrived in their colonies, and working with the appropriate colonial interests to put local pressure on them.

The influence of the London interests and, equally important, the perception of their influence varied among the provinces depending in turn upon the strength of local interests. A study of the three most important governors in the period—Joseph Dudley (Massachusetts, 1702–1715), Robert Hunter (New York, 1710–1720) and Alexander Spotswood (Virginia, 1710–1720)—shows the variety of ways in which London-American interests functioned from colony to colony and the variety of ways in which the governors responded.

The actual appointment of governors was rarely susceptible to the influence of these interests in this period: the governors still owed their appointment to individual patrons—generally the principal officers of state—who were more concerned in finding jobs for unemployed military officers in this generation of intermittent war than they were with gratifying particular London interests. Only occasionally were the London or provincial interests consulted in the selection of a colonial governor. . . .

---

Reprinted by permission of the publisher from *Making the Empire Work: London and American Interest Groups, 1690–1790* by Alison M. Olson, Cambridge, Mass; Harvard University Press. Copyright © 1997 by the president and fellows of Harvard College.

Once the governors were nominated, however, various interests in London and America went to work on them at once. The minister of New York City's Anglican Church wrote to express his hope that "the Bishop of London with other friends will recommend me and my church to the favor and protection of the new Govr, and that affectionately," and dissenting ministers, merchants, and leaders of the Quaker meeting all expected their English associates to do the same. As the period wore on it became the custom for representatives of London interests to call upon governors before their departure, urging support for their colonial correspondents.

When the governor arrived in his colony, he was bound to be greeted by spokesmen for various interests offering food and entertainment, lodgings while his house was put in order, gold boxes, or simply addresses. . . . Typical was the experience of Virginia's Governor Spotswood, greeted by "abundance of Company" within hours of his arrival at Williamsburg, or New York's Lord Cornbury who wrote, on the very day of his arrival, that "I find at my coming hither great complaints of hardships suffered by many people." Clearly, Cornbury had been besieged by various interested parties from the moment he got off the ship.

In time provincial interests found various ways of exerting local influence on the governors, as well as on their councils and legislatures. Their technique centered mainly on offers of electoral support, political sermons, petitions, coffee house speeches, club meetings, and addresses of praise, whose main value was that the governor could send copies on to the Board of Trade or his English patrons as evidence of his local popularity; he could also send them to the relevant London interests to help gain their active support in keeping him in office.

The churches were particularly adept at applying pressure. When the governor was already a member of a church (most governors were Anglican), the church had considerable leverage over him from the beginning. The Bishop of London instructed vestries to appoint Anglican governors to memberships immediately upon their arrival. As a member of the congregation the governor had regularly to listen to sermons on church politics; if he paid insufficient heed to them he could be ostracized from the church's activities. . . .

If the governor was not considered sufficiently supportive, the local groups could turn their meetings, resolutions, petitions and addresses, and their other local weapons against him. Ministers could preach against him (the minister of Trinity Church in New York City preached so effectively against Governor Bellomont's efforts to convict some political leaders of treason that the trial was speeded up to give the minister fewer days on which to preach), and they could leave him out of their prayers. They might meet together to draw up pamphlets or broadsides against him.

In any event, well before they had exhausted their local resources, interest groups who were disappointed with a governor would have appealed back to London for help, seeking to destroy the confidence that his patrons, the Board, and the Privy Council had in him.

Just as governors forwarded favorable addresses and publicized favorable comments, their opponents sent copies of local petitions and addresses to concerned interests in London and gave local publicity to the Londoners' responses. . . .

By the late 1690s some of the London-American interests were sophisticated enough in their techniques to go beyond complaining on particular issues and attempt the total discrediting of certain governors with an eye to bringing them down. Governor Bellomont of New York was probably the first governor so targeted. Soon after his arrival in New York, Bellomont alienated the principal merchants of New York City by cracking down on their collusion with pirates. Soon after that he alienated both the Church of England and part of the Dutch Church by sponsoring legislation to take back lands granted to them with questionable wisdom, if not legality, by his predecessor, and by refusing to the Anglican minister the subsidy from the colony's treasury which Bellomont's predecessor had also granted. When he failed in his efforts to win over the Huguenots of New Rochelle and New York City by hiring a supporter of his who was also a Massachusetts Huguenot minister to serve them, he also cancelled the government's subsidy to the Huguenot minister. Within a year of Bellomont's arrival in the colony the Bishop of London was opposing him, some of the merchants had already sailed for England in order to work with their London correspondents for the governor's dismissal, the Dutch Church had sent one of its merchant members, Nicholas Bayard, to work against Bellomont with the Dutch Church at Austin Friars, and the Huguenot Church of St. Esprit had opened up correspondence with the French Church on Threadneedle Street. Had Bellomont not died suddenly on March 5, 1701, it is likely that he would have been the first gubernatorial victim of out-and-out interest group hostility.

By the time of Bellomont's death, then, it was clear that colonial governors had to be both opportunistic and defensive in dealing with the increasingly sophisticated London and provincial interests. The dangers and the opportunities varied from colony to colony, governor to governor. The three governors who survived longest in this period—and did so in part because they came to appreciate the need for careful maneuvering in the minefield of London-American interests—were Joseph Dudley of Massachusetts, Robert Hunter of New York, and Alexander Spotswood of Virginia. Each developed an awareness of which provincial interests were important to cultivate, which were marginal, which could be divided and thus neutralized, and which were not worth bothering with. Each used what patronage he had to favor the leaders of important interests, each entertained extensively (when Dudley invited Boston's Congregational ministers to his home, Cotton Mather complained that "they were eating of his Daintees and durst not reprove him"); each went as far as he could to grant the interests' various political demands. In these ways their approaches were similar. But they survived for different reasons and with different experiences. Spotswood dealt with a dominant Virginia tobacco aristocracy, whose English connections were powerful. In the time Dudley governed Massachusetts the Congregational-Presbyterian majority he had to work with actually had weaker London connections than did the minority opposing it, and it was Dudley's objective to make just enough concessions to the opposing interests to be able to utilize their English connections without entirely alienating the Congregational-Presbyterian local majority. Hunter, by contrast, worked among complicated sets of rival New York interests, each articulate locally and well-connected in England. Each governor had constantly to reassess the relations of his political patrons with the leaders of London interests for and against him. And each, for all his dexterity, was either brought down or worn down by the interplay of transatlantic pressures. A brief survey of the three men's gubernatorial careers shows the different ways in which London-American interests functioned from colony to colony.

Of the three Spotswood had the least room to maneuver. Spotswood governed a colony dominated by a homogeneous Anglican tobacco planter aristocracy, and there were few, if any, other interests in the colony that he could use as a counterweight.

The planters, if not deeply committed to Anglicanism as a faith, were at least agreed in their support of the Anglican organization, so there was no chance of building an ecclesiastical power base to rival the Church of England. As for the other churches in the colony, we have Robert Beverley's comment that "They have no more than five conventicles amongst them, namely three small meetings of Quakers and two of Presbyterians. 'Tis observed that those counties where the Presbyterian meetings are produce very mean tobacco and for that reason can't get a minister to stay amongst them." . . .

Similarly, there were no non-English groups with whom Spotswood could usefully ally. A proposed Swiss settlement never materialized, though Spotswood did try to help it; a German settlement that Spotswood himself encouraged finally drifted away, and at Manakin town there were only three hundred Frenchmen, whom Spotswood treated with contempt.

Nowhere, moreover, was there a community of merchants that Spotswood could work with to offset the economic power and mercantile connections of the wealthy planters. The colony included lesser planters in great numbers and with interests quite distinct from those of the great planters, but they were not organized as a group; moreover, the merchants they dealt with in England tended to be far less politicized than the merchant factors of the wealthier tobacco growers.

Lacking any alternative base of power, Spotswood had to try to develop what influence he could within the planter aristocracy. He tried, among other ways, to win over the Anglican clergy. He took up correspondence with the Bishop of London and became a member of the Society for Propagation of the Gospel. By passing an act establishing the value of tobacco in relation to the value of coinage, he helped stabilize clerical salaries that were paid in tobacco in the colony. Perhaps most important, by insisting that parishes must accept and support ministers appointed by himself Spotswood got the clergy's support by freeing them from dependence on the whims of their parishioners. Not all the clergy welcomed the governor's assistance, but enough of them did to keep Commissary James Blair from organizing a clerical offensive against Spotswood. By attempting to weaken the vestries, however, Spotswood raised an issue which was bound to create tensions between the clergy and their parishioners, thereby weakening the local influence of his clerical supporters. Patronage could be used to neutralize the clerical interest, not to bring it to the solid support of the governor.

When Spotswood attempted to build up his own support within the planter aristocracy, first by pushing for a tobacco inspection act and promising inspectorships to key politicians, and then by granting a monopoly of the Indian trade to a company of planters in return for their support, his efforts came to grief. The men who had been promised inspectorships were turned out of office in the next election, and the opponents of the Indian company appealed to England and got the act creating the company disallowed. William Byrd, one of the leading local opponents of the governor's Indian Trade Act and his Tobacco Inspection Act, went to London to work with the London merchants trading to Virginia in getting both acts repealed. He was completely successful. When the hearings were held at the Board of Trade, none of the merchants appeared on Spotswood's behalf, while "several" sent a protest and memorial against him. Byrd wrote smugly of "having a hand" in the merchant's activities. Both acts were disallowed, and Spotswood bitterly complained that "it is very well known that the merchants never ceased teazing your Lordships till both these acts were destroyed whether they were pushed on by the remonstrances of their correspondents here . . . I shall not now determine."

Thus Spotswood, who arrived in Virginia determined to wrest some reforms from the tobacco aristocracy that represented all the important interests of the colony, soon found that he had no local interests worth building up to counterbalance it, no way of using patronage or social influence to work on it from within, and insufficient resources to fight its connections in England. In his final years as governor he did the only thing practical at the time—capitulated and joined the group he could not dominate from outside. . . . Clearly, Spotswood had come to terms with a dominant provincial aristocracy in which all major local interests with London connections overlapped.

In one or two ways Governor Joseph Dudley of Massachusetts was worse off then Spotswood: a colonist himself who had lived for a time in England, he was associated with several Massachusetts interest groups so weak locally that they had little political clout, even on those rare occasions when they worked together. Dudley's associations were with very moderate Puritans, Huguenots, and a small, largely Anglican group within the merchant communities; during his administration he also gave some help to Quakers. These small groups, generally clustered in a few seaboard towns, were no political match for the overwhelming Presbyterian-Congregational majority of the colony, lesser merchants and tradesmen or farmers living in small agricultural towns with one Puritan church. Dudley's conversion to Anglicanism made him anathema to the Congregationalists, his identification with a select group of wealthy merchants was not popular with the farmers and lesser tradesmen, and his earlier support of James II's Dominion of New England had brought him considerable unpopularity among the small townsmen of Massachusetts, who wished to have as little to do as possible with the mother country. So the governor was at a disadvantage locally before he even entered his administration.

Dudley, moreover, lacked Spotswood's patronage: since the Massachusetts Council was elected by the lower house, he lacked the power to nominate its members; he never had any patronage comparable to Spotswood's short-lived tobacco inspectorships; and he lacked the power of appointing and inducting ministers in the established church, a power Spotswood had been able to use to neutralize the clergy of Virginia.

In another sense, however, Dudley was luckier than Spotswood, for the Quakers and Huguenots with whom he cooperated and the Anglicans and wealthy merchants with whom he identified had connections with powerful London interests, while the small-town Congregationalist farmers and tradesmen who were likely to oppose him had far weaker London connections than the tobacco planters Spotswood had to deal with. As yet the dissenters in London were poorly organized for lobbying: their ministers met sporadically and occasionally addressed the Queen, but they lacked sustained political organization. . . . Even by the end of Dudley's administration they still had not developed a lobby comparable to that of their ecclesiastical and mercantile rivals.

Although his circumstances were different, Dudley had little more room to maneuver than Spotswood had. His strategy was soon clear: make the minimum concessions necessary to retain the support of his Massachusetts associates and their London lobbies while trying not to antagonize the Congregational majority. By and large, the strategy worked.

His approach is evident with a number of groups. He managed to retain the support of the bulk of London merchants trading to New England, many of whom he had met earlier during his long periods of residence in England. (Many of them had petitioned for his appointment in the first place.) He did this by giving patronage and contracts to their biggest correspondents in Boston and by supporting their demands that ships in the British navy cease carrying certain commercial goods, but the favors cost Dudley the support of the lesser Boston merchants and cost the larger merchants their newly acquired leadership of Boston politics. Dudley may well have found that the cost of maintaining the friendship of a Boston mercantile clique was greater than the rewards of the London support it brought. . . .

For Anglicans, too, Dudley had kind thoughts and not much practical help. Dudley's administration coincided with a period of steady if not very spectacular growth of the Anglican Church in Massachusetts. In 1702, when Dudley took office, the only organized Anglican Church in the colony was in Boston, though there was a small group of Anglicans in Braintree without a minister. In the next thirteen years Anglican churches were organized in five other towns and the S.P.G. [Society for the Propagation of the Gospel] sent over three missionaries to help them out. By the end of Dudley's administration there was as yet no formal organization of ministers, but it was generally acknowledged that the Reverend Samuel Myles of Boston was their leading spokesman.

Dudley himself, though raised a Puritan, was a convert to Anglicanism, a member of the S.P.G., and a corresponding member of the Society for Promoting Christian Knowledge. . . .

Of actual help to the Anglicans, however, Dudley gave very little. . . .

The religious group that was organizing fastest during Dudley's administration was the Quakers; and they, also, got rather nominal help from the governor. Guided by visitors from the London Meeting for Sufferings, the New England Yearly Meeting began taking over the authority and functions—including appeals to England—that had previously been exercised fairly randomly by various monthly meetings and even by individuals. It was also during Dudley's administration that the New England Yearly Meeting began sending agents to London to work with the London Meeting for Sufferings on the repeal of New England laws offensive to Quakers. In response the London meeting established both a committee to handle parliamentary affairs and a committee (largely composed of Quaker merchants trading to the area) to correspond with New England Quakers.

Here, as with the Anglicans and the Huguenots, Dudley had a delicate line to draw in working with a strong transatlantic lobby on the one hand, and an implacably hostile local majority on the other. His concern to keep on good terms with the English Quakers is shown by his making sure that they knew of his reprimand of a Boston newspaper editor who printed an article critical of Quaker lobbying in England. But the limits of his ability to give practical aid to Quakers also became clear early in his administration: an act passed by the Massachusetts General Court in

November 1706 ordered Justices of the Peace to present the names of all towns destitute of a (Congregational) minister. If towns failed to appoint and support a minister, then the General Court was to appoint one, levy and collect taxes, and pay the minister. The act particularly hit the Massachusetts town of Dartmouth, a Quaker center whose magistrates refused to collect the rates and were, predictably, thrown in jail. When they first petitioned Dudley he greeted them warmly and agreed to write to the Board of Trade about their case (which he did, in fairly neutral terms). Accordingly, the Quakers then sent on to the London Meeting for Sufferings a petition to be forwarded to the Queen. Dudley then had the Quaker assessors discharged from jail. The strategy worked: the London Meeting for Sufferings did not forward the petition, but the Congregational majority in the General Court did not complain. Dudley had done just enough for the Quakers to win their "Salutation of respect" and "acknowledgements of his severall ffavors and kindnesses" and to preserve their good will for the rest of his administration.

Rather than saying that Dudley did the least required to neutralize the increasingly effective transatlantic organization he faced, it might be fairer to say that, confronted with a hostile majority in the court and the council, he found it impossible to do more than use his executive office to advise, serve as a conduit for messages to the Board of Trade, and release prisoners from jail. Like Spotswood, he had confronted a homogeneous majority in his colony; unlike Virginia, the Massachusetts majority was not particularly well connected in London, while its opponents were. Spotswood had virtually no room to maneuver because the dominant group in the colony was the only group with English connections able to help them; Dudley had only slightly more room because the local Congregational majority could bring far more pressure on him than could the English allies of their opponents.

In contrast to both Dudley and Spotswood, Governor Robert Hunter of New York had a good deal of room in which to maneuver. In 1710, when Hunter took up his administration, he found himself operating in a network of London-American interest groups that were certainly the most complex of the period: with its heterogeneous ethnic, religious, and even mercantile background New York contained the richest variety of interest groups in this period, enjoying the most complicated relations with interest groups overseas. Instead of a homogeneous majority (in which several interests overlapped) opposed by hopelessly small alternative groups, New York had a number of large interest groups; in New York City, for example, about 50 percent of the population was still Dutch, 35 percent English, 15 percent Huguenot, and there were about 40 Jewish families. Most of the groups, moreover, were further cross-cut into sub-interests by geographical distinctions, class lines, and party divisions dating back to Jacob Leisler's administration. . . .

The Leislerian and anti-Leislerian banners spread out to cover two groups of roughly comparable local strength. The Church of England members, some wealthy Dutch leaders, wealthy Huguenots, thirty of the forty leading merchants in New York City, and later some of the Palatine settlers were anti-Leislerians in sympathy; Presbyterians, Quakers, less wealthy French and Dutch, and the small but strong group of New York City Jews tended to be Leislerian.

Unlike Governor Dudley, Hunter was not committed to any one set of interests by previous experience in the colony, and well after his arrival he was still trying to play a neutral role. But neutrality could not work forever, and after several months Hunter committed himself to the Leislerian grouping. On the face of it, he appeared to have made a disastrous mistake, for though the two groups were fairly equally balanced in provincial politics, the anti-Leislerian groups had potentially far stronger support in London. The Church of England had the Bishop of London and the S.P.G.; the wealthy Huguenots corresponded with the Threadneedle Street Church in London; the wealthier members of the Dutch Church corresponded with the Classis of Amsterdam and with the London Church at Austin Friars far more than did the less wealthy fragment of the church, the anti-Leislerian merchants had the support of a majority of the politically active London merchants trading to New York, and the Palatines had the support of merchants, court chaplains, the S.P.C.K. [Society for the Propagation of Christian Knowledge], and the remnants of the London committee set up to help them in 1710. Against them Hunter's allies had only a mixed bag of London supporters. Strongest were the Quakers; Hunter had pushed hard for an act allowing them to take a solemn affirmation instead of an oath in New Jersey, even though "Our men of noise have excited their talent against the Act." Behind them were the Presbyterians: they were not very well organized in London but what strength they had went to Hunter, "their particular friend." Jewish support—and this possibly included support from the London synagogue at Bevis Marks—came when Hunter pushed through the assembly special acts giving the Jews naturalization.

Except for the Quakers, this combination did not give Hunter a particularly strong nucleus of support, so he had to maneuver with his potential enemies. If they had all worked together they would have been almost unbeatable. . . . But they never did work effectively. Partly by strategy and partly by good luck Hunter was able to make the most of hitches in the transatlantic cooperation and lack of cohesion within the groups.

Two of the groups he neutralized locally, the French by befriending and entertaining their leaders (he had lunch several times in one week, for example, with John Fontaine, a visitor with distinguished connections in the French L'Eglise du St. Esprit), by pushing through the New York Assembly a bill declaring that the children of aliens who had settled in the colony by 1683 were deemed naturalized respecting their right to hold inherited lands, an act which benefitted Huguenots and Dutch, and by restoring the Huguenot minister's salary which Bellomont had cut off. The Dutch he neutralized by declining to press the governor's right to appoint their ministers, thereby eliminating the main issue of contention with earlier governors. Hunter was helped by the disappointment of the Amsterdam Classis [the governing body of the Dutch Reformed Church], which had expected to work through the Dutch ambassador's influence on the Duke of Marlborough, the leading British minister. Marlborough was dismissed from office in 1710, however, and the Classis had no way to influence his successor. New York Dutch had mixed reactions: they complained to the Classis that the "public Declaration and Confession of your impotence does great harm and is very injurious to the General condition of the church," but they had also to admit that "by a change of administration [in New York] a change for the better came to us."

Rather easily Hunter had disarmed the Dutch and French leadership. But his striking successes came with the Anglican Church, the London merchants, and the Palatines. With the Anglican Church he was quite fortunate in the long run. The local leaders were anti-Leislerian and so opposed to him, but Hunter was able to divide the church and neutralize their power. In both New York and New Jersey the Anglican Church served a small minority of the inhabitants (1,200 out of 45,000 in New York), but this minority included leading politicians with strong English allies. . . .

But Hunter himself was an Anglican, a member of the S.P.G., a friend of leading Anglican bishops such as Swift, and he was just as aggressive in courting Anglican support as were the anti-Leislerians in Trinity Church. By personal appeals he won over to his side the two other leading S.P.G. members in the colony, Lewis Morris and Caleb Heathcote; through them and through his own correspondence with the Society he won over part of the S.P.G.; he rebuilt the old Anglican Chapel in the Fort and set up a rival Anglican Church there, attracting members away from Trinity Church. When Vesey called meetings of the clergy, Hunter summoned rival meetings at the same time. He was careful to present his side of every question in regular correspondence to the S.P.G., and he pressed for an Anglican bishop in the colonies, someone whose authority would supersede that of self-appointed local leaders.

Thus Hunter was able to divide the English bishops, the S.P.G., the New York ministers, and even Trinity Church itself. The long-run result was a stalemate; for the last part of Hunter's administration the Anglican interest in New York was neutralized. . . .

The Huguenots, the Anglicans, and the merchants were the core of the governor's opposition. By taking them on at different times, by capitalizing on differences with the New York merchants to narrowly provincial grounds, Robert Hunter was the most successful of the governors in neutralizing the efforts of his local opponents to capitalize on London connections. His successes showed that there were limits to the help provincials could expect from Londoners—but those limits were likely to be realized with an exceptionally able and lucky governor, working with a variety of interest groups so his opposition could be fragmented.

Thus in the quarter-century after 1689, the very effort to placate London-American interests taught the colonial governments some of the limits of their power. But for the interest groups, too, the period was one of learning, of trial and error. In attempting to influence governors the interests experimented with methods that revealed their own limits.

Several factors were responsible for these limits. For one thing, governors were appointed and removed by the leading ministers of state; as most London-American interests of the period lacked influence at the ministerial level, they had no direct leverage over the appointments. In a period of intensely partisan Whig-Tory strife in English politics the ability of patrons to get colonial governorships for their clients depended on their party's power and on their own influence within the party, rather than on their connections with interests.

In this period, moreover, interest groups were still experimenting with techniques for influencing newly appointed governors before they left London; by 1715, for example, they had not yet developed forms of public entertainment which they later used to extract expressions of open support from the new appointees. The fact that many governors appeared to have been caught by surprise by the complaints of various interests when they arrived in their colonies suggests that Londoners had been less than urgent about acquainting the new governors with the needs of their provincial colleagues.

Once the governors arrived in the colonies, they found interest group pressures less strong than they might have been because the London interests were themselves often divided along Whig-Tory lines, coinciding to some extent with High Church-Low Church divisions. Hunter in particular was able to escape the full weight of their influence for this reason. With the exception of the Chesapeake merchants, London merchants trading to America were divided roughly along the lines of the colonists they traded with—pro- and anti-Leislerian in New York, pro- and anti-Proprietary in Philadelphia, Anglican versus dissenter in Boston and Charles Town—as Anglican and Huguenot merchants were moving up the social ranks in the seaport towns and were joining or supplanting Dutch merchants, English Puritans, or English Quakers at the top of the social scale. Divisions of other kinds among the non-English ethnic groups also kept them from concentrating their efforts in the period. In London there was a three-way social division between the French of the Threadneedle Street Church, those of the Savoy, and those of Spitalfields; an ecclesiastical division between those who became Anglican and those who became Presbyterian; and a political division between colonial Huguenots who tended to be Tory and Londoners who were Whig. Jews divided their allegiance between the Sephardic leaders at Bevis Marks and the Ashkenazic ones of small synagogues; Germans were either aristocrats with their own society or poorer people with no connections there. All of them were in various stages of assimilation and as such had different ideas about supporting the demands of their provincial counterparts for isolation and autonomy within their colonies. Indeed, in this period only the Quakers and the Virginia merchants seem to have enjoyed unity, and even the Quakers were temporarily split by the Keithian schism.

A far more important factor in the equation was that governors in colonies still dominated by a homogeneous majority lacked the power to do much for minority interests, however much pressure their colleagues applied from London. Dudley could do little for Massachusetts minorities except release them when they were imprisoned for breaking provincial law; Spotswood rarely tried to do anything. Significantly, more was done for minorities in New York, where the blocs in the assembly were closely matched. In assemblies where particular minorities could produce swing votes on crucial issues (as was true of the Huguenots in South Carolina) they were in a strong position, but this was rare. Thus before 1715 the influence of London interests was strongest on the middle colonies and on South Carolina, societies too varied to be dominated by any single group in which a variety of interests overlapped.

In 1715 an American colonist visiting London would easily have noticed the recent proliferation of London interest groups with American connections. Half a century before, there had been no such groups; thirty years before only three or four. Now there were well over a dozen. With the exception of the Moravians, the Dissenting Deputies, and interests clustered around the founding of Georgia, all of the London-American interests that remained important down to the Revolution were established by 1715. Interests in the provinces looked to Londoners for help on questions they could not handle at the provincial level. They were learning, with some resentment, that Londoners were better equipped to handle such problems because of their proximity to the capital, their position at the center of an information-gathering network, their enhanced ability to function in London's pluralistic society, their greater concentration of wealth and numbers. Londoners, meanwhile, were learning that they could still influence decision-making on American as well as English issues, and some political value attached to serving as spokesmen for interests throughout the provinces.

As one would expect from their development, most of the connections between interests were in the experimental stage, a stage that involved trial and error with the means of communication, forms of organization, and types of pressure, as the groups tested the various institutions of government to find which were most responsive and probed the limits of their influence. As one would also expect, their successes were uneven. They had proved more successful in dealing with the British government at home than with the governors in the provinces, more successful in working with the Board of Trade than with Parliament, the King, or the ministers, and more successful in the pluralistic middle colonies than in the homogenous colonies of the Chesapeake and New England. But rough though they were, the groups were ready to press further with their transatlantic lobbying in the years after 1715. Thanks to the responsiveness of English institutions, interests in England and America were beginning to establish that stable relationship with the government so essential to the placid administration of Walpole, Henry Pelham and the Duke of Newcastle in the heyday of London-American interests that was soon to come.

## British Imperial Policy and the Frontier

### WARREN R. HOFSTRA

During the 1730s, in Virginia west of the Blue Ridge, a settlement frontier developed whose society and culture contrasted sharply with those already established in the colony. A large majority of the new western inhabitants, unlike Virginians elsewhere, were non-English, predominantly German and Scotch-Irish. Called "foreign Protestants" and Irish Protestants, they were almost exclusively white—few Africans or African Americans were among them. Settlers practiced dissenting and sectarian faiths, most stressing a common humanity. Elsewhere, not only was Virginia organized under the Church of England but conforming Virginians largely subscribed to the deferential social practice of the established church. Moreover, western settlers were not tobacco producers. They were yeoman farmers instead of planters—smallholders raising grains and livestock, employing family more often than slave labor, practicing handcrafts, and trading locally in the context of community self-sufficiency.

. . . European refugees wanted land, and Virginia let them have it on very attractive terms. Pouring into Pennsylvania after 1720 from straitened circumstances in Europe and frustrated by high land prices and political disputes, German and Scotch-Irish immigrants turned south to the Shenandoah Valley, where land was good and land prices low. . . .

To explain the movement of peoples to the Virginia frontier during the eighteenth century requires a new perspective that connects the concerns of settlers and the interests of speculators with the geopolitical and imperial forces that defined

Warren R. Hofstra, "'The Extension of His Majesty's Dominions': The Virginia Backcountry and the Reconfiguration of Imperial Frontiers," *Journal of American History* 84(4), March 1998, pp. 1281–1312.

frontiers and made their settlement both possible and expedient. The buffer settlements of European Protestants that the colonial government established west of the Blue Ridge between 1730 and 1745 were part of a larger effort to check French expansion across the interior of North America, extend English dominion, secure a western periphery destabilized by Indian conflict, and occupy mountain fastnesses otherwise a refuge to runaway slaves. What met the needs of Europeans looking for land and economic competence in property ownership also served the interests of colonial officials. Events in the Virginia backcountry from 1730 to 1750, moreover, reflected imperial responses to developments between 1700 and 1722 when France laid the basis for a continental empire, northern and southern Indians resumed disruptive wars across that continent, and African slavery came to define the southern colonial labor system. English colonial governments sought ways to secure established, plantation regions from the threats posed by those changes. Williamsburg and London therefore provide the perspective for explaining why a society that differed so significantly from Virginia traditions developed on a strategically sensitive frontier and under the auspices of the elite that governed the colony in its own interest.

Developments in Virginia compose a case study of change in the eighteenth-century backcountry, conceived for the first time as extending continuously from Nova Scotia south to the Carolinas and, eventually, to Georgia. As William Gooch and the Virginia Council began issuing orders for land west of the Blue Ridge, the Board of Trade and the governor of South Carolina matured plans to lay out frontier towns surrounding that colony's Low Country plantations. Similarly, the board and the government of New York were negotiating the establishment of a chain of forts and settlements that would extend English control north and west from Albany to the centers of French power along the St. Lawrence River and the Great Lakes. Farther east, on the coasts of present-day Maine and Nova Scotia, colonial agents were formulating additional settlement projects. The distinctiveness of the entire backcountry was in part the inevitable consequence of the cultures immigrant peoples brought to the region. But in reconfiguring frontiers, British officials on both sides of the Atlantic Ocean came to see predominantly white, Protestant, yeoman societies as distinctively advantageous to securing a continental frontier. Elsewhere, as in Virginia, backcountry settlement developed out of a coincidence of interests among settlers, speculators, and imperial authorities, but the key to the social construction of this frontier lay with the imperatives of empire.

In Virginia those interests and imperatives met in the forces that transformed what Europeans called wilderness or waste land into property. From the viewpoint of imperial officials, land grants west of the Blue Ridge represented the extension of sovereignty over unorganized territory through the authority of the state in the person of the king to fabricate property. From the viewpoint of European immigrants, however, rights to land meant economic competence and independence from the subject relations of feudal society. Once on the land, these men and women established dispersed communities of enclosed or self-contained farms and household economies lacking the centers of power and forms of administrative control English authorities associated with what the Virginia Council described as "the Extention of His Majesties Dominions." . . .

Insofar as England settled its Virginia frontier through the extension of property rights from the Crown to those taking up land and through the authority of county governments to secure property, facilitate economic development, and provide for the common defense, it was colonial officials, not settlers, who defined the process. Officials could exploit it for their speculative interests, but they also had to act on behalf of the Crown. . . .

The frontier then was an imperial story. . . .

The forces that set the European occupation of the Virginia backcountry in motion can be traced to three sets of developments in the interlude between the close of the War of the League of Augsburg in 1697 and the opening of the War of the Spanish Succession five years later. Those developments set the stage upon which imperial officials reconceptualized English frontiers in colonial North America. In its influential report of September 8, 1721, the Board of Trade moved beyond a colony-by-colony consideration of defense issues and set forth proposals about the security of English colonies based on a continental reconfiguration of the American backcountry. The implementation of these proposals in the decades after 1720 helps explain events in Virginia and elucidates connections between imperial decision making and the evolution of backcountry society.

The first development occurred in Virginia during the peace of 1697–1702, when a boom in the tobacco economy stimulated investments in land and slaves bringing more than one million acres into private hands and three thousand slaves to the colony. Within two decades the number of slaves brought annually to Virginia approached two thousand, and the black population nearly doubled. Territorial expansion and the continuing threat of war in Europe led to an increased concern for colonial defenses. . . .

In a second set of developments, the region between English Carolina and Spanish Florida became contested ground for European powers and Native Americans. From 1698 to 1699 France initiated colonizing efforts in the Gulf of Mexico, Spain responded by establishing the presidio of San Carlos de Austria at Pensacola, South Carolina attempted to extend its Indian trade to the Mississippi, and the English colonizer Daniel Coxe endeavored to plant a Huguenot colony at the mouth of that river. Within three years France had extended its grasp on the North American interior with posts and forts at Cahokia and Kaskaskia in the Illinois Country and along the Great Lakes at Detroit. Native Americans strove to keep all these forces at bay. Virginia governors during the ensuring half century fretted increasingly over the possibility of a French commercial link—an imperial "communication"—between outposts in Canada and Louisiana. But the influence among western Indians that France could achieve through trade and the trouble these Indians could make for Virginia represented a far greater peril to the colony's security than French military power, at least until 1750.

Thus the French threat magnified the third development of the European peace: the entanglement of the Five Nations of Iroquoia in the imperial contentions of the Southeast. In separate agreements concluded in Montreal and Albany in 1701, the Five Nations abandoned violent efforts to engross the northern peltry trade and adopted instead a policy of neutrality between France and England. The Five

Nations then resumed domestic mourning-wars against the Cherokees, Catawbas, Creeks, and Yamasees. These conflicts were intended to replenish kinship circles with captives and to vitalize tribal leadership through opportunities for young warriors to gain stature in feats of bravery. The Five Nations could also use threats of southern warfare as a bargaining chip in diplomatic efforts to maintain neutrality with France and England. . . .

War parties crossing Virginia territory threatened the colony's frontier inhabitants and disrupted Virginia Indians. . . . Entwined affiliations inevitably drew Virginia Indians into distant wars, and their tributary agreements with Williamsburg enmeshed the colonial government in those wars. The movement of non-English Europeans into the region west of the Blue Ridge during the next interval in the imperial wars of England and France, 1713–1744, resulted from attempts by Virginia's governors to resolve the costly conflicts on the colony's frontiers developing out of Indian hostilities and the French connection. . . .

The governor . . . asked the assembly, not to fortify, but to possess the mountain passes. He pointed to the "naked State" of the frontiers and called on the members to give "Encouragement for Extending your Out Settlements to the high Ridge of Mountains [as] the best Barrier that nature could form to Secure this Colony, from the Incursions of the Indians and more dangerous Incroachments of the *French.*" The assembly responded by creating two new counties. Spotsylvania County was to command the northern gap over the Blue Ridge at Swift Run while Brunswick defended Rockfish Gap to the south. Incentives for settling the areas spreading eastward from these gaps included a ten-year remission of local taxes, colonial appropriations for military supplies and public buildings, deferral of land payments, and provision of arms and ammunition at public expense. Spotswood then demonstrated his seriousness about uniting the interests of empire and colonial landowners by obtaining warrants for forty thousand acres of land for himself and petitioning the Crown to exempt everybody who settled in the new counties from quitrents. Rightly concerned that some Virginians would exploit these incentives to engross large speculative tracts in the Piedmont, the Privy Council limited grants to one thousand acres but concurred with the need to secure the mountain passes and granted the quitrent exemption.

Spotswood and the assembly also took decisive steps to end the violence on the Virginia frontier by establishing the Blue Ridge as a barrier between the Five Nations and Indians living in Virginia. Spotswood had already presented the Five Nations with a plan for limiting their travel to a corridor west of the Blue Ridge. He promised that the Virginia Indians would remain to the east. By 1721 all parties had come to terms, and Spotswood traveled to Albany the next year to conclude negotiations personally, making the Albany Treaty the last act of his administration.

By 1722, when Spotswood left office, his administration had hammered out principles that would shape how royal officials established new settlements in Virginia. Spotswood's experiences demonstrated that threats to the colony from the Indians and the French came separately. But trade and diplomacy inextricably linked the fortunes of all nations, Indian and European. Virginia, however, lacked sufficient trade to forge alliances with Native Americans that could secure the colony's frontiers. Military force by itself was also inadequate to safeguard Virginia. Only settlement buffers could accomplish the task. . . . Only subject Europeans could be mobilized into settlement buffers through land grants; foreign Protestants seemed most likely to lend themselves to this use. Finally, the Blue Ridge formed a natural barrier against both the French and Indians. Securing it with settlement buffers was a primary objective.

While Governor Spotswood of Virginia pursued the plan of fortifying and settling the Blue Ridge barrier, the Board of Trade conceived its program of defense and security for a continuous English colonial frontier stretching from Nova Scotia to the Carolinas. In that program Spotswood's barrier ridge played a critical role. . . .

The Board of Trade queried colonial governors and agents and others knowledgeable on colonial affairs about the "number of the Militia" or "forts and places of defense" in each colony, the "number of Indians . . . and how are they inclined," their "strength," and the "strength of your neighbouring Europeans." "What effect," the board wanted to know, "have the French Settlements on the Continent of America upon H.M. Plantations?" The construction of a fort by the French at Niagara and the growing French influence among the Seneca that blocked the Albany trade were major concerns of New York. From William Keith, lieutenant governor of Pennsylvania, the board heard that only in cultivating the Indian trade could the English hope to preserve themselves and break the hold of the French on the interior and its inhabitants. Keith drew heavily upon a paper provincial secretary James Logan had prepared in 1718. Logan had observed that the French have "with great care settled a communication between Canada and the Southern countries" on the Mississippi River. He suggested that "to prevent the designs of the French" the English government must "preserve the Iroquese," "encourage the Government of Virginia to Extend their settlements beyond the mountains," and advise colonial governors to "take special care of the commerce with the Indians." "By these means all the Indians . . . may be very much united to the British interest," he concluded. The board learned from John Barnwell and Joseph Boone, agents for South Carolina, that the "Method of the French" was to "build Forts on their Frontiers." The English ought "to do likewise, not only to preserve Our Trade with the Indians and their Dependance upon Us, but to preserve our Boundaries." Of immediate concern to South Carolina was the exposed region between the Savannah and Altamaha rivers recently vacated by the defeated Yamasees.

After deliberating nearly a year, the board on September 8, 1721, forwarded to the king a report on the "state of your Majesty's Plantations on the Continent of America." In most respects the report mirrored the recommendations of colonial governments. . . .

For Virginia, where "strength and security . . . in a great measure, depend upon their Militia; their plantations being usually at too great a distance from one another to be cover'd by forts or towns," the board endorsed Spotswood's "scheme for securing ye passes over the great ridge of mountains." . . .

. . . The board . . . addressed common defense and security issues. Because French encirclement threatened all the colonies collectively and the destabilizing influences of Indian conflicts engulfed the intercolonial interior, the frontier had to be conceived on the scale of the continent. Thus the board called for "making ourselves considerable at the two heads of your Majesty's Colonies north and south; and [for] building of forts, as the French have done, in proper places on the inland frontiers. . . . naturally fortify'd by a chain of mountains, that run from the back of South Carolina as far as New York, passable but in few places." . . .

Indian relations likewise had to be approached as a matter of imperial interest, and the board reasoned that "the Indian trade, if properly carried on, would greatly contribute to the increase of your Majesty's power and intrest in America." Indians ought to be furnished "at honest and reasonable prices with the several European commodities they may have occasion for," and commerce with Native Americans ought to be extended "westward upon the lakes and rivers behind the mountains [where] forts should be built and garrisons settled in proper places." To implement all its proposals and "render the several provinces on the Continent of America, from Nova Scotia to South Carolina, mutually subservient to each other's support," the board in conclusion recommended that the king "put the whole under the Government of one Lord Lieut. or Captain General" who with two councilors from each colony would possess the power to issue orders to colonial governors "in all cases for your Majesty's service."

Not only did the board reconfigure the North American frontier as a single entity with an interior mountain barrier and zones of contention at northern and southern perimeters, but the periphery of colonial settlement came to be regarded as an area of internal as well as external threat. Any frontier presented a constant temptation to enslaved Africans to rise up and seek asylum beyond the bounds of British authority. Alexander Spotswood placed this construction on the mountains he himself explored when he reported to the Virginia Council in 1721 that "diverse Negro's . . . have lately run away & suspected to be gone towards ye Great Mountains, where it may be hard to apprehd 'em, & if they shou'd encrease there, it might prove of ill consequence to ye Peace of this Colony." . . .

By the early 1720s, therefore, the Board of Trade had succeeded in redefining North American frontiers according to the natural and political geography of English, French, Spanish, and Native American settlement. To counter the threats posed by the frontier, the board had developed an arsenal of weapons including forts, garrisons, British regulars, and manipulation of the Indian trade. But most important for the social construction of the emerging backcountry were the numerous proposals for settling vacant and sensitive areas with dependents of the English Crown. From the perspective of imperial officials in London and the colonial capitals, new immigrants annually increasing in numbers during the late 1710s and 1720s from the north of Ireland and central Europe possessed characteristics ideal for these backcountry buffer settlements. They were white, Protestant, and yeoman.

The Board of Trade and colonial governors made explicit their intention to populate the backcountry with white people. The report of September 1721 had recommended white servant immigration as an antidote to South Carolina's black majority. Eleven years later the board could advise the Privy Council that "it has been the *constant sense* of this Board, that all ye British Colonies and especially the two frontiers, should be peopled as amply and as soon as soon as possible wh. white inhabitants." . . .

Protestantism . . . was a required asset for English buffers against the Catholic monarchies of France and Spain. Imperial wars for territory and trade waged from the seventeenth to the eighteenth centuries were also religious wars between the cultures of Protestantism and Catholicism for the souls, lands, and wealth of the uncommitted. The dangers posed by Catholic inhabitants of an English frontier were made plain in Nova Scotia, where the Acadians threatened English dominion. . . .

Other qualities of white, Protestant immigrants rendered their communities natural buffers against both internal and external threats to the settled areas of English America. Most came from diversified, small-farm economies in Europe and migrated to the English colonies as families seeking the independence that a competence in landholding, family labor, and diversified agriculture could provide. A mentality of competence combined with modest means to encourage the formation of socially and economically integrated communities of middling landholdings averaging usually less than four hundred acres. Slavery was neither alien or antithetical to these yeoman peoples, but mixed farming on small holdings did not generate a significant demand for bonded labor beyond what could be provided by white indentured servants. Yeoman societies did not produce black majorities. And communities of independent smallholders had long been recognized as the essential element of the best militia forces.

If eighteenth-century backcountry societies were culturally diverse and characterized by freeholding yeoman farm families pursuing an array of interdependent economic activities, these traits owed as much to the cultures of constituent peoples as to the use made of those cultures by imperial officials engaged in a struggle for colonial security. The qualities that made the backcountry a distinctive region in early America were not, however, the product of an explicit British colonial policy. The report of September 1721 was not a policy paper. But in effecting a continental reconfiguration of North American frontiers, it accomplished for all the British mainland colonies what Spotswood achieved for Virginia in the 1720 land act and the Albany Treaty. Moreover, most of the report's recommendations, with the notable exception of the proposal for a captain general, were eventually realized in practice, not because the board imposed its proposals as policy, but because they represented working assumptions widely shared by officials at all ranks in the British colonial system. Insofar as colonial governors and members of colonial councils also shared those assumptions, they possessed a remarkably free hand in acting on them. Thus imperial efforts varied from colony to colony and from one decade to another. . . .

On June 8, 1728, William Gooch, in office as lieutenant governor for less than twelve months, informed the Board of Trade that the "great number of Petitions for Land . . . will be an Evidence of the Increase of the colony, and the flourishing Condition of the King's Revenue." It was one year later that this governor defended large grants in Spotsylvania County on the social theory that the "Shade & Protection of the Greater" gave "encouragement to the meaner sort." But from 1730 to 1732 the governor and Council issued nine grants to individuals and groups for a total of 385,000 acres in the Shenandoah Valley outside the bounds of Spotsylvania County. With the exception of William Beverley, an Essex County planter with close ties to the Council, and his partners, none of these grantees were Virginians, English, or the "men of substance" that Virginia governors and the Council had depended upon to organize settlement in the Piedmont. The governor therefore fixed upon them a requirement to recruit and settle one family for every one thousand acres granted. Settlers were to receive patents for their land through the colony's grantees. That these men's ties lay largely among recent immigrants from the German Palatinate and the north of Ireland practically guaranteed cultural diversity on the Shenandoah Valley frontier. . . .

Gooch perhaps felt an additional pressure to hasten settlement west of the Blue Ridge—the possibility that unoccupied mountain lands would become a haven for runaway slaves and a stimulus for slave uprisings. Spotswood had earlier pointed to this possibility. The English colony of Jamaica lay in the grips of a maroon war that would not be resolved for another decade. Concern for the internal security of black-majority colonies such as South Carolina had produced the "constant sense" among members of the Board of Trade that colonial frontiers must be white. Virginia's slave population had reached thirty thousand, the largest of any in the English mainland colonies. In June 1729 the governor reported to the board that approximately fifteen refugees from a James River plantation "formed a Design to withdraw from their master and to fix themselves in the fastnesses of the neighbouring Mountains." Stealing arms and tools, they settled themselves in a "very obscure place among the 'Mountains', where they had already begun to clear the ground" when they were discovered and forcibly returned to slavery. "So [was] prevented for this time a design," Gooch observed, "which might have proved as dangerous to this country, as is that of the negroes of the mountains of Jamaica to the inhabitants of that island." The governor concluded that "Tho' this attempt has happily been defeated, it ought nevertheless to awaken us into some effectual measures for preventing the like hereafter." In 1728 the assembly had passed an act "for making more effectual provision against Invasions and Insurrections," and the governor had subsequently commissioned an adjutant to train local militias against slave uprisings. The mountains unfortunately lay beyond the pale of militia organization. . . .

Gooch's efforts to establish buffer settlements of white, Protestant, yeoman peoples west of the Blue Ridge by relying upon the attractions of property holding had important consequences for the emerging social landscape of the eighteenth-century frontier. Reflecting the aggregate outcome of individual searches for good land, the morphology of Gooch's settlements was, in an immediate sense, the collective expression of those people who took up the land. The governor's policies, for instance, did not require the concentration of population around fortifications, towns, or townships. . . . Colonial authorities, however, never lost sight of the larger purposes for which backcountry settlements existed. Having drawn people to the Virginia frontier with the allurement of "free" land and allowed for their "disorderly" dispersal, the governor and Council then overlaid the institutions of county government on the frontier incrementally, during two decades, in a pattern that ordered the backcountry according to the interests of the colony and coincidentally with the concerns of settlers.

The first description of settlements in the Shenandoah Valley came from the Philadelphia naturalist John Bartram. On October 22, 1738, while on a botanizing venture for the British scientist Peter Collinson, this meticulous observer stood on the Blue Ridge and described a "fine prospect of A spacious vail & ye next great ridge northward." During the following two days he traveled through the vale and the Opequon Settlement there, noting that it was "very thinly inhabited with [people] that is lately settled there & lives A lazy life & subsists by hunting." By 1735 the Virginia government had issued eighty-seven patents throughout a broad territory stretching forty-five miles south from the Potomac River and occupied by a total of perhaps 160 families. As a later Virginia governor put it, they "scattered for the Benefit for the best Lands."

Open-country neighborhoods of dispersed small farms clustered fanlike around the drainages of Opequon Creek or tributaries such as Mill Creek. Situated within property holdings and reflecting close attention to topography and resources, dwellings for single families stood at one-quarter- to one-half-mile intervals on

stream terraces or rudimentary roads. Subsistence farming yielded a familiar patchwork of fields and woodlands. Although by the end of the 1730s many households
produced hides, butter, and even linen for market, most families organized the land
in a ramshackle pattern of small enclosures, fencing livestock out of planted land
around dwellings. "Ye people most of them came from Jersey or Pensilvania," observed Bartram, "sows wheat & oats flax & hemp on ye high ground & hath fine
meadows on ye low." Although slavery was not unknown, the large majority of laborers were white, and even by the 1750s blacks constituted less than 4 percent of
the population in the Shenandoah Valley.

The process of fabricating property out of waste land revealed most clearly
how the world of Opequon evolved as the interests of settlers were made to meet
the security needs of colonial authorities. Acknowledging "his Majesty having by
his Governour & Council agreed to grant us those Lands upon the Consideration of
settling so many Families . . . for the Defence and Extension of the Frontier of his
Government," Jost Hite formed "a Guard to protect them agt. small parties of Hostile Indians, while they were surveying & settling in this Rugged Wilderness." . . .

The surveying and dispensing of land in the Shenandoah Valley occurred
squarely in the path of the Six Nations, whose right to travel west of the Blue Ridge
had been defined by the Albany Treaty in 1722. Ensuring conflicts between settlers
and Native Americans drove the colony to complete the settlement process and impose its own order on the backcountry by progressively erecting the institutions of
county government. . . . Later in 1734 the assembly created Orange County out of
the Spotsylvania piedmont and extended it "westerly, by the utmost limits of Virginia" thus incorporating the Shenandoah Valley settlements for the first time
within the bounds and protections of Virginia counties.

When the Williamsburg government subsequently established counties exclu-
sively within the Shenandoah Valley, however, it was responding, not to increases
in western population, but to Indian conflicts. During the mid-1730s Gooch and the
Council sought a negotiated end to the wars of the northern and southern Indians.
On May 5, 1736, the Council noted "the dangers which may happen to the Inhabitants of this County by the Northern Indians Marching through the Frontiers . . . in
Order to Attack the Cattawbaws, & other Southern Indians with whom they were at
War" and ordered that "the Southern & Northern Indians be severally Invited to
meet here next April for setling a peace between those Nations as the best way for
securing the quiet of Our Frontier Inhabitants." But the Six Nations refused to treat
anywhere except Albany, and the Cherokees declined to travel that far north into
the heart of Iroquoia. The war continued unabated, so that in April 1738 inhabitants
on the Shenandoah River petitioned the Council for arms and ammunition because
the "Northern Indians frequently passing through their plantations Commit frequent
Outrages and have lately killed one of their men." . . .

On November 8 the House of Burgesses took up a measure "For making more effectual provision against Invasions and Insurrections," which the governor signed into
law on December 21. That same day he approved "An Act, for erecting two new
Counties, and Parishes; and granting certain encouragements to the Inhabitants." . . .

The establishment of local government in the two new counties, however, was
delayed until ordered by the governor and Council. The administration was in something of a bind. In conflicts with the Indians the best means of defense clearly lay in

settlement and county organization. Gooch assured the Board of Trade that "enlarging the frontier Settlements and Strengthening them by proper encouragements for Co-habitation hath always proved the most effectual Method Securing the Country against the Indians." But in a candid explanation for delaying the appointment of a court, Gooch admitted to the board that "because most of the People likely to settle there are illeterate and many of them not yet understanding the English Language, it is left to the Governor and Council to fix the time, when Justices and other officers are to be established." . . . What the administration wanted was the power to move quickly, without relying on the legislature, to install local governments and provide for the common defense in case an all-out Indian war engulfed Virginia. But it also needed to buy time in view of doubts about the ability of the new inhabitants to govern themselves. . . .

Other Virginians shared both the government's advocacy of backcountry settlement and its mistrust of the settlers. As early as 1728 William Byrd had written that "it therefore concerns his Majesty's Service very nearly, and the Safety of His Subjects in this part of the World, to take Possession of so important a Barrier [the Blue Ridge] in time, lest out good Friends, the French, and the Indians, thro' their Means, prove a perpetual Annoyance to these Colonies." By the mid-1730s, however, he was complaining to his correspondents Collinson and Bartram about the "Scots-Irish . . . who flock over thither in such numbers, that there is not elbow-room for them. They swarm like Goths and Vandals of old, & will over-spread our continent soon." But hoping to populate his own western lands, Byrd admitted he would be "glad" to tempt Germans "to remove hither."

Within two months of the passage of the militia and county measures, Gooch was explaining to the Board of Trade that he knew "not in what state they [the Cherokees and Catawbas] are in with the Northern Nations, . . . But if Spring tempts them to renew their Hostilitys, and to make the like return of Barbarity through our inhabitants, 'tis not to be imagined that People who have now Arms in their hands, will suffer the Heathens to insult them with Impunity." In July 1739 Gooch received word from the governor of New York that a combined French and Indian force was on its way south to attack Indians friendly to Virginia. New and even more serious difficulties were also developing with the Six Nations. Not only did they now "insist upon it as agreed by the Treaty [of Albany] that as they were not to Pass to the Eastward, the English were not to get to the Westward" of the Blue Ridge, but the Indians also laid exclusive claim "to the Lands on Shenando River." This position varied considerably from the colony's understanding that the treaty conferred only rights of travel, not claims to land. When the Iroquois acted on their interpretation, the Gooch administration moved quickly to effect the final stage of settlement organization west of the Blue Ridge. . . .

Virginia . . . , at least temporarily, settled its differences with the Six Nations at the 1744 Treaty of Lancaster. There the Indians were compensated for land claims in the Shenandoah Valley and agreed to restrict travel to the so-called Warriors Path along its length. Gooch could tell the legislature that he had "concluded a Treaty of Peace and Friendship with the *Northern Indians;* and procured for our Inhabitants seated to the Westward of the Mountains, a quiet Possession of all the Lands to which those Nations claimed a Right." A good thing it was, too, because England was by then at war with France. Possessing the land and organizing a county court to secure the rights of property and to provide for its development and for common

defense would afford Virginia the best protection the colonial and imperial governments could command. Decades of experience had indicated that county militias,
when properly trained, could best secure frontier areas and that those militias were
natural to settlement buffers of white Protestant smallholders. If European settlers
were for the most part Scotch-Irish or German Palatinates, so much the better, because both groups had long served the interests of European states by occupying the
contested areas of national and imperial struggle.

By the mid-1740s the period when speculative interests were muted by the coincidence of settler demands for land and the pursuit of imperial and colonial security was over; new land grants were overtly speculative and firmly controlled by
Virginia elites. . . .

. . . A new frontier narrative requires a different perspective encompassing the entirety of British North America and beginning at the onset of the eighteenth century.
Faced with potential French encirclement and, more immediate to this story, with real
conflict waged by Native Americans across the continent, colonial governors and
their councils explored various defensive strategies to secure their frontiers. Most attractive were the opportunities presented by European migrants uprooted by imperial
strife and seeking land and opportunity in America. The interests of white Protestant
yeoman peoples stimulated settlement schemes from Nova Scotia to the Carolinas.
That speculative interests also helped drive the settlement process is no surprise. . . .

 # F U R T H E R    R E A D I N G

Robert M. Bliss, *Revolution and Empire: English Politics and the American Colonies in the
    Seventeenth Century* (1990).
Patricia U. Bonomi, *The Lord Cornbury Scandal: The Politics of Reputation in Colonial
    America* (1998).
Jack P. Greene, *Negotiated Authorities: Essays in Colonial Political and Constitutional His-
    tory* (1994).
David Hancock, *Citizens of the World: London Merchants and the Integration of the British
    Atlantic Community 1735–1785* (1995).
Richard R. Johnson, *Adjustment to Empire: The New England Colonies, 1675–1715* (1981).
John Gilman Kolp, *Gentlemen and Freeholders: Electoral Politics in Colonial Virginia*
    (1998).
Robert C. Ritchie, *Captain Kidd and the War Against the Pirates* (1986).
Ian K. Steele, *The English Atlantic, 1675–1740: An Exploration of Communication and
    Community* (1986).
Alan Tully, *Forming American Politics: Ideals, Interests, and Institutions in Colonial New
    York and Pennsylvania* (1994).
Stephen Saunders Webb, *Lord Churchill's Coup: The Anglo-American Empire and the Glo-
    rious Revolution Reconsidered* (1995).

C H A P T E R
13

# *New Realities in the Backcountry*

By the middle of the eighteenth century, American colonists increasingly looked west. Settlers hemmed in behind the mountains looked longingly at the fertile land beyond them. People from many parts of Europe, including Scots-Irish, Scottish Highlanders, French, and Germans, poured into the backcountry. These planters came in groups, building communities designed to sustain their own heritage in the new environment. Although the backcountry was within the colonial patents of the established colonies, in many ways it was a region with a unity of its own. Settlers who arrived at the port of Philadelphia flowed southward along the foothills, adding to populations moving directly west, and built chains of settlement. These communities had uneasy, suspicious relationships with English populations and colonial governments on the eastern seaboard.

Europeans were preceded by American Indians, who also moved west. Eastern groups who had been deprived of their land moved into western Pennsylvania and beyond into the Ohio Valley, where they formed communities of mixed heritages and found new ways of thinking about their identities as Indians. The governments of New York and Pennsylvania tried to work through the great Iroquois League in relating to these new entities, but increasingly the western groups rejected Iroquois League control.

In the West native groups came into closer proximity to the other European power active there—the French. French Jesuits made many converts to Roman Catholicism, as did Moravians and Presbyterians to Protestantism, and these new religious experiences affected the new polyglot cultures forming in the West. French forts began to dot the Great Lakes and Ohio Valley; Detroit and New Orleans provided the French with a pervasive presence in the continent's interior and gave American Indians alternative sources of trade goods and access to European culture. Tensions between England and France led to the French and Indian War, which began with frontier fighting in 1754. The fighting ended in the early 1760s and the defeated French gave up their claims to American territory in the treaty of 1763. Indians in the West now found themselves much worse off because the English government no longer had incentives to woo them as allies. New revivalist movements arose in the West and natives attacked the entire frontier in the series of uprisings collectively described as Pontiac's Rebellion.

Frontier regions have always had a special place in American folklore. The national myth has portrayed frontier settlers as men and women who, impatient with *the constraints of life in the hierarchical East, struck out to find a place where they could live as individuals. In the eighteenth century commentators portrayed the western colonists as "white savages," people who first chose to live outside society and then were further corrupted by living in close proximity to the American natives. But new scholarship is reevaluating both native and European communities on the frontier and delineating their sophistication. The most successful people, European or Indian, were those who were capable of moving across cultures and negotiating the multiple realities of the region.*

### D O C U M E N T S

Conrad Weiser kept a journal of his 1737 journey through the backcountry; document 1 records his visit with Madame Montour and his observations on her generosity and her style of life. The Moravian leader Count Zinzendorf kept a journal of his travels to Shamokin in 1742 and document 2 records his impressions of Madame Montour and Andrew Montour as well as his estimate of the future of the Moravians' mission.

Continuing frontier conflict melded with the worldwide contest between France and England in the mid-1750s with the beginning of the French and Indian War. Mary Jemison and her family were captured in 1755 and only twelve-year-old Mary survived the early days of captivity. She was adopted into a loving Seneca family and lived the rest of her life as a Seneca woman. Her story was collected in the early nineteenth century when she described herself as an old woman. Document 3 is her own story of capture and adoption.

In 1754 representatives of nine of the thirteen colonies came together in Albany to meet with the Six Nations of the Iroquois League, a continuation of the colonial policy of attempting to deal with the western Indians through the League. At this meeting, Benjamin Franklin proposed a formal union of the colonies, and his plan is document 4. As the French and Indian War ended Indians found the supply of trade goods cut off. Document 5, a record of a meeting between the British government's Indian supervisor, Sir William Johnson, and representatives of the Iroquois League shows the desperate situation the Indians found themselves in and the English scorn for their religious movements. Each statement was punctuated by laying down a wampum belt.

Document 6 is a contemporary journal kept during Pontiac's War in 1763, which gives a full account of the vision of Neolin, the Delaware (here called Wolf) prophet. David Brainerd, who was a missionary among the Delawares, also describes in document 7 his encounter with a Delaware prophet. His reaction was a mixture of horror and respect.

## 1. Conrad Weiser Describes Madame Montour, 1737

The Indians at this place were out of provisions; our little stock was soon exhausted, as there was a numerous family in the house where we lodged. We had expected on leaving home to supply ourselves with provisions at this place, in which we were entirely disappointed. I saw a new blanket given for about one-third of a bushel of Indian corn. Here we began already to suffer the pangs of hunger, and other troubles

---

Conrad Weiser, "Narrative of a Journey, made in the Year 1737 . . . from Tulpehocken to Onondago," trans. Hester H. Muhlenberg, *Collections of the Historical Society of Pennsylvania* I (1853): 8.

forced themselves on us. It was with great difficulty that I procured a small quantity of corn meal and a few beans for the journey.

The 21st we ventured to proceed on our journey to *Onontago.* There were now five of us, as Shikelimo accompanied me, and we were joined by a warrior who had been on a war expedition to Virginia, and was going home in the same direction as we were travelling. In the forenoon we reached the large creek *Canusorago;* it was very high; we were taken over in a canoe, not without great danger. The next day two English traders attempted to cross, and their canoe was overturned by the force of the current, one of them was drowned, and the other only escaped by swimming.

To day we passed a place where the Indians in former times had a strong fortification on a height; it was surrounded by a deep ditch, the earth was thrown up in the shape of a wall, about nine or ten feet high and as many broad. But it is now in decay, as from appearance it had been deserted beyond the memory of man.

The 22d we came to a village called *Olstuago,* from a high rock which lies opposite. However, before we came in sight of the village, we reached a large creek which looked more dreadful than the one of yesterday. After repeated firing of our guns, two Indians came from the village to see what was to be done; they brought at our request a canoe from the village and took us across. We quartered ourselves with Madame Montour, a French woman by birth, of a good family, but now in mode of life a complete Indian. She treated us very well according to her means, but had very little to spare this time, or perhaps dared not let it be seen on the account of so many hungry Indians about. She several times in secret gave me and Stoffel as much as we could eat, which had not happened to us before for ten days; and showed great compassion for us, saying that none of the Indians where we were going had anything to eat, except the Onontagers, which my Indian fellow travellers refused to believe, until we found it true by experience.

The 23d we lay still on account of rainy weather. Two Indians arrived by water in a canoe made of elk skins, who said that in the high wilderness the snow was still knee deep. I received from Madame Montour some provisions for the journey. We have now advanced one hundred and thirty miles. . . .

### 2. Moravian Leader Count Zinzendorf Records his Impressions of Madame Montour and Andrew Montour, 1742

We camped out twice on the journey. During the second night there was a sudden and heavy fall of rain, and all our horses excepting one strayed away. As we were not far from Otstonwakin, Conrad rode to the village. He soon returned in company with Andrew, Madame Montour's oldest son. Just then our horses came in.

Andrew's cast of countenance is decidedly European, and had not his face been encircled with a broad band of paint, applied with bear's fat, I would certainly have taken him for one. He wore a brown broadcloth coat, a scarlet damasken lappel-waistcoat, breeches, over which his shirt hung, a black Cordovan neckerchief,

William C. Reichel, ed., *Memorials of the Moravian Church* I (Philadelphia, 1870): 95–97.

decked with silver bugles, shoes and stockings, and a hat. His ears were hung with pendants of brass and other wires plaited together like the handle of a basket. He was very cordial, but on addressing him in French, he, to my surprise, replied in English.

When a short distance from the village, Andrew left us and rode ahead to notify the inhabitants of our approach. As soon as they saw us, they discharged their firearms by way of salute, and repeated this mode of welcome on our arriving at the huts. Here we dismounted and repaired to Madame Montour's quarters. Her husband, who had been a chief, had been killed in battle with the Catawbas. When the old woman saw us she wept. In course of conversation, while giving her a general account of the Brethren and their circumstances, I mentioned that one of our towns was named Bethlehem. Hereupon she interrupted me and said: "The place in France where Jesus and the holy family lived was also named Bethlehem." I was surprised at the woman's ignorance, considering she had been born and brought up a Christian. At the same time I thought I had evidence of the truth of the charge brought against the French missionaries, who are said to make it a point to teach the Indians that Jesus had been a Frenchman, and that the English had been his crucifiers. Without attempting to rectify her misapprehension, I in a few words stated our views, replying to her inquiries with sincerity of purpose, without, however, entering into an explanation, as I had purposed remaining retired for a few days. She was very confidential to Anna, and told her, among other things, that she was weary of Indian life. . . .

P. S. We will probably resume our journey about the 9th inst. At times we have observed signs of grace in Andrew. Anna has experienced the same in the case of Madame Montour's granddaughter. Andrew has concluded to give his hunting companions the slip, and to forego the great annual hunt which the Indians are accustomed to prolong into the month of February, and to accompany us to Skehandowana.

## 3. Mary Jemison Recounts Her Experience of Capture and Adoption as a Seneca, 1755

My education had received as much attention from my parents, as their situation in a new country would admit of. I had been at school some, where I learned to read in a book that was about half as large as a Bible; and in the Bible I had read a little. I had also learned the Catechism, which I used frequently to repeat to my parents, and every night, before I went to bed, I was obliged to stand up before my mother and repeat some words that I suppose was a prayer.

My reading, Catechism and prayers, I have long since forgotten; though for a number of the first years that I lived with the Indians, I repeated the prayers as often as I had an opportunity. After the revolutionary war, I remembered the names of some of the letters when I saw them; but have never read a word since I was taken prisoner. It is but a few years since a Missionary kindly gave me a Bible, which I am very fond of hearing my neighbors read to me, and should be pleased to learn to

*A Narrative of the Life of Mrs. Mary Jemison* (1824; Reprint American Scenic and Historic Preservation Society, 1982).

read it myself; but my sight has been for a number of years, so dim that I have not been able to distinguish one letter from another. . . .

. . . Our family, as usual, was busily employed about their common business. Father was shaving an axe-helve at the side of the house; mother was making preparations for breakfast;—my two oldest brothers were at work near the barn; and the little ones, with myself, and the woman and her three children, were in the house.

Breakfast was not yet ready, when we were alarmed by the discharge of a number of guns, that seemed to be near. Mother and the women before mentioned, almost fainted at the report, and every one trembled with fear. . . .

. . . They first secured my father, and then rushed into the house, and without the least resistance made prisoners of my mother, Robert, Matthew, Betsey, the woman and her three children, and myself, and then commenced plundering. . . .

The party that took us consisted of six Indians and four Frenchmen, who immediately commenced plundering, as I just observed, and took what they considered most valuable; consisting principally of bread, meal and meat. Having taken as much provision as they could carry, they set out with their prisoners in great haste, for fear of detection, and soon entered the woods. On our march that day, an Indian went behind us with a whip, with which he frequently lashed the children to make them keep up. In this manner we travelled till dark without a mouthful of food or a drop of water; although we had not eaten since the night before. Whenever the little children cried for water, the Indians would make them drink urine or go thirsty. At night they encamped in the woods without fire and without shelter, where we were watched with the greatest vigilance. Extremely fatigued, and very hungry, we were compelled to lie upon the ground supperless and without a drop of water to satisfy the cravings of our appetites. As in the day time, so the little ones were made to drink urine in the night if they cried for water. Fatigue alone brought us a little sleep for the refreshment of our weary limbs; and at the dawn of day we were again started on our march in the same order that we had proceeded on the day before. About sunrise we were halted, and the Indians gave us a full breakfast of provision that they had brought from my father's house. Each of us being very hungry, partook of this bounty of the Indians, except father, who was so much overcome with his situation—so much exhausted by anxiety and grief, that silent despair seemed fastened upon his countenance, and he could not be prevailed upon to refresh his sinking nature by the use of a morsel of food. Our repast being finished, we again resumed our march, and before noon passed a small fort that I heard my father say was called Fort Canagojigge.

That was the only time that I heard him speak from the time we were taken till we were finally separated the following night.

Towards evening we arrived at the border of a dark and dismal swamp, which was covered with small hemlocks, or some other evergreen, and other bushes, into which we were conducted; and having gone a short distance we stopped to encamp for the night.

Here we had some bread and meat for supper: but the dreariness of our situation, together with the uncertainty under which we all labored, as to our future destiny, almost deprived us of the sense of hunger, and destroyed our relish for food.

Mother, from the time we were taken, had manifested a great degree of fortitude, and encouraged us to support our troubles without complaining; and by her conversation seemed to make the distance and time shorter, and the way more smooth. But fa-ther lost all his ambition in the beginning of our trouble, and continued apparently lost to every care—absorbed in melancholy. Here, as before, she insisted on the necessity of our eating; and we obeyed her, but it was done with heavy hearts.

As soon as I had finished my supper, an Indian took off my shoes and stockings and put a pair of moccasins on my feet, which my mother observed; and believing that they would spare my life, even if they should destroy the other captives, ad-dressed me as near as I can remember in the following words:—

"My dear little Mary, I fear that the time has arrived when we must be parted forever. Your life, my child, I think will be spared; but we shall probably be toma-hawked here in this lonesome place by the Indians. O! how can I part with you my darling? What will become of my sweet little Mary? Oh! how can I think of your being continued in captivity without a hope of your being rescued? O that death had snatched you from my embraces in your infancy; the pain of parting then would have been pleasing to what it now is; and I should have seen the end of your trou-bles!—Alas, my dear! my heart bleeds at the thoughts of what awaits you; but, if you leave us, remember my child your own name, and the name of your father and mother. Be careful and not forget your English tongue. If you shall have an opportu-nity to get away from the Indians, don't try to escape; for if you do they will find and destroy you. Don't forget, my little daughter, the prayers that I have learned you—say them often; be a good child, and God will bless you. May God bless you my child, and make you comfortable and happy."

During this time, the Indians stripped the shoes and stockings from the little boy that belonged to the woman who was taken with us, and put moccasins on his feet, as they had done before on mine. I was crying. An Indian took the little boy and myself by the hand, to lead us off from the company, when my mother exclaimed, "Don't cry Mary—don't cry my child. God will bless you! Farewell—farewell!"

The Indian led us some distance into the bushes, or woods, and there lay down with us to spend the night. The recollection of parting with my tender mother kept me awake, while the tears constantly flowed from my eyes. A number of times in the night the little boy begged of me earnestly to run away with him and get clear of the Indians; but remembering the advice I had so lately received, and knowing the dangers to which we should be exposed, in travelling without a path and without a guide, through a wilderness unknown to us, I told him that I would not go, and per-suaded him to lie still till morning.

Early the next morning the Indians and Frenchmen that we had left the night before, came to us; but our friends were left behind. It is impossible for any one to form a correct idea of what my feelings were at the sight of those savages, whom I supposed had murdered my parents and brothers, sister, and friends, and left them in the swamp to be devoured by wild beasts! But what could I do? A poor little de-fenceless girl; without the power or means of escaping; without a home to go to, even if I could be liberated; without a knowledge of the direction or distance to my former place of residence; and without a living friend to whom to fly for protection, I felt a kind of horror, anxiety, and dread, that, to me, seemed insupportable. I durst not cry—I durst not complain; and to inquire of them the fate of my friends (even if I could have mustered resolution) was beyond my ability, as I could not speak their language, nor they understand mine. My only relief was in silent stifled sobs.

My suspicions as to the fate of my parents proved too true; for soon after I left them they were killed and scalped, together with Robert, Matthew, Betsey, and the woman and her two children, and mangled in the most shocking manner.

Having given the little boy and myself some bread and meat for breakfast, they led us on as fast as we could travel, and one of them went behind and with a long staff, picked up all the grass and weeds that we trailed down by going over them. By taking that precaution they avoided detection; for each weed was so nicely placed in its natural position that no one would have suspected that we had passed that way. It is the custom of Indians when scouting, or on private expeditions, to step carefully and where no impression of their feet can be left—shunning wet or muddy ground. They seldom take hold of a bush or limb, and never break one; and by observing those precautions and that of setting up the weeds and grass which they necessarily lop, they completely elude the sagacity of their pursuers, and escape that punishment which they are conscious they merit from the hand of justice.

After a hard day's march we encamped in a thicket, where the Indians made a shelter of boughs, and then built a good fire to warm and dry our benumbed limbs and clothing; for it had rained some through the day. Here we were again fed as before. When the Indians had finished their supper they took from their baggage a number of scalps and went about preparing them for the market, or to keep without spoiling, by straining them over small hoops which they prepared for that purpose, and then drying and scraping them by the fire. Having put the scalps, yet wet and bloody, upon the hoops, and stretched them to their full extent, they held them to the fire till they were partly dried and then with their knives commenced scraping off the flesh; and in that way they continued to work, alternately drying and scraping them, till they were dry and clean. That being done they combed the hair in the neatest manner, and then painted it and the edges of the scalps yet on the hoops, red. Those scalps I knew at the time must have been taken from our family by the color of the hair. My mother's hair was red; and I could easily distinguish my father's and the children's from each other. That sight was most appaling; yet, I was obliged to endure it without complaining.

In the course of the night they made me to understand that they should not have killed the family if the whites had not pursued them. . . .

At the place where we halted, the Indians combed the hair of the young man, the boy and myself, and then painted our faces and hair red, in the finest Indian style. We were then conducted into the fort, where we received a little bread and were then shut up and left to tarry alone through the night. . . .

The night was spent in gloomy forebodings. What the result of our captivity would be, it was out of our power to determine or even imagine.—At times we could almost realize the approach of our masters to butcher and scalp us;—again we could nearly see the pile of wood kindled on which we were to be roasted; and then we would imagine ourselves at liberty; alone and defenceless in the forest, surrounded by wild beasts that were ready to devour us. The anxiety of our minds drove sleep from our eyelids; and it was with a dreadful hope and painful impatience that we waited for the morning to determine our fate.

The morning at length arrived, and our masters came early and let us out of the house, and gave the young man and boy to the French, who immediately took them away. Their fate I never learned; as I have not seen nor heard of them since.

I was now left alone in the fort, deprived of my former companions, and of everything that was near or dear to me but life. But it was not long before I was in some measure relieved by the appearance of two pleasant looking squaws of the Seneca tribe, who came and examined me attentively for a short time, and then went out. After a few minutes absence they returned with my former masters, who gave me to them to dispose of as they pleased. . . .

On our way we passed a Shawanee town, where I saw a number of heads, arms, legs, and other fragments of the bodies of some white people who had just been burnt. The parts that remained were hanging on a pole which was supported at each end by a crotch stuck in the ground, and were roasted or burnt black as a coal. The fire was yet burning; and the whole appearances afforded a spectacle so shocking, that, even to this day, my blood almost curdles in my veins when I think of them!

At night we arrived at a small Seneca Indian town, at the mouth of a small river, that was called by the Indians, in the Seneca language, She-nan-jee, where the two Squaws to whom I belonged resided. There we landed, and the Indians went on; which was the last I ever saw of them.

Having made fast to the shore, the Squaws left me in the canoe while they went to their wigwam or house in the town, and returned with a suit of Indian clothing, all new, and very clean and nice. My clothes, though whole and good when I was taken, were now torn in pieces, so that I was almost naked. They first undressed me and threw my rags into the river; then washed me clean and dressed me in the new suit they had just brought, in complete Indian style; and then led me home and seated me in the center of their wigwam.

I had been in that situation but a few minutes, before all the Squaws in the town came in to see me. I was soon surrounded by them, and they immediately set up a most dismal howling, crying bitterly, and wringing their hands in all the agonies of grief for a deceased relative. . . .

"Oh our brother! Alas! He is dead—he has gone; he will never return! Friend-less he died on the field of the slain, where his bones are yet lying unburied! Oh, who will mourn his sad fate? No tears dropped around him; oh no! No tears of his sisters were there! . . .

. . . His spirit has seen our distress, and sent us a helper whom with pleasure we greet. Dickewamis has come: then let us receive her with joy! She is handsome and pleasant! Oh! she is our sister, and gladly we welcome her here. In the place of our brother she stands in our tribe. With care we will guard her from trouble; and may she be happy till her spirit shall leave us."

In the course of that ceremony, from mourning they became serene—joy sparkled in their countenances, and they seemed to rejoice over me as over a long lost child. I was made welcome amongst them as a sister to the two Squaws before mentioned, and was called Dickewamis; which being interpreted, signifies a pretty girl, a handsome girl, or a pleasant, good thing. That is the name by which I have ever since been called by the Indians.

I afterwards learned that the ceremony I at that time passed through, was that of adoption. The two squaws had lost a brother in Washington's war, sometime in the year before, and in consequence of his death went up to Fort Pitt, on the day on which I arrived there, in order to receive a prisoner or an enemy's scalp, to supply their loss.

It is a custom of the Indians, when one of their number is slain or taken prisoner in battle, to give to the nearest relative to the dead or absent, a prisoner, if they have chanced to take one, and if not, to give him the scalp of an enemy. On the return of the Indians from conquest, which is always announced by peculiar shoutings, demonstrations of joy, and the exhibition of some trophy of victory, the mourners come forward and make their claims. If they receive a prisoner, it is at their option either to satiate their vengeance by taking his life in the most cruel manner they can conceive of; or, to receive and adopt him into the family, in the place of him whom they have lost. All the prisoners that are taken in battle and carried to the encampment or town by the Indians, are given to the bereaved families, till their number is made good. . . .

## 4. The Albany Plan of Union, 1754

PLAN OF A PROPOSED UNION *of the Several Colonies of Massachusetts Bay, New Hampshire, Connecticut, Rhode Island, New York, New Jerseys, Pensylvania, Maryland, Virginia, North Carolina, and South-Carolina; for their mutual defence and Security, and for extending the British Settlements in North America.*

That Humble Application be made for an Act of the Parliament of Great Britain, by Virtue of which one General Government may be formed in America, including all the said Colonies, within and under which Government each Colony may retain its present constitution, except in the particulars wherein a Change may be directed by the said Act as hereafter follows.

That the said General Government be administered by a President General, to be appointed and supported by the Crown

And a Grand Council to be Chosen by the Representatives of the People of the Several Colonies, met in their respective Assemblies

That within— Months after the passing of such Act, The house of Representatives in the Several Assemblies that happen to be sitting within that time, or that shall be specially for that purpose Convened, may and shall choose Members for the Grand Council, in the following Proportions; that is to say.

| | |
|---|---|
| Massachusetts Bay | 7 |
| New Hampshire | 2 |
| Connecticut | 5 |
| Rhode Island | 2 |
| New York | 4 |
| New Jerseys | 3 |
| Pensylvania | 6 |
| Maryland | 4 |
| Virginia | 7 |
| North Carolina | 4 |
| South Carolina | 4 |
| | 48 |

"Franklin's Plan of Union," in *The Documentary History of the State of New-York,* E.B. O'Callaghan (Albany: Weed, Parsons, and Co., Public Printers, 1850), II, 357–359.

Who shall meet for the first time at the City of Philadelphia in Pennsylvania, being called by the President General as soon as conveniently may be after his Appointment.

That there shall be a new Election of Members for the Grand Council every Three Years; and on the Death or Resignation of any Member, his place shall be Supplyed by a new Choice at the next Sitting of the Assembly of the Colony he represented.

That after the first Three Years when the Proportion of Money arising out of each Colony to the General Treasury can be known the Number of Members to be chosen for each Colony shall from time to time in all ensuing Elections be regulated by that Proportion (Yet so as that the Number to be chosen by any one Province, be not more than Seven nor less than two.)

That the Grand Council shall meet once in every Year, and oftner if Occasion require, at such time and place as they, shall adjourn to, at the last preceeding Meeting, or as they shall be called to meet at by the President General on any Emergency, he having first obtained in writing the consent of Seven of the Members to such Call, and sent due and timely notice to the whole.

That the Grand Council have power to chuse their Speaker and shall neither be desolved, prorogued, nor continue sitting longer than Six weeks at one time, without their own consent or the Special Command of the Crown.

That the Members of the Grand Council shall be allowed for their Service Ten Shillings Sterling p Diem during their Sessions, and Journey to and from the place of Meeting; Twenty Miles to be reckoned a Days Journey.

That the Assent of the President General be requisite to all Acts of the Grand Council; and that it be his Office and Duty to cause them to be carried into Execution.

That the President General with the Advice of the Grand Council, hold or direct all Indian Treaties in which the General Interest or Wellfare of the Colonies may be concerned, and make peace or declare War with Indian Nations.

That they make such Laws as they Judge Necessary for regulating all Indian Trade.

That they make all Purchases from Indians for the Crown, of Lands now not within the Bounds of particular Colonies, or that shall not be within their Bounds when some of them are reduced to more Convenient Dimensions.

That they make new Settlements on such purchases, by granting Lands in the Kings Name reserving a quit Rent to the Crown for the use of the General Treasury.

That they make Laws for regulating and Governing such new Settlements, till the Crown shall think fitt to form them into particular Governments.

That they raise and pay Soldiers, and Build Forts for the defence, of any of the Colonies, and Equip Vessells of Force to guard the Coasts and protect the Trade on the Ocean, Lakes or Great Rivers: But they shall not Impress Men, in any Colony without the consent of its Legislature—That for these purposes they have power to make Laws and lay and leavy such general Duties, Imposts or Taxes as to them shall appear most equal and just, Considering the Ability and other Circumstances of the Inhabitants in the several Colonies and such as may be collected with the least Inconvenience to the People, rather discouraging Luxury, than loading Industry with unnecessary Burthens.

That they may appoint a General Treasurer, and a particular Treasurer in each Government when necessary, and from time to time may order the sums in the Treasuries of each Government into the General Treasury, or draw on them for Special Payments as they find most convenient. Yet no money to issue but by joint orders of the President General and Grand Council, Except where sums have been appropriated to particular purposes, and the President General is previously impowered by an act to draw for such sums.

That the General accounts shall be yearly settled and reported to the several Assembly's.

That a Quorum of the Grand Council impowered to act with the President General, do consist of Twenty five members among whom, there shall be one or more from a Majority of the Colonies;

That the Laws made by them for the purposes aforesaid shall not be repugnant, but as near as may be agreeable to the Laws of England, and shall be transmitted to the King in Council for approbation as soon as may be, after their passing, and if not disapproved within Three Years after presentation to remain in Force.

That in case of the Death of the President General, the Speaker of the Grand Council for the time being shall succeed and be vested with the same powers and Authorities to continue until the Kings Pleasure be known.

That all Military Commission Officers whether for Land or Sea Service to act under this General Constitution shall be nominated by the president General; but the approbation of the Grand Council is to be obtained before they receive their Commissions. And all Civil officers are to be nominated by the Grand Council, and to receive the president Generals approbation before they officiate: But in Case of a vacancy by Death or removal of any officer Civil or Military under this Constitution, The Governor of the Province in which such vacancy happens, may appoint till the pleasure of the President General and Grand Council, can be known. That the Particular Military as well as Civil Establishments in each Colony remain in their present State this General Constitution notwithstanding; and that on sudden Emergencies, any Colony may defend itself, and lay the accounts of Expence thence arisen before the president General and Grand Council, who may allow and order payment of the same, as far as they judge such accounts just and reasonable.

After Debate on the foregoing Plan

RESOLVED

That the Commissioners from the Several Governments, be desired to lay the same before their Respective Constituents for their Consideration, and that the Secretary to this Board transmit a Copy thereof with this vote thereon, to the Governor of each of the Colonies which have not sent their Commissioners to this Congress.

His Honour proposed to the Board, that agreeable to their Resolutions of the 24 June they would now consider, the Expediency of Building Forts in the Indian Country. It was determined that considering the present wavering Disposition of the Sennecas, it was expedient that a Fort should be Built in their Country at a place called Irondequat or Tierondequat. Ordered

That a Committee be appointed to consider what further Forts may be necessary in the Country of the Six Nations, and that each Colony name a Member for this Committee.

ORDERED

That Mr Chambers and Mr Peters be a Committee to revise the Minutes settled and agreed to by this Board.

Adjourned till to Morrow Morning at 9 aClock.

# 5. Sir William Johnson Confers with Iroquois Leaders, 1762

*An Indian Conference*

[September 8–10, 1762]

Proceedings with the Sachems, and Great Warriors of the United Six Nations, at Johnson Hall, Beginning Sept[r]. 8th. 1762. . .

Brother;

We cannot help laying our present case before you.—The Officers at the several Posts, when we want to Say anything to them on Business, Trade, &c[a]. will not hear Us, or look upon Us, but tell us they have nothing to say, or do with Us, nor with the Trade; So that really we are in a very bad Situation, and wish that there were such Officers as wou'd behave more friendly to Us, and Who, wou'd see we were not Impos'd on in our Trade. We also wish there may be a good man reside there as Interpreter, which will prevent Misunderstandings arising between Us and our Brethren.

A Belt.—

Brother;

One of our People lately, in a vision, was told by the Great Spirit above, that when He first made the World, He gave this large Island to the Indians for their Use; at the same time He gave other Parts of the World beyond the great Waters to the rest of his creating, and gave them different languages: That He now saw the white People squabbling, and fighting for these Lands which He gave the Indians; and that in every Assembly, and Company of Governors, and Great Men, He heard nothing scarce spoke, or talk'd of, but claiming, and wanting, large Possessions in our Country. This He said, was so contrary to his Intention, and what He expected wou'd be the Consequence at the time when the white People first came, like Children, among Us, that He was quite displeas'd, and would, altho their Numbers were ever so great, punish them if They did not desist.

A Belt with five Squares.—

Brother;

This Belt, or Covenant Chain, was given to Us Several years ago by Nine Governments hereon represented, and His Majesty King George at the Top, Assuring Us then that they were, and wou'd remain our Friends; insomuch, that if any

---

"An Indian Conference at Johnson Hall, September 8–10, 1762" in Milton W. Hamilton and Albert B. Corey, eds., *The Papers of Sir William Johnson* 10 (Albany: SUNY Press, 1951): 500, 505–511.

Nation, either French, or Indians, or others, shou'd quarrel with Us, they wou'd rise, and Assist Us; at the same time assuring Us, that the Great King wou'd protect Us in the possession of our Lands. — They then also shew'd a Space in said Belt, which They desired We wou'd Fill with as many Nations of Indians, as we cou'd bring into their, and our Alliance. This Belt We only shew you, to let you know that, we constantly look at it, and repeat the purport of it to our old and young, so as never to forget the Promises you then made, as We are determin'd inviolably to abide by those made on our Side.

The Covenant large Belt. — · · ·

Brother;

We are asham'd to make so many Complaints, but our unexpected and miserable Situation, obliges Us to lay our Grievances before you, as it concerns our very Existence. Some of our People were lately repairing a Fishing Wear, (where we have fished time out of mind for our Support) near where you have now a Fort at the lower End of the Oneidoe Lake, when an Officer came up and forbid them, telling them, He wou'd order his Men to break down what They had made. — We did not think it hard while our Brothers, and We, shared alike; which was the Case when the former Officer commanded there: but the present Officer acts an unbrotherly part, which We hope will be taken Notice of, and prevented for the time to come. We are told by a Man, (who speaks our Language) at the East End of Oneida Lake, that there were a number of Men, going the next Day, to build three Houses on the north side of the said Lake, about mid-way, by a Creek, which is one of our best Fishing Places: We desire to know of You, Brother, by whose order these Houses are to be built: what can be intended by it, we cannot See, unless to Starve Us, by taking all our Hunting Places from Us.

A Belt. —

Brother;

We have now open'd our Minds to you, and laid before you what We were charged with from our Nations, and We hope you will take the whole into Consideration, and afford Us such Redress as We think we have a right to Expect from Brethren.

Here the Speaker ended.

Then Sir William told them He had closely attended to what They had said; wou'd consider seriously of it, and when ready to answer, wou'd acquaint them of the time. Then the Meeting ended for this Day. . . .

### An Indian Conference

*[Johnson Hall, September 13–14, 1762]*

At a Meeting with the Six Nations, on Monday the 13th day of Septem$^r$. 1762, at Johnson Hall, . . .

Sir William made the following Answer to what the Onondago Speaker said two days ago.

Brethren of the Six Nations;

I am glad to find you so desirous to remove all evil Thoughts which were occasioned by the late Behaviour of the Oneidoes; and, I cannot but approve of your Sachems conduct in sending you hither, for that purpose.

Gave three Strings.

Brethren;

You were certainly in the right to advise the Oneidoes to come down immediately, to Apologize for their Behaviour; at which time, I own I told them, that I shou'd not continue the Management of their Affairs, if they ever repeated their Crime, which I must certainly do, if I hear more Complaints against them, as I cannot answer it to the Great King, to undertake the conducting of a People's affairs, who will not be govern'd by my advice: but I am in hopes, you will not reduce me to the Necessity of Slighting you, or neglecting your Affairs: And as I am glad to find your promise to correct your Children the Oneidoes, and prevent such Behaviour for the future, you may always expect me to be your Friend, whilst you continue to put your present Resolutions in Execution, and observe all your Engagements with the English. — Such Conduct will be the best means of Securing the General's Esteem, and I shall be always your advocate with him, whilst you in any wise deserve it.

A Belt. —

### Sir William Johnson Replies

Brethren;

I am perfectly well acquainted with your Behaviour during the whole course of the War, and very Sensible you might have done more, if you had Engaged in it with Spirit: however, I cannot but approve of the good Conduct of all such faithful Ind$^s$. as afforded their Assistance to the English, which I hope you will always be ready to do, if there is a necessity for it.

I am glad to hear of your sending down the English prisoners, and I expect you will not let one remain in your Nations, and that you will never give the least Encouragement to Deserters, (but deliver all such up at some of His Majesty's Garrisons) who may endeavour to Screen themselves amongst You. Such people, being void of principle, will always do harm amongst you, and Create Disturbances. By adhering to this my advice, and duly observing all your Treaties with Us, you may be assured of our giving due Attention to all Engagements on our Parts, and that the English will never break their Compacts with any people who do not compel them to it.

A Belt. —

Brethren;

What you tell me of the Commanding Officer at the Detroit, greatly Surprizes me, and I cou'd wish you had not laid such a thing before me, untill you were well assured of the Authenticity of your Intelligence, as I cannot think any Officer wou'd have deliver'd such Sentiments: the several Posts are absolutely necessary, and of Use to both English and Indians. I shou'd be very sorry any differences might arise, or that you had any reason to think your Selves Slighted by the Officers, who, I hope will always treat such Indians as behave well, in a friendly manner, and prevent any Impositions in Trade: and as an Interpreter may be of some Use at Oswego, I shall take your request into Consideration.

A Belt. —

Brethren;

Your romantic Notions, Custom of Dreaming, and Seeing visions, however usual amongst you, cannot but appear in a very ridiculous Light to White People, who will, Consider it, only as a Scheme set on foot by some designing Persons to answer their Purposes; and I hope you cannot but be convinced that the Divine Being is satisfied with the Justice of our Cause, from the great Successes with which He has crowned the British Arms. — I hope therefore, you will not Suspect Us of defrauding you of your Lands, after what I formerly acquainted you concerning His Majesty's Intentions to protect you in all your just Rights, and observe all his Treaties with You.

A Belt. —

Brethren;

The Belt which you produced from the several Governments, I have formerly seen. — I am glad to find you preserve it in remembrance, and repeat the Purport thereof to your people, So that your Posterity may be acquainted with the Engagements You, and We have enter'd into .— Continue to act in this wise manner, and you may always rely on our Friendship, and Observance thereof. —

A Belt. —

## 6. Neolin's Journey to the Master of Life, Described in 1763

An Indian of the Wolf nation, eager to make the acquaintance of the Master of Life,— this is the name for God among all the Indians—resolved to undertake the journey to Paradise, where he knew He resided, without the knowledge of any of his tribe or village. But the question was how to succeed in his purpose and find the way thither. Not knowing anyone who had been there and was thus able to teach him the road, he had recourse to incantation in the hope of deriving some good augury from his trance. As a rule all the Indians, even those who are enlightened, are subject to superstition, and put a good deal of credence in their dreams and those things which one has a good deal of trouble to wean them from. This episode will be proof of what I say.

This Wolf Indian in his dream imagined that he had only to set out and by dint of travelling would arrive at the celestial dwelling. This he did the next day. Early in the morning he arose and equipped himself for a hunting journey, not forgetting to take provisions and ammunition, and a big kettle. Behold him then setting out like that on his journey to Heaven to see the Master of Life.

---

[Anonymous], *The Journal of Pontiac's Conspiracy* (1763), in Milo Milton Quaife, ed., *The Siege of Detroit in 1763* (Chicago: The Lakeside Press, 1958): 8–17.

The first seven days of his journey were quite favorable to his plans; he walked on without growing discouraged, always with a firm belief that he would arrive at his destination, and eight days went by without his encountering anything which could hinder him in his desire. On the evening of the eighth day he halted at sunset as usual, at the opening to a little prairie upon the bank of a stream which seemed to him a suitable camping place. As he was preparing his shelter for the night he beheld at the other end of this prairie where he camped, three roads, wide and plainly marked. This struck him as singular, nevertheless, he went on working on his shelter so as to be protected from the weather, and made a fire. While doing his cooking he thought he noticed that the three roads became all the brighter the darker it grew, a thing which surprised him to the point of fear. He hesitated for some time over what he should do, whether to remain in his present camp, or move and camp elsewhere; but as he pondered he recalled his incantations, or rather his dream, and that he had undertaken this journey from no other reason than to see the Master of Life. This led him to believe that one of the roads was the one he must take to reach the spot he desired. He concluded to remain where he was till the next day, when he would choose one of the three routes at random. However, his curiosity hardly allowed him time to reflect upon it before he abandoned his camp and set out along the road which seemed to him the widest. He continued in it for half a day without seeing anything to stop him, but, pausing a little to take breath, he saw suddenly a great fire coming out of the earth. This aroused his curiosity. He drew nearer to see what this fire was, but the closer he approached the more the fire appeared to increase. This frightened him and caused him to retrace his steps and take another road which was narrower than the first one.

After following this road the same length of time as the other be beheld the same spectacle, and his fear which had been quieted by the change of route was again aroused. He was once more obliged to turn about and take the third road which he followed for a day without discovering anything. Suddenly he saw before him what appeared to be a mountain of marvellous whiteness and he stopped, overcome with astonishment. Nevertheless, he again advanced, firmly determined to see what this mountain could be, but when he arrived at the foot of it he no longer saw any road and was sad. At this juncture, not knowing what to do to continue his way, he looked around in all directions and finally saw a woman of this mountain, of radiant beauty, whose garments dimmed the whiteness of the snow. And she was seated.

This woman addressed him to his own tongue: "Thou appearest to me surprised not to find any road to lead thee where thou wishest to go. I know that for a long while thou hast been desirous of seeing the Master of Life and of speaking with Him; that is why thou hast undertaken this journey to see Him. The road which leads to His abode is over the mountain, and to ascend it thou must forsake all that thou hast with thee, and disrobe completely, and leave all thy trappings and clothing at the foot of the mountain. No one shall harm thee; go and bathe thyself in a river which I shall show thee, and then thou shalt ascend."

The Wolf was careful to obey the words of the woman, but one difficulty yet confronted him, namely, to know how to reach the top of the mountain which was perpendicular, pathless, and smooth as ice. He questioned this woman how one should go about climbing up, and she replied that if he was really anxious to see the Master of Life he would have to ascend, helping himself only with his hand and his left foot. This appeared to him impossible, but encouraged by the woman he set about it and succeeded by dint of effort.

When he reached the top he was greatly astonished not to see anyone; the woman had disappeared, and he found himself alone without a guide. At his right were three villages which confronted him; he did not know them for they seemed of different construction from his own, prettier and more orderly in appearance. After he had pondered some time over what he ought to do, he set out toward the village which seemed to him the most attractive, and covered half the distance from the top of the mountain before he remembered that he was naked. He was afraid to go farther, but he heard a voice telling him to continue and that he ought not to fear, because, having bathed as he had, he could go on in assurance. He had no more difficulty in continuing up to a spot which seemed to him to be the gate of the village, and here he stopped, waiting for it to open so he could enter. While he was observing the outward beauty of this village the gate opened, and he saw coming toward him a handsome man, clothed all in white, who took him by the hand and told him that he was going to satisfy him and let him talk with the Master of Life. The Wolf permitted the man to conduct him, and both came to a place of surpassing beauty which the Indian could not admire enough. Here he saw the Master of Life, who took him by the hand and gave him a hat all bordered with gold to sit down upon. The Wolf hesitated to do this for fear of spoiling the hat, but he was ordered to do so, and obeyed without reply.

After the Indian was seated the Lord said to him: "I am the Master of Life, and since I know what thou desirest to know, and to whom thou wishest to speak, listen well to what I am going to say to thee and to all the Indians:

"I am He who hath created the heavens and the earth, the trees, lakes, rivers, all men, and all that thou seest and hast seen upon the earth. Because I love you, ye must do what I say and love, and not do what I hate. I do not love that ye should drink to the point of madness, as ye do; and I do not like that ye should fight one another. Ye take two wives, or run after the wives of others; ye do not well, and I hate that. Ye ought to have but one wife, and keep her till death. When ye wish to go to war, ye conjure and resort to the medicine dance, believing that ye speak to me; ye are mistaken,—it is to Manitou that ye speak, an evil spirit who prompts you to nothing but wrong, and who listens to you out of ignorance of me.

"This land where ye dwell I have made for you and not for others. Whence comes it that ye permit the Whites upon your lands? Can ye not live without them? I know that those whom ye call the children of your Great Father supply your needs, but if ye were not evil, as ye are, ye could surely do without them. Ye could live as ye did live before knowing them,—before those whom ye call your brothers had come upon your lands. Did ye not live by the bow and arrow? Ye had no need of gun or powder, or anything else, and nevertheless ye caught animals to live upon and to dress yourselves with their skins. But when I say that ye were given up to evil, I led the wild animals to the depths of the forests so that ye had to depend upon your brothers to feed and shelter you. Ye have only to become good again and do what I wish, and I will send back the animals for your food. I do not forbid you to permit among you the children of your Father; I love them. They know me and pray to me, and I supply their wants and all they give you. But as to those who come to trouble your lands,—drive them out, make war upon them. I do not love them at all; they know me not, and are my enemies, and the enemies of your brothers. Send them back to the lands which I have created for them and let them stay there. Here is a prayer which I give thee in writing to learn by heart and to teach to the Indians and their children."

The Wolf replied that he did not know how to read. He was told that when he should have returned to earth he would have only to give the prayer to the chief of his village who would read it and teach him and all the Indians to know it by heart; and he must say it night and morning without fail, and do what he had just been told to do: and he was to tell all the Indians for and in the name of the Master of Life:

"Do not drink more than once, or at most twice in a day; have only one wife and do not run after the wives of others nor after the girls; do not fight among yourselves; do not 'make medicine,' but pray, because in 'making medicine' one talks with the evil spirit; drive off your lands those dogs clothed in red who will do you nothing but harm. And when ye shall have need of anything address yourselves to me; and as to your brothers, I shall give to you as to them; do not sell to your brothers what I have put on earth for food. In short, become good and ye shall receive your needs. When ye meet one another exchange greeting and proffer the left hand which is nearest the heart.

"In all things I command thee to repeat every morning and night the prayer which I have given thee."

The Wolf promised to do faithfully what the Master of Life told him, and that he would recommend it well to the Indians, and that the Master of Life would be pleased with them. Then the same man who had led him by the hand came to get him and conducted him to the foot of the mountain where he told him to take his outfit again and return to his village. The Wolf did this, and upon his arrival the members of his tribe and village were greatly surprised, for they did not know what had become of him, and they asked where he had been. As he was enjoined not to speak to anybody before he had talked with the chief of his village, he made a sign with his hand that he had come from on high. Upon entering the village he went straight to the cabin of the chief to whom he gave what had been given to him, — namely, the prayer and the law which the Master of Life had given him.

This adventure was soon noised about among the people of the whole village who came to hear the message of the Master of Life, and then went to carry it to the neighboring villages. The members of these villages came to see the pretended traveller, and the news was spread from village to village and finally reached Pontiac. He believed all this, as we believe an article of faith, and instilled it into the minds of all those in his council. They listened to him as to an oracle and told him that he had only to speak and they were all ready to do what he demanded of them. . . .

## 7. Missionary David Brainerd Describes His Encounter with a Delaware Prophet, 1745

. . . But of all the sights I ever saw among them, or indeed any where else, none appeared so frightful, or so near akin to what is usually imagined of *infernal powers;* none ever excited such images of terror in my mind, as the appearance of one who

---

David Brainerd, *The Life of David Brainerd,* ed. Jonathan Edwards (1818): 350–353.

was a devout and zealous reformer, or rather restorer of what he supposed was the ancient religion of the Indians.

He made his appearance in his pontifical garb, which was a coat of bear's skins, dressed with the hair on, and hanging down to his toes; a pair of bear-skin stockings, and a great *wooden* face, painted the one half black and the other tawny, about the colour of an Indian's skin, with an extravagant mouth, cut very much awry; the face fastened to a bearskin cap, which was drawn over his head. He advanced toward me with the instrument in his hand that he used for music in his idolatrous worship, which was a dry tortoise-shell, with some corn in it, and the neck of it drawn on to a piece of wood, which made a very convenient handle. As he came forward, he beat his tune with the rattle, and danced with all his might, but did not suffer any part of his body, not so much as his fingers, to be seen: and no man would have guessed by his appearance and actions, that he could have been a human creature, if they had not had some intimation of it otherwise. When he came near me, I could not but shrink away from him, although it was then noon-day, and I knew who it was, his appearance and gestures were so prodigiously frightful. He had a house consecrated to religious uses, with divers images cut out upon the several parts of it; I went in and found the ground beat almost as hard as a rock with their frequent dancing in it.—I discoursed with him about Christianity; some of my discourse he seemed to like, but some of it he disliked entirely. He told me that God had taught him his religion, and that he never would turn from it, but wanted to find some that would join heartily with him in it; for the Indians, he said, were grown very degenerate and corrupt. He had thoughts, he said, of leaving all his friends, and travelling abroad, in order to find some that would join with him; for he believed God had some good people somewhere that felt as he did. He had not always, he said, felt as he now did, but had formerly been like the rest of the Indians, until about four or five years before that time. Then, he said, his heart was very much distressed, so that he could not live among the Indians, but got away into the woods, and lived alone for some months. At length, he says, God comforted his heart, and showed him what he should do; and since that time he had known God, and tried to serve him; and loved all men, be they who they would, so as he never did before.

He treated me with uncommon courtesy, and seemed to be hearty in it. I was told by the Indians, that he opposed their drinking strong liquor with all his power; and if at any time he could not dissuade them from it, by all he could say, he would leave them, and go crying into the woods. It was manifest he had a set of religious notions that he had examined for himself, and not taken for granted upon bare tradition; and he relished or disrelished whatever was spoken of a religious nature, according as it either agreed or disagreed with his standard. While I was discoursing he would sometimes say, "Now that I like: so God has taught me," &c. And some of his sentiments seemed very just. Yet he utterly denied the being of a *devil*, and declared there was no such a creature known among the Indians of old times, whose religion he supposed he was attempting to revive. He likewise told me, that departed souls all went southward, and that the difference between the good and bad was this, that the former were admitted into a beautiful town with spiritual walls, or walls agreeable to the nature of souls; and that the latter would for ever hover round those walls, and in vain attempt to get in. He seemed to be sincere, honest and conscientious in his own way, and according to his own religious notions, which was more than I ever saw in any other Pagan. I perceived he was looked upon, and derided amongst most of the Indians as a precise zealot, that made a needless noise about religious matters. But I must say, there was something in his temper and disposition that looked more like true religion than any thing I ever observed amongst other Heathens.

But alas, how deplorable is the state of the Indians upon this river. The brief representation I have here given of their notions and manners, is sufficient to shew that they are "led captive by Satan at his will," in the most eminent manner. It might likewise be sufficient to excite the compassion, and engage the prayers of pious souls for these their fellow men, who sit in "the regions of the shadow of death."

Sep. 22. Made some further attempts to instruct and christianize the Indians on this island, but all to no purpose. They live so near the white people, that they are always in the way of strong liquor, as well as the ill examples of *nominal* christians; which renders it so unspeakably difficult to treat with them about Christianity.

Forks of Delaware, 1745.

## E S S A Y S

No one in the backcountry could impose a settlement or one version of reality on the varied peoples in the region. Every arrangement involved negotiation and constant adjustment and these processes required people who were knowledgeable about and at home in a variety of settings. These brokers, some of European descent and others of Indian parentage, were constantly traveling, carrying news and offers or threats to people whose interests were concerned in the cauldron of events. Historian James Merrell of Vassar College examines the career of one notable member of this category, Andrew Montour, in the first essay. Montour was a successful broker—at least for a time—but his undoubted ability in these endeavors led all sides to doubt him at the same time they relied on him. Ultimately, his vision of a region of mixed populations living together and forging new identities failed as another frontier reality of fixed boundaries came into being.

In the second essay Gregory Dowd, historian at Notre Dame University, looks beyond the frontier of European settlement to examine the mixed native communities of the Ohio Valley. New religious movements began to spring up there in the mid-eighteenth century. These movements grew in part out of pan-Indian sentiment, as former enemies came together and saw their common plight. Inspired native preachers, many of whom had experienced visions in which they received divine instructions, began to draw hearers. All these preachers called on Indians to eliminate the poison of European ways that was destroying their lives and to return to the ways of their ancestors. Some, like Neolin the Delaware Prophet, founded large movements. To what extent did they incorporate aspects of the Christianity they had learned from missionaries at the same time they rejected European life?

## Reading Andrew Montour

### JAMES H. MERRELL

On the morning of October 25, 1755, a band of forty-nine men sat on their horses at a fork in the road along the east bank of the Susquehanna River. They were discussing how best to get downstream. The path to the right led to a ford across the river, an easy ride down the western shore, and another ford taking them back across the Susquehanna to their homes at Paxton, some fifty miles away. Straight ahead was "the old Road" down the east side, a shorter but harder ride.

Ordinarily the choice would have been easy; the right-hand path was the conventional route, and the one the men had come up two days before. But this was no ordinary time. Just nine days earlier, Indian war had come to Pennsylvania, igniting a conflagration of hatred, bloodshed, and sorrow that would last for a generation. In the Susquehanna Valley, the first blows had fallen upon the Penn's Creek settlements on the west side of the river. On hearing the terrible news, these forty-nine "Paxton people," led by the fur trader and storekeeper John Harris, had come north to bury the dead, search for the missing, and scout the enemy. From Penn's Creek the burial party had forded the river and headed to Shamokin, an Indian town at the confluence of the North and West Branches of the Susquehanna. "There is a Body of Indians assembled" in that village, it was said, Indians who had sent word that they "want to see their [Pennsylvania] Brethren's faces" in these dark times. So the band of Pennsylvanians pushed on upstream in order "to know their [the Indians'] minds." Were those natives preparing to help colonists stop the invasion, or plotting to join it?

It was hard to tell from the look of things at Shamokin, where Harris's party arrived on the evening of October 24. On the one hand, the Paxton men—some of them, like Harris and the fur trader Thomas McKee, well acquainted with the Susquehanna Valley Indian peoples—saw a number of familiar faces and were "seemingly well received." On the other hand, amid the familiar faces were many "strange Indians, . . . all painted Black" for war. Worse still, during the night some of Harris's men overheard Delawares plotting to call in reinforcements against these colonial visitors, talk followed by "the War Song" and then by four Indians, "well armed," paddling off into the darkness. The next morning, Harris and his companions, no fools, "got up early in order to go back." As the party prepared to leave, another familiar face in those parts, a man named Andrew Montour, stepped forward to warn the travelers "not to go the same Road they came, but to keep this side Sasquehannah and go the old Road" in order to slip a trap. And so, at "the parting of the Roads" just outside Shamokin, the forty-nine men talked, that autumn day, about the safer course to take.

The question framing the discussion was simple: Can we trust Andrew Montour? Some in the party, having known the man for more than a decade, said yes. Over the years, Montour had traveled hundreds of miles on errands for Pennsylvania and her sister colonies. His work on behalf of the English—carrying messages, delivering gifts, translating speeches—earned him the dubious distinctions of having a French bounty on his capture (or his scalp), serving with George Washington at Great Meadows, and marching toward even worse disaster with Edward Braddock. So trusted was Montour by Pennsylvanians that, when he had arrived at the Paxton settlements late in 1754 bearing a commission to raise a body of Indian troops for the English, so many "River Men" volunteered (including John Harris's brother, William) that Montour filled his ranks with Pennsylvania colonists instead. Interpreter, adviser, soldier— Montour, some of the Paxton men argued, had proved his loyalty too many times to be doubted now. Heed his warning; stay on this side of the Susquehanna.

Others disagreed. After all, this "French Andrew," this "Monsieur Montour," was the son of a "Madame Montour," with a brother who acted like "a perfect French

Man" and a cousin called "French Margaret." Moreover, the man's recent behavior clearly betrayed him. "Montour knew many days of the Enemy's being on their March against us before he informed me," John Harris said. And, if such silence did not speak loudly enough, when Montour came forward at Shamokin that morning to warn the Pennsylvanians about the risks of the river's west side, he was "painted as the rest." Although admitting that "tis hard to tell," colonists urging the western route insisted that Montour could not be trusted; he was "an Enemy in his heart."

And so the men argued, knowing that their lives might depend upon their reading of Montour. Ultimately, those mistrusting him won the day; the horsemen, "fearing a snare might be laid on that [east] side," forded the river—and rode straight into the ambush that Montour knew was there. Four men fell to the first volley; several more drowned trying to make it back to Montour's side of the Susquehanna. The rest staggered home to Paxton to tell their story to family, to neighbors, to provincial officials, and to us.

The men who misread Andrew Montour that day were neither the first nor the last to make this mistake; they just paid a higher price than others. Richard Peters, an Anglican clergyman and provincial secretary to the Penn family who was deeply involved in the colony's Indian affairs, considered Montour "really an unintelligible person"; many others felt the same way. Conrad Weiser, Pennsylvania's Iroquois specialist who knew Montour even better than Peters did, "found him faithful, knowing, and prudent" in June 1748, but, by summer's end, was "at a lost [*sic*] what to say of him."

Historians, like Peters, have generally thought Montour unintelligible, and, like Weiser, they are often at a loss for what to say about him. Most confine themselves to a sketch of Montour's colorful family and his checkered career: his birth to the Oneida leader Currundawanah and "the celebrated" Madame Montour, a Canadian métis who, among other adventures that brought her fame from Albany to Philadelphia to Detroit, dined with an English governor and bedded a French commandant; his attachment to French Margaret, who once traveled from the Susquehanna Valley to New York accompanied by "her Mohawk husband and two grandchildren, . . . with an Irish groom and six relay and pack-horses"; his appearance on the Susquehanna frontier in 1742 as an interpreter and guide for Moravian missionaries; his performances over the years that followed at councils and other intercultural conversations in Pennsylvania, Iroquoia, New York, Virginia, and the Ohio country; his status as a commander of colonial or Indian troops and a member of the Iroquois council; his bitter arguments with provincial officials; his battles with the bottle; his narrow escapes from debtor's prison; and his murder by a Seneca in 1772, thirty years after he first stepped onto the public stage.

That Montour has befuddled both his contemporaries and later scholars is not surprising. Because he rarely spoke for himself, because he usually translated words others uttered and marked pages others wrote, it is hard to get beneath the surface of his career—this trip, that treaty—in order to study the man, to look upon his face or see into his heart.

More than the lack of sources, Montour's anomalous life gets in the way of a clear view. His very existence goes against the habit of thought, then and since, accustomed to consider the colonial frontier a dividing line between Europeans and native Americans. Trying to locate Montour on either side of that frontier—like the related guessing game devoted to determining whether he favored France or England—preoccupied British colonists, who seemed to spend as much time trying to label Montour as they did trying to understand him. Richard Peters considered him an Indian, but others called him "white," and Conrad Weiser even referred to Montour as Indian on one page of a letter and white on another.

The first encounter with Montour to find its way into the historical record reveals one important source of the confusion about him: his appearance. "Andrew's cast of countenance is decidedly European," wrote the Moravian leader Count Nikolaus Ludwig von Zinzendorf after meeting Montour in September 1742,

> and had not his face been encircled with a broad band of paint, applied with bear's fat, I would certainly have taken him for one. He wore a brown broadcloth coat, a scarlet damasken lappel-waistcoat, breeches, over which his shirt hung, a black Cordovan neckerchief, decked with silver bugles, shoes and stockings, and a hat. His ears were hung with pendants of brass and other wires plaited together like the handle of a basket. He was very cordial, but on addressing him in French, he, to my surprise, replied in English.

To people like Zinzendorf, accustomed to reading European badges of identity—such as color of skin and cut of hair, language (or accent) and literacy, kin and clothes—Montour sent out mixed signals. Even his reply to Zinzendorf's greeting is hard to read: was Montour showing off his English? Trying to avoid being thought French? Relishing the visitor's surprise? No easier to decipher is the fashion statement Montour made by combining hat and waistcoat with earrings and paint. Nor does his impressive collection of names—not just Andrew Montour and French Andrew but Henry Montour, Andrew (or Andreas) Sattelihu, and Echnizera (or Oughsara)—help to fix his identity.

No wonder those skeptical Paxton men, like others reading Montour in their day and our own, admitted that it is "hard to tell" about him. Hard, yes, but not impossible. By venturing into the shadowy Susquehanna world that Montour called home, by listening with care when he did speak his mind, by letting his actions speak as loudly as his words, one can attempt a reading of Andrew Montour. Those shadows, those words, those actions suggest that Montour, nurtured in a distinctive cultural milieu, fashioned himself into a new sort of person, someone who drew from several traditions in order to craft a life. More than that, he might have been groping his way toward a new sort of society, one nestled in the interstices between Indians and colonists, one inhabited by people like him. Reading Andrew Montour, then, offers a sense of the possibilities open to people in that place at that time and a sense, too, of the limits of the possible, the harsh realities on which Montour foundered.

The best way to approach Montour is to visit the Susquehanna River Valley where he spent much of his life. When Montour lived there, from the 1720s to the 1760s, the Susquehanna country was a debatable land, a place marked by confusion and contention. Too few "natives" remained there to serve as a charter group that could determine the character of life in the region, the Susquehannocks having been all but destroyed by their Iroquois neighbors in the late seventeenth century. The Six Nations—Mohawks, Oneidas, Cayugas, Onondagas, Senecas, and (after 1722) Tuscaroras—claimed the area by virtue of that victory and, after 1700, oversaw a repeopling of the valley's lower reaches not only by Seneca, Oneida, and Cayuga emigrants but also by Indian refugees fleeing European colonial intrusions. From Maryland came Conoys and Nanticokes, from Carolina Tutelos and Tuscaroras; from farther south still, and from the west, came Shawnees, and from the east came Delawares.

Out of the east, too, came colonists from various European lands. English and French, German and Scots-Irish, Swiss and Welsh moved into the valley during the first half of the eighteenth century, pursuing their own versions of happiness and drawing sustenance from faiths as various as Catholic, Quaker, Presbyterian, and Moravian. Added to this mix were African Americans, some of them runaway slaves, others owned by colonial fur traders, still others bought or stolen by Indians. Whatever their status, like "Delaware Negroes" visiting a provincial fort on the riverbank one winter day in 1758, African Americans were an everyday feature of the Susquehanna social landscape. . . .

. . . To a person of his background and upbringing, the future must have looked rich in possibilities, for Montour was singularly well equipped to chart a life's course that would take him in a number of different directions.

One of those directions led, through his mother, toward European colonial society. From Madame Montour Andrew picked up more than French and English; he also learned how to behave in polite provincial circles. . . .

. . . With his appearance and his knowledge of European ways, he could have wiped the paint off his face, pulled the spangles from his ears, and found a home in the colonial world.

Alternatively, Montour could have recast his countenance, adding more paint and turning his face away from Philadelphia or Bethlehem and toward Logstown or Onondaga, deeper into the Indian cultures and countries. After all, along with French and English he could speak Delaware, Shawnee, and one or more Iroquois languages. In addition, his mother, whatever her longings for colonial company, was to all appearances "in mode of life a complete Indian," and, in his youth, Montour was apprenticed in his father's trades of hunting and war. An added incentive to look west or north rather than east was the knowledge that colonial society, too, could be a dangerous place. . . . The suspicions Andrew faced at Shamokin in October 1755 had been part of his life since the very beginning.

A third possibility was that Montour could choose neither path. Instead, he could stay in the Susquehanna Valley, where a person like him was, if not common, at least not some freak of nature and culture. As it turned out, Montour did just that. Although he never stayed in one spot for long, his life remained centered in those parts of the Susquehanna where he had grown up. There, the rhythms of his existence resembled those of most other Susquehanna peoples, whether their native soil was along the Delaware or the Rhine, the Savannah or the Thames. Montour hunted and traded, grew corn and raised sheep, and went off to war against both the Susquehanna Indians' traditional enemies, like Catawbas, and England's old foes, the French. And, like many Susquehanna colonists of every description, he drank a lot and piled up debts, habits that sometimes took him from tavern to jail and back again.

At the same time, however, Montour was no ordinary inhabitant of the valley. What distinguished him from his neighbors was not only his exceptional linguistic skill but also his ability to fashion himself from more than one template: genteel colonist, Iroquois warrior, frontiersman. Moreover, he drew on those resources to make connections to peoples near and far. Some of those connections he inherited and then nurtured; others, he manufactured. . . .

. . . Besides Count Zinzendorf, Montour cultivated Conrad Weiser, the expert on all things Iroquois who in 1748 "presented Andrew to the Board [Pennsylvania Council] as a Person who might be of Service to the Province," George Croghan, a prominent fur trader and Pennsylvania's man across the Appalachians, the Virginia land speculators of the Ohio Company, and, after 1755, Sir William Johnson of New York, the crown's superintendent of Indian affairs for the northern department.

Montour's pursuit of all of these relationships sharpened his ability to negotiate the cultural terrain of colonial America. At home in a longhouse and at a governor's dinner table, able to perform the Iroquois condolence ceremony and explain baptism to Indians, bearing a provincial captain's commission and a wampum belt with his credentials as an Iroquois leader, wearing a hat on his head and paint on his face—Montour made a name for himself as "a very useful Person" with "a good Character, both amongst White people and Indians." "Montour would be of singular use to me here at this present, in conversing with the Indians," a worried George Washington wrote from the frontier in June 1754; "I am often at a loss how to behave and should be reliev'd from many anxious fear's of offend[in]g them if Montour was here to assist me." Many people involved in similar conversations during these years sought in Montour the same assistance, the same relief from "anxious fear's."

No one serving so many masters was going to please all of the peoples all of the time, however. Amid the testimonials to Montour were tirades, sometimes by the very people praising him, about his behavior. . . .

When war came to the Susquehanna in the fall of 1755, the grumbling and laughter turned ugly. A month after the first strike at Penn's Creek, riding with the Oneida Scarouyady from Philadelphia to Iroquoia in order to enlist the Six Nations' help, Montour waded into an elemental sea of hatred and anger. Lining the Susquehanna road were several hundred armed colonists, "enraged against all the Indians" and eager to "kill them without Distinction." "Why must we be killed by the Indians and we not kill them!" they shouted as the two rode past under guard. "Why are our Hands so tied?" . . .

. . . Many peoples had plenty of reasons to hate Andrew Montour. Part of the problem was that the man kept changing the cast of his countenance. . . .

Montour's abrupt changes bespoke more than the rum in his belly or the interests of his audience. They were one expression of a habit he had—a nasty habit, in the view of the people he ostensibly served—of changing not only his countenance but his mind. In 1751, he said nothing when George Croghan happily announced to his Pennsylvania superiors that Indians had given the British permission to build a fort in the Ohio country to counter the French, then infuriated Croghan (and, presumably, pleased Ohio Indians) by claiming the opposite: the tribes there had expressly forbidden a fort. A year later, Montour was instrumental in getting Ohio leaders gathered at Logstown to accept Virginia's expansive interpretation of a land sale, then reversed himself again, embarrassing Weiser (and, again, pleasing Ohio nations) by insisting that "the Indians never Sold nor released it [the Ohio land]. If they did they were imposed upon by the Interpreter"—none other than Weiser himself.

Such bold assertions of Indian rights misled those who saw in Montour a consistently staunch defender of native sovereignty, however. In December 1758, when British troops had taken Fort Duquesne and were determined to remain there, Montour helped George Croghan twist Ohio Indian speeches demanding the army's withdrawal into an invitation to stay. Similarly, at Easton four years later, he helped Sir William Johnson side with the Pennsylvania proprietors against Delaware charges of land fraud by condensing a four-hour reading of the proprietary defense into a brief summary for the Delaware ambassadors.

No wonder so many people despised Montour. The man was more than hard to read; he was, in some alarming way, unfathomable. His true nature, the wellsprings of his behavior, remained hidden. Indeed, what made Montour so mistrusted is also what made him so indispensable. His gift, and his curse, was that his habits of dress and address allowed many different readings of him. People saw in him what they hoped (or feared) to see: French spy or British puppet, Christian convert or Iroquois warrior, land agent or defender of Indian domain, "Dupe" of "low Company" (according to colonial authorities) or of the provincial elite (according to Indians defending their lands). Montour could be all things to all peoples—he got along with governors and "Woods Men," led war parties and missionaries, negotiated Indian land sales and then renounced them—but he belonged to no one. His behavior frustrated attempts to label him, to co-opt him, to render him loyal to someone or something, to make him predictable and safe.

There were, then, as many reasons to doubt Montour as there were reasons to rely on him. But perhaps the truest source of the dislike and distrust he inspired, the real reason he rubbed so many people the wrong way, ran deeper than his drinking or his spending, his impertinence or his pride, his changes of countenance or changes of mind, his affinity for "low Company" or for provincial elites. That reason is the way Montour tried to define himself and to shape the future character of Susquehanna society. His vision, inchoate and never stated outright, can be retrieved from an unlikely place: his land dealings at midcentury. In these negotiations, Montour's signature, his hand, can be read more clearly—and clearly puts him at odds with most native Americans and most European colonists of his day. . . .

That Montour might become the landlord and neighbor of European colonists, that he might start a society in which Indian peoples and European peoples lived peaceably together, was Conrad Weiser's worst nightmare. . . . As Peters and Weiser came to see, they were in a contest with Montour not just for land but for the power to determine what sort of society was to be born on the Susquehanna—and, perhaps, beyond it. Would it resemble the Delaware Valley, now virtually empty of Indians? Or would it be something new, forged by various refugee and emigrant groups—European and Indian—from the common Susquehanna experience of the past generation and led by men like Montour?

The answer to these questions came at Albany in July 1754 when Weiser and Peters purchased from the Six Nations the land beneath Montour's feet. Pennsylvania won in part because the Iroquois were as unhappy with Montour's plan as Weiser and Peters were. In the past, Iroquois sales of land had served to affirm the

Six Nations' authority over other native peoples and to keep European colonists at arm's length. No wonder Onondaga refused to go along with his scheme. . . . It was to be a land of lines dividing Indians from Europeans, not a place where lines blurred and peoples came together. . . .

That Anglo-American colonists had no intention of living in "the woods" or becoming one people with Indians is clear enough. Less well known is the Indians' own resistance to such an idea. Beneath the metaphors of harmony and unity that decorated the treaty minutes—the talk of becoming one people with one body, one heart, and one mind—ran a chorus of dissonance and dissent. During a council at Lancaster in 1744, an Iroquois speaker informed his audience: "The World at the first was made on the other side of the Great water different from what it is on this side, as may be known from the different colour of Our Skin and of Our Flesh. . . . You have your Laws and Customs and so have we." "You know I am not as you are," an Oneida from the upper Susquehanna reminded Pennsylvania officials in 1762. "I am of a quite different Nature from you."

Not only were natives different, but they wanted to stay that way. "We are Indians," one Susquehanna headman replied when a missionary broached the subject of conversion, "and don't wish to be transformed into white men. The English are our Brethren, but we never promised to become what they are. As little as we desire the preacher to become Indian, so little ought he to desire the Indians to become preachers." . . .

In the years to come, Susquehanna peoples, native American and Euro-American alike, would scrawl in blood the epitaph for Montour's dream by using knowledge acquired during a generation of peaceful intercourse to kill each other without mercy. *"Be still we wont hurt you,"* an Indian warrior herding German children together a month after Penn's Creek said in "High Dutch"—before burying a hatchet in their mother's head, stepping on her neck to tear off her scalp, and joining his companions to cut down the fleeing boys and girls.

In the Susquehanna Valley eight years later, the tables were turned when some troops from Paxton came upon three Indians. "Dont shoot brothers, dont shoot," the three cried; they proclaimed their friendship for Pennsylvania, and, personifying it, one was even "named George Allen," a Paxton man recalled, "after the George Allen that was with us." Blind to such signs of attachment, the soldiers took the Indians prisoner and, after ordering them to walk on ahead, shot them in the back. George Allen (the Indian), wounded in the arm, played dead while they scalped him; then, as the killers began to strip his leggings off, he jumped up and escaped, even though "the skin of his face, the scalp being off, came down over his eyes so that he cou'd not see." This George Allen, recovering his vision and his health, lived to talk of gaining revenge on his namesake.

In a world where George Allen shot George Allen, where Indians spoke German while killing Germans, where was Montour to fit? He had set about defining himself as a denizen of this debatable land. Only after Montour had made it his life's ambition to become the leading citizen of the territory between the woods and the inhabited parts, only then did he discover that he had pitched his camp, had pitched his life, in a no-man's-land.

Montour was not completely alone, of course. Besides his extended family, besides those peoples on the east side of the Susquehanna living together amicably enough (or so it seemed to Weiser), a few others did articulate this search for a meeting of minds, hearts, and souls that, in Indian metaphor, bound societies one to the other. Among the Iroquois in 1750, the Moravian bishop John Christian Frederick Cammerhoff mused that he "sometimes felt like saying to myself: [']I am dwelling among my own people,['] and when I shall be able to say that in its true meaning, my heart will rejoice." But Cammerhoff never saw that happy day; indeed, virtually no one did. Although many crossed the cultural divide between Indians and Europeans, few really felt at home on the far side. Croghan, Weiser, the Oneidas Shickellamy and Scarouyady—these and the other go-betweens of the Pennsylvania theater were firmly anchored on one side of the frontier or the other. Like Thomas Gist, a frontiersman whom the Wyandots in 1758 captured, stripped, shaved, painted, and adopted, European colonists in the Indian countries were only "acting the part of an Indian." "I could do [this acting] very well," Gist boasted after he—"determined to be what I really was"—made good his escape.

. . . It is as hard to read the man now as it was 250 years ago. What can be said is that Montour was never able to borrow or to fashion a vocabulary that would define him as neither Indian nor European but something new, something else altogether. Lacking that working vocabulary, Montour spent his life maintaining his credentials as both an Indian and a European. . . .

Trying to be both Indian and European, Montour ended up being neither. The life that he made for himself, the path he traveled, turned out to be a dead end in English America, not an avenue to some new social order. There was no place in between, there were no words to describe the sort of person he was, there was no critical mass of people like himself sufficient to weave new social patterns from the fraying edges of the old. . . .

## The Indians' Great Awakening

GREGORY E. DOWD

A nativistic movement that would last a generation to become the religious underpinning of militant pan-Indianism first developed most clearly in the polyglot communities on the Upper Susquehanna. Refugees from earlier dispossessions in New Jersey and eastern Pennsylvania, these peoples began again to fall back before the Anglo-American advance of the 1750s and 1760s. The movement accompanied refugees as they fled northwest and then west from the Susquehanna to the headwaters of the Allegheny, from whence it descended upon the Ohio country. Here it found inviting souls among the already established refugees who inhabited the polyglot villages . . . Laid low during the Seven Years' War, the Indians provided the movement with deep basins of support. The Ohio River issued from mountain springs, snows, and rains. The currents of nativism issued from the reckonings of the several thousand souls, and from the many prophets who gave those souls voice. Because the movement roughly coincided with British America's Christian revival, I have chosen to call it the Indians' Great Awakening. But it was not a "revival" of a religious spirit that had lain, somehow, dormant. In its most important aspect, it was an "awakening" to the idea that, despite all the boundaries defined by politics, language, kinship, and geography, Indians did indeed share much in the way of their pasts and their present. It was an awakening to the notion that Indians shared a conflict with Anglo-America, and that they, as Indians, could and must take hold of their destiny by regaining sacred power.

Between 1737 and 1775, a time of economic dislocation and much warfare in the Susquehanna and Ohio valleys, a cluster of men and women came into direct contact with the usually remote Master of Life. Styled "prophets" by the least hostile of their Christian observers and "impostors" by others, these people differed from the more common shamans or conjurers only in the level of their experience. Although their spiritual encounters may have represented departures from, or elaborations upon, more ordinary shamanistic experiences, they were not new phenomena in the mid-eighteenth century. Over a full century before, Hurons reported spiritual encounters that led them to perform new ceremonies. Indian myths, moreover, are replete with similar journeys to the sky world.

In its mid-eighteenth-century manifestations prophetic nativism first appears, mildly, in the 1737 journals of Pennsylvania's Indian agent, Conrad Weiser. Weiser found starving Shawnees and Onondaga Iroquois at the Susquehanna River town of Otseningo discussing the recent visions of "one of their seers." In "a vision of God," the seer learned that God had "driven the wild animals out of the country" in punishment for the crime of killing game for trade in alcohol. The seer convinced his listeners that if they did not stop trading skins for English rum, God would wipe them "from the earth." Weiser did not dwell on the matter; we do not learn of any ensuing reformation. But by 1744, the Susquehanna Valley, increasingly populated by polyglot refugees from dispossession in the East, swelled again with prophecy.

That year, lower down the river, the Presbyterian missionary David Brainerd encountered religious nativists among the Delawares and Shawnees. He reported that "they now seem resolved to retain their pagan notions and persist in their idolatrous practices." Beset by disease, the Indians looked to the sacred powers "to find out why they were then so sickly." Among the inhabitants of one Delaware town Brainerd met "a devout and zealous reformer, or rather restorer of what he supposed was the ancient religion of the Indians." Like the seer at Otseningo, the holy man claimed that his people "were grown very degenerate and corrupt," and he emphatically denounced alcohol. But he also claimed that his people must revive what he believed were the ceremonies of their ancestors. Although the sight of the Delaware holy man stirred "images of terror" in Brainerd's mind, the shaman did not reveal any hostility toward Anglo-Americans, and Brainerd admitted that "there was something in his temper and disposition that looked more like true religion than anything I ever observed amongst other heathens."

Neither Weiser's "seer" nor Brainerd's "reformer" mounted a political challenge discernible in the record. They did stand against the alcohol trade and therefore against a most visible and physical form of dependence upon Europeans. That is all. . . .

The first of the prophets to mount a political challenge was a young Delaware woman. Noted in 1751 by Brainerd's younger brother, John, she lived in the increasingly militant Susquehanna River town of Wyoming, which was choked with refugees. We know little of her, not even her name; indeed the Indians "seemed somewhat backward to tell" John Brainerd about her at all. But the scanty evidence is tantalizing. Her vision "was a confirmation of some revelations they had had before." She had been told by the "Great Power that they should destroy the poison from among them." The woman worried about the sickness and death of so many of her people and blamed it on that "poison," probably a witch bundle, allegedly held by "their old and principal men." The evidence, though thin, suggests a challenge to the local leadership of the town of Wyoming, a leadership bound to the powerful Six Nations Iroquois to the north and, through their cooperation, to the British colonies. Her people would attack that bondage openly and violently during the Seven Years' War.

The people of this Delaware village asserted their Indian identity. They drew distinctions that separated Indians from blacks and whites. The distinctions, they felt, were God-given. Rejecting Presbyterian attempts to establish a mission among them, they explained, "God first made three men and three women, viz: the indians, the negro, and the white man." Because Europeans were produced last, "the white people ought not to think themselves better than the Indians." Moreover, the Bible was for Europeans alone; since God gave no such book "to the Indian or negro, and therefore it could not be right for them to have a book, or be any way concerned with that way of worship."

This idea of the separate creation of Indians, blacks, and whites, an idea that sanctioned separate forms of worship, was widely reported in the Susquehanna and Ohio regions, where it became commonplace. On the eve of the American Revolution, it would be shared as well by the southern Indians, who described it to Anglo-Americans. The notion of the separate creation gave legitimacy to the Indians' way of life. It explicitly challenged not only those Indians who had converted to Christianity but also those few who had grown too close to the Anglo-Americans. It played in harmony with the Wyoming woman's dissent from the accommodating leadership of her village. Claiming that only Indian ways could lead Indians to salvation, the theology of separation implicitly attacked Indian clients of the Anglo-Americans.

The notion had radical implications for Indian identity. Attachments to the older, local, linguistic, and lineage-oriented conceptions of one's people now competed with a decidedly innovative pan-Indianism. The notion reflected the growing cooperation of militant factions from different peoples in political efforts to unite Indians against the Anglo-American menace. It also reflected the heightening of local tensions, as Indians who rejected nativism and urged accommodation with the British found themselves accused of abomination.

The year after the younger Brainerd first encountered this separatist theology, a group of Munsee Delawares settled a new town some seventy miles up the winding Susquehanna. Munsees increasingly identified with their Unami Delaware-speaking cousins, and like many Unamis they had maintained friendly relations with the Moravians and Quakers. This particular group of Munsees displayed a marked ambivalence toward both Christianity and nativism. Its leader, Papoonan, had once been "a drunken Indian." At the age of about forty-five he "underwent a sorrowful period of reformation, including a solitary sojourn in the woods & a vision following the death of his father." Like other Indian prophets, Papoonan emerged from the vision with a message of love and reformation. He preached against the use of alcohol, as would most prophets, and he preached that the Master of Life, angered by the sins of the Indians, had met them with punishing visitations.

Unlike many of the other prophets, Papoonan refused to countenance war—a stand he may have absorbed from the Moravians and Quakers. The prophet once told a Pennsylvanian that in his heart he knew "the Quakers are Right." He and his followers remained at peace with Pennsylvania throughout the 1750s, and toward the end of the war they sought out Quakers to mediate their talks with the suspicious British authorities.

But even sincere protestations of friendship and interest in Christianity could not mask Papoonan's frustration with the social changes wrought by the Indian-Anglo trade. Recognizing the increasing importance in Indian society of access to British trade goods, Papoonan aimed his message primarily at the greedy. His own people, he worried, "grow proud & Covetous, which causes God to be Angry & to send dry & hot Summers & hard Winters, & also Sickness among the People." He also aimed the message at Anglo-Americans, telling the Pennsylvania Provincial Council that their raising of the prices of manufactured goods created tensions: "You alter the price that you say you will give for our Skins, which can never be right; God cannot be pleased to see the prices of one & the same thing so often alter'd & Changed." While challenging the greed of British colonists, Papoonan, like other prophets, urged his followers to purify themselves of similar greed by "adhering to the ancient Customs & manners of their Forefathers." He and his followers resisted, for a time, Christian efforts to establish missions among them, for they were "much afraid of being seduced & [brought] off from their ways by the White People."

In spite of its attempt to live in peace, Papoonan's community could not escape the massive troubles that surrounded it. Christian Frederick Post found the villagers troubled and quarrelsome in 1760. The town still existed as a native, non-Christian religious community the following year, but as Pontiac's War of 1763 embroiled the region, Papoonan, who held to the peace, lost influence. British colonial lynch mobs, having killed neutral Indians in the Paxton Massacre, forced Papoonan to flee with others to the safety of barracks under Quaker protection in Philadelphia. At the war's end, he was there numbered among the "Christian Indians." Some among his followers invited the Moravian missionaries to come among them. Others went off to joint the nativistic communities that were, by then, abundant on the Upper Ohio. It would not be the last failure of studied neutrality.

Further up the Susquehanna, not far from what is now New York State, Wangomend, or the Assinsink Prophet, experienced his first visions in the early 1750s, probably in 1752, the year Papoonan settled his new town. Unlike Papoonan, this Munsee showed open hostility toward the British. Indeed his message closely resembles the separatist beliefs of the Unami Delaware woman downstream at Wyoming who received her visions the previous year. The Assinsink Prophet encouraged the Indians to abandon British ways, emphatically denouncing rum drinking. . . .

Wangomend, like other Susquehanna country prophets, introduced or reintroduced ceremonies in an effort to gain power. Post reported that the prophet had revived "an Old quarterly Meeting," during which the participants recited the "Dreams and Revelations everyone had from his Infancy, & what Strength and Power they had received thereby." The meeting, which lasted all day and all night, involved walking, singing, dancing, and, finally, cathartic weeping. . . .

Following the Seven Years' War, refugee Munsee and Unami Delawares fled the Susquehanna for the Ohio, and the Assinsink Prophet was among them. There he undoubtedly encountered, if he had not done so previously, the thoroughly compatible teachings of another advocate of Indian separation from Britain, the Delaware Prophet, Neolin. The Ottawa warrior Pontiac would claim inspiration from Neolin for his siege of Detroit in 1763, and Neolin would rapidly emerge as the spiritual leader of a militant movement with political overtones. But it is important to recall that he neither invented nor was solely responsible for the spiritual quest for unity.

### The Delaware Prophet, Neolin

One night in the eighteen months or so of only relative calm that followed the French evacuation of the Upper Ohio Valley, Neolin sat alone by his fire, "musing and greatly concerned about the evil ways he saw prevailing among the Indians." Strangely, a man appeared and "told him these things he was thinking of were right" and proceeded to instruct him in religion. By the fall of 1761 Neolin had gained a considerable following as he relayed the will of the Master of Life to the Delawares. . . . Neolin drew a path from earth to heaven, along "which their forefathers use'd to assend to Hapiness." The path, however, was now blocked by a symbol "representing the White people." Along the right side of the chart were many "Strokes" representing the vices brought by Europeans. Through these strokes the Indians now "must go, ye Good Road being Stopt." Hell was also close at hand, and "there they are Led irrevocably." The programs offered by the Assinsink Prophet and Neolin were identical in many particulars. Each preached strenuously against the use of rum, chief among "ye vices which ye Indians have learned from ye White people," and which each depicted on his chart as strokes through which the difficult way to heaven now led.

Neolin not only drew a cosmographic distinction between Anglo-Americans and Indians, he preached a rejection of dependence on the British through the avoidance of trade, the elaboration of ritual, and the gradual (not the immediate) abandonment of European-made goods. In 1763, Delaware councils agreed to train their boys in the traditional arts of warfare, and to adopt, for seven years, a ritual diet that included the frequent consumption of an herbal emetic, after which they would be purified of the "White people's ways and Nature." The ritual brewing, drinking, and vomiting of this tea became a regular feature of Ohio Valley nativism in the 1760s. . . . The practice repelled missionaries and other visitors to the Ohio country. Shawnees drank and spewed the beverage with such literal enthusiasm that one of their towns, Wakatomica, was known to traders in the late 1760s as "vomit town." Wakatomica became a center of resistance to Anglo-American expansion and cultural influence. Here is where the Delaware Prophet took refuge, in fact, when British troops threatened to invade his hometown on the Tuscarawas River in 1764.

Neolin's message clearly entailed armed resistance to Anglo-American expansion. As early as 1761, Neolin predicted that "there will be Two or Three Good Talks and then War." Neolin's words struck a chord among Indians who suffered from or looked with foreboding upon three major threats to their economies: the disappearance of game, land encroachments by settlers . . . , and the British abandonment of customary presentations of gunpowder to the Indians. . . . Neolin explained the exhaustion of the deer herds as the Great Spirit's punishment for the Indians' embrace of Anglo-American vices. He berated Indians for allowing the colonists to establish settlements west of the Appalachians and for the Indians' humiliating dependence: "Can ye not live without them?" And he threatened continued disaster if they did not both reform and revolt: "If you suffer the English among you, you are dead men. Sickness, smallpox, and their poison will destroy you entirely."

The prophet's message spread among the nations. When the French commander of Fort Chartres (Illinois) learned of the prophet late in 1763, he wrote that Neolin "has had no difficulty in convincing all his own people, and in turn all red men, that God had appeared to him." Commandant Neyon de Villiers was "perfectly convinced of the effect that it has had on the Potawatomi." In 1764, the Wyandots of Sandusky, militants who associated closely with the Shawnees and Delawares, openly joined the crusade against the English. The combined Shawnee, Delaware, and Wyandot inhabitants of Sandusky declared that they had no fear of English numbers. Of the English they claimed that one Indian was "as good as a thousand of them, and notwithstanding they are but *Mice* in Comparison to them, they will bite as hard as *they* can." In addition to the Potawatomis, Wyandots, Shawnees, and Delawares, the prophet's message raised spirits among the Miamis, Senecas, Ottawas, Chippewas, and beyond.

Many spin-off revivals occurred, just as Neolin's had spun off from the earlier Susquehanna episodes. A Delaware of Kuskuski visited Heaven in 1762. He used charts in his ministry and communicated with the Great Spirit through intermediaries, or, as James Kenny put it, through "a little God." A great chief of the Ottawas, Katapelleecy, had personal encounters with the Great Spirit in 1764. In the heart of the Six Nations country an Onondaga received revelations critical of the Anglo-Americans and laced with separation theology on the eve of Pontiac's War. With no end in sight to the British threat, these prophets, despite their many innovations, offered a solution to Indian problems that came out of Indian traditions. Reform the world through ritual; recapture sacred power. The message took hold.

### Prophetic Resistance, 1760–1775

In the spring of 1763, thirteen of the British posts that stood north of the Ohio and the Potomac and west of the Susquehanna, in the heartland of religious nativism, came under devastating Indian attacks. From Senecas in New York to Chippewas in Minnesota and the Indians of Illinois, militant factions joined in a struggle to remove the British from posts so recently French. By 1765 this war, commonly known as Pontiac's War, had ended, and only four of the posts remained, most notably Detroit and Pitt.

Prophecy has long been acknowledged as having had a role in Pontiac's War, a colorful but incidental role. Generally, the prophet's message is a historian's addendum to a list of substantive causes of the war: British abuses in the trade, colonial encroachments on Indian land, Jeffrey Amherst's orders curtailing the customary dispensing of gifts to Indians, and French encouragement to the Indians. A common view is that Neolin's message was a slogan employed by militants to attract warriors. Howard Peckham, calling Neolin a "psychopathic Delaware," sees the prophet as providing a justification for Pontiac's attack on the British at Detroit. Suggesting that Pontiac manipulated "the Prophet's message slightly to support his own ambitions," Peckham implies that the Ottawa leader was too sophisticated to have believed in the prophet's visions, but used prophecy to inspire his more gullible followers.

Pontiac, however, portrayed himself as a true believer in the nativistic movement, and there seems little reason to doubt his claim. Even addressing the Catholic French he spoke in prophetic terms. Visiting Fort Chartres in 1764 to reject de Villiers's request that he stop the war, Pontiac declared that the Master of Life "put Arms in our hands, and it is he who has ordered us to fight against this bad meat that would come and infest our lands." He warned the French not to speak of "Peace with the English," for in doing so they went "against the orders of the Master of Life." Indeed, there is other evidence that Pontiac acted upon Neolin's initiative. . . .

But the extent of the prophet's influence on Pontiac or of Pontiac's influence on the war that now bears his name is less important for an understanding of Indian militancy than is the spiritual nature of militancy itself. The Delaware Prophet was not the single leader of the movement any more than was Pontiac. Both drew upon widespread beliefs in their efforts to confront the problems of 1763. The Delaware Prophet, and many other prophets who preceded and followed him, provided Indians with an explanation for their misfortunes that squared well with their traditions: Indian abominations, including cooperation with the British, caused their loss of sacred power. Construed in this manner, the disturbance could be rectified by ritual and by steadfast, united opposition to British expansion.

When the Indians failed to drive the British from Fort Detroit and Fort Pitt, when smallpox—deliberately disseminated in hospital blankets by Fort Pitt's British officers—broke out among the Ohio peoples, and when British columns marched within striking distance of Indian towns, the military unity of the Indians temporarily collapsed and the war ended. But neither prophetic nativism nor the idea of unity collapsed with it. Prophets and diplomats grew more active. . . .

Paradoxically, it was . . . divisions that permitted the survival of the nativist movement for unity. Nativism depended upon its Indian opponents. Infighting extended the life of the movement. Nativists could attribute the failure of Native American arms not to British numbers, technology, or organization, but to the improper behavior of the accommodating Indians. As long as nativists faced serious opposition within their own communities, they could explain Indian defeat as the consequence of other Indians' misdeeds. . . .

With every twenty-fifth Delaware attending to the Moravian Brethren, and with others attending to the likes of Wangomend, Delaware fissures deepened. Nativist sentiment surfaced regularly in the two major Unami Delaware towns, Kuskuski and Newcomer's, into the early 1770s. Like other advocates of Indian separation, these nativists stressed the distinction between Indians and the eastern settlers. One, visiting the Moravian Munsees in 1771, laid out his categories of understanding before Zeisberger. Christianity, the nativist said, was "for the white people. . . . God has made different kinds of men and has made each kind for a different purpose." The Indian clearly worried that to worship in the Christian manner was to violate the cosmic order. Another Indian, claiming to be a literate ex-Christian, told his townspeople "that he has read the Bible from beginning to end and that it is not written in it that the Indians should live like white people, or that they should change their lives." The nativists of Kuskuski never threatened the mission with violence, but they worried at its success and sought to convince the Christian converts to return to the nativist fold. One nativistic "new preacher" used images of Anglo-American society as the symbols of danger to Indians, declaring that the Moravians sought to have the Indians "transported as slaves, where they would be harnessed to the plough, and whipped to work. . . .

The nativist conviction that Indians were one people under God, at least equal to but quite different from Anglo-Americans, had serious diplomatic consequences. It certainly provided a measure of unity during Pontiac's War, and it continued to influence Indians even beyond their defeat in that struggle. For militants who sought to oppose Anglo-American expansion with armed resistance, it provided justification in their struggles against leaders who cooperated with the British. It also gave an opportunity, through cooperation with the militants of other Indian peoples, to nullify the authority of leading advocates of accommodation. The popularity of the doctrine meant that dissenters from one village or people could find a ready home among the nativists of another. . . .

 # FURTHER READING

Richard R. Beeman, *The Evolution of the Southern Backcountry: A Case Study of Lunenburg County, Virginia, 1746–1832* (1984).

John Demos, *The Unredeemed Captive* (1995).

Erick Hinderaker, *Elusive Empires: Constructing Colonialism in the Ohio Valley, 1673–1800* (1997).

Amy R. W. Meyers and Margaret Beck Pritchard, *Empire's Nation: Mark Catesby's New World Vision* (1998).

Gregory H. Nobles, "Breaking Into the Backcountry: New Approaches to the Early American Frontier," *William and Mary Quarterly,* 3rd ser., XLVI (1989), 641–670.

Ian K. Steel, *Warpaths: Invasions of North America* (1994).

Alan Taylor, *Liberty Men and Great Proprietors: The Revolutionary Settlement on the Maine Frontier, 1760–1820* (1990).

Anthony F. C. Wallace, *The Death and Rebirth of the Seneca* (1969).

Richard White, *The Middle Ground: Indians, Empires, and Republics in the Great Lakes Region, 1650–1815* (1991).

C H A P T E R
14

# Colonial America at Mid-Century

*O*

*By the middle of the eighteenth century, with France officially out of North America from 1763, new possibilities loomed for England's colonies. Americans of European descent saw the rich interior opening before them, presenting an opportunity that dispossessed Indians had already taken up. Settlers assumed a new style of life and comfort and saw themselves assuming a more prominent role in international commerce. On the British side leaders also looked for fuller participation by Americans; in particular they wanted the colonists to pay their share of the costs of empire. The royal government's Proclamation of 1763, forbidding settlement in the lands beyond the mountains until a government had been designed for that mixed and turbulent region, was an ominous sign that the interests of both sides might not always be identical.*

*Colonial styles of life achieved new standards. Among the wealthy, imported fine furniture and china dishes found places in newly elegant homes. Whereas even the most successful seventeenth-century colonist had lived in a structure that was basically a large farmhouse, eighteenth-century elite homes began to be built around a central hall flanked by large rooms. The new house plan provided a setting for entertaining on a grand scale; at the same time it fostered a new emphasis on privacy in family life. Formerly guests walked through the front door directly into the living space; now family activities were hidden away and only selected individuals were admitted to it. Similar shifts occurred at all levels of society, as prices of imported English goods fell after 1740 and the volume of imports went up. Modest families replaced wooden dishes with pottery, and added chairs to their homes. Literacy grew as education was more widely available.*

*Many Americans, even those from other parts of Europe, were beginning to think of themselves as English in various new ways. Not only did they increasingly use products from across the Atlantic in their daily lives, but their newspapers reprinted articles from English newspapers and the sons of wealthy planters went to England for their educations. Travel and contact within the thirteen colonies, on the other hand, accentuated notions of differences among the colonial regions. Few would have predicted that they would irrevocably throw in their lots together a little over a decade after the end of the French and Indian War; fewer still would have foreseen that they could form a national government that would actually forge a single American nation. The failure of delegates to consider seriously Benjamin*

*Franklin's Plan of Union in 1754 at Albany (see Chapter 13) was one example of
how impossible unity seemed.*

## DOCUMENTS

In document 1, Benjamin Franklin's *Autobiography,* he describes his concern as a
young businessman to appear industrious, frugal, and businesslike. He also gives a vivid
impression of the shift taking place in households across the colonies to a higher standard of living, for example, his wife suddenly insisting that he eat his porridge with a
silver spoon from a china bowl.

Letters and diaries from the colonial period demonstrate an abiding interest in the
defining characteristics of American culture, and also of their sources. Contemporaries
often wrote to refute the charge that they had become less cultured or civilized than
their European counterparts, and travelers scrutinized the communities they passed
through for signs of change. Dr. Alexander Hamilton of Maryland traveled northward in
1744. His travels put him in close contact with people of all sorts, sometimes in the
same bed at an inn. In document 2 he gives a particularly acute picture of the ways in
which wealth had come to supply some of the place of inherited gentility in American
society. At the conclusion of his journey, he commented on the variety he had seen.

Jean-Bernard Bossu wrote home from French Louisiana in document 3, comment-
ing on how the colonists had learned from the Indians and recommending a regimen for
a healthy life in hot regions. Pelatiah Webster sailed from Philadelphia to Charleston,
South Carolina, in 1765 and observed this very different scene with great curiosity in
document 4. Janet Schaw, who traveled from Scotland to Wilmington, North Carolina,
in 1774, ridiculed the social pretensions of the people she met. She described a Wilmington version of the Boston Tea Party in document 5. William Eddis was sent to the
colonies as a colonial official in the late 1760s. He sent home his impressions of American society in Maryland and his speculations on the fate of the American Indians. He
dismissed the idea that any cruelty on the part of the English could have played a part in
the shrinking of the native presence in the East.

## 1. Benjamin Franklin on How to Get
## On in Philadelphia (c. 1730–c. 1750), 1793

. . . I now opened a small stationer's shop. I had in it blanks of all kinds; the cor-
rectest that ever appeared among us. I was assisted in that by my friend Breintnal. I
had also paper, parchment, chapmen's books, etc. One Whitemarsh, a compositor I
had known in London, an excellent workman, now came to me, and worked with
me constantly and diligently; and I took an apprentice, the son of Aquila Rose.

I began now gradually to pay off the debt I was under for the printing-house. In
order to secure my credit and character as a tradesman, I took care not only to be in
*reality* industrious and frugal, but to avoid the appearances to the contrary. I dressed
plain, and was seen at no places of idle diversion. I never went out a fishing or
shooting; a book indeed sometimes debauched me from my work, but that was sel-

Benjamin Franklin, *Autobiography* (London: Hutchinson & Co., 1903): 81–92.

dom, was private, and gave no scandal; and, to show that I was not above my business, I sometimes brought home the paper I purchased at the stores, through the streets on a wheelbarrow. Thus being esteemed an industrious, thriving young man, and paying duly for what I bought, the merchants who imported stationery solicited my custom; others proposed supplying me with books, and I went on prosperously. In the meantime, Keimer's credit and business declining daily, he was at last forced to sell his printing-house, to satisfy his creditors. He went to Barbadoes, and there lived some years in very poor circumstances.

His apprentice, David Harry, whom I had instructed while I worked with him, set up in his place at Philadelphia, having bought his materials. I was at first apprehensive of a powerful rival in Harry, as his friends were very able, and had a good deal of interest. I therefore proposed a partnership to him, which he fortunately for me rejected with scorn. He was very proud, dressed like a gentleman, lived expensively, took much diversion and pleasure abroad, ran in debt, and neglected his business; upon which, all business left him; and, finding nothing to do, he followed Keimer to Barbadoes, taking the printing-house with him. There this apprentice employed his former master as a journeyman; they quarrelled often, and Harry went continually behind-hand, and at length was obliged to sell his types and return to country work in Pennsylvania. The person who bought them employed Keimer to use them, but a few years after he died. . . .

At the time I established myself in Pennsylvania, there was not a good bookseller's shop in any of the colonies to the southward of Boston. In New York and Philadelphia, the printers were indeed stationers; but they sold only paper, almanacs, ballads, and a few common school-books. Those who loved reading were obliged to send for their books from England; the members of the Junto had each a few. We had left the ale-house, where we first met, and hired a room to hold our club in. I proposed that we should all of us bring our books to that room, where they would not only be ready to consult in our conferences, but become a common benefit, each of us being at liberty to borrow such as he wished to read at home. This was accordingly done, and for some time contented us.

Finding the advantage of this little collection, I proposed to render the benefit from the books more common by commencing a public subscription library. I drew a sketch of the plan and rules that would be necessary, and got a skilful conveyancer, Mr. Charles Brockden, to put the whole in form of articles of agreement to be subscribed; by which each subscriber engaged to pay a certain sum down for the first purchase of the books, and an annual contribution for increasing them. So few were the readers at that time in Philadelphia, and the majority of us so poor, that I was not able with great industry to find more than fifty persons, mostly young tradesmen, willing to pay down for this purpose forty shillings each, and ten shillings per annum. With this little fund we began. The books were imported. The library was opened one day in the week for lending them to subscribers, on their promissory notes to pay double the value if not duly returned. The institution soon manifested its utility, was imitated by other towns, and in other provinces. The libraries were augmented by donations, reading became fashionable; and our people having no public amusements to divert their attention from study, became better acquainted with books, and in a few years were observed by strangers to be better instructed and more intelligent than people of the same rank generally are in other countries.

When we were about to sign the above-mentioned articles, which were to be binding on us, our heirs, etc., for fifty years, Mr. Brockden, the scrivener, said to us, "You are young men, but it is scarcely probable that any of you will live to see the expiration of the term fixed in the instrument." A number of us, however, are yet living; but the instrument was after a few years rendered null, by a charter that incorporated and gave perpetuity to the company.

The objections and reluctances I met with in soliciting the subscriptions made me soon feel the impropriety of presenting one's self as the proposer of any useful project that might be supposed to raise one's reputation in the smallest degree above that of one's neighbours, when one has need of their assistance to accomplish that project. I therefore put myself as much as I could out of sight, and stated it as a scheme of a *number of friends,* who had requested me to go about and propose it to such as they thought lovers of reading. In this way my affair went on more smoothly, and I ever after practised it on such occasions; and, from my frequent successes, can heartily recommend it. The present little sacrifice of your vanity will afterwards be amply repaid. If it remains a while uncertain to whom the merit belongs, some one more vain than yourself may be encouraged to claim it, and then even envy will be disposed to do you justice, by plucking those assumed feathers, and restoring them to their right owner.

This library afforded me the means of improvement by constant study, for which I set apart an hour or two each day, and thus repaired in some degree the loss of the learned education my father once intended for me. Reading was the only amusement I allowed myself. I spent no time in taverns, games, or frolics of any kind; and my industry in my business continued as indefatigable as it was necessary. I was indebted for my printing-house; I had a young family coming on to be educated, and I had two competitors to contend with for business who were established in the place before me. My circumstances, however, grew daily easier. My original habits of frugality continuing, and my father having, among his instructions to me when a boy, frequently repeated a proverb of Solomon, *"Seest thou a man diligent in his calling, he shall stand before kings, he shall not stand before mean men,"* I thence considered industry as a means of obtaining wealth and distinction, which encouraged me—though I did not think that I should ever literally *stand before kings,* which, however, has since happened; for I have stood before *five,* and even had the honour of sitting down with one, the King of Denmark, to dinner.

We have an English proverb that says, *"He that would thrive must ask his wife."* It was lucky for me that I had one as much disposed to industry and frugality as myself. She assisted me cheerfully in my business, folding and stitching pamphlets, tending shop, purchasing old linen rags for the papermakers, etc. We kept no idle servants, our table was plain and simple, our furniture of the cheapest. For instance, my breakfast was for a long time bread and milk (no tea), and I ate it out of a two-penny earthen porringer, with a pewter spoon. But mark how luxury will enter families, and make a progress, in spite of principle; being called one morning to breakfast, I found it in a china bowl, with a spoon of silver! They had been bought for me without my knowledge by my wife, and had cost her the enormous sum of three and twenty shillings; for which she had no other excuse or apology to make but that she thought *her* husband deserved a silver spoon and china bowl as well as any of his neighbours. This was the first appearance of plate and china in our house; which afterwards, in a course of years, as our wealth increased, augmented gradually to several hundred pounds in value. . . .

## 2. Dr. Alexander Hamilton Surveys the Variety of Pennsylvania, 1744

. . . The lower ferry of Susquehanna, which I crossed, is above a mile broad. It is kept by a little old man whom I found att vittles with his wife and family upon a homely dish of fish without any kind of sauce. They desired me to eat, but I told them I had no stomach. They had no cloth upon the table, and their mess was in a dirty, deep, wooden dish which they evacuated with their hands, cramming down skins, scales, and all. They used neither knife, fork, spoon, plate, or napkin because, I suppose, they had none to use. I looked upon this as a picture of that primitive simplicity practiced by our forefathers long before the mechanic arts had supplyed them with instruments for the luxury and elegance of life. I drank some of their syder, which was very good, and crossed the ferry in company with a certain Scots-Irish man by name Thomas Quiet. The land about Susquehanna is pritty high and woody, and the channell of the river rockey.

Mr. Quiet rid a little scrub bay mare which he said was sick and ailing and could not carry him, and therefor he 'lighted every half mile and ran a couple of miles att a footman's pace to spell the poor beast (as he termed it). He informed me he lived att Monocosy and had been out three weeks in quest of his creatures (horses), four of which had strayed from his plantation. I condoled his loss and asked him what his mare's distemper was, resolving to prescribe for her, but all that I could gett out of him was that the poor silly beast had choaked herself in eating her oats; so I told him that if she was choaked, she was past my art to recover.

This fellow, I observed, had a particular down hanging look which made me suspect he was one of our New Light biggots. I guessed right, for he introduced a discourse concerning Whitfield and inlarged pritty much and with some warmth upon the doctrines of that apostle, speaking much in his praise. I took upon me, in a ludicrous manner, to impungn some of his doctrines, which, by degrees, put Mr. Quiet in a passion. He told me flatly that I was damnd without redemption. I replyed that I thought his name and behaviour were very incongruous and desired him to change it with all speed, for it was very impropper that such an angry, turbulent mortall as he should be called by the name of Thomas Quiet.

### Principio Iron Works—North East

In the height of this fool's passion, I overtook one Mr. B[axte]r, a proprietor in the iron works there, and, after mutual salutation, the topic of discourse turned from religious controversy to politicks; so putting on a little faster, we left this inflammed

Dr. Alexander Hamilton, "Itinerarium" (1744), ed. Carl Bridenbaugh, *Gentleman's Progress* (Chapel Hill: University of North Carolina Press for Institute of Early American History and Culture, 1948).

bigot and his sick mare behind. This gentleman accompanied me to North East and gave me directions as to the road.

### Elk Ferry

I crossed Elk Ferry att 3 in the afternoon. One of the ferry men, a young fellow, plyed his tongue much faster than his oar. He characterized some of the chief dwellers in the neighbourhood, particularly some young merchants, my country-men, for whom he had had the honour to stand pimp in their amours. He let me know that he understood some scraps of Latin and repeated a few hexameter lines out of Lilly's Grammar. He told me of a clever fellow of his name who had com-posed a book for which he would give all the money he was master of to have the pleasure of reading it. I asked him who this name sake of his was. He replied it was one Terence, and, to be sure, he must have been an arch dog, for he never knew one of the name but he was remarkable for his parts.

### Bohemia

Thus entertained, I got over the ferry and rid to Bohemia, and calling att the mannor house there, I found no body att home. I met here a reverend parson who was some-what inquisitive as to where I came from and the news, but I was not very commu-nicative. I understood afterwards it was Parson W[y]e.

### Bohemia Ferry

I crossed Bohemia Ferry and lodged att the ferry house. The landlord's name I can-not remember, but he seemed to be a man of tollerable parts for one in his station. Our conversation run chiefly upon religion. He gave me a short account of the spirit of enthusiasm that had lately possessed the inhabitants of the forrests there and in-formed me that it had been a common practise for companys of 20 or 30 hair brained fanaticks to ride thro' the woods singing of psalms. I went to bed att 9 att night; my landlord, his wife, daughters, and I lay all in one room.

Saturday, June 2d. In the morning there was a clear sky over head but a foggy horizon and the wind att south, which presaging heat, I set out very early.

### Sassafrax Ferry

I took the road to Newtown upon Chester River, crossed Sassafrax Ferry att 7 o'clock in the morning, where I found a great concourse of people att a fair. The roads here are exceeding good and even, but dusty in the summer and deep in the winter season. The day proved very hot. I encountered no company, and I went three or four miles out of my way.

### Newtown

I reached Newtown att 12 o'clock and put up att Dougherty's, a publick house there. I was scarce arrived when I met severall of my acquaintance. I dined with Dr. Anderson and spent the rest of the day in a sauntering manner. The northeren post arrived att night. I read the papers but found nothing of consequence in them; so after some comicall chat with my landlord, I went to bed att eleven o'clock att night.

Sunday, June 3d. I stayed all this day att Newtown and breakfasted with Th. Clay, where I met with one W———b, a man of the law, to appearance a civil, good natured man but set up for a kind of connoiseur in many things. I went to visit some friends and dined att the taveren where I was entertaind by the tricks of a female baboon in the yard. This lady had more attendants and hangers on att her levee than the best person (of quality as I may say) in town. She was very fond of the compliments and company of the men and boys but expressed in her gestures an utter aversion att women and girls, especially negroes of that sex—the lady herself being of a black complexion; yet she did not att all affect her country women.

Att night I was treated by Captain Binning of Boston with a bowl of lemmon punch. He gave me letters for his relations att Boston. Whiele we put about the bowl, a deal of comicall discourse pass'd in which the landlord, a man of a particular talent att telling comic storys, bore the chief part.

Monday, June 4th. The morning being clear and somewhat cool, I got up before 5 a'clock and soon mounted horse. I had a solitary route to Bohemia and went very much out of my way by being too particular and nice in observing directions.

### Sassafrax and Bohemia Ferries

I reached Mr. Alexander's house on the mannor att 12 o'clock. There I stayed and dined and drank tea with Miss C[ours]ey. After some talk and laugh, I took my leave att 5 a'clock designing 12 miles farther to one Vanbibber's that keeps a house upon the Newcastle road, but instead of going there, I went out of my way and lay att one Hollingsworth's att the head of Elk.

### Head of Elk

There is a great marsh upon the left hand of his house, which I passed in the night, thro the middle of which runs Elk. The multitude of fire flys glittering in the dark upon the surface of this marshe makes it appear like a great plain scattered over with spangles.

In this part of the country I found they chiefly cultivated British grain, as wheat, barley, and oats. They raise, too, a great deal of flax, and in every house here the women have two or three spinning wheels a going. The roads up this way are tollerably levell but, in some places, stony. After a light supper I went to bed att 10 a'clock.

### Pensylvania—Newcastle

Tuesday, June 5th. I took horse a little after 5 in the morning, and after a solitary ride thro stony, unequall road, where the country people stared att me like sheep when I enquired of them the way, I arrived att Newcastle upon Delaware att 9 a'clock in the morning and baited my horses att one Curtis's att the Sign of the Indian King, a good house of entertainment.

This town stands upon stonny ground just upon the water, there being from thence a large prospect eastward towards the Bay of Delaware and the province of the Jerseys. The houses are chiefly brick, built after the Dutch modell, the town having been originally founded and inhabited by the Dutch when it belonged to New York government. It consists chiefly of one great street which makes an elbow att right angles. A great many of the houses are old and crazy. There is in the town two publick buildings, viz., a court house and church.

Att Curtis's I met company going to Philadelphia and was pleased att it, being my self an utter stranger to the roads. This company consisted of three men: Thomas Howard, Timothy Smith, and William Morison. I treated them with some lemmon punch and desired the favour of their company. They readily granted my request and stayed some time for me till I had eat breakfast. Smith, in his hat and coat, had the appearance of a Quaker, but his discourse was purged of thee's and thou's tho his delivery seemed to be solemn and slow paced. Howard was a talkative man, abounding with words and profuse in compliments which were generally blunt and came out in an awkward manner. He bestowed much panegyrick upon his own behaviour and conduct.

Morison (who, I understood, had been att the Land Office in Annapolis enquiring about a title he had to some land in Maryland) was a very rough spun, forward, clownish blade, much addicted to swearing, att the same time desirous to pass for a gentleman; notwithstanding which ambition, the conscientiousness of his naturall boorishness obliged him frequently to frame ill tim'd apologys for his misbehaviour, which he termed frankness and freeness. It was often, "Damn me, gentlemen, excuse me; I am a plain, honest fellow; all is right down plain dealing, by God." He was much affronted with the landlady att Curtis's who, seeing him in a greasy jacket and breeches and a dirty worsted cap, and withall a heavy, forward, clownish air and behaviour, I suppose took him for some ploughman or carman and so presented him with some scraps of cold veal for breakfast, he having declared that he could not drink "your damnd washy tea." As soon as he saw his mess he swore, "Damn him, if it wa'n't out of respect to the gentleman in company," (meaning me) he would throw her cold scraps out at the window and break her table all to pieces should it cost him 100 pounds for dammages. Then taking off his worsted night cap, he pulled a linnen one out of his pocket and clapping it upon his head, "Now," says he, "I'm upon the borders of Pensylvania and must look like a gentleman; 'tother was good enough for Maryland, and damn my blood if ever I come into that rascally province again if I don't procure a leather jacket that I may be in a trim to box the saucy jacks there and not run the hazard of tearing my coat." This showed, by the bye, that he payed more regard to his coat than his person, a remarkable instance of modesty and self denyall.

He then made a transition to politicks and damnd the late Sr. R[obert] W[alpole] for a rascall. We asked him his reasons for cursing Sr. R[obert], but he would give us no other but this, that he was certainly informed by some very good gentlemen, who understood the thing right well, that the said Sr. R[obert] was a damnd rogue. And att the conclusion of each rodomontade, he told us that tho he seemed to be but a plain, homely fellow, yet he would have us know that he was able to afford better than many that went finer: he had good linnen in his bags, a pair of silver buckles, silver clasps, and gold sleeve buttons, two Holland shirts, and some neat night caps; and that his little woman att home drank tea twice a day; and he himself lived very well and expected to live better so soon as that old Rogue B——t dyed and he could secure a title to his land.

The chief topic of conversation among these three Pensylvanian dons upon the road was the insignificancy of the neighbouring province of Maryland when compared to that of Pensylvania. They laid out all the advantages of the latter which their bungling judgement could suggest and displayed all the imperfections and dissadvantages of the first. They inlarged upon the immorality, drunkeness, rudeness and immoderate swearing so much practised in Maryland and added that no such vices were to be found in Pensylvania. I heard this and contradicted it not, because I knew that the first part of the proposition was pritty true. They next fell upon the goodness of the soil as far more productive of pasturage and grain. I was silent here likewise, because the first proposition was true, but as to the other relating to grain, I doubted the truth of it. But what appeared most comical in their criticisms was their making a merit of the stonnyness of the roads. "One may ride," says Howard, "50 miles in Maryland and not see as many stones upon the roads as in 50 paces of road in Pennsylvania." This I knew to be false, but as I thought there was no advantage in stonny roads, I even let them take the honour of it to themselves and did not contradict them.

Att Newcastle I heard news of Mr. H[asel]l, my intended fellow traveller. They told me he was att Willmington upon Cristin River. . . .

## Philadelphia

The country round the city of Philadelphia is level and pleasant, having a prospect of the large river of Delaware and the province of East Jersey upon the other side. You have an agreeable view of this river for most of the way betwixt Philadelphia and Newcastle. The plan or platform of the city lyes betwixt the two rivers of Delaware and Skuylkill, the streets being laid out in rectangular squares which makes a regular, uniform plan, but upon that account, altogether destitute of variety.

Att my entering the city, I observed the regularity of the streets, but att the same time the majority of the houses mean and low and much decayed, the streets in generall not paved, very dirty, and obstructed with rubbish and lumber, but their frequent building excuses that. The State House, Assembly House, the great church in Second Street, and Whitefield's church are good buildings.

I observed severall comicall, grotesque phizzes in the inn wher[e] I put up which would have afforded variety of hints for a painter of Hogarth's turn. They talked there upon all subjects—politicks, religion, and trade—some tollerably well, but most of them ignorantly. I discovered two or three chaps very inquisitive, asking my boy who I was, whence come, and whether bound.

I was shaved by a little, finicall, hump backd old barber who kept dancing round me and talking all the time of the operation and yet did his job lightly and to a hair. He abounded in compliments and was a very civil fellow in his way. He told me he had been a journyman to the business for 40 odd years, notwithstanding which, he understood how to trim gentlemen as well (thank God) as the best masters and dispaired not of preferment before he dyed.

I delivered my letters, went to dine with Collector Alexander, and visited severall people in town. In the afternoon I went to the coffee house where I was introduced by Dr. Thomas Bond to severall gentlemen of the place, where the ceremony of shaking of hands, an old custom peculiar to the English, was performed with great gravity and the usuall compliments. I took private lodgings att Mrs. Cume's in Chestnut Street.

Thursday, June 7th. I remarked one instance of industry as soon as I got up and looked out att my chamber window, and that was the shops open att 5 in the morning. I breakfasted with Mrs. Cume and dined by invitation with Dr. Thomas Bond where, after some talk upon physicall matters, he showed me some pritty good anatomical preparations of the muscles and blood vessels injected with wax.

After dinner Mr. V[ena]bles, a Barbadian gentleman, came in who, when we casually had mentioned the free masons, began to rail bitterly against that society as an impudent, assuming, and vain caball pretending to be wiser than all mankind besides, an *imperium in imperio,* and therefor justly to be discouraged and suppressed as they had lately been in some foreign countrys. Tho I am no free mason myself, I could not agree with this gentleman, for I abhorr all tyrannicall and arbitrary notions. I believe the free masons to be an innocent and harmless society that have in their constitution nothing mysterious or beyond the verge of common human understanding, and their secret, which has made such a noise, I imagine is just no secret att all.

In the evening att the coffee house, I met Mr. H[asel]l, and enquiring how he did and how he had fared on his way, he replied as to health he was pritty well, but he had almost been devoured with buggs and other vermin and had met with mean, low company which had made him very uneasy. He added that he had heard good news from Barbadoes concerning his friends there—from one, who he imagined called himself Captain Scrotum, a strange name indeed, but this gentleman had always some comicall turn in his discourse. I parted with him and went to the taveren with Mr. Currie and some Scots gen[t]lemen where we spent the night agreeably and went home sober att eleven a'clock.

Friday, June 8. I read Montaign's Essay in the forenoon which is a strange medley of subjects and particularly entertaining.

I dined att a tavern with a very mixed company of different nations and religions. There were Scots, English, Dutch, Germans, and Irish; there were Roman Catholicks, Church men, Presbyterians, Quakers, Newlightmen, Methodists, Seventh day men, Moravians, Anabaptists, and one Jew. The whole company consisted of 25 planted round an oblong table in a great hall well stoked with flys. The company divided into comittees in conversation; the prevailing topick was politicks and conjectures of a French war. A knott of Quakers there talked only about selling of flower and the low price it bore. The[y] touched a little upon religion, and high words arose among some of the sectaries, but their blood was not hot enough to quarrell, or, to speak in the canting phraze, their zeal wanted fervency. A gentleman that sat next me proposed a number of questions concerning Maryland, understanding I had come from thence. In my replys I was reserved, pretending to know little of the matter as being a person whose business did not lye in the way of history and politicks.

In the afternoon I went to see some ships that lay in the river. Among the rest were three vessels a fitting out for privateers—a ship, a sloop, and a schooner. The ship was a large vessel, very high and full rigged; one Capt. Mackey intended to command her upon the cruise. Att 6 a'clock I went to the coffee house and drank a dish of coffee with Mr. H[asel]l.

After staying there an hour or two, I was introduced by Dr. Phineas Bond into the Governour's Club, a society of gentlemen that met at a taveren every night and converse on various subjects. The Governour gives them his presence once a week, which is generally upon Wednesday, so that I did not see him there. Our conversation was entertaining; the subject was the English poets and some of the foreign writers, particularly Cervantes, author of Don Quixot, whom we loaded with elogiums due to his character. Att eleven a'clock I left this club and went to my lodging.

Saturday, June 9th. This morning there fell a light rain which proved very refreshing, the weather having been very hot and dry for severall days. The heat in this city is excessive, the sun's rays being reflected with such power from the brick houses and from the street pavement which is brick. The people commonly use awnings of painted cloth or duck over their shop doors and windows and, att sun set, throw buckets full of water upon the pavement which gives a sensible cool. They are stocked with plenty of excellent water in this city, there being a pump att almost every 50 paces distance. There are a great number of balconies to their houses where sometimes the men sit in a cool habit and smoke.

The market in this city is perhaps the largest in North-America. It is kept twice a week upon Wednesdays and Saturdays. The street where it stands, called Market Street, is large and spacious, composed of the best houses in the city. . . .

**Annapolis**

I arrived att Annapolis att two o'clock afternoon and so ended my perigrinations.

In these my northeren travells I compassed my design in obtaining a better state of health, which was the purpose of my journey. I found but little difference in the manners and character of the people in the different provinces I passed thro', but as to constitutions and complexions, air and government, I found some variety. Their forms of government in the northeren provinces I look upon to be much better and happier than ours, which is a poor, sickly, convulsed state. Their air and living to the northward is likewise much preferable, and the people of a more gygantick size and make. Att Albany, indeed, they are intirely Dutch and have a method of living something differing from the English.

In this itineration I compleated, by land and water together, a course of 1624 miles. The northeren parts I found in generall much better settled than the southeren. As to politeness and humanity, they are much alike except in the great towns where the inhabitants are more civilized, especially att Boston.

## 3. Jean-Bernard Bossu Advises Newcomers on the Way to Health in Louisiana, 1762

. . . Since it is natural for man to want to live a long time, I think that it would be appropriate for me, with my experience, to indicate briefly the way to conserve and prolong life in America.

I shall finish my letter with a little dissertation on cures. . . . I am certain that you will agree with me, sir, that perfect health is brought about by exercise and sobriety.

Jean-Bernard Bossu, *Travels in the Interior of North America, 1751–1762,* trans. and ed. Seymour Feiler (Norman: University of Oklahoma Press, 1962): 217–220.

When Europeans first came here 260 years ago, the Indians had neither wine nor brandy. The natives, as I have already said, lived on dried and smoked game, roasted or boiled with corn ground in a hardwood mortar. This food, called chili, is very tasty and healthful. When I went up the Mobile River with the Indians, I lived for about two months on this food. I can assure you that I never felt better than I did during that period. The best of all the Latin proverbs is: *Plures gula occidit quam gladius.** Voluptuousness and intemperance in eating and drinking kill more people than the sword. You should lead a life of moderation, especially in the warm regions of America.

First of all, you must allow yourself to become slowly accustomed to the climate, and you must avoid all fruit and liquor until your body gradually becomes adjusted. People with a great deal of blood should have some drawn from time to time to prevent apoplexy, and gentle laxatives should be taken occasionally. You should avoid exposing yourself to the burning heat of the sun and to the wind.

When you have drunk too much wine, eat things with acid in them, such as lemons, which are plentiful here. This will clear your head and keep the vapors from getting you drunk after meals. If you become overheated because you have drunk too much liquor, take something refreshing and be careful not to eat hot food. Spirits should be drunk as little as possible because they burn the blood and cause high fever.

When you have eaten too much, strong liquor is good for fortifying the stomach and aiding digestion, but if, on the other hand, you are overheated because you have drunk too much, alcohol can become very dangerous.** Those who drink to excess are almost always tormented by fantastic dreams which tire them so much that their minds become disturbed. The wine fumes in their bodies excite their imagination. We know from experience that sober people, especially those who drink water, sleep peacefully, without waking too easily or falling into a stupor . . .

After overeating, if you feel so stuffed and lethargic that the nutritive juices bloat and exhaust your entire body, I believe you would do well to imitate the Indians, who find sweating an infallible cure. Increasing the heat of the body is a certain cure, if done at the first signs of discomfort. Europeans who use the perspiration cure lie between two blankets and cover themselves completely, except for their faces. They do not get up until they have perspired for a full hour. When this treatment is continued for several days, the patient's recovery is so remarkable that he regains his strength and his appetite. He is surprised to find himself agile and alert once again. Perspiring purifies the internal organs painlessly and naturally. Ordinary medicines cannot do this. In order to remain healthy, one should undergo this treatment three times a year: in spring, summer, and winter. My conclusion, sir, is that diet and sweating are general cures.

I would say that nature ought to be our guide in everything and should teach us the true means of remaining in good health. Otherwise, we are condemned to great suffering and even to death. I have already mentioned that the North American Indians' great physical activity, such as dancing, ball-playing, hunting, fishing, and fighting, overheats them so that they perspire and thus eliminate body waste. Why

---

*"The gullet kills as many people as the sword."—ED.

**I should mention that since the Americans have begun to drink wine and liquor, they have shortened their lives, just as we have.

do the peasants live so long and remain healthy without the aid of doctors? It is because of their work and exercise that they do not have the gout, kidney stones, and other infirmities to which wealthy Europeans are prone because they eat rich food and walk as rarely as do sick old men. I have known some of them who have turned their stomachs into a drug store.

It has been observed that young people who migrate from Europe to the warm regions of America die more quickly than the old. This is because the young eat all kinds of fruit which cause diarrhea. Very little fruit should be eaten until the body becomes accustomed to the climate of the country. After one year there is no further inconvenience of this sort.

If these precautions are taken, I am sure that one could live longer in the New World than in the Old. There are at present a number of people in Louisiana who have been there since the founding of the colony. I have met a settler named Graveline who is 118 years old. He came here with Monsieur d'Iberville in 1698 and served as a soldier in Canada for about thirty years during the reign of Louis XIV. . . .

## 4. Pelatiah Webster Describes the Uniqueness of Charleston, 1765

**May 1765**

. . . MONDAY 27. Spent in viewing the town. It contains abt. 1,000 houses, with inhabitants, 5,000 whites and 20,000 blacks; has 8 houses for religious worship, viz. St. Philip's and St. Michael's, Church of England, large stone buildings with porticos with large pillars and steeples. St. Michael's has a good ring of bells. I Scotch presbyterian church; 1 independent, called the New England Meeting; 1 Dutch church, and two Baptist meetings, and one French church: these 3 last very small.

The Statehouse is a heavy building of abt. 120 by 40 feet. The council chamber is about 40 feet square, decorated with many heavy pillars and much carvings, rather superb than elegant. The assembly room is of the same dimensions; but much plainer work. 'Tis convenient enough. There are sundry publick offices kept in small apartments below; there are two flights of stairs, one leading to the council chamber, the other to the assembly room. Below stairs is a court house where the courts of common pleas and pleas of the crown are kept, but is yet unfinished.

The streets of this city run N. and S., and E. and W., intersecting each other at right angles; they are not paved except the footways within the posts, abt. 6 feet wide, which are paved with brick in the principal streets.

There are large fortifications here but mostly unfinished and ruinous. There is a pretty fort on James Island called Johnson's Fort which commands the entrance of the harbour, and a great number of breastworks and cannon all round the town with a fosse much filled up. There are also mounds thrown up and ditches round the back part of the town but all ruinous and nearly useless.

Pelatiah Webster, "Journal of a Voyage from Philadelphia to Charlestown in South Carolina, begun May 15, 1765," in H. Roy Merrens, ed., *The Colonial South Carolina Scene: Contemporary Views, 1697–1774*, Tricentennial Edition No. 7 (Columbia: University of South Carolina Press, 1977).

The town stands on a neck of land formed by the two rivers, Ashley on the S. and Cowper on the north, fronting the bay abt. 9 miles within the bar. The two rivers are not more than a mile apart at several miles north of the town, and the only considerable road which leads from the city is up the neck and called The Path and at six or seven miles from the town it forks and runs into the various parts of the country.

The laborious business is here chiefly done by black slaves of which there are great multitudes. The climate is very warm. The chief produce is rice and indigo. The manufacture of hemp is set afoot and like to succeed very well. They have considerable lumber and naval stores. They export annually 100,000 barrels of rice and 60,000 lbs indigo (rice worth on average 6 shillings per ct. i.e. 30/- per bbl., indigo from 3/- to 3/6 per lb.), with considerable pine boards, tar, turpentine, hemp, staves, etc.; have very few mechanic arts of any sort, and very great quantities of mechanic utensils are imported from England and the northward colonies.

They have no considerable seminaries of learning, but many youth of quality go to London for an education. The people are vastly affable and polite, quite free from pride, and a stranger may make himself very easy with them.

The whites in this province are computed at abt. 20,000 and the blacks at 4 times that number. The English settlements extend two or three hundred miles into the country westward into the Cherokee and Catawba's country, and those distant westward parts of the province are settled by great numbers of people that travel from the northward for lands from the back parts of Pensylvania, Maryland and Virginia, and consist mostly of Dutch and Irish families. The pine sandy plains extend two hundred miles westward before any mountains rise, nor is there a mill or any other water works to be found in all that space.

There is a little wheat raised in this province, but poor in quality, nor will it produce more than two thirds of the price of the northward flour which is the principal supply of bread. Few apples grow here, all the cyder used here is imported. There are a few vessels built here, and are all planked with pitch pine plank, and the crooked timbers are live oak, (a wood of great firmness and great durableness) and the beams, keels, and all other strait timbers are of pitch pine. 'Tis said that a ship well built here will last thirty years.

There is a pretty well chosen library in town purchased by private subscriptions of a number of gentlemen, by the name of the Charlestown Library Society.

The most active season of the year is from December to May by which time most of their crops of rice and indigo are brought to town and shipped off, so that during the great heat of the succeeding summer months the merchants in town have little to do. There are but few country seats near the town, and many people move to considerable distances up into the country to spend the summer and avoid the intense heats and confined air of the town: the winds generally blowing during the summer months from the south and S. W., from off the hot sands of Florida and Georgia, are much warmer than the Westindia breezes which come in from the sea.

Dined this day with Mr. Thomas Shirley, a very polite English gent., residing here in very genteel fashion; is an ingenuous ready man; was bread a merchant, has travelled much, understands several modern languages; passed the afternoon agreably with him.

TUESDAY 28. Still viewing the town with some attention. Dined with Mr. William Glen, a reputable merchant in the town who deals largely in the London trade; in the afternoon took an airing into the country with him in his chair several miles; the road is level and sandy and would be very hot were it not shaded by fine avenues of large trees growing close by each side of the road and shading it.

WEDNSDAY 29. Still sauntring abt. town as much as the great heats will permit. Dined with Mr. Tho. Smith, a reputable merchant in this town and in very fine business; is an agreable sensible kind man; passed my time with him very pleasantly several hours.

THURSD. 30. Dined this day with Mr. John Poaug, a Scotch merchant in this city, a very genteel polite man.

FRID. 31. Dined with Reverend Robt. Smith, rector of St. Philips's in this city, an English gent., educated at University of Cambridge, a very sociable and polite clergyman.

## June 1765.

SAT. 1. Rode into the country seven miles with Mr. Tho. Laughton Smith to the country seat of Col. Benjn. Smith. Dined there. Spent the afternoon very pleasantly; the Col. is a gent. of abt. 50, cheerful, easy, and generous, has a great fortune and declines business, having turned over his mercantile affairs into the hands of his son Tho.

SUND. 2. Attended divine service at St. Michael's. Dined at Mr. Torrans's on the bay, a reputable merchant, with Col. Howard and sundry European gent. Mr. Torrans is a sensible man and deals largely as a merchant in partnership with Mr. Poaug 'fore mentioned.

MONDAY. 3. Dined this day with Mr. Thomas Liston, a reputable merchant born here; is a man of great openess and politeness, of generous sentiments and very genteel behaviour; passed the afternoon very agreably in his sumer house with him and Mr. Lindo, a noted Jew, inspector of indigo here.

TUESD. 4. The militia all appeared under arms, abt. 800, and the guns at all the forts were fired, it being the king's birthday. The artillery co. made a good appearance and performed their exercises and firings very well. The militia were not so well trained and exercised, but made a pretty good and handsome appearance. N. B. The militia and artillery of Charlestown are said to consist of 1,300 men in the whole list from 16 to 60 years old. Dined with Mr. Wm. Glen afore mentioned.

WEDS. 5. Rode out to Mr. George Marshal's country seat 3 miles from town on Ashley River. Dined there; viewed his plantation; saw his rice and indigo growing in the field, and his Negroes howing it. The rice grows much like rye but somewhat finer and paler. The indigo is a dark colored weed growing on a clumsy stalk which branches much and bears single leaves somewhat like buckwheat and abt. as high. I viewed also his vats for steeping, beating and lyming his indigo, the trough for pressing it, conveniences for drying, etc., in short the whole process, but it not being the season for making it, I could not have an opportunity of seeing the process performed.

Mr. Marshal is a Scotch gentleman of great humanity and courtesy. . . .

Now I have left Charlestown an agreable and polite place in which I was used very genteelly and contracted much acquaintance for the time I staid here. The heats are much too severe, the water bad, the soil sandy, the timber too much evergreen; but with all these disadvantages, 'tis a flourishing place, capable of vast improvement; will have I fear some uncomfortable bands of banditti on its frontiers soon, it's distance from proper authority having already drawn there great numbers of very idle dissolute people who begin to be very troublesome. . . .

## 5. Janet Schaw Visits Wilmington, North Carolina, 1774

I have been in town a few days, and have had an opportunity to make some little observations on the manners of a people so new to me. The ball . . . was intended as a civility, therefore I will not criticize it, and tho' I have not the same reason to spare the company, yet I will not fatigue you with a description, which however lively or just, would at best resemble a Dutch picture, where the injudicious choice of the subject destroys the merit of the painting. Let it suffice to say that a ball we had, where were dresses, dancing and ceremonies laughable enough, but there was no object on which my own ridicule fixed equal to myself and the figure I made, dressed out in all my British airs with a high head and a hoop and trudging thro' the unpaved streets in embroidered shoes by the light of a lanthorn carried by a black wench half naked. No chair, no carriage—good leather shoes need none. The ridicule was the silk shoes in such a place. I have however gained some most amiable and agreeable acquaintances amongst the Ladies; many of whom would make a figure in any part of the world, and I will not fail to cultivate their esteem, as they appear worthy of mine.

I am sorry to say, however, that I have met with few of the men who are natives of the country . . . and as their natural ferocity is now inflamed by the fury of an ignorant zeal, they are of that sort of figure, that I cannot look at them without connecting the idea of tar and feather. Tho' they have fine women and such as might inspire any man with sentiments that do honour to humanity, yet they know no such nice distinctions, and in this at least are real patriots. As the population of the country is all the view they have in what they call love, and tho' they often honour their black wenches with their attention, I sincerely believe they are excited to that crime by no other desire or motive but that of adding to the number of their slaves.

The difference between the men and the women surprised me, but a sensible man, who has long resided here, in some degrees accounted for it. In the infancy of this province, said he, many families from Britain came over, and of these the wives and daughters were people of education. The mothers took the care of the girls, they were train'd up under them, and not only instructed in the family duties necessary to the sex, but in those accomplishments and genteel manners that are still so visible amongst them, and this descended from Mother to daughter. As the father found the labours of his boys necessary to him, he led them therefore to the woods, and taught the sturdy lad to glory in the stroke he could give with his Ax, in the trees he felled, and the deer he shot; to conjure the wolfe, the bear and the Alligator; and to guard his habitation from Indian inroads was most justly his pride, and he had reason to boast of it. But a few generations this way lost every art or science, which their fa-

Janet Schaw, *Journal of a Lady of Quality,* ed. Evangeline Walker Andrews and Charles Mclean Andrews (New Haven: Yale, 1923), 153–156. Copyright © 1923 by Yale University Press.

thers might have brought out, and tho' necessity no longer prescribed these severe occupations, custom has established it as still necessary for the men to spend their time abroad in the fields; and to be a good marksman is the highest ambition of the youth, while to those enervated by age or infirmity drinking grog remained a last consolation.

The Ladies have burnt their tea in a solemn procession, but they had delayed however till the sacrifice was not very considerable, as I do not think any one offered above a quarter of a pound. The people in town live decently, and tho' their houses are not spacious, they are in general very commodious and well furnished. All the Merchants of any note are British and Irish, and many of them very genteel people. They all disapprove of the present proceedings. Many of them intend quitting the country as fast as their affairs will permit them, but are yet uncertain what steps to take. This town lies low, but is not disagreeable. There is at each end of it an ascent, which is dignified with the title of the hills; on them are some very good houses and there almost all my acquaintances are. They have very good Physicians, the best of whom is a Scotchman, at whose house I have seen many of the first planters. I do not wish however to be much in their company, for, as you know, my tongue is not always under my command; I fear I might say something to give offence, in which case I would not fail to have the most shocking retort at least, if it went no further. . . .

## 6. William Eddis Praises the Society of Annapolis, Maryland, and Speculates on the Fate of the American Indians, 1771

### Annapolis, December 24, 1771

The intense heat which prevails during the summer and the extremity of cold in winter I well know has been asserted to be highly prejudicial to the constitution; though for my own part I have not been sensible of any material inconvenience from the opposite quality of the seasons but have continued to enjoy uninterrupted health and spirits.

The variations of the weather are certainly more sudden in this part of America than even in the changeable climate of Britain. During one part of the day I have frequently thought the lightest apparel scarcely supportable, when in a moment a northwest wind has created sensations of a very different nature and a substantial suit of broadcloth has scarcely been sufficient to repel the cold.

Whatever you have heard relative to the rigid puritanical principles and economical habits of our American brethren is by no means true when applied to the inhabitants of the southern provinces. Liberality of sentiment and genuine hospitality are everywhere prevalent; and I am persuaded they too frequently mistake

William Eddis, *Letters from America,* ed. Aubrey C. Land (Cambridge: Harvard University Press, 1969): 57–60.

profuseness for generosity, and impair their health and their fortunes by splendor of appearance and magnificence of entertainments.

The quick importation of fashions from the mother country is really astonishing. I am almost inclined to believe that a new fashion is adopted earlier by the polished and affluent American than by many opulent persons in the great metropolis; nor are opportunities wanting to display superior elegance. We have varied amusements and numerous parties which afford to the young, the gay, and the ambitious an extensive field to contend in the race of vain and idle competition. In short, very little difference is, in reality, observable in the manners of the wealthy colonist and the wealthy Briton. Good and bad habits prevail on both sides the Atlantic.

It is but justice to confess that the American ladies possess a natural ease and elegance in the whole of their deportment; and that while they assiduously cultivate external accomplishments, they are still anxiously attentive to the more important embellishments of the mind. In conversation they are generally animated and entertaining, and deliver their sentiments with affability and propriety. In a word, there are, throughout these colonies, very many lovely women who have never passed the bounds of their respective provinces and yet, I am persuaded, might appear to great advantage in the most brilliant circles of gaiety and fashion.

In this country the marriage ceremony is universally performed in the dwelling houses of the parties. The company who are invited assemble early in the evening, and after partaking of tea and other refreshments, the indissoluble contract is completed. The bride and bridegroom then receive the accustomed congratulations; cards and dancing immediately succeed; an elegant supper, a cheerful glass, and the convivial song close the entertainment.

There are few places where young people are more frequently gratified with opportunities of associating together than in this country. Besides our regular assemblies, every mark of attention is paid to the patron saint of each parent dominion; and St. George, St. Andrew, St. Patrick, and St. David are celebrated with every partial mark of national attachment. General invitations are given, and the appearance is always numerous and splendid.

The Americans on this part of the continent have likewise a saint whose history, like those of the above venerable characters, is lost in fable and uncertainty. The first of May is, however, set apart to the memory of Saint Tamina, on which occasion the natives wear a piece of a buck's tail in their hats or in some conspicuous situation. During the course of the evening, and generally in the midst of a dance, the company are interrupted by the sudden intrusion of a number of persons habited like Indians, who rush violently into the room singing the war song, giving the whoop, and dancing in the style of those people, after which ceremony a collection is made and they retire well satisfied with their reception and entertainment.

In this province there are scarce any vestiges of the original inhabitants, but it does not appear that their numbers have been reduced by any inhuman or indirect practices of the British settlers. In Dorset County on the eastern shore of Maryland, there are indeed the remains of a nation, once populous and powerful, who to this day retain considerable tracts of valuable land for which they receive an annual consideration but by no means equivalent to the real value. When every other Indian nation thought it necessary to retire beyond the range of the European settlements, these people it seems determined to continue on their native spot. But being precluded from their former occupations and pursuits, they became totally indolent and inactive; and a different habit of living, a violent propensity to spirituous liquors, and the havoc occasioned by the smallpox and other disorders, to which they were unaccustomed, reduced their numbers to such a degree that at this time not twenty of their descendants remain.

Since no charge of cruelty can justly be adduced, it becomes a natural enquiry what is become of those numerous tribes that formerly occupied this fertile territory?

Maryland, comparatively, is a small province, bounded on the west by the interior counties of Virginia and Pennsylvania; the Indians, from their particular mode of living, require an extensive circuit, depending principally on hunting for their support; and wherever their game becomes scarce, they instantly quit that country for a more eligible situation. As this colony became populous by the arrival and natural increase of the new adventurers, the aborigines were circumscribed in their ancient limits and were consequently induced to relinquish their possessions, for a supposed equivalent, and retire to a more extensive field of action.

From what cause I cannot ascertain, but the North American Indians have never yet been known to incorporate with Europeans; nor has any progress yet been made in civilizing their manners or in reclaiming them from that ignorance in which they are universally involved. Their habits appear rooted beyond the possibility of conviction to remove; the present moment engrosses every thought, regardless of the events of futurity.

 *E S S A Y S*

Historian T. H. Breen of Northwestern University examines the American consumer revolution of the mid-eighteenth century in the first essay. Americans began to buy and use items made in Britain to replace homemade American wares, and they developed the capacity to discriminate among a wide variety of styles, qualities, and types. Americans wanted the latest fashions and the best quality they could afford. And this was true of colonists at all levels of society—the period saw a general upward shift in styles of life. As Breen points out, this consumption of British goods led to greater American consciousness of themselves as British, but it also, paradoxically, led to the possibility of a sense of mutual identity among the colonists and unified resistance to Britain.

In the second essay John M. Murrin of Princeton University analyzes both the prospects for any kind of unified action on the part of American colonists after the French and Indian War and the grounds on which such unity was built. Pointing to the extreme variety of cultural traditions, languages, and religious allegiances settlers brought to America and the dramatically different cultures and economic systems that had arisen in the different regions, he highlights contemporaries' doubts that any concerted action could ever be organized and, if undertaken, sustained for any period of time. Mutual suspicion, even hostility, seemed more likely. Like Breen, Murrin sees the colonists as becoming more British as the century progressed, and this growing sense of Britishness helped lead to national identity.

# Consumption, Anglicization, and the Formation of American Identity

### T. H. BREEN

. . . At mid-century almost no one would have predicted such as occurrence [American unity]. Some two million people had scattered themselves over an immense territory. They seemed to have little in common. In fact contemporary observers concluded that should the colonists ever achieve political independence, they would immediately turn on each other. "In short," declared one English traveller in 1759, "such is the difference of character, of manners, of religion, of interest, of the different colonies, that I think . . . were they left to themselves, there would soon be a civil war from one end of the continent to the other." John Adams agreed. Reflecting in 1818 on the coming of revolution, he marvelled that the Americans had ever managed to unite. Their own separate histories seemed to have conspired against the formation of a new nation. The colonies, Adams explained, had evolved different constitutions of government. They had also experienced:

> so great a variety of religions, they were composed of so many different nations, their customs, manners, and habits had so little resemblance, and their intercourse had been so rare, and their knowledge of each other so imperfect, that to unite them in . . . the same system of action, was certainly a very difficult enterprise.

Very difficult indeed! And yet in 1776 these colonists surprised the world by successfully forming a new nation. In Adams's words, "Thirteen clocks were made to strike together." Somehow Americans had found a means to communicate effectively with each other, to develop a shared sense of political purpose, to transcend what at mid-century had appeared insurmountable cultural and geographic divisions. . . .

The eighteenth century witnessed the birth of an Anglo-American "consumer society." Though the Industrial Revolution was still far in the future, the pace of the British economy picked up dramatically after 1690. Small manufacturing concerns scattered throughout England began turning out huge quantities of consumer goods—cloth, ceramics, glassware, paper, cutlery—items that transformed the character of everyday life. Merchants could hardly keep up with expanding demand. The domestic market hummed with activity. People went shopping, gawking at the wares displayed in the "bow-windows" that appeared for the first time along urban streets. Advertisements in the provincial English journals fuelled consumer desire, and to those middling sorts who wanted to participate in the market but who did not possess sufficient cash, tradesmen offered generous credit.

Americans were quickly swept up in this consumer economy. These were not the self-sufficient yeomen of Jeffersonian mythology. Eighteenth-century colonists demanded the latest British manufactures. Few would have disagreed with the members of the Maryland general assembly who once announced, "We want the British Manufactures." In order to pay for what they imported, the Americans har-

---

Extracts from T. H. Breen, "'Baubles of Britain': The American and Consumer Revolutions of the Eighteenth Century," *Past and Present,* no. 119 (May 1988), pp. 73–104, are reprinted with kind permission (World Copyright: The Past and Present Society, 175 Banbury Road, Oxford, England).

vested ever larger crops of tobacco, rice and indigo. Northern farmers supplied the West Indian plantations with foodstuffs. . . . At a time when the American population was growing at an extraordinary rate, per capita consumption of British imports was actually rising. In other words, more colonists purchased more manufactured goods every year. Since this was a young population—half of the colonists were under the age of sixteen—one must assume that adults were responsible for this exploding demand. Their consumption raised per capita rates for the entire society. After mid-century the American market for imported goods took off, rising 120 per cent between 1750 and 1773. Throughout the colonies the crude, somewhat impoverished material culture of the seventeenth century—a pioneer world of homespun cloth and wooden dishes—was swept away by a flood of store-bought sundries.

These ubiquitous items transformed the texture of everyday life in provincial America. Even in the most inaccessible regions people came increasingly to rely on imports. One English traveller discovered to her surprise that in rural North Carolina women seldom bothered to produce soap. It was not a question of the availability of raw materials. Good ashes could be had at no expense. But these rural women were consumers, and they preferred to purchase Irish soap "at the store at a monstrous price." In more cosmopolitan environments, the imports were even more conspicuous. Eighteenth-century Americans situated other men and women within a rich context of British manufactures. John Adams betrayed this habit of mind when he visited the home of a successful Boston merchant:

> Went over [to] the House to view the Furniture, which alone cost a thousand Pounds sterling. A seat it is for a noble Man, a Prince. The Turkey Carpets, the painted Hangings, the Marble Table, the rich Beds with crimson Damask Curtains and Counterpins, the beautiful Chimny Clock, the Spacious Garden, are the most magnificent of any Thing I have ever seen.

Like other Americans, Adams had obviously developed a taste for British imports.

How does one make sense out of this vast consumer society? There is much that we do not know about eighteenth-century colonial merchandizing. Still, even at this preliminary stage of investigation, it is possible to discern certain general characteristics that distinguished the colonial market-place at mid-century: an exceptionally rapid expansion of consumer *choice,* an increasing *standardization* of consumer behaviour and a pervasive *Anglicization* of the American market. . . .

Whatever the psychological impact of this change may have been, there is no question that Americans at mid-century confronted a range of choice that would have amazed earlier generations. A survey of New York City newspapers revealed, for example, that during the 1720s merchants seldom mentioned more than fifteen different imported items per month in their advertisements. The descriptions were generic: cloth, paper, ceramics. But by the 1770s it was not unusual during some busy months for New York journals specifically to list over nine thousand different manufactured goods. And as the number of items expanded, the descriptive categories became more elaborate. In the 1740s New York merchants simply advertised "paper." By the 1760s they listed seventeen varieties distinguished by colour, function and quality. In the 1730s a customer might have requested satin, hoping apparently that the merchant had some in stock. By the 1760s merchants advertised a dozen different types of satin. No carpets were mentioned in the New York advertisements before the 1750s, but by the 1760s certain stores carried carpets la-belled Axminster, Milton, Persian, Scotch, Turkey, Weston and Wilton. One could purchase after the 1750s purple gloves, flowered gloves, orange gloves, white gloves, rough gloves, chamois gloves, buff gloves, "Maid's Black Silk" gloves, "Maid's Lamb Gloves," and even "Men's Dog Skin Gloves." There is no need to continue. Everywhere one looks, one encounters an explosion of choices.

If, as many scholars currently argue, human beings constitute external reality through language, then the proliferation of manufactures during the eighteenth cen-tury may have radically altered how Americans made sense out of everyday activi-ties. The consumer market provided them with an impressive new vocabulary, thousands of words that allowed them not only to describe a changing material cul-ture but also to interpret their place within it. Adams demonstrated this point when in his diary he recorded his reactions to the possessions of the wealthy Boston mer-chant. This language of goods was shared by all who participated in the market. It was not the product of a particular region or class, and thus furnished colonists with a means of transmitting experience across social and geographic boundaries. As we have seen, a visitor could engage the women of North Carolina in a discourse about imported soap. It was a conversation that the women of Virginia and Massachusetts would also have understood.

An example of this kind of cultural exchange occurred in a Maryland tavern in 1744. A travelling physician from Annapolis witnessed a quarrel between an innkeeper and an individual who by his external appearance seemed "a rough spun, forward, clownish blade." The proprietor apparently shared this impression, because she served this person who wore " a greasy jacket and breeches and a dirty worsted cap" a breakfast fit "for some ploughman or carman." The offended customer vehe-mently protested that he too was a gentleman and to prove his status, pulled a linen hat out of his pocket. He then informed the embarrassed assembly that "he was able to af-ford better than many who went finer: he had good linnen in his bags, a pair of silver buckles, silver clasps, and gold sleeve buttons, two Holland shirts, and some neat night caps; and that his little woman att home drank tea twice a day." What catches our attention is not the man's clumsy attempt to negotiate status through possessions—people have been doing that for centuries—but rather that he bragged of owning spe-cific manufactured goods, the very articles that were just then beginning to transform American society. He assumed—correctly, in this case—that the well-appointed stranger he encountered in a country tavern understood the language of shirts, buckles and tea.

This expanding consumer world of mid-eighteenth century led almost in-evitably to a *standardization* of the market-place. To be sure, as the previous anec-dote suggests, Americans had begun to define status in relation to commodities. In this they were not especially unique. Throughout the Atlantic world choice created greater, more visible marks of distinction. Nevertheless by actually purchasing manufactured imports as opposed to making do with locally produced objects, by participating in an expanding credit network and by finding oneself confronted with basically the same types of goods which were now on sale in other, distant commu-nities, Americans developed a common element of personal experience.

One can only speculate, of course, why colonial shoppers purchased certain items. They may have been looking for status, beauty, convenience or price. Whatever the justification may have been, the fact remains that people living in different parts of America were exposed to an almost identical range of imported goods. . . .

The standardization of taste affected all colonial consumers. This is an important point. It is easy for modern historians to concentrate on the buying habits of the gentry. Their beautiful homes—many of which are now preserved as museums—dominate our understanding of the character of daily life in eighteenth-century America. This interpretive bias is not a problem peculiar to the colonial period. The consumer behaviour of the wealthy has always been more fully documented than that of more humble buyers. But however much we are drawn to the material culture of the colonial élite, we should realize that the spread of the consumer market transformed the lives of ordinary men and women as fundamentally as it did those of their more affluent neighbours. Though wealthy Americans purchased goods of superior quality, poorer buyers demanded the same general range of imports. Rural pedlars, urban hawkers, Scottish factors responded to this eager clientele, providing farmers and artisams with easy credit, the ticket to participation in this consumer society. These people became reliant on imported manufactures, so much so in fact that Francis Fauquier, lieutenant-governor of Virginia, could note in 1763, "These imports daily encrease, the common planters usually dressing themselves in the manufactures of Great Brittain [sic] altogether."

Tea provides an instructive example of the standardization of consumer taste. Early in the eighteenth century this hot drink became the preferred beverage in gentry households. Polite ladies—perhaps as a device to lure gentlemen away from tavern society—organized elaborate household rituals around the tea service. In fact the purchase of tea necessitated the acquisition of pots, bowls, strainers, sugar-tongs, cups and slop-dishes. One writer in a New York newspaper suggested the need for a school of tea etiquette. The young men of the city, finding themselves "utterly ignorant in the Ceremony of the Tea-Table," were advised to employ a knowledgeable woman "to teach them the Laws, Rules, Customs, Phrases and Names of the Tea Utensils."

Though less well-to-do Americans did not possess the entire range of social props, they demanded tea. As early as 1734 one New Yorker reported:

> I am credibly informed that tea and china ware cost the province, yearly, near the sum of £10,000; and people that are least able to go to the expence, must have their tea tho' their families want bread. Nay, I am told, they often pawn their rings and plate to gratifie themselves in that piece of extravagance.

It did not take long for this particular luxury to become a necessity. "Our people," wrote another New York gentleman in 1762, "both in town and country, are shamefully gone into the habit of tea-drinking." And when Israel Acrelius visited the old Swedish settlements of Delaware at mid-century, he discovered people consuming tea "in the most remote cabins." During the 1750s even the inmates of the public hospital of Philadelphia, the city poor-house, insisted on having bohea tea. All these colonists drank their tea out of imported cups, not necessarily china ones, but rather ceramics that had originated in the English Midlands where they had been fired at very high temperature and thus made resistant to the heat of America's new favourite drink.

Ordinary Americans adopted tea for reasons other than social emulation. After all, it was a mild stimulant, and a hot cup of tea probably helped the labouring poor endure hard work and insubstantial housing. Nevertheless in some isolated country villages the desire to keep up with the latest consumer fads led to bizarre results, the kind of gross cultural misunderstanding that anthropologists encounter in places where products of an alien technology have been introduced into a seemingly less-developed society. In 1794 a historian living in East Hampton, New York, interviewed a seventy-eight-year-old woman. "Mrs. Miller," he discovered, "remembers well when they first began to drink tea on the east end of Long Island." She explained that none of the local farmers knew what to do with the dry leaves: "One family boiled it in a pot and ate it like samp-porridge. Another spread tea leaves on his bread and butter, and bragged of his having ate half a pound at a meal, to his neighbor, who was informing him how long a time a pound of tea lasted him." According to Mrs. Miller, the arrival of the first tea-kettle was a particularly memorable day in the community:

> It came ashore at Montauk in a ship, (the *Captain Bell*). The farmers came down there on business with their cattle, and could not find out how to use the tea-kettle, which was then brought up to old "Governor Hedges". Some said it was for one thing, and some said it was for another. At length one, the more knowing than his neighbors, affirmed it to be the ship's lamp, to which they all assented.

Mrs. Miller may have been pulling the historian's leg, but whatever the truth of her story, it reveals the symbolic importance of tea in this remote eighteenth-century village.

Standardization of consumer goods created a paradoxical situation. As Americans purchased the same general range of British manufactures—in other words, as they had similar consumer experiences—they became increasingly Anglicized. Historians sometimes refer to this cultural process as "the colonization of taste." The Anglo-American consumer society of the eighteenth century drew the mainland colonists closer to the culture of the mother country. In part, this was a result of the Navigation Acts which channelled American commerce through Great Britain, a legislative constraint that made it difficult as well as expensive for Americans to purchase goods from the Continent. There is no reason to believe, however, that parliament passed these acts in a conscious attempt to "colonize American taste." That just happened. And during the eighteenth century this process is easy to trace. For most people, articles imported from the mother country carried positive associations. They introduced colour and excitement into the lives of the colonists. Their quality was superior to that of locally made goods, silverware and furniture being two notable exceptions. It is not surprising that the demand for British manufactures escalated so quickly after mid-century. The market itself created new converts. Advertisements, merchants' displays, news of other people's acquisitions stoked consumer desire and thereby accelerated the spread of Anglicization. Booksellers—just to note one example—discovered that colonial readers preferred an English imprint to an American edition of the same title. "Their estimate of things English was so high," reports one historian, "that a false London imprint could seem an effective way to sell a local publication."

Anglicized provincials insisted on receiving the "latest" English goods. They were remarkably attuned to even subtle changes in metropolitan fashion. "And you may believe me," a young Virginia planter named George Washington lectured a British merchant in 1760, "when I tell you that instead of getting things good and fashionable in their several kinds[,] we often have Articles sent Us that could have been usd[*sic*] by our Forefathers in the days of yore." Washington may have envied his neighbours in Maryland. According to one visitor to Annapolis:

> The quick importation of fashions from the mother country is really astonishing. I am almost inclined to believe that a new fashion is adopted earlier by the polished and affluent American than by many opulent persons in the great metropolis [London]. . . . In short, very little difference is, in reality, observable in the manners of the wealthy colonist and the wealthy Briton.

No doubt this man exaggerated, but as he well understood, after mid-century American consumers took their cues from the mother country. Certainly that was the case of the people whom William Smith observed in New York. "In the city of New-York," he wrote in 1762, "through the intercourse with the Europeans, we follow the London fashions." . . .

Nevertheless the totality of these private consumer experiences deeply affected the character of eighteenth-century provincial society, for in a relatively short period following 1740 this flood of British manufactures created an indispensable foundation for the later political mobilization of the American people. Though these highly Anglicized men and women were not fully aware of this shared experiential framework, it would soon provide them with a means to communicate across social and spatial boundaries. . . .

The importation of British goods on such a vast scale created social tensions that the colonists were slow to appreciate. The very act of purchasing these articles—making free choices from among competing possibilities—heightened the Americans' already well-developed sense of their own personal independence. The acquisition of manufactures also liberated them from a drab, impoverished, even insanitary folk culture of an earlier period. But consumption inevitably involved dependency. The colonists came increasingly to rely upon British merchants not only for what they now perceived as the necessities of daily life but also for a continued supply of credit. So long as the Anglo-American economy remained relatively prosperous and stable, it was possible to maintain the fiction of personal independence in a market system that in fact spawned dependence. But those days were numbered. An increasingly volatile international economy coupled with parliament's apparent determination to tax the colonists sparked an unprecedented debate about the role of commerce within the empire. Comfortable relations and familiar meanings were no longer secure. That was the burden of John Dickinson's troubled remark in 1765, "under all these restraints and some others that have been imposed on us, we have not *till lately* been unhappy. Our spirits were not depressed."

As Dickinson's observation suggests, the colonists' experiences as consumers no longer yielded the satisfaction that they had at an earlier time. The rising level of personal debt made the Americans' growing dependence upon British merchants increasingly manifest, and in this context of growing consumer "disappointment", the meaning of imported goods began to shift. A semiotic order was changing. Articles that had been bound up with local cultures, with individual decisions within house-holds, were gradually thrust into public discourse, and during the constitutional crisis with Great Britain these "baubles" were gradually and powerfully incorporated into a general moral critique of colonial society that traced its origins in part to radical country pamphleteers such as John Trenchard and Thomas Gordon and in part to the evangelical preachers of the Great Awakening. . . .

Considering the growing ambivalence of the colonists towards consumer goods—these items were immensely desirable, but also raised unsettling questions about economic dependency—it is not surprising that the Stamp Act crisis sparked a boycott of British manufactures. . . .

. . . As early as 1765 many colonists had begun to realize that patterns of consumption provided them with an effective language of political protest. In that sense, Americans discovered political ideology through a discussion of the meaning of goods, through observances of non-consumption that forced ordinary men and women to declare where exactly they stood on the great constitutional issues of the day. British manufactures thus took on a new symbolic function, and the boycott became a social metaphor of political resistance. If the mainland colonies had not already been transformed into a consumer society, the Stamp Act protesters would have found it extremely difficult to communicate effectively with each other at this moment of political crisis. The purchase of British manufactures was the one experience that most of them shared, and by raising the possibility that they could do without these goods patriotic Americans strained the bonds of Anglicization.

Revolution did not occur in 1765. The bonds of empire withstood the challenge, and as soon as parliament repealed the Stamp Act the Americans returned to the import shops. The confrontation with the mother country had eroded but not destroyed the traditional meaning of consumer goods. Newspaper advertisements carried the familiar words "just imported from England," a clear indication that many colonists still took their cultural cues from Great Britain. Until that connection could be severed, independence was out of the question. . . .

# The Dilemma of American National Identity

### JOHN M. MURRIN

. . . The seventeenth century created, within English America alone, not one new civilization on this side of the Atlantic, but many distinct colonies that differed as dramatically from one another as any of them from England. . . .

For the English, the Atlantic functioned much as a prism in the seventeenth century, separating the stream of immigrants into a broad spectrum of settlements from the Caribbean to New England. Most colonies shared many important traits with immediate neighbors (Massachusetts with Connecticut, Maryland with Virginia, St. Kitts with Barbados), but differences became cumulative as one advanced farther along the spectrum. At the extremes—Barbados and Massachusetts, for instance—the colonies had almost nothing in common.

Historical demography suggests the larger pattern. For complex reasons that included climate and settler motivation, the farther north one went, the greater that life expectancy generally became, the higher the percentage of women in the colony, and the sooner population growth by natural increase set in. The extent of population mixture also followed the spectrum. New Englanders really were English. The Middle Atlantic colonies threw together most of the peoples of northwestern Europe. The Chesapeake added a significant African population, which would expand dramatically from the 1690s on. Africans eventually outnumbered Europeans by two to one in South Carolina and by much greater ratios in the islands. Climate and demography also affected local economies. Apart from the fur trade, few settlers north of Maryland engaged in economic activities strange to Europeans. As rapidly as possible, they even converted to European crops (without abandoning maize), grown mostly through family labor. But the staple colonies specialized in the growth and export through unfree labor of non-European crops, especially tobacco and sugar. The West Indies did not even try to raise enough food to feed the settlers and their servants and slaves.

Government and religion also followed the spectrum. At the province level, New England gloried in its corporate autonomy, which Rhode Island and Connecticut would retain until the Revolution. Royal government, by contrast, really defined itself in the Caribbean during the Restoration era. On the mainland south of New England, most settlers lived under proprietary governments that eventually became royal, but Virginia had been royal since 1624, and Maryland and Pennsylvania regained their proprietary forms after losing them for a time following the Glorious Revolution. In local government, the New England town—a variation of the traditional English village—spread no farther south than East Jersey. English counties, not villages, became the dominant form of local organization from West Jersey through North Carolina, and parishes prevailed in South Carolina and the islands. In general, the farther north one traveled, the higher became the percentage of local resources that settlers were willing to spend on religion. Formally, the Old World established church, the Church of England, became the New World establishment everywhere from Maryland south by 1710. In the Middle Atlantic region, dissent and establishment fought to a standstill, with toleration the big winner. In New England except for Rhode Island, Old World dissent became New World establishment.

Some uniformities different from England's did emerge to bridge these cultural chasms. Except in the smaller sugar islands, all of the colonies enjoyed a more widespread distribution and ownership of land. No colony successfully reproduced a hereditary aristocracy. Indeed, younger sons enjoyed liberties in North America hard to match in any European society. Similarly, England's complex legal system was everywhere simplified and streamlined. And except in Quaker communities, the settlers also adopted a ferocious style of waging war. For Europe's more limited struggles among trained armies, they substituted people's wars of total subjection and even annihilation. Their methods were deliberately terroristic. They, not the Indians, began the systematic slaughter of women and children, often as targets of choice. Finally, the English language became more uniform in America than in England simply because no colony was able to replicate the mother country's rich variety of local dialects.

Nevertheless, the overall differences stand out more starkly than the similarities. The spectrum of seventeenth-century settlement produced, not one, but many Americas, and the passage of time threatened to drive them farther apart, not closer together. Most of what they retained in common—language, Protestantism, acquisitiveness, basic political institutions—derived from their shared English heritage, however institutionally skewed, and not from their novel encounters with the continent of North America.

Between the Glorious Revolution of 1688–1689 and the Peace of Paris of 1763, the colonies grew more alike in several respects. As newer generations adjusted to climate, life expectancy improved south of Pennsylvania, population became self-sustaining, and family patterns grew more conventional. Warfare retained its original brutality in conflicts with Indians, but it too Europeanized as the primary enemy became the settlers and soldiers of other European empires. The widespread imposition of royal government through the 1720s gave public life structural similarities it had lacked in the seventeenth century.

As these examples suggest, British North America in fundamental ways became more European, more English, in the eighteenth century. The growth of cities, the spread of printing and newspapers, the rise of the professions, and the emulation of British political culture all encouraged this trend. But the colonies did not all change in the same way. New England anglicized at the core. On the fringes of the social order, it retained much of its original uniqueness, such as the Puritan Sabbath and annual election sermons. The southern colonies anglicized on the fringes while remaining unique at the core, which now more than ever was characterized by plantations and slave labor. A planter's economic base had no English counterpart, but his daily behavior closely imitated gentry standards. In the Middle Atlantic region, where emulation of England always had ethnic and class overtones, the pattern was less clear.

A few examples will have to suffice in illustrating this process. New England increasingly replicated basic European institutions. Southern provinces, by contrast, imported much of what they needed and did not acquire the same capacity to produce their own. Thus, for instance, every college but one was north of Maryland in 1775. New England trained virtually all of its own clergy, lawyers, and physicians. By contrast, no native-born South Carolinian (and only a few dozen Virginians out of the several hundred men who took parishes in the colony) became Anglican clergymen. All of South Carolina's bar and much of Virginia's was trained in England. Similarly, New Englanders wrote their own poetry, much of it bad, while Maryland imported poets, a few of them quite good. . . .

Perhaps the change was most conspicuous in public life. In the seventeenth century many colony founders had tried quite consciously to depart from and improve upon English norms. They attempted to build a city upon a hill in Puritan Massachusetts, a viable autocracy in ducal New York, a holy experiment of brotherly love in Quaker Pennsylvania, a rejuvenated feudal order in Maryland, and an aristocratic utopia in Carolina. But from about the second quarter of the eighteenth century, colonial spokesmen expressed ever-increasing admiration for the existing British constitution as the human wonder of the age. Improvement upon it seemed scarcely imaginable. North American settlers read British political writers, absorbed their view of the world, and tried to shape their provincial governments into smaller but convincing replicas of the metropolitan example.

One conspicuous consequence was imperial patriotism. The generation in power from 1739 to 1763 fought two global wars and helped to win the greatest overseas victories that Britain had ever seized. Despite frequent disputes in many colonies, royal government achieved greater practical success in America than at any other time in its history to 1776. Colonial expressions of loyalty to Britain became far more frequent, emotional, intense, and eloquent than in earlier years. To the extent that the settlers were self-conscious nationalists, they saw themselves as part of an expanding *British* nation and empire. Loyalty to colony meant loyalty to Britain. The two were expected to reinforce one another.

Occasionally a new vision of a glorious future for the American continent would appear in this rhetoric, but almost without exception these writers confined their exuberance to an Anglo-American context. North America would thrive *with* Britain, Nathaniel Ames's almanacs excitedly told New Englanders. Because population grew faster in America than in Europe, mused Benjamin Franklin, the colonies would one day surpass the mother country, and perhaps crown and Parliament would cross the ocean to these shores.

In other words, political loyalties to an entity called America scarcely yet existed and could not match the intensity with which settlers revered either their smaller provinces or the larger empire. Despite the frequent worries voiced in the British press or expressed by British placemen in America, native-born North Americans showed no interest in political union, much less independence. Every colony involved rejected the Albany Plan of Union of 1754 regardless of the manifest military peril from New France.

This reality was far from obvious to the British. They, not the settlers, imagined the possibility of an independent America. Imposing new patterns of uniformity on colonies that they had to govern routinely, few London officials grasped the extent or significance of local differences three thousand miles away. The British worried about the whole because they did not understand the parts, and they reified their concerns into a totality they called America. . . .

In a word, America was Britain's idea. Maybe it was even Britain's dream, but if so, it soon became her nightmare. Every countermeasure taken to avert the horror seemed only to bring it closer. Nothing is more ironic in the entire span of early American history than the way in which Britain finally persuaded her North American settlers to embrace a national destiny that virtually none of them desired before the crisis of 1764–1776.

There was, in short, nothing inevitable about the creation and triumph of the United States. Rather, the American nation was a by-product that at first nobody wanted. . . .

Perhaps we can now appreciate the dilemma of American national identity. To the extent that North Americans were more alike by 1760 than they had been in 1690 or 1660, Britain had been the major focus of unity and the engine of change. To repudiate Britain meant jeopardizing what the settlers had in common while stressing what made them different from one another. Older patriots quickly sensed the danger. If goaded into the attempt, the colonies would indeed be able to win their independence, John Dickinson assured William Pitt in 1765. "But what, sir, must be the Consequences of that Success? A Multitude of Commonwealths, Crimes, and Calamities, of mutual Jealousies, Hatreds, Wars and Devastations; till at last the exhausted Provinces shall sink into Slavery under the yoke of some fortunate

Conqueror." Younger patriots were more confident about America. They welcomed the chance to become fabled heroes in their ironic quest to prove that the British had been right about America all along and that their own doubts and hesitations were unworthy of their lofty cause. . . .

. . . Not only would an American national identity have to be forged in a brutal war with the world's mightiest maritime power, but the settlers would have to do so without the usual requisites of nationhood.

Sir Lewis Namier has contrasted two basic types of European nationalism from the eighteenth century to the present. Both reduce to a question of human loyalties. To what social collectivity do people choose or wish to be loyal? One pattern was traditional and, at root, institutional. England was a nation because it possessed reasonably well defined boundaries and a continuity of monarchical rule for about nine hundred years. The crown had created Parliament, which became both a reinforcing and a competing focus for loyalties as the two, together with their public, defined England's distinct political culture in the seventeenth century. . . .

The other model, just beginning to find important spokesmen in late-eighteenth-century Germany, was linguistic nationalism. Among a people who shared no common institutional links, language seemed an obvious focus for loyalty. Even though the boundaries between competing languages were by no means clear-cut, this type of nationalism would come to dominate Central and Eastern Europe in the nineteenth and twentieth centuries. Whereas institutional nationalism had the potential to absorb waves of reform without internal upheaval, linguistic nationalism recognized no obvious geographical boundaries and had to replace existing political institutions with new ones to achieve full expression. Although it began with warm sentiments of benign humanitarianism, it was far more likely to become militaristic and destructive, and by the twentieth century it could be deflected into overt racism whenever it seemed necessary to distinguish true Germans, for example, from outsiders who had merely mastered the language over several generations.

The most fascinating and troubling feature about the American case is that neither model could work here. The American continent could boast no common historic institutions other than crown and Parliament. It had acquired no shared history outside its British context. Likewise, the American settlers possessed only one language in common: English. In both cases, the logic of national identity pointed back to Britain. . . .

As . . . North Americans (often for the first time) came into intimate contact with each other. . . . [t]he shock of recognition was uncomfortable and disturbing, for it was just as likely to expose differences as similarities. It revealed, in effect, the underlying spectrum of settlement. Too often the Americans discovered that they really did not like each other very much, but that they needed common trust to survive. Mutual suspicion and fascination jostled for preeminence in the hearts of patriots. The language of virtue may have intensified the sense of hostility, for it became all too easy to explain any annoying cultural differences as someone else's lack of virtue and commitment. The terms of opprobrium that Americans hurled at each other may even have contained more venom than did the anti-British polemics of the period, many of which reflected the anguish of an ancient and real affection now inexplicably betrayed.

The most conspicuous fault line divided New Englanders from everyone else, although other antagonisms surfaced as well. Yankees could not conceal their sense of moral superiority, which often seemed rankly hypocritical to observers from other regions. "We Pennsylvanians act as if we believe that God made of one blood all families of the earth," complained William Maclay; "but the Eastern people seem to think that he made none but New England folks." One New York merchant, Gerard G. Beekman, thought that nearly everyone in Connecticut "has proved to be d——d ungreatfull cheating fellows." Thirteen years later he was still denouncing "the best of them out of that damd Cuntry" for defaulting on their debts. Lewis Morris, Jr., could not even keep a similar sense of disgust out of his last will and testament in 1762. He ordered that his son Gouverneur Morris (the later patriot) receive

> the best Education that is to be had in Europe or America but my Express Will and Directions are that he be never sent for that purpose to the Colony of Connecticut least he should imbibe in his youth that low Craft and cunning so Incident to the People of that Country, which is so interwoven in their constitutions that all their art cannot disguise it from the World tho' many of them under the sanctified Garb of Religion have Endeavored to Impose themselves on the World for honest Men.

When John Adams passed through New York City in 1774, he heard Yankees castigated as "Goths and Vandalls," infamous for their "Levelling Spirit." He retaliated in the privacy of his diary by speculating on the shocking lack of gentility and good breeding among the New York elite. To Abigail Adams, Virginia riflemen seemed every bit as loathsome and barbaric as British propaganda claimed.

American national identity was, in short, an unexpected, impromptu, artificial, and therefore extremely fragile creation of the Revolution. . . .

## FURTHER READING

Joyce Appleby, "A Different Kind of Independence: The Postwar Restructuring of the Historical Study of Early America," *William and Mary Quarterly,* 3rd ser., L (1993), 245–267.

T. H. Breen, *Tobacco Culture: The Mentality of the Great Tidewater Planters on the Eve of Revolution* (1985).

Richard L. Bushman, *The Refinement of America: Persons, Houses, Cities* (1992).

Jack P. Greene, *The Intellectual Construction of America: Exceptionalism and Identity From 1492–1800* (1993).

Ned C. Landsman, *From Colonials to Provincials: American Thought and Culture, 1680–1760* (1997).

Richard K. Matthews, *Virtue, Corruption, and Self-Interest: Political Values in the Eighteenth Century* (1994).

Margaret Ellen Newell, *From Dependency to Independence: Economic Revolution in Colonial New England* (1998).

David S. Shields, *Civil Tongues and Polite Letters in British America* (1997).

Peter Thompson, *Rum Punch & Revolution: Taverngoing & Public Life in Eighteenth-Century Philadelphia* (1999).

Michael Warner, *The Letters of the Republic: Publication and the Public Sphere in Eighteenth-Century America* (1990).